MARTHA:
HERE'S SOME GOOD
READING TO PREPARE YOU
FOR YOUR "GOLDEN YEARS"!

LOVE
MARILIN
BILL
& HOUSTON
& LOU ××

Mental Health and the Elderly

A SOCIAL WORK PERSPECTIVE

Francis J. Turner,
Editor

With a Foreword by Naomi Golan

THE FREE PRESS
A Division of Macmillan, Inc.
NEW YORK

Maxwell Macmillan Canada
TORONTO

Maxwell Macmillan International
NEW YORK   OXFORD   SINGAPORE   SYDNEY

The Free Press
A Division of Macmillan, Inc.
866 Third Avenue, New York, N.Y. 10022

Maxwell Macmillan Canada, Inc.
1200 Eglinton Avenue East
Suite 200
Don Mills, Ontario M3C 3N1

Macmillan, Inc. is part of the Maxwell Communication Group of Companies.

Printed in the United States of America

printing number
1 2 3 4 5 6 7 8 9 10

Library of Congress Cataloging-in-Publication Data

Mental health and the elderly : social work perspective/Francis
    J. Turner, editor ; with a foreword by Naomi Golan.
        p.   cm.
    Includes index.
    ISBN 0–02–932795–4
    1. Aged—Mental health.   2. Geriatric psychiatry.
3. Psychiatric social work.   I. Turner, Francis J. (Francis
Joseph)
    [DNLM: 1. Mental Disorders—in old age.   2. Social
Work, Psychiatric.   WT 150 M54936]
RC451.4.A5M442   1992
362.2′0425—dc20
DNLM/DLC
for Library of Congress   92–14579
                                                                CIP

In memory of Grandmothers Corwin and Turner,
whose renown will no longer go unsung

Contents

Foreword

When Francis Turner announced that he was planning to edit a third book in his series on psychopathology throughout the life cycle, to be entitled *Mental Health and the Elderly*, it seemed entirely appropriate. For years, Dr. Turner has been one of the most prolific and thorough writers on the theory and practice of social work. From the time that his first book on social work treatment was published in 1968, his works have appeared consistently in bibliographies of courses on social work practice and life-span development. The works that he has edited and that he has written have been of a high caliber and directly responsive to the knowledge needed by social work students and practitioners.

The subject of the current volume, how older people affect and, in turn, are affected by their environment is a welcome one. It has been my observation that social workers tend to base their professional practice with the elderly on a combination of social, psychological, and physiological information; years of experience in the field; and a mishmash of old-wives' tales, personal prejudices, and paths of least resistance. The proliferation of research in the area of gerontology over the past twenty-odd years has been welcome reading, but has provided little basis for day-to-day interactions with this population. As we refine our practice wisdom, it seems that we will have to pay much more attention to both the similarities and differences between older persons and those in earlier stages of development. Several years ago, when I was teaching at a university in California, I was pleased to hear that the school of social work offered a joint degree with the university's Institute of Gerontology. However, when I asked students what they were learning in gerontology, I was dismayed to hear that little had to do with actual practice with older individuals and much had to do with the research interests of their teachers, largely sociologists and psychologists.

I am convinced that professional practitioners, who come into daily contact with elderly persons in mental health clinics, retirement centers, and family agencies—to mention just a few of the settings in which they interact—have something solid to say and should be listened to. I hope that in this book we will gain a broader perspective on how older persons in our society function, how they continue to operate despite their advancing years, and at which point they tend to "go off the track."

This volume, as can be seen, covers many areas. I am somewhat troubled by the use of psychopathological terms, although I recognize that we have not found suitable substitutes for them. Certainly, it behooves us to keep in mind that as the individual grows older, the division between physiological and psychological processes tends to blur, as do the demarcations between normal and abnormal behavior. Again, I urge readers to pay more attention not to the weakness in thinking, feeling, and behaving, but to the strengths—the areas in which the elderly person still functions and functions well, despite the pressures put upon him or her.

My final suggestion is to consider, in the various case examples that are given, what the particular behavior described serves. It is well to keep in mind that the elderly balance their limitations with years of accrued experience and a ripeness of wisdom that are not always recognized. The social worker's particular function in multidisciplinary settings is to provide the team with the familial and social background that is necessary to understand the individual. It is hoped that in the chapters of this book, readers will find a broad canvas from which they can take appropriate information and understanding.

Naomi Golan

Preface

It would be easy, and indeed tempting, to begin this book by smugly saying that it is the final component of a long-planned trilogy addressing the major aspects of social work's contribution to mental health problems: practice with children, practice with adults, and finally, practice with the elderly. Unfortunately, this is not the case. The fact that this third book on this topic has emerged and rounds out an ages-and-stages approach to psychopathology is surprising to me.

I had long thought that there was a need for a book on psychopathology in general from a social work perspective. Thus, several years ago, with the assistance of a group of highly competent and enthusiastic colleagues, I began work on just such a text. Early in that project it became evident that trying to do a single book that encompassed all ages was too mammoth a task. The first authors kept finding it necessary to draft major sections on the different implications of various syndromes from the perspective of children and adolescents. Therefore, a decision was soon made to limit the first book to adults and to reflect this decision in the final title: *Adult Psychopathology: A Social Work Perspective.*

The idea of a companion volume, focusing on children, emerged soon after the publication of the first. Several authors had already done some work from this perspective in the early drafts of chapters for the first book. Furthermore, practitioners indicated that more material on children was needed, especially since social workers are often the first persons in the helping network to come in contact with and to identify mental health problems in children. Hence, *Child Psychopathology: A Social Work Perspective* was a logical follow-up to the first book.

During the evolution of these two works, at no time was I aware that a third book, focusing on the elderly as a particular subset of adulthood, might be useful. The first inkling of this possibility came during the process of proofreading the manuscript for the book on children, when my son Francis, who was helping me, remarked during a coffee break from our work: "Dad, I suppose the next book will be about old people."

ix

I did little with this comment for several months except to note that it kept emerging into consciousness. Initially, I was not enthused with the idea, nor were my colleagues at The Free Press. However, the idea kept reappearing, both here and in New York.

On looking back, I believe that the very need for this book was the very reason why I and others were resisting the idea. What was evident to my son, a non-social worker was less clear to me. Like others, I was reluctant to consider the elderly as a special developmental category requiring focused attention and consideration. We are all too aware of the unfortunate consequences of the misuse of diagnostic categories and labels with the all-too-often resultant stereotyping. As well, we know that for many the terms *aged* and *senescence* are almost coterminous. Thus, would not a book that focused on this life stage serve only to reinforce and perpetuate this perception? This concern was very much to the fore in the early discussions with the publishers and the consultants to whom they turned for opinions on the book.

In the initial submission to The Free Press, I used the same format for the working title as in the first two books, namely, "Aged Psychopathology: A Social Work Perspective." There were two strong responses to this title. One to the term *aged* and the second to the word *psychopathology*. I learned that unlike the other two labels, *children* and *adults*, the term *aged* is, in much of North America, clearly pejorative. I was quite surprised at this view; it certainly was not my perception in regard to my Canadian colleagues. The various reviewers of the proposal were strong in their support of the idea, but adamant that the word *aged* needed to be changed to *elderly*. This I have done.

Of equal conviction was that the term *psychopathology* was not to be used. Again, a strong opinion was voiced that including this term in a title would only reinforce the all-too-common attitude just mentioned that being over age 65 is equated with illness and deterioration.

Language is a complex way to communicate, but it is the best medium we have at present. In recent years social work has become particularly sensitive to the way that society often applies pejorative meanings to particular descriptors or labels. Indeed, we are just emerging from a period in which all who used "labels" were themselves "labeled." I think we have finally learned that it is not labels that are bad and to be avoided, but the misuse of labels or the use of certain labels. There is no way to escape using labels in language. Thus, instead of railing against labels, we need to become sensitive to the ways in which words can be negatively stereotyped by being loaded with ideology or distortion. When necessary, we need to substitute a troublesome word with another. In so doing, as we look back on the past two centuries of terminology in the mental health field, we need to remember that this is an ongoing process.

This problem with words may be seen in how the terms *aged* and *psychopathology*, once valid and useful, now appear to many to have a pejorative implication and, as was just mentioned, have been avoided. Throughout this book we have tended to use the term elderly, although there is not full consistency among the various authors. In doing so, I am well aware that soon this term, like many other terms in our field, may take on a negative meaning and thus need to be replaced.

However, in substituting terminology, we always need to be careful that the terms that are used as substitutes are ways not of distorting or denying reality, but of describing phenomena precisely. As well, we must learn to become comfortable with terms that create discomfort in others. For example, it is interesting to note how sensitive we have had to be even to talk about problems in the elderly.

That some of our elderly clients have problems of a mental health nature is obvious. That these problems need to be understood from a differentially diagnostic perception is certain. That the special biopsychosocial-political realities of those over age 65 in our society require the specific targeting of our traditional classifications of mental health problems is critical. That this field of practice is expanding and not receiving sufficient attention is of concern.

Hence, there was strong support for the book. But it was continuously emphasized that we must not overstress pathology from a traditional mental health perspective. There were frequent caveats from all sides that much of what may be seen as pathology in the elderly is best understood as reactive to insensitve and rejecting societal attitudes. In fact, much of this so-called inappropriate behavior is frequently adaptive. Only by understanding the biopsychosocial realities of the elderly in our society can we sensitively and accurately assess the nature and causes of various components of functioning and respond sensitively and appropriately with needed services and interventions.

Over and over again we were reminded that we must be aware of, facilitative with, and responsive to strengths and health. All elderly persons do not have mental health problems, just as all children and all adults do not. Many achieve the full flowering of the lifelong developmental process in their senior years. As social workers, we need to keep these realities before us to ensure that our diagnostic perspective with the elderly (indeed with all clients) must be from a position of strength and shaped by a biopsychosocial perspective.

Hence, this theme has marked the contributions of the various colleagues who have contributed to this volume. It is also reflected in the topics covered in the different chapters. Although the outline of the book is based generally on the terminology of DSM-III-R,* this terminology has been used only in a background thematic way. The authors were encouraged to go beyond the traditional subdivisions of mental illness and to address other factors, such as the family and general psychosocial topics.

This book has a strong problem focus because of an awareness that elderly people in our society frequently experience problems specific to their age group that require specific responses. It is our task and responsibility to recognize problems, pain, and suffering; to know the underlying cause; and to search out the potentials for relief and growth and change, so we can intervene sensitively and effectively. To do so requires that we use agreed-upon labels with precision to ensure that we neither overassess or underassess strengths and potential. But just as the latter years of life can be filled with pain and pathology and problems, for most they can also be filled with joy, achievement, and satisfaction. Since these are the goals we have for all persons, even though this is a problem-focused book, it is written from a health-oriented, positive perspective, based on our professional value that our task is to build from strength and the potential for strength and to foster growth and achievement.

Each author has been asked to focus on some particular area of problem functioning that we encounter in our practice with elderly clients and to consider what we social workers need to know to intervene, when appropriate, in as growth-enhancing and facilitative a way as possible.

Once the commitment to the book was made, the search for appropriate authors was begun. This proved to be a highly satisfying experience. Three things struck me during this process. The first was the extent of social work expertise on this topic. From the beginning, the challenge was not to find potential authors, but to select from the richness of all-too-often hidden resources among our colleagues. This fact reinforced my conviction that not only are we expert in this field of work with the elderly, but we appear to be determined to keep this expertise hidden. As a profession, we seem bent on ignoring the scriptural admonition not to hide our candles under bushels. There is just such a richness of knowledge, experience, and expertise contained in our body of practice wisdom. As this area of practice becomes increasingly important, we will need to find more effective ways of tapping what we know and dispersing it widely in the field.

---

*American Psychiatric Association, *Diagnostic and Statistical Manual of Mental Disorders, Third Edition, Revised* (Washington, DC: American Psychiatric Association, 1987).

Second, I was impressed with the enthusiasm of the persons to whom I turned. As I mention in the acknowledgments, both those I knew and those I searched out were most responsive to my approach—not only in regard to the need for the book but in the provision of helpful ideas about content, needed chapters, and suitable titles.

Third, I was impressed with the level of responsibility in the responses. On several occasions persons replied that they would be pleased to participate, but suggested other colleagues whom they thought would be more appropriate to deal with specific topics.

I mentioned earlier that the final selection of topics was strongly influenced by the conceptual base of DSM-III-R. In a different way the attitudinal bases of much of the content were influenced by Dr. Naomi Golan's book *The Perilous Bridge* and its emphasis on transitions.

Throughout the book, the theme is that social workers need to be the predominant professionals in the provision and coordination of treatment and services to the elderly, both those who are healthy and need only the occasional assistance of particular services and those at the other end of the health continuum, who are suffering from the range of conditions we call mental illness.

We have much to offer but, of even more importance, much to learn. It is this latter point that will keep us humble in our attitudes and committed to the search for knowledge that translates into effective, enabling, enriching social work intervention that is based on a differential diagnostic perspective that begins with an assessment of strength.

Francis J. Turner
York University,
Toronto, Canada

About the Contributors

Daniel C. Andreae, *M.S.W., C.S.W.,* was the former and first executive director of the Alzheimer Society of Metropolitan Toronto, the first such society formed anywhere in the world. Prior to this, he served as executive assistant to the principal secretary to a former prime minister of Canada. He has also been director of a health education agency and has practiced as a clinician in the Family Service Association. He is currently the director of a provincewide campaign to achieve legislatively based regulation of social work in Ontario.

Robert L. Barker, *D.S.W.,* is professor at the National Catholic School of Social Service, Catholic University of America, Washington, D.C., and a social worker specializing in family therapy in private practice. He is founder and editor of the *Journal of Independent Social Work* and author of fourteen books, including *Social Work in Private Practice, The Business of Psychotherapy, Treating Couples in Crisis,* and *The Green Eyed Marriage.* He has just completed the second edition of his *Social Work Dictionary* for the National Association of Social Workers.

Sondra Brandler, *D.S.W.,* is assistant professor at New York University School of Social Work. She is the former executive director of the Jay Senior Citizens' Center and the Council Senior Citizens' Center, both in Brooklyn, New York, and is a fellow of the Brookdale Center on Aging. She has served as a consultant for training in nursing homes, is the author of a number of journal articles dealing with aging and with group work, and has coauthored a textbook on groups.

Ann Burack-Weiss, *D.S.W.,* is adjunct associate professor at Columbia University School of Social Work. She is engaged in agency consultation and in-service training and development and participates nationally in workshops and seminars to advance practitioners' skills. A 1989 recipient of the Social Worker in Aging award of the New York City chapter of the National Association of Social Workers, Dr. Burack-Weiss is coauthor, with Barbara

Silverstone, of *Social Work Practice with the Frail Elderly and their Families* (Charles C Thomas, 1983) and coauthor, with Frances Coyle Brennan, of *Gerontological Social Work Supervision* (Haworth Press, 1991). She has also written several papers and chapters in professional journals and books.

Pat Conway, *Ph.D.*, is associate professor at the University of South Carolina School of Social Work. She participates in teaching, writing, and practice in the area of loss and grief. Her work involves diverse populations of clients, including older persons, people with AIDS, women who are battered, and people who are experiencing divorce.

Joan Davies, *C.S.W.*, is an independent consultant specializing in innovative program planning and development and the provision of adult educational services. Her career in gerontology spans twenty years and includes experiences as a clinician and social work manager at Baycrest Centre for Geriatric Care in Toronto. She is active on many professional committees that identify gaps in services and advocate for the needs of seniors living in the community. She is currently president of the Toronto branch of the Ontario Association of Professional Social Workers.

Ruth E. Dunkle, *M.S.W.*, *Ph.D.*, is associate dean of the School of Social Work at the University of Michigan and the past director of the Center on Aging and Health and faculty member at the Mandel School of Applied Social Sciences, Case Western Reserve University. Her current teaching, practice, and research interests are in gerontology, and her recent articles have been "Decision Making for Long Term Care Among Hospitalized Older Persons" and the "Effect of Stress on the Functioning of the Oldest Old." In addition, she has published widely in this field, including books and articles, among which is an article in the *Encyclopedia of Social Work* (National Association of Social Workers, 1987) entitled "Protective Services for the Aged." She is project director of the training program, "Social Research Training on Applied Issues of Aging," of the National Institute on Aging.

Kathleen Joyce Farkas, *Ph.D.*, is assistant professor of social work at the Mandel School of Applied Social Sciences, Case Western Reserve University. Her articles have appeared in *Health and Social Work, The Gerontologist, Mental Retardation,* and *Family Relations.* She is a licensed independent social worker in Ohio and consults both nationally and regionally on service delivery and evaluation issues.

Nora Gold, *Ph.D.*, is assistant professor of social work at McMaster University, Hamilton, Ontario. Over the past ten years, she has specialized in social work in the field of autism. Her professional activities in this area include teaching, research, a private clinical practice, and consultation to several agencies that serve people with autism and their families. Dr. Gold is on the board of the Autism Society of Canada and is actively involved in the Ontario College of Certified Social Workers.

Eda G. Goldstein, *D.S.W.*, is professor at New York University School of Social Work, where she is chairperson of the Social Work Practice Curriculum Area. She has authored numerous publications, including two books, *Ego Psychology and Social Work Practice* and *Borderline Disorders: Clinical Models and Techniques.* She is a consulting editor to the *Clinical Social Work Journal* and engages in agency consultation and staff development and in private practice with individuals and couples.

Edith S. Lisansky Gomberg, *Ph.D.*, is professor of psychology, Department of Psychiatry, School of Medicine, at the University of Michigan. She is one of several principal investigators in the Alcohol Research Center, focused on alcohol problems among the elderly. She has authored several books, the most recent being *Drugs and Human Behavior.* Her edited works include *Gender and Disordered Behavior: Sex Differences in Psychopathology; Alcohol, Science and Society Revisited; Current Issues in Alcohol and Drug Studies;* and *Women and Substance Abuse.* She serves on the editorial boards of the *Journal of Substance Abuse, Drugs and Society, Health Values,* and the *Journal of Social Work and Policy* in Israel and is an editorial referee for many journals. Her adjunctive appointments include adjunct professor of psychology, Rutgers University Center of Alcohol Studies, and research consultant in neuropsychiatry, Ann Arbor Veterans Medical Center.

David Guttman, *D.S.W.*, is dean of the School of Social Work at the University of Haifa, Israel, and the director of the school's Center for Research and Study of Aging. A graduate of the National Catholic School of Social Service of Catholic University of America, he is the author of several books on aging and ethnicity and numerous articles in professional journals. He is organizer of two White House miniconferences on the European-American elderly for the 1981 White House conference on Aging. He has been engaged in teaching, training, and consultation for the past two decades, and his main areas of academic activities and interest are related to social work education, gerontology, ethics, and logotherapy. He is a former director of the Center for the Study of Pre-retirement and Aging at Catholic University.

Ariela Lowenstein, *Ph.D., M.P.A.*, holds a doctorate from the Hebrew University of Jerusalem, and a master's degree form New York University.

She is the director of the Undergraduate Social Work Program and coordinator of the Center for Research and Study in Aging at the School of Social Work, Haifa University, Israel. She is also the national chairperson of the Israeli Gerontological Association. She has written several book chapters and numerous journal articles in the areas of aging and the family, policy, and service development. She is the recipient of several major research grants and is involved in a variety of research projects on widows in various stages of the life cycle, the evaluation of services, and intergenerational relations. She is engaged in teaching and the creation of innovative educational and training programs in institutional management and long-term care. She serves as a consultant to national and local health and welfare agencies and has been instrumental in the development and advancement of the services for the aged in Haifa.

Glenda E. McDonald, *M.S.W., C.S.W.,* is director of social work at Sunnybrook Health Science Centre and part-time instructor at the School of Social Work, York University, Toronto. She has been a professional social worker since 1975 and has worked primarily in the field of psychogeriatrics. She has conducted workshops and lectures and participated in research on the cognitively impaired elderly and their families.

Susan O. Mercer, *M.S.S.W., D.S.W.,* is professor, Graduate School of Social Work, at the University of Arkansas at Little Rock. She teaches in the areas of clinical practice, aging, health, and women's issues. In addition to teaching, she is engaged in private practice and agency consultation. Dr. Mercer has authored or coauthored numerous articles, chapters, and books in the areas of aging and long-term care. She has served on the editorial boards of the *Journal of Gerontological Social Work* and the *Journal of Women and Aging.* She has consulted in long-term care facilities for over twelve years and served three years on the Arkansas governor's Long Term Care Advisory Board. She recently completed a national study examining elder suicide and the availability of prevention and intervention programs. This research was funded by the American Association of Retired Persons and was initially published as a monograph. Dr. Mercer is currently working with two nursing colleagues on a four-year funded research project studying the promotion of functional independence in cognitively impaired nursing home residents, using dressing behavior as a model.

Theresa Norgard, *M.A., M.S.W.,* is currently a National Institute on Aging predoctoral trainee at the University of Michigan in social work and sociology. Her former studies were completed at the University of Toledo, where her emphasis was in sociology and aging.

Desmond L. Pouyat, *M.S.W., C.S.W.*, is director of social work services, Hamilton Psychiatric Hospital, and assistant clinical professor in the Department of Psychiatry at McMaster University, Hamilton, Ontario. He is a consultant and private practitioner in the Kitchener-Waterloo Region who works with families of the mentally ill and a variety of mental health problems. He is also an associate of the PACE Consulting Group of Mental Health Professionals.

Gary B. Seltzer, *M.S.S.W., Ph.D.*, is associate professor, School of Social Work, at the University of Wisconsin–Madison, where he is the chair of the doctoral program. He is currently the director of the Clinic on Aging and Developmental Disabilities, cosponsored by the Waisman Center on Mental Retardation and Human Development and the Section on Geriatrics of the University of Wisconsin Medical School. His research interests are the functional assessment of persons with disabilities and the age-related changes manifested by adults with mental retardation.

Marsha Mailick Seltzer, *Ph.D.*, is professor, School of Social Work, at the University of Wisconsin–Madison, and coordinator of the Applied Research and Technology Unit of the Waisman Center on Mental Retardation and Human Development. Her current research project is on aging parents who continue to provide in-home care to their adult children with mental retardation and the impact of this normative parenting responsibility on the development and well-being of the parents.

Ahuva Soifer, *M.S.W.*, is a part-time associate professor at the School of Social Work, McMaster University, Hamilton, Ontario. She has practiced in health and children's service settings in Canada and the United States. Her particular practice interest is the impact of culture on the lives of families, particularly of the elderly.

Joy Spalding, *Ph.D.*, is a licensed clinical social worker in Portland, Oregon, specializing in clinical gerontology. She has taught and carried out research in the United States and Australia. Her major areas of interest are mental health in long-term-care settings and older women.

Francis J. Turner, *D.S.W., C.S.W.*, is professor and chair, School of Social Work, York University, Toronto. He has been dean, vice president, and professor at several universities in Canada, the United States, and England and was the Moses Distinguished Visiting Professor at Hunter College in 1984–85. He is the author and editor of several books and is currently the editor of *International Social Work*. He has practiced in community and hospital mental health settings, family service agencies, and Children's Aid Societies and has been in private practice.

Joanne C. Turner, M.S.W., C.S.W., is assistant professor at the School of Social Work, King's College, University of Western Ontario. She is a clinical social worker in private practice, specializing in mental health disorders. She is past chairperson of the Ontario College of Certified Social Workers and coeditor of *Canadian Social Welfare.*

Susan Watt, D.S.W., is professor and director of the School of Social Work, McMaster University, Hamilton, Ontario. She has written extensively concerning social work practice and social policy issues in the provision of health care. Her current research examines the use of social workers in emergency departments to influence the care of the elderly. Dr. Watt is a consultant to the Department of Social Work Services at Chedoke McMaster Hospitals in Hamilton.

Lilian M. Wells, M.S.W., Dip. Adv. S.W., C.S.W., is professor and associate dean at the Faculty of Social Work, University of Toronto. She has extensive practice, research, and teaching experience in health, illness, disability, and gerontology. She is particularly interested in the quality of life, empowerment, and a range of social work practice methods to meet the needs of older people and their families. She teaches social work practice, policy, and research.

Margaret Whelan, M.S.W., C.S.W., is executive director of the Geneva Centre for Autism in Toronto. She has been actively involved in the children's mental health sector in Ontario and is currently chairperson of a communitywide association of agencies serving individuals with developmental disabilities.

1

The Elderly: A Biopsychosocial Overview

Francis J. Turner

Of the many dramatic developments taking place in our society, one of the most exciting, and perhaps most important, is the changing attitudes toward the elderly. Although many pejorative views still abound, overall we are beginning to appreciate and welcome that the period of life traditionally designated as beginning at age 65 can be highly satisfying and productive for many persons. Clearly, there are differences of opinion as to how pervasive this attitudinal change is and differential evaluations of whether we are or are not making sufficient progress.

The reasons for these changing attitudes are, of course, varied. Certainly, in this part of the world at least, we have realistic expectations for a much longer life than people had even a generation ago. Not that we are living longer as a race, only that more of us can expect to reach our eighties and nineties. This change in life expectancy is the result of many interrelated factors, including improved standards of living, reductions in many public health risks, dramatic advances in medicine, a more positive outlook toward health, and healthy patterns of living. Increasingly people are aware that with proper attention to their present life-styles and to planning for the future, they may expect to live longer, more comfortable and productive lives.

A more positive perspective on the elderly is not always based on unselfish humanitarian motives. There is a growing awareness that the elderly are rapidly becoming a strong economic force and that there are attractive economic opportunities to supply the large range of desired and required goods and services to this cohort of society. There is also the realization

1

that these persons are rapidly becoming a powerful societal force that needs to be taken into account when various political agendas are being devised or enacted.

For many, but certainly not all, the existence of improved pension plans and various forms of social benefits make the prospect of a financially secure old age a reality. As well, the wide range of technology available to an ever-increasing component of this population can bring considerable comfort, entertainment, and pleasure to persons in their senior years.

These opportunities are as yet not universal. We need to be aware that we are talking only of one part of the world and particularly of the more affluent in this part of the world. However, as social workers, it is important that we are cognizant of these changing attitudes and sensitive to all aspects of the positive and important potentials for the elderly in our society. In doing so, we will ensure that as a profession, we will respond appropriately to our immediate clients and will seek to broaden this trend to include other components of society here and in other parts of the world.

❑ ❑ ❑

From the perspective of social work itself, there are many positives to this important societal change toward the elderly. New services and a wide range of new practice positions have emerged. This trend has brought about and, indeed, has been brought about by new policy challenges; values issues; and, perhaps what is most important, a conceptual understanding of the human potential, not only in our elderly years, but in all ages and at all stages of the life cycle.

It has been professionally satisfying to observe the gradual positive change in attitudes toward the elderly. As social workers, we have been long aware of the damage to current functioning and to the potential for enhanced functioning that may result from a limited, pessimistic, and frequently pathological perspective of aging and the aging process. Although it would be naive for us to claim all the credit for changing attitudes, we have had some influence on this positive trend. Many of our colleagues have contributed to this societal change by sharing their rich and satisfying experiences in working with the elderly from a positive developmental perspective. Some of the rich theoretical developments of recent years that have enhanced social work practice in general have also contributed to this process.

Thus a growing appreciation of the full import of ego psychology and the Eriksonian concept that the eighth stage of life is a stage of development, not of pathology, has helped. Too long have we overstressed the earlier developmental stages and, in so doing, paid only lip service to the side of the continuum that speaks to full maturity.

In addition, existential theory has subtly but powerfully influenced our practice in this area much more than we have acknowledged. This theory, based on the concept of the lifelong potential and, indeed, responsibility of people to achieve the full flowering of their capabilities, has helped us look for potential and growth, rather than concentrate on pathology.

Other more pragmatic approaches to practice, such as problem solving and task-centered theories, have helped us develop a present and future orientation to intervention, rather than an emphasis on developmental issues. This orientation, in turn, helps us to work more positively and enthusiastically with older clients.

Crisis intervention has also helped us to appreciate the reality that all of us, both helpers and the helped, can and do respond in all life stages to unmanageable overloads of stress in upsetting and, at times, bizarre ways that are, for the most part, time bound. This theory has assisted us to recognize that many situations that hitherto were frequently interpreted as symptoms of psychopathology in the elderly are, in fact, normal and easily understood crisis reactions to highly stressful assaults on one's person, possessions, and dignity.

Overall our tradition of psychosocial theory, now enriched with a broader biological sensitivity, has helped us to view this period of life much more positively. Indeed, all the current twenty-five practice theories would support these concepts of growth in different ways.

Hence, as professionals who are highly committed to respecting the individuality and worth of each person, we can take some comfort in this societal shift to a growing respect for and optimism about the elderly. However, this shift is not without its clinical risks. In our enthusiasm for struggling against the "overpathologizing" of any aspect of the human condition, we must maintain a watchful clinical awareness to ensure that we recognize and respond to need when it exists.

If we can posit that there is a potential for healthy functioning in the elderly, we also must accept the possibility of unhealthy and problem-filled functioning. We should remind ourselves of some of the overenthusiasm in the anti-mental-illness movement of the late sixties that sometimes seemed to be moving to a position that there was no such thing as mental illness. In its extreme, this movement suggested that the business of mental illness was really only a strategy for creating legitimate categories of persons to keep the members of the helping professions occupied.

In a similar way, some popular articles and enthusiastic orators seem to want to convince their audiences that the developmental period of aging is a form of Nirvana for all, even though for many, it is a tough, highly problem-laden, stressful period, full of pain, suffering, and despair that stem from physical, psychological, and sociological factors. It can be a time that often is endured only with the concerned, knowledgeable, and ongoing response to society and its human service professionals.

I raise this issue because of an observed tendency to minimize the problems of the elderly, apparently out of a wish to stress a more positive outlook. In all stages of development, including aging, there are not only societal and psychological advantages and payoffs, but risks and challenges that can be highly distressing and based on pathology.

Thus, a more positive attitude toward the elderly requires that, in addition to emphasizing strength and potential, we recognize problem functioning when it exists and be ready to respond to it with the maximum impact of our knowledge and skills at whatever stage of development it may occur.

As was mentioned in the Preface, the reviewers of the original proposal for the book strongly opposed using the word *psychopathology*—and even *aged*—in the title. I think this resistance is unfortunate. Our constant challenge as practitioners is, as it has always been, to locate our clients as accurately as possible on the health–pathology spectrum. As diagnosticians, it is just as serious an error in judgment for us to overestimate strength as it is to overstress pathology or problems. An accurate balance of both positives and negatives is our goal.

The stage of life that we call aging is, indeed, filled with risks of a wide and highly complex set of situations, realities, and attitudes that make it highly vulnerable and painful for many individuals and their significant others. Many of the stress-producing situations arise from the complex interaction of biological, psychological, interpersonal, cultural, situational, sociological, and environmental factors. This intersystemic reality makes this component of society the natural and appropriate sphere of interest of social workers.

The complexities and gravity of these problems is vast, as may be seen in the content of the following chapters. Unfortunately, in some instances we are much better able to identify and describe the problems and their origins than we are to offer fully satisfactory interventions or services to remediate them. However, this is the reality of practice in all the human services, given the limitations of our knowledge and skills, and it should not deter us. Rather, it should spur us to even more stringent efforts to understand the realities of our clients and, on the basis of our understanding and empathy, to strive to devise and evaluate interventions, services, and policies that will permit our elderly clients to achieve their optimum level of human functioning.

This sense of both optimism and realism about the potential and impact of problems is reflected in the writings of the contributors to this volume.

The authors of all the chapters stress that in our work with the elderly we must start from, and build on, an understanding of and commitment to health and potential. But we must also be highly sensitive to the fragility of many situations and the lurking possibilities of the problems that our clients may encounter which may require intervention by us or by some other component of the helping system.

Intermixed with the twofold theme of health and pathology that marks the various contributions is a third highly important theme: complexity. Each chapter reminds us that in our practice with the elderly and their significant others we need to be vigilant to the reality that similar problems may be manifested in a variety of ways and that problems that look similar may, in fact, have different causes. Thus, what may appear to be a classical manifestation of an antisocial personality may have as its base a variety of causes, such as a lifelong personality defect, an ill-fitting denture, misuse of a prescription, an unrecognized gastric upset, or a religiously based existential wish to distance oneself from the hurly-burly of day-to-day living and prepare for a life beyond. The sequellae of this is, of course, the essential and compelling importance of diagnostic skill to ensure that we are adequately sensitized to the wide range of interconnecting factors. Our growing understanding of the therapeutic applications of systems theory has been helpful in assessing critical intersystemic influences.

Although the case for and against labeling has long been debated elsewhere, it is an issue that needs to be addressed here. I hope we are now long past the stage where labeling is seen as an either-or issue. Mature practitioners are aware that it is impossible to describe any human situation without using some labels or categories. Our problem is not with labels, but with the misuse of them. Diagnostic categories are essential to responsible practice with any type of client. But as with any method of intervention, to make effective use of labels, we must be aware of the risks inherent in their misuse, of the degree of precision that the label carries or does not carry. As well, we need to be aware of the temptation to find comfort in applying a label as a way of avoiding a more precise and careful assessment of other possible explanations of complex phenomena.

In this regard, two concepts from systems theory may be particularly helpful: equifinality and multifinality. These formulations remind us that different phenomena or inputs can have similar outcomes and, conversely, that similar phenomena can have differential outcomes. Thus diagnostic categories are useful, at times essential, in helping us to be precise about the various aspects of a person's reality with which we are confronted. But, as was mentioned earlier, labels can be blinders and ways to oversimplify much more complex realities. In the following chapters, our colleagues have been careful to keep this reality before us by providing examples of how difficult it can be to sort out the precise nature and cause of some aspect or aspects of a client's life for which we have assumed professional responsibility.

An idea that is only obliquely addressed in most of the chapters is the implied assumption that no one of the interventive theories in our broad biopsychosocial approach is adequate in itself to equip us for the quality of practice needed in this area. Rather, the premise is that to practice responsibly and effectively in this area we need to function from both a multitheory and multimethod orientation.

Several times in the preceding comments, I have referred to the multifaceted complexities with which we are usually faced in working with the elderly and their significant others and significant social systems. Although they are touched on in most of the following chapters in an episodic way, it seems useful to comment in general on some significant observed themes in the overall life situations of the elderly in this part of the world.

On the positive side, when all is well, there are many advantages to this stage of life. One can be free of many roles that in an earlier day were highly demanding, such as the role of a parent of young children and of a worker in the home or in the work force, including the many subroles of these complex role sets, such as the role of taxpayer and the role of homeowner.

In a maturational way, many satisfactions can come with existential success, in whatever manner we have defined it or let it be defined for us. Thus, one can find considerable satisfaction in the fact that one has done well with one's life—that one has been a good parent, a good spouse, a good citizen, a devoted companion, and a success in one's chosn occupation or in any one of the myriad of ways in which success is viewed.

One can find satisfaction that one has succeeded economically, especially if one has lived through an era in which economic survival was highly tenuous or an ever-present challenge.

Indeed, one can feel satisfied that one has survived at all. This satisfaction may be related to one's physical health, which may be free of any limiting aspects. Or it may be more of a sense of having survived some of the complex periods in history through which one lived. Although we are aware of the phenomenon of survivor guilt that can mark some persons, many live in ongoing gratitude and satisfaction that they have come through some of the most horrendous chapters of world history that have ever been experienced in the evolution of the human race.

Still others will gain satisfaction in an existential way from the idea that they have lived up to a set of values, beliefs, ideals, or principles that have guided their lives and from which they have derived direction, security, identification, and ego satisfaction.

Although social work does not always appear to be too comfortable with things spiritual, many persons in their older years find considerable satisfaction in their religious beliefs and in the awareness that they are approaching the beginning of the eternity, the promise of which has given them hope and direction throughout their lives.

Certainly, in this part of the world at least, another important source of satisfaction for the elderly is the possibility of retiring, either in the formal sense of leaving one's accustomed place in the marketplace or in the informal sense of changing role sets. Retirement may bring many satisfactions. It may relieve one from a wide spectrum of duties and responsibilities, as well as permit one to assume new roles and do many hitherto impossible things. Thus, studying new areas of interest; traveling; reading; embarking on new activities, new hobbies, or a new career; resuming activities long untouched; and meeting new friends or renewing old friendships become important and possible.

One activity that is of particular interest to some people, especially in this part of the world, has been tracing one's ancestral origins. Clearly, discovering one's roots has been such a large area of interest for many senior citizens that it has become a developing industry.

For others, the retirement years present the opportunity to take on a much more active role in the community, from volunteering in a particular service center to actively participating in the political process in a variety of ways. As the elderly become a more cohesive group in some parts of Canada and the United States, many may well, for the first time in their lives, experience some degree of empowerment that permits them to take effective action in causes of concern to them. Certainly, politicians at all levels are beginning to appreciate the potential of *gray power*.

Also at times the elderly person gains increased power in the extended family, especially when there are financial realities over which he or she has control, such as the disposition of possessions or the anticipation by family members of inheriting in the future. This power may give some elderly persons tremendous control over issues that affect the extended family.

However, it would be wrong to overidealize this phase of life. As social workers, we know it is a period of considerable stress and suffering for many. Hence the need for a volume such as this. Both the elderly and those associated with them have a growing sense of their mortality when a significant portion of their social life is taken up in attending the funerals of friends and associates.

There is a more existential concern about what lies ahead, reminiscent of the lyrics to the song "My Way": The end approaches, and one has to "face the final curtain." This awareness of one's mortality may raise complex ethical and theological issues, doubts, and anxieties, including whether one wishes or not to prolong one's life or that of a loved one who may be suffering. It is interesting that many social workers are not comfortable dealing with these issues and hence may not respond sensitively to these needs in their clients.

For many, indeed perhaps for all, there is a realistic fear of the increasing risk of injury and disease. This fear is evidenced in some of the popular cynical humor around Alzheimer's disease that has become symbolic of the risks of being old.

For many persons in this stage of life, there may well be some or much unfinished personal and family "business," such as a long-standing feud with a friend or a relative, an unconfessed failing, or the wish to undo some wrong. In addition to past concerns, many elderly people face real current day-to-day challenges as their resources become depleted and their problem-solving abilities become limited.

Personal as these problems are, they, in turn, create challenges and problems in the elderly person's significant networks that are related to roles, responsibilities, values, goals, and attitudes. Depending on how these difficulties are handled, they can be either a source of help or a source of further strain on the elderly person.

❏ ❏ ❏

In sum, this book seeks to help our colleagues in social work practice and in related professions find a way between two extremes. At one extreme being old is coterminous with senescence in the old usage of that word, and at the other extreme, it is naively believed to be *wunderbar*, with no problems except society's refusal to understand.

As professionals who are committed to the individuality of all persons, including ourselves, we have deep down a thankful awareness that much of our behavior is predictable and understandable. Problems and behaviors have patterns and solutions. And thus there are useful and helpful diagnostic categories and labels that help us to understand and direct us to appropriate, sensitive, and dependable interventions.

We have an accumulated repertoire of knowledge and experience in working with the elderly. What we have not done well is to present our accumulated knowledge in a way that our colleagues in our and allied professions can make use of it. We need to do so in two ways: to understand what we know about various types and patterns of difficulty for the aged and to identify the limitations and gaps in our knowledge so we will know when we need to be cautious and inquiring.

Thus, in the following chapters this body of knowledge is looked at from a highly focused perspective, making full use of the power and potential of diagnostic labels and with a full appreciation of the limitations and risks of the misuse of such labels. In addition to specifying what we know, these chapters should also help us to identify the gaps in our knowledge more clearly. The chapter content, in turn, should lead us to more focused and disciplined research that will help us to serve more effectively those fellow global villagers we call the elderly.

2

The Losses of Late Life: Elder Responses and Practice Models

Ann Burack-Weiss

A biopsychosocial framework forms the core of social work practice. The organization of this book around DSM-III-R categories addresses the "psycho" part of the configuration. It affirms the fact that elders are as prone to mental health problems and benefit as much from differential assessment and intervention by skilled clinicians as do younger adults. An emphasis on the psychological aspects of aging is a necessary corrective to the often prevailing view that the provision of concrete services and a kind heart are all that are needed to help the elderly.

However, there are dangers to the unilateral embrace of a psychological perspective. One possible danger is that the normative life crises and losses that form the context of the elder's world will be obscured. The lack of attention to physical realities may distort clinical judgments. For example, an 83-year-old woman who arranges her toiletries in a clockwise fashion and becomes agitated when one is moved from place may have an obsessive-compulsive personality disorder. Or she may just as likely have no mental health problem, but be justifiably upset when the method she has devised to compensate for her visual impairment is thwarted.

In addition to the danger of an inappropriate psychiatric diagnosis is the situation in which some pathology does exist, yet the diagnosis does not reflect the adaptive nature of the behavior. A 66-year-old man who is preoc-cupied with an old "case" against the army and spends his days searching, clipping, and filing newspaper articles he thinks support his claims of maltreatment may well suffer from paranoia. But he is also filling his day with gratifying purposeful activity at a time of life when more mentally healthy peers may be despondent over the loss of their work roles.

The sole reliance on a psychiatric diagnosis also poses the danger of overshadowing clients' strengths and coping capacities. Although this aspect of diagnosis is true at any age, it is especially relevant in old age, when dormant abilities of a lifetime may be masked by the frailties of the moment.

Whatever we don't know about the past of the individual older person who sits before us, we do know that she or he has already endured change and loss. No one can survive six or more decades of life without experiencing some measure of trouble: disappointments and failures in work and personal relationships, financial concerns, accidents, one's or a loved one's illness, and the death of a close friend or relative.

Some individuals handled problems by relying on the advice of a powerful authority figure. Other sought solace in prayer or activity. Some survived through fierce independence and keeping a stiff upper lip, while others leaned on the nearest available person.

With older persons, the goal of social work treatment more often is the restoration of past abilities and the maintenance of current functioning than of personality change. This is not to say that age in itself is a barrier to insight or to improved psychosocial functioning; it clearly is not. However, the cumulative effects of losses in late life exact a toll. Simply "holding one's own" may involve a maximum effort. As one 84-year-old woman put it, "I could handle the pain of arthritis. I even got to the point that I could inject the insulin for diabetes. But just last year my husband died, and I had to give up the house and move in with my daughter. Now they say I need an operation for my eyes. It is just too much."

The mental health practitioner who collects the history of a younger adult will most likely be searching for sources of the client's problems. With the elder, the practitioner looks to the past for evidence of the client's solutions. Although the specific problems of old age may not have been experienced before, they resonate with past meanings to the individual elder. And even with diminished inner and outer resources, the elderly client will attempt to meet them in a way that has worked before.*

A primary focus of the practitioner, then, is to identify the ways in which difficulties were handled in the past and to utilize that knowledge in designing current intervention strategies. For the 84-year-old woman who was overwhelmed with problems, the goal was to help her recollect the coping

*Thanks to Charlotte Kirschner for a clinical intervention that has proved valuable over the years.

strategies she had shown in managing a serious chronic illness while caring for her ill husband and then to mobilize these strengths in the present.

Research on personality in late life confirms the clinical experience that elders do not perceive that their values or characteristics change as they grow older; rather, they carry within them an "ageless self" (Kaufman, 1986) that seeks a continuity from the past to the present (Atchley, 1989) as they negotiate the tasks of aging.

What are these tasks? Peck (1968) enlarged upon the Eriksonian notion of the older person's need for ego integrity, rather than ego despair (Erikson, 1963), positing three additional challenges. The first task is ego differentiation versus work-role preoccupation, as the family and vocational roles of the workplace or home must be replaced by alternatives that fill the same needs for self-esteem and satisfaction. The second task, body transcendence versus body preoccupation, speaks to the fact that the inevitable physical decline need not be accompanied by the loss of social and emotional sources of pleasure. The third task, ego transcendence versus ego preoccupation, refers to an interest and investment in what will come after one's death, the sense that one lives on through contributions to family and community.

Theoretical frameworks on the tasks of aging and the fact that they are negotiated by each elder, in keeping with a sense of self that has been acquired and reinforced through a lifetime of experiences, help the practitioner place the problems of an individual client into context.

Two powerful predictors of the way elders may face late-life problems are ethnic-cultural influences and cohort group. Ethnic-cultural beliefs affect almost every aspect of the elder's daily life. Ideas about diet; medical care; receiving help from persons outside the family; the proper relationship of adult children and their aged parents; and, not infrequently, prejudices against those of another ethnic group are deeply ingrained and fiercely maintained. Ethnic-cultural identification is, for many elders, a buffer against the changes of old age. In fact, a return to religious observance or one's native language is not uncommon among those who abandoned them in earlier years. This identification is a strong tie to the past and an affirmation of "roots" that should be respected as such.

To understand the influence of the cohort group on the individual elder, the practitioner needs to be familiar with the major social and political events of the past century, as well as the human growth and development of the individual. For example, a 90-year-old client and a 70-year-old client were at different ages and were struggling with different developmental tasks during such historical events as immigration, World Wars I and II, and the Great Depression. Their world view has surely been shaped as much by these influences and the times in their lives when they occurred as by their personal experiences.

In summary, the mental health needs of the elderly are both the same as and different from those of other adults. While the following chapters of this book address differential psychiatric diagnoses, this chapter addresses commonalities among elders.

LOSSES OF LATE LIFE

Old age is a time of loss. Although there is great chronological and individual variation, the beginning of the process is usually evident around the life event of retirement, which takes place at about age 65.

Late-life losses may be biologically determined (arising from genetically programmed cellular changes) or socially determined (arising from societal attitudes and policies toward the aged). In most instances, both sets of factors interact.

Chronic physical illnesses are likely to be manifest first during the sixties and to accelerate in number and severity thereafter. Hypertension, heart disease, and arthritis are the most common of these illnesses. There is also an increase in cancers, strokes, various diseases of the central nervous system, and diabetes, among others.

In the early stages of many chronic illnesses, management may be more of an irritation than a crisis. Changes in diet, exercise, medication, and other noninvasive treatments may hold the effects at bay. However, the progressive nature of many of these conditions, the decreasing abilities of the immune system to ward off diseases, and a general lowering of the energy level in the seventies and eighties contribute to increasingly more serious functional consequences.

As the years go by, the elder is more prone to acute illnesses, such as influenza and, especially in the case of older women, osteoporosis, which leads to falls and fractures. The healing process may be extended, and residual effects often remain. Older people also take somewhat longer to recover from surgical procedures.

The loss of vision and hearing affects a majority of older people, as does a decrease in mobility that accompanies many physical illnesses.

For the mental health practitioner, the most salient fact is the consequences of the biologically determined losses for the physical and social functioning of the elderly. The elderly person's dependence on others for performing activities of daily living that were once handled independently and the cessation of social and recreational activities that once gave life meaning have far-reaching psychological effects.

The need to have one's bodily needs cared for by someone else may be a source of shame or result in a regression to a childlike state in other areas of life. Decreased mobility because of arthritis, stroke, or fractures may render the elder homebound and isolated.

The older person with vision loss may have to stop driving and with it, participation in many activities. He or she often cannot read as easily or often as before and so receives less information. The world shrinks further when the person gives up such seemingly unrelated activities as dining out in restaurants or participating in senior center activities because of embarrassment or fear of vulnerability.

Hearing loss separates the elder still further from others. The older person with this deficit may withdraw physically from social encounters that are frustrating or may remain in them only to misunderstand what is being said. At times this loss of hearing is so gradual that the person fails to appreciate it is happening and thus projects other explanations on those in his or her midst. Isolation, depression, and paranoid ideation are common consequences. As may be imagined from the foregoing discussion, the combined functional effects of hearing and vision impairments are devastating.

The benefits of medications must be weighed against the side effects. Often the treatment of choice for one condition may not be possible because of the existence of another. Or elders may become confused or noncompliant with medical regimes, under- or overmedicating themselves.

Mental impairments, specifically dementia and delirium, are discussed elsewhere in this book and so will not be treated here except to note that they rarely occur alone, but usually interact with the forementioned conditions. The foregoing physical losses typically interact with a host of simultaneously occurring social losses and changes.

The life event of retirement may signal losses of income, outlet for energy and ideas, socialization opportunities, and status. Married women who have never been employed may experience a loss of autonomy because their husbands are now home during the day. For those with good health, financial resources, and adequate preparation, retirement may well be, as the slogan of the American Association of Retired Persons (AARP) puts it, "the beginning of a new lifetime." Travel, second careers, new interests, and moving to more hospitable climes or to be nearer to children and grandchildren are all positive choices. Yet they may also occasion dislocation and stress. By the time elders reach their late seventies, many who have made these retirement choices will no longer be physically able to sustain them.

When they are in their sixties, women often become widows. For those who came of age at a time when women defined themselves through the marital relationship, the death of a husband is more than the loss of a crucial significant other—as devastating as that may be. For many women, it also marks the diminution of income, social standing, activities, and friendships and the cessation of opportunities for sexual expression. Men are widowed less frequently and are more likely to remarry. Nevertheless, the death of a wife occasions a host of other losses, some the same as and some different from those suffered by a woman. Men in this cohort are frequently unacquainted with basic housekeeping skills, which, combined with reactive depression to the loss of a wife, may lead to their neglect of nutrition and hygiene.

As both married and single people age, there are fewer and fewer people in their lives. Their parents, in-laws, siblings, friends, lovers, and even children may have died. Their friends may have relocated or become homebound because of illness and thus are less able to socialize. As their physical mobility decreases, so does the opportunity to form new relationships. At a time when they most need the help of others, such help is least likely to be available.

Over three decades of research have confirmed that families do not "dump" their elderly relatives into nursing homes or otherwise depend upon formal agencies or governmental assistance. Over 80 percent of care to the elderly is provided by family members; outside help is usually sought only when the financial and emotional resources of the family are exhausted.

Most often the primary caregiver is a middle-aged daughter who is struggling to reconcile the needs of her husband and children with those of her aged parent (Horowitz, 1985). More women are entering the work force than in previous generations, and more women are feeling entitled to time for themselves, creating a generation of caregivers who feel squeezed by demands on all sides.

Adult children who may have been distanced from their parents or each other because of geographic or emotional reasons often find themselves reconnected as their elderly parents' need for care increases. Planning with and for an older parent reawakens old conflicts and rivalries, as well as provides opportunities for their resolution.

There is also a significant amount of spousal care, usually of wives for disabled husbands, but also of husbands for wives. A more common picture in late-life marriage is the mutual dependence of two individuals who are impaired in different ways. The visually impaired wife and arthritic husband may boast of being a good "team" in the supermarket; he reads the labels while she provides an arm to lean on. Although such an alliance is touching to onlookers, it is also exceedingly fragile. The slightest change in the physical functioning of either partner may place them both in jeopardy.

Lest the preceding discussion leave the erroneous impression that late life is an inevitable unmitigated disaster, the point that not every loss befalls everyone must, though obvious, be made. General trends are not individual destinies.

There are elders who endure into their eighties and nineties with great vigor and a minimum of life stresses; with the assistance of medical technology and social supports, their numbers may be expected to increase.

Most often, the course of late-life losses is not a steep downhill slide, but a meandering road with many plateaus of functioning and even significant gains along the way. The ever-shifting nature of the elder's physical and social world requires ongoing assessment and frequent revisions of clinical plans for mental health problems.

ADAPTIVE AND MALADAPTIVE RESPONSES

To survive one or many of the losses just described, the elders cannot simply continue living as they have done before. They must adapt in some way.

The overarching goal of all physical and mental health treatment is to ensure that the individual has reached the highest possible level of adaptation, given his or her circumstances. Adaptive responses enable older persons to live as fully as possible, given their disabilities and the limitations of their life situations. Maladaptive responses compound and worsen the effects of the original losses and accompanying problems.

Whether an individual will choose an adaptive or maladaptive response to loss depends on many factors, some of whose roots are within the individual's personality and life experience, some that originate in the present.

Emotional Responses to Loss

Mental health practitioners are all familiar with the concept of mourning as a process over time. In most conceptualizations, mourning refers to the period during which the individual slowly comes to terms with the loss of a loved one. Kübler-Ross (1969), Simos (1979), and others have eloquently discussed the feeling states and behavioral manifestations of mourning. Whether or not one believes that mourning inevitably takes place in a sequence of stages or that those who do not mourn a loss at the time it occurs are in jeopardy of mental dysfunction later (views that are contested by professionals), there is a consensus that the loss of a significant other must be mourned before a new relationship can take hold.

Understanding of the mourning process is less widespread when it refers to the loss of one's health and abilities. Mental health practitioners who would not dream of suggesting that elderly women try to meet new men after the death of their husbands often have no reservations about urging their clients to obtain home health care immediately following the loss of physical functioning and are often puzzled by their clients' "resistance" to accepting help, as obvious as the need for it may be.

Mourning losses of the self is at least as important as mourning losses of significant others. Dependence in activities of daily living in a society that prizes independence is a severe narcissistic injury. The elder may feel (and be treated as if) he or she has regressed to a childlike state. Just as the process of letting go of a loved one involves reminiscences of the time spent together, so the process of adapting to physical losses is marked by recollections of times when the elder was able to manage not only his or her life but often care for others.

Many emotions that accompany the mourning process fall short of meeting the criteria of a DSM-III-R classification, but require the skilled intervention of mental health professionals. Sadness over losses may blend into a state of inertia and hopelessness that does not meet the criteria for clinical depression, yet is very painful. Frustration and anger at being deprived of a loved one or of one's abilities may be completely appropriate, given the circumstances, yet alienate those who are closest to the elder. The fear of future losses may reflect a realistic appraisal of one's options, but prevent the elder from making the most of the present.

The denial of unpleasant truths is a common response to the losses and changes of late life. A complex phenomenon in old age, denial has a variety of manifestations—some adaptive and some not. The denial of a health problem that prevents the elder from receiving needed care is clearly maladaptive, as is the denial of an environmental situation that places the person at risk. However, when we move from such obvious examples, it is difficult to assess whether denial fills an adaptive function.

The most frequently occurring and adaptive form of denial is a time-limited response to a catastrophic life event; a serious illness and the death of a loved one are prototypical situations. A state of disequilibrium ensues during which the individual, in great emotional pain, moves back and forth from rejection toward acceptance of the reality. As the mourning process goes on, denial lessens.

Another adaptive form of denial is the "one day at a time" philosophy adopted by many of the elderly. Although these elders are intellectually aware that they are in a vulnerable situation, they choose not to dwell on situations they can do nothing about.

With the exception of the severely mentally impaired, who may totally deny an evident impairment, maladaptive denial in the elderly may be partial and difficult to identify. For example, an older man may freely discuss his inability to walk independently, yet in the next breath maintain that he can manage without a cane or a walker. Or an elderly woman who can no longer prepare meals for herself may fire one homemaker after another on the grounds that they cannot cook as well as she does.

Paradoxes of Adaptation

Clinical experience with younger adults suggests that the more pathological the client's diagnosis, the more maladaptive his or her responses will be. Practice with the elderly does not uphold this logic.

The more bizarre manifestations of psychoses are often muted as the individual becomes more physically frail, allowing the person to "fit in" in congregate settings where he or she previously may have been shunned.

The case is particularly strong with regard to elderly people with personality disorders. The schizoid personality will not suffer the losses of relationships he or she never had. The narcissistic personality is often unable to recognize the changes in physical appearance that agonize more intact peers. The obsessive-compulsive personality may find it easier to follow a complicated regimen of diet and medication than an individual who is less rigid. Such paradoxes alert the mental health practitioner to the importance of looking beyond the diagnostic label to the behavior it reflects.

ENABLING ADAPTIVE RESPONSES: PRACTICE MODELS

Social gerontology is a relatively new field. While empirically based knowledge about the aging population and its needs has increased in the past three decades, the attempt to combine this knowledge with clinical experience to construct models for practice has occurred only recently.

A forerunner of practice models for the aged was a slim monograph by Wasser, published in 1966. This monograph presented the findings of a four-year demonstration project in family service agencies in selected communities throughout the country.

Although this pioneer text fell short of constructing a practice model, it was the first to identify many components of contemporary models: the themes of loss and grief in old age, the need for mastery over one's life and adaptive strategies, a family-centered approach, and the personal demands on the social worker. The practice wisdom and inductive nature of the inquiry give this book a timeless validity (Wasser, 1966).

The four practice models selected for discussion in this section were all developed within the past decade.* They are framed within an ecosystems perspective, that is, they recognize both the older person's losses and the environment that supports or thwarts his or her efforts at mastery. Each represents an attempt to integrate empirical and clinical knowledge about the elderly into a useful framework that practitioners may use. The models differ in the emphasis that the authors place on the assessment of various components of the elder's life situation.

Brearly (1982) selected "vulnerability" as his operative concept, arguing that the multiple losses of age contribute to an endangered state. Thus, the practitioner's primary task, when assessing the elder's needs, is to analyze the overall risk. In this analysis, four factors are weighed: predisposing hazards (in the individual and social network), situational hazards (in the environment), strengths (in the person's inner and outer resources), dangers (negative outcomes). The results of this analysis are then used to assign priorities for work. They may also be useful in professional decision making in protective service situations.

Greene (1986) presented a "functional-age model of intergenerational family treatment." This model is seen as an approach for evaluating the client system that is a composite of one particular member's bio-psycho-social functioning within a family context and allows for adaptive and maladaptive patterns to be identified and appropriate interventions made. It is unique in its incorporation of life-cycle and family-cycle theory.

Maluccio (1981) introduced a practice model for all ages—a competence-oriented approach that facilitates natural adaptive processes. Libassi and Turner (1982) applied this model to the elderly person's need for mastery. They stressed the importance of providing "prerequisite conditions" at the environmental level and at the individual level. At the environmental level, these conditions include restructuring the person's physical and social life space, meeting concrete needs, and facilitating social networks. At the individual level, they include bringing about satisfactory internal states, providing information, enhancing skills, and exercising autonomy and choice.

Silverstone and Burack-Weiss (1983a, 1983b) proposed the auxiliary function model of practice with the frail elderly and their families. The auxiliary function fills in for the depletions and losses of the elder. Just as an auxiliary power system is activated by the failure of a regular system and shuts off

*Thanks to Dr. Elizabeth Ozanne for the idea of analyzing a single case from the point of view of a range of practice models.

when the power is restored, the auxiliary function provides the elder with the borrowed strengths he or she needs in the area and for the time in which they are needed. The auxiliary function is filled by the social worker in partnership with the family or alone, when necessary. It consists of case management and affective components. Particular emphasis is given to the social worker's role and skills throughout the model.

Each of the models just outlined is illustrated by intervention strategies that purportedly flow from the model itself. In fact, the differences among the models are more of degree than of kind. The approach to case examples is not dissimilar. This similarity is most notable in the application of social work values, such as enabling clients to work on their own behalf and respecting their autonomy and individuality. Brearly and Libassi and Turner stressed environmental interventions, while Greene and Silverstone and Burack-Weiss emphasized psychodynamically based treatment skills. Furthermore, since the models complement each other, the applicability of one or another model may depend on the practice setting and the theoretical preference of the practitioner.

With regard to these practice models, it is important to conclude with the caveat that mental health treatment of the elderly is not limited to issues of loss and adaptation. While the vast majority of problems that reach the practitioner are *precipitated* by these issues, they generally coexist with unresolved conflicts of the past. Surviving separation and loss, balancing needs for dependence and independence, responsibilities to oneself versus responsibilities to others, all are issues that are negotiated throughout the life span. Thus, it is the task of the mental health practitioner to integrate knowlege about the special needs of the elderly population with what has been learned in work with other age groups.

PRACTICE CHALLENGES

Mental health practice with the elderly offers special challenges, ranging from logistical issues, such as timing and the site of interviews, to existential concerns, such as the forced confrontation with one's mortality.

Elders are not likely to present themselves to a mental health setting for counseling or therapy. Those who do usually have received such help earlier in their lives or are from a younger, better-educated cohort who are aware of the benefits to be gained. More typically, elders present themselves or are referred by others because of concrete problems involving access to and use of services. Because mental health problems tend to be acted out in this arena, it is not advisable to dichotomize elders' concerns as either "concrete" or "emotional."

Social service agencies that assign paraprofessionals to handle case-management tasks and professional workers to conduct counseling are, in this author's opinion, operating from the assumption that the two are separate. In fact, elders are far more likely to act out their problem of accepting their dependence by firing one home attendant after another than to talk about the problem with a therapist. It is by helping with the concrete task that the practitioner gains an elder's trust and then can attempt to look at the underlying issues.

Starting "where the client is" assumes literal significance in practice with the elderly, who are frequently in a hospital, are homebound, or are in a congregate setting when they are seen by practitioners. Interviews are as likely to take place at the bedside, at a kitchen table, or in the corner of a hallway as in the traditional office setting. Being on the client's "turf" shifts the balance of power somewhat from practitioner to client, discomfiting some practitioners while freeing others to be more authentic in the encounter.

Similarly, the fifty-minute hour is not appropriate for many elderly persons whose physical or mental state is such that they cannot tolerate such a long session. Shorter, more frequent meetings, sometimes interspersed with telephone conversations, are often more useful.

Another logistical issue to be decided is who to see, in what combinations, and for what purpose. The elder alone? The elder and spouse? The primary caregiver? All the adult children? There are no guidelines beyond the primacy of elders and their right to participate in any planning that involves them. Practitioners who are at ease with couple and family interventions will find many occasions when these interventions usefully augment one-to-one counseling.

Interdisciplinary work, particularly with health care providers, is an important aspect of mental health practice with the elderly. This approach to treatment, which requires its own set of skills, is actually beyond the scope of this chapter. However, its value should not be disregarded.

Practitioners sometimes have trouble focusing interviews with an older person. Even in the absence of cognitive impairment, elders are apt to wander verbally from the topic at hand, interspersing social conversation or reminiscences. These clients are not necessarily being resistant. It is just as likely that they are lonely and value the therapeutic encounter as much for the human warmth it provides as for any insights they may gain. Moreover, stories from the past that may appear irrelevant often reveal underlying content that is closely related to the issue being discussed. When elderly clients repeat the same few reminiscences at each meeting, they are trying to tell practitioners something about themselves. In such cases, it is useful to explore more about the incident: how old the client was, other people who were present and their relationship with the client, and the outcome of the incident. As the underlying content or theme emerges, it often sheds light on the situation of the moment.

When the elder first presents a problem, it is usually helpful to find out how long it has been going on and what he or she has done about it until now. This information is valuable, especially in the absence of an extensive history of the client, in getting an immediate grasp of the client's coping style.

Perhaps the greatest differential in work with the elderly is the practitioner's use of self. The older person may well interpret professional distance and objectivity as not caring. At the same time, the practitioner cannot play the part of a surrogate family member or friend. Expressions of warmth and caring that respect the boundaries of the relationship, an ease with "small talk" that validates the client's interests without patronizing them, even asking the client's advice on matters about which he or she has expertise are all ways in which the practitioner can be "real" to the client without overstepping the professional role.

Transference and countertransference issues loom as large in work with the elderly as they do in work with other age groups. The fact that practitioners are often at least one generation younger than their clients facilitates the identification with a parent or a child. At the same time, the unconscious is not bound by such linear distinctions. Therefore, it is important for practitioners to understand how they are viewed by individual elders (they may well represent a parent as well as a child or many people at one time). It is also important that they be in touch with and in control of their own feelings about the aging process and the care of older people. It is a rare practitioner who does not carry the residue of personal experiences with elderly relatives or friends into the therapeutic encounter.

Mental health practice with the elderly is a direct confrontation with one's vulnerability. Practitioners are confident that, in their personal lives, they can escape the problems of mental retardation, schizophrenia, or chemical dependence that they meet in their clients. But if they live long (as most wish to), they will face many of the problems that their clients are encountering, such as depression, anxiety, confusion, and loss of autonomy.

Elderly clients are more likely than are younger ones to deteriorate physically and mentally and, sometimes, to die during the course of their treatment. The appropriate response in a given situation may well be to step out of the professional setting: to make hospital visits, attend funerals, and pay condolence calls. Deciding upon actions is easier than handling the feelings aroused by these events. Supervision, consultation, and peer support are invaluable aids to self-aware practitioners who are trying to maintain the necessary balance between hope and sorrow.

A minority of older people have long-standing mental health problems or have acquired them in old age. The majority of older people are not only free of mental illness but have coped well with the hand that life has dealt them. It is only now, when they have outlived their inner and outer resources, that they approach the professional service system for help. Each set of survivors has something to teach practitioners about the meaning of life.

There is hope in work with the elderly, as strange as this assertion may seem at the conclusion of a chapter on late-life loss. All who are old today are survivors of life events that overwhelmed less sturdy peers. They have survived immigration, discrimination, world wars, poverty, and the untimely death of parents, siblings, and children. Whether their defenses were pathological or their coping skills were superb matters less in the final analysis than does the fact that they have survived.

REFERENCES

Atchley, R. (1989). A continuity theory of normal aging. *The Gerontologist, 29,* 183–190.

Brearly, C. P. (1982). *Risk and ageing.* London: Routledge & Kegan Paul.

Erikson, E. (1963). *Childhood and society* (2nd rev. ed.). New York: W. W. Norton.

Greene, R. (1986). *Social work with the aged and their families.* New York: Aldine de Gruyter.

Horowitz, A. (1985). Family caregiving to the frail elderly. In M. P. Lawton & G. Maddox (Eds.), *Review of gerontology and geriatrics* (pp. 194–246). New York: Springer.

Kaufman, S. (1986). *The ageless self.* Madison: University of Wisconsin Press.

Kübler-Ross, E. (1969). *On death and dying.* New York: Macmillan.

Libassi, M. F., & Turner, N. (1982). The aging process: Old and new coping tricks. In A. Maluccio (Ed.), *Promoting competence in clients* (pp. 264–289). New York: Free Press.

Maluccio, A. (Ed). (1982). *Promoting competence in clients.* New York: Free Press.

Peck, R. (1968). Psychological developments in the second half of life. In B. Neugarten (Ed.), *Middle age and aging.* Chicago: University of Chicago Press.

Silverstone, B., & Burack-Weiss, A. (1983a). The social work function in nursing homes and home care. In G. Getzel & J. Mellors (Eds.), *Gerontological social work practice in long-term care*. New York: Haworth Press.

Silverstone, B., & Burack-Weiss, A. (1983b). *Social work practice with the frail elderly and their families: The auxiliary function model*. Springfield, IL: Charles C Thomas.

Simos, B. (1979). *A time to grieve: Loss as a universal human experience*. New York: Family Service Association of America.

Wasser, E. (1966). *Creative approaches in casework with the aging*. New York: Family Service Association of America.

3

Neurological Disorders

Glenda E. McDonald

INTRODUCTION

It is well established that the borders between psychiatry and neurology frequently overlap. Diseases that affect the central nervous system often affect not just one but multiple brain functions. Emotional, affective, and cognitive functions, just as much as sensory and motor functions, are controlled by the brain (Johnson & Hart, 1984). Within the field of psychiatry, a number of disorders that were considered psychogenic have been discovered to have a biological origin. Most significant among them are mania, depression, and schizophrenia. In fact, this borderland area ranks among the most rapidly expanding areas of research in both neurology and psychiatry (Benson & Blumer, 1982).

For the elderly, the similarity in the symptomatology of various psychiatric and neurologic conditions is further evidence of the close relationship between these two specialties. Some neurological disorders are misdiagnosed as psychiatric disorders—Huntington's disease is misdiagnosed as schizophrenia, Parkinson's disease is misdiagnosed as depression, and some types of stroke are misdiagnosed as manic excitement or schizophrenia (Johnson & Hart, 1984). The coexistence of neurological and psychiatric symptoms has been identified in many illnesses of old age, including Alzheimer's disease, Huntington's disease, Parkinson's disease, and cerebrovascular disease. In addition, coping with a chronic neurological problem may contribute to psychiatric symptomatology in many patients and families.

To intervene appropriately, social workers who work with the elderly must have knowledge of some of the more common neurological disorders in old age. They should be able to distinguish between psychological manifestations of neurological disorders and psychosocial stressors associated with being disabled. They must consider the entire response of the patient system and be aware of three aspects of neurological disorders: the actual disease process, the personal reaction to the disease, and the consequences of the disease process for the patient's social and family situation.

This chapter focuses on the following neurological disorders: cerebrovascular disease, Parkinson's disease, intracranial tumor, head injury, alcoholic neurological disorders, and Huntington's disease. These diseases have been identified as the most common neurological diseases associated with the elderly (Caird, 1982). Readers are referred to textbooks on neurology for information about less common conditions.

Dementia is also a major disorder that crosses the border of neurology and psychiatry. However, in this chapter, it is discussed only as a consequence of the neurological conditions presented, rather than as a distinct entity. Chapter 4 discusses dementia, specifically Alzheimer's disease, in detail.

This chapter is organized into three sections. The first section describes the major characteristics of each disease, including common psychiatric symptomatology, and briefly discusses the management of each disease. The reader should note that a discussion of psychopharmacological interventions has been deliberately avoided, exept for Parkinson's disease. Psychopharmacology is a rapidly changing field and is thought to be beyond the scope of this book. The second section outlines the issues for patients and families associated with these illnesses. The final section focuses on social work interventions, targeted at the issues identified in the preceding section.

CEREBROVASCULAR DISEASE: STROKE

Although its incidence and mortality rates in most westernized countries have been falling for all ages and both sexes since before World War II (Bonita, Stewart, & Beaglehole, 1990), cerebrovascular disease, or stroke, is still considered to be the most important neurological disorder for three reasons: It is the most common, it ranks third behind heart disease and cancer as a cause of death, and it is a major cause of disability in those who survive.

The risk of stroke rises after age 60, and 75 percent of strokes occur in persons over age 65 (Scheinberg, 1986). About 500,000 people in the United States have a new stroke annually. Of this number, 40–50 percent die within the first thirty days, 20 percent require special care, 20 percent have mild problems, 5 percent are unimpaired, and 5 percent require institutional care (Scheinberg, 1986). Stroke is a major cause of hospital admissions, and bed utilization is high for stroke patients, especially the elderly. Some say that patients with a stroke will occupy up to 18 percent of all available hospital-bed days by the end of the century (Akhtar & Garraway, 1982).

A stroke is a sudden interruption in blood flow, and subsequently oxygen, to the brain. When brain tissue is deprived of oxygen-rich blood, irreparable damage may occur. Such interruption is caused by a blockage (thrombus, embolus) or hemorrhage. A hemorrhage is caused by the bursting of a diseased artery, an aneurysm, or a head injury (Scheinberg, 1986). Approximately 20 percent of strokes are due to hemorrhage and 80 percent are due to blockage by clots of blood, fat, or air (Andrews, 1982; Johnson & Hart, 1984; Scheinberg, 1986).

Symptoms of a stroke include weakness or paralysis (hemiplegia) in two or more limbs in 92 percent of the patients who are admitted to the hospital. Marked confusion is evident in 25 percent of the patients with stroke, but it subsides in 66 percent of those who survive the first year. The presence of such confusion is a poor prognostic indicator for functional recovery. Bladder function may be lost initially, but it returns in 50 percent of the cases within six months and a further 18 percent within a year. Fecal incontinence is less common, occurring in 25 percent, with recovery in 83 percent within six months. Other symptoms include deficits in the visual field, an inability to concentrate, and personality changes (Andrews, 1982).

Aphasia and dysphasia are evident in one-third of stroke survivors. These communication disorders present complex problems: Patients may be unable to interpret the spoken word, the written word, or both. They may be able to repeat words or may speak without comprehension or understand but be unable to find names, or they may have expressive language difficulties (Andrews, 1982).

The specific syndromes that may result from stroke depend on where in the brain the damage has occurred. A right hemiplegia means an injury to the left side of the brain and is associated with speech and language deficits and a behavioral style that is slow, cautious, anxious, and disorganized when attending to a new task. A left hemiplegia means an injury to the right side of the brain and is associated with spatial and perceptual deficits, performance difficulties, and a behavioral style that may be impulsive and careless (Andrews, 1982; Fowler & Fordyce, 1974).

Almost any injury to the brain produces memory problems. The right hemiplegic tends to have more memory difficulties associated with language, and the left hemiplegic tends to have more memory problems with spatial-perceptual information. Either may have more global memory deficits, evidenced by a reduced retention span, an inability to learn new tasks, and an inability to transfer learning from one setting to another (Fowler & Fordyce, 1974).

Emotional Reactions

Depression is a common consequence of stroke, but it is difficult to assess. It is difficult to distinguish between neurological damage that may result in depressive symptomatology and unhappiness at the change in life-style and body image. Depression at the outset of the stroke is more commonly related to neurological damage, especially in the right hemisphere, and has a poor prognosis (Andrews, 1982; Dam, Pedersen, & Ahlgren, 1989).

Depression after the first few months is more often correlated with a change in life-style, such as restricted social activity and the loss of independence, self-respect, and self-esteem. It has been reported that psychosocial factors predict depression even when the effects of the severity and site of the stroke are controlled (Thompson, Sobolew-Shubin, Graham, & Janigian, 1989). There is limited information about the prevalence of depression in stroke patients (Malec, Richardson, Sinaki, & O'Brien, 1990), but it is known that, when untreated, depression in such patients may be prolonged and severe. Poststroke depression may be accompanied by suicidal ideation, although reports of suicide in this population are rare (Garden, Garrison, & Jain, 1990). Risk factors for suicide include depression, severe insomnia, chronic illness, and organic brain syndrome. The reader is referred to Chapters 10 and 20 for further information on the symptomatology and treatment of depression and suicide.

A stroke may also release preexisting conflicts, drives, and fantasies that have been contained by social inhibitions. Adverse emotional reactions that have been cited include aggression, irritability, uncooperativeness, regressive behavior, and withdrawal (Andrews, 1982; Fowler & Fordyce, 1974).

Other emotional reactions associated with stroke include emotional lability, emotional incontinence, and catastrophic reactions. These reactions are likely to be related to the neurological damage associated with the stroke. Emotional lability causes the patient to show emotions easily in response to circumstances and to move quickly from happiness to sadness. Emotional incontinence is an outburst of weeping (or laughter) that is inappropriate to the circumstance and without provocation. A catastrophic reaction is an excessive form of anxiety in a patient who is confronted with a situation that is beyond his or her ability; the patient becomes excessively anxious, agitated, mute, and unable to respond. Patients may have insight into and be embarrassed and depressed by these incidents.

Management

Recovery from stroke depends on factors other than just the nature and extent of impairment. Although functional recovery of muscle power usually occurs within six months, it is unlikely if there is no improvement within one month (Andrews, 1982).

The focus of stroke management is on the patients who survive the immediate period of mortality. Many inpatient settings have stroke rehabilitation units that have a multidisciplinary focus on the comprehensive and concentrated rehabilitation of functional, sensory, and cognitive deficits. The theory is that with early and concentrated rehabilitation, functional ability can be maximized. The difficulty is to determine, at an early stage, which patients will benefit from such comprehensive inpatient rehabilitation because there is no certain way of predicting the potential for recovery in the early stages after a stroke (Shah, Vanclay, & Cooper, 1990). Factors that have been found to be predictive of successful rehabilitation include the extent of impairment, the patient's self-perception, the extent of family support, and the patient's age (Shah et al., 1990; Smith, 1990).

There continues to be some controversy in the literature regarding the effectiveness of stroke units. Some have found that stroke units had no impact on patients' functioning, while others have pointed to an increase in the percentage of patients who are discharged home (Akhtar & Garraway, 1982). Garraway, Akhtar, Prescott, and Hockey (1980) attempted to resolve the controversy via a randomized controlled trial that compared the management of elderly patients with acute stroke on a stroke unit and on medical units. The study concluded that the stroke unit improved the natural history of stroke during the acute phase of rehabilitation by increasing the proportion of patients who were returned to functional independence.

There is general agreement that stroke rehabilitation should begin early and be reassessed often. Day hospitals for geriatric patients who need continuing rehabilitation after discharge from a hospital have existed for approximately thirty years. Such facilities are often a valuable resource for stroke patients.

Another focus of stroke management is prevention—reducing the risk factors associated with stroke through public education. However, although the great majority of strokes occur among elderly people, most of the knowledge about associated risk factors relates to people under age 60. Thus, although it is clear that blood pressure is the dominant risk factor for stroke in younger people, there is no evidence that the control of high blood pressure in patients over age 60 confers any benefit. Data on the relationship between obesity and stroke are inconsistent and are related mainly to the young and middle aged. There seems to be no relationship between serum cholesterol and stroke in the middle aged and elderly. Likewise, cigarette smoking has not been shown to contribute to stroke in the elderly. The importance of all recognized risk factors probably declines with age, but the reasons for this decline are not clear. If this hypothesis is correct, there are fewer benefits to controlling risk factors in the old than in the young. These facts reinforce the need for public education that is targeted at the young and middle aged to improve their chance of health in old age (Andrews, 1982; Birket-Smith et al., 1989; Scheinberg, 1986).

PARKINSON'S DISEASE

Parkinson's disease is the second most common neurological disease in the elderly. It was named for James Parkinson, who first recorded the distinctive tremors or "shaking palsy" that are associated with the disease (Pearce, 1989). Parkinson's disease primarily affects older people; it is rare before age 40, and incidence rates increase until the sixth and seventh decade of life. Men and women are affected equally; the Parkinson's Foundation of Canada reports that currently, in Canada, there are about 70,000 people suffering from the disease.

Its cause is not known. Parkinson's disease is not inherited or contagious. It is related to a decrease in dopamine, a chemical produced in the substantia nigra area of the brain. A decrease in dopamine is a normal occurrence in aging. One hypothesis of causation is that this process accelerates in some individuals to produce Parkinson's disease (Langston, 1989). There are others who think the decrease in dopamine may be due to aging plus an environmental insult or toxin. However, neither hypothesis explains why some people get it and others do not. The cause of the decrease in dopamine continues to be the focus of recent research in Parkinson's disease (Langston, 1989).

In addition to the tremor, which occurs in the limbs even when at rest, other symptoms include muscle rigidity, bradykinesia (slowness of movement), akinesia (the inability to initiate movement), difficulty with fine motor movement, disorder of posture/balance, disturbance of gait, a mask-like face, loss of volume in speech, decreased bladder control, and constipation. Parkinson's disease is a progressive disorder, that is, the symptoms gradually worsen. Its onset is slow and subtle, and it is often misdiagnosed as arthritis or depression in its early stages (Calne, 1989; Langston, 1989; Pearce, 1989).

Emotional Reactions

Depression is a well-known feature of Parkinson's disease and has been reported in 40 percent of the patients (Celesia & Wanamaker, 1972). As with stroke patients, however, it is not known if the incidence of depression is related to the neurological changes caused by the disease or to the patients' reactions to the changes in their lives as a consequence of the disease. The biochemical changes (e.g., the decrease in dopamine) that cause the disease are also associated with depression. In addition, the clinical aspects of depression are sometimes difficult to distinguish from the symptoms of Parkinson's disease. Thus, mood change must be considered an important accompaniment of the disease, but it may be unrelated to the degree of disability. The presence of depression in Parkinson's disease continues to be of clinical and theoretical interest (Serby, 1980).

Another significant psychiatric disturbance associated with Parkinson's disease is dementia. For decades, however, reports of organic mental changes have been inconsistent, citing prevalence rates ranging from 20 to 40 percent (Celesia & Wanamaker, 1972; Reid et al., 1989; Serby, 1980).

Recently investigators have begun to examine the relationship between depression and dementia. For example, Starkstein, Bolduc, Mayberg, and Preziosi (1990) found that intellectual decline was severer and the progression of motor symptoms was faster for depressed than for nondepressed patients. These researchers suggested that the treatment of depression could forestall further cognitive decline.

Management

The diagnosis of Parkinson's disease may require hospitalization, but afterward management of the disease occurs primarily in the community. A multidisciplinary focus is necessary to ensure comprehensive management of the disease and its consequences.

Levodopa (or L-dopa) is the drug of choice for the treatment of Parkinson's disease. However, levodopa only alleviates the symptoms of the disease and does not halt its progress. Furthermore, chronic levodopa therapy may increase the incidence of vivid nightmares, visual hallucinations, and paranoid delusions, as well as acute confusional states. These are essentially toxic effects of the drug and are more likely with high-dose therapy.

In addition to medication, patients with Parkinson's disease are encouraged to remain as physically active as possible and to engage in therapeutic exercises to maximize their functional independence.

INTRACRANIAL TUMOR

Although intracranial tumors are uncommon compared with strokes or Parkinson's disease, they are important to review, albeit briefly, because their prognosis and management are difficult. The incidence of primary intracranial tumors increases with age to a peak at ages 60–70, whereas the incidence of metastatic intracranial tumors increases with age to a maximum at 50–80 years and has a poor prognosis. Nearly half the metastatic tumors versus one-quarter of the primary tumors occur over age 60 (Caird, 1982).

The effects of an intracranial tumor depend on its location in the brain, its size, and whether it is malignant. Medical management often includes neurosurgery, with all the related risks for the elderly, such as the reaction to anesthesia, and the sensory deprivation associated with intensive care units.

HEAD INJURY

In the elderly, head injury is a common event that causes more physical complications and has a higher mortality rate than in younger patients. Falls are the main cause of head injuries for older people, and about half are related to alcohol. Less common causes of head injuries for the elderly than for younger people are car accidents and assaults (Jennett, 1982).

In the elderly, the effects of brain damage may exacerbate preexisting, age-related cognitive decline. The consequences of a head injury may include hemiparesis, epilepsy, and dementia. Those who survive a severe head injury may suffer for the rest of their lives. It is usually the mental changes that prove the most disabling and that may interfere with or inhibit the potential for rehabilitation (Lambert, 1974).

The management of head injuries may include neurosurgery. Further management is based on the severity of the head injury and whether or not there will be permanent deficits. Such defects may resemble those of a stroke, and long-term management may be similar.

ALCOHOLIC NEUROLOGICAL DISORDERS

Alcohol is one of the most potent and common causes of psychiatric morbidity. In the elderly, although the incidence and prevalence is difficult to determine, alcohol consumption is known to contribute to three neurological disorders: Wernicke's encephalopathy, alcoholic dementia, and Korsakoff's syndrome (see Chapter 16).

Wernicke's encephalopathy is an acute organic reaction with transient ophthalmoplegia (paralysis of the eye muscles), ataxia (incoordination), peripheral neuropathy (wasting, weakness, numbness, tingling, and burning pain in extremities). Individuals will have difficulty climbing stairs, turning keys in locks, and doing buttons. The disorder is caused by thiamine deficiency, which is nearly always a consequence of prolonged heavy alcohol consumption. Fortunately, with prompt and adequate thiamine replacement, the condition is resolved completely within two months (Cutting, 1982; Exton-Smith, 1982).

Alcoholic dementia is a chronic reaction produced by the direct insidious effect of alcohol on cerebral function. Approximately 6 percent of dementias are thought to be of this type (Katzman & Terry, 1983). The major symptoms are a global deterioration of intellectual functioning, emotional lability, impaired judgment, the lack of drive, and a poor appreciation of social cues (Cutting, 1982). The cause is not straightforward and is related to the interrelation of age, sex, and certain aspects of a person's drinking pattern. Those who are more at risk are older, female, and drink regularly, rather than periodically. The surprising and encouraging feature of alcoholic dementia is its tendency to remit during abstinence. However, despite this improvement in symptoms, psychological functioning remains below what it would have been if the person had never drunk heavily (Cutting, 1982).

Korsakoff's syndrome is a chronic organic reaction in which disorders of memory predominate over other forms of mental impairment. Some researchers have reported a greater preservation of intelligence in persons with Korsakoff's syndrome than in those with alcoholic dementia, although this area is still considered to be controversial. Korsakoff's syndrome has an acute onset and is more common in men, and ophthalmoplegia can be detected at the outset. Unfortunately, the prognosis for this disorder is poor (Cutting, 1982).

Emotional Reactions

Heavy alcohol consumption increases the risk of affective disorders, specifically depression. In fact, an increase in alcohol consumption may be a coping response to feelings of depression. Other personality changes may include low vitality, emotional lability, denial or the minimization of behavior and disability, and a loss of social skills.

Management

An important component in the management of any of these conditions is the reduction in alcohol consumption. This is a difficult goal to achieve. The elderly do not fit easily into current alcohol treatment programs, which are usually geared to younger and middle-aged alcoholics. Several aspects of these programs are not appropriate for elderly participants (e.g., exercise programs, group therapy, and return-to-work programs). In fact, many programs restrict their services to younger people.

Any reduction in alcohol consumption should be done under medical supervision. Depending on the severity of the drinking problem, sudden withdrawal may result in delirium tremens, convulsions, psychoses, and acute confusional states.

HUNTINGTON'S DISEASE

Huntington's disease is not technically considered to be a neurological disease of the elderly. However, it is included in this chapter because, although the age of onset may be in the forties or fifties, the disease lasts from ten to thirty years. It is also such a devastatingly progressive disease, with significant implications for patients and their families, that social workers who work in a neurological or psychogeriatric setting should be familiar with it.

Huntington's disease is a genetic disorder, characterized by disordered movement, progressive intellectual impairment, and a spectrum of psychiatric and behavioral disturbances. It is an autosomal dominant inherited disease such that each child of an affected parent has a 50 percent risk of inheriting the gene and developing the illness.

The primary symptom is the movement disorder chorea, consisting of sudden, arrhythmic, involuntary movements that increase during stress and decrease during sleep. Associated abnormalities include speech and swallowing difficulties, emotional disturbance, and a slow, progressive decline in all functional and intellectual capacities (Shoulson & Behr, 1989).

Emotional Reactions

Depression is the most frequent affective disorder attending Huntington's disease and may constitute the most striking feature of the early clinical presentation. Delusional, hallucinatory states; suicidal ideation and behavior; mania; and schizophreniclike illness may also be observed in the early phases. (Depression and psychosis are observed in 40–50 percent of the patients.) Some cases are misdiagnosed as schizophrenia, particularly when there seems to be no family history of the disease (Shoulson & Behr, 1989).

Management

There is no clear management protocol for Huntington's disease. There is no cure, so treatment must focus on the symptoms of the disorder, as well as support and treatment for the family. The complexity and chronicity of the disease requires that a skilled clinician address the needs of the patient and family. It is recommended that a multidisciplinary team of care providers attend to the variety of issues presented, but that one clinician direct the therapeutic program to avoid the fractionation of care and misinterpretation. The prevalence of psychiatric symptoms will influence the clinical approach to the patient and family.

Presymptomatic detection is now available for family members who are "at risk." In 1983 a group of researchers identified a genetic marker located close to the gene responsible for Huntington's disease. This type of analysis can be used to inform at-risk persons of their gene status with 95 percent reliability. The reliability is dependent upon several factors, including a pedigree structure (present in one-third to one-half the at-risk individuals) that is suitable for presymptomatic testing. This information can aid people in planning their careers and finances and in deciding whether to marry and bear children. It can also have negative consequences, such as depression, guilt, marital and family stress, and suicide. Thus, such presymptomatic testing requires an ongoing process of care and support (Shoulson & Behr, 1989).

In addition, the use of the same genetic marker, in combination with amniocentesis or chorionic villi sampling, during early pregnancy may further clarify whether a fetus is at risk. This procedure is still experimental, however (Shoulson & Behr, 1989).

ISSUES FOR PATIENTS AND THEIR FAMILIES

The neurological disorders described in this chapter present great challenges to both patients and their families. The majority of these disorders produce chronic conditions that require permanent and significant changes in the life-styles of patients and their families. In the case of the elderly, these changes occur at a time when other losses also cluster, placing them in multiple jeopardy. Adult children of persons afflicted with a stroke, Parkinson's disease, Huntington's disease, or a tumor may find themselves torn between the demands of their nuclear families and the obligations to their elderly, disabled parents.

Specific issues associated with neurological disorders that may require significant adjustment for patients and families include

1. physical limitations-deterioration in the patient
2. emotional reactions of the patient and family
3. changes in family roles and relationships
4. sexuality
5. competence
6. institutionalization.

Physical Limitations-Deterioration in the Patient

Potentially, all the neurological conditions described in this chapter will result in a significant degree of physical disability. In some, deterioration occurs over a period of time, while in others, death comes sooner than may otherwise be expected.

Patients with Huntington's disease face total physical disability and death. Patients with a stroke may be partially paralyzed, unable to communicate, and be dependent on others for all or part of their activities of daily living. Patients with Parkinson's disease face deteriorating physical abilities that cause them to have extreme difficulty walking and feeding and dressing themselves. Patients with long-standing alcoholic neurological disorders may have problems of balance, mobility, and coordination. Those with intra-cranial tumors and head injuries may face problems similar to those of patients with strokes. Both the patient and family must make necessary adjustments to compensate for the loss of physical functioning. In many cases, patients are aware of these disabilities, which significantly lowers their self-esteem.

Emotional Reactions of the Patient and Family

Depression appears to be the most common emotional reaction of elderly patients who are suffering from neurological disorders and is often resistant to treatment. It may be that depression increases as dependence and help-lessness increase or that depression is a consequence of the neurological changes related to the disease. Depressive symptomatology may also be present in family members, in reaction to the many changes in the patient and their life-style as the result of the neurological disorder.

There is a significant body of literature on the stress or "burden" experienced by family caregivers, especially caregivers of dementia patients, and the subsequent impact of this stress on their mental health. It is not unreasonable to expect similar reactions from families of neurologically disabled persons who suffer from a coexisting dementia; in fact, there have been recent reports in the literature of increased depression in these family members (Dura, Haywood-Niller, & Kiecolt-Glaser, 1990; Shoulson & Behr, 1989). For family members, this decline in their elderly relative's cognitive functioning is often the most difficult change to experience. The essence of the person they knew and loved is lost, and a reciprocal relationship may no longer be possible. Families may feel ambivalent, angry, rejecting, and guilty as the previous harmony in the family is disrupted.

Denial is also a common emotional reaction in both the patient and the family. It is important to remember that it is frequently an appropriate coping mechanism, particularly in the initial stages of the illness, when the patient or family is not yet able to face the illness and its implications. Denial may serve a useful purpose and should not be aggressively challenged unless it interferes with treatment. It is important to remember that patients and their families have their own timetables for acceptance and adjustment.

Diseases such as Huntington's and Parkinson's may cause overpowering anxiety in both the patient and family as they contemplate the long, slow course of the disease. These patients may know of others with the same diagnosis whose condition is more advanced. Years ahead, families of Huntington's patients may be faced with dread as they contemplate contracting the disease while caring for an afflicted family member.

Changes in Family Roles and Relationships

The extent of the impact of an elderly relative's neurological disorder on other members of the family depends on the degree of adjustment required by the family system to accommodate the patient's needs. Often, new roles have to be assumed, and relationships are significantly altered as a result of the disease process. For patients with combined cognitive and physical deficits, a greater reallocation of family roles is required than for these who retain their cognitive faculties.

Rolland (1987) presented a unique conceptual framework from which to view the interface between the illness, the individual, and the family system. He suggested that it is helpful to consider several components of the illness (e.g., onset, course, and outcome) in conjunction with the stages of individual development and the family life cycle. The purpose is to gain an appreciation of the meshing of the various life tasks of the individual and family to be viewed in concert with the components of the illness.

Neurological disorders may be divided into those whose onset is acute, such as strokes and head injury, and those whose onset is gradual, such as Parkinson's and Huntington's diseases. Although the total amount of family adaptation may be about the same for both types of disorders, acute-onset disorders require the family to mobilize its crisis-management skills more rapidly than with gradual-onset disorders, which allow for a more protracted period of adjustment.

The course of the disorder may take different forms—progressive or constant. Patients and families who are faced with a progressive disorder are likely to have little relief from it and thus may frequently need to adapt and change roles. A constant-course disorder requires an adjustment during the initial phase of rehabilitation, but then the family is faced with a semipermanent change that is stable over time.

The most significant outcome to consider is the extent to which a neurological disorder is a likely cause of death. A terminal illness, such as Huntington's disease or a malignant tumor, presents issues related to separation, death, grief, bereavement, and the resumption of a "normal" family life after the loss.

This model allows for speculation about the importance of strengths and weaknesses in various components of individual and family functioning at various phases of different types of disorders or diseases.

Sexuality

Although sexuality is related to the roles and relationships within a family, it is presented here as a separate issue. Although it is an extremely important issue for many elderly neurological patients, it has received scant attention from health care professionals. This lack of professional interest may be related to the persistent myth that persons over age 65 are essentially asexual. Although the frequency of sexual intercourse may decrease with age, this should not be interpreted to mean that sexuality plays no role in the lives of the elderly. Research has consistently indicated that older patients welcome open and frank discussions of their sexual needs and concerns (Novak, 1988) (see Chapter 18).

Sexual problems of the elderly seem to be discussed primarily in the literature on stroke and Parkinson's disease. However, many of the issues probably can be generalized to other neurologically disabled elderly persons as well.

With regard to the issue of sexuality, it is important to distinguish between physiological sexual dysfunction and changes in patterns of sexuality and intimacy.

Physiological dysfunctions that are associated with neurological disorders include impotence in male stroke patients; reduced orgasmic function in female Parkinson's patients; reduced arousal in both stroke and Parkinson's patients; and erectile and ejaculatory-problems in Parkinson's patients, as well as hypersexuality, which results from levodopa treatments (Ballivet, Marin, & Gisselmann, 1973; Barrett, 1990; Brown, Jahanshahi, Quinn, & Marsden, 1990; Burgener & Logan, 1989). Data on the prevalance of sexual dsyfunction related to neurological disorders in the elderly are not readily available.

Factors that contribute to secondary sexual dysfunction may be more significant than physiological problems, however. Changes in sensation, mobility, speech, and appearance may affect psychological desire and self-image, as well as the enjoyment of sexual activity. The motor symptoms of Parkinson's disease or Huntington's disease may make sexual intercourse difficult. Fatigue may also play a role; a patient's illness may cause a couple to sleep in separate beds or rooms, which will decrease the opportunity for spontaneous sexual contact. Anxiety and depression in the patient or partner may affect libido and sexual performance. Strain on the "well" spouse may negatively affect desire. Difficulties may be exacerbated in couples who are unwilling to make adaptive changes to previous patterns of sexual behavior, either in timing or in the roles played by individual partners (Brown et al., 1990).

The resolution of these problems will depend partly on the couple's ability to discuss them. Such discussions may be difficult, if not impossible, however, if the patient's ability to communicate has been compromised by such disorders as Parkinson's disease or a stroke.

Competence

As a result of significant memory impairment and diminished judgment, an older person may no longer be able to process information to make "competent" decisions about legal, financial, or personal-care matters. Questioning a person's competence profoundly affects the person's sense of dignity and self-esteem, as well as the family's sense of responsibility and obligation. In addition to the emotional consequences of the label "mentally incompetent," the determination of mental incompetence usually requires both medical and legal consultation.

A medical assessment is often required to determine the extent of impairment and the ability to make decisions. If a patient is determined to be incompetent, a family often requires legal advice regarding the procedures necessary to make decisions on behalf of the patient. In Canada, these procedures differ from province to province, but usually involve some form of legal appointment of a "power of attorney" or "committee" of the estate or person to authorize a person to make "substitute decisions" on behalf of the patient. In some provinces, people can appoint their own substitute decision makers before their cognitive status deteriorates. This option could be exercised by persons with Huntington's or Parkinson's disease. However, as is true with wills, few people plan for such an eventuality in their lives. Thus, in the case of neurological disorders with an acute onset (e.g., stroke or head injury), families must obtain a legal appointment themselves or have an authorized governmental official, such as public trustee or an official guardian, appointed. This process is often fraught with emotional overtones because a family resents or distrusts a publicly appointed official yet may be unable to agree on which family member to appoint.

The determination of mental incompetence should not lead families or health care professionals to treat the patients as if they are small children. The increased dependence of old people has fostered the use of clichés, such as "role reversal" and "second childhood." These are inaccurate and demeaning descriptions, which should not be used just because the balance of giving help and protection has shifted between the parent and the adult child.

Institutionalization

The institutionalization of an elderly family member is an emotionally charged issue for the total family system. It is rarely a decision that families treat lightly. Decades of gerontological research have challenged the myth that families "abandon" their elderly relatives to institutions at the first hint of dependence and have found that the institutionalization of an elderly family member is a significant interactional event in the life of a family.

The decision to institutionalize is complex and is not based solely on the physical and cognitive status of the patient. However, when physical impairment and cognitive impairment coexist, eventual institutionalization is more likely.

Many family and community variables have been cited as contributing to the decision to institutionalize. The caregiver's age, sex, relationship to the patient, health, coping style, and duration of caregiving are important considerations, as are such social factors as other supports, services used, and satisfaction with social supports. The placement decision is complex and overshadowed by emotions, family values, and outside pressures. There is no simple way to predict the point at which institutionalization will occur. However, families should not be made to feel guilty because they have come to this decision.

SOCIAL WORK INTERVENTIONS

A variety of interventions have been developed by social workers and other health care professionals to confront individual and family issues that are associated with neurological disorders in the elderly. Here, the discussion is limited to interventions that are related to the issues presented in the previous section. For all the disorders presented, a multidisciplinary approach to care is recommended. Such an approach usually identifies social work as one of the key disciplines in recognition of the extensive emotional and social impact that neurological problems have on the patient and family. Family dynamics change as a result of physical, cognitive, and perceptual difficulties. Thus, although the family can promote rehabilitation, it can also have a negative influence if family members are uninformed or uninvolved.

It is suggested that one use the acronym APPEARS to ensure that all components of a comprehensive social work intervention have been addressed:

A: Assess the patient and family.
P: Provide information about the disorder.
P: Plan with the patient and family.
E: Explore feelings and concerns via counseling techniques.
A: Acknowledge the reality of the disorder.
R: Refer the patient and family to community services or institutional care.
S: Support social action.

Assess the Patient and Family

Although this component of intervention may be considered obvious, it bears emphasizing that a thorough assessment of the patient and family is essential before any plans for psychosocial treatment can be recommended or implemented. This is no less true for the elderly than it is for a younger population. Unfortunately, few models have been developed for working with families of elderly relatives. However, the work of those who view the development of families according to a series of life stages, as well as the work of family systems theorists, can provide useful frameworks from which to assess the family as an interactive and multigenerational entity.

McGoldrick and Carter (1980) have identified six developmental stages common to most families. These encompass the life cycle of the family from the unattached young adult to the family in later life. In assessment it is important to identify the meshing of the various family life tasks associated with these stages. This becomes more complicated as families age. It is often the blending of the later stages that we must be alerted to when working with the families of the neurologically impaired elderly.

In the fifth stage, the launching of the last child from the home sets the stage for family relationships in later years. The family moves from a two-generation household to a marital dyad. The major tasks include parent-child separation and reinvestment in the marital relationship.

The sixth stage continues the redevelopment of the marital relationship and involves new ways of communication between parent and adult child. Major tasks for the older individual include adjustments related to retirement, grandparenthood, widowhood, and declining physical abilities (McGoldrick & Carter, 1980).

In the assessment, it is helpful to review these stages with families to determine how the transitions were negotiated. Although most families adjust well, if these stages were not negotiated, a delayed impact may occur when a family is faced with the illness of a member that demands new adjustments or reorganization. For example, an unhappily married middle-aged couple may avoid dealing with the reality of their dissatisfaction with each other by shifting the blame for their misery to a disabled parent. Alternately, the illness of a parent may prevent a middle-aged child from successfully negotiating a stage; when this adult child is trying to reinvest in the marital relationship, he or she is faced with increased demands from and responsibilities for the parent.

The family systems work of Minuchin (1974) also offers valuable insights for the assessment of elderly families. Although Minuchin based most of his work on families with children, his view of the family as an interactive system is applicable to the aging family. The identification and assessment of family subsystems, boundaries, and transactional patterns give a comprehensive framework from which to assess and treat families with elderly members.

The assessment of subsystems highlights a number of potential issues for families who are coping with their elderly members' neurological disorders. Elderly parents remain the executive subsystem of the family and thus often continue to retain their authority even when their insight and judgment are significantly impaired. Adult children are frequently caught between the competing responsibilities of two subsystems—the executive subsystem in their nuclear family and the sibling subsystem in their family of origin.

The assessment of boundaries includes evaluating whether boundaries are rigid or flexible, clear or enmeshed. Such a perspective assesses a family's way of interacting, its connections with the external community, and its ability to solve problems by allowing a helping subsystem to enter theirs.

The assessment of transactional patterns looks at established patterns of how, when, and to whom the family members relate.

In times of stress, such as the need to deal with any form of impairment, family members often revert to their "old ways" of interacting, reactivating old loyalties, rivalries, hurts, and misconceptions. Historical questioning is a way to track key events and transitions to gain an understanding of the family system's organizational shifts and coping strategies in response to past stressors (Rolland, 1987). How families communicate information, feelings, and ideas and what content and affective responses are permitted and valued or avoided, consciously or unconsciously, are factors that should be considered during assessment.

The life stage of the family and the age and position of the member who is ill affect the degree to which the hopes and values of all members are threatened and alterations in life-styles are required. From a systems perspective, at the time of diagnosis, it is important to know the phase of the family life cycle and the stages of individual development of all family members, not just the ill one. A goal is for the family to deal with the developmental demands presented by the illness or disorder without the need for family members to sacrifice their own or the family's development as a system. Therefore, it is important to ask what life plans the family or individual members had to cancel, postpone, or alter as a result of the diagnosis (Rolland, 1987).

The assessment should also include concrete information that may be necessary for future planning, including information on living arrangements, religious affiliation, financial resources, and the social support networks of both the patient and the family.

Provide Information about the Disorder

The provision of comprehensive information about the neurological disorder to patients and their relatives is essential. Studies have shown that the majority of patients react positively to the frank disclosure of information (Johnson & Hart, 1984). The initial communication of the diagnosis and prognosis of the disorder is the purview of the physician. Social workers, particularly in a medical setting, may be present when this information is presented because they frequently continue to work with the individual and the family beyond the initial diagnosis. In this capacity, they often provide further information about the disorder and its consequences, particularly in more general, less medical terms. Hence, they need to have comprehensive knowledge about neurological disorders to work with this population of patients. However, social workers should be cautious about providing new information about the disease or its symptoms without discussing it with the patient's physician. They should also resist the temptation to present the initial diagnosis and prognosis to the family when a physician is unable or unwilling to do so. They must remain clear that their role is to address the interface of illness, individual development, family life cycle, and community support, not to function as pseudophysicians.

Social workers should regularly elicit feedback from the patients and their families to ensure that they understand the information they have received. Often, repeated discussions about the disorder and its probable course and outcome are necessary before all family members can internalize the information and proceed to make appropriate plans for the future.

Advocacy and self-help groups exist for most of the neurological disorders. A stated goal of most of these organizations is to disseminate up-to-date information about a particular disorder in "lay terms" in the form of booklets or regular newsletters. Social workers should contact the local chapters of these organizations and obtain a supply of their brochures or newsletters to give to patients and their families. They should also encourage families to join such organizations, which are a valuable source of support as well as information.

Plan with the Patient and Family

Again, at the risk of stating the obvious, it must be emphasized that all planning must be done *with both the patient and the family*, who must receive detailed information about the disorder and its prognosis to make realistic plans for the future. Health care professionals often have to be reminded of this fact, especially in work with the elderly. They sometimes present information and discuss plans with adult children separate from the elderly patient. The worst-case scenario is to discuss such information and plans with the adult children and not with the elderly patient. The rationale for such practice is usually the patient's cognitive impairment. An unconscious or unstated rationale may be that health care professionals identify with and feel more comfortable with the adult children than with the elderly patient. Discussions with elderly persons who have some physical or cognitive deficits require health care professionals to be patient and self-aware. However, it is important to remember that even in the face of cognitive impairment, patients may be able to participate, albeit in a limited fashion, in discussions regarding their future. The rule of thumb should be to include patients in all discussions unless they clearly demonstrate their inability to appreciate and comprehend the discussions because of their advanced cognitive impairment.

Explore Feelings and Concerns via Counseling Techniques

As was previously stated, few models have been developed for working with families with elderly members. This limitation has been compounded by the frequently single-minded focus on increasing a family's ability to continue to support its elderly relative in the community with concrete supports (e.g., home care, homemaking, and transportation). Although this is a worthwhile and necessary intervention, its narrow focus may cause social workers to avoid dealing with the emotional consequences of neurological disorders. Clinical experience has taught us that while many families are able to provide for the concrete needs of their elderly relatives, they may be unable to resolve the affective problems associated with coping with the aftermath of neurological disorders. Research has also confirmed the significance of the stress associated with the caregiving role (Evans, Matlock, Bishop, Stranahan, & Pederson, 1988; Evans, Noonan, Bishop, & Hendricks, 1989; Lambert, 1974; Shoulson & Behr, 1989). Thus, there seems to be some support for a variety of treatment options for these families.

In determining the need for counseling interventions with elderly families, it is important to keep in mind that, for the most part, social workers work with healthy adaptive families who are able to respond when faced with a crisis. Unlike many other disorders presented in this book, the presence of a neurological disorder in an elderly family member is not related to earlier or long-standing family dysfunction. Crisis intervention techniques and supportive psychotherapy will be useful for these families. If the family is assessed as having relatively open and flexible emotional systems, its members will probably be able to process information and use community resources and offers of emotional support when needed.

A major therapeutic intervention for both patients and families of elderly people with neurological disorders is the peer support group. Such groups have been established for most of the neurological disorders. The format is usually a closed group with a consistent membership of eight to twelve persons (either both patients and family members or one group or the other) who meet regularly for eight to ten sessions. Such groups disseminate information about the disorder and about resources, discuss coping strategies, and provide the type of support that comes from others who are in a similar situation. It is believed that peers may be more effective than professionals in helping each other in these areas. However, professional skills are essential in planning and convening groups, in providing structure and direction when needed, in facilitating communication, and in resolving conflict or alleviating disruption when it occurs (Johnson & Hart, 1984).

In the case of Huntington's disease, genetic counseling should be considered. Shoulson and Behr (1989) recommended that the following should be emphasized in genetic counseling for this disease:

1. The mode of inheritance and the risk of occurrence must be presented clearly and carefully.
2. Mature "at-risk" individuals need to be informed of the possibility that their children could be "at risk" for HD.
3. The distinction between marriage and parenthood should be addressed. There should be discussion about childbearing alternatives (e.g.: adoption; artificial insemination by donor, etc.).
4. Indicate that the "at risk" status may be a lifelong dilemma, although "risk" diminishes by the sixth of seventh decade.
5. Information about potential presymptomatic and prenatal testing should be provided.
6. Provide information about DNA banking options for older and affected individuals.
7. Discuss the importance of postmortem studies of the brain (p. 24).

These issues should be presented and discussed by a trained genetic counselor over several sessions. Genetic counseling for Huntington's disease should be based on the needs and concerns of the individual and family members.

If a couple is experiencing sexual difficulties as a result of a neurological disorder, sex therapy may be indicated. As with any form of counseling, one must be careful not to exclude this population because of advanced age. Modern methods of sex therapy are multifaceted and are adapted to fit the demands of individual couples. Physical illness and disability are just extra factors in the overall picture that can be taken into account when planning a program of sex therapy. Patients with neurological diseases and their partners stand just as much chance of obtaining benefits from such therapy as does any other couple (Brown et al., 1990).

The assessment may also indicate the need for family therapy. Such feelings as anger, frustration, and guilt may reach pathological proportions and have to be addressed within the context of the family. Likewise, conflicts over the decision to declare the elderly member incompetent or to institutionalize him or her may trigger dysfunctional family interactions. The following therapeutic techniques are recommended when working with these families:

1. Include all family members, whenever possible.
2. Respect the hierarchy of relationships in the family, but be aware of the probable shift in power that has taken place between the elderly parent and the adult children.
3. Clarify the boundaries of the nuclear family and the family of origin for each adult child.
4. Do not attempt to resolve all past issues within the family. Keep the purpose of the sessions focused and directed.
5. Increase the strength of the sibling subsystem as a decision-making and responsibility-taking system, in the absence of a "well" spouse and when the neurologically impaired elder is too cognitively impaired to participate.

Acknowledge the Reality of the Disorder

This intervention is more broad than is the provision of information. It is the acknowledgment by the health care professional of the realistic reactions to neurological disorders. Families and individuals have to be reassured that their feelings of anger, guilt, embarrassment, resentment, and frustration are normal reactions to an abnormal situation.

The use of euphemistic language only reinforces the initial denial that may be present and may prevent the individual and family from appreciating the full significance of the disorder. Overoptimism is often interpreted to mean that the disorder is too terrible to consider. Honesty should be the sine qua non of a helping relationship (Johnson & Hart, 1984).

Refer the Patient and Family to Community Services or Institutional Care

Although society places a high premium on self-reliance and productivity, sooner or later, patients and families who are coping with a neurological disorder will have to receive community services or even face the prospect of institutionalization. The social work function of linking consumers with community resources is essential. To be effective, social workers must become knowledgeable about such resources and assist with referral and access, when necessary.

Referral for institutionalization will usually involve social work intervention. Medical social workers in hospitals have been providing this service within the context of discharge planning since the beginning of hospital social work in 1910. Discharge planning should be seen as an integral part of the process of assessing and treating the patient and family. Both the needs of the patient and family and the availability of resources should determine the recommendations for discharge planning. It is hoped that most social workers will view this service from a clinical perspective, rather than from a purely instrumental one.

Because of the pressure to promote the optimal utilization of hospital beds, social workers may find themselves in a position of encouraging families to take home their impaired relatives to be cared for with the help of community resources, rather than to "resort" to institutionalization. Unfortunately, in many communities, community supports are not yet at a level to be a viable alternative to long-term care in an institution. Thus, one may continue to burden an already depleted family, and such a plan should be considered with caution. To convince relatives who are unable to cope to take home a severely incapacitated patient is not only dishonorable but lacks foresight. If a patient has to be readmitted, a second discharge will be more difficult because the relatives, feeling let down, will distrust the hospital and be reluctant to let the patient return home again.

Frequently, social workers will have to be advocates for patients and families to ensure their access to the health care or social service systems. These systems continue to be complex and bureaucratic. Families or patients with depleted emotional or physical resources may find it difficult to overcome, on their own, the obstacles to obtaining services.

Support Social Action

Because no amount of counseling or therapy can prevent some of the serious casualties of the system, social workers should, as part of their practice, be skilled in social action or advocacy skills for elderly persons in general or neurologically disabled elderly persons in particular (Johnson & Hart, 1984). Our human service systems continue to be ill equipped to deal with the consequences of the rapidly aging population, their illnesses and disabilities. Social workers are in a unique position to offer advocacy consultation to families or groups. The combination of clinical expertise and knowledge of the systems should enhance this advocacy role.

Although advocacy groups are skilled at gaining power by putting pressure on governmental officials and the elderly themselves have become more politically active and astute, many families still feel reluctant to confront the system. The role of social work should be to encourage or facilitate the empowerment of such groups or individuals. Munro (1991) presented a teaching model for effective advocacy by families of people with severe disabilities.

CONCLUSION

This chapter has reviewed some of the more common neurological disorders in the elderly, the issues these disorders present for patients and families, and the social work interventions that are appropriate for this client group. No section is considered to be exhaustive; there are other disorders, issues, and interventions that could have been discussed had space permitted. It is hoped that the most significant ones have been put forward.

Social work with neurologically disabled elderly people can contribute to a rewarding and challenging career. There continues to be more to learn, to research, and to teach to replace myth with fact, fear with knowledge, and confusion with understanding (Novak, 1988). Social work with this population continues to be a clinical frontier.

REFERENCES

Akhtar, A. J., & Garraway, W. M. (1982). Management of the elderly patient with stroke. In F. I. Caird (Ed.), *Neurological disorders in the elderly* (pp. 99–114). London: Wright PSG.

Andrews, K. (1982). Clinical features of stroke. In F. I. Caird (Ed.), *Neurological disorders in the elderly* (pp. 85–98). London: Wright PSG.

Ballivet, J., Marin, A., & Gisselmann, A. (1973). Aspects of hypersexuality observed in Parkinsonian patients treated with L-dopa. *Annals of Medical Psychology, 2,* 512–522.

Barrett, M. (1990, January–February). Sexuality and stroke recovery—Who cares? *Phoenix* (newsletter of the Stroke Recovery Association), p. 1.

Benson, D. F., & Blumer, D. (1982). *Psychiatric aspects of neurologic disease* (Vol. 2). New York: Grune & Stratton.

Birket-Smith, M., Knudsen, H. C., Nissen, J., Belgvad, N., Kohler, O., Ramussen, D., & Worm-Petersen, S. (1989). Life events and social support in prediction of stroke outcome. *Psychotherapy and Psychosomatics, 54* (1–3), 146–150.

Bonita, R., Stewart, A., & Beaglehole, R. (1990). International trends in stroke mortality: 1970–1985. *Stroke, 21,* 989–992.

Brown, R. G., Jahanshahi, M., Quinn, N., & Marsden, C. D. (1990). Sexual function in patients with Parkinson's disease and their partners. *Journal of Neurology, Neurosurgery and Psychiatry, 53,* 480–486.

Burgener, S., & Logan, G. (1989). Sexuality concerns of the post-stroke patient. *Rehabilitation Nursing, 14,* 178–181.

Caird, F. I. (Ed.). (1982). *Neurological disorders in the elderly.* London: Wright PSG.

Calne, D. B. (1989). Is Parkinson's "disease" one disease? *Journal of Neurology, Neurosurgery and Psychiatry* (Special Suppl.), 18–21.

Celesia, G. G., & Wanamaker, W. M. (1972). Psychiatric disturbances in Parkinson's disease. *Diseases of the Nervous System, 33,* 577–583.

Cutting J. (1982). Alcoholic dementia. In D. F. Benson & D. Blumer (Eds.), *Psychiatric aspects of neurologic disease* (Vol. 2, pp. 149–165). New York: Grune & Stratton.

Dam, H., Pedersen, H. E., & Ahlgren, P. (1989). Depression among patients with stroke. *Acta Psychiatrica Scandinavica, 80,* 118–124.

Dura, J. R., Haywood-Niller, E., & Kiecolt-Glaser, J. K. (1990). Spousal caregivers of persons with Alzheimer's and Parkinson's disease dementia: A preliminary comparison. *The Gerontologist, 30,* 332–336.

Evans, R. L., Matlock, A. L., Bishop, D. S., Stranahan, S., & Pederson, C. (1988). Family intervention after stroke: Does counselling or education help? *Stroke, 19,* 1243–1249.

Evans, R. L., Noonan, W. C., Bishop, D. S., & Hendricks, R. D. (1989). Caregiver assessment of personal adjustment after stroke in a Veterans Administration Medical Centre Outpatient Cohort. *Stroke, 20,* 483–487.

Exton-Smith, A. N. (1982). Disorders of the autonomic nervous system. In F. I. Caird (Ed.), *Neurological disorders in the elderly* (pp. 182–201). London: Wright PSG.

Fowler, R. S., & Fordyce, W. E. (1974). *Stroke: Why do they behave that way?* Dallas: American Heart Association.

Garden, F. H., Garrison, S. J., & Jain, A. (1990). Assessing suicide risk in stroke patients: A review of two patients. *Archives of Physical Medicine and Rehabilitation, 71,* 1003–1005.

Garraway, W. M., Akhtar, A. J., Prescott, R. J., & Hockey, L. (1980). Management of acute stroke in the elderly: Preliminary results of a controlled trial. *British Medical Journal, 280* (April), 1040–1043.

Jennett, B. (1982), Head injuries in the elderly. In F. I. Caird (Ed.), *Neurological disorders in the elderly* (pp. 202–211). London: Wright PSG.

Johnson, H. C., & Hart, E. J. (1984). Neurological disorders. In F. J. Turner (Ed.), *Adult psychopathology: A social work perspective* (pp. 73–118). New York: Free Press.

Katzman, R., & Terry, R. (1983). *The neurology of aging*. Philadelphia: F. A. Davis.

Lambert, G. (1974). Patients with progressive neurological diseases. *Social Casework, 55*, 154–159.

Langston, J. W. (1989). Current theories on the cause of Parkinson's disease. *Journal of Neurology, Neurosurgery and Psychiatry* (Special Suppl.), 13–17.

Malec, J. F., Richardson, J. W., Sinaki, M., & O'Brien, M. W. (1990). Types of affective response to stroke. *Archives of Physical Medicine and Rehabilitation, 71*, 279–284.

McGoldrick, M., & Carter, B. (1980). *The Family life cycle*. New York: Gardiner Press.

Minuchin, S. (1974). *Families and family therapy*. Cambridge, MA: Harvard University Press.

Munro, J. D. (1991). Training families in the "Step Approach Model" for effective advocacy. *Canada's Mental Health, 39* (1), 1–6.

Novak, M. (1988). *Aging and society: A Canadian perspective*. Toronto: Nelson Canada.

Pearce, J. M. S. (1989). Aspects of the history of Parkinson's disease. *Journal of Neurology, Neurosurgery and Psychiatry* (Special Suppl.), 6–10.

Reid, W. G., Broe, G. A., Hely, M. A., Morris, J. G., Williamson, P. M., O'Sullivan, D. J., Rail, D., Genge, S., & Moss, N. G. (1989). The neuropsychology of de novo patients with idiopathic Parkinson's disease: The effects of age of onset. *International Journal of Neuroscience, 48*, 205–217.

Rolland, J. S. (1987). Chronic illness and the life cycle: A conceptual framework. *Family Process, 26*, 203–221.

Scheinberg, P. (1986). *An introduction to diagnosis and management of common neurologic disorders* (3rd ed.). New York: Raven Press.

Serby, M. (1980). Psychiatric issues in Parkinson's disease. *Comprehensive Psychiatry, 21*, 317–322.

Shah, S., Vanclay, F., & Cooper, B. (1990). Efficiency, effectiveness and duration of stroke rehabilitation. *Stroke, 21*, 241–246.

Shoulson, I., & Behr, J. (1989). *Care of the patient and family with Huntington's disease: A guide for clinicians*. Cambridge, Ontario: Huntington Society of Canada.

Smith, D. S. (1990). Outcome studies in stroke rehabilitation: The South Australian Stroke Study. *Stroke, 21*, 1156–1158.

Starkstein, S. E., Bolduc, P. L., Mayberg, H. S., & Preziosi. (1990). Cognitive impairment and depression in Parkinson's disease: A follow-up study. *Journal of Neurology, Neurosurgery and Psychiatry, 53*, 597–602.

Thompson, S. C., Sobolew-Shubin, A., Graham, M. A., & Janigian, A. S. (1989). Psychosocial adjustment following a stroke. *Social Science Medicine, 28*, 239–247.

4

Alzheimer's Disease:
The Family Affliction
Daniel C. Andreae

Alzheimer's disease is a progressive neurological illness for which there is no known cause or cure. The disease is characterized by the loss of memory and changes in mood and behavior. Ten years ago it was rare if persons knew or talked openly about this fatal affliction. However, because of the extensive coverage of this illness in recent years through books, films, documentaries, and television specials; increased public awareness and education; the work of Alzheimer Societies; and the escalating number of cases and more accurate medical diagnoses, most individuals have by now personally experienced the trauma of Alzheimer's disease either through caring for a victim or knowing someone who has.

It is estimated that Alzheimer's disease is the fourth leading cause of death after heart disease, cancer, and stroke. It affects primarily those over age 65, but can strike as young as age 40. The chance of succumbing to Alzheimer's disease increases with age (Alzheimer Society of Canada, 1987). Considerably less than 1 percent of the population is cognitively impaired by age 65, but this proportion increases to 5 percent of the population over age 65 and escalates to approximately 20 percent or more by age 85.

The course of the disease can last anywhere from two to twenty years, with an average of ten years beyond the diagnosis. It is not a contagious illness, nor is it the result of excessive strain or emotional stress. No one is immune from this insidious killer. It strikes both men and women, although women are 1½ times more likely to develop it, primarily because they outlive men by seven to twelve years. Alzheimer's disease transcends all income and educational levels, professional groups, and ethnic and racial groups

53

and is uniquely a disease of the human species. As our populations continue to age, increasing numbers will fall prey to it.

Alzheimer's disease is perhaps the most pernicious disease of modern times in that, unlike any other illness however hideous, every family member is scarred by its devastating impact. The biopsychosocial life of the family or support network is dramatically altered and thrown into continuous disarray. The title of Mace and Rabins' (1984) book for caregivers, *The 36-Hour Day*, aptly encapsulates the seemingly endless nightmare of the caregiving experience.

The continued projected increase in the number of cases of Alzheimer's disease makes it imperative that social workers, whether clinicians, community developers, administrators, or policy analysts, become familiar with all aspects of the disease, its etiology, epidemiology, symptomatology, progressive stages of deterioration; its emotional impact on the patient and family; and case management and techniques of intervention on the clinical, community, and policy levels.

Social workers are actively involved in counseling Alzheimer's patients and their families; providing case management; leading support groups in institutional and community settings; referring patients and families to appropriate community resources and allied professionals; and developing policies in hospitals, nursing homes, homes for the aged, and governmental agencies to ensure high-quality care. However, they will be increasingly called upon to assume a leadership role in the battle against this baffling condition because they have a unique professional knowledge base and set of skills that blend the clinical and social-environmental perspectives.

EPIDEMIOLOGY

In 1906, German physician Alois Alzheimer first defined Alzheimer's disease clinically and neuropathologically in a 51-year-old female patient. In his description of the case he remarked upon the patient's aphasia, amnesia, apraxia, paranoid delusions, and relative preservation of motor function, and at the autopsy he demonstrated that she suffered from a "unique illness, involving the cerebral cortex," characterized by neurofibrillary tangles and miliary foci (Miner, Winters-Miner, Blass, Richter, & Valentine, 1989, p. 57). Because the patient was younger than age 65, he referred to her condition as presenile dementia, but it is now known that Alzheimer dementia, whether presenile (under age 65) or senile, is the same condition and is commonly referred to as senile dementia of the Alzheimer type, usually abbreviated to SDAT or DAT.

Certainly, Alzheimer's disease existed long before Alzheimer first identified the symptoms. The medical literature had referred to other dementias, and Esquinol outlined a condition similar to Alzheimer's disease in a French textbook on psychiatry in 1838 in which he referred to *demence senile* as an illness that is characterized by a weakening of the memory for recent experiences, drive, and willpower. Esquinol stated that the condition appears gradually and may be accompanied by emotional disturbances (Reisberg, 1986, p. 4).

In the past, Alzheimer's disease was commonly referred to as senility, or hardening of the arteries. Often when an elderly person or relative began to act strangely, he or she was labeled senile, crazy, or demented. This unfortunate individual was probably suffering from a dementia, of which Alzheimer's disease is the most prevalent nonreversible type, accounting for approximately two-thirds of all dementias. Alzheimer's disease and multiinfarct dementia account for up to 90 percent of all organic brain disorders. The remaining approximately 10 percent of dementias are the result of infections; metabolic and nutritional disorders; cardiovascular and pulmonary disease; high blood pressure; brain tumor; abnormal thyroid function; medication; pernicious anemia; abnormalities in the spinal fluid, which is a form of hydrocephalus; and isolation and sensory deprivation. Some individuals with Parkinson's disease develop dementia in the late stages of the illness. Over sixty conditions mimic the symptoms of Alzheimer's disease, and up to 30 percent of all individuals with symptoms of dementia have a condition that can be treated and most likely reversed. Potentially treatable causes of dementia include the following:

1. Drugs and alcohol; beta-blockers, methyldopa, clonidine, haloperidol, chlorpromazine, phenytoin, bromides, phenobarbital, cimetidine, steroids, procainamide, disopyramide, atropine
2. Tumors
   a. Direct CNS invasion
   b. Remote effect: mostly lung, but occasionally ovary, prostate, rectum, or breast
3. Nutritional disorders
   a. B_{12} deficiency (dementia may precede anemia)
   b. Folate, pellagra, Wernicke-Korsakoff's syndrome
4. Infection: syphilis, abscess, encephalitis
5. Metabolic disorders: electrolytes, hepatic, renal, pulmonary
6. Inflammatory disorders: systemic lupus erythematosis
7. Endocrine disorders: thyroid (hypo- or hyper-), adrenal, parathyroid
8. Trauma: subdural hematoma

9. Psychiatric/neurological disorders
   a. Schizophrenia
   b. Seizures
   c. Normal-pressure hydrocephalus (dementia, ataxia, incontinence)
   d. Depression (Miner et al., 1989, p. 61).

The word *dementia* is derived from two Latin words meaning away and the mind and refers to a group of symptoms, not to the name of the disease that causes the symptoms. DSM-III-R presents the most widely utilized criteria for dementia. These criteria are that the patient must be socially or occupationally disabled by intellectual losses, exhibit memory impairment, have at least one neuropsychological deficit (loss of abstracting abilities, impaired judgment, aphasia, apraxia, agnosia, constructional disturbances, or personality change), and have no delirium. In addition, there must be either physical or laboratory evidence of a cause of the syndrome or evidence to warrant the conclusion that the disorder is an idiopathic condition. DSM-III-R emphasizes the etiologically nonspecific nature of the dementia syndrome and the need for a careful evaluation to determine its cause. The DSM-III-R criteria for primary degenerative dementia include the diagnosis of DAT, as well as of other less common related disorders, such as Pick's disease, which is similar to Alzheimer's disease and difficult to diagnose clinically, and Creutzfeld-Jakob disease, which is caused by an infectious agent and progresses rapidly. The patient must meet the critera for dementia, the disorder must have an insidious onset and progressive course, and other causes of dementia must have been eliminated.

Alzheimer's disease is not an inevitable part of the aging process, but a distinct disease entity. Everyone knows of elderly people whose intellectual functioning remains vibrant and alert well into their eighties and nineties and who are never debilitated by serious cognitive impairment. It is estimated that 5 percent of elderly individuals suffer from a severe cognitive impairment, but that 80 percent never suffer a marked deterioration in cognitive abilities. Indeed, some degree of memory loss is normal and inevitable during the aging process and is in no way attributable to Alzheimer's disease. Everyone at some point has experienced lapses in memory because of anxiety, depression, disease, or another underlying cause and has questioned whether he or she has Alzheimer's disease.

POSSIBLE CAUSES: RESEARCH

Why do some people develop Alzheimer's disease, while others with similar genetic makeups and social histories do not? An adult's chance of succumbing to Alzheimer's disease is approximately one or two in a hundred after age 65, but the odds increase by a factor of four if a close relative has the disease. This factor, combined with evidence that the disease may be linked to other diseases such as Down's syndrome or mongolism, which are known to be caused by a defect in Chromosome 21, and the fact that Down's syndrome patients over age 40 invariably develop Alzheimer's disease, indicates that there is a genetic predisposition in at least some of the cases (Mace & Rabins, 1984; Kociol & Schiff, 1989). It has been estimated that familial Alzheimer's disease accounts for approximately 10 percent of all cases, which makes genetics an important but not exclusive factor. Other possible causes that are currently under investigation include biochemical imbalances in the brain, such as a shortage of the enzyme acetyltransferase, which is necessary to produce the vital neurotransmitter acetylcholine; the possibility of a slow virus that may lie dormant for many years only to express itself later in life, although no evidence has yet been found to validate this etiology; and the high concentration of certain proteins in, and the decreased blood and oxygen supply to, the brains of Alzheimer's patients.

Aluminum in acidic drinking water may also be a contributor to the development of Alzheimer's disease. Epidemiological studies conducted in Norway and Britain indicate that the risk of developing the disease in areas in which water contains high levels of aluminum is 1.8 times greater than it is in geographic regions with low levels of aluminum in the drinking water (Kociol & Schiff, 1989). Researchers continue to debate whether an elevated level of aluminum in the brains of Alzheimer's patients is a cause or an effect of the disease and whether aluminum pots and pans and products containing high levels of aluminum, such as deodorants and lipstick, should be discarded.

Interesting studies have determined other possible risk factors for the onset of Alzheimer's disease, including a previous head injury, which increases the risk factor by three times, and the possibility of thyroid gland dysfunction, which raises the risk by 1.5 times over those who do not manifest signs of thyroid gland disease. Thus an understanding of the effect of thyroid gland disease upon brain function may prove extremely important in determining the causes of Alzheimer's disease (Kociol & Schiff, 1989). Ultimately it is likely that a series of cofactors, rather than a single factor, will be shown to cause the disease. The challenge is to identify these various factors and to determine how they interrelate with and affect each other. Canada is among the world's leaders in research on Alzheimer's disease, and several excellent research centers have been established across the country, including the Centre for Research in Neurodegenerative Diseases at the University of Toronto.

DIAGNOSIS

No definitive tests are available to determine whether a person has Alzheimer's disease, although a physician can make a highly accurate diagnosis, based on the exclusion of other possible diseases or dementias, after conducting extensive tests. Alzheimer's disease can be verified only at the time of autopsy through a biopsy of brain tissue from which the neuropathologist looks for the telltale signs of neurofibrillary tangles and senile plaques. A postmortem diagnosis is not simple to make because these neurological changes also occur to some extent in the brains of normal patients, so the pathologist must be certain to locate affected tissue from the frontal and temporal lobes of the brain that are most ravaged by this affliction. In Europe a brain biopsy is occasionally performed on living patients, who are administered a local anesthetic while a small piece of brain is removed for the examination of pathological trademarks under the microscope. Since a brain biopsy involves some risk of infection or hemorrhage, as does any surgical procedure, it is performed only when a clinical diagnosis of Alzheimer's disease is indicated. This procedure is never performed in Canada exclusively to validate a diagnosis of Alzheimer's disease, but a biopsy may be done when another medical condition, such as a brain tumor or abscess, is indicated.

Therefore, it is essential that a person who is suspected of having Alzheimer's disease undergo a thorough examination, including physical, neurological, psychiatric, and psychogeriatric evaluations, under the supervision of a physician. The complete evaluation of a patient who is suspected of having Alzheimer's disease should indicate

1. the exact nature of the person's illness
2. whether or not the condition can be reversed or treated
3. the nature and extent of the disability
4. the areas in which the person can still function successfully
5. whether the person has other health problems that require treatment and that might be making the cognitive problems worse

6. the social and psychological needs and resources of the ill person and the family or caregiver

7. changes one can expect over time (Mace & Rabins, 1984).

Although each physician or hospital will utilize different procedures for diagnosis, a good evaluation will include a medical or neurological examination, an assessment of the person's support network, and an evaluation of his or her remaining abilities. The physical examination should include a complete medical history; blood tests, including tests for detecting metabolic disorders; X rays and electrocardiograms; and other tests for problems that result in the symptoms of Alzheimer's disease, such as special studies of the spinal fluid system.

Neurological testing would include an electroencephalogram, computerized axial tomography, magnetic resonance imagery, and other neurological tests to determine reflexes, motion, and sensory functions. Psychiatric testing to assess a patient's mental condition may include an in-depth clinical interview and tests to determine the person's memory for numbers or misplaced items and general emotional well-being.

Once this battery of tests has been completed, the physician will need some time to evaluate and determine the results. The physician will then be in a position to state that he or she strongly suspects Alzheimer's disease, but will undoubtedly request that the patient return in approximately six months and on a continuing basis to gauge whether and how much further cognitive deterioration has occurred. At that time the physician will be in a better position to confirm the original diagnosis or decide which additional tests are required to determine the cause of the symptoms.

It is difficult enough for families to cope with the shock of learning the diagnosis and so the question arises as to whether, and what, to tell the Alzheimer's patient if the physician has not already informed him or her. There is no correct answer to this question, and the merits of both disclosing and withholding the diagnosis from a patient can be contested. There may be an advantage to informing the patient if he or she is in the earliest stages because the patient still has time to participate in planning the rest of his or her life. It also discourages the formation of a barrier to communication between the family and patient and provides the patient with an explanation for his or her condition and the fact that he or she is not "crazy." Some patients prefer to know and are reassured by the labeling of a specific medical diagnosis. The key is to take the lead from the Alzheimer's patient and to base the decision to tell or not to tell on the patient's personality and behavior in previous circumstances, as well as on the types of questions that the patient has asked. Different approaches are appropriate for different patients.

TREATMENTS

Although the progression of Alzheimer's disease is irreversible, there are limited treatments, including drugs, that can alleviate the symptoms in the absence of an effective cure. However, there are always risks and unpleasant side effects with drugs, some of which may result in further cognitive impairment.

Tranquilizers can help to control outbursts, but the prolonged use of major tranquilizers may cause serious and chronic effects. For example, tardive dyskinesia, a syndrome resulting from the prolonged use of antipsychotic drugs, results in involuntary rapid uncontrolled jerky movements and lip smacking. Haloperidol (Haldol) is an antipsychotic medication that appears to have an effect in managing such symptoms as depression, agitation, anxiety, and sleep disturbances; however, the fact that it is a sedative and anticholinergic means that it can increase memory loss (Powell & Courtice, 1983). Indeed, several medications that are commonly prescribed for heart disease, hypertension, diabetes, or anxiety may also exacerbate cognitive impairment.

It has been estimated that persons aged 65 and older who are living in the community are taking an average of five medications per day and that those in nursing homes are consuming more than ten drug mixtures (Cohen & Eisdorfer, 1989). This mixture of drugs may be dangerous because many drugs interact with each other to cause a wide variety of physical problems in addition to agitation, sedation, drowsiness, or memory loss. The result of multimedication may be symptoms that mimic Alzheimer's disease, but once the patient is taken off the drugs or has the dosages decreased, the symptoms subside or disappear. This is not to indicate that drugs do not have a positive purpose and effect, but it is important for the physician, caregiver, and patient, when appropriate, to weigh the potential benefits of particular drugs against their possible adverse side effects.

In addition to drugs, exercise may help to reduce a patient's restlessness and anxiety. The Alzheimer's patient may engage in such activities as walking, dancing, or basic calisthenics. Also, a well-balanced nutritious diet can increase the patients's resistance to disease and alleviate digestive problems, such as diarrhea and constipation, as well as dehydration, malnutrition, anemia, or vitamin and mineral deficiencies.

STAGES OF DETERIORATION

Each Alzheimer's patient progresses through a series of stages of deterioration; however, the duration and intensity of each of the three major stages is idiosyncratic to the patient. Some individuals decline rapidly in the initial phases, but then reach a plateau for a while, and even show occasional glimmers of improvement, before they lapse into further deterioration. Others may decline more slowly in the early stages, but then degenerate more quickly toward the end. Every individual does not suffer the same symptoms during the course of the disease or suffer them at the same time or to a similar degree. There is no way to predict the rate at which a patient will move through the stages that make Alzheimer's disease so frustrating, unpredictable, and frightening for patients, families, and lay and professional caregivers.

In addition to the generally utilized three-stage model, a seven-stage model, developed by Reisberg (1986), is used by professionals primarily for diagnostic and assessment purposes. Reisberg's research demonstrates that Alzheimer's patients lose abilities in the reverse order that they were initially learned. This knowledge may assist professionals in deciding whether an individual has Alzheimer's disease. For example, according to the Reisberg model, if a person is able to function in a difficult work environment, yet forgets appointments and major responsibilities, one would suspect that Alzheimer's disease is not the cause of memory loss.

THE SEVEN STAGES OF ALZHEIMER DISEASE

Stage 1: No cognitive decline	No functional problem
Stage 2: Very mild cognitive decline	Forgets names and location of objects
Stage 3: Mild cognitive decline	Has difficulty travelling to new locations
	Has difficulty in demanding employment settings
Stage 4: Moderate cognitive decline	Has difficulty with complex tasks (finances; marketing; planning dinner for guests)
Stage 5: Moderately severe cognitive decline	Needs help to choose clothing
	Needs coaxing to bathe properly
Stage 6: Severe cognitive decline	Needs help putting on clothing
	Requires assistance in bathing; may have fear of bathing
	Has decreased ability to handle toileting
	Is incontinent

Stage 7: Very severe cognitive decline	Has vocabulary of six words
	Has single word vocabulary
	Loss of ambulatory ability
	Loss of ability to sit
	Loss of ability to smile
	Stupor and coma

(Kociol & Schiff, 1989)

The onset of Alzheimer's disease is gradual and at times imperceptable. The person may begin to suspect that something may be wrong, but often hides this suspicion from family members, other relatives, friends, and co-workers. Since there is little or no physical sign of deterioration until the late stages, it is difficult to determine in the early stages whether a person has Alzheimer's disease because he or she appears physically normal. Thus, in the early stages, people in the community may think that the person is simply intoxicated, upset, or emotionally unstable.

The first stage is characterized by slow subtle changes in the person's ability to learn, problems in communcation, memory loss for recent events, difficulty making decisions, impaired judgment, a shortened attention span, problems in coping with new situations, and a decreased desire to attempt new things and to meet people.

A typical characteristic of all examples of Alzheimer's disease is its effects on recent memory, which involves recollections of events that occurred a few minutes to several days in the past. Recent memory is distinct from immediate memory, which refers, for example, to the short time it takes to look at an address and write it down. Not all recent memory is affected during Alzheimer's disease; for instance, the person still remembers the sensation of pain. Recent memory is also different from remote memory—the remembrance of events and people from childhood or adolescence. Remote memory is usually permanent, but it may deteriorate. This variable memory loss is both random and unpredictable. Indeed, it is not unusual for a patient to forget where he or she has just left the keys to the house but be able to recall in detail some aspect of childhood sixty, seventy, or eighty years before. Some examples contributed by caregivers to illustrate the first stage include these:

Since my wife had always described herself as being absentminded, it was easy for her to excuse and laugh off memory lapses such as forgetting names of grandchildren and missing appointments. It was only after she became anxious after getting lost on the way home that we were able to persuade her to see a doctor.

My wife was cooperative and when it was suggested that she wash up for dinner, she would go to the appropriate place. However, she would consistently emerge from the bathroom without having washed. We realized later that she had forgotten what "wash" meant, so she had not been able to carry out this task.

My husband was a bus driver. He began coming earlier and earlier for work because he couldn't remember what time his shift started (Kociol & Schiff, 1989, p. 21).

Another wife related that the first thing she noticed in her 55-year-old husband was "poor memory, slow movements and occasional weak legs" (*About Alzheimer's Disease*, 1987, p. 7).

During the second or middle stage, memory continues to deteriorate. The ability to concentrate lessens, errors in judgment increase, and word-finding problems emerge. There are also marked difficulties in speech, language, and communication and a decreasing ability to conduct daily activities without supervision or guidance. There is a disconnection between time and place, and the person may not be able to recognize himself or herself in the mirror. The Alzheimer's victim may still be able to read aloud and repeat words, but numerical functions and other cognitive abilities decline. It is difficult to know what is still intact and what the person can feel, understand, interpret, and experience because further intellectual and behavioral changes are occurring.

During the second stage, it is important to reduce the amount of stimulation and to establish as predictable a schedule as possible. The patient may respond to people or objects in an aggressive manner because he or she misperceives what is happening. For example, someone who approaches the person suddenly to assist with dressing may be perceived as a threat, particularly if the approach is made from behind or from one side at the edge of the person's peripheral vision.

In this stage there is often a struggle to maintain bodily functions, some of which are retained longer than are others. The loss of dexterity and the slowing down of bodily movements may impede such tasks as dressing and other self-care routines, but the patient physically resists help. Some Alzheimer's victims may begin to wander from home, often just in a housecoat and in the middle of the night, and may be unaware that they are wandering and that they are placing themselves in potential danger. Wandering can cause extreme anxiety and upset for family members and caregivers.

Typical problems associated with the middle stage are illustrated in the following examples:

Mrs. S stated that her 53-year-old husband showed an "inability to concentrate and work at figures." She added that he seems a different person but is not too hard to handle. Later, however, she said that he had visual and speech impairments, as well as the loss of bladder and bowel control (*Alzheimer's Disease*, 1987, p. 7).

Mr. W said: "When the phone rings I don't let my dad answer it anymore because it could be business. He can't take messages even. The person at the other end of the phone will ask 'Where's Jim' and I'll be standing next to him, and he'll say 'He's not here today' " (Powell & Courtice, 1983, p. 170).

Mrs. L remarked that her brother now shows so much impairment that "comprehension is too poor to determine if there is still memory." She added that he is "fearful, suspicious, has episodes of depression and weeping—and sometimes of giggling. He needs to be guided for he has just fallen down and broken his hip" (*About Alzheimer's Disease*, 1987, p. 7).

In the third and final stage, twenty-four-hour nursing care is usually required. The patient may need complete assistance with daily self-care routines, such as feeding, toileting, and dressing. In addition, the patient may require hospitalization to treat the increasing occurrence of physical infirmities and illness. The ability to speak or communicate disappears and may consist of only randomly spoken phrases with no apparent meaning, as well as immobility. Bowel and urine control decrease greatly, leading to incontinence, and twitching and jerking may develop. Seizures, delusions, and delerium may occur. There may be virtually no spontaneous movements or reactions to people or other stimuli as the patient assumes an almost vegetative state. Reflexes may develop, such as the one that causes the patient to suck anything put in his or her mouth. The person with Alzheimer's disease becomes increasingly susceptible to bedsores, pneumonia, and heart failure, the last two of which eventually result in death. Although the immediate cause of death is in reality Alzheimer's disease, often a secondary cause of death is listed on the certificate; however, this practice is slowly changing as physicians become better educated about Alzheimer's disease.

This difficult final stage was described by two members of an Alzheimer Society:

Mr. G stated that his 69-year-old wife is now showing a "general slowing of movement and recently has become bedridden due to a complete loss of mobility."

Mrs. G reported that she has been nursing and caring for her 65-year-old husband at home for about two years, "but finally I could no longer stand the physical and emotional strain and was able to have him placed in a nursing home three months before he died" (*About Alzheimer's Disease*, 1987, p. 7).

IMPACT ON PATIENTS AND FAMILIES

Alzheimer's disease has a devastating psychological, emotional, social, and even financial and legal impact on the family system that often extends over a period of years. Marion Roach, the daughter of an Alzheimer's patient wrote: "It goes on and on, and just when we can't stand another phase, we don't have to, because it's succeeded by another one—a worse phase, a more outrageous phase, a quieter phase, a sloppier phase, a more confused phase, a phase of hushed panic—seen in the eyes of the victim, seen by us" (quoted in Ronch, 1989, p. 35). Both the patient and family members and caregivers will experience a myriad of emotional responses to the consistently evolving and challenging conditions associated with this unpredictable disease. These feelings and reactions are perfectly normal and should be openly acknowledged, accepted, and resolved to ensure that they will not become barriers to caregiving in the future, according to Eva Philipp, a psychotherapist in private practice in Toronto (interview, July 15, 1991). Often these emotions seem overwhelming, conflicting, and confusing, but they are shared by many others who are witnessing the gradual disappearance of the traits that make up the unique personality of the sufferer.

It is important for family members to realize that although the patients are increasingly unable to articulate what is occurring inside them, they require constant compassion, support, and understanding, however difficult it is to provide them. In the beginning, Alzheimer's patients feel confused as they realize that something is happening to their memory or ability to work but are unsure what is occurring or why. They feel frustrated because, regardless of how diligently they try, they are unable to perform the same tasks that they once could. Many patients feel angry at the loss of their abilities and question, "Why is this happening to me?" They experience fear as the loss of memory makes the world seem a frightening place and feel uncertain because the symptoms and progression of the illness are so unpredictable that they do not know what the future will hold. Alzheimer's victims also experience grief and depression as they mourn the loss of their abilities and feel hopeless about their future.

Family members experience similar emotional reactions. In the early stages, denial is common when the symptoms begin to appear and are diagnosed. Families frequently express hope that the diagnosis is incorrect and that the patient will recover. Indeed, denial may be functional in protecting against the traumatic reality of the disease. However, if families continue to deny, they may suffer serious problems of coping and adjustment in the long run. As the disease progresses and the patient becomes increasingly dependent, role adjustments become necessary in the family (Lezak, 1978, cited in Dobrof, 1986). The spouse, children, or caregiver must assume the role of guardian. As the Alzheimer's patient becomes too debilitated to do previously simple tasks, such as cooking, cleaning, or money management, the family must take over these chores.

As a result of memory loss, Alzheimer's patients begin to display many behavioral symptoms, such as wandering, forgetfulness, the continued repeating of questions, paranoia, and occasionally violence (Mace, 1981, cited in Dobrof, 1986, p. 28). Family members are constantly uncertain as to when the patient will exhibit aggressive behavior or inappropriate outbursts that are due to the patient's distorted view of reality. Often these behaviors are seen as rude and unacceptable, but they are caused by the patient's misperception of the situation. Caregivers may feel guilty because they are embarrassed by the person's bizarre behavior or need for constant reminders in public. These unpredictable behaviors, in conjuction with disrupted family routines and the exorbitant amount of time, energy, and money that are involved in the care of the Alzheimer's patient, lead to anger, frustration, and resentment.

Family members may feel guilty because they believe they are somehow responsible for the illness, although it is not a result of anything they have done or could have prevented, or because they are angry at the patient's inability to perform even the most routine tasks. Caregivers also often experience unresolved guilt when they contemplate the possibility of placing a loved one in a nursing home and feel fear as they watch their loved one gradually lose his or her personality and memory. During the later stages of the disease, when the patient becomes immobilized, families may go through a grieving process in which they mourn the loss of their loved one. However, they often need permission to begin the mourning process because the patient is still alive. They need to be able to grieve the loss of a personal relationship that no longer exists (Mace, 1981, cited in Dobrof, 1986, p. 29).

The feelings of sadness, anger, fatigue, guilt, and despair associated with grief are reactivated each time another element disappears that makes that unique patient a person. The loss of the person while he or she is physically present inspires such feelings as those expressed by a family caregiver:

> Sometimes I feel like I have a big hole in my stomach. It's open and empty and so painful. It aches and begs to be filled with a touch, some sign of understanding, something that will somehow bond Ray and me again. . . . He doesn't know that I hurt and can't make the emptiness and loneliness go away. And yet he is physically there. I know I lost Ray long before he actually died. I lost the part of him that made him the man I found so satisfying. We complimented [sic] each other. As he deteriorated, we lost that (Ronch, 1989, p. 36).

In fact the grieving process experienced by family members has been compared to the process described by Kübler-Ross (1969) in her five stages of mourning: denial and isolation, anger, bargaining, depression, and acceptance.

Throughout the course of the disease, caregivers often experience depression, isolation, and physical deterioration. They are left feeling emotionally drained as a result of the continued care of the patient without relief or encouraging changes. Isolation exacerbates the problem, since the twenty-four-hour care required prevents the caregivers from continuing their hobbies and outside interests. As a result, it is not unusual for caregivers to become physically ill and to develop stress-related disorders. Both friends and extended family members may shun the caregivers because of the often bizarre characteristics associated with the disease. Their rejection augments the caregivers' feelings of loneliness and depression (Lezak, 1978, cited in Dobrof, 1986, p. 51). These overwhelming and at times conflicting feelings may result in strained relationships among family members that may become inflamed if some family members believe that others are not contributing fairly to the care of the patient.

It is wise that caregivers address their own physical and emotional needs on an ongoing basis by building support networks; learning more about the disease; joining a support group; seeking counseling; organizing for occasional respite care; and remaining healthy through exercise, rest, and nutritionally balanced meals.

PRACTICAL SUGGESTIONS FOR CAREGIVERS

Family members can learn to be supportive of the Alzheimer's patient and thus make a substantial difference in the patient's comfort, safety, and some level of involvement, if possible. For example, caregivers can engage the patient in physical exercise, such as accompanying them on regular walks around the block or arranging time for dancing or calisthenics. In addition, they can arrange for social activites at community centers, churches and synagogues, senior citizens' centers, hospitals, or adult day care centers whose programs provide the needed socialization and stimulation with individuals with similar problems. They can allow the patient to assist in household chores that are not too mentally taxing and that give the patient a sense of purpose and a feeling of helpfulness. And although the cognitive capabilities of the Alzheimer's patient are deteriorating, many in the early stages can still appreciate and benefit from a visit to a museum, a sporting event, or a zoo or from a walk in the woods.

At home, family members can make the life of the Alzheimer's patient more bearable by employing memory aids, such as a calendar that displays the date, day of the week, and any appointments; written reminders of often-forgotten tasks; large labels on frequently used items; safety instructions to help protect the patient and family; lists to keep things in order; and directions to help find necessary items.

In the late stages, safety precautions, such as locking up poisons and disconnecting gas burners that could be left on, are essential. Additional safety precautions include these:

Stairs: A wrought-iron or wooden expanding gate at the top or bottom of the stairs should be placed to keep a family member from going up or down the stairs.

Bathing: Baths and showers should be made easier by using a detachable head and hose.

Dead bolts: If there is a dead-bolt lock without a front latch, a key should be kept in a nearby location for an emergency.

Mirrors: Mirrors can frighten the patient, so they should be turned around or removed.

Playthings: If the patient likes to fiddle with things, he or she should be given pieces of string or large plastic beads, baby toys, a stuffed animal, or other objects that he or she likes to handle.

Recreation: Simple arts and crafts, like watercolors or large playing cards, should be used.

Breakables: Breakable objects should be packed away because patients can injure themselves if these objects are broken.

Eating: One food item should be offered at a time because a choice may be confusing. Ample time for eating and chewing should be allowed.

Utensils: A utensil may have to be put in the patient's hand to get him or her to begin eating. A baby plate with a suction bottom to keep the plate in one spot should be used, as well as a baby cup with a cover to minimize spills.

Dressing: In general, clothes that can be put on and taken off easily should be worn. If a man is unable to tie his tie, a clip-on tie should be used or a turtleneck or open-collar shirt. Laces should be avoided. If the patient cannot operate buttons and zippers, Velcro strips should replace them. The caregiver should help the patient select clothing to avoid unnecessary and inappropriate choices.

Changes: Changes should be made gradually. The patient must be well prepared for any physical, emotional, drug, nutritional, or geographic changes or a change of caregivers. In this context, counseling is very important.

Exercise: A daily exercise routine, such as a walk, should be established. It is important to keep the patient mobile for as long as possible.

Crowds: Large crowds or large spaces without boundaries should be avoided.

Environment: The patient should be given concrete sources of information that help him/her to establish daily time and place as these help to ground the patient in reality. For example, he or she should be given calendars with huge figures, clocks with all numbers for hours, and reminders of such special events as birthdays, anniversaries, and holidays.

Cooking: The utilities company should be consulted about making the stove inoperable when no one else is around. It is easy to turn on an unlit burner, to put flammable materials in the oven, or to create a number of other fire hazards.

Hot water: The hot water heater should be adjusted so the temperature is low enough to prevent scalding.

Small appliances: The patient should be supervised in using essential electrical appliances, and other small but potentially dangerous ones should be hidden in a safe place.

Poisons and medications: Poisons and medications should be locked up or should be difficult to open because the patient may exercise poor judgment in handling them as the disease progresses.

Safety devices: A public health nurse, social worker, or occupational therapist should be able to provide the caregiver with information on a whole range of innovative safety devices and procedures, including proper aids and handrails.

Driving: The patient must not be permitted to drive as soon as indications of deteriorating driving ability appear. The driver who forgets where he or she is going and how to get there is a hazard both to himself or herself and to others.

Smoking: The patient should give up smoking, both for health reasons and to eliminate a fire hazard. The patient may forget that he or she is smoking, and a smoldering cigarette could start a fire. If the patient is unable or unwilling to give up smoking, then he or she should be supervised while smoking (*About Alzheimer's Disease*, 1987, p. 11).

Toothbrushing: Caregivers should ensure that the patient's teeth are brushed. When the patient is unable to do it, the caregiver should do so gently and reassuringly.

Personal hygiene: It is preferable to allow the patient to perform whatever personal-hygiene tasks he or she is able to accomplish, but the caregiver should be ready to intervene when necessary. In some instances, simple reminders may be sufficient, but at other times, the task should be broken down into small steps, so the patient can manage it.

Toilet accidents: If toilet accidents occur, then a regular toilet schedule should be established, and the patient should be reminded of it (*About Alzheimer's Disease*, 1987, p. 11).

CAREGIVING AND PLANNING GUIDE SUMMARY

Stage 1: Early Stage

Physician	A professional diagnosis should be obtained. A family physician should be chosen or confirmed. A record of medications should be set up.
Talking about Alzheimer's Disease	Relatives, friends, neighbors, employers, and shopkeepers should be informed.
Community Resources	The caregiver should build a support network and identify key persons, including the public health nurse, information centers, and the Alzheimer Society. Services that will be needed in the future should be identified (i.e., meals, homemaking, day care, and respite care).

Informal Helpers	The caregiver should identify key persons (relatives, neighbors, and friends) who can help.
Legal Issues	A lawyer should be chosen or confirmed, and power of attorney should be obtained. Also, the will should be reviewed, and valuable papers should be collected and stored.
Financial Issues	Assets should be listed. Credit cards should be removed, and insurance policies should be reviewed. Bank accounts should be simplified, and a chartered accountant should be chosen or confirmed.
Home Environment	Changes that are needed immediately and those that will be required in the long term should be identified, and workers should be called to provide estimates.
Emergency Planning	Someone should be designated to be contacted in an emergency. The caregiver should find out if a long-term-care facility has respite beds on an emergency basis.

Stage 2: Middle Stage

Physician	The caregiver should work closely with the physician.
Community Resources	A checklist should be used to choose appropriate services, such as day care and respite care. These services should be used when needed.
Informal Helpers	The caregiver should stay connected with friends and relatives and activities to prevent social isolation and should plan for new roles that will be assumed later.
Home Environment	Changes should be made in the home as required.
Long-term Care	The caregiver should visit available long-term-care facilities and place the patient on their waiting lists.

Stage 3: Late Stage

| *Staying Healthy* | The caregiver should plan his or her future as a single person. |

(Adapted from Kociol & Schiff, 1989)

COMMUNICATING WITH THE ALZHEIMER'S PATIENT

The caregiver can also alleviate stress by learning to communicate as effectively as possible with the Alzheimer's patient. Communication becomes increasingly difficult as the patient gradually loses the ability to speak and communicate. Several strategies should be utilized to facilitate this difficult process, and the social worker should be prepared to give the family or caregiver guidance on the following communication techniques:

1. It is important not to assume that the patient does not know what you are talking about. The patient retains the capacity to understand language well after he or she no longer can speak intelligently and can understand the emotional content or facial and other cues that indicate anger, rudeness, and the like. Thus, you should assume that the patient understands more than he or she can say, especially with regard to emotional messages.

2. As you would not speak about any person to another in the person's presence, do not do so with the patient.

3. Do not hold conversations with another person in close proximity to the patient as if he or she was not there. Because the patient has difficulty understanding what is being said, the patient may think he or she is the subject of the conversation. For example, if you are talking to a social worker about someone at whom you are angry and the patient believes you are referring to him or her, the patient may become angry. Such a misperception can lead to aggressive or other emotional reactions by the patient.

4. Sentences and questions should be kept short and simple.

5. The use of pronouns should be avoided, and proper names that the patient can recognize and is familiar with should be used.

6. Conversations should revolve around observable, actural occurrences, not abstract or philosophical ideas that may be difficult to understand or communicate. Your use of abstract ideas may lead the patient to feel "stupid" or less than he or she used to be.

7. When talking to the patient, you should position yourself at the patient's eye level, so the patient does not think that the conversation may be quickly terminated. This fear increases the pressure to "perform," in this instance to be verbally fluent, and may heighten the patient's anxiety and diminish his or her functional memory.

8. The patient should be allowed time to listen, comprehend, think, formulate, and express a response to what you have said. You should be careful not to communicate impatience or annoyance if communication takes longer, as it undoubtedly will. If you show impatience, the patient

may feel that you are angry or disappointed. If you show anger, the patient may respond with anger; if you show impatience, the patient may choose not to risk the loss of self-esteem that comes with disappointing someone he or she respects and hence may stop communicating.

9. Background noise and other stimuli that compete for the patient's attention and make it difficult to pay attention to your message should be reduced. Noisy jewelry, telephone ringing, public-address systems, and busy nurses' stations and hallways further impede the patient's already-compromised ability to communicate.

10. Messages should be stated directly. The patient should not be expected to draw inferences from what is said. For example, if you are too busy to speak with the patient, but will be able to talk to him or her in an hour, say, "I can't talk now, but I will see you at twelve-thirty," rather than, "Does it look like I have time now? See me later when I'm free."

11. Metaphor and analogy should be avoided. The patient is unable to abstract the properties of two things and establish their similarity or their membership in the same class (i.e., that apples and bananas are fruit).

12. The patient thinks literally. Such statements as, "Why don't you jump into the shower" may elicit a response like "I'm afraid to; I may fall." Use clear descriptive terms, for example, "Put on your green blouse," rather than "get dressed now."

13. If your message is not understood, it should be restated and paraphrased. Doing so will allow you to formulate communication in a way that the patient understands as best as he or she can, given the progression of his or her dementia.

14. You should talk in a low-pitched, audible tone of voice and use appropriate animation and intonational cues, and it is helpful for the patient to receive a stream of communication that contains as many of the normal channels of meaning as possible. The patient can then utilize a number of different cues to decode the message if he or she has forgotten the meaning of individual words.

15. The nonverbal components of communication should be remembered and used to enhance the patient's readiness to listen or to understand your message. Touch, facial expression, posture, head movements, eye contact, gesture, and position relative to the patient help communicate emotional messages about how you regard the patient and what feelings you are conveying. It is important not to touch the patient until you have established trust, and you should touch the patient slowly, gently, and in full sight of him or her.

16. You should ascertain whether the patient can hear you by watching

the patient's face for signs of comprehension. Many older persons suffer an age-related hearing loss, and it must be remembered that Alzheimer's patients may have physical as well as cognitive difficulties. In addition, you should be aware of the existence of visual defects and be prepared to compensate for them by changing lighting, relying less on visual cues, removing sources of glare, and making sure that the patient can see you.

17. You should avoid becoming overexcited, using wild gestures, or being overly demonstrative because doing so can cause the patient to become alarmed and anxious. Alzheimer's patients readily absorb their caregivers' moods.

18. You should provide cues and assist the patient to find the "lost" word while he or she is talking. When a patient describes a concept instead of using a noun, you should tell him or her the correct word. For example, if the patient says, "I'm looking for my, you know it's on my arm and I look at it," you can say, "Your watch?"

19. Alzheimer's patients can read words even after they have lost some of the meaning of a word or phrase. Ambiguous sentences may cause particular difficulty. For example, the sign "Exit" may be interpreted as a command, rather than simply as a label for a means of egress.

20. You should attend to the words and emotional message that is being conveyed. If the patient sounds upset while he or she is talking or begins to cry, it is important to react to the affective response.

21. You should ask only one question or give one direction at a time and use short sentences (five to ten words in sequence), rather than make paragraph-length utterances.

22. If the patient loses the thread of a story or is unable to complete a sentence (i.e., he or she pauses, looks at you, and then digresses to another topic), it is important to repeat the last phrase he or she said to prompt the memory. If the patient cannot retrieve the sentence, you should paraphrase it and help him or her to continue. If these techniques are unsuccessful, you should not pressure the patient too long. The patient will probably have forgotten the idea by then.

23. You should ask yes-or-no questions (i.e., Do you like the food? Is this upsetting?) when appropriate, but you should not restrict all communication to this category. The patient should be allowed to use his or her remaining communication abilities in the framework of conversation with you (e.g., "How do you like this music?")

24. You should observe the patient for signs of restlessness or withdrawal, such as agitation (foot movements and handwringing), restless eye move-

ments or continuous scanning of the room, becoming loud or argumentative, and frowning.

25. You should help the patient become tolerant of his or her communication difficulties by supporting the patient's remaining skills and encouraging their use. You should reassure the patient that you will take the time to listen.

26. You should observe Alzheimer's patients to monitor how they communicate with each other and with their caregivers. Get to know the patient's vocabulary, sentence structure, and normal conversational patterns, so a context can be developed for greater understanding. You should remember that the patient is using a language, i.e., rule-governed communication. It is your task to learn the idiosyncratic rules of the patient's communication and become more adept at helping the patient use all his or her remaining communication abilities as a means of personal expression and social adaptation (Ronch, 1989, p. 70).

THE ROLE OF THE SOCIAL WORKER

The social worker plays an indispensable role in the ongoing care of the Alzheimer's patient and family members. Working in concert with a multidisciplinary team of allied professionals, such as general practitioners, neurologists, psychiatrists, psychologists, neuropsychologists, nurses, physiotherapists, occupational therapists, speech pathologists, rehabilitation counselors, recreational therapists, and the clergy, the social worker contributes a set of intervention skills that combine clinical and community foci. Social workers, especially those with some training in gerontology, can help family members with emotional difficulties arising from the illness and to cope with the changing disease process, offer practical suggestions and techniques to improve caregiving, provide case management, educate and provide information about the condition, and conduct support groups for patients and families in the community and in institutional settings. They can also engage in ongoing psychotherapy with family members, when required; assist families to resolve disagreements about caregiving; help families plan for the legal and financial consequences of the disease; assist in the diagnostic process by conducting a thorough family history to ascertain the family's strengths and deficits and to identify needs; refer the patient and family to appropriate community resources and allied professionals, when required; conduct research on psychosocial issues associated with Alzheimer's disease; and help the family to plan for and select an appropriate long-term-care facility.

The choice of an institutional facility is one of the most traumatic and agonizing decisions a family has to make, and the social worker can provide much-needed support and practical assistance in this regard. At some point, the overwhelming majority of Alzheimer's patients require institutional care. There are several circumstances in which residential care must be considered. For example, the patient may be residing alone and not be able to handle violent episodes or incontinence, or the patient's need for medical attention may require the family to place him or her in residential care. Family members should deal openly with the circumstances of, and options for, long-term care and should talk about them in advance because institutions often have long waiting lists and the number of facilities that accept patients may be restricted. Indeed, many institutions are reluctant or even refuse to admit Alzheimer's patients. Options for residential care may include homes for the aged; chronic care hospitals; nursing homes, both private and non-profit; and psychiatric institutions (for brief assessments).

As well as helping the family to deal with the emotional turbulence associated with this decision, the social worker can also help the family with admissions procedures; assist the patient to adjust to the institutional environment; and consult with the institution's staff concerning the psychological and social needs of the patient, including the selection of a roommate and a dining partner. If appropriate, the social worker can help the family look at alternatives to institutionalization.

Most families consult a social worker in a time of high stress—once the diagnosis has been made or when they feel they are no longer able to cope with the strain of caregiving. This situation presents the social worker with a unique opportunity to intervene. Often a physician refers the family to a social worker who works in a hospital (if the patient is hospitalized), in a home for the aged or nursing home, in a senior citizens' center, in a family service agency, in a public housing project, or in private practice.

When they visit a social worker, most families require both information and education about the disease and emotional reassurance and support. It is imperative that the social worker attend to both areas, for providing only one type of assistance will prove ineffective, since it neglects the holistic needs of the caregiver.

Individual Counseling

Most social work intervention involves individual counseling with the primary caregiver; in this type of counseling, it is important that the social worker keep focused on the caregiver's ability to cope with the daily rigors of caring for the Alzheimer's patient. Family counseling may also be effective in facilitating decision making and thus may prevent conflicts from emerging over such issues as finances and placement and allow the family members to cathect and resolve feelings that could stand in the way of cooperative behavior.

However, the social worker's main objective is to ensure the well-being of the patient and caregivers and to avoid being sidetracked into dealing with other difficulties in family members' relationships. The social worker should focus on improving functioning and problem-solving abilities and not become a forum for long-standing unrelated conflicts.

The social worker should be internally secure enough to deal with the caretaker's intense feelings of anger and depression and to remain focused on these feelings.

It is important to remember that the social worker also has feelings that he or she will experience during the counseling sessions. All feelings should be accepted nonjudgmentally, and if the social worker has difficulties accepting feelings, then he or she will have problems accepting the caregiver's feelings. The social worker should provide a comfortable and secure haven in which the caregiver can talk openly about the difficulties and experience, express and resolve feelings, so the caregiver's energy is liberated to focus on practical issues (Eva Philipp, psychotherapist in private practice, Toronto).

In addition to providing the necessary clinical support, the social worker is equipped to engage in community intervention, such as referring the patient and caregiver to a local Alzheimer Society, a support group, outside respite care, in-home respite care, and a day program, if appropriate. Adult day care for patients provides stimulation and socialization, as well as a link to services that maintain or enhance their health status. It is a positive long-term alternative to institutionalization that increases the options available to the cognitively impaired elderly and thus improves the quality of their lives. In addition, the social worker may assist with legal and financial planning by identifying available options and resources, especially for elderly women who may not have had to deal with legal and financial matters in the past.

Social workers should also utilize their advocacy skills throughout the counseling process on both the individual level and the macrolevel. Individual advocacy provides caregivers with the courage and means to regain control and adjust to unpredictable circumstances. By giving support and information, the social worker is in a position to empower patients and families to engage in macrolevel activites in relation to policy and care issues through letter-writing campaigns, telephone blitzes, petitions, and visits to governmental officials and representatives. The personal and political empowerment of caregivers is a key element in the counseling process, since it helps caregivers focus their anger outward toward social change.

The social worker also should be in the forefront of meeting the needs of multicultural communities. Currently, the vast majority of information on Alzheimer's disease is available only in English, even though both Canada and the United States are rich, diverse, multicultural mosaics. Because Alzheimer's disease affects all cultures and ethnic groups, families, caregivers, and practitioners from every linguistic group must be able to receive information, support, medical assistance, and vital community services in the appropriate language. For many reasons, some ethnic groups often prefer to care for their elderly relatives and utilize the services available solely within their own communities. Also for valid reasons, many ethnic groups are wary of outside interventions from established institutions, community agencies, and other sources that they view as being unsympathetic or insensitive to their unique concerns. It is the róle of the social worker to attempt to overcome these barriers, to facilitate the training of culturally appropriate practitioners to provide sensitive information and support, and to promote awareness of multicultural issues and foster attitudinal changes in the society at large. These are challenging tasks, but fortunately several ethnic groups have already begun to initiate steps to deal with Alzheimer's disease in their own environments.*

Support Groups

Many social workers conduct or facilitate support groups for caregivers, as well as for patients, primarily in institutional settings. They and other health care professionals have successfully employed group work techniques with the elderly for years (Burnside, 1978, & Shore, 1952, cited in Dobrof, 1986, p. 16).

Support groups are an invaluable resource for family members who are seeking information and emotional solace. At least at the beginning of their relative's illness, some caregivers may choose to participate in a support group, rather than attend formal group therapy. Support groups may be utilized in conjunction with traditional clinical interventions and offer an additional avenue of support for desperate people. These groups provide a forum through which caregivers can share ideas and experiences, learn

*While executive director of the Alzheimer Society for Metropolitan Toronto, the author initiated the translation of information on Alzheimer's disease into Chinese and Italian. Other ethnic groups are beginning to look at this need, but at this time their work is still formulative.

practical caregiving tips, receive emotional support, and realize that their pain and loneliness are not unique. Most caregivers feel isolated and believe that no one can really comprehend their feelings of loss. The support group both reduces and validates these feelings and allows caregivers to become helpers and receivers of assistance.

The result of the support group may include adaptive coping through emotional support, information, and guidance. As the group begins to function more cohesively, the need for concrete information is replaced by the need to share personal experiences and feelings, leadership occasionally emerges, and members gain confidence in their ability to help others.

Support groups may be found in hospitals, community centers, homes for the aged, nursing homes, family service agencies, and churches and synagogues and through local Alzheimer Societies. Groups differ widely in their composition, focus, size, leadership style, goals, content, and duration. Some groups provide mainly information and education, while others concentrate on emotional support while still others combine these two foci. Certain groups have closed memberships, while others allow participants to enter and leave as they please. Some groups adopt an open-ended format, while others are structured for a limited number of meetings. Some groups may invite guest presenters to address a variety of related topics, while others do not use outside resources. Some groups are led or co-led by facilitators who are often social workers, while others do not employ a formal leader and are nondirective. Some groups schedule meetings on a regular basis, while others meet as required. There is no one modality or correct way to organize and conduct a support group because the needs of various populations differ over time. It is important for the social worker to help the caregiver select an appropriate support group that meets his or her specific needs at a particular time and that complements the individual counseling.

Social workers also conduct groups with Alzheimer's patients in institutional settings. The goals of these groups are to enhance the patients' self-esteem, to increase stimulation through interaction, and to improve the group's social skills. Working in groups with the cognitively impaired elderly is a highly rewarding but frustrating experience that tests the social worker's skills. The success of the group depends, in significant part, on the expectations of the group leader. The leader should realize that there is no hope of long-term improvement and that the goals should be realistic, with a focus on the maintenance or maximization of function. Thus, he or she should strive to appreciate the individual moments of success.

Patients with Alzheimer's disease are more docile than are the well elderly, so the leader must consistently encourage them to participate. The leader must focus on tangible, concrete facts or memories because of the patients' limited ability to think in conceptual terms. Since the patients in the group are easily distracted, it is important to limit the use of visual aids or handouts that may divert their attention. Also, the patients' reaction time is greatly diminished, and patients are more sensitive to and aware of nonverbal cues, such as others' moods or facial expressions, as their communication deteriorates.

Alzheimer's patients often experience chaotic mood swings, regardless of efforts to ensure a tranquil environment, and their moods fluctuate from meeting to meeting. Therefore, the leader must adjust his or her expectations of the patients' responses. Since the leader has minimal control over these unpredictable variations in mood, he or she should not personalize this emotional volatility.

The leader should also be sensitive to the social and environmental milieu (anything outside the individual) of the group meetings. Hiatt (1978, cited in Dobrof, 1986, p. 18) pointed out that the greater the individual's cognitive impairment, the more significant the environment is for independent coping and for sustaining other aspects of well-being. It is therefore essential that group sessions are conducted in a closed, quiet place that contains no unnecessary distractions. A calm environment allows the patients to pay greater attention, to respond more quickly, and to keep track of the sequence of events. To facilitate communication, the meeting room should have good acoustics and be set up to permit the group leader to maintain eye contact with the patients.

In addition, the leader must be familiar with each patient's idiosyncracies. During the sessions, potential wanderers should sit close to the leader, so they can be reminded that they are valuable members of the group and be assured of the passing of time. Occasionally, the leader may have to hold a wanderer's hand to keep his or her attention. No Alzheimer's patient should be forced to attend group sessions against his or her will because such a patient will be disruptive to other participants and to the group process.

Other types of patients' groups that have been successful include a current-events group held at the Alzheimer Unit at the Dallas Home for the Aged. This group allows residents to discuss and debate current news items, provides reality testing for those who have been isolated or not able to stay in contact with the outside world, and encourages residents to read news magazines and newspapers. These activities have increased the patients' self-esteem, alertness, and orientation and improved their social skills, although these gains cannot be maintained outside the group.

Reminiscence groups have also been used. In her reminiscence group of demented elderly patients, Cook (1984, cited in Dobrof, 1986, p. 16) discovered that the group fostered active and spontaneous participation, which encouraged socialization and personal interactions. Group psychotherapist Linden (1953, cited in Dobrof, 1986, p. 16) found that group intervention with elderly regressed women could improve the participants' alertness and orientation and diminish their confusion. The group leader could hope for occasional momentary improvements in some group members at some times, but these temporary improvements could not be seen as long-term goals.

Policy Development

Social workers also can contribute enormously to policy development, both in institutional settings and in the government. Silverstone and Weiss (1981, cited in Dobrof, 1986, p. 74) indicated that the challenge of the social worker is heightened by the changes that inevitably occur in long-term care in which "goals are defined by the problem and the needs of the frail impaired client wherever encountered along the continuum."

The involvement and expertise of social workers in the planning, conceptualization, and development of these environments is crucial. Social workers must play key roles in the decision-making and organizational processes to achieve institutional change. They must expand their role from their traditonal work with individual clients to include work with the systems and staffs of long-term-care facilities to influence the establishment and maintenance of positive, pleasurable, and supportive environments.

Social workers should also encourage governmental policymakers at all levels to pay serious attention to the looming crisis of Alzheimer's disease in Canada and the United States. Governments in a pluralistic democracy have an obligation to arbitrate among many different societal interests, but it is difficult to capture the attention, interest, and financial commitment of politicians and policymakers. However, the costs of ignoring this silent epidemic will be exorbitant. Social workers, employing their array of advocacy skills, must mobilize patients, caregivers, and allied health professionals to insist that governments provide much greater funding for such areas as long-term-care facilities, hospital beds, respite and in-home respite care, day care centers, transportation, and biomedical and psychosocial research. The future well-being of tens of thousands of Canadians and Americans will literally depend on it.

The stigma associated with Alzheimer's disease is still evident, although the situation is changing, thanks to the work of public education programs and the Alzheimer Societies. The future with regard to Alzheimer's disease is grim yet hopeful. Despite the pain, loss, and tragedy that lie in its wake, there is hope because of recent medical discoveries throughout the world and because of the caring, compassion, strength, and concern shown by caregivers, citizens, families, and friends.

The profession of social work, armed with a theoretical base and practical understanding of the biopsychosocial dimensions of human behavior, combined with a wealth of knowledge of community-based resources and services, is poised to make this unbearable situation brighter and more tolerable. There are challenges that must be faced, but social workers, steeped in a commitment to human values, will be in the forefront of caregiving and in the vanguard of institutional and societal change.

REFERENCES

About Alzheimer's disease: A family handbook. (1987). Toronto: Alzheimer Society of Canada.

Alzheimer's disease: A family information handbook. (1987). Toronto: Alzheimer Society of Canada.

Aronson, M. K. (1988). Understanding Alzheimer's disease: What it is, how to cope with it, future directions. New York: Macmillan.

Cohen, D., & Eisdorfer, C. (1989). The loss of self: A family resource for the care of Alzheimer's disease and related disorders. New York: Plenum Press.

Dobrof, R. (Ed.). (1986). Social work and Alzheimer's disease: Practice issues with victims and their families. New York: Haworth Press.

Kociol, L., & Schiff, M. (1989). Alzheimer: A Canadian family resource guide. Toronto: McGraw-Hill Ryerson.

Kübler-Ross, E. (1969). On death and dying. New York: Macmillan.

Mace, N. L., & Rabins, P. V. (1984). The thirty-six-hour day: A family guide to caring for persons with Alzheimer's disease, related dementing illnesses, and memory loss in later life. New York: Warner Communications.

Miner, G. D., Winters-Miner, L. A., Blass, J. P., Richter, R. W., & Valentine, J. L. (1989). Caring for Alzheimer's patients: A guide for family and healthcare providers. New York: Plenum Press, p. 59.

Powell, L. S., & Courtice, K. (1983). Alzheimer's disease: A guide for families. Don Mills, Ontario: Addison-Wesley.

Reisberg, B. (1986). A guide to Alzheimer's disease for families, spouses, and friends. New York: Free Press.

Ronch, J. L. (1989). Alzheimer's disease: A practical guide for those who help others. New York: Continuum.

5

Schizophrenia in the Elderly

Desmond L. Pouyat

Schizophrenia is an illness that develops in both men and women usually in their late teens or early twenties, with the vast majority of cases occurring before age 35. Late-life disorders, whose symptoms appear to be like those of schizophrenia, are called *"paraphrenia"* (Lurie, Swan, & Associates, 1987, p. 20). Cases of schizophrenia in elderly persons are extremely rare, affecting "less than 1% in the geriatric population" (Lurie, Swan, & Associates, 1987, p. 21). Thus, paraphrenia may be different from schizophrenia in that its "symptomatology is unique to old age" (Lurie, Swan, & Associates, 1987, p. 23); this is certainly an area for further research. For the purposes of this chapter, the important point is that schizophrenia develops in the young, and, in long-term cases of schizophrenia, follows them into old age. It is important to keep this point in mind because this chapter focuses on the elderly person with schizophrenia.

DIAGNOSING SCHIZOPHRENIA

Schizophrenia affects at least one person in one hundred (1 percent of the population) and affects both men and women equally. (Turns, 1978.) Often the illness encroaches on the individual slowly, almost imperceptibly, so that the individual and his or her family are unaware of its presence. In other cases, it strikes suddenly and with dramatic impact, producing mind-boggling symptoms.

When the illness develops gradually, the person may lose interest in typical pursuits and withdraw from friends or family, spending much of his or her time alone. The person may become easily confused, have difficulty con-

83

centrating, feel listless and apathetic, and become intensely preoccupied, often with religious or philosophical thoughts. Family members and friends may be upset by this behavior and begin to think that the person is lazy and unambitious, disorganized, or on drugs, rather than ill. At times, these symptoms level off and do not get worse, but usually they lead to another phase of the illness: the acute episode.

In the acute phase, the person may experience delusions, hallucinations, disturbances in behavior and feeling, and major distortions in thinking. This phase may take a long period to develop or may appear suddenly.

After this first acute episode, some people begin a journey of prolonged trouble with schizophrenia. The symptoms during this phase typically resemble those of the gradual-onset stage, although for many, this prolonged phase (traditionally referred to as chronic schizophrenia) is followed by additional acute episodes that often result in hospitalization.

Because the symptoms of schizophrenia resemble those of other conditions, differential diagnosis is necessary. Some other conditions that should be considered are the organic mental disorders, paranoid disorders, major depressive and manic episodes in which psychotic features are dominant, borderline disorders, and paranoid personality disorders. DSM-III-R, the standard diagnostic reference, should be consulted carefully when there are diagnostic concerns. The DSM-III-R criteria for diagnosing schizophrenia must be adhered to as described. The requirements are specific and broken into sections. The clinician must be rigorous in observation, analysis, and history taking to apply the criteria accurately.

TREATMENT ISSUES

Once a family member has been diagnosed as having schizophrenia, a sense of dread usually envelopes the family, particularly the parents. Much of this fear is due to the still-prevailing view that schizophrenia is a lifelong devastating illness, with little hope of recovery and limited forms of treatment. However, tremendous advances have been made in the use of medications (antipsychotics) and psychosocial rehabilitation techniques. It is in this latter area, along with individual, group, and family interventions of various types that social workers, along with other professionals in the mental health field, are making significant contributions.

Before the advent of chlorpromazine in the 1950s, many patients with schizophrenia who were not fortunate enough to recover or to have mild forms of the illness were sentenced to horrible lives in institutions for the insane, with little prospect of improvement. It is also worth noting that patients were misdiagnosed as having schizophrenia and hospitalized, so that they eventually became institutionalized. The institutionalization resulted in a similar psychosocial outcome for these patients as for those who suffered the dreaded dementia praecox, which became known as schizophrenia. What was often ignored was that many patients got well or improved significantly (on their own) and were able to live in their communities without psychiatric care.

Many first-admission patients never return to the hospital. Hence, professional judgments are often made from a distorted frame of reference, usually using the worst cases as the basis for judgment, research, and exploration about this patient group. Nevertheless, advances in the technology of medication since the introduction of chlorpromazine in the 1950s, in conjunction with improvements in psychosocial therapies, have definitely led to more effective treatments for the most difficult cases. The result has been a depopulation of the psychiatric hospitals in most Western countries, especially Canada, the United States, Italy, and Great Britain. Much has been learned about deinstitutionalization since the great surge of the 1970s, and this information has contributed to an improvement in current approaches to treatment.

Some of these improvements have included the expanded use of case-management services that are usually employed postdischarge after a generally much shorter stay in a hospital. Community infrastructures are improving, including increased recreational opportunities and more and generally better housing. Opportunities to work and to enter employment-focused rehabilitation programs still remain limited. However, there is increased awareness that major strides are needed in these two areas.

The recognition that people with long-term schizophrenia have frequently not been allowed to exercise independence and autonomy because of the illness itself, as well as the adverse effects of institutionalized care, is leading to the increased awareness that these individuals must be helped to be empowered. Thus, the mental health establishment in some jurisdictions has begun to consult with and involve consumers of mental health services regarding decisions about the evolution of the mental health care system. An example of this is The Provincial Mental Health Committee in Ontario, chaired by Robert Graham, which released a report on mental health care (1988). In 1990 throughout the Province of Ontario, the Graham Committee sought input from consumers and providers of services about proposed legislation on community health services. In one memorable example, the committee came to the grounds of the Hamilton Psychiatric Hospital in Hamilton, Ontario, for a summer gathering with an outdoor barbecue. Some 120 consumers (patients) attended, many of them with schizophrenia, young and old. After an informal outdoor lunch, many came one by one to outdoor microphones to voice their opinions. These views all had a common theme: the wish, the dream, to live as independent and fulfilling a life as possible, secure that their basic needs would be met through a dependable long-term system of psychiatric care that would follow them from hospital to community, to hospital, to community.

Members of the mental health professions are now in a position to acknowledge that the treatment of the long-term mentally ill, notably those with schizophrenia, must be considerably different from what it was in past decades. A major difference will be a changing role for large institutions. No longer will it be acceptable to keep patients in hospitals for years, for entire lifetimes. These institutions will continue to be downsized, and some will close. Some will become specialized in working with particular patient types such as forensic patients, or in providing certain types of service to the long-term mentally ill within an organized system of care that works in an increasingly coordinated and truly collaborative fashion with providers, consumers, and families to provide a system of treatment, care, and service that is truly sensitive to the patients' desire for as independent, productive, and fulfilling lives as possible, in which autonomy is encouraged and respected.

With changes in the service systems, advances in brain research, and improvements in medications, particularly the development of longer-acting medications with fewer side effects, by the next century, young people who develop long-term schizophrenia will spend the bulk of their lives in the community. No longer will these patients grow old in psychiatric hospitals and then go to the infirmaries of these hospitals to die or to nursing homes. They will be residents of our communities. Hence, the challenge for the remainder of this decade and into the twenty-first century will rest with the community. It will require major efforts to ensure that these individuals receive the type of coordinated, dependable, facilitative care they require to live fuller lives. It will mean that more attention must be paid to quality-of-life issues.

Because long-term sufferers of schizophrenia will live more of their lives in the community, gainful employment and income support will be major issues. Most people who suffer from long-term schizophrenia are poor, generally because they have not worked. There are many reasons for their exclusion from the labor force, including long stays in hospitals and the resulting institutionalization, the illness itself, and discrimination by employers and the larger society.

Clearly, innovative thinking is necessary to create a flexible income-support system that allows for governmental support, with the flexibility to earn reasonable amounts of money to supplement this support, and social workers should be at the forefront in developing such proposals. In this regard, the idea of a guaranteed annual income, a seemingly long-forgotten enlightened social policy proposal, is worth reviewing. There could be tremendous advantages to replacing the complicated, outdated, and expensive income-support programs with a guaranteed annual income that would allow earning above the ceilings that exist in many jurisdictions. The progressive income tax system could be used as a means of adjusting income gradually, as the ceiling was exceeded.

Work must also be done with the business community to create more flexible job opportunities in the free-market economy. Although there will continue to be a need for publicly funded sheltered work environments, perhaps these environments have been overemphasized. Certainly, encouraging businesses to make the workplace more flexible and attuned to the needs of the long-term mentally ill is an exciting challenge, and one that social workers are well equipped to lead. Organizations like the Canadian Mental Health Association and the National Institute of Mental Health should be at the forefront of this challenge.

As these changes continue to occur in the treatment structures that provide services to the long-term mentally ill, particularly those with prolonged schizophrenia, we will see improved levels of functioning by the more difficult cases.

SCHIZOPHRENIA AND OLD AGE

Thus far, this chapter has discussed what schizophrenia is, the criteria for its diagnosis, and the fact that it is a disease that generally afflicts young people, but that becomes chronic (prolonged) for many. In addition, some of the current and future treatment issues, particularly those that are salient to social work, have been examined. This section focuses on issues and concerns that challenge the elderly person who has managed to survive a lifetime of battling this illness and, at times, those who treat it.

Outcome

In order to gain a better understanding of these issues, the author examined the mental health literature's most well-known long-term follow-up studies, the important results of which are discussed here. In addition, because of the general paucity of information on elderly people with schizophrenia, the author developed a survey questionnaire and circulated copies of it to his colleagues in the ten provincial psychiatric hospitals in Ontario. (The

questionnaire and a summary of responses are available from the author.)
The major issues noted by the respondents (multidisciplinary professionals
working with the elderly) are addressed in this section.

The results of recent outcome studies, short and long term, all point to
varied outcomes, with marginal or deteriorated status the exception, rather
than the norm (Bheuler, 1968; Harding & Brooks, 1980; Huber, Gross,
Schuttler, et al., 1980; Winokur, Morrison, Clancy et al., 1972). They are
different from those of earlier studies, which demonstrated contradictory
outcomes. The recent investigations addressed those earlier contradictory
results by "outlining numerous methodological reasons why such contradictions have existed" (Harding, Zubin, & Strauss, 1987, p. 478). They
have helped to correct former illusions about the course and outcome of
schizophrenia by accounting for the outcome of everyone who once had
the disorder, instead of only patients who remain in systems of care.

Of the five long-term follow-up studies reported since 1972, all have
found that at least 50 percent of their cohorts had significantly improved or
recovered when assessed at twenty-, thirty-, or forty-year follow-ups. For
example, Bluer (1968, quoted in Harding et al., 1987, p. 478) followed
208 patients over twenty-three years who were admitted to Burgholzi Hospital in Zurich during 1942–43 and found that "23% of the first admission
group had achieved full recovery, and an additional 43% had sustained
significant improvement." Brook's (1981, quoted in Harding et al., 1987,
p. 479) thirty-two year investigation of a cohort of 269 chronic patients at
Vermont's only state hospital also demonstrated positive outcome results:
"At follow up in the 1980's, one-half to two-thirds of all the cohort sub
samples achieved significant improvement, or recovery; for the living DSM
III schizophrenia sub sample, 34% achieved full recovery in both psychiatric
status and social functioning, and an additional 34% were significantly
improved in both areas."

Other studies, such as Ciompi and Mueller's (1976, cited in Harding et
al., 1987, p. 479) assessment of a cohort of 289 subjects an average of thirty-
seven years after admission, have shown similar results. Ciompi and Mueller
noted that 29 percent of these patients achieved an end state of recovery,
and an additional 24 percent significantly improved. In the Bonn study,
Huber and associates (1975, cited in Harding et al., 1987, p. 479) reported
that of the 502 subjects they studied an average of twenty-two years after
admission, 26 percent had achieved complete recovery in both psychological
and social functioning and 31 percent had sustained significant improvement. These German researchers concluded that schizophrenia does not
appear to be a disease of slow progressive deterioration (as conventional
wisdom would have it). They noted, rather, that even in the second and

third decades of the illness, there is still a potential for full or partial recovery.

A U.S. study, the "Iowa 500" (Winokur et al., 1972, cited in Harding et al., 1987, p. 479), yielded much the same findings. Of 186 patients who were admitted to University Hospital in Iowa City from 1934 to 1944 and followed 35 years later, 20 percent were said to have recovered from psychiatric symptoms and an additional 26 percent had significantly improved.

HOPE. Although these studies looked at outcome, rather than at treatment methods, the positive results must be examined in the context of the times. Since deinstitutionalization took place only in the 1970s, a large number of patients would have lived great parts of their lives in psychiatric hospitals. With the recent emphasis on keeping patients in the community and with gradual improvements in the community infrastructure that are necessary for long-term rehabilitation and treatment, the prospects of substantial recovery for the person with long-term schizophrenia look positive, indeed. The fact that long-term studies indicate significant improvements for patients over time tends to support the view that even the elderly with schizophrenia, who were in hospitals most of their lives, could hope for significant improvements in their psychological and social functioning, particularly if the problems of institutionalization could be overcome. For these patients, the possibility of leaving the psychiatric hospitals for residence in a community-based setting is still viable and likely their best opportunity to sustain further improvements in their functioning.

OBSTACLES TO IMPROVEMENT. It is not always easy, however, to see hope for improvement in elderly individuals who have been branded with a diagnostic label as damaging as schizophrenia. Certainly, the stigma of this disorder is a major obstacle to overcome. Institutionalization, which frequently robs individuals of autonomy, motivation, and a reason to think, is another major barrier. Often these obstacles must be challenged vigorously and creatively to make a difference, and much ongoing education of both mental health professionals and the public is needed.

For many elderly people with schizophrenia, the physical infirmities of old age begin to take precedence over psychiatric symptomatology and may ultimately dictate what happens to and for them. However, the myths of the lack of potential because of age and no possibility of improvement because of the diagnosis of schizophrenia stand in the way of any hope for enhanced functioning. Of course, other myths also impede possible progress, such as, that all people with schizophrenia including the elderly, are dangerous. This myth may be a particular problem for the elderly person who requires care in a nursing home or other setting besides a psychiatric one. Social workers who try to obtain nursing-home beds for their clients who are patients in psychiatric hospitals or residential facilities know all too well how elusive those beds become when their patients arrive at the top of the waiting list only to find that the beds disappear and they must again be put on the list.

ETHNIC CULTURAL GROUPS. Other errors in thinking about prognosis and outcome concern results for ethnic groups from developing countries. The outcome of schizophrenia for these groups may be better, and the course more benign. The developing countries that have been studied include Mauritius, Saint Thomas, Sri Lanka, India, Colombia, Nigeria, Hong Kong, and Taiwan (Bland, 1982). A ten-year follow-up study by Lo and Lo (cited in Murphy, 1978) of Chinese schizophrenics in Hong Kong found that 65 percent had achieved remittance or suffered only mild deterioration. In Sri Lanka, (Wayler, 1979, pp. 144–58), where it is expected that the illness will be short lived, with a quick return to normality, the expectations seem to be fulfilled. The situation in Sri Lanka may be explained by Murphy's (1978) argument that the prevailing societal views on the causation of mental illness and society's expectations of its citizens are factors that may influence the outcome in schizophrenia. These studies point out that for elderly schizophrenics from other countries, cultural variables must be seriously examined, particularly in relation to their impact on treatment and service strategies.

❑ ❑ ❑

From the long-term follow-up studies, there is considerable evidence that changes in the severity of the illness occur over time. The psychiatric and social functioning of many people improves, but for many others, serious problems emerge. There is usually an increase in diseases that afflict the elderly, as well as those that afflict many long-term mentally ill persons, namely, chronic lung disease, cancer, and heart disease, which are due largely to a lifetime of heavy smoking. Social and housing problems also head the list of difficulties faced by elderly schizophrenics, as do problems with finances (managing their own estates).

Case Vignettes

The following case illustrations highlight these and other issues. Certainly, they show that working with elderly persons who have suffered lifelong schizophrenia is a challenging and rewarding endeavor.

The first two cases present examples of community living situations that followed years of psychiatric inpatient care. They demonstrate some of the typical needs of elderly schizophrenic patients who have been residing in the community for a long time. These case illustrations are actual ones, managed in the Home for Special Care (HSC) program of the Hamilton Psychiatric Hospital, Hamilton, Ontario. HSC is a special housing program, developed by the Ontario Ministry of Health to assist with deinstitution-alization. It consists of 2–13-bed residential and nursing homes, supervised by the social work staff of the hospital. Indentifying information has been changed.

Case A

Leroy is a 70-year-old single man, born June 11, 1920, in a small southwestern Ontario town. He became a patient at the hospital in 1942 and, except for a few brief interludes, remained a patient until 1968. At that time, he was discharged to the HSC program. He has remained in the HSC program since 1968 and has been at his current address since 1975. He has had no psychiatric admissions since his discharge from the hospital in 1968.

At the time of discharge, clinical notes indicated that his family members were not interested in Leroy. Indeed, Leroy felt "bossed around" by family members. However, the family was interested, and over time the members have become more involved. They were reinvolved more actively when Leroy turned 65 (in 1985), and his brother requested assistance for Leroy in applying for old-age security. Family visits were increased at the request of the family, but Leroy's prolonged visits to his family had to be managed in such a way that he could retain his place in the residential home. This issue often arises because the system's regulations limit the amount of time and the reasons why a bed may remain vacant; operators of these homes are not paid for beds left vacant beyond a certain cutoff point. These regulations hamper a social worker's plans for a resident to leave a home for an extended period and create problems when a resident must be hospitalized for a long time. Thus, social workers must play an active role in this area.

In 1986, when Leroy was admitted to the hospital for emergency surgery, the social worker functioned as a link among Leroy, his physicians, and his family, who resided in another town. She kept Leroy's family involved throughout the medical crisis, and her contact with them resulted in their continuing interest in Leroy afterwards.

Following Leroy's treatment for cancer, which included a colostomy, the social worker participated in a case conference in which it was recommended that he transfer to a nursing home. It became apparent that this recommendation was made because it was assumed that Leroy would not learn to care for his colostomy because of his diagnosis of schizophrenia.

The social worker explained the recommendation to Leroy, his family, and his landlady and said she would follow up on the anticipated application to the nursing home. Because of her knowledge of Leroy's capabilities and the nature of his home environment, however, the social worker thought that there was another option: Leroy could return to the residential home. Since she knew that the hospital discharge plans do not often follow through on recommendations for home care once the elderly patient with schizophrenia is discharged, she arranged for home care herself and provided support to the home care worker, Leroy, and the residential home staff during the period when Leroy was learning to care for the colostomy. Leroy's family members were also involved and were introduced to the home care nurse, and his visits to them were resumed. Today, Leroy continues to live in the residential home where he has resided since 1975.

Case B

Marilyn is a 67-year-old widow, born October 24, 1923. Until 1977, she had multiple admissions to Hamilton Psychiatric Hospital, where she was treated for schizophrenia. In case notes at the time, she was described as "subject to spontaneous regression into psychotic states" and with "no possibility of rehabilitation to self-sufficient living outside [the] hospital." In 1977, Marilyn was admitted to the HSC program. She remained in the same home for thirteen years, after which she had to be moved because the operator of the home could not continue to meet the psychiatric and physical challenges she presented.

Because of a combination of schizophrenia and alcoholism, Marilyn has been a particular challenge. She is unkempt; has problems handling money; resists medication; and has recently suffered falls, heart disease, pneumonia, and periodic urinary incontinence. However, she is friendly and has an independent nature.

Marilyn's second HSC living arrangement lasted fewer than three months; then she was moved to another home. After a short while, however (between April and October 1990), she fell and broke her ankle, for which she was hospitalized. After a week of hospitalization, Marilyn was pronounced ready for discharge. It was suggested that she could be returned to the infirmary at Hamilton Psychiatric Hospital or that a ground-floor room with an adjoining bathroom could be located for her in a lodging home. The pronouncement of her readiness for discharge ignored the recommendation that she should receive physiotherapy, the difficulty she had walking even a short distance, and her history of falls. The physiotherapist's second recommendation for physiotherapy was also ignored, and the surgeon pressured for Marilyn's release. Marilyn was finally discharged to an out-of-town facility to meet her need for a ground-floor room with an adjacent bathroom and twenty-four-hour staff who could care for her physical needs. Since the new facility was in the country, Marilyn was now cut off from her friends in the city. In addition, she would not be acceptable to day programs because of her careless smoking, frequent absences, and other psychiatric symptomatology.

The social worker intervened by arranging to have Marilyn and her city friends get together regularly for coffee. By maintaining these relationships, Marilyn no longer feels so isolated in her new country residence.

In this case, the social worker, by attempting to link Marilyn to her natural and informal network, is using resources that are immediately accessible to ensure that the social disruption created by the recent moves, especially the most recent move to the country, is minimized. The importance of maintaining the social relationships and natural support structures of those with schizophrenia, particularly the more vulnerable elderly, cannot be overemphasized.

Case C

Joan, aged 76, was institutionalized from 1936 to 1970 for the treatment of schizophrenia. She was discharged in 1970 and has lived in her present home since 1975. This home has seven residents, including four women, aged 68 through 79, who have been together for many years and who have developed strong bonds and a system of mutual support. Although all have some family connections, their great fear is that they will be separated from one another as they continue to age and their physical health deteriorates. During the six years that the present social worker has worked with Joan and the other women, they have had difficulties related to pensions, eyesight, hearing, mobility, and general access to the community at large. These issues have all be handled through a variety of means, including discussions in regular group meetings. The group meetings have not only helped the women to manage their fears more effectively, but have resulted in solutions to problems, some practical, and some innovative.

Joan has been showing signs of memory loss for some years, but has managed to function and at times has tried to cover up signs of her memory loss by fabricating responses to questions. Recently, however, Joan has insisted on visiting a nearby house "to be with her family." On one occasion, she was found packing her clothes for a possible move to this house. The occupants of the home, who were not related to Joan, were understanding of Joan's plight and agreed to inform her landlady whenever Joan turned up at the home. There was no major concern about Joan getting lost because she seemed to know the area well and always returned safely. Inquiries to Joan's family revealed that the home that Joan was intent on visiting and possibly moving into, had been her family home when she was a child.

Because of Joan's behavior, the social worker requested a psychiatric evaluation to determine the possible reasons for it. Of particular interest was whether dementia had actually established a firm hold.

The psychiatric consultation confirmed that Joan was experiencing signs of dementia and would probably deteriorate. The issue then became whether Joan should be moved to a more structured environment now or supported and cared for in her present home. It was decided to keep Joan where she was.

The social worker increased Joan's attendance at a senior citizen's program by one day per week and contacted her family, who agreed to write more often and to increase Joan's visits with them. In the home steps were taken to prevent Joan from making unplanned excursions by removing her coat and boots because she would not leave the home without them. In addition, the help of her support group of elderly women residents was solicited. The women agreed to watch Joan and to inform the house staff if she attempted to leave. A latch was also installed on the door as a deterrent. Although the other residents preferred to have the door unlocked, they were able to accept a latch to protect Joan.

These actions have enabled Joan to remain in her home, to be in a familiar environment with supportive friends and staff. This arrangement is not only beneficial from a social and human perspective, but it has prevented the more rapid deterioration in memory and confusion that would surely come from a move to new surroundings. Therefore, the goal is to keep Joan in this home setting for as long as is feasible.

Other Issues of Care

By now it should be clear that the elderly person with schizophrenia has far greater problems from a host of other situations, not the least of which are the many physical health problems of old age, than from schizophrenia. Those who still suffer schizophrenia in the final decades of life have many social and systemic problems associated with their illness, including the lack of access to appropriate and high-quality care for their physical ailments and to other levels of care, such as nursing homes. Frequently, these difficulties exist because of stereotypes about people with schizophrenia that militate against their getting appropriate care. In some cases, persistent symptoms of the illness alarm others. These symptoms usually take the form of some type of behavioral outburst, especially acts of physical aggression. (Of course, the behavioral responses of some elderly patients with other conditions, such as Alzheimer's disease and deteriorating dementia, are similar.)

In addition, the elderly person with schizophrenia may have received care from the same people for years—a situation that has positive aspects, but may also result in these caretaker's limited vision of the person: whether he or she is or is not changing, the person's potential or lack thereof, and so on (the not being able to see the forest for the trees phenomenon). In the responses to the author's questionnaire, "Schizophrenia and the Elderly," these individuals were described in such terms as "unhappy, worn out, lacking in life! lonely alienated human beings"; "fairly isolated individuals with little or no family-supportive network"; "very regressed"; "poor social skills"; "they appear burnt out, much older than their age"; "it is difficult to distinguish between the dementing process and symptoms of schizophrenia."

The issues that face elderly persons with schizophrenia have much in common with those of people who suffer from any long-term chronic illness. According to the responses to the author's questionnaire by professionals who work with these patients, the following problems are common: the side effects of the long-term use of neuroleptic medications, such as tardive dyskinesia; chronic physical illnesses that often complicate or limit the use of psychotropic medications; and increased neuropsychological deficits that become more prominent and obvious. Because many of today's elderly persons with schizophrenia live in the community, the need for adequate supportive housing and coordinated, integrated programming is another major issue. A related issue is the need for appropriate and adequate post-hospital follow-up, including ongoing case management and supportive care that is humane and cognizant of concerns related to quality-of-life issues— programs and services that provide stimulation to help individuals function at their highest levels.

Some patients are considered not to be suitable for nursing homes because of a history of episodic, unprovoked physical aggression that is associated with limbic cortex dysfunction and the lack of frontal-system inhibition. These patients present great challenges and often require continuing care in a psychiatric hospital.

For elderly patients who are still cared for by their families, often their own elderly parents, usually their mothers, there are other issues, including the need for respite care or relief care and, in many cases, ongoing assistance. In these situations, there is also the reality that care may have to be provided elsewhere as the parents or other family members themselves grow older and gradually or suddenly become unable to provide the care they may have provided for most of a lifetime. Professionals who work with these families must help them prepare to let go of their caretaking role and to plan for the continuing care needs of their relative, rather than to act precipitously in the midst of a crisis.

Role of the Social Worker

Working with elderly persons with schizophrenia who have remained in the mental health care system much of their lives poses a significant challenge to all the professionals who are usually involved, but especially to social workers, who are involved at every level in the system of care. Social workers are found in the psychiatric units of general hospitals; on the inpatient and outpatient teams of psychiatric hospitals; on the medical floors of general hospitals; and in the community in mental health clinics, case-management agencies, and in the social welfare agencies that provide income-maintenance assistance of all types, from general welfare to disability, and old-age pensions. Because of this all-encompassing role, social workers are in the best position to have an overall view and hence to determine the type, quality, and humaneness of care provided to this population. Because they work closely with patients and families, they are also in a position to hear what families are saying about their relatives' needs and should be acutely aware of the patients' needs as consumers.

Of course, utilizing this knowledge effectively and taking the time to do so are themselves a challenge because it is easy to become frustrated with a system that views elderly persons with schizophrenia in a negative way, that thinks that these people should remain in psychiatric hospitals for treatment, and that has had limited success with this chronic group.

Because of the inescapable, gradual demise that occurs with these elderly patients as they develop additional maladies in conjunction with their psychiatric condition, it is easy to become discouraged. Discouragement may lead to burnout, or a resigned state in which opportunities for improvement in patients and systems are ignored. However, by focusing on some of the principal functions of their profession that are clearly necessary for work with this population and by striving for excellence, social workers can overcome their despair. Some of these functions include discharge planning; community-integration efforts; community consultation; linking the system and the community; manipulating the environment, advocacy, education, and mediation; counseling and support for patients, caregivers, family, and friends; and the traditional social welfare role.

Most of these functions are carried out in the community. The focus of care has shifted from large institutions to a variety of community-living arrangements, from independent living to the high-care protective environment of nursing homes. In ensuring that they effectively develop and implement discharge plans that place patients in community-living arrangements that most appropriately meet their needs, social workers have a tremendous responsibility. When there are no appropriate resources in the community, they have the opportunity, through a community development approach, to garner the necessary support to develop what is needed. Social workers are best positioned to take on such roles because of their role as liaisons between institutions and all persons in the community who are involved in the system of care. Thus, social workers establish linkages, consult, educate, provide support for new ventures, join and initiate advocacy ventures on behalf of client groups, help change micro- and macroenvironments, and develop new systems of care.

Finally, social workers have an obligation to conduct research, including evaluations of new approaches to care. Elderly people with schizophrenia are a neglected group; considerable opportunities exist to examine this population and the structures that are involved in the provision of treatment and care.

Basic demographic data are needed on the population of elderly persons with schizophrenia. How many exist, and where are they located? How many still live with caregivers who are themselves elderly? What is the potential for change? How many can still be discharged from psychiatric hospitals to community living arrangements? Should some live out their lives in psychiatric hospitals? If so, who are they? How many have recovered from schizophrenia, but continue to be treated with antipsychotic medications and are given little or no medical review? What about normal medical care that elderly people require? Does this population of patients receive it, or are they victims of medical (health care) discrimination, simply because they have schizophrenia and are poor, as well as elderly? Are they overmedicated?

The questions and research possibilities are many; what is required are dedicated professionals who are willing to devote themselves to work in this field and to the discipline and hard slugging of the practitioner-researcher, so that knowledge of this tragic group of people can be expanded, documented, and studied. Social workers can, and should, take the lead.

REFERENCES AND SUGGESTED READINGS

Bheuler, M. (1968). A 23-year longitudinal study of 208 schizophrenics and impressions in regard to the nature of schizophrenia. In D. Rosenthal, & S. S. Kety, (Eds.), *The transmission of schizophrenia*. Oxford: Pergamon, 1968.

Bland, R. C. (1982). Predicting the outcome of schizophrenia. *Canadian Journal of Psychiatry, 27*, 52–62.

Blixen, C. E. (1988). Aging and mental health care. *Journal of Gerontological Nursing, 14*(11), 11–15.

Brugha, T. S., Wing, J. K., & Smith, B. L. (1989). Physical health of the long-term mentally ill in the community. Is there unmet need? *British Journal of Psychiatry*, 155, 777–781.

Buckwalter, K. C., & Light, E. (1989). New directions for psychiatric mental health nurses: The chronically mentally ill elderly. *Archives of Psychiatric Nursing*, 3(1), 53–54.

Buckwalter, K. C., McLeran, H., Mitchell, S., & Andrews, P. H. (1988). Responding to mental health needs of the elderly in rural areas: A collaborative geriatric education center model. *Gerontology Geriatric Education*, 8(3–4), 69–80.

Ciompi, L. (1980). Catamnestic long-term study on the course of life and aging of schizophrenics. *Schizophrenia Bulletin*, 6, 606–616.

Cohen, C. I., Stastny, P., Perlick, D., Samuelly, I. & Horn, L. (1988). Cognitive deficits among aging schizophrenic patients residing in the community. *Hospital and Community Psychiatry*, 39, 557–559.

Daum, C. M., Brooks, G. W., & Albee, G. W. (1977). Twenty year follow-up of 253 schizophrenic patients originally selected for chronic disability: Pilot study. *Psychiatric Journal of the University of Ottawa*, 2(3), 129–132.

Draper, R. J. (1989). The chronically mentally ill: Planning a future. *Psychiatric Journal of the University of Ottawa*, 14(3), 463–466.

Fellin, P. A., & Powell, T. J. (1988). Mental health services and older adult minorities: An assessment. *The Gerontologist*, 28, 442–447.

Fischer, P. J., Shapiro, S., Breakey, W. R., Anthony, J. C., & Kramer, M. (1986). Mental health and social characteristics of the homeless: A survey of mission users. *American Journal of Public Health*, 76, 519–524.

Freeman, H., & Alpert, M. (1986). Prevalence of schizophrenia in an urban population. *British Journal of Psychiatry*, 149, 603–611.

Goldstrom, I. D., Burns, B. J., Kessler, L. G., Feuerberg, M. A., Larson, D. B., Miller, N. E., & Cromer, W. J. (1987). Mental health services use by elderly adults in a primary care setting. *Journal of Gerontology*, 42, 147–153.

Gomez, E. (1977). Clinical observations in the treatment of tardive dyskinesia with dihydrogenated ergot alkaloids (Hydergine), preliminary findings. *Psychiatric Journal of the University of Ottawa*, 2(2), 67–71.

Grau, L. (1989). The changing context of mental health care for the elderly. *Gerontology Geriatric Education*, 9(3), 7–15.

Haber, S., & McCall, N. (1989). Use of nonphysician providers in the Medicare program: Assessment of the Direct Reimbursement of Clinical Social Workers demonstration project. *Inquiry*, 26, 158–169.

Harding, C. M., & Brooks, E. W. (1980). Longitudinal assessment of a cohort of chronic schizophrenics discharged twenty years ago. *Psychiatric Journal of the University of Ottawa*, 5, 274–278.

Harding, C. M., Zubin, J., & Strauss, J. S. (1987). Chronicity in schizophrenia:

Fact, partial fact, or artifact? *Hospital and Community Psychiatry, 38,* 477–486.

Huber, G., Gross, G., Schuttler, R., et al. (1980). Longitudinal studies of schizophrenic patients. *Schizophrenia Bulletin, 6,* 592–605.

Jennings, J. (1987). Elderly parents as caregivers for their adult dependent children. *Social Work, 32,* 430–433.

Koenig, H. G., & Meador, K. G. (1987). Psychiatric megatrends and the elderly (editorial). *Geronology Geriatric Education, 7*(3–4), 43–53.

Kuipers, L., MacCarthy, B., Hurry, J., & Harper, R. (1989). Counselling the relatives of the long-term adult mentally ill. II. A low-cost supportive model. *British Journal of Psychiatry, 154,* 775–782.

Levy, A., Davidson, S., & Elizur, A. (1987). The elderly patient in the emergency psychiatric unit. *Harefuah, 112,* 112–114.

Lurie, E. E., Swan, J. H., & Associates. (1987). *Serving the mentally ill elderly: Problems and perspectives.* Lexington, MA: D. C. Heath.

McGlashan, T. H. (1984). The Chestnut Lodge follow-up study. *Archives of General Psychiatry, 41,* 586–601.

Milazzo-Sayre, L. J., Benson, P. R., Rosenstein, M. J., & Manderscheid, R. W. (1987). Use of inpatient services by the elderly age 65 and over, United States, 1980. *Mental Health Statistical Note, 181,* 1–37.

Murphy, H. B. M. (1978). Cultural influences in incidence, course, and treatment response. In W. L. Cromwell & R. L. Matthysse (Eds.), *The nature on schizophrenia* (pp. 586–594). New York: Grune & Stratton.

Newman, F. L., Griffin, B. P., Black, R. W., & Page, S. E. (1989). Linking level of care to level of need: Assessing the need for mental health care for nursing home residents. *American Psychologist, 44,* 1315–1324.

Nielsen, J. A., & Nielsen, J. (1989). Prevalence investigation of mental illness in the aged in 1961, 1972 and 1977 in a geographically delimited Danish population group. *Acta Psychiatrica Scandinavica* (Suppl.), *348,* 95–104, 167–178.

Owens, D. G. C., & Johnstone, E. C. (1980). The disabilities of chronic schizophrenia—their nature and the factors contributing to their development. *British Journal of Psychiatry, 136,* 384–395.

Perez, E. L., & Blouin, J. (1986). Psychiatric emergency consultations to elderly patients in a Canadian general hospital. *Journal of the American Geriatric Society, 34*(2), 91–94.

Persky, T., Taylor, A., & Simson, S. (1989). The network trilogy project: Linking aging, mental health and health agencies. *Gerontology Geriatric Education, 9*(3), 79–88.

Provincial Mental Health Committee, The. (1988, July). Building community support for people: A plan for mental health in Ontario. (Also called The Graham Report.)

Reifler, B. V., Larson, E. G., & Teri, L. (1987). An outpatient geriatric psychiatry assessment and treatment service. *Clinical Geriatric Medicine. 3,* 203–209.

Rickards, L. D. (1989). Conference on Interdisciplinary Issues in Mental Health and Aging: Workshop issues and recommendations. *Gerontology Geriatric Education*, 9(3), 61–77.

Roybal, E. R. (1988). Mental health and aging: The need for an expanded federal response. *American Psychologist*, 43, 189–194.

Smith, D. A. (1987, May 1). The family practitioner and psychiatric problems in the old (letter). *Journal of the American Medical Association*, 257, 2292–2293.

Smyer, M. A. (1989). Nursing homes as a setting for psychological practice. *American Psychologist*, 44, 1307–1314.

Snowdon, J. (1987). Psychiatric services for the elderly. *Australian and New Zealand Journal of Psychiatry*, 21, 131–136.

Swan, J. H. (1987). The substitution of nursing homes for inpatient psychiatric care. *Community Mental Health Journal*, 23, 3–18.

Thusholt, F. J., Antonsen, J., Jorgensen, F., & Nguyen-Ba-Thuan. (1989, June 12). Social psychiatric therapeutic possibilities for long-term psychiatric patients. *Ugeskr-Laeger*, 151, 1544–1549.

Tourigny-Rivard, M. F., & Drury, M. (1987). The effects of monthly psychiatric consultation in a nursing home. *The Gerontologist*, 27, 363–366.

Turns, D. M. (1978) The epidemiology of schizophrenia. In H. C. Denber (Ed.), *Schizophrenia: Theory, diagnosis, and treament*. New York: Dekker.

Wayler, N. E. (1979). Is outcome for schizophrenia better in non-industrialized societies? The case of Sri Lanka. *Journal of Nervous and Mental Disorders*, 167, 144–158.

Wells, J. E., Bushnell, J. A., Hornblow, A. R., Joyce, P. R., & Oakley-Browne, M. A. (1989). Christchurch Psychiatric Epidemiology Study: Part 1. Methodology and lifetime prevalence for specific psychiatric disorders. *Australian and New Zealand Journal of Psychiatry*, 23, 315–326.

Winokur, G., Morrison, J., Clancy, J., et al. (1972). The Iowa 500 II: A blind family history comparison of mania, depression, and schizophrenia. *Archives of General Psychiatry*, 27, 462–464.

Woodruff, J. C., Donnan, H., & Halpin, G. (1988). Changing elderly persons' attitudes toward mental health professionals. *The Gerontologist*, 28, 800–802.

6

Elderly People with Autism:

Defining a Social Work Agenda for Research and Practice

Nora Gold • Margaret Whelan

T here is no documented information about the needs of elderly people
with autism. Therefore, it is essential that social workers begin immediately to identify the questions to be asked and then pursue the answers,
so the profession may play a meaningful role in planning for the needs of
elderly people with this condition. This chapter represents a crucial first
step in defining an agenda for research and practice with this population.

This chapter was written with equal collaboration, and the names of the authors are listed
alphabetically.
   Since the writing of this chapter, there have been significant developments in the field of
autism. Although the criteria for diagnosing this disorder remain unchanged so far, the
introduction of a technique called facilitated communication is challenging many of the
prevailing assumptions about autism and is prompting a re-examination of both the nature
and implications of the disorder. Through facilitated communication, many people with
autism are now able to communicate more fully than ever before. They are also demonstrating
levels of comprehension, reading, math skills, and awareness of their environments previously
considered far beyond the capacities of these people. Unfortunately, as so often happens with
clinical breakthroughs of this kind, it takes time for the research to catch up with the field.
Research on facilitated communication is only now being conducted, and it will be some
time before what are expected to be fundamental redefinitions of autism stand on an empirical
basis. Until that time, the authors are forced to rely on the knowledge base of what has been
empirically established about autism to date, while recognizing that much of this may be
obsolete in the very near future.

THE CURRENT UNDERSTANDING OF AUTISM

There is little doubt that there have always been children with autism. The work of Kanner (1943) resulted in the recognition that these children have a constellation of deficits that are different from those of mentally retarded children and children with schizophrenia. Upon reflection, many have wondered if tales and myths were actually describing children with autism. For example, Wing (1971) reviewed the story of Victor, the Wild Boy of Aveyron, discovered by Dr. J. M. G. Itard in 1799 and concluded that the descriptions of Victor's behavior were consistent with the current knowledge of autism.

The most current perspective on autism is articulated in DSM-III-R, which lists autism as one of two subtypes of the classification of Pervasive Developmental Disorders (PDD) and part of the broader grouping called Developmental Disorders. The term *pervasive* denotes that the disorder affects several areas of development (socialization, communication, and the repertoire of interests and activities). The term *developmental* conveys the fact that this disorder originates in infancy and childhood and rules out injury or disease. *Disorder* indicates that there is a delay in development, as well as a deviance from the pattern of normal development (Geneva Centre, 1988).

This categorization incorporates a number of previously used diagnoses in DSM-III-R, including Atypical Development, Symbiotic Psychosis, Childhood Psychosis, Childhood Schizophrenia, Infantile Autism, and Kanner's Syndrome. DSM-III-R focuses on three central areas of impairment that are of importance when the diagnosis of autism is to be considered. These include impairments in social interaction and communication, as well as highly limited interests (pp. 38–39).

Considerable research and academic debate have challenged and redefined autism since Kanner's (1943) original formulation. Although the original descriptions of the unique characteristics of autism have withstood the test of time (Kanner, 1971; Rumsey, Rapoport, & Sceery, 1985; Szatmari, Bartolucci, Bremner, Bond, & Rich, 1989), many of the accompanying, and subsequent, hypotheses of causation and prognosis have not. Over the past forty-nine years there has been a shift from the erroneous view of autism as a psychiatric disorder akin to psychosis to the recognition that autism is a developmental disorder. It was not until 1980, almost forty years after Kanner's work first appeared, that autism, as a category distinct from schizophrenia, was included in the DSM code system.

Autism frequently coexists with other disorders, most notably mental retardation. Approximately 75 percent of individuals with autism also have

a diagnosis of mental retardation. However, even persons with severe retardation do not present with the essential cluster of symptoms of autism
(DSM-III-R). In DSM-III (1980), the incidence rate for autism was noted
as 4 in 10,000. The more specific and inclusive criteria in DSM-III-R
(1987) have recently raised the estimated rate to 12 in 10,000 (Bryson,
Clarke, & Smith, 1988). The implications of this incidence rate are not yet
clear, but obviously will be significant for planning and providing services
to a much larger population than before.

The impairments evidenced in autism are assumed to be lifelong, based
on follow-up studies of young adults with autism. In his follow-up study,
twenty-eight years after his original treatise, Kanner (1971) found that the
central qualities that designated the autistic disorder had remained essentially
intact. Similarly, two more recent follow-up studies (Rumsey et al., 1985;
Szatmari et al., 1989) of high-functioning adults with autism (all under age
36) showed the constancy of the central elements of the diagnosis, even
though there may be considerable changes in the manifestation of these
impairments. These findings mean that persons with autism may be expected
to live into older adulthood without a significant diminution of the chief
symptoms of the disorder.

THE UNIQUE CHALLENGE IN THE STUDY OF ELDERLY PEOPLE WITH AUTISM

Who are the elderly people with autism? And where are they? The oldest
persons known to have autism, according to Kanner's definition, are
now only in their forties and fifties, since this diagnosis has been available
only since 1943. Thus, no elderly people currently have a diagnosis of
autism.

Obviously, however, there are elderly persons with autism (even if they
have not been formally diagnosed as such), since it is understood to be a
lifelong disorder. Many of these adults probably can be found in the institutions for the developmentally handicapped (Geneva Centre, 1988; Munro
& Duncan, 1984), since prior to 1943, children and adults with autism
were viewed as severely mentally retarded or seriously emotionally disturbed.
Some of the higher-functioning adults with autism (whose IQs are above
70) may also be in psychiatric institutions, since high-functioning children
with the symptoms of autism were then served by the facilities for the
psychiatrically impaired, as well as by those for the developmentally disabled.
The authors know of only one attempt to establish an incidence rate of

autism among adults who have the symptoms, but not the diagnosis, of autism. The results suggest that as many as 10 percent of the residents in an institution for the developmentally disabled may qualify as having autism (Munro & Duncan, 1984). It is probable that similar numbers of elderly people in these institutions would also meet these criteria.

In spite of the obvious difficulty of not having a population that can be directly and readily studied, it is possible to begin discussing the needs of older people with autism. This chapter relies on two sources of data as the basis for generating questions and defining the issues for study: (1) the experience in the field of mental retardation, specifically related to aging, and (2) the extensive clinical expertise regarding persons with autism, particularly in the area of planning for previous developmental transitions (i.e., childhood to adolescence and adolescence to adulthood).

With regard to the first knowledge base, there is a wealth of research and experience in the field of mental retardation (e.g., Janicki, Knox, & Jacobson, 1985; Janicki, Otis, Puccio, Rettig, & Jacobson, 1985; Krauss & Seltzer, 1986; Seltzer, 1985; see also Chapter 8, this volume). This body of knowledge has obvious relevance to the study of elderly persons with autism and can contribute to our understanding by helping us to articulate and focus our questions and research. However, it is important to remember that although the questions explored may be similar, the answers to these questions will differ in many cases because of the differences between the two disabilities (see, e.g., Goldberg, Marcovitch, MacGregor, & Lojkasek, 1985; Holroyd & McArthur, 1976).

Regarding the second source of data, there has been a growing recognition in the field of autism about the importance of special professional supports during transitions in the life cycle. Persons with autism experience great difficulty with change in general, and the changes associated with transitions (such as the move from home to school and then from school to work) are challenging for them. These transitions can be relatively smooth if there is careful planning, attention to pacing, and preparation of the individual. A study of transitional issues related to young adults with autism concluded that the main factor in the success of planning for transitions is the commitment to interagency collaboration and long-term planning and the involvement of the clients (parents, guardians, and persons with autism) in the decision-making process (Geneva Centre, 1988). The same study found that having trained staff available to assist the individual is essential to successful transitions. The focus on planning for transitions for persons with autism provides a strong foundation for beginning to assess and deal with the needs of people with autism as they age.

THE SOCIAL WORKER'S ROLE

Social workers will have a central role to play in planning for this population. Their principal tasks will include, in sequential order,

1. assessing and defining the needs of elderly people with autism
2. developing and providing the necessary services
3. monitoring and evaluating these services on an ongoing basis and initiating modifications to improve them.

These three social work tasks can be most clearly conceptualized as two prongs of mutually enhancing professional activity: research and service development. This section discusses both these functions, although it gives greater weight to research in light of the lack of knowledge about elderly people with autism and their needs.

Defining a Research Agenda

A crucial first step in conducting research on this population will be to acquire some basic descriptive data. Specifically, we need to know how many elderly people with autism there are and whether their numbers are growing, decreasing, or remaining constant. A profile of the characteristics of this population, in terms of their physical and mental health, residential arrangements, and occupational activities, is also essential. Finally, the needs of this population for supports and services must also be examined. Studies in all these areas must be started as soon as possible if they are to serve as the foundation for systematic and rational planning.

A major challenge in conducting this research, as was already mentioned, is not having a population of elderly people with autism who can be studied at this time. One solution may be to begin research with the first cohort who were diagnosed with autism according to Kanner's definition and to start the first longitudinal studies now. In these studies, in addition to using secondary data (medical reports, census data, agency statistics, and information from professionals and relatives), it will be crucial, insofar as possible, to begin asking people with autism what they want and to involve them in planning. Because many persons with autism have major communication deficits, they have consistently been excluded from the research process, and their wishes have not been heard (the one notable exception being the study by Rumsey et al., 1985). Higher-functioning persons with autism who can communicate their wishes, either verbally or nonverbally (through the use of augmentative communication systems, such as signing and computers), should be partners with planners and researchers in defining their own difficulties, needs, and solutions, even if these factors cannot be generalized to persons with autism at other functional levels.

Four main areas relevant to elderly people with autism need to be addressed by research: (1) physical health, (2) mental health, (3) occupational planning, and (4) residential alternatives. These areas are discussed next in relation to issues and questions for research.

PHYSICAL HEALTH The critical questions to be explored in this area concern the interaction between the normal processes of aging and the manifestations of autism over the life span and any unique medical or neurological patterns that may emerge. The questions asked with regard to aging and mental retardation are equally applicable here (see Chapter 8). Specifically, we would want to find out whether the health care needs of elderly people with autism differ from those of other elderly people; whether their life span is shorter (as is the case, for example, with persons with Down's syndrome); and whether there are differences in the rate of deterioration in their functional abilities, in the diseases associated with their aging, or in the causes of their death. Another important issue is whether changes in the symptom profile in the main deficit areas of autism (social, communicative, cognitive) occur as these persons age. Given that recent research has indicated that autism is a disorder with multiple causes (DSM-III-R, 1987; Ritvo, 1987), it is possible that there will be a wide range of answers to these questions.

MENTAL HEALTH Assessing the mental health of persons with autism is possibly the most difficult and underdeveloped area of research related to this population. Because many persons with autism experience severe deficits in the areas of communication and social interaction, little is understood about their affective patterns or disorders. The presence of depression or anxiety may be overlooked or misdiagnosed because of assumptions about the disorder, a reluctance to examine these possibilities in the absence of previous research or clinical understanding, or the severity or overwhelming nature of an individual's other problems. The development of a descriptive profile of affective norms would therefore be essential before the mental health needs of this population could be met.

Research in this area could begin by examining the kinds of gratifications (activities, objects, or social relationships) that exist for elderly people with autism and that thereby contribute to their enhanced emotional well-being and mental health. The deficits experienced by persons with autism in forming and maintaining social connections may have resulted in some lack of attention by professionals to the social variable when planning. For example, whereas the relationships with others may be considered a crucial factor in selecting a certain residential placement for a person with mental retardation, in the case of autism, usually only the individual's functional level or educational needs have been considered (since it is often assumed that people with autism do not connect with others, anyway).

On the other hand, there are reports of higher-functioning persons with autism who have married or intend to marry and who are apparently capable of a long-lasting relationship (Szatmari et al., 1989). The issue of the affective potential of persons with autism, at all functional levels, is becoming a focus of interest in the field, especially in light of emerging data (e.g., Wing, 1981) about persons with dual diagnoses (a developmental disorder and a psychiatric disorder). In the meantime, until more is known, perhaps our assumptions about what persons with autism may achieve in relation to intimacy, love, marriage, or sexual relations should be questioned more carefully in research, and sensitive attention to social connections that have been formed and valued (such as intense and meaningful relationships with family members) should constitute a significant aspect of our plans for treatment and services. It is also important to examine more closely the relationships of elderly people with autism with peers and professionals and the significance of these connections to them.

With regard to high-functioning persons with autism, it is worth exploring the extent to which emotional issues arise that are similar to those for some mentally retarded persons (for example, the awareness of "being different" and of having "missed out" on some aspects of "normal life"). For the elderly person with autism who is capable of both higher cognitive processes and has the capacity to articulate them, the opportunity to discuss these feelings and losses would be important.

OCCUPATIONAL PLANNING Determining the kinds of daily activities that would be most appropriate for this population takes on a special significance in light of some of the characteristics of autism. Most of the programs for elderly people (in the mainstream and in the mental retardation sectors) involve a variety of leisure-time activities that are, for the most part, relaxed, loosely structured or not structured, and highly social in content. Most children and adults with autism tend to withdraw socially and to engage in perseverating or self-stimulatory behavior in response to unstructured situations. They may also have no interest in, and even discomfort with, social interactions. Should these characteristics persist into older adulthood, the usual programs for the elderly in both the mainstream and the mental retardation sectors would be contraindicated for elderly people with autism.

More suitable activities for this population would then be those that are highly structured and predicable, with flexibility regarding the degree of social interaction required. The need for such activities may render the usual distinctions between retirement and leisure and work irrelevant and may suggest that we consider extending whatever work, vocational, or occupational arrangements that characterized the preceding period into this stage of life. This is not to suggest that older adulthood is conceived of as a mere holding period in which people are maintained, rather than encouraged to develop and grow. It merely speaks to the intense needs of persons with autism for structure in their daily activities, as well as the importance of sensitive planning regarding the degree of social interaction these activities assume. Whatever the findings of the research, it is likely that given the wide range in functional ability and social competence among persons with autism, a variety of activities and programs will be necessary to meet their needs. For example, elderly people with autism who are high functioning may be able to benefit from some of the programs in the mainstream or mental retardation sectors, but would likely still require careful planning and professional support to facilitate their involvement.

RESIDENTIAL ALTERNATIVES Living with a person with autism is, in most cases, extremely stressful for families (Bristol, 1979; DeMyer, 1979; Gold, 1990; Marcus, 1977), considerably more so, for example, than living with a person with Down's syndrome (Holroyd & McArthur, 1976). Consequently, by early adulthood, most persons with autism are living apart from their families, usually in group homes (Bryson, 1991), in contrast to persons with mental retardation, many of whom live at home until the death of their parents (see Chapter 8). Therefore, it seems evident that, with few exceptions (those who continue to live with their families or the small high-functioning group who are able to live independently in the community), the great majority of elderly people with autism will live in residential facilities. This situation poses a considerable challenge to planners and professionals, since residential alternatives for persons with autism are scarce, waiting lists are long (five years or longer) for those that do exist, and arrangements lack variation and flexibility. The September 1990 issue of the *Journal of Autism and Developmental Disorders*, devoted exclusively to residential services for persons with autism, reflects the current concerns in the field.

Research would be an essential part of the planning process and would involve the following tasks:

1. Exploring the range of different residential needs and preferences of elderly people with autism.
2. Assessing existing residential facilities in the community (in both the mainstream and the mental retardation sectors) that could be appropriate and made accessible to elderly people with autism.

3. Developing criteria for determining which type of residence would best suit a given individual (the person's functional level being only one variable).
4. Estimating how many new residences of each type would have to be created to meet the need.

The residential needs of elderly people with autism will necessarily differ from those of adolescents and young adults with autism. Certain additional supports (e.g., safety and emergency measures) are required for an aging population (even for the well elderly), as well as, of course, progressively intensive medical and nursing supports to respond to the predictable deterioration of people as they age. Usually, residential facilities are defined by the residents' functional level; therefore, if a resident's medical condition worsens, he or she will be transferred to another type of facility, such as a nursing home. This discontinuity of care has damaging effects on elderly people in general (Chappell, Strain, & Blandford, 1986) and may be particularly distressing to elderly people with autism, in light of their need for constancy in their surroundings and their difficulty adjusting to change. One innovative proposal is that residential facilities should be developed that can adapt to elderly people as their needs change, rather than obliging them to adapt to the services. So, for example, as an individual required more medical supports, more supports would be brought into the residence, and he or she would be cared for there (*Strategies for Change*, 1990). Such an approach to residential services would represent "permanency planning" at its best.

Implications for Practice

Social work practice at all levels is significantly challenged by the needs of a special aging population that has been largely unrecognized until now. Social workers have an essential role to play in the delivery of service to families who are struggling to deal with an aging family member with autism. There are also important functions for social workers as advocates for these individuals and their families and as agents of social change at the policy and service development levels.

The impact of autism on the family is now known to be both devastating and pervasive (DeMyer, 1979; Gold & Whelan, 1989). On the basis of what we know from working with children and adolescents with autism and their families, it is possible to identify crucial areas in which these families would need support. Central among them is help with long-term planning. The lifelong nature of the disorder of autism and the severity of its impairments require that families remain actively involved in planning and caring well beyond the ages usually expected for normally developing children. The caregiving expectations do not necessarily diminish with the increasing age and maturity of the child with autism.

The current policies of community care have thus far not established a sense of partnership between families and the state. Therefore, there is reason to be concerned about whether the burden of caregiving will remain with the family, especially in light of the movement toward deinstitutionalization and community-based care. It cannot, and should not, be assumed that siblings will be willing or able to step in and assume the caregiving responsibilities that were previously borne by parents. An important role for social work with these families, then, would be to support parents and siblings as they define (or seek to define) the roles, if any, they can or want to play in relation to the aging person with autism. The social worker's role also includes advocating for policies that would allow family members the flexibility to take an active part in the lives of their aging relatives with autism without having to assume the full burden of care.

Advocacy is also necessary in regard to issues of financial and legal protection. Elderly people in general are increasingly vulnerable to poverty (Ross & Shillington, 1989), and elderly people with disabilities are all the more so, since most will not have a lifetime of paid work that can provide them with security in old age. Furthermore, elderly people with disabilities may be particularly vulnerable to violations of various human rights and freedoms. Legal issues that have been relevant in the past to persons with mental retardation and that may also become important to elderly people with autism, include the right to marry, the right to have children, and the right to have or to refuse certain kinds of treatment. Social workers have an important role to play in collaborating with families in advocacy efforts to protect elderly people with autism, as well as other disabilities, against abuses of their financial or legal rights.

Before they develop new services in each of these four areas, social workers must closely examine which formal supports exist that may be relevant and helpful to elderly people with autism. The service sectors that cater to the mainstream elderly and to elderly people with other developmental disabilities (notably, mental retardation) may be valuable resources to elderly people with autism, as much as these two sectors are for children and adults with autism. With reference to these earlier stages of development, there is a growing body of knowledge about both the advantages and the limitations of utilizing services that are not designed specifically for persons with autism (Geneva Centre, 1988; *Journal of Autism and Developmental Disorders*, 1990). One obvious advantage is that services are not duplicated, so the limited available resources can be channeled in a focused way to respond to the specific and unique needs of those with autism. If services to children and adults with autism are any indication, it is likely that services in the mainstream and mental retardation sectors will be most useful to elderly people with autism when they are used selectively, with clearly defined goals, close monitoring, and professional support. Balancing the benefits of both integrated and specialized autism-only services is an essential part of the planning process with this population. Social workers should also be prepared to help train and consult with generic service providers, so these providers can tailor their services to meet the special needs of elderly people with autism. Effective advocacy through lobbying for the needs of these individuals will ensure that the families of persons with autism, and autistic persons themselves, when possible, are true partners in the development and provision of services to this population.

CONCLUSION

Services to individuals with autism and their families have emerged primarily in the past two decades. The efforts of parents and professionals have focused on the development of services for children, and as these children and their families have grown and needed new and changing services, the system has tried to adjust accordingly. Because of the numerous and urgent demands for service, much of the professional activity during this period has been reactive, rather than proactive. As a result, there is now an increased commitment in the field to long-term planning from a proactive perspective. Such an approach to assisting elderly people with autism and their families is particularly urgent as the movement toward deinstitutionalization continues and as the entire society faces the burgeoning demand for services to all persons who are aging.

This chapter has defined a preliminary research agenda for the profession and for the field in general and identified some of the major issues in planning services for this population. Although it is by no means an exhaustive projection of the complexities and challenges that lie ahead, the authors hope that it will help spur the research and planning that are urgently necessary if we are to be well prepared when we greet the first cohort of people with autism as they enter older adulthood.

BIBLIOGRAPHY

American Psychiatric Association. (1980). *Diagnostic and statistical manual of mental disorders* (3rd ed.) (DSM-III). Washington, DC: Author.

American Psychiatric Association. (1987). *Diagnostic and statistical manual of mental disorders* (3rd ed., rev.) (DSM-III-R). Washington, DC: Author.

Anglin, B. (1981). *They never asked for help: A study on the needs of elderly retarded people in Metro Toronto.* Maple, Ontario: Belsten.

Bristol, M. M. (1979). Maternal coping with autistic children: Adequacy of interpersonal support and effects of child's characteristics. *Dissertation Abstracts International, 40,* 3943A–3944A. (University Microfilms No. 79-25, 890)

Bryson, S. E. (1991). *Our most vulnerable citizen: Report of the Adult Task Force.* Guelph, Ontario: Autism Society Ontario.

Bryson, S. E., Clarke, B. S., & Smith, I. M. (1988). First report of a Canadian epidemiological study of autistic syndromes. *Journal of Child Psychology and Psychiatry, 29,* 433–445.

Chappell, N. L., Strain, L. A., & Blandford, A. A. (1986). *Aging and health care.* Canada: Holt, Rinehart & Winston.

DeMyer, M. K. (1979). *Parents and children in autism.* New York: John Wiley & Sons.

Geneva Centre for Autism (1988). *Report to the Toronto Area Office, Ministry of Community and Social Services: The Adult Services Project.* Toronto: Author.

Gold, N. (1990). *A gender analysis of families of autistic boys: Depression and social adjustment.* Unpublished doctoral dissertation, Faculty of Social Work, University of Toronto.

Gold, N., & Whelan, M. (1989). Autism: A pervasive developmental disorder. In F. J. Turner (Ed.), *Child psychopathology: A social work perspective* (pp. 35–71). New York: Free Press.

Goldberg, S., Marcovitch, S., MacGregor, D., & Lojkasek, M. (1985, April). *Family responses to a developmentally delayed preschooler: Etiology and the father's role.* Toronto: Psychiatric Research Unit, Hospital for Sick Children.

Holroyd, J., & McArthur, D. (1976). Mental retardation and stress on the parents: A contrast between Down's syndrome and childhood autism. *American Journal of Mental Deficiency, 80,* 431–436.

Janicki, M. P., Knox, L. A., & Jacobson, J. W. (1985). Planning for an older developmentally disabled population. In M. P. Janicki & H. M. Wisniewski (Eds.), *Aging and developmental disabilities* (pp. 143–159). Baltimore, MD: Paul H. Brookes.

Janicki, M. P., Otis, J. P., Puccio, P. S., Rettig, J. H., & Jacobson, J. W. (1985). Service needs among older developmentally disabled persons. In M. P. Janicki & H. M. Wisniewski (Eds.) *Aging and developmental disabilities* (pp. 289–304). Baltimore, MD: Paul H. Brookes.

Journal of Autism and Developmental Disorders (1990, September). (Special Issue on Residential Services), 20(3).

Kanner, L. (1943). Autistic disorders of affective contact. *Nervous Child, 2,* 217–250.

Kanner, L. (1971). Follow-up study of eleven children originally reported in 1943. *Journal of Autism and Childhood Schizophrenia. 1,* 119–145.

Krauss, M. W., & Seltzer, M. M. (1986). Comparison of elderly and adult mentally retarded persons in community and institutional settings. *American Journal of Mental Deficiency, 91,* 237–243.

Marcus, L. M. (1977). Patterns of coping in families of psychotic children. *American Journal of Orthopsychiatry, 47,* 388–399.

Metro Agencies Representatives Council. (1989). *A continuum of service for persons with dual diagnosis: Report of the Task Force on Mental Health for Persons with Developmental Handicaps.* Toronto: Author.

Munro, J. D., & Duncan, H. G. (1984). *Preliminary identification of adult autistic persons in a mental retardation facility.* Woodstock, Ontario: Oxford Regional Centre.

One Voice—The Canadian Seniors Network. (1988). *Habitat: New perspectives—new choices—senior Canadians speak on housing issues.* Ottawa: Author.

Ritvo, E. R. (1987). Keynote address, delivered at the conference of the *Autism Society of America,* New Orleans.

Ritvo, E. R., & Freeman, B. J. (1984). A medical model of autism: Etiology, pathology and treatment. *Pediatric Annals, 3,* 298–305.

Ross, D., & Shillington, R. (1989). *Canadian fact book on poverty.* Ottawa: Canadian Council on Social Development.

Rumsey, J. M., Rapoport, J. L., & Sceery, W. R. (1985). Autistic children as adults: Psychiatric, social and behavioral outcomes. *Journal of the American Academy of Child Psychiatry, 24,* 465–473.

Schreiber, M. (1970). *Social work and mental retardation.* New York: John Day.

Seltzer, M. M. (1985). Research in social aspects of aging and developmental disabilities. In M. P. Janicki & H. M. Wisniewski (Eds.), *Aging and developmental disabilities* (pp. 161–173). Baltimore, MD: Paul H. Brookes.

Strategies for change: Report of the Long-term Task Force (1990). Ontario: Ministry of Health, Government of Ontario.

Szatmari, P., Bartolucci, G., Bremner, R., Bond, S., & Rich, S. (1989), A follow-up study of high-functioning autistic children. *Journal of Autism and Developmental Disorders, 19,* 213–225.

Van Bourgondien, M. E., & Elgar, S. (1989). *The relationship between existing residential services and the need of autistic adults.* Unpublished manuscript, University of North Carolina, Division TEACCH.

Wing, L. (1971). *Autistic children: A guide for parents.* London: Constable.

Wing, L. (1981). Asperger's syndrome: A clinical account. *Psychological Medicine, 11,* 115–129.

7

Paranoia in the Elderly

Joan Davies

Paranoia in late life poses a complexity of problems for persons who suffer the paranoid symptoms, their families, and others who make up their world. The subjective experience of this condition, demographic trends, and increasing concerns about the particular vulnerability of the elderly to paranoid illness, all combine to make paranoia an area of growing clinical interest to social workers.

The term *paranoia* refers to excessive suspiciousness or jealousy, combined with an exaggerated fear of harm that is unjustified or based on limited evidence. Although most people occasionally draw the wrong conclusions from facts that are presented, their misperceptions are readily corrected by the availability of new or clarified information and thus it would be inaccurate to call them paranoid. Similarly, people who share belief systems with others who consititute their generation, race, culture, or religious group would not be considered paranoid in this context. Instead the term refers to people who hold a rigid view of reality and who are constantly searching for data that support this bias, while consistently discarding information to the contrary. Since paranoia exists on a continuum, it is examined in this chapter as it presents from excessive suspiciousness of a nondelusional nature to conditions in which paranoid delusions are found in elderly people.

DSM-III-R notes that the incidence of paranoid illness is relatively uncommon, yet a review of the literature on mental illness in late life suggests a different picture. Although statistics are not available for Canada, in the United States it has been reported that paranoia is the second most common psychiatric illness in late life following depression (Pfeiffer, 1972), and there is little reason to believe that the prevalence of paranoia is different in Canada. Some authors have also observed that the actual incidence of

115

paranoia seems to increase with age and that it escalates significantly after age 65 and increases again after age 75 (Butler & Lewis, 1982). One U.S. study reported that as many as 40 percent of elderly patients who were referred for psychiatric hospitalization had some form of paranoid ideation (Roth, 1955). These figures support a view that paranoid illness is and will increasingly present as a practice issue for social workers.

Paranoia in late life is not easily understood and precise assessments of its cause are often difficult because of the complexity of factors associated with it. Like anxiety, paranoia is a nonspecific symptom and may be found in a variety of medical, neurological, and psychiatric disorders. Social workers therefore need to have sound knowledge of the broad range of conditions in which paranoia is commonly found. Similarly, they need to be attuned to the particular vulnerabilities that stem from the experience of living into late life and the variety of factors that singly or in combination load the dice for some elderly people.

Although many social workers have had extensive clinical experience with the paranoid elderly, little has been written about this area from a social work perspective. It is important that social workers share their practice wisdom with others in the field, since the paranoid elderly are to be found in most caseloads. In attempting to further the knowledge of frontline workers who serve this client group, this chapter brings together information on conditions in which paranoia emerges as a primary symptom and conditions in which paranoid ideation is secondary to another disease process. The essential features, causes, prevalence, prognosis, and treatment of paranoia are discussed as they arise in paranoid personalities, delusional (paranoid) disorders, and late-onset schizophrenia, or paraphrenia. Similarly, paranoia is examined as it appears secondary to organic brain disorders and mood disorders. Attention is also paid to the impact of paranoid illness on the elderly and their families and to how it relates to social work practice and policy.

HISTORICAL PERSPECTIVE

Unlike paranoid disorders that first appear in early to midlife, there has been limited information on, interest in, or agreement about the etiology of paranoid illness in late life. In part, the absence of systematic research in this area has simply been a reflection of the general pessimism that has surrounded work with the psychiatrically disturbed elderly. Influenced by early psychoanalytic thought and the work of Anna Freud, researchers and theoreticians viewed the elderly personality as a reactive set of processes and thus described normal aging in terms of rigidity, regression, and ego disintegration (Pincus, 1967). Given this bleak perspective, it is not surprising that there was limited optimism about work with the elderly in general. Although theoretical and empirical knowledge of the normal aging process has increased dramatically over the past thirty years, methodical research on the causes and treatment of paranoia in late life has remained limited (Berger & Zarit, 1978).

A number of theories have been put forth to explain the genesis of paranoia in late life. Some theorists hold that old age itself predisposes some people to the risk of paranoid ideation. A variety of psychosocial factors, in addition to the loss of visual and auditory senses, have been listed as precipitants (Berger & Zarit, 1978). Unfortunately, however, sensory loss is one of the few areas in which there has been systematic research on etiology.

Other theorists suggest that paranoia that emerges for the first time in late life may serve as an adaptive mechanism to preserve the person's self-image against the narcissistic assaults of aging. From a psychodynamic perspective, projecting blame or failure on the outside world wards off feelings of depression and helps the older person maintain a view of himself or herself as strong and intact, rather than as weak and in a decline (Savitsky & Sharkey, 1972; Verwoerdt, 1976).

Some authors have further postulated that certain personality types may be especially subject to paranoid ideation. It has been suggested, though unsubstantiated by research, that people with premorbid personality traits of compulsiveness, suspiciousness, and litigiousness in early life may develop paranoid symptoms in the initial stages of Alzheimer's disease (Raskind, 1982). Similarly, there is speculation that paranoid styles of relating that may be taught in early childhood make some older people prone to delusional disorders and late-onset schizophrenia.

Until the publication of DSM-III-R in 1987, the American Psychiatric Association effectively denied the existence of late-onset paranoia by setting the cutoff age for the onset of schizophrenia in early- to midlife. As a consequence, many psychiatrists believed that the cause of severe paranoid delusions was organic. By raising the age of onset of schizophrenia to late midlife the American Psychiatric Association finally acknowledged that late-onset psychosis occurs.

Various authors have noted that despite the growing interest in the paranoid elderly and the increasing optimism about work with this client group, pessimism still overshadows the area and custodial care remains the major treatment (Newhill, 1989).

CONTINUUM OF PARANOID CONDITIONS

Paranoia is a primary symptom in three major psychiatric disorders in the elderly. DSM-III-R lists these disorders as Paranoid Personality Disorders, Delusional (Paranoid) Disorders, and Schizophrenia (Paranoid Type). The literature frequently refers to this latter condition as late-onset schizophrenia, or paraphrenia, a term that will be used in this chapter (see also, Chapter 5).

Paranoid Personality Disorders

Older people who suffer from paranoid personality disorders are often described as having gone through life with a "chip on their shoulders." Their personalities have been characterized by abnormal suspiciousness or jealousy that has been devoid of delusional content. Quarrelsome and emotionally aloof, they tend to be unduly sensitive to slights, either real or imagined. People who enter late life with paranoid personality disorders have poor interpersonal relationships, and although they may have functioned relatively independently in the community, their work and family relationships are likely to have been poor (Pitt, 1982). Frequently well-known to local agencies and authorities because of their constant complaints, they often do not seek or receive treatment. For this reason, little is known about the prevalence of this disorder. The actual relationship between this disorder and delusional (paranoid) disorder and schizophrenia (paranoid type) is unclear, but DSM-III-R suggests that hypersensitivity and suspiciousness may predispose them to these psychotic disorders. It is also speculated that under extreme stress, they may experience transient psychotic symptoms.

Unlike delusional (paranoid) disorders and schizophrenia (paranoid type), which sometimes originate for the first time in late life, personality disorders have their beginnings in adolescence or early adulthood and persist throughout life. Complaints about being controlled by external forces are usually vague, but they occasionally become focused on families, neighbors, or others who enter the person's world, such as superintendents of apartment houses. It has been noted that these people's problems may increase with age either because they become "more like themselves" because their alienation of family and friends puts them at risk or because they have particular difficulties in situations in which they are dependent on others, for example, when placement is required (Pitt, 1982).

Case Example

Mr. Smith, aged 84, lived alone in an apartment until he was hospitalized with a heart attack. Never married, he always kept to himself, preferring music and books to people. Emotionally cold and highly critical of others, he fought with his neighbors and frequently registered complaints with the apartment superintendent about the state of his apartment, the condition of the building, and the behavior of other tenants. Despite his quarrelsome personality, he managed fairly well on his own until his hospitalization. Following his admission to the hospital, his complaints escalated markedly. In reality, the Food Services Department did make mistakes in his diabetic menu and several new medical residents were unfamiliar with his physical condition. Mr. Smith became extremely upset by these incidents, however, and would eat only the food that he purchased from the cafeteria. He constantly grilled the staff about their knowledge of his care and often became belligerent with staff when there were unforeseen changes in routines. When he saw several staff laughing in the hallway, he became convinced that they were laughing at him.

Delusional (Paranoid) Disorders

Delusional (paranoid) disorders, previously known as paranoid disorders, are characterized by persistent, nonbizarre delusions. These delusions are relatively self-contained and, aside from times when the delusions are being discussed or acted upon, the person's behavior does not stand out as being unusually odd. Also striking is the absence of serious disruptions in the person's intellectual and emotional functioning or a disintegration of the personality. Although auditory or visual hallucinations may occur, they are of a secondary nature. The DSM-III-R notes that specific themes commonly emerge in the delusional ideation of individuals who suffer from this disorder. The delusional disorder then derives its name from the type of primary delusion that is manifest. The delusional themes commonly observed are those of an erotic, somatic, jealous, persecutory, or grandiose nature.

Although the actual cause of delusional disorders is not known, various authors have suggested that predisposing factors may include deafness, social isolation, extreme stress, low socioeconomic status, immigration or emigration, and certain types of premorbid personality (Berger & Zarit, 1978). The usual age of onset is mid- to late adulthood, with the intensity of the delusions varying over time.

Treatment is rarely sought because daily functioning is often not impaired. Since interpersonal relationships are usually poor, however, persons with a delusional disorder, like those with paranoid personalities, frequently run into difficulties when failing health forces them into dependent relationships with others.

Case Example

Mrs. Allen had complained for some years about toxic odors that were pumped into her apartment by a neighbor whom she believed was intent on driving older people from the building. When an elderly man on her floor died suddenly and several people moved from her floor, Mrs. Allen became convinced that her neighbor was responsible and that she was at physical risk if she did not voluntarily find new accommodations.

The literature does not always clearly distinguish between delusional disorders and late-onset schizophrenia. Some authors see these conditions as simply representing different points on the same continuum, while others see them as distinctly different entities. The latter position is represented by DSM-III-R, which acknowledges a distinction between nonbizarre and bizarre delusions and recognizes the existence of late-onset bizarre symptoms. It is this very quality of the delusion that distinguishes delusional disorders from late-onset schizophrenia. Other conditions that may also be confused with delusional disorders are organic brain syndromes, in which simple persecutory delusions may be present in the early phase, or organic delusional syndrome, a condition caused by a brain tumor or amphetamines.

Late-Onset Psychosis (Paraphrenia)

Controversy has long surrounded late-onset psychosis. Much of the debate has centered on whether such a condition actually exists in the absence of an organic or affective etiology and if it does exist, whether it represents a form of schizophrenia or a condition in its own right. For many years European psychiatrists have maintained that late-onset psychosis is a condition resembling schizophrenia, but is distinctive from this disorder and worthy of separate classification. The term *paraphrenia* was initially used to describe mostly elderly patients who resembled paranoid schizophrenics, yet displayed a minimum of the debilitating hallucinations and personality disorganization that are common to this condition. Persecutory delusions that frequently were prominent were, typically, of a bizarre nature. Despite the European psychiatric community's clarity about its definition of the term paraphrenia, a similar consensus has not occurred in North America. Here the term has variously been used to describe late-onset forms of schizophrenia and has overlapped or been used interchangeably with delusional (paranoid) disorders. At different times, the nature of the contentious issues surrounding paraphrenia has caused the term to fall in and out of favor.

Despite the many areas of disagreement about late-life psychosis, the psychiatric literature has consistently associated a number of features with it. The core manifestation of this illness is invariably described as persecutory delusions and, usually but not always, hallucinations. The delusional and hallucinatory symptoms are frequently of a bizarre nature and often involve plots about being spied on, being poisoned, or being subjected to physical attacks, including rape. Unlike other forms of psychosis, however, there is an absence of personality disorganization or changes in thought and affective processes. Factors often associated with the etiology of paraphrenia are social isolation and sensory deficits, particularly deafness, as well as premorbid personalities of hypersensitivity, eccentricity, and stubbornness.

The onset of paraphrenia tends to be after age 60. Although the literature consistently observes the high proportion of women suffering from paraphrenia, Newhill (1989) suggested that studies have not adequately taken into account the fact that more women than men survive into late life.

It is widely held that the overall prognosis for paranoid illness is poor. Despite this guarded perception, many paranoid older people manage to live relatively comfortable lives in the community and never come to the attention of social workers or other professionals (Newhill, 1989). Although the literature suggests that individuals' insight into their paranoid behavior is usually limited, some authors maintain that the potential for even slight changes in behavior through counseling should not be overlooked. The benefits to be derived from the therapeutic and supportive relationship, as well as the opportunities to find alternative ways of coping, should not be minimized.

PARANOID SYMPTOMS SECONDARY TO OTHER DISORDERS

Paranoid ideation also appears as a secondary feature in disorders that are common in the elderly. These conditions are organic brain syndrome and mood disorders.

Organic Brain Syndrome: Delirium and Dementia

DELIRIUM Delirium, or acute organic brain syndrome, is reported to occur in 10 to 15 percent of elderly patients who are admitted to general and medical units in hospitals. Of the elderly patients who are diagnosed as suffering from delirium, an estimated 40–50 percent experience paranoid and persecutory delusions. Futhermore, a recent study of referrals to the psychiatric unit in a general hospital observed that approximately 17 percent received a diagnosis of organic brain disorder, most of whom were older people diagnosed with delirium (Stoudemire & Riether, 1987).

Delirium is characterized by sensory misperceptions and disrupted thought processes. The onset of this confusional state is sudden, the course of the condition may fluctuate, and the duration is typically brief (Raskind, 1982). Unable to understand, organize, and process what is seen and heard, the person misidentifies, misperceives, and misinterprets what is happening. Since the unknown is often experienced as frightening, florid delusions and hallucinations often occur, and the elderly person feels at risk. Illusions, confabulation, and altered states of consciousness are also common, as are sleep disturbances and psychomotor abnormalities.

Acute brain syndromes in the elderly are often associated with general medical illness; metabolic disorders; reactions to medications; postoperative states; acute physical assaults to the brain, such as strokes; and alcohol and drug intoxication. It is believed that the elderly are more prone to delirium than are other age groups because of preexisting sensory losses and dementia (Stoudemire & Riether, 1987). Delirium frequently presents problems for caregivers, since the fear and anxiety that occur from this condition may result in aggressive and noncompliant behavior. To treat this condition, it is essential that the medical cause be found.

Paranoid and persecutory ideation may be diminished by reducing opportunities for misperceptions, such as providing care in a well-lighted room; ensuring that eyeglasses and hearing aids, if prescribed, are available; offering reassuring information and orientation; and providing regular routines and permanent caregivers, when possible.

DEMENTIA Paranoid symptoms often complicate chronic organic brain syndrome or dementia. The essential features of the dementia syndrome are changes in intellectual capacity, judgment, memory, and personality; the paranoid reaction occurs in relation to the decline in memory. It is believed that the syndrome of paranoid forgetfulness arises during the early stages of dementia when the person has some awareness, either at a conscious or an unconscious level, that changes are occurring in cognitive functioning (Wasylenki et al., 1987).

The literature makes particular reference to paranoid ideation in three conditions: neuronal degeneration of the Alzheimer's type, cerebrovascular disease (strokes), and Parkinson's disease. It has been reported that delusional symptoms may emerge at some stage of their illness in as many as half the elderly with Alzheimer's disease (Casey, 1989).

It is widely held that the paranoid projections, in the form of denial of the memory impairment, may serve to protect the person's sense of self-esteem and competence. Rather than acknowledge that one has forgotten an event or misplaced an object, the idea of deception or theft is formed. Others have suggested that paranoid projection may fill the gap in information that is missing because of the memory loss. Various authors have suggested that the previous personality may predispose the person with dementia to paranoid ideation (Pitt, 1982; Raskind, 1982). Others have observed that previous personality may also influence the type of delusional thinking that will be manifest. For example, habitually jealous persons may develop delusions about the fidelity of their mates (Wasylenki et al., 1987). The most common types of delusions reported are delusions of theft, that the spouse is an imposter, or that strangers have entered or are living in the house (Stoudemire & Riether, 1987).

Paranoid symptoms associated with dementia are usually simple and poorly organized (Pitt, 1982). They typically exist briefly and disappear in direct relationship to the anxiety felt by the older person. Despite the simplicity of the paranoid symptoms, the paranoid ideation may nonetheless present troubling management problems to caregivers. Although the paranoid symptoms usually do not require treatment on their own, it is important to reduce the older person's anxiety by making the surroundings as understandable and predictable as possible, through environmental manipulation and emotional reassurance.

Mood Disorders and Paranoid Symptoms

Mood disorders in the elderly, namely depression and mania, commonly have a paranoid component. Psychotic symptoms, often of a paranoid nature, are reported in 15–20 percent of depressed elderly people (Stoudemire & Riether, 1987). Delusions are predominantly of a persecutory nature, and hallucinations, when present, frequently involve critical voices that point out the person's inadequacies. Hallucinations tend to be simple and transient (Wasylenki et al., 1987). Other types of delusions may relate to anxieties about serious illness or poverty. Obsessional behavior may also be present. Although upset by the tone of the delusions and hallucinations, the depressed person often believes that the hostility is justified (Wattis & Church, 1986). Many authors believe that some forms of depression, the most common type of mental illness in the elderly, are caused by age-related stress (Jacobson, 1981; see also, Chapter 10). This observation seems to support the finding that the frequency of depression with psychotic and delusional symptoms increases with age.

The literature warns that psychotic depression may be life threatening in the elderly because of nutritional and compliance problems. The prognosis is generally seen as poor unless treatment is obtained.

Mania, though less common than depression in the elderly, also appears in late life and may have psychotic symptoms (Shulman & Post, 1980). When delusions are present, they frequently are of a persecutory nature. In these instances, the manic person may imagine that she or he is the object of envy or jealousy by those who are less fortunately endowed (Pitt, 1982). It is generally believed that the etiology of new-onset mania in late life is organic (Shulman & Post, 1980). As was noted earlier, affective symptoms may also appear as part of paraphrenia.

IMPACT OF PARANOIA ON FAMILIES

Even in its mildest form, paranoia often has a devastating affect on family members. Paranoid individuals typically focus paranoid thoughts on people who enter their world and, in the case of the elderly, these people are often family members, although they may be neighbors, shopkeepers, apartment superintendents, and so on. A devoted daughter or grandchild can feel troubled when she or he is the target of accusations of physical abuse, theft, or plots to assume control of financial resources. Although older people are sometimes the prey of greedy, abusive relatives, families of paranoid individuals are often the innocent victims of paranoid projections. The family members' frustration and feelings of vulnerability because of their fear that they may become the butt of suspicious ideation causes their communication with the elderly paranoid relative to break down. When communication is not clear or is limited, opportunities are ripe for misinterpretation, and families may find that they have unwittingly confirmed their relative's paranoid ideas. The following case example illustrates how a family member can get caught in this trap.

Case Example

Mrs. David, an 80-year-old widow, lived alone in an old apartment building that was undergoing renovations. As work on the building progressed, her complaints about people lurking in the hallways and trying to break into her apartment increased to the point where she refused to leave the apartment except for medical appointments. Feeling desperate about the unsanitary conditions in the apartment, her daughter arranged for cleaning help to come in on the afternoon that she was taking her mother to see the doctor. After much resistance Mrs. David reluctantly agreed to keep the doctor's visit, but was very agitated when she returned home and discovered that "strangers had entered her apartment with a special key" and had rearranged her furniture. She would not be comforted by her daughter's explanation about the cleaning help and dismissed factors that were in keeping with this interpretation—the freshly scrubbed floor and the clean sink, for example. Her accusations of plots to break into her apartment escalated, and she subsequently refused to venture from her apartment.

Family members may also feel helpless and frustrated as a result of accusations directed at nonfamily members, especially since they often rely on neighbors, friends, and others who live locally to provide informal support, particularly to the dependent elderly. When a nonfamily member becomes the focus of paranoid accusations, family members often feel caught between their paranoid relative and the person who is the target of the paranoia. Not knowing how much or what to explain to others, they may feel conflict about what to say and may believe that explanations betray family loyalties. Feelings of frustration are often heightened when the older person has led a lifelong paranoid style of relating to others.

It has been noted that paranoid behavior, particularly in older women, often goes undetected until the death of a spouse. Although families often are aware of the paranoid thoughts, a spouse may cover up or even share the delusional thinking (Ledbetter Hancock, 1990). With the death of the spouse or the removal of the paranoid older person from the home to a residential facility, the paranoia suddenly becomes exposed to the outside world.

The very nature of institutional placement may increase paranoid thinking. The lack of control over what happens in the environment, the close physical proximity of communal living, the lack of privacy, and so forth all afford opportunities for misinterpretation and misperception. Insensitive or unskilled staff may feel angry or hurt by the older person's mistrust and accusations, as may roommates, and families, in turn, often become the focus of the staff's and residents' upset. Feelings of dependence upon the service network may increase families' feelings of vulnerability.

SOCIAL WORK INTERVENTIONS

Implications for Social Work Practice

Social workers play an important role in work with the paranoid elderly and the caregiving network. For this reason, it is vital that they understand the complexity of issues that paranoia presents in regard to assessment and intervention strategies.

ASSESSMENTS The literature notes that assessments with this client group must go beyond the traditional psychiatric evaluation and include the biological, psychological, and social context of the paranoia (Berger & Zarit, 1978). As a member of the assessment team, the social worker can help further an understanding of the paranoid symptomatology by providing a thorough personal and family history that identifies, among other things, areas of healthy functioning, previous patterns of relating to the world, and social supports and resources (Butler & Lewis, 1982). Similarly, the social worker must be attuned to the effects of past or present losses or other factors that may have played a part in bringing on the paranoid ideation (Berger & Zarit, 1978). Special attention must also be paid to the impact of historical events and nonnormative experiences suffered in earlier life. Immigrants who have fled harsh political regimes, who have lost family and friends, or who have experienced persecution may harbor ongoing feelings of distrust or persecution or may have these feelings reactivated in late life. In these instances, it will be important to understand the nature of the experience, the persons' initial and subsequent reactions to the event or events, and the nature and quality of their functioning before the experience. In a similar vein, the evaluation needs to take into consideration the impact of the paranoia on the older person and the impact on those involved in the older person's life. Some paranoid people continue to function fairly well on a daily basis despite their paranoia, whereas family and friends may be distressed by even mildly paranoid ideation. The ability of the older person's environment to tolerate the paranoia and to provide support is crucial in formulating intervention strategies that will ameliorate, rather than exacerbate, the paranoid symptoms. If the older person is living in the community and cannot receive the support required to function, the issue of institutional placement will need to be addressed. Unless the person is at risk of harming himself or herself or others or is acutely anxious and thus requires a carefully monitored regimen of medications, institutional placement should be considered only after all other strategies have been explored. By their very nature, institutional settings may increase paranoid behavior, whereas a predictable home environment may be assisted in providing support that will reduce the symptomatology (Newhill, 1989).

Noncompliance with drug regimens is a typical problem with paranoid clients and presents particular difficulties when older clients live in the community (Newhill, 1989). It is around these issues that the social worker must exercise creative problem-solving skills and his or her extensive knowledge of both the formal and informal networks of service delivery. Other professionals often look to social workers to convince the older person of the need to comply with a variety of helping interventions. Although the importance of compliance is often beyond question, social workers need to give careful thought to taking on this role in the initial phase of the relationship with the older person, when an alliance with the client may be tenuous. In the absence of a trusting relationship, little may be served by the social worker trying to obtain the older person's compliance in an area that is contentious for the client. Indeed, the fledgling relationship may be seriously undermined. However, a thorough assessment that includes information about the quality of the older person's past and present relationships may reveal resources that can be drawn on, such as a trusted church leader or a family friend.

The assessment also needs to examine the reality base of paranoid accusations. At times older people are the prey of unscrupulous landlords or family members and friends who would wish to deprive them of their property or finances (Ledbetter Hancock, 1990). Some authors have noted that the very term *paranoia* can serve to restrict older people's rights and should be used cautiously (Pitt, 1982).

There is general consensus in the literature that the overriding goal of all initial work with paranoid clients, regardless of age, is the development of a trusting, supportive relationship. To establish this relationship, the social worker must be sensitive to the client's view of the world, as well as to the potential threat posed by the helping relationship. It is crucial for social workers to have a sound understanding of the paranoid client's subjective experience, since it is this paranoid perspective and the style of relating that the worker will be attempting to alter in counseling sessions. Central to this paranoid style is an intensity of observation and a constant scrutinizing of the environment for signs of danger. The uncertainty of a new relationship is likely to heighten the ongoing sense of risk that the paranoid client feels (Zentner, 1987). The social worker needs to be prepared for the fact that the client's fear of harm will be played out with particular intensity during the early phases of the helping relationship. Paranoid clients are especially watchful for behavior that does not ring true and is unwarranted. Thus, the paranoid elderly client will be quick to detect hollow reassurances, superficiality, and simplistic explanations of his or her concerns. Any interpretations of the client's world, therefore, must be based on a solid understanding of the circumstances surrounding the complaint. Furthermore, the social worker must guard against being vague or tentative in his or her responses, since this lack of decisiveness is likely to arouse suspicion and anger. Since social workers are often one of many service providers involved in the paranoid person's life, the social worker needs to know how these services are structured and delivered. An older person who is living in the community may complain, for example, that the volunteer drivers in the Meals-on-Wheels program do not like them and offer as proof the fact that recently the drivers have changed frequently and that there was a mix-up of the days on which meals were to be delivered on two occasions. In this instance, it is important for the social worker to indicate that getting used to new people is difficult and that not receiving meals on the prescribed day is inconvenient. An alternate explanation for the changes in service should also be offered, such as the difficulty in obtaining drivers at specific times of the year. The social worker should also alert the Meals-on-Wheels coordinator to the problem.

The paranoid person's intensity of observation frequently contains a bias and a rigidity of perception that flagrantly ignores information that contradicts the underlying suspicion and instead picks out only those facts that support the paranoid beliefs (Zentner, 1987). While it may be tempting to address the often-glaring contradictions posed by the paranoid formulation, the social worker must avoid direct challenges of the reality of the delusional content. Instead, he or she should, in a matter-of-fact manner, offer other interpretations of the experience or help the client draw on alternate coping strategies that interfere less with day-to-day functioning. An elderly woman who eats in a communal dining room in a home for the aged may, for example, become convinced that the waitresses are conspiring against her by regularly overlooking her table when they serve meals. The social worker's sensitivity to difficulties in waiting one's turn and an explanation about the rotating schedule for serving tables may be of help. By maintaining a sense of impartiality about the delusional content, while trying to understand the anxiety underlying the belief system, the social worker attempts to build an alliance with the elderly person. This alliance is crucial for a number of reasons. First, it affords an opportunity to find alternative coping mechanisms for the paranoid behavior and, second, the worker's empathic response can break down the pervasive sense of social isolation experienced by the paranoid elderly client (Casey, 1989). The literature is inconclusive regarding the extent to which true insight is possible, given severe paranoid ideation, but various authors have noted that some degree of insight and change in behavioral patterns may be possible in less severe forms of paranoid illness (Newhill, 1989).

STRATEGIES FOR INTERVENTION Understanding the causes of the paranoia is imperative in formulating strategies for intervention. If, for example, the paranoia is secondary to Alzheimer's disease, the simplicity of the client's belief system and his or her forgetfulness may combine to enable the social worker to acknowledge the client's underlying feelings and then to changing the subject tactfully to something more concrete (Wattis & Church, 1986). As with other forms of paranoia, it is essential to reduce the anxiety that underlies the paranoia.

Environmental manipulation may play an important part in reducing anxiety and lessening opportunities for misinterpretation. Eyeglasses and hearing aids, if prescribed, should be provided, and emphasis should be placed on ensuring that the clients' surroundings are familiar and predictable and afford clients a sense of control over their lives. If, for example, the paranoid person lives in an institution, a single room will be beneficial, since the anxiety stemming from roommates, their family, and staff impinging on the paranoid person's world will be lessened. The dilemma that sometimes arises is that strategies that reduce anxiety, such as a separate table in a communal dining room, may increase social isolation. It is here that a balance needs to be struck to ensure that optimal opportunities for both self-control and social involvement are explored.

Besides supportive counseling, the social worker also needs to address the elderly person's social isolation. Although the relationship with the social worker may in itself lessen the isolation that the older person may be experiencing, other avenues for social contact also need to be found. The social worker should attempt to connect the older client to group activities or day programs that are available through senior citizens' clubs, Elderly Person's Centres, or recreational programs that are connected to institutions and to support the client's participation.

In addition to direct work with elderly clients, social workers also play an important role in working with the informal support network. Family, friends, and neighbors often need a great deal of support and information to understand the nature of the paranoid experience. Without this understanding, members of the informal caregiving network frequently react with anger or hurt and may withdraw their support or challenge the content of the paranoid ideation.

Though the paranoid behavior may continue to be difficult for and frustrating to the informal caregiver, an understanding of its meaning may reduce the upset experienced. Similarly, knowledge of the feelings underlying the behavior can free families and others within the support system to be innovative in finding ways to address problems; for example, a trusted family member can taste food in the nursing home to ensure that the food is not poisoned. Furthermore, social workers can model ways of behaving toward the suspicious person that include the person in planning and decision making. The paranoid person should, for example, hear reasons why the physician is suggesting certain medications, how these medications will be helpful, and so on. All too often older persons are excluded from discussions that involve their care because of their paranoid ideation. Except in instances of severe psychosis or paranoia secondary to dementia, the issues of compliance will best be served by ensuring that older clients are present when discussions that will affect their lives take place.

The social worker may also play an instrumental role with families and older clients by connecting them to required services to which they otherwise may have difficulty gaining access and by acting as an intermediary between the client system and the service delivery network. Family and friends are often overwhelmed by the complexity of the service delivery network. They do not know what services are needed, what services are available, and how one gains access to the appropriate service once it has been identified. Similarly, the clergy, family physicians, and the staff of home-supports programs often need information and assistance to understand the older person's behavior and needs. By providing insights into the meaning underlying the paranoid behavior, the social worker can help strengthen and mobilize the service network to offer services in a manner that is sensitive to the older persons' anxieties and is supportive of their needs.

WORK IN INSTITUTIONAL SETTINGS As a team member in an institutional setting, the social worker will have a more formalized role than he or she would have in the community. Within the institution the social worker's role with the older person is likely to center on providing an empathic hearing for the client's concerns, while trying to assist the person to find alternate coping strategies to alleviate the complaints. Though sensitive to the client's issues, the social worker will need to be careful not to become overly allied with the client and inadvertently undermine other members of the team who may be the target of the client's complaints or suspicions. Here the neutrality of the social worker to the delusional content is vital. Furthermore, the social worker is likely to play a key role with members of the team, as well as with the family, in furthering an understanding of the paranoid behavior and in helping the environment adapt to the needs of the client. A partnership must be forged between the staff and the family to ensure that care is provided in a way that reduces anxiety and shores up self-esteem. If institutional staff can be helped to see families as part of the caregiving team, families can be drawn on as a valuable resource. Not only are families a source of vital knowledge about the older person's past, they also can assist in the provision of care. For example, if the older person is fearful of baths, a devoted family member may need to be present on bath days; similarly, a trusted friend may need to accompany the older person to an appointment at a clinic.

Although the use of groups with the paranoid elderly has been limited primarily to institutional settings, the literature suggests that group therapy may prove to be a useful adjunct to work with individual clients. Some authors have suggested that the paranoid elderly are less likely than are younger paranoid adults to benefit from the interaction with other group members, whereas they may derive support from the relationship with the group leader (Jacobson, 1981). Other authors have noted that cognitive and sensory impairments can be addressed in group therapy, since through the group process, older persons can become aware of how the impairment affects their lives (Jette & Winnett, 1987).

Social Policy Issues

A number of social policy issues emerge in relation to the service delivery needs of the paranoid elderly and their families. The most striking policy issues are in the areas of coordination of services, particularly as they pertain to the availability of and access to services, case management, and discharge policies.

COORDINATION OF SERVICES The coordination of services is particularly important in serving the paranoid elderly because of the multitude and complexity of their needs. Unfortunately, the structural divisions imposed by the involvement of the federal, provincial or state, and municipal governments make such coordination difficult. Various levels of government often have overlapping areas of responsibility, and at each level services are carried out by a number of ministries or governmental agencies with different mandates and philosophies. "Psychiatric" and "support" services for example, are under different jurisdictions, as are services to the well and the frail elderly. At the interministerial or interagency level, joint policies need to be developed to ensure that there are no duplications and gaps in services, resources, and information. At the agency level, there is also a great need for coordinating services and devising joint policies on eligibility criteria, catchment areas served, the range of services offered, and the like.

AVAILABILITY OF AND ACCESS TO SERVICES Currently, specialized psychogeriatric services are thinly spread in most communities, which means that many paranoid elderly people go untreated or have limited treatment options, such as drug therapy or institutional placement. Although urban areas are much better served than are less populated regions, the elderly with special language needs are poorly served, regardless of where they live. The inability of service providers to communicate directly with the paranoid elderly heightens the clients' sense of social isolation and increases their potential to misperceive the helping relationship.

The absence of a single point of entry to the existing service delivery system further compounds this client group's problems in gaining access to services. Partnerships need to be struck and policies established to ensure that the bureaucratic maze of services is demystified and that referral to appropriate services is simplified. In addition to single-entry delivery systems, case managers also play an important role in the coordination of services at the level of individual cases when a multiplicity of services are required.

DISCHARGE POLICIES The general trend toward decreasing the length of psychiatric stays in hospitals has often been detrimental to the elderly, who frequently require longer periods of hospitalization than do younger adults because of the complexity of their needs. Since the psychiatrically ill elderly are not eligible for chronic care, the options available to them upon their discharge from hospitals are limited. Often nursing homes and homes for the aged are reluctant to admit older people with psychiatric illnesses and, in reality, staff in these institutions are often ill equipped to understand the needs of the paranoid elderly. To serve this client group, staff need specialized training; beds should be allocated in long-term care facilities for the mentally ill; and ongoing treatment, follow-up, and consultation services must be provided by psychogeriatric services. Placement problems also exist for the elderly who are chronically mentally ill, since psychiatric facilities often see age 65 as a cutoff point for services and attempt to transfer these patients to facilities or programs for the aged.

Elderly patients who are discharged back to the community often deteriorate emotionally, owing to the absence of necessary follow-up and support services. Ironically the very nature of their psychiatric illness often weakens their informal support system, and in the absence of checks within the service delivery system, the paranoid elderly are often poorly served. Without people to help establish a familiar, predictable environment, they are likely to fall through the cracks in the system, only to come to public attention again when their paranoid behavior places them or others at risk of harm.

CONCLUSION

Paranoid illness is an issue of considerable clinical significance to social workers and other health care professionals who work with the elderly. This chapter has provided an overview of a range of conditions in which paranoia commonly occurs as either a primary or a secondary feature. It is vital that social workers know about these conditions and have a sound understanding of the paranoid elderly person's subjective view of the world, since they play a key role in providing services to this client group and their families. However, social work interventions need to go beyond direct work with the paranoid elderly and to include strategies to strengthen the formal and informal support networks surrounding the older person. Such strategies will be particularly important as more and more older people live into late life and an increasing number remain in the community.

Governmental and organizational policies also need to be developed to support the needs of the paranoid elderly and their families. Particular attention should be paid to the coordination of existing services, as well as to ensuring access to these services. Furthermore, policies need to be developed within institutions to ensure that discharge policies take the special needs of this client group into consideration.

BIBLIOGRAPHY

Berger, K. S., & Zarit, S. H. (1978). Late life paranoid states: Assessment and treatment. *American Journal of Orthopsychiatry, 48*, 528–537.

Butler, R. N., & Lewis, M. I. (1982). *Aging and mental health* (2nd ed.). Saint Louis, MO: C. V. Mosby.

Casey, D. A. (1989). Paranoid disorders in the elderly. *Journal of the Kentucky Medical Association, 87*, 283–285.

Health and Welfare Canada. (1988). *Guidelines for comprehensive services to elderly persons with psychiatric disorders*. Ottawa: Ministry of Supply and Services Canada.

Jacobson, S. (1978). Geriatric psychiatry today. *Bulletin of New York Academic Medicine, 54*, 568–572.

Jacobson, S. (1981). Psychiatric treatment of the aged. *New York Journal of Medicine, 81*, 802–804.

Jette, C. C., & Winnett, R. (1987). Late-onset paranoid disorder. *American Journal of Orthopsychiatry, 57*, 485–494.

Ledbetter Hancock, B. (1990). *Social work with older people* (2nd ed.). Englewood Cliffs, NJ: Prentice-Hall.

Molinari, V., & Chacko, R. (1983). The classification of paranoid disorders in the elderly: A clinical problem. *Clinical Gerontologist, 1*, 31–37.

Monk, A. (1983). Social work with the aged: Principles of practice. In F. J. Turner (Ed.), *Differential diagnosis and treatment in social work* (pp. 129–143). London: Collier Macmillan.

Newhill, C. E. (1989). Paranoid symptomatology in late life. *Clinical Gerontologist, 8*, 13–29.

Pfeiffer, E. (1972). Psychopathology and social pathology. In J. E. Birren & W. K. Schaie (Eds.), *Handbook of the psychology of aging*. New York: Van Nostrand Reinhold.

Pfeiffer, E., & Busse, E. W. (1973). Mental disorders in later life—Affective disorders: Paranoid, neurotic and situational reactions. In E. Busse & E. Pfeiffer (Eds.), *Mental illness in later life* (pp. 127–141). Washington, DC: American Psychiatric Association.

Pincus, A. (1967). Toward a developmental view of aging for social work. *Social Work, 12*, 33–41.

Pitt, B. (1982). *Psycho-geriatrics: An introduction to the psychiatry of old age* (2nd ed.). Edinburgh: Churchill Livingstone.

Raskind, M. (1982). Paranoid syndromes in the elderly. In C. Eisdorfer & W. Fann (Eds.), *Treatment of psychopathology in the aging* (pp. 184–191). New York: Springer.

Roth, M. (1955). The natural history of mental disorder in old age. *Journal of Mental Science, 101*, 281–301.

Savitsky, E., & Sharkey, H. (1972). The geriatric patient and his family: Study of family interaction in the aged. *Journal of Geriatric Psychiatry, 5*(1), 3–24.

Shulman, K., & Post, F. (1980). Bipolar affective disorders in old age. *British Journal of Psychitry, 136,* 26–32.

Stoudemire, A., & Riether, A. (1987). Evaluation and treatment of paranoid symptoms in the elderly: A review. *General Hospital Psychiatry, 9,* 267–274.

Verwoerdt, A. (1976). *Clinical geropsychiatry.* Baltimore, MD: Williams & Wilkins.

Wasylenki, D., et al. (1987). Paranoid disorders. In *Psycho-geriatrics: A practical handbook* (pp. 91–103). Toronto: Gage.

Wattis, J., & Church, M. (1986). Hallucinations and persecutory states. In *Practical psychiatry of old age* (pp. 109–121). New York: New York University Press.

Whitehead, T. (1979). Paranoid reactions. In *Psychiatric disorders in old age: A handbook for the clinical team* (pp. 50–59). New York: Springer.

Zentner, M. (1987). Paranoia. In F. J. Turner (Ed.), *Adult psychopathology. A social work perspective* (pp. 365–383). London: Collier Macmillan.

8

Aging in Persons with Developmental Disabilities

Marsha Mailick Seltzer · Gary B. Seltzer

Many more persons with developmental disabilities are living to old age than did in the past. As a result, social workers and other service providers, as well as researchers and policy analysts, have become increasingly interested in how the aging process is manifested in persons with developmental disabilities and how these people's extended life span affects their families. Information about this population and their families has only recently become available. It is clear, however, that persons with developmental disabilities are a growing portion of the aging population (Janicki & Wisniewski, 1985). It is therefore necessary for social workers to understand the characteristics of this subgroup of the aging population, their needs for formal and informal support, and the needs of their families.

This chapter reviews the literature about aging in persons with developmental disabilities and identifies issues that are relevant to social work practice. First, it considers the demographic trends that characterize this group, including its size, life expectancy, and projections of the future population. Second, it describes age-related changes that are characteristic of older persons with developmental disabilities, including changes in functional abilities, cognitive abilities, and physical and mental health status. Third, it examines this group's need for support with respect to the use of both formal services and family and other informal supports. Last, it presents recommendations for future practice, policy development, and research on this population. Throughout, special attention is paid to older persons with Down's syndrome, because they have an increased risk for and earlier onset of Alzheimer's disease. First, however, it is necessary to define the basic terms that are used throughout this chapter, including developmental disabilities and aging.

A *developmental disability*, as defined by P.L. 85-602 (the Rehabilitation, Comprehensive Services, and Developmental Disabilities Amendments of 1978) is a severe chronic disability of a person, that

(A) is attributable to a mental or physical impairment or combination of mental and physical impairments;

(B) is manifested before the person attains age 22;

(C) is likely to continue indefinitely;

(D) results in substantial functional limitations in three or more of the following areas of major life activity: (i) self-care, (ii) receptive and expressive language, (iii) learning, (iv) mobility, (v) self-direction, (vi) capacity for independent living, and (vii) economic self-sufficiency; and

(E) reflects the person's need for a combination and sequence of special, interdisciplinary, or generic care, treatment, or other services which are of lifelong or extended duration and are individually planned and coordinated.

Developmental disabilities are thus defined on the basis of the functional characteristics of the affected individual, rather than on the basis of his or her categorical diagnosis. Nevertheless, the most commonly included categories of developmental disability are mental retardation, cerebral palsy, epilepsy, and autism.

The largest subgroup of the population with developmental disabilities consists of persons with mental retardation. Most available knowledge about older persons with developmental disabilities has been generated from research on older persons with mental retardation. According to the American Association on Mental Retardation (Grossman, 1983), *mental retardation* is defined as significantly subaverage general intellectual functioning (an IQ score of approximately 70 or below), existing concurrently with deficits in adaptive behavior and manifested during the developmental period (before age 18). The diagnostic and classification nosology of mental retardation utilizes measures of adaptive behavior as well as IQ tests because there is much behavioral variability among persons with identical IQ scores. Measures of adaptive behavior provide information about the functional correlates of mental retardation, namely, a person's ability to perform activities of daily living (G. B. Seltzer, 1988). The most prevalent known cause of mental retardation is Down's syndrome, a chromosomal anomaly in which there is an extra twenty-first chromosome.

The definition of *old age* in the general population poses conceptual challenges for gerontologists and social workers who work with the elderly. Although old age is generally defined in years (Siegel, 1980), there is variation in the specific age used to define the onset of this stage of life—age 60, 62, or 65. The "young-old" have been differentiated from the "old-old" (Streib, 1983), although the age that separates these two groups has been inconsistently applied from program to program and from study to study. Some gerontologists have developed functional definitions of old age (Birren, 1959; Eisdorfer, 1983), stressing the different trajectories of biological, psychological, and social aging.

Defining old age in the population with developmental disabilities has been even more challenging than in the general population. Definitions based on age alone are problematic because some subgroups of the population with developmental disabilities, notably those with Down's syndrome, age prematurely, with age-related declines observable in their forties and fifties (Evenhuis, 1990; Zigman, Schupf, Lubin, & Silverman, 1987). Functional definitions of aging are especially problematic for this population because the definition of developmental disabilities includes functional limitations, which would make a functional approach to defining the onset of old age in this group redundant with the group's basic definition. Most studies of older persons with developmental disabilities have used age 55 as the lower age boundary in an attempt to include at least some of those who age prematurely (see M. M. Seltzer & Krauss, 1987, for a review of the literature on this issue).

The definition of old age in persons with developmental disabilities remains unresolved. From a policy perspective, it has been argued that age 60 should be used to be consistent with the Older Americans Act (Rose & Janicki, 1986). From a clinical perspective, it has been argued that a single chronological cutoff age is not useful in that there is so much heterogeneity in the point of onset of old age in this population (Cotten & Spirrison, 1986; G. B. Seltzer, 1985). The use of age 60 would virtually exclude persons who age prematurely, such as those with Down's syndrome. From a research perspective, it is recognized that there is a need to measure age-related changes in cognitive, functional, and health characteristics for each subgroup of the population with developmental disabilities to gain an empirically sound understanding of the process of aging in this diverse group (M. M. Seltzer & Krauss, 1987).

CHARACTERISTICS OF THE POPULATION AND DEMOGRAPHIC TRENDS

Size of the Population

The size of the older population with developmental disabilities in not precisely known. Several factors make this population difficult to count. First, there is the unresolved problem of defining the lower age boundary of this population, as was just described. Second, all counts of this population are based on older persons with developmental disabilities who are known to the formal mental retardation–developmental disabilities (MR-DD) service system in each state (Janicki, Knox, & Jacobson, 1985). These individuals total about 200,000 persons nationally (Jacobson, Sutton, & Janicki, 1985). However, individuals who have not been recipients of formal MR-DD services in adulthood or who receive generic (non–MR-DD) services are generally not identified in enumerations of this group (Krauss, 1988). Third, in some states, individuals with developmental disabilities other than mental retardation (e.g., cerebral palsy) are less consistently counted than are those with mental retardation.

Efforts have been made to estimate (rather than to count) the size of the older population with developmental disabilities on the basis of prevalence rates. However, age-adjusted prevalence rates are not available for either the population with developmental disabilities as a whole or for the various diagnostic groups included in the population with developmental disabilities. For example, in childhood about 3 percent of the population is diagnosed as having mental retardation, while in adulthood, the prevalence is believed to be only about 1 percent (M. M. Seltzer, 1989). This decrease is believed to occur because fewer intellectual challenges are encountered in adulthood than during the school years. Many adults with mild mental retardation do not have a continual need for formal services (Edgerton, 1988). In old age, some persons who were classified as having mental retardation during their childhood but who were not so labeled in adulthood may reenter the formal service delivery system if they become frail or socially isolated.

Two additional factors have an effect on the size of the older population with developmental disabilities: (1) the life expectancy of the population and (2) the aging of cohorts of different sizes.

Life Expectancy

As was noted earlier, there has been a marked increase in the life expectancy of persons with developmental disabilities (Janicki, 1988). This increase is due, in part, to new medical technology and the improved health care provided to this population. For example, fully one-third of all children born with Down's syndrome have congenital heart defects (Pueschel, 1987). In the past, these children generally died at a young age. However, because of improved surgical procedures and changed social attitudes toward medical intervention with persons with disabilities, their length of life has been extended considerably.

Little data are available about the current life expectancy of persons with each of the various causes of developmental disabilities. It is believed that individuals with an organic basis of their disability and severe–profound retardation have a shorter life expectancy than do persons in the general population, but the differences in life expectancy among the specific disorders (e.g., chromosomal anomalies versus metabolic disorders versus teratogenic effects) have not been adequately described (Granger, G. B. Seltzer, & Fishbein, 1987). However, those who have no organic basis for their disability and mild or moderate retardation have a life expectancy that is close or equal to that of persons in the general population (Lubin & Kiely, 1985).

Eyman, Call, and White (1989) described the life expectancy of persons with mental retardation in California. They reported that the death rate in this population is curvilinear, with the highest death rate occurring before age 5 and after age 55. Those with severe or profound retardation have a higher death rate at all ages than do those with mild or moderate retardation.

Persons with Down's syndrome have a reduced life expectancy compared to those in the general population and to most other persons with retardation. Those with Down's syndrome can be divided into two groups with respect to their life expectancy (Eyman, Call, & White, 1991). Those who have no ambulation or feeding skills have a shorter life expectancy—usually fewer than 30 years. However, most persons with Down's syndrome are ambulatory and can feed themselves; these individuals have a life expectancy of about 50 or 55 years. A primary reason that the latter group has a shorter life span than does the general population is their increased risk for Alzheimer's disease (Wisniewski & Merz, 1985). Nearly all persons with Down's syndrome who survive to age 35 manifest the neuropathology of Alzheimer's disease (detected upon autopsy) (Lott & Lai, 1982), although only about 45 percent manifest the behavioral symptoms (Thase, 1982). Among middle-aged adults with Down's syndrome, the risk of the behavioral manifestations of Alzheimer's disease appears to increase with advancing age.

The Aging of Cohorts

In addition to the effects of increased longevity, the increase in the size of the population with mental retardation is attributed to the aging of larger cohorts of persons with developmental disabilities than in the past. In particular, the members of the baby-boom generation with developmental disabilities are currently approaching midlife and will reach old age during the beginning of the next century (Baird & Sadovnick, 1985). Owing to the large size of this cohort, the population of older persons with developmental disabilities will increase as they age. In addition, during the past two decades, the most dramatic reductions in mortality have been in infant mortality (Lubin & Kiely, 1985). This cohort will increase the size of the older population with developmental disabilities when it reaches old age.

Summary

To summarize, although the size of the population of older persons with developmental disabilities is difficult to estimate precisely, we do know that at a minimum, there are about 200,000 persons, aged 55 or older, with developmental disabilities in the United States. Two interrelated trends have a continuing and dynamic effect on this group's size: (1) changes in the life expectancy of various subgroups of the population with developmental disabilities and (2) changes in the size of successive cohorts with developmental disabilities. There is a great need to understand age-specific prevalence rates for the major subgroups of the population with developmental disabilities for the planning and development of services and to clarify our understanding of the processes of development and aging in this group. The increase in the size of the older population with developmental disabilities will result in greater demands on families and other informal supports, as well as a greater need for professional personnel, including social workers, to provide services to them.

AGE-RELATED CHANGES

Development across the life span is characterized by both stability and change. This is true for older persons with developmental disabilities, as well as for the general population, although the paucity of longitudinal research on this group makes it difficult to characterize their trajectories of stability and change in various behavioral and social domains. The confounds of cohort effects and true age effects have been described for the general population (Schaie, 1988) and for those with developmental disabilities (M. M. Seltzer, 1985b; in press). In that true age effects and cohort effects have not been disentangled in much of the literature on older persons with developmental disabilities, some descriptions of age-related changes in this population remain confounded by differences in the cohorts.

Cognitive Abilities

Of particular interest to social workers who provide services to older persons with developmental disabilities and their families are age-related changes in cognitive abilities. As in the general population, most persons with developmental disabilities maintain their cognitive abilities throughout their adult years and may even show evidence of intellectual development (Eyman & Widaman, 1987; Hewitt, Fenner, & Torpy, 1986; Janicki & Jacobson, 1986; G. B. Seltzer, 1985), with declines manifested only after age 60 or 70.

An exception is that persons with Down's syndrome are at an increased risk for Alzheimer's disease, and those who manifest the behavioral symptoms of the disease show a pattern of cognitive decline starting in their forties or fifties. Dalton (1982) reported that the average age of onset of memory loss in persons with Down's syndrome was 49. However, he noted that the heterogeneity of this group with respect to memory loss was great and that there are persons with Down's syndrome in their sixties who do not show evidence of cognitive decline. Thase (1982) compared older persons with Down's syndrome with age- and IQ-matched controls. The subjects with Down's syndrome had significantly greater impairment that did the controls on measures of orientation, attention span, digit-span recall, visual memory, and object identification.

Functional Abilities

The pattern of age-related changes in functional abilities parallels the trajectories for cognitive abilities. Persons with retardation continue to develop new functional abilities throughout their adult years, but the acquisition of new skills levels off and begins to decline in older age. In persons with mild and moderate retardation who do not have Down's syndrome, declines in activities of daily living are not routinely observed until the mid-seventies, but motoric skills tend to begin to decline two decades earlier (Bell & Zubek, 1960; Janicki & Jacobson, 1986). In persons with severe and profound retardation who survive to old age, the declines in functional abilities are not as marked as in those who are less impaired, perhaps because of their more limited initial abilities (Janicki & Jacobson, 1986). Persons with Down's syndrome who manifest the symptoms of Alzheimer's disease begin to decline in their functional abilities in their forties and fifties (Evenhuis, 1990; Zigman et al., 1987). At all levels of retardation, regression in self-care skills and mobility is a significant predictor of mortality (Eyman et al., 1989).

Several studies have compared the patterns of functional decline manifested by older persons with mental retardation and those of other older at-risk or disabled groups. For example, Sherwood and Morris's (1983) study of older persons with mental retardation, mental illness, and no disabilities, all of whom were participants in the Pennsylvania Domiciliary Care Program, found that those with mental retardation declined in functional abilities, while the other two groups did not. Callison et al.'s (1971) comparison of the changes in visual ability, hearing, and grip strength in elderly persons with mental retardation, elderly persons with schizophrenia, and elderly persons who were not disabled concluded that although all three groups declined, those with mental retardation declined the most in hearing and vision. These studies suggest that persons with mental retardation manifest more pronounced age-related declines than do those in other diagnostic groups and in the general population, but their results should be generalized with caution because these studies were conducted on local samples that may not be representative of the population with developmental disabilities. Furthermore, the members of these samples undoubtedly received poorer social, educational, and health services in their childhood and early adulthood than would be the case today. Therefore, it is difficult to separate the true differences in aging patterns between the general older population and persons with developmental disabilities from artifactual differences associated with poor services and poor health care.

It is interesting that even though older persons with developmental disabilities manifest a more marked pattern of age-related declines in functional and cognitive abilities than does the general population, cross-sectional comparisons of younger and older adults with developmental disabilities reveal unexpected patterns. When Krauss and M. M. Seltzer (1986) compared adults with mental retardation aged 18–54 with those aged 55 and older in both institutional and community-based settings, they found that the younger individuals were significantly more impaired cognitively and functionally than were the older ones. The explanation for these unexpected findings was that the younger and older cohorts were composed of a different mix of persons. These differences were the result of changes in diagnostic practices, placement patterns, and mortality that have occurred during the past century. The members of the younger cohort included a higher proportion of persons with severe and profound retardation, who in the past were less likely to survive beyond childhood. The older cohort included a higher proportion of persons having "borderline" mental retardation, who would not be included in the younger cohort as a result of contemporary diagnostic practices. This example illustrates the distinction between true influences of aging and cohort effects, which are particularly marked in the population with developmental disabilities. Furthermore, these findings caution social workers and other service providers to refrain from making service plans solely on the basis of the chronological age of the clients.

Functional abilities determine, in part, residential placement patterns, although not always in the expected direction. G. B. Seltzer, Finaly, and Howell (1988) investigated the differences in functional characteristics of older persons with developmental disabilities who lived in two types of placements: community-based settings and nursing homes. All had some physical or psychological problem that required diagnostic attention. The researchers explored the "goodness of fit" between the functional competence of the person and the setting in which he or she was placed. Contrary to their expectation, nursing home residents had fewer medical and behavioral problems than did community-based residents. However, medications for behavioral problems were used more frequently in nursing homes. These findings suggest that social workers may expect to find less-than-optimal matches between some older persons with developmental disabilities and their residential placements.

Physical and Mental Health Care Needs

With selected exceptions, the health status and health care needs of older persons with developmental disabilities are similar to those of their age peers without disabilities (Anderson, Lakin, Bruininks, & Hill, 1987). Older persons with developmental disabilities manifest the expected age-related increases in chronic diseases and medical problems (Janicki & Jacobson, 1986), as well as increases in the extent to which they utilize health care services (Janicki & MacEachron, 1984). However, access to health care services tends to be a function of living arrangement, with older persons who live in community-based group homes having more frequent contact with physicians than those who live with their families (Janicki, Jacobson,

& Ackerman, 1985). A history of institutionalization is associated with more medical problems and a shorter life span (Krauss & M. M. Seltzer, 1986; Lubin & Kiely, 1985; Tait, 1983). However, these studies do not separate the effects of the possible differential characteristics of the individuals placed in institutions (e.g., severer retardation) from the negative impact of the institutional setting on the health and longevity of residents.

Persons with Down's syndrome have a number of medical problems in addition to Alzheimer's disease and congenital heart disease. They have a higher-than-average incidence of acquired cataracts, leukemia, hypothyroidism, and skeletal abnormalities (Pueschel, 1987). In addition, a number of investigators have reported that persons with Down's syndrome manifest a marked pattern of impaired auditory abilities associated with advancing age (Brooks, Wooley, & Kanjilal, 1972; Kaiser, Montague, Wold, Maune, & Pattison, 1981).

Another important domain of age-related stability and change that is of particular interest to social workers pertains to the mental health of older persons with developmental disabilities. Although it has been well documented that there is an increased prevalence of mental health problems among persons with developmental disabilities (Cohen & Bregman, 1988; Menaloscino & Potter, 1989; Reiss, 1990), not much is known about the age-related manifestation of such problems. It is known, however, that memory losses and other cognitive declines may be associated with increases in anxiety and depression in older persons with developmental disabilities (G. B. Seltzer, 1985). When increased anxiety is present, it is likely to have a negative effect on the person's sense of well-being, behavior, and even memory and other cognitive processes. In addition, psychological problems are often overlooked by professionals, who tend to focus primarily on cognitive changes in this group. Pseudodementia occurs in older persons with mental retardation, although it is often not recognized as an affective disorder and is wrongly assumed to be some form of organic brain disorder. Diagnostically, it is important to recognize that older persons with developmental disabilities do experience such major mental disorders as depression and that these disorders will further compromise their cognitive and behavioral status.

In sum, most persons with developmental disabilities manifest the patterns of declines in cognitive and functional abilities and physical and mental health status that are characteristic of the general aging population. There is some evidence that the declines may begin somewhat earlier or are somewhat steeper in persons with developmental disabilities, but, for the most part, there appear to be more similarities than differences. The exceptions include those whose developmental disabilities are due to specific disorders, notably those with Down's syndrome, who manifest accelerated and atypical patterns of aging.

FORMAL AND INFORMAL SUPPORTS

For a number of reasons, older persons with developmental disabilities have a greater need for formal and informal supports than does the general older population. First, these individuals, by definition, have impairments in their functional abilities and need compensatory supports to manage their daily activities, maintain their health, and enjoy a reasonable quality of life. Second, since most older persons with developmental disabilities do not marry or have children, they lack the basic supports that are provided to most older persons by spouses and adult children. Instead, they must depend on their aging parents or on siblings. Third, their disabilities and advancing age may interfere with their ability to develop meaningful relationships with friends, who could provide support to them (Berkson & Romer, 1980; Krauss, 1989; Landesman-Dwyer, Sackett, & Kleinman, 1980). For all these reasons, older persons with developmental disabilities may be especially vulnerable and socially isolated and therefore have a high need for formal support, as well as for continued informal support from their family of origin and from friends.

Formal Supports

Older persons with developmental disabilities receive services from three formal service sectors (M. M. Seltzer & Krauss, 1987): (1) the age-integrated developmental disabilities service sector, (2) the age-specialized developmental disabilities service sector, and (3) the generic aging service sector. All three sectors are multidisciplinary, with social workers and other human service professionals providing the services.

The dominant approach to providing services to older persons with developmental disabilities in the United States is the age-integrated developmental disabilities service sector. Age-integrated services include older clients in residential and day programs without establishing age-based eligibility criteria or modifying the programs. One study that examined the patterns of service utilization of older persons with retardation in Massachusetts found that about two-thirds of the services received by these older persons were provided by this service sector (M. M. Seltzer, 1988).

There are advantages and disadvantages to the use of age-integrated services by older persons with developmental disabilities. Regarding the advantages, this option avoids making chronological age *the* issue in service delivery. In addition, individuals who receive services in this sector can continue their activities and friendship groups and have the opportunity to participate in active treatment programs that are stimulating and challenging. The disadvantages include the inability of many programs to be responsive to age-related needs as they emerge, the absence of retirement options in most employment-oriented day programs, and the limited number of age peers.

The second service sector utilized by older persons with developmental disabilities is the age-specialized developmental disabilities service sector. In the Massachusetts analysis of patterns of service utilization (M. M. Seltzer, 1988), it was found that only 5 percent of the services utilized by the population of older persons with mental retardation were in this sector. In this sector, special services are provided to older persons with developmental disabilities to respond specifically to their age-related needs. Programmatic features of these day and residential services include a slower pace, more room for personal choice, a greater emphasis on recreational and leisure-time activities, and increased attention to health care services. A national survey of age-specialized services for older persons with mental retardation (M. M. Seltzer & Krauss, 1987) identified a total of 529 programs in forty-three states and the District of Columbia, about 60 percent of which were located in community-based settings and 40 percent of which were institution based. Of all the programs, about 65 percent were residential programs and 35 percent were day programs. The likelihood that a social worker would be a member of the staff of these programs varied considerably, from 26 percent of the institutional day programs to 29 percent of the community residential programs to 40 percent of the community day programs to 81 percent of the residential programs in institutions.

As with age-integrated services, age-specialized services have both advantages and disadvantages. The advantages include the potential to create flexible, individualized, and age-appropriate services, such as retirement options. Also, such programs appear to be particularly effective in establishing a context in which peer relationships will flourish because participants interact with others who are similar to them in age and level of skills. The weaknesses of this sector include the possibility that programs may be isolated or segregated by age and disability. Participants may be separated from their past friends and placements, which may be particularly troublesome at a time in life when new relationships are often difficult to form.

The third service sector that provides services to older persons with developmental disabilities is the generic aging service sector. In this sector, older persons with developmental disabilities are included in services that were designed for the general elderly population. These services include all the services in the aging network: home health services, day health services, senior centers, congregate housing, home-delivered meals, and nutrition sites. Older persons with developmental disabilities who are less severely disabled participate widely in such services, usually in conjunction with, rather than as a substitute for, services sponsored by the developmental disabilities services system (M. M. Seltzer, Krauss, Litchfield, & Modlish, 1989).

The advantages of generic aging programs include the high level of social integration in them. Participation in such programs is believed to be normalizing and beneficial for developing relationships with age peers. However, the disadvantages include a lack of professional staff with expertise in serving individuals with disabilities and the negative attitudes of both staff and other participants, who may not welcome the participation of older persons with developmental disabilities. In addition, the level of tasks required of participants may involve intellectual or motoric capacities that are beyond all but the most mildly disabled.

During the next decade, three trends will affect the patterns of service utilization of older persons with developmental disabilities. First, as was noted earlier, the growth in the absolute size of this population will necessitate an increase in the service options available to them. Second, as the population of older persons with developmental disabilities continues to age, these individuals may be expected to be more frail, which will result in an increase in the intensity of services that are needed. Third, human service professionals, including social workers, will become more familiar with the needs of older persons with developmental disabilities, which, it is hoped, will result in more appropriate services to these individuals.

Family and Informal Supports

It is common for persons with developmental disabilities to live with their families, in many cases for their entire lives (Fujiura, Garza, & Braddock, 1989; Lakin, 1985). A great deal of attention is being paid to aging parents who have provided long-term care to their adult children with developmental disabilities (Engelhardt, Brubaker, & Lutzer, 1988; Heller & Factor, 1988; M. M. Seltzer, 1985a). This interest is the result of several factors. First, social workers and other human service professionals, researchers, and policymakers are all concerned about the impact on parents of the increased longevity of persons with developmental disabilities. The demographic shifts described earlier pose new challenges to family caregivers, the effects of which are not yet well understood.

Second, social workers and gerontologists are increasingly interested in the capacity of older persons to be family resources. In much past research and clinical service, elderly persons were viewed as burdens on their families. This perspective is changing (Greenberg & Becker, 1988; Rowe & Kahn, 1987). It is now recognized that intergenerational relationships are often reciprocal, with the older generation providing assistance to, as well as receiving assistance from, the younger generation. However, it is necessary to understand how the aging process affects parents' ability to give care, particularly when the parents are in their seventies and eighties.

Although family caregiving is not an unusual role, especially for women, several factors distinguish the experiences of aging parents who care for an adult child with developmental disabilities. First, whereas the provision of care by a mother for a child is normative when the child is young, this arrangement is not normative when the mother is approaching or has reached old age and the son or daughter has reached adulthood. The family life cycle for these families is "off cycle" (Farber, 1959; Turnbull, Summers, & Brotherson, 1986). It is often assumed that the effects on parents of off-cycle caregiving responsibilities are negative, but this assumption has not yet been tested. It is possible that there are also positive effects, especially when the adult with developmental disabilities provides assistance to a physically impaired or infirm parent or when the parent derives a continued purpose in life from caregiving.

Another unique aspect of the caregiving experiences of aging parents who care for their adult son or daughter with developmental disabilities is the duration of the caregiving responsibilities. National data indicate that the period of family caregiving for an elderly relative who is not developmentally disabled averages about five years (Stone, Cafferata, & Sangl, 1987). In contrast, the period of care for an aging son or daughter with developmental disabilities may span five or six decades.

In a longitudinal study of 450 mothers (aged 55–85) who provide care to their sons or daughters with mental retardation (aged 15–66), M. M. Seltzer and Krauss (1989) are examining a number of the issues just discussed. The overall purpose of the study is to investigate the correlates of well-being in the sample of older caregiving mothers, to identify the predictors of continuing in-home versus out-of-home placement for their adult children with retardation, and to describe the patterns of stability and change in the adults with retardation.

The preliminary findings of this study suggest that the older women are coping surprisingly well with their continuing caregiving responsibilities.

Although it was hypothesized that they would be at risk for poor physical and mental health because of their long years of caregiving, it was found that they compared favorably with samples of age peers and samples of other caregivers. Specifically, the aging mothers in this study were substantially healthier and had better morale than did other samples of caregivers for the elderly. Furthermore, they reported no more burden or stress than did other caregivers. Thus, despite the long duration of their caregiving roles and despite the unique characteristics of their children, many of these mothers appear to be resilient, optimistic, and able to function well in multiple roles.

The second hypothesis of the study that was tested in preliminary analyses pertained to the mothers of the sons and daughters with Down's syndrome (37 percent of the total sample). It was hypothesized that these mothers would have poorer physical and mental health than would the other mothers in the sample because adults with Down's syndrome have a higher rate of chronic health problems and are at risk for premature aging. Contrary to these expectations, the mothers of the adults with Down's syndrome manifested *better* overall well-being than did those of adult children whose retardation was due to other factors (M. M. Seltzer, 1990). Even when between-group differences on socioeconomic and disability factors were controlled, the mothers of the adults with Down's syndrome perceived their families to be more cohesive and less conflictual, were more satisfied with their social supports and with the services provided to their adult children, and were less stressed and less burdened by their caregiving responsibilities than were the other mothers in the sample.

These differences mirror patterns that have been reported for young families with a child with Down's syndrome compared with other groups with developmental disabilities (Holroyd & McArthur, 1976; Krauss, 1989; Mink, Nihira, & Meyers, 1983). Although it was not expected that well-being of the mothers of the adults with Down's syndrome would be superior in older age, these differences may be persistent sequelae of the diagnosis. Possible reasons include the greater level of scientific knowledge about Down's syndrome than about other diagnostic groups, the greater prevalence of Down's syndrome than other diagnoses and therefore the possibly greater public familiarity with it, and tempermental differences between children with Down's syndrome and comparison groups of children whose mental retardation is caused by other factors. These "protective factors" may buffer some of the stresses associated with having a child with retardation that are manifested more negatively by families of children with other diagnoses.

The third hypothesis of the study concerned the involvement of aging siblings with their brother or sister with retardation. It was hypothesized that the involvement of siblings would be positively related to maternal well-being (G. B. Seltzer, Begun, M. M. Seltzer, & Krauss, 1991). It was found that a mother had significantly better health, was more satisfied with her life, and had less stress and burden associated with caregiving when at least one of her other children provided either affective or instrumental support to her adult child with retardation. Over 80 percent of the families in which there were siblings reported at least some involvement of siblings, with affective support much more common than instrumental support. However, the extent to which siblings are prepared to assume primary responsibility for their brother or sister with retardation when the mother is no longer able to do so was not assessed and remains an important question for future research. Also, the families in which there were no children other than the adult with retardation or in which no sibling was involved with the son or daughter with retardation appear to be particularly vulnerable and in need of assistance from social workers with planning for the future.

In sum, only a little is known about families of older persons with developmental disabilities. However, preliminary data from the study by M. M. Seltzer and Krauss suggest that both resiliency and vulnerability may be characteristic of these families' coping style. Therefore, social workers are challenged to avoid the assumption of negative outcome and instead to respond to the range of needs of families at this stage of life.

Permanency Planning

The vulnerability of older persons with developmental disabilities—physically, socially, cognitively—and the limited resources available to them may precipitate crises of care and adjustment. The effects of such crises may be minimized if families do careful long-range planning.

Permanency planning, often used in foster care services for children, involves the development of a plan whose goal is to place a foster child in a permanent home—a home in which the child can live until he or she reaches adulthood. By extension, permanency planning can be used to develop plans to ensure as secure a lifestyle as possible for the older person with developmental disabilities.

The result of permanency planning is not an unchangeable plan, but a plan that will be in force until it is amended. Such plans for individuals with developmental disabilities should include three components: residential security, legal protection, and financial security.

In relation to residential security, some families are interested in making plans that ensure that the aging person with developmental disabilities will have a permanent place to live, but do not know how to go about creating such a plan. In contrast, other families are reluctant even to discuss the possibility that a time will come when the parents are no longer able to care for their adult child. Social workers can make an important contribution to both types of families by helping them to acknowledge this difficult problem and to begin to make appropriate plans. Still other types of families have distanced themselves from their family member with developmental disabilities, often through institutional placement. Years later, and often with great ambivalence, some families have attempted to reconnect with their adult children, often following deinstitutionalization. Assisting families to address the issue of the future residential security of the adult with developmental disabilities is perhaps most challenging with these families because once before—usually upon the advice of the professionals—they had attempted to arrange a secure residential placement for their children and have since been told—again by professionals—that the arrangement they chose is neither appropriate nor will provide a lifelong home.

Although private residential facilities are often prohibitively expensive and generally do not ensure permanence beyond the time that funding for the resident is available, families who do have sufficient funds can consider this option. Several examples of such programs are described in M. M. Seltzer and Krauss (1987). The trade-off made when a family places an adult child in a private residential setting is that security and a sense of community are ensured in return for limitations in opportunities to encounter new experiences and to take risks. The social worker can help the family members consider the appropriateness of this decision, to involve the adult child in the decision to the extent possible, and to help them select the best option.

With regard to legal protection, although adults with developmental disabilities are assumed to be legally competent, many need assistance in money management and in making important decisions. In some cases, a guardian may be appointed by the court following a competency hearing. The guardian serves as the person's advocate and attempts to protect him or her from exploitation. Parents ordinarily fill this role, but as they age, their capacity to function in this role may diminish. In preparation for such a time, some parents appoint a testamentary guardian, often a sibling of the adult with developmental disabilities, who will assume responsibility for him or her when the parents are no longer able to do so.

Many persons may be involved in the decision to establish guardianship: the judge, the lawyer, the guardian, the social worker, the family, and the person with developmental disabilities. The social worker can provide support to the person with developmental disabilities and the family as they evaluate the plans for guardianship. When the family perceives that the person with developmental disabilities needs a guardian, but professional opinion suggests that the adult could manage independently, the social worker can help the family recognize that their relative with developmental disabilities is competent.

As for financial security, there are many obvious reasons why it is important to arrange for as much of it as possible. First and foremost, there is the welfare of the person with developmental disabilities. In addition, the relatives or guardian may not be in a position to assume all the financial burden of caring for the person. Although a few families will be able to leave an estate that is sufficiently large to cover all or most of the costs incurred by or on behalf of their son or daugher with disabilities, most will not. An alternative source of financial security is Supplemental Security Income (SSI), for which most persons with developmental disabilities are eligible. SSI, which is accompanied by Medicaid benefits, provides a modest but regular income that can constitute or be part of a permanent financial plan for the person.

In sum, there are three key components of permanency planning for older persons with developmental disabilities: residential security, legal protection, and financial security. The extent to which any family or person with developmental disabilities needs the support and expertise of a social worker in arranging for each of these components varies from case to case, depending upon the capacities and resources of the retarded person and the family. Often, however, some professional intervention is desirable to minimize anxiety about the future and to maximize the extent to which the family can provide support so that the person with developmental disabilities can face a secure old age.

Case Examples

The following two case vignettes illustrate the range of characteristics and needs of older persons with developmental disabilities and their families.

The Peterson Family

Mrs. Peterson, aged 73 years, is a widow who lives with Matthew, her 48-year-old son with profound mental retardation. She also has a 39-year-old married daughter who lives nearby with her husband and young children. Matthew attends a day program on weekdays.

Other than the time spent at the day program, he goes out of the house only when he is accompanied by his mother.

Matthew's health status is poor and has become worse during the past few years. He can dress himself but needs assistance from his mother with a variety of daily living skills, including bathing and remembering to use the bathroom. He does not perform any household chores. Mrs. Peterson provides all the needed support to Matthew. In light of the intensity of the care that Mrs. Peterson provides to Matthew, they receive little formal and informal support. Other than social security, Mrs. Peterson receives no services for herself. Matthew participates in the day program, but his mother thinks that not all his needs are met there. Specifically, she thinks that her son needs physical therapy, occupational therapy, a visiting nurse, and some sort of recreational program. Regarding informal support, Mrs. Peterson turns only to her daughter and son-in-law for help. She said she has no friends she can really count on when help is needed.

Mrs. Peterson is in poor health. She has a heart condition and arthritis. Her main concern is to find a "special home" for Matthew because she believes she cannot take care of him much longer. Although she hopes her daughter will provide this special home, a plan has not yet been fully worked out.

The Sullivan Family

Mrs. Sullivan, aged 58, lives with her husband and two children in a suburban community. The Sullivans also have three grown children who do not live at home. The Sullivan's eldest child, Sharon, has mild mental retardation.

Sharon is 35 years old and has always lived at home with her parents. Last year she completed a vocational training program, but she does not attend any program or engage in any kind of work. She goes out with friends or other family members for social activities about twice a week and goes out on her own several more times each week. Sharon is independent and requires no assistance with personal care or with many housekeeping tasks. Her mother told us that Sharon makes a real contribution to the family by cleaning the house and doing errands for other family members.

Mrs. Sullivan is in good health. She holds a part-time job and has a large circle of friends and extended family members. She turns for support to her husband, to her sisters, and to several close friends. Except for one sister, all nine people who comprise Mrs. Sullivan's support network live within an hour's drive of her home; most live within a few miles.

Mr. and Mrs. Sullivan strongly believe that their other children should not have to accept the full responsibility for Sharon. Mrs. Sullivan states that she wants each of her children to be able to "live their own lives." Although she and her husband respect Sharon's determination to be independent, they also fear that it may prevent her from accepting needed help.

Although Sharon has a social worker, she refuses to participate in any formal services. However, her mother thinks she would benefit greatly from vocational guidance and from participating in a structured recreational program. Both Mr. and Mrs. Sullivan are concerned that Sharon lacks an adequate support network and worry that her refusal to accept services will become a much greater problem when they are no longer around to provide for her. Mr. Sullivan expects that Sharon will have to live out her life in some type of special setting, but his wife is uncomfortable with this possibility. Although the Sullivans have accepted Sharon's limitations, they have had difficulty deciding about her future.

CONCLUSIONS

Knowledge about aging in persons with developmental disabilities has only recently begun to accumulate. Compared with just a decade ago, a great deal is now understood about the characteristics of this population and the extent to which they are similar to and different from the larger population of older Americans. This knowledge has formed the basis of social work practice with older persons with developmental disabilities and their families.

Many clinical, policy, and research issues regarding aging in the population with developmental disabilities warrant additional attention, and social workers can play an important role in resolving them. One particularly important clinical issue pertains to the mental health characteristics and needs of older persons with developmental disabilities. Despite the preliminary understanding of the age-related changes in the cognitive, functional, and health statuses of older persons with developmental disabilities reviewed here, there has been no systematic investigation of the mental health status of this population. Some have hypothesized that there is an increased risk of depression in this group because of their social isolation and advanced age, but this hypothesis has not been tested in research or clinical practice.

From a policy perspective, it is necessary for older persons with developmental disabilities to gain greater access to services provided by the aging network, as well as by the developmental disabilities service system. Although these clients are at risk of "falling through the cracks," successful case management and advocacy can result in the improved coordination of services. Policies that foster interagency collaboration would facilitate this process.

From a research perspective, more descriptive and analytic studies about older persons with developmental disabilities and their families are needed. Both qualitative and quantitative methods are required to enhance our understanding of the course and consequences of the aging process for this group. This research should be multidisciplinary, so it can address the range of biopsychosocial issues that have emerged in the past decade.

REFERENCES

Anderson, D. J., Lakin, K. D., Bruininks, R. H., & Hill, B. K. (1987). A *national study of residential and support services for elderly persons with mental retardation* (Report No. 22). Minneapolis: University of Minnesota, Department of Educational Psychology.

Baird, P. A., & Sadovnick, A. D. (1985). Mental retardation in over half-a-million consecutive live births: An epidemiological study. *American Journal of Mental Deficiency, 89,* 323–330.

Berkson, G., & Romer, D. (1980). Social ecology of supervised communal facilities for mentally disabled adults: I. Introduction. *American Journal of Mental Deficiency, 85,* 219–228.

Bell, A., & Zubek, J. P. (1960). The effect of age on the intellectual performance of mental defectives. *Journal of Gerontology, 15,* 285–295.

Birren, J. E. (1959). Principles of research on aging. In J. E. Birren (Ed.), *Handbook of aging in the individual* (pp. 3–42). Chicago: University of Chicago Press.

Brooks, D. N., Wooley, A., & Kanjilal, G. C. (1972). Hearing loss and middle ear disorders in patients with Down's (mongolism). *Journal of Mental Deficiency Research, 16,* 21–29.

Callison, D. A., Armstrong, H. F., Elam, C., Cannon, R. L., Paisley, C. M., & Himwich, H. (1971). The effects of aging on schizophrenic and mentally defective patients: Visual, auditory, and grip strength measurements. *Journal of Gerontology, 26,* 137–145.

Cohen, D. J., & Bregman, J. D. (1988). Mental disorders and psychopharmacology of retarded persons. In J. F. Kavanaugh (Ed.), *Understanding mental retardation: Research accomplishments and new frontiers* (pp. 319–330). Baltimore, MD: Paul H. Brookes.

Cotten, P. D., & Spirrison, C. L. (1986). The elderly mentally retarded (developmentally disabled) population: A challenge for the service delivery system. In J. S. Brody & G. E. Ruff, (Eds.), *Aging and rehabilitation: Advances in the state of the art.* New York: Springer.

Dalton, A. J. (1982). *A prospective study of Alzheimer's disease in Down's syndrome.* Paper presented at the Sixth Meeting of the International Association for the Scientific Study of Mental Deficiency, Toronto.

Edgerton, R. (1988). Aging in the community—A matter of choice. *American Journal of Mental Retardation, 92,* 331–335.

Eisdorfer, C. (1983). Conceptual models of aging: The challenge of a new frontier. *American Psychologist, 38,* 197–202.

Engelhardt, J. L., Brubaker, T. H., & Lutzer, V. D. (1988). Older caregivers of adults with mental retardation: Service utilization. *Mental Retardation, 26,* 191–195.

Evenhuis, J. M. (1990). The natural history of dementia in Down's syndrome. *Archives of Neurology, 47,* 263–267.

Eyman, R. K., Call, T. L., & White, J. F. (1989). Mortality of elderly mentally retarded persons in California. *Journal of Applied Gerontology, 8,* 203–215.

Eyman, R. K., Call, T., & White, J. F. (1991). Life expectancy of persons with Down's syndrome. *American Journal of Mental Retardation, 95,* 603–612.

Eyman, R. K., & Widaman, K. F. (1987). Life-span development of institutionalized and community-based mentally retarded persons revisited. *American Journal of Mental Deficiency, 91,* 559–569.

Farber, B. (1959). Effects of a severely mentally retarded child on family integration. *Monographs of the Society for Research in Child Development, 24* (2, Serial No. 71).

Fujiura, G. T., Garza, J., & Braddock, D. (1989). *National survey of family support services in developmental disabilities.* Unpublished manuscript, University of Illinois at Chicago.

Granger, C. V., Seltzer, G. B., & Fishbein, C. (1987). *Primary care of the functionally disabled: Assessment and management.* Philadelphia: J. B. Lippincott.

Greenberg, J., & Becker, M. (1988). Aging parents as family resources. *The Gerontologist, 28,* 786–791.

Grossman, H. J. (Ed.) (1983). *Classification in mental retardation.* Washington, DC: American Association on Mental Deficiency.

Heller, T., & Factor, A. (1988). Permanency planning among black and white family caregivers of older adults with mental retardation. *Mental Retardation, 26,* 203–208.

Hewitt, K. E., Fenner, M. E., & Torpy, D. (1986). Cognitive and behavioral profiles of the elderly mentally handicapped. *Journal of Mental Deficiency Research, 30,* 217–225.

Holroyd, J., & McArthur, D. (1976). Mental retardation and stress on the parents: A contrast between Down's syndrome and childhood autism. *American Journal of Mental Deficiency, 80,* 431–436.

Jacobson, J. W., Sutton, M. S., & Janicki, M. P. (1985). Demography and characteristics of aging and aged mentally retarded persons. In M. P. Janicki & H. M. Wisniewski (Eds.), *Aging and developmental disabilities: Issues and approaches* (pp. 115–142). Baltimore, MD: Paul H. Brookes.

Janicki, M. P. (1988). Aging: The new challenge. *Mental Retardation, 26,* 177–180.

Janicki, M. P., & Jacobson, J. W. (1986). Generational trends in sensory, physical, and behavioral abilities among older mentally retarded persons. *American Journal of Mental Deficiency, 90,* 490–500.

Janicki, M. P., Jacobson, J. W., & Ackerman, L. J. (1985). *Patterns of health and support services among elderly mentally retarded persons living in community group home settings.* Paper presented at the 13th International Congress of Gerontology, New York.

Janicki, M. P., Knox, L. A., & Jacobson, J. W. (1985). Planning for an older developmentally disabled population. In M. P. Janicki & H. M. Wisniewski (Eds.), *Aging and developmental disabilities: Issues and approaches* (pp. 143–160). Baltimore, MD: Paul H. Brookes.

Janicki, M. P., & MacEachron, A. E. (1984). Residential, health, and social service needs of elderly developmentally disabled persons. *The Gerontologist, 24,* 128–137.

Janicki, M. P., & Wisniewski, H. M. (Eds.) (1985). *Aging and developmental disabilities: Issues and approaches.* Baltimore, MD: Paul H. Brookes.

Kaiser, H., Montague, J., Wold, D., Maune, S., & Pattison, D. (1981). Hearing of Down's syndrome adults. *American Journal of Mental Deficiency, 85,* 467–472.

Krauss, M. W., (1988). Long-term care issues in mental retardation. In J. Kavanagh (Ed.), *Understanding mental retardation: Research accomplishments and new frontiers* (pp. 331–340). Baltimore, MD: Paul H. Brookes.

Krauss, M. W. (1989). *Parenting a young child with disabilities: Differences between mothers and fathers.* Paper presented at the 22nd Annual Gatlinburg Conference on Research and Theory in Mental Retardation and Developmental Disabilities, Gatlinburg, TN.

Krauss, M. W., & Seltzer, M. M. (1986). Comparison of elderly and adult mentally retarded persons in community and institutional settings. *American Journal of Mental Deficiency, 75,* 354–360.

Lakin, K. C. (1985). Service system and settings for mentally retarded people. In K. C. Lakin, B. Hill, & R. Bruininks (Eds.), *An analysis of Medicaid's ICF-MR program* (4-1–4-37). Minneapolis: University of Minnesota.

Landesman-Dwyer, S., Sackett, G. P., & Kleinman, J. S. (1980). Relationship of size to resident and staff behavior in small community residences. *American Journal of Mental Deficiency, 85,* 6–17.

Lott, I. T., & Lai, F. (1982). Dementia in Down's syndrome: Observations from a neurology clinic. *Applied Research in Mental Retardation, 3*, 233–239.

Lubin, R. A., & Kiely, M. (1985). Epidemiology of aging in developmental disabilities. In M. P. Janicki & H. M. Wisniewski (Eds.). *Aging and developmental disabilities: Issues and approaches* (pp. 95–114). Baltimore, MD: Paul H. Brookes.

Menaloscino, F. J., & Potter, J. F. (1989). Mental illness in the elderly mentally retarded. *Journal of Applied Gerontology, 8*, 192–202.

Mink, I. T., Nihira, K., & Meyers, C. E. (1983). Taxonomy of family life styles: I. Homes with TMR children. *American Journal of Mental Deficiency, 87*, 484–497.

Pueschel, S. M. (1987). Health concerns in persons with Down syndrome. In S. M. Pueschel, C. Tingey, J. E. Rynders, A. C. Crocker, & D. M. Crutcher (Eds.), *New perspectives on Down syndrome* (pp. 113–134). Baltimore, MD: Paul H. Brookes.

Rehabilitation, Comprehensive Services, and Developmental Disabilities Amendments of 1978, P.L. 85-602,92 Stat. 2955 (1978).

Reiss, S. (1990). Prevalence of dual diagnosis in community-based day programs in the Chicago metropolitan area. *American Journal of Mental Retardation, 94*, 578–585.

Rose, T., & Janicki, M. P. (1986). Older mentally retarded adults: A forgotten population. *Aging Network News, 3*, 17–19.

Rowe, J. W., & Kahn, R. L. (1987). Human aging: Usual and successful. *Science, 237*, 143–149.

Schaie, K. W. (1988). The impact of research methodology on theory building in the developmental sciences. In J. E. Birren & V. L. Bengston (Eds.), *Emergent theories of aging* (pp. 41–57). New York: Springer.

Seltzer, G. B. (1985). Selected psychological processes and aging among older developmentally disabled persons. In M. P. Janicki & H. M. Wisniewski (Eds.), *Aging and developmental disabilities: Issues and approaches.* Baltimore, MD: Paul H. Brookes.

Seltzer, G. B. (1988). *The use of functional assessment with elderly persons with mental retardation* (pp. 23–26). Paper presented at the Best Practices Conference, Cincinnati, OH.

Seltzer, G. B., Begun, A., Seltzer, M. M., & Krauss, M. W. (1991). The impacts of siblings on adults with mental retardation and their aging mothers. *Family Relations, 40*, 310–377.

Seltzer, G. B., Finaly, E., & Howell, M. (1988). Functional characteristics of elderly mentally retarded persons in community settings and nursing homes. *Mental Retardation, 26*, 213–217.

Seltzer, M. M. (1985a). Informal supports for aging mentally retarded persons. *American Journal of Mental Deficiency, 90*, 259–265.

Seltzer, M. M. (1985b). Research in social aspects of aging and developmental disabilities. In M. P. Janicki & H. M. Wisniewski (Eds.), *Aging and developmental disabilities: Issues and approaches* (pp. 161–173). Baltimore, MD: Paul H. Brookes.

Seltzer, M. M. (1988). Structure and patterns of service utilization by elderly persons with mental retardation. *Mental Retardation, 26,* 181–185.

Seltzer, M. M. (1989). Introduction to aging and lifelong disabilities: Context for decision making. In E. F. Ansello & T. Rose (Eds.), *Aging and lifelong disabilities: Partnership for the 21st century.* College Park: University of Maryland Center on Aging.

Seltzer, M. M. (1990). *Continuing effects of etiology in adulthood: Down syndrome vs. other diagnostic groups.* Paper presented at the 23rd Annual Gatlinburg Conference on Research and Theory in Mental Retardation, Brainerd, MN.

Seltzer, M. M. (in press). Family caregiving across the full life span. In L. Rowitz (Ed.), *Mental retardation in the year 2000.* New York: Springer.

Seltzer, M. M., & Krauss, M. W. (1987). *Aging and mental retardation: Extending the continuum.* Washington, DC: American Association on Mental Retardation.

Seltzer, M. M., & Krauss, M. W. (1989). Aging parents with mentally retarded children: Family risk factors and sources of support. *American Journal of Mental Retardation, 94,* 303–312.

Seltzer, M. M., Krauss, M. W., Litchfield, L. C., & Modlish, N. J. K. (1989). Utilization of aging network services by elderly persons with mental retardation. *The Gerontologist, 29,* 234–238.

Siegel, J. S. (1980). On the demography of aging. *Demography, 17,* 245–364.

Sherwood, S., & Morris, J. N. (1983). The Pennsylvania domiciliary care experiment: I. Impact on quality of life. *American Journal of Public Health, 73,* 646–653.

Stone, R., Cafferata, G. L., & Sangl, J. (1987). Caregivers of the frail elderly: A national profile. *The Gerontologist, 27,* 616–626.

Streib, G. (1983). The frail elderly: Research dilemmas and research opportunities. *The Gerontologist, 23,* 40–44.

Tait, D. (1983). Mortality and aging among mental defectives. *Journal of Mental Deficiency Research, 27,* 133–142.

Thase, M. E. (1982). Longevity and mortality in Down's syndrome. *Journal of Mental Deficiency Research, 26,* 117–192.

Turnbull, A. P., Summers, J. A., & Brotherson, M. J. (1986). Family life cycle: Theoretical and empirical implications and future directions for families with mentally retarded members. In J. J. Gallagher & P. M. Vietze (Eds.), *Families of handicapped persons: Research, programs, and policy issues* (pp. 45–65). Baltimore, MD: Paul H. Brookes.

Wisniewski, H. M., & Merz, G. S. (1985). Aging, Alzheimer's disease, and developmental disabilities. In M. P. Janicki & H. M. Wisniewski (Eds.), *Aging and developmental disabilities: Issues and approaches* (pp. 177–184). Baltimore, MD: Paul H. Brookes.

Zigman, W. B., Schupf, N., Lubin, R. A., & Silverman, W. P. (1987). Premature regression of adults with Down syndrome. *American Journal of Mental Deficiency, 92,* 161–168.

9

Anxiety and Anxiety Disorders

Lilian M. Wells

Mrs. H was a 94-year-old widow who had been living in a nursing home for one month. She had arthritis, high blood pressure, mild congestive heart failure, and a skin irritation subsequent to a shingles infection that had occurred some time previously. She was an alert, dignified woman who was able to walk short distances with the aid of a walker. She had been having increasing difficulty living in her own apartment and decided to move to a home after major surgery for a perforated intestine. She chose a four-bed room because it was more spacious and had a large window with a view.

One evening the nurse thought that Mrs. H's rash might be infectious and had her moved to a semiprivate room. The new roommate drew the curtain between the beds so that Mrs. H was, in effect, in a small windowless cubicle. Suddenly, Mrs. H felt overwhelmed with a sense of foreboding. Her heart began to race, and she became short of breath, sweaty, and tremulous. She needed to go to the bathroom, but felt dizzy as she got out of bed and had to call for help. She told the assistant that she felt unwell, but did not elaborate. The night wore on. Mrs. H was terrified. She felt trapped, tears slipped from her eyes. She knew her feelings were irrational and felt angry that she couldn't control them. She also thought the move was illogical: If she was infectious, her new roommate would also be at risk. Her agitation grew. She wanted to escape. With her stiff and painful joints, she couldn't even toss and turn in her bed.

She tried to relax, to soothe her pounding heart. Nothing worked. As soon as it was morning she desperately phoned her nephew. She knew that he experienced claustrophobia and would understand. He came over at once and accompanied his aunt to the lounge, where they discussed her experiences and she became calmer. He talked with the staff, who decided to move her back to her own room. He invited Mrs. H to his home for dinner that evening. Later the nurse phoned to tell him Mrs. H would be unable to go out because her blood pressure was too high. The nephew asked that Mrs. H be advised of the pros and cons and that she be allowed to decide what to do. She went to her nephew's and, in this instance, her blood pressure regained its usual reading by the next morning.

OVERVIEW OF ANXIETY

Anxiety is an affect that has normal as well as pathological or maladaptive forms. The foregoing vignette illustrates that anxiety reactions incorporate somatic, emotional, and cognitive features and include a behavioral component. As Kaplan (1984) noted, most people do not usually experience such extreme feelings of anxiety. Adaptive anxiety involves feelings of apprehension and tension before an examination, job interview, marriage, golf tournament, annual driver's test for elderly persons, and so on. There is a heightened sense of alertness, an anticipation of things that may go wrong, and a range of physical symptoms. In such situations there is a realistic threat or challenge, and the individual retains some sense of control and can carry through with appropriate behavior. This anticipatory or "signal anxiety" serves to motivate the individual to achieve his or her goal. Maladaptive anxiety and anxiety disorders are associated with a "state of anxiety," in which constructive functioning is hampered (Kaplan, 1984).

The term *anxiety* is related to *angina*, both words have the same Latin root *angere*—to constrict or distress. A dictionary definition of anxiety is a painful concern for an uncertain future. Angina, which is chest pain related to an insufficient supply of blood to the heart muscle, and anxiety are linked etymologically as they are linked by similar experiences, with anxiety attacks frequently associated with a suffocating feeling in the chest. In French, comparable terms are *angine* (angina) and *angoisse* (anguish, agony, heart rending). Portuguese describe *osh i gneish*, which encompasses a chest discomfort and a sense of desperation.

Many people with severe anxiety try to carry on and conceal it; however, the physical symptoms are similar to those of diseases and may thus increase their concern and anxiety about their health and well-being. It is noteworthy that even people with severe anxiety wait an average of twelve years after the onset of symptoms to seek treatment (Shader, Goodman, & Gever, 1982). Older people could be expected to fit into this general pattern, and it is therefore important for social workers to understand the dynamics and be able to explore for and to assess anxiety and anxiety disorders in their elderly clients. Verwoerdt (1981) emphasized the importance of early recognition and treatment of anxiety to interrupt what he termed the vicious cycle of anxiety–depression, physical illness, and other negative outcomes that feed anxiety.

Brenner (1974, 1976) distinguished between anxiety and depression by describing anxiety as an anticipatory sensation about doom in the future and depression as the sensation of disaster that has already occurred. However, symptoms of anxiety and depression often occur together, and Salzman (1977, as cited in Patterson, 1988) argued that the distinction between anxiety and depression may become blurred in older people.

Although anxiety is a prevalent and significant problem in the elderly, it is given much less attention than are dementia and depression (Patterson, 1988). Kuhlen (1959, as cited in Patterson, 1988) contended that successful aging may depend on the management of anxiety, while Belsky (1990) suggested that people who have anxiety disorders in middle age may be less likely to survive to old age.

Psychologically, older people must be able to adapt to physical changes and to changes in their social states (Bloom, 1980). Optimum growth and development can occur throughout the life course, when the individual's strengths and potentials are recognized, reinforced, and encouraged by the social and physical environment (Butler, 1980). However, older people experience more stressors than do those in any other age group, and these stressors are often devastating.

According to Erikson's developmental theory, mature age is the stage in which there is a heightened potential to develop ego integrity and an increased vulnerability for despair (Anderson & Carter, 1990; Peck, 1968). During this stage, people normally reevaluate and review their lives, a process that is characterized by the progressive return to consciousness of past experiences, in particular, the resurgence of unresolved conflicts, which can lead to anxiety and despair.

Butler, with social work colleagues (Butler, 1980; Butler & Lewis, 1983), developed a "life review therapy" that can be used for both therapeutic and preventive purposes. Outcomes of the process of recounting and reviewing memories and responses can lead to a restructuring that includes the extirpation of guilt, the exorcism of problematic childhood identifications, the resolution of intrapsychic conflicts and family relationships, the transmission of knowledge and values, and the renewal of the ideals of citizenship. "Personal construct therapy," another approach, has been shown to lead to reduced anxiety and depression, less indirectly expressed anger, and more feelings of competence than are found in control groups (Viney, Benjamin, & Preston, 1989).

The ego analytic perspectives of Erikson (in Anderson & Carter, 1990) and Peck (1968) are helpful in addressing intrapsychic issues of anxiety in that they emphasize the growth and resolution of problems in earlier stages of life. However, as Glenwick and Whitbourne (1980) noted, while Erikson's first seven stages are rooted in the individual's current activities and experiences, the eighth stage—"integrity versus despair"—centers on the future (the inevitability of death) and the past (the evaluation of one's life). Therefore, a transactional model is required to understand how the individual deals constructively and positively with current psychological, physical, and social changes. An ecological social work practice model that addresses the individual, the social and physical environment, and the transactions between them is a useful framework. The following is an example of such an approach to dealing with a common anxiety of residents (and prospective residents) in senior citizens' apartments and long-term-care institutions, that is, anxiety about the use of elevators:

When two people moved into a nursing home with this problem, the social worker used the opportunity to institute a group program including three others who also experienced such extreme anxiety in elevators that they restricted their activities. They began each session by meeting in a quiet alcove and the worker used her knowledge of yoga to teach the members relaxation strategies. They discussed their fears and things that made it easier for them to cope. At the first session the worker had arranged to have the key of one elevator so that people could practice getting on and off, opening and shutting the door, without the elevator moving. Each session included a ride to the main floor where the group had coffee in the lounge. The worker arranged one session to coincide with the visit of the maintenance man who serviced and inspected the elevators. He was very interested in explaining and showing how the elevator worked. One resident subsequently recounted his experience as a youngster when his teacher would shut him up in a storage cupboard as punishment. The group was supportive in validating his feelings and discussed their own past frightening experiences. They also considered "worst case" scenarios in using the elevator. By the end of the program (held twice a week for five weeks) three people felt comfortable when alone in the elevator, one wanted someone with her but was comfortable in asking, and one, though unable to use the elevator alone because of a disability, was not anxious anymore.

This outcome was found to correspond to a similar program (Hussian, 1981) that used "stress inoculation training."

TYPES OF ANXIETY DISORDER

Anxiety disorders are particularly severe and pervasive forms of maladaptive anxiety. Five major categories of anxiety disorder are described in DSM-III-R: panic disorder, obsessive-compulsive disorder, generalized anxiety disorder, phobia, and post-traumatic stress disorder. Phobias are discussed in Chapter 14 and post-traumatic stress disorder is covered in Chapter 19 of this book.

Panic Disorders

These disorders are characterized by recurrent panic attacks, that is, discrete periods of intense fear or discomfort, with at least four associated symptoms. These symptoms, as listed in the DSM-III-R (American Psychiatric Association, 1987, p. 238), include discomfort or difficulty in breathing; a lightheaded or unsteady feeling; rapid heartbeat; quivering or tremulousness; perspiring excessively; queasiness, upset stomach, or indigestion; detached or distorted ways of relating to one's environment; moments of feeling extremely hot or extremely cold for no apparent cause; tightness in the chest; and a "fear of going crazy or of doing something uncontrolled."

A panic attack is sudden, unexpected, and unpredictable and reflects anxiety in its most intense form. It may last minutes or hours. "Panic" itself is named after the Greek god Pan, who would terrify travelers by springing at them unexpectedly (Tyrer, 1982). People with panic disorder may associate their *first* attack with a period of life stress, but usually there is no precipitating event. After experiencing several attacks, they often develop a chronic but less intense level of anxiousness in anticipation of further attacks. In attempts to prevent these sensations, some people avoid situations in which they believe an attack is more likely to occur or restrict their lives to what they think will be "safe" limits. Such avoidance can lead to phobic disorder.

Panic disorder is associated with pervasive social and health consequences. These consequences include feelings of poor physical and emotional health, alcohol and drug abuse, increased suicide attempts, impaired social and marital functioning, financial dependence, and the increased use of health services (Markowitz, Weissman, Ouellette, Lish, & Klerman, 1989).

Shader, Scharfman, and Dreyfus (1986) cited evidence to support the concept that panic disorders have a biophysiological base in certain people who have a genetic predisposition, reporting on studies of twins (Klein, 1980), families (Shader et al., 1982) and a range of biochemical studies. Therefore, they suggested that a multimodal approach to treatment is the most appropriate.

In psychoanalytic theory, panic attacks are attributed to the failure of the ego defenses to control unacceptable impulses or to a threatened or experienced loss of support (Atwood & Chester, 1987). Klein (1980) proposed that panic anxiety in adults is analogous to severe separation anxiety in children and that the panic response is like the protest response that Bowlby (1969, 1973) described in children who are separated from their mothers. Research by Thyer and his colleagues (Thyer, Nesse, Cameron, & Curtis, 1986; Thyer, Nesse, Curtis, & Cameron, 1985) has not supported this hypothesis.

TREATMENT STRATEGIES In some people panic attacks are alleviated with medication (imipramine, monoamine oxidase inhibitors, or benzodiazepine alprazolam). Shader et al. (1986) stated that psychosocial treatment, psychodynamic or behavioral, is usually more effective after the panic attacks are initially alleviated with medication.

There is little in the literature on specific psychosocial treatments of panic disorders and none on older people. Particularly if medication is being used, a close liaison between the social worker and the physician is required. A number of organic conditions can cause paniclike states, including hyperventilation, inner-ear problems, hypoglycemia, thyroid conditions, and organic mental disorders. Visual problems, common in older people, may contribute to disorientation in poorly lighted malls and feelings of incompetence and anxiety. The fear of falling may also be heightened, especially at street crossings, on stairways, or in buses.

Cognitive-behavioral strategies of anxiety management using relaxation training that the client can apply at the onset of a panic attack are generally useful. A psychodynamic approach to working through past conflicts associated with separations may be indicated. It may be particularly important for older people when new losses and separations reactivate previous conflicts.

Mrs. H may be said to have experienced a panic attack, as far as is known, her first. It was atypical in that it was directly related to the change in rooms, but was associated with a period of stress in giving up familiar surroundings to move to a nursing home. Although one panic attack does not constitute an anxiety disorder, her nephew's response illustrates important concepts. His strong, warm relationship and empathic support provided reassurance that she was a valued family member. He truly understood her feelings and was able to normalize them. He held to values of autonomy and self-determination and used an educational and advocacy approach with the nursing and medical staff. He reaffirmed Mrs. H's right and ability to make her own decisions about both psychosocial and medical issues. Did this response forestall further attacks or alleviate her intense fear of having more? One cannot know.

Generalized Anxiety Disorder (GAD)

The DSM-III-R (APA, 1987, pp. 252–253)* defines this disorder as "unrealistic or excessive anxiety and worry (apprehensive expectation) about two or more life circumstances," during most days over a minimum of six months. At least six of the following symptoms are often present:

Motor tension
(1) trembling, twitching, or feeling shaky
(2) muscle tension, aches or soreness
(3) restlessness
(4) easy fatigability
Autonomic hyperactivity
(5) shortness of breath or smothering sensations
(6) palpitations or accelerated heart rate (tachycardia)
(7) sweating or cold, clammy hands
(8) dry mouth
(9) dizziness or lightheadedness

*Reprinted with permission from the *Diagnostic and Statistical Manual of Mental Disorders, Third Edition, Revised*. Copyright 1987 American Psychiatric Association.

(10) nausea, diarrhea or other abdominal distress
(11) flushes (hot flashes) or chills
(12) frequent urination
(13) trouble swallowing or "lump in throat"
Vigilance and scanning
(14) feeling keyed up or on edge
(15) exaggerated startle response
(16) difficulty concentrating or "mind going blank" because of anxiety
(17) trouble falling or staying asleep
(18) irritability

Particularly in older people, it is necessary to consider whether the disorder is due to organic causes, such as thyroid conditions or low blood sugar; to overstimulation by substances, such as caffeine; or to withdrawal from alcohol, sedatives, and other medications. Less commonly, certain brain tumors, chronic obstructive pulmonary disease, pulmonary embolus, neurological diseases, intolerance of aspirin, and vitamin B_{12} deficiency are examples of conditions that may lead to an organic anxiety syndrome. Frequently, people have a "sense of something wrong" before their organic condition develops to the point where it can be diagnosed, and they may develop symptoms of anxiety. It is thus important to continue to monitor a client's physical health status even after an assessment of anxiety disorder has been determined. In addition, the symptoms may be identified as part of a concurrent physical condition, such as arthritis, heart problems, or dementia.

Another complication is to define what is unrealistic or excessive anxiety in an older person. An elderly widow, dependent on the support of a daughter, may realistically worry about her daughter's health and continuing ability to assist her. Someone who has lived through the depression of the 1930s may reasonably worry about finances, inflation, and the cost of care more than may someone of a younger generation.

With a GAD, mild depressive symptoms are common, and an unrelated panic or depressive disorder is often present. The age of onset is usually before the midthirties, but onset at later ages has been reported. Gorman and Liebowitz (1986) stated that adequate data on the actual age at onset, course, and prognosis are not available. In clinical situations the disorder is apparently equally common in men and women. Since people frequently use alcohol to deal with their anxiety, the social worker should consider an underlying anxiety disorder when treating people with problems of alcoholism and other substance abuse. GAD is a factor that could contribute to the relapse in a "recovering" addict and should be addressed as soon as abstinence begins.

A major study found that, across age groups, two-thirds of people with

GAD reported two or more somatic health problems and a large majority reported two or more stressful life events (Uhlenhuth, Balter, Mellinger, Cisin, & Clinthorne, 1983). Impaired social role performance, reported by 67 percent, was attributed to psychological factors by 22 percent and to somatic illness and other factors by 45 percent of the respondents. These findings illustrate how social, psychological, and somatic factors intertwine in such conditions and indicate the impact of these conditions on social functioning. The following case example illustrates some features of GAD in an older woman:

Mrs. P was referred to a public health nurse by the hospital emergency department, where she had been taken after a fall in her apartment. She was 73 years old and lived with an elderly friend in drab, poorly maintained public housing.

Mrs. P was a complainer and preoccupied with possible misfortunes. She felt isolated and alone, complained sarcastically about the stupidity, incompetence, and lack of concern she saw in her friend. She said she had always suffered from "bad nerves" and had taken tranquilizers off and on for many years. She spent most of her day on the sofa, and was often troubled by dizziness. She thought she had a bladder infection because she had to urinate so frequently. Her arthritis had become much more disabling over the past two years, particularly in her knees and feet, and her hands had become weak and misshapen. She was able to walk around her apartment with difficulty, but did not leave it. She was afraid she would be physically unable to walk the long distance to the elevator and that nobody would be able to help her if she got in trouble, or that she would get diarrhea and be unable to get to a bathroom. She was too embarrassed to use a wheelchair or walker, but was comfortable going out if someone she felt confidence in accompanied her. She had no friends to visit and had never invited people to her home. She tended to be brusk and impatient with people she met. She enjoyed television and became talkative and relatively animated when discussing her life. From time to time she said she was fed up with life, although she was not suicidal.

Like many people with GAD, Mrs. P had low self-esteem, felt dependent on others for the resolution of her problems, and had a difficult family life. Her mother had a chronic illness when Mrs. P was a child, her first husband was killed during World War II, and her second husband died after a long illness and disability. Mrs. P had two children, both of whom lived at a great distance and had infrequent contact with her.

TREATMENT STRATEGIES The central component is to establish a realistic, positive therapeutic approach that involves the client's active participation. People with GAD are often sensitive and have difficulty handling failures and setbacks. They may also expect and need to have rapid and dramatic improvement, which sets the scene for disappointment. It is important to build in opportunities for success, to reduce failures, and to work on small steps. Deffenbacher and Suinn (1987) highlighted the importance of self-monitoring, as well as practicing and promoting the client's self-control. They cautioned that termination of treatment should not be considered until the client has been stable for a period and suggested longer intervals between sessions, periodic follow-ups, booster sessions, and regular self-reviews by the client as strategies to maintain and consolidate gains.

On the basis of her analysis of treatment approaches, Seligman (1990) stated that a combination of cognitive and behavioral techniques seem particularly powerful and suggested beginning with feelings and behavior and then moving on to autonomic thoughts, underlying assumptions, and major concerns. The client is helped to develop new views of the problems, to reframe distorted and dysfunctional beliefs about self and situation, and to acquire new coping skills.

Obsessive-Compulsive Disorder (OCD)

OCD, as described in DSM-III-R, is marked by recurrent obsessions or compulsions that are sufficiently severe to cause marked distress, to be time consuming, or to disrupt normal social roles or relationships significantly. Obsessions are persistent thoughts, ideas, impulses, or images that the person recognizes as a senseless product of his or her own mind. The person resists them by trying to ignore, suppress, or neutralize them with some other thought or action. The most common obsessions are repetitive thoughts of violence (killing a spouse); of contamination (becoming infected by shaking hands); of doubt (Did I harm someone?); or of disgusting, sexual, or blasphemous subjects.

Compulsions are repetitive, purposeful, and intentional behavior, performed in response to an obsession according to certain rules or in a stereotyped way. The ritual behavior is designed to neutralize or prevent discomfort or a dreaded event, but the activity is either clearly excessive or is not related realistically to what it is designed to prevent. It is not pleasurable, although it may reduce tension. The person usually recognizes that his or her behavior is unreasonable and may be sufficiently embarrassed to hide such actions from others. Some people's obsessions have evolved over time into over-valued ideas, and thus they see their behavior as appropriate.

Typically, OCD begins early in life; its onset after age 35 is seen in less than 10 percent of the cases (Shear & Frosch, 1986). It is equally common in men and women. The course is usually chronic, with the symptoms waxing and waning. People with OCD tend to have rigid consciences; to feel driven and pressured; to be indecisive and perfectionistic; to be concerned with control; to ruminate and doubt themselves; and to have a high need for reassurance, support, and help with social anxiety (Seligman, 1990).

Depression and anxiety are commonly associated factors, as is substance abuse. Frequently, persons may develop a phobic avoidance related to their obsession, such as the avoidance of public rest rooms if they are obsessed with cleanliness. The avoidance of public rest rooms may be a special problem for an older man with urinary urgency because of an enlarged prostate or for someone using a diuretic.

A search of the literature revealed little information specifically on OCD in elderly populations. However, clinical experience suggests several factors that may be relevant. Because OCD is more common than was previously thought (Thyer, 1987), as older people come into closer contact with social and health care services, their OCD may become evident to professionals. It is also possible that the strategies the person has developed to conceal and cope with symptoms are no longer available in retirement or with failing health. Life-stage tasks of reflection and review, rather than of establishing a sense of integrity and meaning, may facilitate excessive rumination and obsessive thoughts. Moreover, the person's life situation may make long-standing obsessions more upsetting.

The following examples illustrate some of these factors. A woman who has always harbored obsessional ideas of killing or harming her husband finds these ideas more distressing now that he has Alzheimer's disease and she is caring for him at home than she did when he was working and away much of the time. If she confides in formal or informal helpers, she thinks they, too, may become concerned.

A person who normally had several showers a day is greatly stressed after moving into a nursing home where scheduled showers are given once a week; the staff may be irritated and unsympathetic to the resident's concerns. A person who is compulsively meticulous will have problems accepting help from a housekeeper who does not understand the importance of having clothes folded in a particular way. A compulsive checker, who would spend over an hour repeatedly checking that everything was in order before leaving home, may have increasing problems if he or she develops some memory deficit. The obsessional slowness found in some people with OCD may increase with age. Compulsive hoarding is a category of OCD (Marks, 1981) that can bring an older person to the attention of the public health, social, or mental health services.

The basis for OCD is poorly understood. Psychoanalytic theory relates OCD to the repression of sexual and aggressive impulses and to the use of defense mechanisms of isolation, undoing, displacement, and magical thinking that are common in earlier stages of development. Shear and Frosch (1986) proposed that this theory facilitates empathic understanding of the "haunted, lonely" obsessional person, but does not lead to treatment strategies. Interpersonal theory suggests that the obsessions and compulsions reflect an underlying fear of humiliation or loss of control in a person with strong feelings of inadequacy. The ritual behavior thus serves to maintain self-esteem (Atwood & Chester, 1987; Seligman, 1990). According to learning theory, the obsessions and compulsions are learned responses that reduce anxiety. There is increasing evidence that OCDs have a biological and genetic base (Shear & Frosch, 1986).

TREATMENT STRATEGIES It seems that a substantial number of clients with OCD respond to treatment (Seligman, 1990; Thyer, 1987). Although an older person's symptoms may be entrenched over time, the life-review process and the need to adapt to new circumstances may provide an impetus for treatment.

The quality of the client-worker relationship is important. It must be open and trusting to overcome resistance to disclosure (Seligman, 1990) and sufficiently strong to provide the intense support needed for the reduction of maladaptive thoughts and behavior (Thyer, 1987). Firm support and the promotion of self-control, problem solving, the expression of feelings, and anxiety reduction are essential characteristics (Atwood & Chester, 1987). Medication may be useful either for a direct antiobsessional effect or for reducing the severity of anxiety or depression and thus facilitating psychosocial treatment. Active collaboration with a physician who understands substance abuse is required.

There is general support in the research literature for the use of behavioral models as an important component of treatment. Seligman (1990) stated that multiple modes of intervention seem more effective than does single-focus treatment and recommended that attention should be paid to the source as well as the symptoms. One would expect that such attention would be especially important in older people because of their more complex biopsychosocial situations.

The plan, therefore, should be set in the context of the person's life situation and life-stage tasks. The following strategies to increase self-esteem and effectiveness and to reduce anxiety may be helpful: practice in assertiveness, coping skills, relaxation, cognitive rehearsal, modeling, role playing, attention focusing and distraction, and problem solving.

Thyer (1987) described a program to reduce compulsive rituals that involves prolonged exposure to ritual-provoking cues combined with the prevention of ritualistic responses. He recommended the Maudsley Obsessional-Compulsive Inventory (Hodgson & Rachman, 1977) as a useful tool for assessment and for evaluating outcome. The following summarizes some of the key features of Thyer's approach to treating compulsive rituals; more details with examples are given in his book (Thyer, 1987, pp. 99–108).

The first step is a careful mapping to determine the precise cues that lead to the ritual. Each ritual needs to be treated separately, and a clinical decision must be made regarding the first target for treatment: It is best for psychologically fragile clients or those with few psychosocial resources to start with less demanding or pervasive rituals. After the worker and client jointly agree on the target ritual, several hours should be scheduled for the first treatment session. The client needs to be induced to come in contact with the ritual-provoking cues or to think ritual-provoking covert equivalents and then to tolerate the intense anxiety they engender until he or she becomes calm. During this habituation, the client must be persuaded to forgo all ritualistic activities used to reduce anxiety, to avoid surreptitious rituals designed to relieve anxiety (e.g., subtle touching, covert self-reassurance) and to tell the worker when they occur. Such treatment sessions should continue until the client can demonstrate calmness and refrain from the target ritual. Reassurance by the worker and network members is contraindicated. Family members and formal and informal helpers can assist the client with response prevention. However, their help requires the client's agreement plus careful instruction and involvement, as described by Thyer (1987, pp. 101–102). Support groups or help from a person who has recovered from OCD can serve a maintenance function.

Thyer (1987) emphasized that a good client-worker relationship is essential and noted that the sessions of therapeutic exposure and response prevention are psychologically and physically demanding for the client. Despite relatively intense levels of initial discomfort, he reported that most clients lose the overwhelming urge to ritualize in several minutes or hours after exposure begins. Long and frequent sessions are the most beneficial. Clients should be aware that symptoms commonly reemerge and that booster treatment sessions may be necessary.

The treatment of obsessions in people who do not have compulsions has received less attention, and less success has been reported. However, Thyer (1987) described a behavioral technique that involves the client in re-creating obsessional material for prolonged periods to undertake therapeutic exposure and habituation. Emmelkamp and Van der Hyden (1980) tested the hypothesis that obsessional thoughts of harming others are caused by unexpressed aggressive feelings and associated guilt. In a study of six patients, they found assertiveness training to be an effective component of treatment.

There are reports of successful treatment of OCD in older people. Pruitt, Miller, and Smith (1989) described the treatment of a 71-year-old woman who had had a severely debilitating OCD that had been unresponsive to numerous hospitalizations and a wide range of treatment approaches. After an intensive behavioral treatment program of exposure and response prevention, her obsessive-compulsive symptoms and her overall quality of life improved dramatically and was enduring.

PREVALENCE OF ANXIETY DISORDERS

Ackerknecht (1968) dated the serious study of "affections of the nervous system" in Western medicine to the eighteenth century. In 1733 Dr. Cheynne published *The English Disease*, reporting that a third of his patients were "nervous" and that the English were particularly susceptible to this illness.

The DSM-III-R states that according to recent studies, anxiety disorders are the most frequently found mental disorders in the general population, with panic disorder being the most common among people seeking treatment. As was mentioned earlier, strong familial links have been found among patients with panic disorder (Crowe, Noyes, Pauls, & Slyman, 1983), and there is likely a higher risk of alcoholism as well. Genetic studies have indicated that identical twins have a higher incidence of panic attacks than do fraternal twins (Klein, 1980) and that one-quarter of close relatives of patients with panic attacks also have such attacks (Shader, Goodman, & Gever, 1982). The nature of this genetic link is not yet understood.

A major psychiatric epidemiological study (Myers et al., 1984) reported that anxiety disorders are the most common form of mental illness in the United States, with 60–150 out of every 1,000 people meeting the DSM-III criteria. Another national sample (Barlow et al., 1984) found that 30–40 percent of the general U.S. population had marked anxiety.

A nationwide American household survey of adults aged 18–79 (Uhlenhuth et al., 1983) found that the generalized anxiety syndrome occurred at an increased rate with older people (aged 50–79). The prevalence of the agoraphobic-panic syndrome rose slightly, while other phobias were most prevalent in people under age 35. By contrast, major depression was distributed fairly evenly over age groups. For people aged 65–79, great distress was caused by anxiety for 5.7 percent and by mixed anxiety and depression for 9.5 percent (Mellinger & Balter, 1981).

Other studies have reported that rates of depression decrease with age (Chappell & Barnes, 1982; Hirshfield & Cross, 1982) and therefore that anxiety may be the greater problem. These findings are compatible with an earlier British study which found that anxiety disorders are the most common mental disorder in old age (Kaye, Beamish, & Roth, 1964, 1965). Misery, tension, anxiety, loss of self-esteem, and hypochondriasis are the most common symptoms in this group, whereas phobic and obsessional symptoms are less common.

The Canadian Health Survey (1982) found that people over age 65 who live in the community have almost three times more self-reported mental health problems than do people aged 15–64. Symptoms of anxiety and depression increase slightly throughout adulthood, with 4 percent of men and 7.7 percent of women over age 65 reporting frequent symptoms of anxiety and depression. Since a much higher proportion of those over age 65 did not respond to this question, the survey report estimated that a more realistic picture would be that 14–17 percent of older people have anxiety and depression.

Anxiety disorders seem to occur at similar levels across cultures, but the emphasis may be on different symptoms in different cultures, with people in nonindustrialized societies tending to have more somatic symptoms (Good & Kleinman, 1985).

LIAISON WITH PHYSICIANS AND MEDICAL KNOWLEDGE

It is necessary for social workers to understand the medical conditions of their clients, to collaborate with physicians in biopsychosocial assessments, to know the impact of their clients' medications, and to be alert for adverse effects and changing physical and mental conditions. Developing a foundation of medical knowledge is particularly important for five major reasons: (1) elderly people frequently have concomitant physical illnesses, (2) anxiety reactions include physical symptoms, (3) drug treatment is frequently an adjunct to psychosocial treatment, (4) older people are often more susceptible to paradoxical reactions and side effects of medication, and (5) drug effects may be compounded by polypharmacy.

To avoid the buildup of medications in the body, older people are frequently prescribed lower doses of drugs or shorter-acting drugs. Some of the latter may produce severe withdrawal reactions and require multiple daily doses. With many drugs, tapered withdrawal is necessary to avoid symptoms of irritability, agitation, and so on. Although medication may be used by itself, many writers state that the role of drug therapy is to provide transient relief while other treatments are used to achieve more lasting benefits (Kocsis & Mann, 1986). Caution is needed so that the medication is not used to mask the symptoms, for such relief may lead to addiction, thus compounding the original problem.

Depression, like anxiety, also has symptoms in three areas: somatic, emotional, and psychic. Although anxiety and depression often occur together, one clue in differentiating between them is that depressed people often feel worse in the morning, while anxious people feel worse as the day goes on. Also, like Mrs. P, people with anxiety may become more responsive and animated when engaged in conversation.

DISCUSSION AND CURRENT ISSUES

Anxiety in the elderly is a complex issue, since symptoms of several physical and mental conditions, as well as socioenvironmental problems, are frequently present and complicate assessment and treatment. The vignette of the group program for anxiety in using the elevator illustrates the broad range of approaches that are required. In that example, the social worker considered the clients' physical and social life space, practical needs for movement through the building, information and coping skills, social support, autonomy, and a more satisfactory internal state of reduced anxiety (Libassi & Turner, 1981).

Generally, the social worker's educational and team-building functions are critical in working with formal and informal helpers to develop a coherent treatment plan in conjunction with the client. Mediation, brokerage, and advocacy are also essential. Attention to policies and procedures and to the attitudes and behavior of the personal and caregiving network that disempower the elderly is important as well (Wells & Singer, 1988).

Psychotherapy (psychodynamic, cognitive, and behavioral) may be helpful to older people (Abramson, Quam, & Wascow, 1986; Hartman and Laird, 1983; Kahana, 1979; Newton, Brauer, Gutmann, & Grunes, 1986; Turnbull, 1989). Since social support can be of great consequence, group and family work, in addition to individual counseling, may be appropriate. Advanced age is not, in itself, an indication for a different treatment approach (Turnbull & Turnbull, 1985).

Relaxation-meditation training modifies the body's response to stress, directly acting on the physical components of the anxiety reaction and indirectly on the affective, cognitive, and behavioral factors. It has an impact in a relatively short time. Cognitive restructuring and assertiveness training focus mainly on the cognitive, behavioral, and affective components of the biopsychosocial spectrum that take more time to be altered and are more dependent on ego functioning (Viney, Benjamin, & Preston, 1989). The objectives of cognitive restructuring, assertiveness training, and the problem-solving approach are to develop adaptive coping skills; to decrease the helplessness and low self-esteem associated with chronic anxiety; to increase respect for one's rights; and to improve communication, self-esteem, and confidence. Psychodynamic approaches also address issues of self-esteem and the development of skills, with specific attention to inner conflicts and the life-stage developmental components of ego integrity.

For all modalities, most authors stress the importance of relationship in assessing and treating anxiety. This may be especially critical in providing support to help older people address anxiety. People generally try to conceal their anxiety, and this tendency may be even more prevalent in older people, as the Canadian Health Survey (1982) suggested. It should be noted that the terms "nervousness" or "bad nerves" tend to be used rather than "anxiety" by older people at this time, and stoicism may be more highly valued. It is important also to evaluate clients' use of alcohol and other drugs and to consider the role these substances have in masking or protecting the individual from anxiety. As mentioned previously in this chapter, people from nonindustrialized cultures tend to express anxiety through physical symptoms. Older people with life experience in rural or less complex cities may do the same. Consequently, since it is expected that the elderly will have physical health problems, anxiety may be overlooked.

It should be emphasized that relatively few studies of maladaptive anxiety and its treatment focus on elderly populations. Of those that do, most consider people only up to age 75. This lack of research reflects the general neglect of the needs of the elderly. To understand and treat anxiety in older people better, we must conduct research that concentrates on this population, but that includes comparisons with other age groups and longitudinal studies of people with anxiety disorders. The current literature is based on expert opinion, case studies, and a few outcome studies. It is clearly time to use carefully documented single-case designs and other research strategies that will determine when results are due to planned interventions.

On the one hand, social workers and others often address only the instrumental or practical needs of older people. On the other hand, social workers have developed effective treatment methods, but have tended not to share their work. For example, an account of the group program to combat anxiety in elevators was not published previously, while a similar program, implemented by a psychologist, was reported as a contribution to knowledge building. The role of the social work profession in assessing and treating anxiety and anxiety disorders is recognized (Abramson, Quam, & Wascow, 1986; Cooper, Frances, & Sacks, 1986; Patterson, 1988; Seligman, 1990; Sketetee & White, 1990; Thyer, 1987; Turner, 1984). Our traditional attention to biopsychosocial variables has direct applicability to anxiety conditions. Social workers have an obligation to study systematically the effectiveness of their practice, to document when and with whom specific strategies work or do not work, and to engage in research to develop practice-related knowledge for social work and mental health care in general.

As with other mental disorders in older people, anxiety and anxiety disorders are frequently accompanied by multiple physical illnesses, the need to adjust to a series of life changes, and problems in the socioenvironmental context. The social worker must be comfortable with ambiguity and complexity in dealing with a combination of problems, be humble in recognizing his or her inexperience with being old, and be able to extend professional roles and to use himself or herself and other resources creatively.

Community studies (Tyrer, 1982; Weissman, 1985) have indicated that although many people do not receive treatment for their anxiety disorders, they tend to be high users of health care. The identification and treatment of these disorders may therefore reduce medical costs, as well as enhance the quality of these people's lives.

BIBLIOGRAPHY

Abramson, N. S., Quam, J. K., & Wascow, M. (1986). *The elderly and chronic mental illness.* San Francisco: Jossey-Bass.

Ackerknecht, E. H. (1968). *A short history of psychiatry* (2nd ed.). New York: Hafner.

American Psychiatric Association. (1987). *Diagnostic and statistical manual of mental disorders* (3rd ed., rev.). Washington, DC: Author.

Anderson, R. E., & Carter, I. (1990). *Human behaviour in the social environment* (4th ed.). New York: Aldine de Gruyter.

Atwood, J. D., & Chester, R. (1987). *Treatment techniques for common mental disorders.* New York: Jason Aronson.

Barlow, D. H., Cohen, A. S., Waddel, M. T., Vermilyea, B. B., Klosko, J. S., Blanchard, E. B., & DiNardo, P. A. (1984). Panic and generalized anxiety disorders: Nature and treatment. *Behaviour Therapy, 15,* 431–449.

Belsky, J. K. (1984). *The psychology of aging: Theory, research and practice.* Monterey, CA: Brooke-Cole.

Bloom, M. (Ed.) (1980). *Life span development.* New York: Macmillan.

Bowlby, J. (1969). *Attachment and loss: Vol. 1.* New York: Basic Books.

Bowlby, J. (1973). *Attachment and loss: Vol. 2.* New York: Basic Books.

Brenner, C. (1974). Depression, anxiety and affect theory. *International Journal of Psychoanalysis, 55,* 25–36.

Brenner, C. (1976). On the nature and development of affects: A unified theory. *Psychoanalysis Quarterly, 43,* 532–556.

Butler, R. N. (1980). Successful aging. In M. Bloom (Ed.), *Life span development* (pp. 352–360). New York: Macmillan.

Butler, R. N., & Lewis, M. (1983). *Aging and mental health, positive psychological approaches* (3rd ed.). St. Louis: C. V. Mosby.

The Canadian Health Survey. (1982). *The Health of Canadians* (No. 82–538E). Ottawa: Health and Welfare Canada & Statistics Canada.

Chappell, N. L., & Barnes, G. E. (1982). The practicing pharmacist and the elderly client. *Contemporary Pharmacy Practice, 5,* 170–175.

Cooper, A. M., Frances, A. H., & Sacks, M. H. (Eds.). (1986). *Psychiatry: Vol. 1. The personality disorders and neuroses.* New York: Basic Books.

Crowe, R. R., Noyes, R., Pauls, D. L., & Slyman, D. (1983). A family study of panic disorder. *Archives of General Psychiatry, 40,* 1065–1069.

Crowe, R. R., Pauls, R., Slyman, D., & Noyes, R. (1980). A family study of anxiety neurosis. *Archives of General Psychiatry, 40,* 77–79.

Deberry, S., Davis, S., & Reinhald, K. E. (1989). A comparison of medication-relaxation and cognitive/behavioral techniques for reducing anxiety and depression in a geriatric population. *Journal of Geriatric Psychiatry, 22,* 231–247.

Deffenbacher, J. L., & Suinn, R. M. (1987). Generalized anxiety syndrome. In L. Michelson & L. M. Ascher (Eds.), *Anxiety and stress disorders* (pp. 332–360). New York: Guilford Press.

Emmelkamp, P. M. G., & Van der Hyden, H. (1980). The treatment of harming obsessions. *Behavioral Analysis and Modifications, 4,* 28–35.

Glenwick, D., & Whitbourne, S. (1980). Beyond despair and disengagement: A transactional model of personality development in later life. In M. Bloom (Ed.), *Life span development* (pp. 373–378). New York: Macmillan.

Good, B., & Kleinman, A. (1985). Culture and anxiety: Cross-cultural evidence for the patterning of anxiety disorders. In A. H. Tuma & J. D. Maser (Eds.), *Anxiety and the anxiety disorders* (pp. 297–324). Hillsdale, NJ: Lawrence Erlbaum Associates.

Gorman, J. M., & Liebowitz, M. R. (1986). Panic and anxiety disorders. In A. M. Cooper, A. J. Frances, & M. H. Sacks (Eds.), *Psychiatry: Vol. 1. The personality disorders and neuroses*. New York: Basic Books.

Hartman, A., & Laird, J. (1983). *Family-centered social work practice*. New York: Free Press.

Himmelfarb, S., & Murrell, S. (1984). The prevalence and correlates of anxiety symptoms in older adults. *Journal of Psychology, 116*, 159–167.

Hirshfield, R. M., & Cross, C. K. (1982). Epidemiology of affective disorders: Psychosocial risk factors. *Archives of General Psychiatry, 39*, 35–46.

Hodgson, R. J., & Rachman, S. J. (1977). Obsessive-compulsive complaints. *Behaviour Research and Therapy, 15*, 389–395.

Hussian, R. A. (1981). *Geriatric psychology: A behavioral perspective*. New York: Van Nostrand Reinhold.

Kahana, R. J. (1979). Strategies of dynamic psychotherapy with a wide range of older individuals. *Journal of Geriatric Psychiatry, 12*, 71–100.

Kaplan, B. (1984). Anxiety states. In F. J. Turner (Ed.), *Adult psychopathology: A social work perspective* (pp. 260–279). New York: Free Press.

Kaye, D. W. K., Beamish, P., & Roth, M. (1964). Old age mental disorders in Newcastle upon Tyne. *British Journal of Psychiatry, 110*, 146–158, 668–682.

Kaye, D. W. K., Beamish, P., & Roth, M. (1965). Old age mental disorders in Newcastle upon Tyne. *British Journal of Psychiatry, 111*, 938–946.

Klein, D. F. (1980). Anxiety reconceptualized. *Comprehensive Psychiatry, 21*, 411–427.

Kocsis, J. H., & Mann, J. (1986). Drug treatment of personality disorders and neuroses. In A. M. Cooper, A. J. Frances, & M. H. Sacks (Eds.), *Psychiatry: Vol. 1. The personality disorders and neuroses* (pp. 129–138). New York: Basic Books.

Kramer, M., & Stoltzman, R. (1984). Six-month prevalence of psychiatric disorders in three communities. *Archives of General Psychiatry, 41*, 959–969.

Libassi, M. F., & Turner, N. S. (1981). The aging process: Old and new coping tricks. In A. N. Maluccio (Ed.), *Promoting competence in clients* (pp. 264–289). New York: Free Press.

Markowitz, J. S., Weissman, M. M., Ouellette, R., Lish, J. D., & Klerman, G. L. (1989). Quality of life in panic disorder. *Archives of General Psychiatry, 46*, 984–992.

Marks, I. M. (1981) *Cure and care of neuroses*. New York: John Wiley & Sons.

Mellinger, G. D., & Balter, M. B. (1981). Prevalence and patterns of use of psychotherapeutic drugs: Results from a 1979 national survey of American adults. In G. Tognoni, C. Bellantuono, & M. Lader (Eds.), *Epidemiological impact of psychotropic drugs: Proceedings of the International Seminar on the Impact of Psychotropic Drugs* (pp. 117–135). Amsterdam: Elsevier–North Holland.

Myers, J. K., Weissman, M. M., Tishler, G. L., Holzer, C. E., Leaf, P. J.,

Orvaschel, H., Anthony, J. C., Boyd, J. N., & Burke, J. D. (1984). Six-month prevalence of psychiatric disorders in three communities. *Archives of General Psychiatry, 41*, 959–967.

Newton, N. A., Brauer, D., Gutmann, D. L., & Grunes, J. (1986). Psychodynamic therapy with the aged: A review. *Clinical Gerontologist, 5*, 205–229.

Patterson, R. L. (1988). Anxiety in the elderly. In C. G. Last & M. Hersen (Eds.), *Handbook of anxiety disorders* (pp. 541–551). New York: Pergamon Press.

Peck, R. (1968). Psychological developments in the second half of life. In B. Neugarten (Ed.), *Middle age and aging* (pp. 88–92). Chicago: University of Chicago Press.

Pruitt, S. D., Miller, W. R., & Smith, J. E. (1989). Outpatient behavioral treatment of severe obsessive-compulsive disorder: Using paraprofessional resources. *Journal of Anxiety Disorders, 3*, 179–186.

Seligman, L. (1990). *Selecting effective treatments.* San Francisco: Jossey-Bass.

Shader, R. I., Goodman, M., & Gever, J. (1982). Panic disorders: Current perspectives. *Journal of Clinical Psychopharmacology, 2*, 25–105.

Shader, R. I., Scharfman, E. L., & Dreyfus, D. A. (1986). A biological model for selected personality disorders. In A. M. Cooper, A. J. Frances, & M. H. Sacks (Eds.), *Psychiatry: Vol. 1. The personality disorders and neuroses* (pp. 41–52). New York: Basic Books.

Shear, M. K., & Frosch, W. A. (1986). Obsessive-compulsive disorder. In A. M. Cooper, A. J. Frances, & M. H. Sacks (Eds.), *Psychiatry: Vol. 1. The personality disorders and neuroses* (pp. 353–362). New York: Basic Books.

Sketetee, G., & White, K. (1990). *When once is not enough: Help for obsessive-compulsives.* Oakland, CA: New Harbinger Press.

Thyer, B. A. (1987). *Treating anxiety disorders: A guide for human service professionals.* Newbury Park, CA: Sage.

Thyer, B. A., Nesse, R. M., Cameron, O. G., & Curtis, G. C. (1986). Panic disorder: A test of the separation anxiety hypothesis. *Behaviour Research and Therapy, 24*, 209–211.

Thyer, B. A., Nesse, R. M., Curtis, G. C., & Cameron, O. G. (1985). Agoraphobia: A test of the separation anxiety hypothesis. *Behaviour Research and Therapy, 23*, 75–78.

Turnbull, J. M. (1989). Anxiety and physical illness in the elderly. *Journal of Clinical Psychiatry, 50* (11, Suppl.), 40–45.

Turnbull, J. M., & Turnbull, S. K. (1985). Management of specific anxiety disorders in the elderly. *Geriatrics, 40*, 75–82.

Turner, F. (1984). *Adult psychopathology: A social work perspective.* New York: Basic Books.

Tyrer, P. J. (1982). Anxiety states. In E. S. Paykel (Ed.), *Handbook of affective disorders* (pp. 59–69). New York: Guilford Press.

Uhlenhuth, E. H., Balter, M. B., Mellinger, G. D., Cisin, I. H., & Clinthorne,

J. (1983). Symptom checklist syndromes in the general population. *Archives of General Psychiatry, 40,* 1167–1173.

Verwoerdt, A. (1981). *Clinical geropsychiatry* (2nd ed.). Baltimore, MD: Williams & Wilkins.

Viney, L. L., Benjamin, Y. N., & Preston, C. A. (1989). An evaluation of personal construct therapy for the elderly. *British Journal of Medical Psychology, 62,* 35–41.

Weissman, M. M. (1985). The epidemiology of anxiety disorders: Rates, risks and familial patterns. In A. H. Tuma & J. D. Maser (Eds.), *Anxiety and the anxiety disorders* (pp. 275–296). Hillsdale, NJ: Lawrence Erlbaum Associates.

Wells, L. M., & Singer, C. (1988). Quality of life in institutions for the elderly: Maximizing well-being. *Gerontologist, 28,* 266–269.

10

Depressive Disorders

Ruth E. Dunkle · Theresa Norgard

EPIDEMIOLOGY

Practitioners and researchers in the field of aging generally agree that depression is a prevalent and serious condition that affects many people in later life. Depending on the diagnostic criteria and the population under study, estimates of the extent of depression in elderly persons vary considerably. Although most older adults enjoy good mental health (Busse, 1987; Cohen, 1988), those who do not often experience painful consequences that may be life threatening (Jenike, 1988).

The reported prevalence of depression in the older age group has been inconsistent. For example, the Duke Longitudinal Study found that at any given time of testing, 20–25 percent of the elderly living in the community were diagnosed as depressed (Blazer, Hughes, & George, 1987), whereas 20–35 percent of elderly patients with concurrent medical illnesses were so diagnosed (Moffie & Paykel, 1975). In addition, about 60 percent of the study population fell into the depressed category at least once by the tenth round of evaluation (Blazer, Hughes, & George, 1987). For many in the Duke Longitudinal Study, depression was often chronic; the same people tended to be depressed at each test period. Although these estimates are for noninstitutionalized elders, there is increasing evidence that the prevalence of mental disorders in nursing homes is substantial as well (Harper & Lebowitz, 1986).

On the other hand, a report prepared by the Senate Special Committee on Aging and the American Association of Retired Persons (AARP), based on epidemiological information gathered by researchers at the National

Institute of Mental Health, concluded that depression was not a major problem of old age (U.S. Senate Special Committee on Aging, 1984).

The use of stringent inclusion criteria may explain some of the difference in the estimates of how many older people suffer from depression (Blazer, Hughes, & George, 1987; Kermes, 1986). The failure to recognize the symptoms associated with depression in the elderly may also result in underreporting. As Cohen (1990) observed, many of the symptoms associated with mental illness are often overlooked or dismissed as inevitable manifestations of the aging process. Since good mental health is the norm in later life, families and health care practitioners need to be rigorous in seeking proper diagnoses and treatment for elderly individuals who display unexplained changes in behavior or affect.

DEMOGRAPHICS

Differences in rates of depression emerge when one examines rates by gender, race, and age, as well as marital status. General population surveys indicate that women are twice as likely as are men to be diagnosed as depressed, which may be due, in part, to their greater likelihood to report depressive symptoms on self-assessment measures (Myers, Weissman, & Tischler, 1984; Weissman, Leaf, & Halzer, 1984; Weissman & Myers, 1978).

Although there is evidence that blacks do not seek or receive treatment at the same rate as do whites (Fellin, 1987), most epidemiological research has found little difference in the prevalence of depression among racial and ethnic minorities. The few studies of older members of racial and ethnic minorities, though, indicate that depressive and organically based psychiatric conditions tend to increase with age (LaRue, Dessonville, & Jarvik, 1985). When racial differences were found, blacks had higher rates of depression than did whites, but these differences disappeared when socioeconomic status was controlled (Comstock & Helsing, 1976).

There do seem to be age and racial variations in suicide rates, an issue that is related to depression. When depression was broadly defined, nearly all the older people who attempted suicide had depressive symptoms (Stenback, 1980). Although prevalence rates of depression among elderly persons tend to mirror those of younger people, there are important differences between the young and the old. Currently, elderly persons constitute 12 percent of the U.S. population, but account for 17–25 percent of all reported suicides (Manton, Blazer, & Woodbury, 1987; Sendbeuhler & Goldstein, 1977). White men, in particular, are at a considerable risk. They account for a disproportionate share of all suicides, regardless of age, with their suicide rate rising dramatically with advancing age. Their rate peaks at about age 85, with aged white men committing suicide three times more often than any other group (Manton, Blazer, & Woodbury, 1987). The suicide rate also increases sharply at higher ages for nonwhite men (see chapter 20).

DEFINITION OF DEPRESSION

To understand depression, it is important to define good mental health. What is mental health? Jahoda (1958) defined mental health as encompassing six criteria: a positive attitude toward self; a sense of growth, development, and self-actualization; integration; autonomy; a perception of reality; and environmental mastery. Obviously, these terms take on different meanings, depending on a person's functional level. For instance, would an older person who is immobilized by arthritis be viewed as capable of mastering the environment? Is growth a concept that is usually applied to older people? The terminology is relative and needs to be reinterpreted in a realistic manner in relation to the functioning of the person in question. For some older people just being able to feed themselves may be a good indication of environmental mastery. Since the standards of good mental health clearly vary, the clinician needs to be attuned to their relevance to the individual at hand.

The definition of good mental health or mental health that is age relevant is not only a professional issue. The elder also has a belief about how one should be feeling as he or she grows older. These beliefs are imposed by the society at large across the life span.

Through the socialization process, age-appropriate behavior should be determined by how people are socialized to view it. The question is really, Does society have expectations of the behavior of those who achieve old age? Neugarten (1980) argued that perceptions in the United States about behaviors that are appropriate at given ages have relaxed somewhat in recent years. There have been changes in the timing of role transitions, that is, getting married, having children, or retiring. Now these events may happen over several decades. These transformations call into question what behavior is appropriate for any group. Professionals and elders alike struggle to identify behaviors that classify behavior, especially mental health behavior, in terms of what is age appropriate and what is not.

ASSESSMENT ISSUES

Just as there is controversy surrounding the prevalence of depression in the elderly, there is also disagreement over how depression should be defined. Depression is usually defined in terms of symptoms and may be classified into two categories: major and minor. Major depression implies severer symptoms with specific physical manifestations and usually (although not always) no apparent environmental or psychosocial event associated with its onset. Often the person has had a history of depression or another family member was diagnosed with depression.

Minor depression tends to be preceded by unhappy life events—physical decline and the loss of roles or a loved one—and physical symptoms are not as predominant. In reality, many depressed people have symptoms that are indicative of both major and minor depressions simultaneously (Gurland et al., 1976; Zarit & Zarit, 1984).

Affective disorders in older people represent both a diagnostic and a therapeutic challenge for clinicians. The elderly patient is often confronted not only by the difficulties associated with the social changes that accompany aging, such as retirement and widowhood, but with more medical problems. Because of the complex interplay between biological and social factors, it is difficult to arrive at an appropriate diagnosis. The treatment of the elderly patient with an affective disorder is equally complex and requires the ability to integrate various health perspectives. For example, since older patients are more prone to the side effects of medications, some of which may be life threatening, the pharmacological treatment of the elderly requires in-depth knowledge of the pharmacokinetic and pharmacodynamic aspects of the antidepressant medications. Knowledge of the interactions between illness and psychiatric diagnosis is equally important. Most diseases of the central nervous system may appear as or be complicated by an affective illness. Of particular importance is the issue of dementia.

This section discusses issues that are relevant to depression in older people. Some years ago, Jarvik (1976) made a statement about the relationship between old people and depression that holds true today:

> Given the biological changes, the rising frequency of somatic illness, physiological decline, physical debilities, malnutrition, overmedication (iatrogenic or self-induced), sensory deficits, reduction in mental agility, economic deprivations, social losses, and the increasing proximity to death, all of which are associated with advancing chronological age, why is not every old person in a profound state of depression? (Jarvik, 1976, p. 326)

Although many older people suffer great losses in their lives, the result is not always depression. This is not to say that they do not experience grief or what may seem to be a continuous grief reaction caused by the increasing loss and death that is associated with advanced age, but this condition is different than being diagnosed as depressed. In fact, while most depressions among older people are reactive, meaning that they are a response to a psychosocial situation, some depressions in old age are biological. Ban et al. (1981) presented a schematic representation of the etiological factors in depressive disorders that illustrates the connection between the reactive and endogenous types of depression.

Biological Factors

Among the physiological factors that have been implicated in depression are abnormalities in neurotransmitters, particularly low levels of norepinephrine (Davis, Segal, & Spring, 1983; Griest & Griest, 1979). Metabolic changes associated with normal aging, such as changes in the sensitivity of receptors, as well as in neurotransmitters, may also be involved (Jenike, 1982; Salzman, 1984; Vestal & Dawson, 1984). Metabolic changes associated with normal aging are also important in the pharmacological treatment of depression (Jenike, 1988).

Social Factors

For many people losses of one kind or another are a frequent part of later life. Blazer (1982) noted that some older people may overreact to significant losses. The experience of one loss may predispose an individual to anticipate future losses, resulting in a heightened sense of threat to security and anticipatory grief. Anticipatory grief does not always result in depression and may have positive consequences for some (Carey, 1977; Fulton & Gottesman, 1980). However, periods of anticipatory grief may carry with them social effects (sensory deprivation, physical illness, social isolation) that may result in depression (Parkes, 1972; Switzer, 1970).

Clinicians have long associated the loss of a meaningful role and of a loved one with depression for persons of all ages (Lipton, 1976). The most frequent loss that results in depression in older people is the loss of physical functioning (Zarit & Zarit, 1984). Social isolation, chronic illness, and the loss of financial resources have also been reported (Friedman & Sjogren, 1981). Zung (1980) suggested that stressful life events, whether they originate from within the person or from the environment, are important components of depression.

The death of a spouse is perhaps the most significant loss (Holmes & Rahe, 1967; Parkes, 1972). The social isolation following the death of a spouse has been reported to be significantly related to a variety of affective disturbances, including depression, as have intense feelings of hopelessness, helplessness, and self-blame (Becker, 1974; Fry, 1986).

Increasingly, researchers are investigating the relationship between control or a sense of self-efficacy and depression. More opportunities for control and a greater sense of personal efficacy may have a beneficial effect on physical and psychological health (Rodin, 1986). Holahan, Holahan, and Beck (1984) reported that the sense of personal efficacy in dealing with day-to-day annoyances and stressful life events is associated with lower levels of depression among both men and women. Similar findings were reported among residents in nursing homes (Banziger & Roush, 1983; Langer & Rodin, 1976).

How a person interprets particular events may be an important factor in depression. Beck (1979) postulated that it is not a particular event per se that causes depression, but unrealistic negative interpretations of events.

Diagnosis

Depression may be defined in terms of five categorical dimensions: emotional-affective; cognitive; motivational; physical; and, at the severest level, delusions and hallucinations (Beck, 1979). Criteria set forth in DSM-III-R are most frequently used as indicators of depression. In brief, these criteria are as follows:

- dysphoric mood
- apathy, loss of interest or pleasure in activities
- change in appetite, significant weight loss or gain
- alteration in sleep patterns
- psychomotor agitation or retardation
- fatigue, reduced energy level
- inappropriate guilt, self-blame, worthlessness
- recurrent thoughts of death, suicidal ideation

Persons in whom at least five of the DSM-III-R symptoms are present during a two-week period are defined as being clinically depressed.

People with depression often complain of insomnia, particularly early morning awakenings, but hypersomnia is less common (Bixler, Kales, & Soldatos, 1987; Blazer, 1982). They also typically display apathy, inertia, and withdrawal, as well as self-depreciation (Epstein, 1976). Many symptoms of depression are associated with a decrease in memory, such as slower physical movement, slowed speech and thinking, anxiety, and low self-esteem (Reisberg, 1981). Deficits in short-term but not long-term memory have also been reported (Sternberg & Jarvik, 1976). Other researchers caution that variability and inconsistency in cognitive functioning are common in older persons with cognitive impairments (Wells, 1979).

Since it is not easy to diagnose depression in older persons, physicians often fail to detect psychiatric symptoms in patients (Waxman & Carner, 1984). Furthermore, the symptoms of depression in the elderly may vary from those in younger people and may be complicated by physical illness. Atypical clinical features are more likely among older than among younger depressed people. Such symptoms as pseudodementia (Epstein, 1976), slowness of cognition, apathy, and somatic complaints without an obvious mood defect are common (Fry, 1986). The older person is less likely to complain of a dysphoric mood, but closer questioning of the person should reveal more common symptoms of feeling sad and blue. With these potential areas of diagnostic confusion, the clinician's task is twofold: "1) to ascertain the presence of depression, especially if it is not immediately apparent from the patient's complaints; and 2) to determine the nature of the syndrome so that appropriate treatment can be instituted" (Christison & Blazer 1988, p. 91).

Types of Depression

UNIPOLAR The criterion used for diagnosing depression in late life is the same as it would be at other stages of life using the DSM-III-R. It should be remembered that depression is not more commonly diagnosed in older people than in other age groups, especially older adolescents, and is just as successfully treated as in other age groups. The criteria for depression listed in DSM-III-R pp. 222–224 suggest that the person has either a depressed mood or a marked disinterest in daily activities. Coupled with either of these symptoms are at least four of the following: significant weight loss or gain or an increase or decrease in appetite, insomnia or hypersomnia, psychomotor agitation or retardation, fatigue or loss of energy, feelings of worthlessness or inappropriate guilt, diminished ability to think, and recurrent thoughts of death. Typically these symptoms occur daily. The main demarcating feature of this type of depression is the disruption in vegetative symptoms. This type of depression is not maintained by an organic factor and is not part of delusional symptoms that have occurred in the past two weeks. Last, a major depressive disorder is not superimposed on schizophrenia, a schizophreniform disorder, or a delusional disorder.

A major depressive episode should not be confused with unhappiness or normal sadness. The increasing loss of friends and relatives through death as one grows older results in grief. With frequent death, a seemingly persistent state of grief can exist. According to DSM-III-R, for older people a diagnosis of depression, rather than sadness, is indicated if symptoms persist for more than six weeks; there is significant weight loss, sleep is disturbed, the degree of sadness exceeds the losses sustained, there is a sense of worthlessness or guilt, and the sadness gets worse over time.

BIPOLAR The second major type of depression is a bipolar disorder (or manic-depressive illness). The onset of this disorder is usually before age 50 and rarely occurs in later life (Angst, Baastrup, Grof, et al., 1973), although a substantial number of older persons have a bipolar disorder. Diagnostic criteria in DSM-III-R (pp. 217–218) identify behaviors associated with the manic episode. The person has an abnormally and persistently elevated, expansive, or irritable mood, and at least three of the following seven features that persist during the mood disturbance are present: inflated self-esteem or grandiosity, a decreased need for sleep, more talkativeness than usual, a flight of ideas or racing thoughts, distractibility, increased goal-directed activity or agitation, or excessive involvement in pleasurable activities with a high potential for painful consequences. Typically, the person has problems in his or her work life or in social relationships. Delusions, which may have existed in the past, have not occurred for the past two weeks. This disorder is not superimposed on schizophrenia, a schizophreniform disorder, or a delusional disorder.

DIFFERENTIAL DIAGNOSIS OF DEPRESSIVE SYMPTOMS

Numerous symptoms of depression may appear to be like those of other problems, such as dementia or an illness. Therefore, it is essential for the clinician to be able to differentiate these symptoms, so an accurate diagnosis can be made and treatment can be directed to the most productive channel.

Depression versus Illness

The elderly often have symptoms that are due to aging that look like depression; nonspecific physical symptoms, such as fatigue or anorexia, that may be a manifestation of a medical problem; or depressive symptoms that actually exacerbate symptoms of a coexisting physical illness (Kane, Ouslander, & Abrass, 1989). Table 10.1 presents examples of somatic complaints that

TABLE 10.1
Examples of Physical Symptoms That Can Represent Depression

System	Symptom
General	Fatigue
	Weakness
	Anorexia
	Weight loss
	Anxiety
	Insomnia (see Table 5.4)
	"Pain all over"
Cardiopulmonary	Chest pain
	Shortness of breath
	Palpitations
	Dizziness
Gastrointestinal	Abdominal pain
	Constipation
Genitourinary	Frequency
	Urgency
	Incontinence
Musculoskeletal	Diffuse pain
	Back pain
Neurological	Headache
	Memory disturbance
	Dizziness
	Paresthesias

Source: R. Kane, J. Ouslander, and J. Abrass, *Essentials of Clinical Geriatrics* (New York: McGraw-Hill, 1989), p. 118. Reproduced with permission of McGraw-Hill, Inc.

may represent depression or be exacerbated by depression (Kane et al., 1989).

Psychological symptoms may also be present in the following medical conditions: brain tumor, anemia, minor strokes, hyperthyroidism, head injury, uremia, diabetes, lupus, leukemia, congestive heart failure, Parkinson's disease, cancer, and cardiovascular illness. Various medications such as psychotropic drugs, sedatives, and antihypertensive medication, may also lead to depressive symptoms, as may the use of alcohol and the discontinuation of stimulants (see Table 10.2; Kane et al., 1989). In general, medical and neurological illnesses play a part in the development of depression in the elderly (Alexopoulos, 1989). In a study of older medical patients, Kinzie,

TABLE 10.2
Drugs That Can Cause Symptoms of Depression

Antihypertensives
  Reserpine
  Methyldopa
  Propranolol
  Clonidine
  Hydralazine
  Guanethidine
Analgesics
  Narcotic
    Morphine
    Codeine
    Meperidine
    Pentazocine
    Propoxyphene
  Nonnarcotic
    Indomethacin
Antiparkinsonism drugs
  Levodopa
Antimicrobials
  Sulfonamides
  Isoniazid

Cardiovascular preparations
  Digitalis
  Diuretics
  Lidocaine
Hypoglycemic agents
Psychotropic agents
  Sedatives
    Barbiturates
    Benzodiazepines
    Meprobamate
  Antipsychotics
    Chlorpromazine
    Haloperidol
    Thiothixene
  Hypnotics
    Chloral hydrate
    Flurazepam
Steroids
  Corticosteroids
  Estrogens
Others
  Cimetidine
  Cancer chemotherapeutic
    agents
  Alcohol

Sources: After Hall, 1980; Levenson and Hall, 1981.
As cited in R. Kane, J. Ouslander, and J. Abrass, *Essentials of Clinical Geriatrics* (New York: McGraw-Hill, 1989), p. 121. Reproduced with permission of McGraw-Hill, Inc.

Lewinson, Marile, and Teri (1986) found that about 50 percent of their sample had depression associated with the illness, with drug use, or with both.

Depression versus Dementia

Dementia in the elderly produces a constellation of symptoms that are characterized by the loss of intellectual abilities that are severe enough to interfere with social and occupational functioning (DSM-III-R). Usually the decline in functioning is of long duration and is progressive. Approximately, 1.5 million Americans have dementia (Crook, 1986), and this number is expected to increase because of the growing number of persons over age 85 and because the incidence of dementia increases with age (Benson, Scherbel, & Spar, et al., 1982). The leading cause of irreversible dementia in the elderly is Alzheimer's disease, and the second-most-common cause is multi-infarct dementia, the result of a series of small strokes.

Until recently, it was believed that depression and dementia existed separately. Research has disproved this notion and demonstrated that they co-exist and can be successfully treated. In fact, major depression has been noted in 20 percent of geriatric outpatients with various forms of dementia (Reifler, Larson, & Hanley, 1982; see also, Alexopoulos, 1989), but estimates of the prevalence of secondary depression in irreversible dementia vary from almost never (Kresevich, Martin, Berg, & Danziger, 1982) to 40 percent (Lazarus, Newton, Cohler, Lesser, & Schereon, 1987; Rovner, 1986). Great optimism was shown for the successful treatment of depression and coexisting reversible dementia (Alexopoulos, 1989), but that is no longer the case. In a study of twenty-three patients with major depression and reversible dementia, 39 percent ultimately developed irreversible dementia over a period of twenty to thirty-seven months (Alexopoulos, Young, Lieberman, & Shamoran, 1987). The important clinical point is that these depressive symptoms respond to treatment even if the cognitive disorder does not (Rabins, 1989). The typical regimens of treatment modalities for depression, such as psychotherapy, electroconvulsive therapy (ECT), and pharmacological therapy, are appropriate.

In the 1970s it was believed that depression was a common cause of reversible dementia and that the symptoms mimicked irreversible dementia (Rabins, 1985). Until recently, clinicians believed that depression-induced dementia was difficult to diagnose. Clinical signs and symptoms have now been identified that may be used to diagnose these patients: a past history of depression, a subacute onset of current symptoms, and a sleep disorder (Reding, Wegforss, et al., 1984; Reding, Haycox, & Blass, 1985). Coupled with these symptoms are the typical depressive symptoms and the absence of neurological problems (Reding et al., 1985). This depression-induced memory disorder exists both in the old and in other age groups (Niederehne & Burt, 1986). A more complete picture of the comparative features of a depression-induced memory disorder and irreversible dementia can be found in studies by Wells (1979, 1980) and Zung (1980). The tables in these works are particularly helpful to the clinician because they suggest the potential results of various tasks and procedures.

Frequently the clinician turns to DSM-III-R for assistance in identifying the symptoms of the disorder.

Unfortunately, these standards are of no help with the overlap in the symptoms of depression and dementia because although problems in memory and concentration are identified in both disorders, a diagnosis of a major depressive disorder cannot be given if the symptoms are due to an organic mental disorder. In the latter case, the primary diagnosis is dementia with a subclassification of depression (Teri & Reifler, 1987).

ASSESSMENT TOOLS

Although clinical skills are a critical component of an accurate assessment, numerous depression inventories are suitable for use with older people. Among the most widely used scales identified by Salzman, Kochansky, Schader, and Cronin (1972) are the Hamilton Rating Scale for Depression (Hamilton, 1960, 1967), the Zung Self-Rating Depression Inventory (Zung, 1965), the Beck Depression Inventory (Beck, Ward, Mendelson, Meck, & Erbaugh, 1961), the Geriatric Mental Status Review (Gurland et al., 1976), and the Geriatric Depression Scale (Yesavage, Brink, Rose, & Adey, 1983).

The Hamilton Rating Scale is widely used, but requires a trained observer to administer the questions during a clinical interview. Some further drawbacks of this scale are that it favors somatic complaints, which may be confused with the symptoms of old age, including anxiety and neurotic complaints, and is time consuming (Gaylord & Zung, 1987). The Zung Self-Rating Depression Inventory is the most widely used scale and is easy to administer, using the elder himself or herself.

TRENDS IN TREATMENT

A range of treatment modalities are available for treating elderly persons who are depressed. The choice or combination of treatment approaches depends on the cause of the depression, the severity of the symptoms, the availability of various treatments, and other medical problems the elder faces (Kane et al., 1989). The main treatment modalities are drugs, ECT, psychotherapy, and supportive approaches, all of which are effective with older depressed people. The success of the treatment rests with the consideration of the elder as an individual who is biomedically, psychologically, and socially different from adults in other age groups.

Drug Treatment

Drugs are used in treating depression when the diagnosis of major depression is made or if the depression is causing major functional limitations (Kane et al., 1989). Unfortunately, if an older person's sleep or eating patterns are disrupted, the physiological consequences of those disruptions may be great, even to the point of irreversible medical problems or death. Intervening to interrupt the cycle of symptoms through the use of drugs or ECT may be life saving.

Tricyclic antidepressant medication is the most widely used antidepressant with the elderly who are suffering from a major affective disorder. Elders with a bipolar disorder find lithium of benefit for manic states (Bernstein, 1983), but unfortunately, the effect of lithium on depression is not well established (Jefferson, 1983). Of course, side effects occur with all drugs, and alternatives are available (Kane et al., 1989).

As with the use of all drugs with the elderly, issues of compliance, polypharmacy because of multiple disease states (Vestal & Dawson, 1984), and the absorption and distribution of drugs jeopardize the successful use of drugs in treating depression in the elderly (Hollister, 1978). For instance, Blackwell (1972) found that 25–50 percent of outpatients failed to follow the clinicians' orders. Therefore, the careful monitoring of the blood levels of the drugs in older patients can provide helpful information to prescribing physicians.

Vestal and Dawson (1984) identified general principles for prescribing drugs to older people. They recommended that physicians should strive for a diagnosis before treatment, take a drug history before prescribing any new drug, know the pharmacology of the drugs being prescribed, titrate the drug dosage with the patients' responses, typically use smaller doses in the elderly, and, when possible, simplify the therapeutic regimen to maximize the patient's efforts to comply with treatment. The frequent review of the drugs being taken simultaneously is necessary to identify those that are no longer needed.

Electroconvulsive Therapy

ECT induces a series of grand mal seizures, by the passage of electric current through the brain, that have a therapeutic effect. Although ECT is used with all age groups, it is more commonly used with the elderly because of other health problems, such as lessened cardiac function, that may make the use of antidepressant drugs less desirable (Weiner, 1982).

ECT is particularly effective with elders who have not responded to drug treatment. Scovern and Kilmann (1980) found that 80–85 percent of the patients who were treated with ECT after not responding to drug therapy for depression went into remission. Follow-up studies showed that 85 percent of the patients improved and remained that way (Abrams, 1972).

Psychological Therapies

The full range of psychological treatments may be used to help depressed older people; individual therapy, group therapy, and family therapy all have a part in the treatment process. Before these treatment modalities are discussed, the special psychological issues of the elderly should be mentioned because they concern overall treatment. For instance, older people more frequently struggle to adapt to the social and physical losses of their lives, and the older the person, the more frequent the losses become. Isolation because of sensory losses or living alone may jeopardize the elder's contact with reality, as well as raise existential concerns that may be less common in a younger person. As was mentioned earlier, organic problems, more frequent in the elderly, cause difficulty in diagnosis as well as treatment. Last, in work with an older depressed person who is having difficulty coping with everyday life, the task of integrating the past, present, and future into a meaningful fabric of life may seem overwhelming. This difficulty is further exaggerated by the elder's realization that so little time remains of his or her life.

Specific factors in therapy include the frequency of contact, the structure and direction of treatment, and the role of significant others in the treatment process. The traditional fifty-minute hour in therapy is frequently ineffective with older people. The elder's concentration and fatigue should be taken into account in determining the duration of sessions; more frequent sessions may be one solution to this problem. As for the structure and direction of therapy, treatment is more helpful to many older people if it is supportive and directive. The provision of advice within the therapeutic context may be helpful to a person with some memory deficit. On frequent therapeutic occasions, family members or close friends should be included in the process because they often are an invaluable source of information for the therapist and a support to the older client. It should be remembered, however, that the elder is the client and therefore that he or she should not be upstaged by significant others who are more coherent or more assertive.

INDIVIDUAL THERAPY The two main theoretical approaches that guide the understanding of and treatment goals for depression are psychoanalytic theory and cognitive theory. Psychoanalytic theory helps the client understand the issue of loss, a common theme in depression. Symbolic loss, premised on the early life experience of loss, is triggered by changes that the older person experiences. These later-life events take on a meaning that is greater than the events per se as the person struggles to deal with what the recent losses represent.

The issues of transference and countertransference are central to the therapeutic psychoanalytic process. In the traditional view of transference, the client places the therapist in the role of parent and thereby gains psychological access to the early parent-child relationship. Belsky (1990) and Lazarus and Weinberg (1980) questioned whether transference actually occurs or whether the older client views the therapist as a child because of the usual age difference between them. On the other hand, this reverse-transference strategy has been disputed and called countertransference by others (Berezin, 1983); that is, the therapist is uncomfortable with the parental role in the face of the client's age.

Many limitations to the use of psychoanalytically oriented therapy with older persons have been identified. Belsky (1990) noted that many older people are not oriented to their feelings because of their socialization during the Great Depression of the 1930s, when rugged individualism was emphasized. Moreover, treatment that is approached as a review of childhood experiences may seem remote to older clients. Furthermore, the approach may violate the traditional view of the therapist-patient relationship (Haug, 1981). Therapists who support this approach with older people suggest modifications, such as more activity by the therapist, a focus on more practical issues of life, and shorter-term therapy (Blum & Tros, 1980; Pfeiffer, 1976).

Cognitive behavioral theory posits that all behavior is learned, and so are emotional problems like depression. The learning that causes emotional problems, though, has been wrong; the person has committed logical errors in interpreting the events in his or her life. In therapy, these misperceptions are identified, examined, and subsequently changed (Beck, 1973; Rush, Khatomi, & Beck, 1975).

This treatment approach is successful with older clients because of its problem orientation and short duration. Furthermore, the therapist is assertive with the client and therefore eliminates some of the problems linked with disrupting the traditional therapist-patient relationship (Belsky, 1990). In studies that have compared the effectiveness of cognitive behavioral therapy and psychoanalytically oriented therapy, cognitive behavioral therapy proved to be more effective (Gallagher & Thompson, 1983; Thompson, Davies, Gallagher, & Krantz, 1986).

GROUP THERAPY Yalom (1975) stated that the purpose of groups is to facilitate interpersonal learning and to help members develop social skills. This approach is especially helpful to elders who are isolated and need support, for it brings them in contact with others and provides a safe vehicle for learning that others experience similar problems.

Groups have been used extensively with older people (Gatz, Poplin, Pino, & Vanden Bas, 1985), although some researchers have found that being in a group may be more difficult for older than for younger persons because older persons have a harder time sharing personal feelings with strangers (Altolz, 1978). Hartford (1980) noted that groups may intensify the sense of isolation that the older person feels if he or she is criticized by other group members for something he or she said.

In general, groups are usually categorized in three ways: social, remedial, or reciprocal. Groups that are organized using a social model provide the means for elders to make a social contribution and engage them in activities that are directed toward social change (Lowy, 1979). Remedial groups are set up to bolster the elder's ability in a certain area, such as memory retraining; elders come to such groups to learn specific skills to improve their functioning. Reciprocal groups, unlike the other two types, function like self-help groups; they have no appointed leader and the purpose is to allow group members to help one another. For instance, in a widow-to-widow group, members whose spouses died come together to help one another cope with the adjustments.

FAMILY THERAPY Unfortunately, family therapy is an infrequent choice of treatment with the elderly. It is not used because extended family members often do not live near each other and elderly family members are sometimes not viewed as an integral part of the family process and therefore are more likely to receive treatment individually or in groups with other elderly people.

ISSUES IN SERVICE DELIVERY

The diagnosis and treatment of elderly depressed persons occur within a service delivery context that either facilitates or impedes the success of treatment. Unfortunately, elders who seek mental health services are more likely to receive medication for their problems and are more likely to leave treatment without their problems being resolved (Goldstrom et al., 1987). Although the elderly are 12 percent of the population, they receive only 6 percent of the psychological services at community mental health centers (Flemming, Buchanan, Santos, & Rickards, 1984) and 4 percent of the outpatient visits to private psychiatrists (Schurman, Kramer, & Mitchell, 1985). By and large, nursing homes have become the repositories for elderly people who are mentally ill (Sherwood & Mor, 1980).

There are several reasons for this low use of psychological services. Both the elderly themselves and the providers of mental health services are responsible. Service providers may underestimate the efficacy of psychological treatment of the aged and may also have negative attitudes toward elderly clients (Dye, 1978; Gatz and Perarson, 1988; Knight, 1986; Setting, 1982). Many older people shy away from psychological services because they believe the services are for "crazy" people (Lazarus & Weinberg, 1980) or that older people cannot benefit from such services. The result is that by the time many older people come for psychological services, their problems are more serious (Gallagher & Thompson, 1982; Lowy, 1979).

Another major deterrent is payment for service. Medicare, the primary health care coverage utilized by older people, provides extensive coverage for inpatient mental health services, but only limited coverage for outpatient psychological services. A small number of outpatient visits with a psychiatrist are covered, a psychologist's services are covered under certain conditions, and the services of a social worker are not covered at all (Belsky, 1990).

These financial limitations are compounded by the reluctance of many professionals to treat older persons. On occasion their reluctance is the result of their psychological training that was rooted in the psychoanalytic view that older persons are mentally recalcitrant. Freud believed that the mental elasticity of older persons was limited and that there was too much psychological territory to cover to make treatment productive (Cath, 1965).

On occasion, professionals believe that treating older people does not allow them to provide care at the level that they were trained to provide. These professionals view themselves as caretakers only, not as therapists with the elderly (U.S. Commission on Civil Rights, 1979). In reality, treating older people often does require arranging for concrete services, as well as providing psychological therapy (Blum & Tros, 1980).

SUMMARY AND CONCLUSIONS

This chapter provides an overview of the key issues in understanding and treating depression in older people. Only recently have practitioners realized that treatment options as well as the success of treatment are the same for adults of all ages. No longer are older people believed to suffer from depression in disproportionate numbers compared with other age groups, although diagnostic concerns and treatment modalities for them may differ from those of younger people. As with any other age group, individual differences need to be considered when assessing an older person's symptoms and choosing a particular treatment approach. Furthermore, the actual provision of service can be different for older people based on training and attitudes of health care professionals as well as the elderly's attitude about themselves. Unfortunately, it is still common for health care professionals to have little interest in treating older people and for older people themselves to believe they are untreatable.

In the future emphasis needs to be placed on the social as well as the medical and educational aspects of appropriate treatment of depressed older people. As the number of people who are old increases the number of those who are depressed will increase as well. The pressure this will bring to bear on the service delivery system will need to be addressed if the needs of older segments of the population are to be met.

REFERENCES

Abrams, R. (1972). Recent clinical studies of ECT. *Seminar in Psychiatry, 4,* 3–12.

Albert, M., & Moss, M. (Eds.). (1988). *Geriatric neuropsychology.* New York: Guilford Press.

Alexopoulos, G. (1989). Biological abnormalities in late life depression. *Journal of Geriatric Psychiatry, 22,* 25–33.

Alexopoulos, G., Young, R. C., Lieberman, K., & Shamoran, C. (1987). Platelet MAO activity in geriatric patients with depression and dementia. *American Journal of Psychiatry, 144,* 1480–1483.

Altolz, J. A. S. (1978). Group psychotherapy with the elderly. In I. M. Burnside (Ed.), *Working with the elderly: Group process and techniques.* North Scituate, MA: Duxbury Press.

American Psychiatric Association. (1980). *Diagnostic and statistical manual of mental disorders* (3rd ed.). Washington, DC: Author.

Angst, J., Baastrup, P., Grof, P., et al. (1973). The course of monopolar depression and bipolar psychosis. *Psychiatra, Neurologia, 76,* 489–500.

Ban, T. A., Gonzalez, R., Jablensky, A. S., Sartouus, N. A., & Vartanian, F. E. (Eds.). (1981). *Prevention and treatment of depression.* Baltimore, MD: University Park Press.

Banziger, G., & Roush, S. (1983). Nursing homes for the birds: A control relevant intervention with birdfeeders. *The Gerontologist, 23,* 527–531.

Beck, A. T. (1973). *The diagnosis and management of depression.* Philadelphia: University of Pennsylvania Press.

Beck, A. T. (1979). *Depression: Courses and treatment* (7th ed.). Philadelphia: University of Pennsylvania Press.

Beck, A. T., Ward, C. H., Mendelson, M., Meck, J., & Erbaugh, J. (1961). An inventory for measuring depression. *Archives of General Psychiatry, 4,* 561–571.

Becker, J. (1974). *Depression: Theory and research.* Washington, DC: V. H. Winston.

Belsky, J. K. (1990). *The psychology of aging: Theory, research, and interventions* (2nd ed.). Pacific Grove, CA: Brooks/Cole.

Benson, D. F., Scherbel, A. B., Spar, J. F., et al. (1982). Dementia in the elderly: The silent epidemic. *Annals of Internal Medicine, 97,* 231–241.

Berezin, M. A. (1983). Psychotherapy in the elderly. In L. D. Breslau & M. R. Haug (Eds.), *Depression and aging: Causes, care and consequences.* New York: Springer.

Bernstein, J. G. (1983). *Handbook of drug therapy in psychiatry.* Boston: John Wright.

Bixler, E. O., Kales, A., & Soldatos, C. R. (1987). Prevalence epidemiology of depression in an elderly community population. *The Gerontologist, 27,* 281–287.

Blackwell, B. (1972). The drug defaulter. *Clinical Pharmacology of Therapeutics, 13,* 841.

Blazer, D. G. (1982). *Depression in late life.* St. Louis, MO: C. V. Mosby.

Blazer, D., Hughes, D. C., & George, L. K. (1987). *The healing.* Nashville, TN: Abington Press.

Blum, J. E., & Tros, S. (1980). Psychodynamic treatment of the elderly: A review of issues in theory and practice. In C. Eisdorfer (Ed.), *Annual review of gerontology and geriatrics* (Vol. 1). New York: Springer.

Busse, E. W. (1987). Mental health. In G. L. Maddox (Ed.), *The encyclopedia of aging* (pp. 438–439). New York: Springer.

Carey, R. G. (1977). The widowed: A year later. *Journal of Counseling Psychology, 24,* 125–131.

Cath, S. H. (1965). Some dynamics of middle and later years: A study in depletion and restitution. In M. A. Berezen & S. H. Cath (Eds.), *Geriatric psychiatry: Grief, loss, and emotional disorders in the aging process.* New York: International Universities Press.

Christison, C., and Blazer, D. (1988). Clinical assessment of psychiatric symptoms. In M. Albert & M. Moss (Eds.), *Geriatric neuropsychology.* New York: Guilford Press.

Cohen, G. D. (1988). *The brain in human aging.* New York: Springer.

Cohen, G. D. (1990). Psychopathology and mental health in the mature and elderly adult. In J. E. Birren and K. Warner Schau (Eds.), *Handbook of the psychology of aging* (3rd ed.). San Diego: Academic Press.

Comstock, G. W., & Helsing, K. J. (1976). Symptoms of depression in two communities. *Psychological Medicine, 6,* 551–563.

Crook, T. (1986). Drug effects in Alzheimer's disease. *Clinical Gerontologist, 5,* 489–502.

Davis, J. M., Segal, N. L., & Spring, G. K. (1983). Biological and genetic aspects of depression in the elderly. In L. D. Breslau & M. R. Haug (Eds.), *Depression and aging: Causes, care and consequences.* New York: Springer.

Dye, C. J. (1978). Psychologists' role in the provision of mental health care for the elderly. *Professional Psychology, 9,* 38–49.

Epstein, L. (1976). Depression in the elderly. *Journal of Gerontology, 31,* 278–282.

Fellin, P. (1987). Perspectives on depression among black Americans. *Health and Social Work, 14,* 245–252.

Flemming, A. S., Buchanan, J. G., Santos, J. E., & Rickards, L. D. (1984). *Mental health services for the elderly: Report on a survey of mental health centers.* Washington, DC: White House Conference on Aging.

Friedman, J., & Sjogren, T. (1981). Assets of the elderly as they retire. *Social Security Bulletin, 44(1),* 16–31.

Fry, P. S. (1986). *Depression, stress and adaptations in the elderly: Psychological assessment and treatment.* Rockville, MD: Aspen.

Fulton, R., & Gottesman, D. J. (1980). Anticipatory grief: A psychosocial concept reconsidered. *British Journal of Psychiatry, 137,* 45–54.

Gallagher, D., & Thompson, L. W. (1982). *Elders' maintenance of treatment benefits following individual psychotherapy for depression: Results of a pilot study and preliminary data from an ongoing replicated study.* Paper presented at the 90th annual meeting of the American Psychological Association, Washington, DC.

Gallagher, D., & Thompson, L. W. (1983). Cognitive therapy for depression in the elderly: A promising mode of treatment and research. In L. D. Breslau & M. R. Haug (Eds.), *Depression and aging: Causes, care and consequences.* New York: Springer.

Gatz, M., & Perarson, C. G. (1988). Ageism revised and the provision of psychological services. *American Psychologist, 43,* 184–188.

Gatz, M., Poplin, S. J., Pino, C. D., & Vanden Bas. (1985). Psychological interventions with older adults. In J. E. Birren & K. W. Schaie (Eds.), *Handbook of the psychology of aging* (2nd ed.) New York: Van Nostrand.

Gaylord, S., & Zung, W. (1987). Affective disorders among the aging. In L.

Carstensen & B. Edelstein (Eds.), *Handbook of clinical gerontology*. New York: Pergamon Press.

Goldstrom, I. D., Burns, B. J., Kessler, L. G., Feurberg, M. A., Larson, D. B., Miller, N. E., & Cromer, W. J. (1987). Mental health services use by elderly adults in a primary care setting. *Journal of Gerontology, 42*, 147–153.

Griest, J. H. & Griest, T. H. (1979). *Anti-depressant treatment: The essentials*. Baltimore, MD: Williams & Wilkins.

Gurland, B. J., et al. (1976). The comparative frequency of depression in various adult age groups. *Journal of Gerontology, 31*, 283–292.

Hall, R. C. W. (Ed.). (1980). *Psychiatric presentations of medical illness—somatopsychic disorders*. New York: SP Medical & Scientific Books.

Hamilton, M. (1960). A rating scale for depression. *Journal of Neurological and Neurosurgical Psychiatry, 23*, 56–62.

Hamilton, M. (1967). Development of a rating scale for primary depressive illness. *British Journal of Social and Clinical Psychology, 6*, 278–296.

Harper, M. S., & Lebowitz, B. D. (Eds.). (1986). *Mental illness in nursing homes* (DHHS Publication No. ADM 86–1459). Washington, DC: U.S. Government Printing Office.

Hartford, M. E. (1980). The use of group methods for work with the aged. In J. E. Birren & R. B. Sloane (Eds.), *Handbook of mental health and aging*. Englewood Cliffs, NJ: Prentice-Hall.

Haug, M. (1981). *Elderly patients and their doctors*. New York: Springer.

Holahan, C. K., Holahan, C. J., & Beck, S. S. (1984). Adjustment in aging: The role of life stress, hassles, and self-efficacy. *Health Psychology, 3*, 315–328.

Hollister, L. E. (1978). *Clinical pharmacology of psychotherapeutic drugs*. New York: Churchill-Livingstone.

Holmes, T. H., & Rahe, R. H. (1967). The social readjustment rating scale. *Journal of Psychosomatic Research, 11*, 213–218.

Jahoda, M. (1958). *Current concepts in positive mental health*. New York: Basic Books.

Jarvik, L. (1976). Aging and depression: Some unanswered questions. *Journal of Gerontology, 31*, 324–327.

Jefferson, J. W. (1983). Lithium and affective disorder in the elderly. *Comprehensive Psychiatry, 24*, 166–178.

Jenike, M. A. (1982). Dexamethasone suppression: A biological marker of depression. *Drug Therapy, 12*, 203–212.

Jenike, M. (1988). Depression and other psychiatric disorders. Status, and mental health. *Social Forces, 51*, 34–44.

Kane, R., Ouslander, J., & Abrass, J. (1989). *Essentials of clinical geriatrics*. New York: McGraw-Hill.

Kermes, M. (1986). *Mental health in late life: The adaptive process*. Boston: Jones & Bartlett.

Kinzie, J. D., Lewinson, P., Marile, R., & Teri, L. (1986). The relationship of depression to medical illness in an older community. *Comprehensive Psychiatry*, 27, 241–246.

Knight, B. (1986). Therapist attitudes as explanations of under service of elderly mental health: Testing an old hypothesis. *International Journal of Mental Health*, 22(4), 261–269.

Kresevich, J., Martin, R., Berg, L., & Danziger, W. (1982). Preliminary report on affective symptoms in the early stages of senile dementia of the Alzheimer type. *Americna Journal of Psychiatry*, 140, 233–235.

Langer, E. J., & Rodin, J. (1976). The effects of choice and enhanced personal responsibility for the aged: A field experiment in an institutional setting. *Journal of Personality and Social Psychology*, 34, 191–198.

LaRue, A., Dessonville, C., & Jarvik, L. F. (1985). Aging and mental disorders. In J. E. Birren and K. W. Schaie (Eds.), *Handbook of the psychology of aging*. New York: Van Nostrand Reinhold.

Lazarus, L. W., Newton, N., Cohler, B., Lesser, J., & Schereon, C. (1987). Frequency and presentation of depressive symptoms in patients with primary degenerative dementia. *American Journal of Psychiatry*, 144, 41–45.

Lazarus, L., & Weinberg, J. (1980). Treatment in the ambulatory care setting. In E. W. Busse & D. G. Blazer (Eds.), *Handbook of geriatric psychiatry*. New York: Van Nostrand Reinhold.

Levenson, A. J., and Hall, R. C. W. (Eds.). (1981). *Neuropsychiatric manifestations of physical disease in the elderly*. New York: Raven Press.

Lipton, M. A. (1976). Age differentiation in depression: Biochemical aspects. *Journal of Gerontology*, 31, 293–299.

Lowy, L. (1979). *Social work with the aging: The challenge and promise of the later years*. New York: Harper & Row.

Manton, K. G., Blazer, D. G., & Woodbury, M. A. (1987). Suicide in middle and later life: Sex and race specific life-table and cohort analyses. *Journal of Gerontology*, 42, 219–227.

Moffie, H. S., & Paykel, E. S. (1975). Depression in the medical epidemiology of depression. *Archives of General Psychiatry*, 34, 98–111.

Myers, J. K., Weissman, M. M., & Tischler, G. L. (1984). *Six features of medical disorders*. New York: Plenum.

Neugarten, B. (1980, April). Acting one's age: New rules for the old. *Psychology Today*, pp. 66–74, 77–80.

Niederehne, G., & Burt, D. (1986). *Depression and memory dysfunction in the aged*. Paper presented at the meeting of the Gerontological Society of America, Chicago.

Parkes, C. M. (1972). *Bereavement*. New York: International Universities Press.

Pfeiffer, E. (1976). Psychotherapy with elderly patients. In L. Bellack & T. B.

Karasu (Eds.), *Geriatric psychiatry: A handbook for psychiatrists and primary care physicians*. New York: Grune & Stratton.

Rabins, P. (1985). Reversible dementia. In T. Arie (Ed.), *Recent advances in psychogeriatrics* (No. 1). London: Churchill-Livingstone.

Rabins, P. (1989). Coexisting depression and dementia. *Journal of Geriatric Psychiatry*, 22, 17–23.

Reding, M., Haycox, J., & Blass, J. (1985). Depression in patients referred to a dementia clinic. *Archives of Neurology*, 42, 894–896.

Reding, M., Wegforss, K., et al. (1984). Follow-up of patients referred to a dementia service. *Journal of the American Geriatrics Society*, 32, 265–268.

Reifler, B., Larson, E., & Hanley, R. (1982). Coexistence of cognitive impairment and depression in geriatric outpatients. *American Journal of Psychiatry*, 139, 623–626.

Reisberg, B. (1981). *Brain failure: An introduction to current concepts of senility*. New York: Free Press.

Rodin, J. (1986). Aging and health: Effects of the sense of control. *Science*, 233, 1271–1276.

Rovner, B. (1986). Prevalence of mental illness in a community nursing home. *American Journal of Psychiatry*, 142, 1446–1449.

Rush, A. J., Khatomi, M., & Beck, A. T. (1975). Cognitive and behavior therapy in chronic depression. *Behavior Therapy*, 6, 398–404.

Salzman, C. (1984). *Clinical geriatric psychopharmacology*. New York: McGraw-Hill.

Salzman, C., Kochansky, G., Schader, R., & Cronin, D. (1972). Rating scales for psychotropic drug research with geriatric patients: 2. Mood ratings. *Journal of the American Geriatrics Society*, 20, 215–221.

Schurman, R. A., Kramer, P. D., & Mitchell, J. B. (1985). The hidden mental health network. *Archives of General Psychiatry*, 42, 89–94.

Scovern, A. W., & Kilmann, P. R. (1980). Status of ECT: A review of the outcome literature. *Psychological Bulletin*, 87, 260.

Sendbeuhler, J., & Goldstein, S. (1977). Attempted suicide among the aged. *Journal of the American Geriatrics Society*, 25, 245–248.

Setting, J. M. (1982). Clinical judgement in geropsychology practice. *Psychotherapy: Theory, Research and Practice*, 19, 397–404.

Sherwood, S., & Mor, V. (1980). Mental health institutions and the elderly. In J. E. Birren & R. B. Sloane (Eds.), *Handbook of mental health and aging*. Englewood Cliffs, NJ: Prentice-Hall.

Stenback, A. (1980). Depression and suicide behavior in old age. In J. E. Birren & R. B. Sloane (Eds.), *Handbook of mental health and aging*. Englewood Cliffs, NJ: Prentice-Hall.

Sternberg, D. E., & Jarvik, M. E. (1976). Memory functions in depression: Improvement with antidepressant medication. *Archives of General Psychiatry, 33,* 215–224.

Switzer, D. K. (1970). *Dynamics of grief: Its sources, pain, and Hispanic Americans.* Paper presented at the NIMH Workshop on Depression and Suicide in Minorities, Bethesda, MD.

Teri, L., & Reifler, B. (1987). Depression and dementia. In L. Carstensen & B. Edelstein (Eds.), *Handbook of clinical gerontology* (pp. 112–119). New York: Pergamon Press.

Thompson, L. W., Davies, R. Gallagher, D., & Krantz, S. (1986). Cognitive therapy with older adults. *Clinical Gerontologist, 5,* 245–280.

U.S. Commission on Civil Rights. (1979). *The age discrimination study: A report of the U.S. Commission on Civil Rights* (Part 2). Washington, DC: U.S. Government Printing Office.

U.S. Senate Special Committee on Aging. (1984). *Aging America: Trends and projections.* Washington, DC: U.S. Department of Health & Human Services.

Vestal, R. E., & Dawson, G. W. (1984). Pharmacology and aging. In C. E. Finch & E. L. Schneider (Eds.), *Handbook of the biology of aging* (2nd ed.) New York: Van Nostrand Reinhold.

Waxman, H., & Carner, E. (1984). Physicians' recognition, diagnosis, and treatment of mental disorders in elderly medical patients. *The Gerontologist, 24,* 593–597.

Weiner, R. D. (1982). The role of electroconvulsive therapy in the treatment of depression in the elderly. *Journal of the American Geriatrics Society, 30,* 710–712.

Weissman, M. M., Leaf, P. L., Halzer, C. E., et. al. (1984). The epidemiology of depression: An update on sex differences rate. *Journal of Affective Disorders, 7,* 179–188.

Weissman, M. M., & Myers, J. K. (1978). Affective disorders in a United States urban community: The use of research diagnostic criteria in an epidemiological survey. *Archives of General Psychiatry, 35,* 1204–1311.

Wells, C. E. (1979). Pseudodemented. *American Journal of Psychiatry, 136,* 895–900.

Wells, C. E. (1980). The differential diagnosis of psychiatric disorders in the elderly. In J. Cole and J. Barrett (Eds.), *Psychopathology in the aged.* New York: Raven Press.

Yalom, I. D. (1975). *The theory and practice of group psychotherapy* (2nd ed.) New York: Basic Books.

Yesavage, J. A., Brink, T. L., Rose, T. L., & Adey, M. (1983). The Geriatric Depression Rating Scale: Comparison with other self-report and psychiatric rating scales. In T. Crook, S. Ferris, & R. Bartus (Eds.), *Assessment in geriatric psychopharmacology* (pp. 153–167). New Canaan, CT: Mark Powley Associates.

Zarit, S. H., & Zarit, J. M. (1984). Depression in later life: Theory and assessment. In J. P. Abrahams & V. Crooks (Eds.), *Geriatric mental health*. New York: Grune & Stratton.

Zung, W. (1965). A self-rating depression scale. *Archives of General Psychiatry*, *12*, 63–70.

Zung, W. W. K. (1980). Affective disorders. In E. W. Busse & D. G. Blazer (Eds.), *Handbook of geriatric psychiatry* (pp. 338–367). New York: Van Nostrand Reinhold.

11

Adjustment Disorders

Joanne C. Turner

Erickson (1963) reminded us that each successive life stage presents developmental tasks to be faced and that the last task for elderly people is ego integrity versus despair. If they are successful in this last stage, elderly individuals synthesize their life experiences; if they are unsuccessful they often withdraw or descend on the epigenetic scale. This chapter is concerned with elderly persons who are suffering from an adjustment disorder and are at least temporarily unable to accept the challenge of the last stage of human development. It explores the dimensions of this type of disorder and discusses the possible treatment modalities that are available to help such elderly persons recover from the disorder, thus freeing the energy necessary to achieve the task of this last developmental phase.

With this elderly population, it is often difficult to distinguish between depression as a basic effect of experience and depressive illness when it presents as a more regressive or a clinical syndrome. It is also often difficult to engage this population in seeking out and carrying through with treatment to explore and, it is hoped, resolve the stressors that have brought about the onset of reactive depression syndrome.

DESCRIPTION OF THE CONDITION

The essential feature of an adjustment disorder, as discussed in DSM-III-R (p. 329), is "a maladaptive reaction to an identifiable psychosocial stressor or stressors that occurs within 3 months after the onset of the stressor and has persisted for no longer than 6 months." DSM-III-R also states that the maladaptive nature of the reaction is indicated either by impairment in

208

occupational functioning or in the usual social relationships or activities with others or by symptoms that are in excess of a normal expected reaction to the stressor. The assumption is that the adjustment disorder will desist soon after the stressor ceases or if the source of stress persists, the symptoms will decrease when the individual achieves a new level of adaptation. Although DSM-III-R characterized adjustment disorders of adulthood as a residual category of maladaptive reactions to psychosocial stressors, it also states that, "the disorder is not an exacerbation of one of the other mental disorders but is clearly a maladaptive reaction to an identified problematic event or set of adverse circumstances within the range of ordinary human experience." (APA, 1987). The disorder and the response associated with it are intense, but they are usually short lived because the impairment is temporary. Thus, the term *adjustment disorder* in essence describes the situation in which a specified stressor has found "a point of vulnerability in a person who normally enjoys considerable ego strength" (Mishne, 1984, p. 49).

The stressors that bring on this disorder may be single, such as the death of a spouse, or multiple, such as change of residence, the loss of a significant other person or persons, or the onset of a chronic illness. They may affect a specific person in a specific situation, as, for example, a psychological reaction to the onset of a chronic illness, or they may affect an entire group or an entire community, as, for example, in response to a natural disaster, such as an earthquake or the persecution of a particular religious group. It is also important to note that the severity of the reaction is not completely predictable when viewed from the intensity of the stressor. Some individuals who are particulary vulnerable may experience a more severe form of the disorder in response to a milder moderate stressor, while others may experience a mild disorder in response to a severe or continuing stressor, according to DSM-III-R.

If the stressor is a sudden event, such as an accident or a loss, the symptoms usually appear within a few days and their duration may be relatively brief, usually no more than a few months. If the sources of stress are persistent, such as those related to the diagnosis of a terminal illness, then the stress will persist for a longer period and the achievement of a new level of adaptation will take a significant amount of time, perhaps up to a year.

While depressive, anxious, and mixed features are common in adults, in the elderly, physical symptoms are often present as well. Again the symptoms are expected to cease or gradually diminish either when the stressor is reduced or ends or when the elderly individual achieves a new level of adaptation.

DIAGNOSTIC CRITERIA

ADJUSTMENT DISORDER WITH DEPRESSED MOOD When such symptoms as tearfulness and feelings of hopelessness and uselessness are present in addition to a depressed mood, this category is the appropriate classification. But it is important to note that with older persons, there is often a connection between physical pain or chronic pain and depression. Also, environmental changes, including the person's removal from his or her home to a nursing home or hospital, may produce sufficient stress to cause this type of symptom. It is also important to remember that the rating given is based on the clinician's assessment of the amount of stress that an average person in similar circumstances and with similar sociocultural values would experience from the particular psychosocial stressor. In addition, the amount of change in the individual's life and the degree to which the event was desired by or under the individual's control need to be considered. Both factors affect the amount of stress and the number of stressors that are affecting the psychosocial functioning of the individual. Again it must be emphasized that this type of disorder is due to a stressor that has contributed to the individual's inability to cope and adapt to change in what was considered a previously normal fashion.

ADJUSTMENT DISORDER WITH ANXIOUS MOOD This subcategory is utilized when worry, nervousness, and generalized anxiety are present. It is similar to symptoms of an anxiety disorder, which is also characterized by generalized anxiety and by symptoms of motor tension, an inability to relax, hyperactivity, distractibility, and sometimes insomnia. Since the symptoms are similiar in these two disorders, it is important to note that the major difference is the existence of a specific stressor that has caused the adjustment disorder.

ADJUSTMENT DISORDER WITH MIXED EMOTIONAL FEATURES When the presenting symptoms involve a combination of anxiety and depression or other emotions and affects, this category is applied. A mix of emotional symptoms may be seen with older persons following the loss of a life partner, the transition from a family home to an apartment or a nursing home, or increased leisure because of retirement. Again this type of disorder may occur at the same time that a physical illness or chronic physical condition is diagnosed.

AJUSTMENT DISORDER WITH MIXED DISTURBANCE OF EMOTIONS AND CONDUCT When the predominant symptoms are both emotional, such as feelings of depression and anxiety, and conduct disturbances, this category should be utilized. In older persons, these symptoms are often observed in connection with a person's failure to fulfill social obligations; to meet financial obligations, including bill paying and banking; and, at times, inappropriate interactions with family members and friends.

ADJUSTMENT DISORDER WITH WITHDRAWAL This grouping refers to the social withdrawal by an elderly person who previously participated in satisfactory social relationships within his or her home environment and community. Concurrently, the person is not demonstrating any significant depression or anxiety, as this case example indicates:

Mrs. H was referred to the local family service agency by a worker at the senior citizens' club. Mrs. H, who had normally been involved in attending university classes, learning French, and playing bridge a couple of times a week, had shown a disinclination to continue attendance and had told the worker that she thought that she might drop out. She seemed to be losing interest. During the intake interview at the agency, Mrs. H disclosed that she had recently been persuaded to move from her family home, in which all her children had grown up and in which her husband had died, to a new senior citizens' apartment. As well, she had a major difference of opinion with her eldest son over the disposition of the house and the investment of the money realized by its sale.

In summary, in adustment disorders, the symptoms are not attributable to another identified mental disorder and they surface within three months of one or more stressful events and are considered to be in excess of a normal and expectable reaction to that event. Clinicians will recognize that it is sometimes difficult to distinguish between a mental disorder and an adjustment disorder and, therefore, that some judgment is required. In this instance DSM-III-R provides guidelines that help to distinguish between a reactive disorder and severer types of depression or other mental illness.

SOME ETIOLOGICAL CONSIDERATIONS

Depression is frequently described as the psychiatric disorder most likely to occur in the elderly (Blazer, 1987; Hale, 1982). It is interesting that although a large percentage of older people demonstrate some evidence of dysphoria, a small percentage of them could be classified as clinically depressed. With regard to the relationship between stress and depressive symptoms in elderly persons, some researchers (Blazer, 1987; Hale, 1982; Lieberman, 1983; W. J. Smith, 1978) have explained that stressful events have always been associated with subsequent dysphoria and that some of these primary events include the loss of a loved one, personal illness, the illness of a family member or a close friend, and problems with interpersonal relationships. Other authors (Billings & Moos, 1985), have mentioned the absence of social supports or their departure from the social system of the person demonstrating the depressive symptoms as causative factors. Furthermore, a number of authors (Raymond, Michels, & Steer, 1980; Waxman & Carner, 1984) have noted that depressive symptoms are often ignored because physicians may be inattentive to the mental state or the behavioral problems of their older patients or because they believe that problems like insomnia or anxiety are a natural part of the aging process. Obviously, recognition of the problem is the first necessary step, and it can be aided by knowledge of the causes of a depressed effect or at least of the factors associated with it. Once professionals are aware of the existence of some of these conditions, they can learn to notice and respond to the symptoms or, in the case of physicians, to make the necessary referral.

When Grant, Patterson, and Yager, (1988) examined the relationship of social support to the physical and psychological well-being of persons aged 65 years or older, they found that patients with more symptoms of dysphoria reported having fewer emotionally satisfying supports from relatives, but that those who suffered from a physical illness reported having more social supports from relatives. They concluded that fewer key supports may indeed contribute to depressive symptoms at an adjustment level, but that all social support and health outcomes must be carefully defined so that the specific differential relationship between them can be understood. A similar finding was described by Murphy (1985), who concluded that as the level of depression becomes severer, the patient is no longer able to maintain close personal relationships and thus that the positive effect of strong and consistent supports is of little benefit to the affected person.

The relationship between depression and negative life events, such as physical impairment, social dissatisfaction, and the loss of social supports, has been well documented. A few researchers have investigated the relationship between these variables and somatic symptoms (Waxman et al., 1985) and concluded that depression is the most important factor in the appearance of somatic complaints. However, whether these factors directly influence somatic complaints or whether they are necessarily mediated by the depressive mechanisms, was the subject of a study by Rozzini, Bian-chetti, Carabellese, Inzoli, and Trabucchi (1988), who concluded that depression in elderly people is strongly related to the appearance of somatic symptoms, which, in turn, are linked with such factors as physical impair-ment, social satisfaction, income, and social support. This literature supports the need for a clearer understanding of the nature of the relationship between depression and health status in this aging population, as well as a greater awareness of the fact that psychological pain is often real for elderly persons. It is hoped that a greater understanding of this factor will result in changed attitudes toward elderly persons who suffer from adjustment disorders and more sympathy for their life experiences by helping professionals.

Chronically heavily stressed persons are another group who often dem-onstrate symptoms of depressivelike reactions. Caregivers, often over age 65, of persons suffering from chronic illness are one large subgroup of this category. Some authors, such as Becker and Morrissey (1988) have con-tended that many of the depressivelike reactions or adjustment disorders in caregiving spouses of Alzheimer's patients should be categorized under the DSM-III-R code-five conditions: "not due to psychiatric disorder." Becker and Morrissey stated that the major difficulty is not in distinguishing nor-mative distress reactions from major depressions, but, rather, in differen-tiating nonspecific distress reactions, adjustment disorders, and milder pathological disorders. They pointed out that research on this assessment process has failed to separate appropriate responses to chronic, severe dis-tressors from the symptoms of a major depressive diagnosis.

IMPLICATIONS FOR TREATMENT

Since the client population for this type of disorder is frequently composed of persons who are normally high functioning and competent, successful individuals, the prognosis for successful intervention is relatively good. Although the adjustment disorder will lessen when the stressors decrease or when a new level of adaptation is achieved, intervention as early as possible in the process is often helpful. Early intervention may also have a preventive component and may obscure the onset of more complicated or serious symptoms.

Different treatment approaches, such as crisis intervention, cognitive ther-apy, or reminiscence, may be appropriately utilized in working with this population. However, the most frequently used theoretical base is a bio-psychosocial model.

As is true of the classification of depression, the diagnosis of affective disorders is not reliable, and no single homogeneous set of symptoms may characterize the presence of such a disorder. As was mentioned earlier, one or more stressors in an older person's environment may bring on the onset of the symptoms.

Individual psychotherapy is frequently cited as the treatment of choice, but some dissention is evident in the literature concerning how much needs to be included in a comprehensive psychodynamic evaluation. Mishne (1984) noted that A. Freud, Nagera, and W. E. Freud (1977) recommended that clinicians assess the client's general characteristics from the viewpoint of the need for treatment, and the person's ability to profit from it. Freud et al. suggested an analytic approach that considers the current strengths and weaknesses in the level of ego functioning, the present and potential level of insight and capacity for self-observation, and the ability to tolerate limits on the amount of wish fullfillment with the transference setting.

The literature also suggests, and we know from our practice, that clients will often come out of an adjustment disorder in a stronger state than they were in before its onset. Therefore, the treatment approach has to be related to the social worker's assessment of the degree to which the disorder is related to the client's earlier attempt to cope and adapt. If the disorder is a first-time occurrence, then brief individual therapy may be sufficient. If an individual has experienced recurring adjustment disorders or prolonged impairment from one, then more intensive treatment is indicated. Both individual and group therapy may be useful, particularly for certain client groups, such as persons who have faced an environmental disaster or families who have just learned that one of their relatives has a terminal illness.

In the case of a first adjustment disorder, treatment would not normally include the identification of preconscious and unconscious meaning (Kaplan & Sadock, 1981), but would focus more on the meaning of the distress and the client's ability to cope with, understand, and adjust to the effects of the stressors on his or her everyday functioning.

Whatever the combination of stressors leading to the onset of symptoms, the person is left with less psychic energy to cope with reality, and, as Sherman (1984) discussed, there is a growing problem for the ego, particularly in coping with the loss of significant object relations. The ego's attempt to cope with such progressive losses, particularly important object relations, all lead to a loss of cathexis and an impoverishment of the ego. This ego depletion can have serious emotional effects, from lowered self-esteem to shame and guilt, to despair. Thus, the psychological construct of depletion–restitution balance (Cath, 1965) is central to the treatment model being used in work with the older person who demonstrates these symptoms. Sherman (1984, p. 71) defined the construct as one in which the ego continually tries to strike a balance between internal and external depleting forces throughout the life span but particularly in old age. Although these efforts at restitution appear regressive (e.g., more hypochondrial, dependent, or attention-seeking behaviour), they serve as defenses against depletion anxiety which seems to be rooted in a more basic dread of abandonment.

The implication of this construct for practice methods is that the social worker has to support defenses that are normally considered maladaptive in younger persons. As Sherman (1984, p. 71) pointed out, "a limited ("restitutive") use of defenses such as regression, denial and dependency is seen as adaptive rather than pathological and the practitioner has to be selectively supportive of them."

Furthermore, according to this viewpoint, attempts should not be made to uncover the use of such defenses for the purpose of gaining insight. Supportive techniques should be utilized to help older persons retain their remaining strengths and resources and to relieve both inner and outer stress; thus support, encouragement, warmth, reinforcement of realistic hope, and acceptance of some regressive and dependent behavior are often the appropriate techniques for treating such symptoms.

In addition, the social worker needs to distinguish between causality and somatic symptoms, particularly when considering physical illness and the onset of an affective disorder. The distinction is critical, since somatic systems that are associated with depression are likely to respond to treatment for depression even if the person is concurrently suffering from a physical illness. It is essential to try to distinguish which is the predominant factor in the onset of symptoms, and a careful physical evaluation as part of a thorough assessment should help the practitioner sort out the major stressor that is responsible for the onset of the symptoms of the affective disorder. Elderly persons with such symptoms often perceive themselves as having little control over their lives, particularly if illness is a prominent factor; thus, an important first step is to help them gain as much control over their lives, particularly over those events that occured in the few months preceding the onset of their symptoms, as is both positive and realistic (Zarit, 1980, p. 201). The following case example illustrates this process:

Mrs. M, an 88-year-old widow with abundant financial resources, had lived alone in an elegant apartment for fifteen years following the death of her husband. A rapid deterioration in her physical health necessitated the presence of a caregiver in the home for several hours each day. Initially, Mrs. M became either abusive or withdrawn when dealing with her family and friends and especially with the caregiver, who was provided by her health insurance plan. The social worker suggested that Mrs. M advertise, interview, and select her own caregiver and pay her a salary. Mrs. M did so, and after a series of interviews selected a person whom she felt was acceptable.

It is unfortunate that so little has been written about adjustment disorders from a social work perspective. We know from our practice that there is a growing knowledge base of clinical experience with this particular population, much of which is stored in the case records of our community agencies and within the practice wisdom of our colleagues.

Adjustment disorders are easily overlooked, especially in the early stage of intervention. They may be misdiagnosed as a more serious type of depression, a health-related problem, or simply as natural side effects of the aging process. Although more serious disorders must be ruled out before an adjustment disorder is diagnosed, the fact that symptoms of depression, anxiety, fatigue, and somatic complaints may all be present complicates the diagnostic process.

As was mentioned earlier, because adjustment disorders are amenable to treatment and persons suffering from this disorder are usually motivated to reduce the stressors, the prognosis for this client group is good. In fact, social work intervention in some cases provides clients with an opportunity to resolve earlier issues and hence to emerge from the disorder in a healthier mental state than they possessed before its onset. If the social worker is the only professional the client has contacted, then in addition to individual therapy, there is often the need to establish a helping network involving other professionals, such as the family physician, group workers, and other community resources.

Generally, treatment for such disorders may be obtained in a variety of agencies or clinics. Family service agencies, outpatient clinics of psychiatric facilities, mental health clinics, and increasingly private practitioners are regularly contacted for service by this well-motivated client group.

At the policy level, the need to have social work consultations and treatment covered by governmental and private health insurance plans becomes more critical each day as shrinking welfare funds result in longer waiting lists and increased pressure for service at community-based family agencies and clinics.

BIBLIOGRAPHY

American Psychiatric Association. (1987). *Diagnostic and statistical manual of mental disorders* (3rd ed., rev.). Washington, DC: Author.

Becker, J., & Morrissey, E. (1988). Difficulties in assessing depressive-like reactions to chronic severe external stress as exemplified by spouse caregivers of Alzheimer patients. *Psychology and Aging, 3,* 300–306.

Blazer, D. (1987). The epidemiology of depression in an elderly community population. *The Gerontologist, 27,* 281–287.

Billings, A., & Moos, R. (1985). In E. E. Beckham & W. R. Leber (Eds.), *Handbook of depression.* Homewood, IL: Dorsey Press.

Cath, S. H. (1965). Some dynamics of middle and later years. In H. J. Parad (Ed.), *Crisis intervention: Selective readings.* New York: Family Service Association of America.

Erikson, E. (1963). *Childhood and society* (2nd ed.). New York: W. W. Norton.

Freud, A., Nagera, H., & Freud, W. E. (1977). Metapsychological assessment of the adult personality: The adult profile. In R. Eissler, A. Freud, M. Kris, et al. (Eds.), *The anthology of the Psychoanalytic Study of the Child—Psychoanalytical assessment: The Diagnostic Profile.* New Haven, CT: Yale University Press.

Grant, I., Patterson, T. L., & Yager, J. (1988). Social supports in relation to physical health and symptoms of depression in the elderly. *American Journal of Psychology, 145,* 1254–1258.

Greengart, B., & Salamon, M. J. (1987). Things have changed here: An adjustment disorder of the long-term nursing home patient. *Clinical Gerontologist, 7*(2), 50–52.

Hale, W. D. (1982). Correlates of depression in the elderly: Sex differences and similarities. *Journal of Clinical Psychology, 38,* 253–257.

Headey, B., & Wearing, A. (1989). Personality, life events, and subjective well-being: Toward a dynamic equilibrium model. *Journal of Personality and Social Psychology, 57,* 731–739.

Jacobs, S., Hansen, F., Berkman, L., Stanislav, K., & Ostfeld, A. (1989). Depressions of bereavement. *Comprehensive Psychiatry, 30,* 218–224.

Kaplan, H., & Sadock, B. (1981). *Modern synopsis of Comprehensive Textbook of Psychiatry* (Vol. 3, 3rd ed.) Baltimore, MD: Williams & Wilkins.

Kirk, S., Siporin, M., & Kutchins, H. (1989). The Prognosis of social work diagnosis. *Social Casework: The Journal of Contemporary Social Work, 70,* 295–304.

Krause, M. (1987). Life stress, social support, and self-esteem in an elderly population. *Psychology and Aging, 2*, 349–356.

Lieberman, M. A. (1983). Social contexts of depression. In L. D. Breslau & M. R. Haug (Eds.), *Depressions and aging: Causes, care and consequences.* New York: Springer.

Magni, G., Palazzolo, O., & Bianchin, G. (1988). The course of depression in elderly outpatients. *Canadian Journal of Psychiatry, 33*, 21–24.

Milinsky, T. S. (1987). Stagnation and depression in the elderly group client. *Social Casework: The Journal of Contemporary Social Work, 68*, 281–289.

Mishne, J. (1984). Adjustment disorders. In F. J. Turner (Ed.), *Adult psychopathology: A social work perspective* (pp. 249–259). New York: Free Press.

Morris, L. W., Morris, R. G., & Britton, P. G. (1989). Cognitive style and perceived control in spouse caregivers of dementia sufferers. *British Journal of Medical Psychology, 63*, 173–179.

Murphy, E. (1985). The impact of depression in old age on close social relationships. *American Journal of Psychiatry, 142*, 3–9.

Rapp, S. R., & Davis, K. M. (1989). Geriatric depression: Physicians' knowledge, perceptions, and diagnostic practices. *The Gerontologist, 29*(2), 252–257.

Raymond, E. F., Michels, T. J., & Steer, R. (1980). Prevalence and correlates of depression in elderly persons. *Psychological Reports, 47*, 1055–1061.

Razavi, D., Delvaux, N., Farvacques, C., & Robaye, E. (1990). Screening for adjustment disorders and major depressive disorders in cancer in-patients. *British Journal of Psychiatry, 156*, 78–83.

Rife, J. C., & First, R. J. (1989). Discouraged older workers: An exploratory study. *International Journal on Aging and Human Development, 29*, 195–203.

Rozzini, R., Bianchetti, A., Carabellese, C., Inzoli, M., & Trabucchi, M. (1988). Depression, life events and somatic symptoms. *The Gerontologist, 28*, 229–232.

Ryff, C. D. (1989). In the eye of the beholder: Views of psychological well-being among middle-aged and older adults. *Psychology and Aging, 4*, 195–210.

Schlesinger, J. L., & Salamon, M. J. (1987). A case of somatization of anxiety and depression. *Clinical Gerontologist, 7*(2), 44–46.

Sherman, E. (1984). *Working with older persons.* Boston: Kluwer-Nijhoff.

Smallegan, M. (1989). Level of depressive symptoms and life stresses for culturally diverse older adults. *The Gerontologist, 29*, 45–50.

Smith, T. W., Peck, J. R., & Ward, J. R. (1990). Helplessness and depression in rheumatoid arthritis. *Health Psychology, 9*, 377–389.

Smith, W. J. (1978). The etiology of depression in a sample of elderly widows. *Journal of Geriatric Psychiatry, 11*, 81–83.

Waxman, H. M., & Carner, E. A. (1984). Physicians' recognitions, diagnosis, and treatment of mental disorders in elderly medical patients. *The Gerontologist, 24,* 593–597.

Waxman, H. M., et. al. (1985). A comparison of somatic complants among depressed and non-depressed older persons. *The Gerontologist, 25,* 501–507.

Zarit, S. H. (1980). *Aging and mental disorder.* New York: Free Press.

12

Borderline Personality Disorders

Eda G. Goldstein

Despite the avid interest that mental health clinicians have shown in recent years in the study of the character pathology known as borderline personality disorder, scant attention has been paid to the diagnosis and treatment of borderline conditions in work with the elderly. The questionable belief that character disorders, specifically borderline conditions, are not common among this age group and unwarranted pessimism regarding the psychotherapeutic treatment of this population (White & Weiner, 1986) have contributed to this state of affairs. Furthermore, there has been a tendency to attribute the problems of the elderly to the impact of the aging process and to an absence of environmental supports, rather than to personality difficulties that lead to vulnerability and maladaptive coping patterns (Sadovy, 1987). That most helping persons are much younger than their aging clients, hold stereotyped views of the aged, or experience a host of countertransference reactions in work with the elderly has made it more difficult to make accurate assessments and to implement appropriate treatment (Greene, 1986) with this population.

Although statistics have shown that the incidence of neuroses and personality disorders reaches a peak during the 25–44 age range and then tapers off, this fact "does not justify the conclusion that such disorders ameliorate with advancing age" (Verwoerdt, 1981, p. 117). The aging process may diminish the intensity of certain impulses and needs, but it can stimulate other types of dysfunction, for example, severe depression, alcoholism, suicide, or somatic difficulties and aggravate underlying personality weaknesses.

220

Thus, it is likely that the number of elderly borderline persons is far greater than we realize. Perhaps unknowingly, practitioners encounter elderly borderline men and women in their work, but usually are baffled, drained, and frustrated by these people's problems. Often angry, complaining, depressed, clinging, impulsive, and self-destructive, elderly borderline persons arouse strong feelings in those with whom they come in contact. Even helping professionals use negatively tinged terms, such as *manipulative, demanding, needy, controlling,* and *provocative,* to describe these individuals and view them as "difficult." Like their young counterparts, elderly borderline persons suffer considerably. They both want and fear closeness with others, are frightened of abandonment, experience intense feelings of aloneness, and are highly sensitive to rejection. Their self-esteem fluctuates dramatically, and they become flooded with anxiety and are often angry and defensive when stressed.

The family relationships of elderly borderline individuals present their own host of difficulties and often reflect shared pathology. Interactions of couples are turbulent and filled with conflict. Parent-child relationships generally are characterized by rejection or enmeshment. Those who work with borderline families frequently experience them as demanding, intrusive, or uncaring and may unintentionally aggravate their pathology.

Most elderly borderline persons do not receive treatment for their particular personality problems, which, nevertheless, affect their functioning wherever they are found in the service delivery system—medical clinics, home care agencies, nursing homes, senior citizens' centers, psychiatric hospitals, and the like. Collaborative difficulties among staff members are common, particularly in residential settings such as nursing or group homes. Disputes typically center on how to work with a particular resident, who is likely to be viewed by one staff member as needy and fragile and by another as hostile and belligerent. Consequently, it is important for helping persons to recognize these individuals' characteristics and areas of vulnerability and to understand current thinking about therapeutic approaches with this population.

What are borderline disorders? How can practitioners recognize their presence in the elderly population? What types of treatment do aging borderline individuals need? After a brief review of historical and current perspectives on borderline disorders and their main clinical features, this chapter discusses the mutual impact of the aging process and borderline personality, appropriate treatment approaches, and selected practice principles in work with elderly borderline individuals. It concludes with comments on implications for research, training, service delivery, and social policy.

222 MENTAL HEALTH AND THE ELDERLY

HISTORICAL PERSPECTIVES

Historically, the borderline designation referred to a diverse group of ill-defined disturbances that did not seem to fit traditional diagnostic criteria and were more severe than the neuroses and less severe than the schizophrenias (Goldstein, 1990). Clinicians considered it a "wastebasket" category that encompassed many different symptoms and personality traits, rather than a distinct disturbance. There was considerable debate over whether it constituted a type of severe character disorder that reflected entrenched and maladaptive traits and defenses—borderline personality—or a milder form of schizophrenic illness—borderline schizophrenia. Although Stern (1938) was credited with coining the term *borderline*, more than ten different diagnostic labels were used to describe these unusual conditions (Chatham, 1985; Stone, 1980).

Knight (1953a), a major psychodynamic theorist who studied so-called borderline persons in this early period, believed that ego weakness was at the root of these disorders. Theorists using other developmental frameworks, such as object relations and self psychology, put forth various formulations (Goldstein, 1990; Meissner, 1988; Stone, 1980). Biologically oriented researchers at this time believed that what seemed to be borderline pathology was linked genetically to schizophrenia (Kety, Rosenthal, Wender, & Schulsinger, 1968). Some clinician-researchers set aside the causality issue and tried to identify borderline characteristics more systemically (Grinker, Werble, & Drye, 1968; Gunderson & Singer, 1975).

Concerned about the regressive or self-destructive potential of borderline individuals, many clinicians argued that they required a highly structured, consistent, supportive, and reality-oriented treatment that maximized their ego functioning and adaptive defenses and that did not foster regression (Knight, 1953b; Zetzel, 1971). Others advocated a more ambitious treatment approach, since they believed that supportive psychotherapy did not substantially change the borderline person's character pathology (Eissler, 1953).

CURRENT PERSPECTIVES

There are four current models in the study of borderline disorders: the DSM-III-R model, the psychodynamic or developmental model, the family model, and the biological model. It is important to consider as well that the social environment is a crucial context in which these models must be viewed.

The DSM-III-R Model

DSM-III-R classifies disorders on the basis of symptoms and traits that commonly cluster into distinct categories. It does not link these disorders to a particular theory of causality or advocate any particular treatment approach. Borderline conditions are classified on Axis II as a type of personality disorder that reflects the presence of at least five of the following eight characteristics (p. 347):

1. A pattern of unstable and intense interpersonal relationships in which the person alternates between extremes of overidealization and devaluation.
2. Impulsiveness in at least two areas that are potentially self-damaging, for example, spending, sex, substance use, shoplifting, reckless driving, and binge eating.
3. Affective instability: marked shifts from baseline mood to depression, irritability, or anxiety, usually lasting a few hours and only rarely more than a few days.
4. Inappropriate, intense anger or lack of control of anger, for example, frequent displays of temper, constant anger, and recurrent physical fights.
5. Recurrent suicidal threats, gestures, or behavior or self-mutilating behavior.
6. Marked and persistent identity disturbance, manifested by uncertainty about at least two of the following: self-image, sexual orientation, long-term goals or career choice, type of friends desired, and preferred values.
7. Chronic feelings of emptiness or boredom.
8. Frantic efforts to avoid real or imagined abandonment.*

Although DSM-III-R attempts to use clear-cut, nonoverlapping criteria for the borderline designation, not everyone agrees with its conception of this disorder (Kernberg, 1984; Kroll, 1988; Stone, 1987).

The Psychodynamic or Developmental Model

Psychoanalytic, ego psychology, object relations, and self psychology formulations have put forth different views of the nature of borderline pathology

---

*Reprinted with permission from the *Diagnostic and Statistical Manual of Mental Disorders, Third Edition, Revised.* Copyright 1987 American Psychiatric Association.

and its origins in early childhood. Most theories stress the role of drives or early relationships with caretakers in the etiology of borderline disorders. They differ in whether they see the borderline individual as having a rigid defensive structure and pathological internalized object relations, ego deficits, or problems in self-cohesion. For example, Kernberg (1975, 1984) thought that the borderline personality reflects an intermediate intrapsychic structure between psychotic and neurotic levels of development at which a child becomes stuck. A malformed defensive structure that protects the child from conflict caused by constitutionally predisposed aggression or early frustration becomes fixed and affects all later personality functioning. Primitive defenses protect the individual from anxiety about the destructive effects of his or her aggressive impulses by keeping "good" views of the self and others separate from "bad" or angry ones. Kernberg's broad conception of borderline conditions cuts across a variety of personality disorders, according to DSM-III-R criteria. Masterson (1972, 1976) and Rinsley (Masterson & Rinsley, 1975) proposed that maternal unavailability during the rapprochement subphase of the separation-individuation process (Mahler, Pine, & Bergman, 1975) results in borderline personality as some children experience maternal withdrawal or punishment for their independent moves and rewards for their dependence. To maintain a connection with the rewarding object and to avoid the withdrawal associated with individuation, these children erect a rigid defensive structure. Later life events that involve increasing independence may reactivate their fears of abandonment, depression, primitive defenses, and dependent behavior.

In contrast to Kernberg and Masterson and Rinsley, Blanck and Blanck (1974, 1979) leaned toward a deficit model of borderline disorders and suggested that the specific nature of an individual's ego development is determined by how the person negotiates each of the separation-individuation subphases. The earlier the difficulties the child-caretaker dyad encounters, the more likely the child will show severe ego impairment. There is a range of borderline functioning that depends on the nature of the specific developmental arrests that have occurred and the level of structuring of the ego that has been attained. Likewise, Kohut (1971, 1977, 1984) argued that true borderline individuals display a core deficiency in the formation of the self as a result of severe protracted failures in parental empathy, and Adler (1985) and Buie and Adler (1982) described the borderline person's main deficit as an inability to evoke a positive mental representation of a sustaining, holding, or soothing caretaker. Lacking good-enough mothering, children fail to acquire the internal resources for self-soothing. Prone to fragmentation and sensitive to abandonment, they feel easily overwhelmed by a sense of aloneness. Panic and rage reactions commonly occur.

The Family Model

Family-oriented theorists view the family of origin and current interpersonal interactions as generating and sometimes perpetuating borderline pathology. The clinical and research findings on family characteristics and dynamics have identified pathological parental personality traits: primitive defenses, such as splitting, denial, and projective identification; conflicts around autonomy and dependence; and the presence of archaic self-object needs. Different family patterns have been observed: triadic sadomasochistic relations (Wolberg, 1982); enmeshment and overinvolvement (Goldstein, 1981; Shapiro, Shapiro, Zinner, & Berkowitz, 1977); underinvolvement, neglect, and rejection (Goldstein, 1981; Grinker et al., 1968; Gunderson, Kerr, & Englund, 1980; Walsh, 1977); parentification and role reversal (Schwoeri & Schwoeri, 1981, 1982); and denial and idealization (Goldstein, 1981). Loss, separations, violence, and sexual abuse (Goldstein, 1981; Herman, Perry, & van der Kolk, 1989; Kroll, 1988; Walsh, 1977; Wheeler & Walton, 1987) have been identified in the histories of borderline individuals. The dynamics of couples include collusion, distortion, and vicious cycles of mutual frustration stemming from the repetition of early internalized self- and object representations and archaic self-object needs (Scharff & Scharff, 1987; Schwartzman, 1984; Slipp, 1988; Solomon, 1985; Stewart, Peters, Marsh, & Peters, 1975).

The Biological Model

The older view that borderline disorders were linked genetically to schizophrenia has been replaced by the belief that they reflect an underlying affective or mood disorder (Akiskal, 1981; Klein, 1977). The evidence for viewing borderline pathology as a form of affective disorder that is treatable with antidepressants is not conclusive, although it seems clear that some borderline patients may also present with a depressive disorder and may benefit from medication (Kroll, 1988).

THE SOCIAL CONTEXT

Although there is no evidence to suggest that minority-group members are more prone to developing borderline disorders, there is general agreement that societal oppression, discrimination, and prejudice; socioeconomic deprivation and the lack of opportunity; and the absence of positive role models engender low self-esteem, self-hatred, and negative self-concepts that affect personality. Ethnic and racial minorities, women, and gays and lesbians are major examples of groups that are subject to cultural conflict, feelings of dissonance or difference with respect to others, and the taking in of unfavorable societal attitudes. The achievement of a stable and integrated identity is more difficult when, at an early age, an individual does not know where he or she belongs culturally or learns that crucial aspects of his or her self-experience are demeaned, derogated, and often punished by the larger society (Chestang, 1980; Comas-Diaz & Minrath, 1985; Lewis, 1984). Thus, the development of symptoms may be a consequence of efforts to cope with identity conflicts that stem from conflicts between the individual and society.

Rigid and narrow role expectations are another source of potential identity difficulties. The impact of poverty and the lack of social justice that deprive people of resources and opportunities cause feelings of rage and impotence in those who are poor and often of minority backgrounds. Likewise, traumatic events, such as parental loss, unemployment, and divorce, affect personality development and psychopathology.

THE CLINICAL PICTURE

How can practitioners who work with the elderly recognize borderline individuals? Drawing upon various psychodynamic models, the next section presents thirteen major characteristics that are common in borderline individuals (Goldstein, 1990). Some of these characteristics will be evident through careful history taking and others will show themselves in the client's current interactions with peers, family members, and helping persons.

Major Characteristics of Borderline Individuals

IDENTITY DISTURBANCES Borderline individuals are confusing and unpredictable. They tend to portray themselves either as "all good" or "all bad," so it is difficult to get a three-dimensional sense of who they are. Some are vague or go from topic to topic without reflecting on the significance of what they are saying. They lack a clear definition or latch onto others for a sense of identity. Abrupt and radical shifts in feelings, attitudes, and behavior may occur within hours, days, or weeks, seemingly without reason. Long-term commitments to work or people may be difficult.

SPLITTING AND RELATED DEFENSES Splitting is the main defense of borderline individuals. It keeps apart two conscious, contradictory feeling states, such as love and anger or admiration and disappointment, so that someone who is viewed as all "good" suddenly may be seen as all "bad." Selected personality traits are associated with "goodness" or "badness"; thus, for example, one views assertiveness negatively and compliance favorably or may acknowledge one's submissiveness and cooperativeness while denying the existence of independent or rebellious thoughts, feelings, or behavior.

Other related borderline defenses are (1) denial, in which one cannot acknowledge selected aspects of the self or of others that conflict with one's image of the self or of others; (2) idealization, in which one tends to see oneself or others as totally "good" to ward off frightening impulses; (3) devaluation, in which one tends to see oneself or others as all "bad"; (4) omnipotent control, in which one has a highly inflated sense of self and attempts to control others totally; and (5) projective identification, in which one continues to have an impulse, generally an angry one, which, at the same time, is projected onto another person, who then is feared as an enemy who must be controlled.

PROBLEMS WITH IMPULSE CONTROL Borderline individuals generally are impulsive in one or more areas of their lives. Their impulsiveness may be chronic and seemingly without environmental triggers or episodic in response to internal or external events, such as blows to their self-esteem, loss, or the threat of abandonment. Often their impulsiveness is shown in alcohol and drug abuse, eating disorders, at-risk sexual behavior, manipulative suicidal threats and acts, financial mismanagement or gambling, other self-destructive behavior, physical abuse, and violence. Some borderline individuals are overcontrolled except for severe episodic outbursts.

PROBLEMS IN TOLERATING ANXIETY Many borderline individuals are anxious most of the time or have recurrent, disabling bouts of diffuse anxiety. They may experience dread when they awake or wake up in the middle of the night. Increases in stress are disorganizing or overwhelming. They may experience panic reactions intermittently in response to life events, especially separations.

PROBLEMS IN THE REGULATION OF AFFECT The feelings of borderline individuals often escalate rapidly, so that, for example, irritation becomes rage, sadness becomes despair, loneliness becomes aloneness, and disappointment becomes hopelessness. They become overwhelmed by too-intense positive or negative feelings and feel great urgency. Seemingly happy at one moment, they plunge into a painful depression the next. It is not easy for those who are close to them to understand, track, or tolerate their fluctuations. They often show intense and inappropriate anger, temper tantrums, or storms of affect. When these displays are coupled with impulsiveness, borderline individuals may become frightening, physically violent, or self-destructive.

NEGATIVE AFFECTS Often complaining of chronic depression, many borderline individuals have persistent feelings of anger, resentment, dissatisfaction, and envy. Sometimes they experience inner emptiness and feel bereft of positive or meaningful connections to others or even to themselves. Without the capacity to love or care about anyone or anything, they feel disconnected, hopeless, and futile.

PROBLEMS IN SELF-SOOTHING Borderline individuals lack the capacity to soothe themselves. They are at the mercy of any upsurge of uncomfortable feelings and have no inner resources to draw upon in moments of stress. They become overwhelmed by feelings of panic, rage, and aloneness. Even minor separations, such as leaving a therapy session, can generate panic that prompts them to engage in desperate efforts to make contact. Some individuals immerse themselves in activities of all sorts or engage in addictive or other types of self-destructive behavior to escape from their feelings.

FEARS OF ABANDONMENT Borderline patients commonly have fears of abandonment. Some attempt to merge with others in efforts to deny or ward off their aloneness and to reassure themselves that they will never be abandoned. They seek constant proximity to or contact with those upon whom they are dependent and need to know their exact whereabouts or minute details of their activities. Intimates experience this behavior as controlling, clinging, or possessive. At the same time, most borderline individuals have a need-fear dilemma that makes them ward off or withdraw from the positive experiences with others for which they long. They may become panicked by and attempt to withdraw from or repel those who respond favorably to them. This oscillating cycle of clinging and distancing behavior is common in many borderline individuals. When they are not feeling intense loneliness, many borderline individuals manage their fears of abandonment by regulating the interpersonal closeness they allow and seem to engage in many superficial relationships and to avoid intimacy with any one individual.

PROBLEMS IN REGULATING SELF-ESTEEM Borderline individuals are extremely dependent upon the approval and recognition of others for the maintenance of positive feelings about themselves. Consequently, their self-regard is highly vulnerable and may undergo radical swings as a function of the degree and nature of the feedback they receive or the degree to which they live up to their own standards of perfection. Some have either highly grandiose or devalued conceptions of their abilities and talents and tend to feel either entitled to special treatment or unworthy or to fluctuate between these extremes. Because of these unrealistic qualities, they have difficulty getting the external affirmation they require or even engaging in pursuits that could bring some rewards. Rage reactions, feelings of worthlessness, or fits of self-loathing and self-hate may result from even seemingly minor events or comments. Shame and humiliation are common.

SUPEREGO DIFFICULTIES Some borderline individuals show an absence of guilt and empathy in their dealings with others and are capable of ruthless and exploitative acts. Many, however, seem to manifest a "split" in their superego functioning. They may show a high degree of impulsiveness in certain areas of their functioning or at certain times in their lives and experience remorse, self-contempt, and self-recriminations as a result. They find themselves unable to stop the very behavior that they hate. Others live by a strict moral and ethical code, but episodically engage in impulsive acts that do not bother them despite their obvious contradictory nature, while some have strict standards for their behavior and are persecuted by their superego if they do not live up to its unrelenting demands.

INTENSE AND UNSTABLE INTERPERSONAL RELATIONSHIPS Intimacy is a problem, since borderline individuals tend to merge with or distance themselves from others or to regulate closeness so it is not threatening. If closeness is attained, it is rarely peaceful or lasting. Moodiness, possessiveness, insecurity, and highly charged interactions are common. Fights, accusations, and sudden breaks frequently occur and are usually related to feelings of being rejected or abandoned. Feelings of victimization are frequent. Separations are difficult, however, and cause anxiety and severe depression. They may lead to desperate and often seemingly manipulative and attention-getting behavior, such as suicidal threats and acts or other types of acting out.

REALITY TESTING AND PSYCHOTICLIKE FEATURES Although borderline individuals have distorted perceptions, these perceptions are usually not bizarre, and they maintain the capacity for reality testing. For example, they may be highly suspicious of friends and associates, but can accept other alternatives that are presented to them. Some may have psychoticlike beliefs or a loosening of ego boundaries, but can modify their false or bizarre ideas at times. For example, they may seem convinced that they are psychic and can predict the future, are dying of an incurable illness, or are being punished for their success. When more reality-based explanations for their perceptions are presented, such individuals often become more realistic.

Showing problems in their sense of reality, as evidenced by feelings of depersonalization and derealization, borderline individuals may feel that they are looking at themselves while being outside their bodies or as if they are walking on a strange planet. They recognize, however, that these experiences, while frightening, are strange. Distortions of body image, such as feeling too fat even if one is thin, are frequent. These phenomena, although they seem bizarre, are compartmentalized and do not reflect more pervasive impairments in reality testing.

PROBLEMS IN SELF-COHESION Some borderline individuals are vulnerable to psychotic decompensation under stress. They have a profound lack of self-cohesion that leaves them susceptible to transient periods of fragmentation that can be quite disturbing. When in equilibrium, they can maintain their self-cohesiveness by regulating the degree of intimacy in their relationships and thus avoid the loss of ego boundaries involved in closeness.

The Mutual Impact of Aging and Borderline Personality

Because of the characteristics just described, most borderline individuals do not enter later life having achieved the emotional stability, self-acceptance and self-esteem, career or occupational achievement, satisfying networks of close family members and friends, financial stability, and social supports that can cushion them against some of the inevitable assaults of old age. Sadovy (1987) suggested that among these assaults are severe and frequent interpersonal losses; physical decline and disability; the loss of external manifestations of the self, such as beauty; the loss of meaningful social roles; the loss of defensive outlets and options; increased dependence on others; confrontation with death; and conflicts over living and dying. Although all individuals must deal with the assaults of aging, the elderly borderline individual usually has few internal and external resources to draw on to cope adaptively. Such persons may be less impulsive and driven than are their younger counterparts, but their needs are still urgent. Many of the ways in which they have characteristically coped are not as possible. Often deprived of a sense of achievement, self-esteem, and security and facing interpersonal losses, narcissistic injuries, and death, they may be more desperate. Thus, the elderly borderline individual "will find himself [herself], as he [she] ages, assaulted by the very things that he [she] has most feared throughout his [her] life" (Sadovy, 1987, p. 186).

Many of these issues are reflected in the following case example.

Ms. B, a 65-year-old unmarried Jewish woman, had no children or close relatives. Her receipt of a plan announcing the intended conversion of the building in which she rented a two-room apartment to a cooperative precipitated her seeking outpatient treatment. In early sessions, she expresseed rage at others or despair about her future. She railed about her "bastard" landlord, the "greedy" tenants in the building, the "fucking city," the "wimp" with whom she had been having an affair intermittently for the past fifteen years, the homeless "beggars" on the subway toward whom she had no pity, and the social worker assigned to her case for being younger than she and undoubtedly owning the apartment in which she resided.

Alternately Ms. B was filled with self-recrimination about having been "stupid" all her life and ending up with "nothing." She regretted not having the money to buy her apartment, and even though she could continue to rent and did not have to move, she feared that she would be harassed by other tenants who purchased theirs. Ms. B also believed that she had only herself to blame for the fact that she had little savings and needed to continue to earn a meager income in a business she hated, rather than be able to retire. She thought that she had spent money "foolishly" all her adult life and had moved from one unsatisfying job to another, usually because of interpersonal conflict.

Disappointed in the "weakness" of her unhappily married male companion, Mr. L, whom she talked to on the telephone briefly several times a week but saw only once every few months, Ms. B condemned herself for not having sought a more suitable partner. She hated being childless and often had fantasies of adopting a child.

Although the social worker was able to empathize with Ms. B at times, she was taken aback by the graphic nature and extent of Ms. B's aggression, which seemed not to spare anyone. "I'd like to see all the homeless hunted down and shot," Ms. B would exclaim, or "I bet you're one of the liberals who have ruined the city." She would add, "I know you think I'm disgusting, but I can't help it; my mother told me I was angry when I was born." Although it was difficult to focus Ms. B, who changed subjects frequently, it was clear as she recounted aspects of her history that her life was riddled with a sense of low self-esteem, a sense of failure, losses, separation anxiety bordering on panic at times, neediness, impulsiveness, angry outbursts, distancing behavior, and a problem with intimacy. When asked about times of her life when she was happy or felt better about herself, Ms. B replied, "Well, there was one week in 1972 when I thought I had breast cancer and people might feel sorry for me."

Ms. B's father died when she was a baby. Her mother, who was supported by welfare, was withdrawn, pessimistic, and critical. She was devoted to Ms. B's older brother, who became financially successful and somewhat well-known professionally but committed suicide at the age of 40 upon learning of his wife's infidelity. Ms. B experienced reflected glory because of his achievements, but envied him. She was bound to her mother in a hostile but enmeshed relationship until her mother's death when Ms. B was in her late forties. Until then, she would become infatuated with men who were flashy but emotionally unavailable and sometimes cruel and broke off relationships with those who were more attentive and needy.

Ms. B had hoped that Mr. L would leave his wife, but he never would, and his relationship with Ms. B was tumultuous. Except for a domineering but somewhat caring aunt with whom she socialized, Ms. B had no women friends for any length of time, since she was easily disappointed by others. Her aunt died when Ms. B was 60. Ms. B. felt she had devoted her life to her mother at the expense of getting married, having children, or building a career and has always feared winding up alone, homeless, and on welfare. She has kept herself going with the hope that her life would turn around one day, although she never actively tried to make it happen. Now time was running out, and except for her two cats, she was alone.

Diagnostic problems are common in work with elderly borderline individuals. Although these individuals may present acute problems and a host of symptomatic reactions that are stimulated by the aging process and life events, these problems and reactions tend to be more complicated than do those that are found in more stable personalities. For example, losses are more difficult to mourn because of highly conflicting feelings and relationships; physical changes may be invested with unusual meaning that destabilize the self; people and social roles cannot be as readily replaced; fears of abandonment cannot be dealt with through usual activities; the need for caretakers heightens conflicts around dependence, autonomy, and abandonment; the restriction of mobility prevents flight and avoidance; and anxiety about death cannot be avoided or modulated through usual channels (Sadovy, 1987; Thomas, 1989). Older borderline persons' negative feelings and dysfunctional personality traits and patterns of relating—for example, depressive withdrawal, bitterness, self-recriminations, combativeness, fears of abandonment, panic states, excess demands, clinging dependence, distancing behavior, paranoid reactions, low self-esteem, somatic preoccupation, and primitive defenses—often seem to escalate. Sometimes these individuals' behavior is misinterpreted as signs of organicity or psychosis, as the following case examples illustrate.

In the case of Mrs. D, a 75-year-old Catholic widow of many years, her need for caretakers, the restriction of her usual activities, and her sense of diminished control over her life escalated her use of primitive defenses to deal with the conflict caused by her increased dependence. The home care agency that was called in to provide services to her during her recovery from hip-replacement surgery was driven to distraction by her reactions to one home health aide after another.

Although Mrs. D seemed mild mannered and friendly when she first requested service, she soon called the agency to complain bitterly about an aide's domineering and controlling behavior, incompetence, and irresponsibility. The aide would be removed and replaced. Again, Mrs. D would initially appear to be happy only to engage in another round of angry telephone calls. The aides were always surprised to be taken off Mrs. D's case, since they found her to be needy but generally pleasant and cooperative.

It was only after four aides were replaced that an agency supervisor visited Mrs. D while a new aide was present to observe what was occurring. To her surprise and relief, she found the aide and Mrs. D getting along well. Consequently, she was shocked when two days later, the agency received another complaint from Mrs. D. The supervisor erroneously concluded that Mrs. D was paranoid and probably suffering from senility. In reality, Mrs. D was having difficulty accepting her own need for dependence, which she allowed to be gratified, on the one hand, only to disavow, split off, and project, on the other hand. Likewise her need to please and maintain a positive connection to her caretakers was split off from her angry and resentful reactions to her plight.

In the case of Mrs. R, a 69-year-old Jewish woman with Parkinson's disease, her increased need for structured environment, loss of bodily intactness, and fear of decreasing mobility and death led to an escalation of her long-standing tendency first to seek closeness and then to fight with and flee from the very human contact that she craved. In addition, her terror at being alone surfaced. After being admitted to a nursing home, Mrs. R went through one roommate after another, leaving a trail of angry residents behind her. Each time she acquired a new roommate, she would attempt to make the roommate into a close friend and confidante only to hurl angry accusations at her for being insensitive and uncaring. Usually, these episodes were precipitated by her feeling rebuffed by her new friend's withdrawal or efforts to set limits on her need for constant attention. After several changes of roommates, the nursing home gave Mrs. R her own room. Rather than resolving the matter, being in a separate room led to further problems. Feeling alienated from others, Mrs. R became terrified, particularly at night, and began to harass the staff with constant demands for attention. Medication was prescribed in the hope that Mrs. R would sleep through the night but she hoarded the pills and took a handful of them one night before calling the nurse and informing her of what she had done.

Because of their complexity and entrenched nature, the problems of elderly borderline individuals are not easily treated, nor do such persons present themselves in ways that make it easy for others to emphathize with their difficulties. These tend not to be the sweet and gentle older men and women who elicit and respond well to support and who are popular with their peers, family members, or helping staff. For these reasons and because whatever close interpersonal relationships they do have are enmeshed and conflict-ridden or estranged and distant, elderly borderline individuals may engage in efforts to coerce those who are part of their social network to provide for them. Attention-getting, manipulative, and divisive types of behavior are common, as are both passive and active suicidal acts (McIntosh & Hubbard, 1988).

In the following example, a 68-year-old divorced, Jewish woman's fears of abandonment and rage over her loss of control precipitated a manipulative suicide attempt aimed at trying to coerce her daughter into devoting herself to the mother's care and to punish her for moving toward greater independence.

Mrs. T had become nearly bedridden following a stroke, but refused to allow anyone other than the woman who cleaned her apartment weekly and family members to help her. Her two daughters-in-law and her only daughter alternated in caring for her, and the daughter eventually took a leave of absence from her job and moved in with Mrs. T. They always had an overtly conflicting and combative relationship that the daughter managed through infrequent contact, on the one hand, and self-sabotaging behavior in her own life that reflected her difficulty freeing herself from their enmeshment. Mrs. T was angry and bitter about her condition, and although her daughter tried to be attentive and responsible, Mrs. T was critical and verbally abusive of her. The daughter became increasingly burdened and exhausted by her mother's anger and demands and stubborn refusal to allow paid help to come in.

Although Mrs. T had regained some mobility, so she was able to manage during the day, she needed help at night. When the daughter decided to assert herself and take a weekend off to attend the wedding of a colleague, her family prevailed upon her to arrange for a home attendant, for whom they would pay. Mrs. T was furious and told the daughter that she was trying to kill her. The daughter almost relented, but became so angry at her mother's behavior that she went ahead with her plans. When she returned early from the trip, she found that Mrs. T had been hospitalized following an overdose of tranquilizers.

TREATMENT APPROACHES

Individual Psychodynamically Oriented Treatment

Individual psychodynamically oriented psychotherapy is the most frequently used modality in the treatment of borderline individuals. Treatment models are contradictory, however, and present the practitioner with a bewildering array of choices. Moreover, accounts of successful treatment do not clarify which approach is optimal (Waldinger & Gunderson, 1987), and no systematic studies have reported on the outcomes of different approaches. Most treatment models give an important role to establishing a therapeutic holding environment, but they differ in whether they emphasize the use or a confrontational, interpretive, limit-setting, and highly structured model or a more empathic, responsive, reparative, and flexible approach (Goldstein, 1990). All but a few of the models that have been put forth are generally long term and applications to shorter-term treatments have not been described systemically, nor is much written that is specific to elderly borderline individuals (Greenes, 1987).

Couple and Family Treatment

There are many instances in which therapeutic success with borderline individuals necessitates work with the family system (Goldstein, 1983). Current interpersonal transactions seem to be perpetuating the problems of the identified patient, and family members are affected by the borderline pathology or need to be involved in the overall treatment plan. Family members bring a host of feelings and attitudes to their interactions with mental health professionals. Among them are a sense of shame and guilt, low self-esteem, frustration, fatigue, helplessness, and hopelessness. Sometimes staff become judgmental and react to such families with increased defensiveness and other dysfunctional responses that make them appear to be highly pathological, difficult, and demanding. Both the family and the borderline patient require a therapeutic holding environment that helps them to contain their anxiety and to become true collaborators in the treatment process.

Group Intervention

Arguing that unstructured groups mobilize regression and stimulate more volatility and primitive defenses in borderline individuals, most clinicians have cautioned against the use of group therapy with this population. Supportive, structured, and task-oriented groups, however, can be used effectively with many elderly borderline individuals. They can be used to promote reality testing and other ego functions, self-esteem, and interpersonal relationships. The other group participants offer opportunities for identification with and the internalization of different attitudes and behavior. Task-oriented groups provide opportunities for the exercise of autonomy and the expansion of ego and social functioning. The nature of community living in structured settings is fertile ground for the formation of a patient-government group and ad hoc special-interest groups, for example, to plan parties or to address problems that affect everyone.

The Role of Psychotropic Drugs

In treating younger borderline adults, clinicians viewed psychotropic drugs as contraindicated because they did not work and often were abused. Since certain other disturbances, including affective disorders, psychosis, severe anxiety, phobic reactions, and panic states, may coexist with borderline disorders, medication may be used selectively. Research on the effects of medication with the borderline population is sparse. The findings of studies are equivocal, and thus indications for the use of drugs are vague. Medication tends to be given to ameliorate certain target symptoms, such as severe anxiety, depression, or disorganized thinking, to see if they are effective. A rule of thumb is to give antidepressants if an affective disorder seems to be present or major tranquilizers if the pathology is close to the psychotic range of symptoms (Berger, 1987; Pack, 1987).

With elderly borderline individuals, the use of medication for specific target symptoms may be beneficial as one part of the treatment. Medication should be used cautiously, however. It should not be used by staff punitively or as a way to avoid dealing with a particularly difficult patient. Furthermore, minor tranquilizers relieve anxiety, but generally are misused. Major tranquilizers, although they are not abused and sometimes helpful in small doses, often have serious side effects. Antidepressants are lethal when used as part of a suicide attempt, and lithium is toxic when combined with alcohol. Noncompliance with drug regimens, as well as the abuse of medication, is common, since borderline patients tend to use drugs in acting out their intense feelings. Drugs also have positive and negative meanings that go beyond their specific utility; they may be seen as an unwanted intrusion, a transitional object, a sign of caring, a magical substance that instills hope, or an indication that there is no hope (Meissner, 1988).

The Role of Psychiatric Hospitalization

A sizable number of elderly borderline persons are admitted to psychiatric hospitals for diagnostic purposes and problems with medication or following suicide attempts, psychotic episodes, or self-destructive behavior. Hospital treatment is usually short term and focuses on resolving the immediate crises that led to hospitalization (Friedman, 1969; Nurnberg & Suh, 1978). A multifaceted treatment approach, partialized goals, and an active approach are necessary. Family members must be involved in the treatment from the beginning, not only as part of the problem but as part of the solution. Medication for target symptoms may be utilized as part of a holistic approach to the patient's difficulties.

Since borderline patients are typically admitted to hospitals at times of crisis when they are extremely agitated, impulsive, or disorganized, the short-term model emphasizes the control function of the setting (Nurnberg & Suh, 1978). It tries to limit disruptive behavior by maintaining a firm, highly structured, unified, and predictable atmosphere in which patients must meet all rules and expectations. While avoiding punitive interactions with patients, the staff nevertheless are encouraged to be strict (Kernberg, 1984). This approach may be useful at times, but it is equally if not more important for the staff to provide an optimal "holding" environment and to relate empathically to, rather than distance themselves from, patients' panic and aloneness, so they can calm the patients and help them to restore their inner controls and sense of self (Adler, 1985).

Discharge planning is paramount, often requiring creativity, advocacy and system-negotiation skills, and persistence. Patients and families need to be involved in the process, and much of the groundwork can be done by family members. Linkages to resources generally should be made before the patient leaves the hospital. There should be ample time to discuss reactions to the plan and specific services.

PRINCIPLES OF INTERVENTION

In the absence of research on the process and outcome of different therapeutic models with borderline patients of all ages, it is difficult to know which approach is optimal or to reconcile often-contradictory treatment recommendations. It is not possible to present a completely integrated or unified set of guidelines to work with this population in general. A flexible and experimental treatment approach is necessary, particularly with elderly borderline persons for whom psychotherapy has usually been neglected. For these individuals, as for their younger counterparts, it is useful to think of borderline pathology as reflecting a range of difficulties that necessitate highly individualized and attuned therapeutic techniques. It is the goodness of fit between the therapist's interventions and the patient's needs that is crucial to successful treatment.

Establishing a Therapeutic Holding Environment

Flexibility, empathy, realness, and structure are vital in establishing a therapeutic holding environment for elderly borderline patients, whether they are in individual outpatient treatment, a nursing home, a hospital, or other type of setting. Despite the emphasis that many clinicians who treat borderline individuals place on setting firm limits for the work, a more flexible approach is necessary. Although stability and consistency always are important in helping borderline individuals to feel safe, the treatment framework should be individualized to a particular client's needs. Certain anxious, demanding, impulsive, and disorganized individuals can benefit from the establishment of clear strict limits and rules to help them maintain control. Others who feel frightened, depressed, intensely alone, and estranged from others may need greater access to staff.

Likewise, although many clinicians have advocated a confrontational approach that draws attention to and attempts to modify the borderline patient's self-defeating and self-destructive behavior, it is important that those who work with borderline individuals see beyond their often-angry presentation and overtly dysfunctional behavior to their underlying anxiety, desperation, diminished self-esteem, fears of abandonment, feelings of being unloveable, and hopelessness. Too great an emphasis on pointing out and controlling maladaptive defenses and behavior may escalate aggressive outbursts or other forms of self-destructive behavior, since the patients are likely to feel attacked and not heard. A better approach is to engage in "experience-near-empathy" (Kohut, 1984; Wolf, 1988), in which one tries to feel what it is like to be in a patient's shoes. This effort to understand a disturbed patient's subjective experience will be calming and soothing to him or her. It is important that those who work with borderline patients address the patient's self-defeating behavior at times, but it is generally preferable to do so in ways that show an understanding of their inner states and difficulties in soothing themselves or getting their needs met in more adaptive ways. When the therapeutic alliance is more secure, it usually is possible to expand the patient's understanding of the impact of his or her behavior on others and to help the patient develop empathy for others' motivations and needs.

Rather than practice from a more traditionally neutral and abstinent position, staff, including psychotherapists, should be more real and selectively meet the client's needs at times. This does not mean that they should always gratify the clients' requests, since doing so may stimulate regressive behavior or eventually lead to staff burnout or angry withdrawal, but it does mean that they should try to provide a type of "optimal responsiveness" (Bacal, 1985) based on what will help the clients function more adaptively.

Unfortunately, borderline individuals' fears of abandonment, problems with closeness, absence of self-soothing mechanisms, and panic and rage reactions, which make them feel more alone and alienated, do not easily permit them to experience being "held" sufficiently by a worker's empathy, accessiblity, or realness. The patients' actual life circumstances may also present stresses that stimulate impulsiveness and that overshadow the therapeutic holding environment, especially at the beginning of treatment. Some individuals may require active and protective interventions, such as the use of hospitalization or other types of limits and external structure. To the degree that limits and structure are needed, staff should attempt to maintain empathy with patients and to engage them collaboratively in a problem-solving effort about what will enable them to contain their impulses and self-destructive behavior. Obviously, crises may occur that call for decisive action, but all too often, therapists and other staff members set limits arbitrarily or in anger or frustration. Limits that are set should be arrived at through shared decision making by the patient and helping personnel.

Ego Building

Most of us take for granted certain capacities that borderline individuals often lack, for example, the ability to recognize and verbalize feelings, soothe themselves, maintain positive connections when alone or frustrated, and empathize with others' motivations and feelings. These deficits impair their ability to cope effectively. Treatment must attempt to help them restore, develop, or strengthen their adaptive coping mechanisms or restructure the environment to be more responsive to their particular personalities (Goldstein, 1984). This approach requires a careful assessment of an individual's deficits, strengths, compensatory structures, and environmental supports. Although it usually is focused on here-and-now issues, some reparative work can occur.

Strengthening the Self

It is not only the elderly borderline individual's ego that needs strengthening, but his or her sense of self (Elson, 1986; Lazarus, 1980; Tobin, 1988). Extremely negative about themselves and their past experiences, borderline patients' self-esteem can be enhanced by empathically helping them to review and reshape the way they view themselves and their own past life experiences. Since loss of self, others, opportunities, time, and the like are such core issues, helping elderly individuals to mourn the past, as well as lost future opportunities, may be a crucial focus of intervention (Conway,

1988; Pollock, 1987). Enabling this mourning process to occur, rather than closing it off through communicating false reassurance or unwarranted optimism, for example, is an important and often painful task of the practitioner.

Pointing out Maladaptive Defenses and Behavior

In addition to providing empathy and support, staff may need to help borderline elderly patients recognize and modify their self-destructive or self-defeating behavior. A nonjudgmental attitude is needed. It may be achieved by empathically relating to the conditions of early and later life and to the urgent needs that led to the patient's style of coping and by pointing out the negative consequences of behavior that may have served a positive function for the person. This emphasis must be accompanied by efforts to help the person expand his or her ego functioning by developing and experimenting with new ways of perceiving and relating to others.

Involving the Family

An approach that is sensitive to the family's needs and defenses and that respects their rights as consumers is important for lessening their extreme reactions and for developing a therapeutic alliance. Avoiding power struggles, providing information and access to professionals, and involving family members in decision making early in treatment facilitates their engagement. Although many families may require treatment for their "pathology," they may perceive that their psychological survival is being threatened by such efforts. Without support, the family's resistance and acting out usually undermines the patient's treatment. On occasion, limits may control the family's behavior, but they do not promote a therapeutic alliance or motivate the family to alter its dysfunctional patterns.

Managing Countertransference

There is a general consensus that therapists are especially vulnerable to troublesome reactions that can obstruct their work with borderline individuals because of the impact of these patients' urgent needs and primitive defenses. The literature has tended to say that borderline patients "induce" particular responses in those around them. Although patients may do so in many instances, it is risky to assume that they always do so, since such an assumption shifts the responsibility for a staff member's feelings to a patient. An individual's provocative and even obnoxious behavior may result in others feeling angry, helpless, or wanting to withdraw, but it is incorrect to assume that a patient is making the therapist experience certain feelings because of his or her internal pathology. Such a view presumes that the therapist has no effect on the patient's reactions or that the therapist has no control over his or her reactions. In many instances, patients bring their past experiences in human relationships with them in ways that may distort current interactions and induce self-fulfilling prophecies, and their characteristic responses may have some degree of autonomy from external triggers. Their urgent needs and pathological defenses can exert enormous force in the therapeutic interaction, but therapists and other staff members must understand rather than act out their reactions.

An important requirement of therapeutic personnel is that they must refrain from (1) retaliating in anger to patients' provocative and attacking behavior, (2) giving too much to the point of exhaustion or frustration, or (3) withholding or withdrawing in the face of overwhelming demands. To provide a therapeutic holding environment, the staff must understand the treatment philosophy that guides their work and have ample opportunity for open communication and for sharing and examining their work, support in managing their intense reactions to patients, and help in recognizing and dealing with borderline patients' needs and primitive defenses, such as splitting and projective identification. When patient-staff interactions seem too "real," countertransference acting out occurs. The most common manifestation of this problem is when staff become polarized. Seemingly "good" staff members fight with those who are "bad" about their perceptions and management of the patient. Therapeutic stalemates occur. Staff-patient meetings, rounds, and team meetings that embody an atmosphere of openness and acceptance provide opportunities for all those involved in the care of patients to share their impressions and to plan individualized treatment strategies. The following case example illustrates this problem.

Mr. F, aged 73, who was admitted to a nursing home following a spinal-cord injury that resulted in his partial paralysis, became the focus of a struggle among the staff. His drinking and contradictory personality traits were denied, and the staff engaged in emotional interchanges about him and dysfunctional behavior toward him. A still-handsome, seemingly charming and mild-mannered individual, he had no family or friends who visited. Many staff members felt sorry for him and were especially attentive to him. After two months in the home, a new staff aide reported in a meeting that he suspected that Mr. F had been nearly intoxicated on several occasions in the past week. Numerous staff members became angry at the aide, defended Mr. F, and suggested that there must be other reasons for his seeming alcoholic behavior. When Mr. F's roommate found him sleeping on the floor near his bed a week later, the roommate confessed that he knew Mr. F had been drinking for many weeks and that Mr. F had been verbally abusive and threatening.

Many staff members did not believe the roommate's story, while others secretly admitted that they had felt intimidated by Mr. F's anger and threats at times. When these discrepancies were brought into the open, staff members who perceived Mr. F one way argued with the others that their views of him were wrong. When a bottle of alcohol was brought in as evidence, those who were pro Mr. F argued that they did not see anything wrong with his "taking a nip" now and then, given his condition. One staff member confessed privately that she had been purchasing alcohol for Mr. F. When a social work supervisor suggested that perhaps it was important to stop arguing about who was right and who was wrong and whether Mr. F was good or bad and start to try to understand the painful feelings he might be trying to deal with through his drinking, as well as his impact on others around him, the staff were gradually able to coalesce.

IMPLICATIONS FOR RESEARCH, TRAINING, SERVICE DELIVERY, AND SOCIAL POLICY

An important question to which the professional community has insufficient answers is what happens to individuals who have been diagnosed as borderline earlier in their lives when they reach the later stages of adulthood. It would be helpful to gain a greater understanding of their coping patterns, characteristic difficulties, and areas of strength and vulnerability. We need better means of identifying the borderline elderly and differentiating their problems and needs from those of individuals with other symptoms or syndromes, so we may intervene more effectively. Studies that seek to establish the effectiveness of specific treatment techniques and modalities and environmental structuring according to the characteristics of particular patients would be useful.

One of the unfortunate aspects of the current system of delivering services to the elderly is that there is a lack of understanding of psychopathology in general and of borderline disorders in particular, as well as a paucity of differential treatment resources and qualified professional staff. Little attention is given in the curricula of programs in nursing, social work, psychology, and medicine to the needs, problems, clinical diagnoses, and treatment of the elderly. Education and training that equip both potential and actual staff with essential knowledge and skills and that challenge negative stereotypes of and pessimistic attitudes toward the elderly are vital. The nature of funding and health care policy must recognize the need for differential treatments for this population.

REFERENCES

Adler, G. (1985). *Borderline psychopathology and its treatment*. New York: Jason Aronson.

Akiskal, H. S. (1981). Subaffective disorders: Dysthymic, cyclothymic and bipolar II disorders in the borderline realm. *Psychiatric Clinics of North America, 4*, 25–46.

Bacal, H. A. (1985). Optimal responsiveness and the therapeutic process. In A. Goldberg (Ed.), *Progress in self psychology* (Vol. 1, pp. 202–227). New York: Guilford Press.

Berger, P. A. (1987). Pharmacological treatment for borderline personality disorder. *Bulletin of the Menninger Clinic, 51*, 277–284.

Blanck, G., & Blanck, R. (1974). *Ego psychology in theory and practice*. New York: Columbia University Press.

Blanck, G., & Blanck, R. (1979). *Ego psychology II: Psychoanalytic developmental psychology*. New York: Columbia University Press.

Buie, O. H., & Adler, G. (1982). The definitive treatment of the borderline personality. *International Journal of Psychoanalytic Psychotherapy, 9*, 51–87.

Chatham, P. (1985). *Treatment of borderline personality*. New York: Jason Aronson.

Chestang, L. (1980). Character development in a hostile environment. In M. Bloom (Ed.), *Life span development: Bases for preventive and interventive helping* (pp. 40–50). New York: Macmillan.

Comas-Diaz, L., & Minrath, M. (1985). Psychotherapy with ethnic minority borderline clients. *Psychotherapy, 22*, 418–426.

Conway, P. (1988). Losses and grief in old age. *Social Casework: The Journal of Contemporary Social Work, 69*, 541–549.

Eissler, K. (1953). The effects of the structure of the ego on psychoanalytic technique. *Journal of the American Psychoanalytic Association, 1*, 104–143.

Elson, M. (1986). *Self psychology in clinical social work*. New York: W. W. Norton.

Friedman, H. (1969). Some problems of inpatient management with borderline patients. *American Journal of Psychiatry, 126,* 47–52.

Goldstein, E. G. (1981). *The family characteristics of borderline patients*. Paper presented at the 58th Annual Meeting of the American Orthopsychiatric Association, New York.

Goldstein, E. G. (1983). Clinical and ecological approaches to the borderline client. *Social Casework: The Journal of Contemporary Social Work, 64,* 353–362.

Goldstein, E. G. (1984). *Ego psychology and social work practice*. New York: Free Press.

Goldstein, E. G. (1990). *Borderline disorders: Clinical models and techniques*. New York: Guilford Press.

Greene, R. R. (1986). Countertransference issues in social work with the aged. *Journal of Gerontological Social Work, 9,* 79–88.

Greenes, J. M. (1987). The aged in psychotherapy: Psychodynamic contributions to the treatment process. In J. Sadovy & M. Leszcz (Eds.), *Treating the elderly with psychotherapy*. Madison, CT: International Universities Press.

Grinker, R. R., Werble, B., & Drye, R. (1968). *The borderline syndrome*. New York: Basic Books.

Gunderson, J. G., Kerr, J., & Englund, D. W. (1980). The families of borderlines: A comparative study. *Archives of General Psychiatry, 37,* 27–33.

Gunderson, J. G., & Singer, M. T. (1975). Defining borderline patients: An overview. *American Journal of Psychiatry, 132,* 1–10.

Herman, J. L., Perry, J. C., & van der Kolk, B. (1989). Childhood trauma in borderline personality disorder. *American Journal of Psychiatry, 146,* 490–495.

Kernberg, O. F. (1975). *Borderline conditions and pathological narcissism*. New York: Jason Aronson.

Kernberg, O. F. (1976). *Object relations theory and clinical psychoanalysis*. New York: Jason Aronson.

Kernberg, O. F. (1984). *Severe personality disorders*. New Haven, CT: Yale University Press.

Kety, S. S., Rosenthal, D., Wender, P. H., & Schulsinger, F. (1968). Mental illness in the biological and adoptive families of adopted schizophrenics. In D. Rosenthal & S. S. Kety (Eds.), *Transmission of schizophrenia* (pp. 345–362). Oxford: Pergamon Press.

Klein, D. F. (1977). Psychopharmacological treatment and delineation of borderline disorders. In P. Hartocollis (Ed.), *Borderline personality disorders* (pp. 365–384). New York: International Universities Press.

Knight, R. P. (1953a). Borderline states. *Bulletin of the Menninger Clinic, 17,* 1–12.

Knight, R. P. (1953b). Management and psychotherapy of the borderline schizophrenic patient. In R. P. Knight & C. R. Freidman (Eds.), *Psychoanalytic psychiatry and psychology* (pp. 110–122). New York: International Universities Press.

Kohut, H. (1971). *The analysis of the self.* New York: International Universities Press.

Kohut, H. (1977). *The restoration of the self.* New York: International Universities Press.

Kohut, H. (1984). *How does analysis cure?* Chicago: University of Chicago Press.

Kroll, J. (1988). *The Challenge of the borderline patient.* New York: W. W. Norton.

Lazarus, W. (1980). Self psychology and psychotherapy with the elderly: Theory and practice. *Journal of Geriatric Psychiatry, 13,* 69–88.

Lewis, L. A. (1984). The coming out process for lesbians: Integrating a stable identity. *Social Work, 29,* 464–469.

McIntosh, J. L., & Hubbard, R. W. (1988). Indirect self-destructive behavior among the elderly: A review with case examples. *Journal of Gerontological Social Work, 13,* 37–48.

Mahler, M. S., Pine, F., & Bergman, A. (1975). *The psychological birth of the human infant.* New York: Basic Books.

Masterson, J. F. (1972). *Treatment of the borderline adolescent.* New York: John Wiley & Sons.

Masterson, J. F. (1976). *Treatment of the borderline adult.* New York: Brunner-Mazel.

Masterson, J. F., & Rinsley, D. (1975). The borderline syndrome: The role of the mother in the genesis and psychic structure of the borderline personality. *International Journal of Psychoanalysis, 56,* 163–177.

Meissner, W. W. (1988). *Treatment of patients in the borderline spectrum.* New York: Jason Aronson.

Nurnberg, H. G., & Suh, R. (1978). Time-limited treatment of hospitalized borderline patients: Considerations. *Comprehensive Psychiatry, 19,* 419–431.

Pack, A. (1987). The role of psychopharmacology in the treatment of borderline patients. In J. S. Grotstein, M. F. Soloman, & J. A. Lang (Eds.), *The borderline patient* (Vol. 2, pp. 177–186). Hillsdale, NJ: Analytic Press.

Pollock, G. H. (1987). The mourning-liberation process: Issues in the inner life of the older adult. In J. Sadovy & M. Leszcz (Eds.), *Treating the adult in psychotherapy.* Madison, CT: International Universities Press.

Sadovy, J. (1987). Character disorders in the elderly: An overview. In J. Sadovy & M. Leszcz (Eds.), *Treating the elderly with psychotherapy* (pp. 175–229). Madison, CT: International Universities Press.

Scharff, D. E., & Scharff, J. S. (1987). *Object relations family therapy.* Northvale, NJ: Jason Aronson.

Schwartzman, G. (1984). Narcissistic transferences: Implications for the treatment of couples. *Dynamic Psychotherapy, 2,* 5–14.

Schwoeri, L., & Schwoeri, F. (1981). Family therapy of borderline patients: Diagnostic and treatment issues. *International Journal of Family Psychiatry, 2,* 237–251.

Schwoeri, L., & Schwoeri, F. (1982). Interactional and intrapsychic dynamics in a family with a borderline patient. *Psychotherapy Theory, Research, and Practice, 19,* 198–204.

Shapiro, E. R., Shapiro, R. L., Zinner, J., & Berkowitz, D. (1977). The borderline ego and the working alliance: Implications for family and individual treatment. *International Journal of Psychoanalysis, 58,* 77–87.

Slipp, S. (Ed.). (1988). *The technique and practice of object relations family therapy.* Northvale, NJ: Jason Aronson.

Soloman, M. F. (1985). Treatment of narcissistic and borderline disorders in marital therapy: Suggestions toward an enhanced therapeutic approach. *Clinical Social Work Journal, 13,* 141–156.

Stern, A. (1938). Psychoanalytic investigation of and therapy in a borderline group of neuroses. *Psychoanalytic Quarterly, 7,* 467–489.

Stewart, R. H., Peters, T. C., Marsh, S., & Peters, M. J. (1975). An object relations approach with marital couples, families, and children. *Family Process, 14,* 161–172.

Stone, M. H. (1980). *The borderline syndromes.* New York: McGraw-Hill.

Stone, M. H. (1987). Systems for defining a borderline case. In J. S. Grotstein, M. F. Soloman, & J.A. Lang (Eds.), *The borderline patient* (Vol. 1, pp. 13–36). Hillsdale NJ: Analytic Press.

Thomas, G. (1989). *Emotional problems of aging.* Springfield, IL: Charles C Thomas.

Tobin, S. (1988). Preservation of the self in old age. *Social Casework: The Journal of Contemporary Social Work, 69,* 550–555.

Verwoerdt, A. (1981). *Clinical geropsychiatry.* Baltimore, MD: Williams & Wilkins.

Waldinger, R. J., & Gunderson, J. G. (1987). *Effective psychotherapy with borderline patients.* New York: Macmillan.

Walsh, F. (1977). Family study 1976: 14 new borderline cases. In R. R. Grinker & B. Werble (Eds.), *The borderline patient* (pp. 158–177). New York: Jason Aronson.

Wheeler, B. K., & Walton, E. (1987). Personality disturbances of adult incest victims. *Social Casework: The Journal of Contemporary Social Work, 68,* 597–602.

White, M. T., & Weiner, M. B. (1986). *The theory and practice of self psychology.* New York: Brunner-Mazel.

Wolberg, A. R. (1982). *Psychoanalytic psychotherapy of the borderline patient.* New York: Thieme-Stratton.

Wolf, E. S. (1988). *Treating the self: Elements of clinical self psychology.* New York: Guilford Press.

Zetzel, E. (1971). A developmental approach to the borderline patient. *American Journal of Psychiatry, 127,* 867–871.

13

Narcissistic Personality Disorder

Eda G. Goldstein

N arcissism is a complicated concept that has diverse meanings (Cooper, 1986; Kernberg, 1986; Pulver, 1986). It is usually judgmental to call someone "narcissistic" in popular parlance, since the term refers to traits such as self-involvement, the need for attention or special treatment, arrogance, and grandiosity. Clinically, much of the confusion regarding the use of the term, *narcissism*, stems from the fact that it describes both healthy and pathological adult character traits, a normal stage of infantile development, an immature type of interpersonal relationship, and a full-fledged personality disorder. Despite numerous theories about its exact nature, origins, and treatment, there is still controversy over all these issues. There is general agreement, however, that pathological narcissism in adults, at the clinical level, "may be defined as the normal or pathologic regulation of self-esteem or self-regard" (Kernberg, 1986, p. 220).

Healthy narcissism is vital for a person's sense of well-being and intactness. It enables the individual to seek and appreciate attention, affirmation, and praise without being driven to obtain them. It allows a person to survive feelings of being hurt by criticism, rejection, disapproval, insults, failures, or setbacks without feeling devastated and to have empathy for others. There are various degrees of narcissistic vulnerability, and its extreme forms may be debilitating, sometimes leading to chronic emptiness, depression, bitterness, envy, and even death. Pathological narcissism limits the capacity for pleasure, love, genuine human concern, empathy, and commitment. It leads to dependence on the affirmation and tribute of others; to being crushed or ashamed by even minor criticisms, disapproval, rejection, and failure;

and to compensatory feelings of superiority to others, coupled with insensitivity to their feelings. Although healthy self-esteem is a relatively stable part of the personality, it also requires a sustaining environment to some degree (White & Weiner, 1986).

Most theorists believe that the origins of healthy and pathological narcissism occur in early childhood and that there are narcissistic issues at every stage of the life cycle. In our society, individuals who are entering old age are particularly vulnerable to blows to self-esteem, since the aging process, unlike processes at other developmental stages, often works against them. The aging process brings multiple losses and ushers in psychologically, physically, and socially assaulting experiences that tax and sometimes erode and even obliterate an older person's self-concept, identity, self-regard, and self-cohesion. Concurrently, customary support and reward systems and productive outlets may weaken. The impact of loss and narcissistic injury on the self varies greatly with the severity of inner and outer stresses, an individual's coping capacities and personality characteristics, and environmental attitudes and resources. Yet even someone who enters old age relatively intact may find it a difficult period (Berezin, 1977). Consequently, narcissistic vulnerability and problems are pervasive among the elderly and require special attention (Berezin, 1987; Breslau, 1980; Goldfarb, 1959; Lazarus, 1980; Sadovy, 1987). However, for aged persons who have characteristically shown moderate to severe narcissistic vulnerability or narcissistic personality disorder per se, this period may be catastrophic.

Despite the prevalence of narcissistic problems among the elderly, helping professionals often fail to recognize or understand the significance of their presence because they appear in the form of other disorders, arouse negative attitudes, or are attributed to the normal process of aging. In many instances, the failure to assess and treat the narcissistic sector of the personality correctly results in some of the more severe depressive, withdrawn, suicidal, somatic, addictive, and otherwise debilitating symptoms that occur among older people. Even when underlying narcissistic vulnerability is correctly assessed, however, successful treatment may be time consuming and difficult.

After reviewing some key historical developments and perspectives in the study of narcissism, this chapter presents the main clinical features of narcissistic personality disorder and considers its manifestations among the elderly. It discusses some major treatment principles that may be used with elderly clients who show narcissistic pathology and then comments on implications of working with this population for staff and agency settings.

HISTORICAL DEVELOPMENTS

Psychoanalytic Theories

According to Greek mythology, the gods punished Narcissus, a handsome young man, for his indifference and callousness to those who loved him by causing him to fall in love with his own reflection in a mountain pool. Gazing enraptured at his own adored face for hours and unable to embrace the object of his love, he soon became melancholy and plunged a dagger through his heart (Chessick, 1985). This legend has been called upon by numerous psychoanalytic writers to describe a form of pathological self-love that has been termed narcissistic. Enlarging upon an earlier view of narcissism as a sexual perversion in which an individual treated his or her own body as a sexual object (Ellis, 1898), Freud (1914/1957) believed that so-called narcissistic individuals defensively withdraw libido (instinctual energy) from the external world of people and things as a consequence of some disappointment or trauma and focus on (cathect) their own egos. He saw them as self-reliant, grandiose, self-centered, and indifferent to the needs of others and unable to form caring attachments to others. In fact, Freud thought that they could not be treated psychoanalytically because of their inability to develop the necessary transference to the therapist. Although Freud also used the term *narcissism* in various ways, for example, to refer to self-esteem or to a type of object choice in which the person loves another as he or she would love himself or herself or for qualities that he or she once had or would like to have, his main contribution was to define narcissism or excessive self-love as the opposite of object love.

Emphasizing ego development and capacities, rather than instinctual conflict, Hartmann (1950), Jacobson (1964), and Reich (1960) helped to identify the self as a separate subsystem of the ego, drew attention to the formation of internal self- and object representations that form the core of an individual's concept of self and others, and introduced more firmly the concept of narcissism as a regulator of self-esteem. Reich thought that the development and maintenance of self-regard is a crucial function of the mature ego. The pathological narcissist defensively resorts to grandiosity to make up for feelings of inferiority and worthlessness. According to Reich's concept, self-love compensates for a defect in the regulation of self-esteem, rather than being a withdrawal from object love, as Freud described, although it affects the way a narcissist will relate to others. Reich recognized that narcissistically vulnerable individuals may turn away from those who have caused them psychological injury, but may turn back to external objects to regain their self-esteem through magical identification, merger, or idealization. Envious rage and devaluation may follow, however, when others fail to provide what these narcissistically vulnerable people feel they need.

In a more current view that attempted to integrate structural theory and object relations theory, Kernberg (1970, 1974) considered the development and defensive rigidification of the grandiose self as being at the core of pathological narcissism. He believed that as a result of early frustration at the hands of external objects, the infant defensively fuses his or her ideal self-representation, ideal object representations, and actual self-representations into a fantastic structure that rigidifies and becomes walled off from reality to some degree. The grandiose self reflects a highly idealized self-concept, and the individual defensively projects his or her split-off aggression, self-hatred, and other negative traits and feelings onto others. Thus, a pathological form of self-esteem is maintained at the expense of realistic perceptions of the self and others. Although they often seem charming, superficially warm, and even successful, narcissistic personalities feel empty; lack empathy for others; are incapable of true love, concern, and dependence; and often envy or hate those upon whom they seem to rely. Suspicious of and guarded with others, they often show paranoid tendencies.

An alternative contemporary view of narcissism comes from the work of Kohut (1966, 1971, 1977), the originator of self psychology, who brought healthy narcissism "out of the closet," so to speak. Rejecting classical drive theory and ego psychology, Kohut argued that the self is the central organizing and motivating force in the personality. Postulating a separate developmental line for the evolution and maintenance of healthy narcissism, Kohut believed that the self emerged as a result of the interplay between the infant's innate potentialities and the selective responsiveness of early caretakers or self-objects.

According to Kohut, the infant is born with rudimentary potentialities that form the basis of the core nuclear self, and three basic needs for mirroring, idealization, and twinship provide pathways to cohesive self-development. The self becomes structured through the processes of parental empathy, optimal frustration, and transmuting internalization, in which the functions of the self-object are taken over by the child, rendering the actual presence of the self-object less vital or even unnecessary. For example, comforting self-object experiences eventually enable the child to soothe himself or herself and to regulate his or her self-esteem under the impact of stress, criticism, or disappointments when others are not present. The normal child's grandiose self emerges in the first year of life. The parents' selective mirroring (approving and confirming) responses to the child's innate and unique unfolding characteristics, sense of omnipotence, and nontraumatic instances of imperfect attunement help the child to transform his or her grandiosity into realistic self-confidence and later to develop life goals and ambitions. At the same time, children begin to lose their sense of omnipotence, but continue to feel powerful by idealizing parental figures. With appropriate attunement, idealization eventually gives way to realistically based self-esteem and the core of a sense of values. Gradually, the self achieves cohesiveness and stability as an enduring structure.

When children experience severe and protracted exposure to a lack of parental empathy, the self remains enfeebled. The grandiose self does not undergo transformation, and the weakness or deficits in self-development may show in inappropriate grandiosity and cool indifference to others. Alternatively, these children may be traumatized as a result of deidealization or suffer from the absence of idealizable parents and may continually seek those who serve to make him or her feel powerful through idealization or likeness while they retain underlying feelings of weakness and imperfection. The narcissistic rage that occurs as a reaction to early self-object failures may be remobilized later in life when these individuals experience losses, traumas, disappointments, rejections, lack of appreciation, misunderstandings, or even minor criticisms from those upon whom they depend as self-objects. Kohut and Wolf (1978) described the range of disorders of the self that may result from traumatic self-object failures.

In Kohut's schema, the child may be able to acquire compensatory structures that strengthen the self. These structures enable the person to make up for or repair deficits in one aspect of the self through the successful development of its other facets. Thus, the child has more than one chance to achieve self-cohesion. Although early self-objects are crucial to the development of the infant's self, the need for others to provide support and sustenance continues all through life.

THE CULTURE OF NARCISSISM

It is commonly believed that today more individuals show narcissistic traits than was true previously, although there are no clear-cut research findings to support this view. In *The Culture of Narcissism*, Lasch (1978) identified certain features of American life that are contributing to increased narcissism. As people devalue the past and dread the future, they live for the moment. They seek gratification, but technology, the rapidity of social change, the nature of work, and the disintegration of family life and the society itself lead to chronic restlessness, emptiness, dissatisfaction, rage, loneliness, self-absorption, feelings of transience in relationships, difficulties in personal commitment, anxiety, depression, and problems with self-esteem. In taking a broader view of the social conditions that may breed narcissism, one has to consider the prevalence of the sexual and physical abuse of children, the insidious effects of racism and oppression, the pervasiveness of violence, and the shrinking of opportunities for occupational and financial success. Although this view may be used to glorify the past and to negate all aspects of social change, it does focus attention on the broader context that predisposes people to develop personality disorders.

THE CLINICAL PICTURE

DSM-III-R (pp. 349–351) defines narcissistic personality disorder as reflecting the following cluster of long-standing and entrenched character traits:

1. A grandiose sense of self-importance or uniqueness.
2. Preoccupation with fantasies of unlimited success, power, brilliance, beauty, or ideal love.
3. Exhibitionism, reflected in the need for constant attention or admiration.
4. Cool indifference or marked feelings of rage, inferiority, shame, humiliation, or emptiness in response to criticism, indifference of others, or defeat.
5. At least two of the following: feelings of entitlement, that is, an expectation of special favors without assuming reciprocal responsibilities; interpersonal exploitation, such as taking advantage of others to indulge oneself or a disregard of the rights of others; relationships that alternate between the extremes of overidealization and devaluation; and the lack of empathy with others.

Psychodynamically oriented clinicians tend to go beyond these particular manifestations of narcissistic pathology and look to structural defects in the self. In their assessment of narcissistic vulnerability, they focus on underlying problems in the regulation of self-esteem and the maintenance of self-cohesion, as well as the defensive structures that form to protect the self (Kernberg, 1970, 1974; Kohut, 1966, 1971, 1977).

Not all individuals with narcissistic personality disorder show the same degree of dysfunction or come for treatment, since the presence of areas of good ego functioning and a responsive environment may make reasonably successful adaptation possible. For example, narcissistic personalities who are intelligent, attractive, talented, and charming may, for the most part, be able to obtain sufficient success, status, and affirmation to sustain themselves without major breakdowns or disruptions of their characteristic mode of functioning. Their drive, perfectionism, opportunism, and sometimes ruthlessness may result in successful careers, financial rewards, power, and a seemingly ideal family life, despite the superficiality and emptiness of human relationships. Although they tend to be driven to reach greater and greater heights, always to conquer new challenges, and continually to acquire more symbols of success and are prone to depression when these are not forthcoming, they have the ability to evoke needed emotional supplies from others and from the environment to sustain them and to balance temporary setbacks and defeats.

Many of these individuals may seek relief from intense internal pressures through the abuse of substances or may develop somatic difficulties, but they usually seek help only when they are depressed because they did not get what they feel they deserve or need. Sometimes they become depressed when they are faced with the loss of someone or something who has been essential to the maintenance of their self-esteem and self-cohesion. When their depression is relieved, however, they often lose their motivation for further psychotherapy. Nevertheless, some narcissistic individuals of this type may realize that they are never satisifed or are missing something from life and want more. They may feel fraudulent despite their overt successes and fear exposure. Others have more chronic difficulties in functioning. Their feelings of entitlement and fantasies of success exceed their actual capacities, or they are so focused on achieving greatness that they cannot or will not engage in the hard work and step-by-step process by which their goals may eventually be realized. Wanting the perfect relationship or to be the most acclaimed, they do not try to meet others, constantly find fault with those who like them, do not look for work, or leave jobs because they perceive them as inferior to their talents. There is a serious risk of suicide with depressed narcissistic individuals who feel empty, embittered, angry, and hopeless. Some narcissistic individuals are overtly borderline and engage in destructive behavior that leads to hospitalization or antisocial acts that result in imprisonment.

NARCISSISM AND AGING

Even those persons who have been able to compensate for their underlying narcissistic vulnerability and to attain a reasonably high level of functioning encounter increasing difficulties in later life, since the aging process creates inevitable stresses that tax their adaptation. In middle age, for example, bodily changes that lessen one's feeling of attractiveness, physical prowess, and sense of immortality occur. In a society that is so youth oriented, growing older often is accompanied by diminished opportunities for advancement and satisfaction in a career and increased competition. It becomes more difficult to attract others and to develop new relationships, and one's time perspective begins to center on how many years one has left. The bubble of perfection, self-sufficiency, and omnipotent control of others and life bursts as individuals and couples experience their underlying emptiness and lack of real intimacy, as problems mount, and as adolescent and adult children begin to show the negative effects of having been raised by narcissistic parents (Goldstein, 1990).

For narcissistic personalities whose dysfunction has been more overt or who have failed to attain necessary supplies from the environment, the past seems to be strewn with lost or failed opportunities, and the long-held illusion that the future will be better dims. The gap between one's fantasies of success and the actual realities of life widens as the possibility of gaining acclaim, status, wealth, the ideal relationship, children, and the like becomes illusive. Although everyone is affected by these issues more or less, narcissistic personalities usually negate their own past achievements and lack the flexibility and internal resources to make new adaptations. Highly dependent on their sense of omnipotence and control or the environment's reward system, they continue to utilize the same coping mechanisms with less success and consequently begin to show more maladaptive defenses, envy, rage, exhibitionism, entitlement, controlling behavior, depression, withdrawal, paranoid thinking, and alienation. Some may rely on denial or continued fantasies of success to keep themselves going and seem to have a disregard for reality that ranges from magical thinking and unrealistic fantasies even to psychotic delusions that nevertheless enable them to feel better and to preserve their self-concepts.

Old age may assault the self-esteem and identity of even healthy individuals, but narcissistic personalities enter this period in a state of heightened vulnerability. The internal and external changes that occur undermine their coping mechanisms. These changes include bodily changes, illness, and disability; the loss of meaningful roles, status, outlets, and people, particularly those who provide affirmation and feelings of being special; the need for increased dependence on others, along with the sense of a loss of control over one's life; changes in self-concept as a result of getting old; the prospect of death; and the actual insults of those who are insensitive to or who have stereotyped views of older persons (Furstenberg, 1989; Sadovy, 1987; Thomas, 1989). Although the effects of narcissistic assaults may be short lived, they become chronic and malignant for narcissistic personalities. Certain illnesses also have devastating effects on a person's self-concept and self-cohesion. For example, Cohen and Eisdorfer (1986) poignantly described the gradual and insidious "deselfing" process that characterizes victims of Alzheimer's disease.

Diagnostic problems are common with narcissistic older persons, largely because helping persons fail to recognize that certain types of depression and rage reactions, "difficult" personality traits, problems in recovering from physical illnesses, or somatic and other types of symptoms stem from narcissistic injury and weaknesses in the self. The DSM-III-R criteria do not fully capture the ways in which narcissistic pathology manifests itself in the here and now with elderly persons. It is important to develop a good history of the individual's characteristic mode of functioning. Furthermore, helping professionals are not immune to negative reactions toward narcissistic traits and stereotyped attitudes toward the elderly in general that impede accurate assessment.

There are two broad groupings of elderly narcissistic individuals: (1) those who made reasonably successful adaptations, but who begin to experience either a gradual erosion or sudden and catastrophic loss of the work, status, role, people, or symbols that have sustained them and (2) those who have had a history of low achievement in selected or all areas of their lives and who become overwhelmed by feelings of failure, worthlessness, a sense of betrayal, and remorse and have few external or internal resources. The issue of multiple losses of internal capacities and external supports that are the mainstays of self-esteem, identity, and hope for the future is paramount in both these instances (Conway, 1988; Pollock, 1987; Tobin, 1988). It is this profound sense of loss, with the resultant rage, despair, and sometimes suicidal rumination and behavior, that is at the root of the most dysfunctional types of reactions in elderly individuals with narcissistic pathology, as is shown in the cases described next. These reactions are compounded by some helping persons' insensitivity and inability to relate to these persons' shattered selves.

Case Examples

Angela was 65 and relatively stable medically when she stopped her hemodialysis treatment and died. Her kidneys had failed two years earlier, secondary to diabetes that was diagnosed when she was 34. Her recent, almost total blindness and the numbness in her limbs interfered with her daily activities. In the past, she had held respon-

258   MENTAL HEALTH AND THE ELDERLY

sible positions in which she felt autonomous and special. Because of her failing condition, she was forced to stop working a year before she started dialysis and remained at home, where she fought with or withdrew from those who were close to her. Although she generally was compliant with her medical regimen, she often was bitter about her condition and sometimes missed her dialysis appointments. On these occasions, she received well-intentioned pep talks from her physician, but was generally ignored by other staff members at the dialysis center, who withdrew from her because of her contemptuous attitude toward them and her feelings that she was entitled to special treatment.

Angela's husband, who worked long hours in a successful law practice, had always provided her with the status of marriage and a financially secure relationship, but they shared little closeness. Despite a large network of business acquaintances with whom they socialized and traveled, they had no close friends, nor did they have children. Angela's husband became increasingly burdened and exhausted by Angela's anger, attempts to control everyone and everything around her, stubborn refusal to allow help to come in during the day, and insistence that he take care of her exclusively.

After a year and a half of dialysis, Angela, who had become increasingly depressed and withdrawn, overdosed on Valium and was hospitalized in a biologically oriented psychiatric unit, where a course of electroshock therapy (ECT) was recommended. Her suicide attempt was viewed as a symptom of an affective disorder, rather than as an outgrowth of the narcissistic assaults imposed by her condition. Before ECT, to which she was opposed, could be given, Angela began to respond to antidepressants to some degree and returned home. She reluctantly agreed to hire caretakers, but was extremely domineering in dealing with them. When some items of her laundry were lost for a few days and she learned they were ruined in the wash, she became inconsolable. She convinced her physician and husband to allow her to terminate dialysis and soon died.

While wishing to end one's life might be understandable in non-narcissistic individuals who face a bleak future, Angela's history showed that the bedrock of her self-concept was her need for control which compensated for underlying feelings of powerlessness and worthlessness. Any challenge to her need for control led to rage reactions. Her autonomy was more important than her health, and she had frequently been noncompliant with her medical regimen all through her life. Her drive to succeed, attractiveness, and intelligence helped her in many areas of her functioning, but Angela was closed off emotionally, capable of superficial attachments rather than true intimacy, and she relied on external admiration and work achievements for her self-esteem. Angela met her husband when he was graduating from law school. Involved in building his career and uninterested in raising a family, he made few demands on her for intimacy. Angela had struggled to control her diabetes over the years. Food was a major source of nurture, and she resented having to curtail her eating and to be on a strict regimen of any kind. In addition to the multiple losses of work, physical function, and bodily intactness imposed by her illness, the loss of control over her life was the source of greatest narcissistic injury and rage. She then experienced the loss of the one activity that she enjoyed the most, reading, and she lacked any interest in finding substitutes or in learning new ways of coping with her blindness. People around her verbally held out hope and offered endless reassurance, rather than empathy with her pain and despair. They expected her to improve the quality of her life when she felt she had no future. Disappointed in her loss of power and in the lack of omnipotence in those around her, she turned her anger against both herself and those close to her.

Diane, a divorced free-lance fashion consultant, was 68 when a malignant tumor of the breast necessitated a mastectomy. Despite a favorable laboratory report, Diane became angry at everyone around her, cried easily, was depressed, refused visitors, was uncooperative with the nurses, and would not discuss the need for further preventive treatment, reconstructive surgery, and attendance at a support group. Initially thinking that she would become more positive over time, the medical and nursing staff tried to encourage her. When Diane was discharged and failed to keep her appointment with the physician, he tried to contact her and persuade her to see him. Since her discharge from the hospital, she had isolated herself from her friends and her two daughters and had not returned to work, a major source of self-esteem.

Diane's history showed that she was the child of alcoholic parents. She lived with her mother, and her father left the family when she was a child. Although her needs were neglected, she was especially attractive, and her appearance was the focus of positive attention from her mother and others. Diane was extremely popular in school, but she always felt that people responded to her only because she was pretty and that she basically had little to offer others. She often felt unattractive, unlovable, and alone, despite the emphasis she herself put on appearing fashionable and perfectly groomed. Men were attracted by her good looks, but eventually disappointed her. She longed for the perfect relationship, but was not interested in men who were caring toward her. Despite this pattern, a failed marriage, and turbulent relationships with two daughters who functioned only marginally, Diane always was able to find a new admirer for a time, and these relationships and her success at work sustained her.

Diane's physician convinced her to see a psychiatrist, an attractive woman in her thirties. Diane filled her initial appointments with angry attacks on the hospital and the physicians for their incompetence and on the psychiatrist herself for being too young and attractive to understand her pain. She felt that she had no identity or future. She was afraid not of dying but of having to live on without any hope of being able to attract men or to look beautiful. The psychiatrist attempted to explore and understand Diane's reactions to the surgery and to her diagnosis and prognosis, but became increasingly annoyed with Diane for being so upset. She had trouble empathizing with why a 68-year-old woman would be so concerned about her inability to attract men and with her sense of doom. She questioned Diane's seeming obsessive emphasis on her appearance and attempted to point out Diane's seemingly unrealistic pessimism and the positives in Diane's situation. Diane became more angry and berated the therapist for her insensitivity. Dreading the sessions with Diane and relieved when she missed appointments, the psychiatrist agreed to terminate the treatment when Diane expressed her doubt that the therapist could do anything for her. The therapist told the referring physician that Diane had been resistant to getting help and that she would be glad to see Diane if she became motivated.

Marvin, a 66-year-old personnel recruiter and recovering alcoholic with a twenty-five-year history of sobriety, began drinking excessively to the point of having blackouts after being laid off from his job because of economic cutbacks and his poor performance. This position was the last of a long series of ill-fated jobs that held the promise of financial rewards that never materialized. Fearing that the few friends he had and other acquaintances would learn of his drinking, Marvin withdrew from everyone on the pretext that he was looking for work. Each day, he spent hours fantasizing about going back into the theater, his original career, or starting a business in which he would make his fortune. He barely survived financially and drew on meager savings to meet his expenses while he incurred considerable debt. He was consumed with anger at himself for having ruined all his opportunities for financial success and personal happiness, as well as his sobriety, the one accomplishment that sustained his self-respect. When an automobile accident that occurred after his drinking resulted in his hospitalization and the suspension of his driver's license, Marvin curtailed his drinking briefly and was referred to an outpatient therapist with the understanding that he would return to Alcoholics Anonymous (AA).

Marvin was raised in a family that was perfectionistic and valued performance, material success, and the opinions of others, but failed to provide Marvin with a sense of his own worth and competence. He was expected to be part of an admiring audience for his parents and to bolster their self-esteem through his achievements. As long as he could remember, his parents told him he was destined for greatness, and he studied music and theater in the hope of becoming an orchestra conductor or a director of Broadway musicals.

For a time Marvin performed in small theater groups, but always was fearful that others would recognize that he was a fraud because (he thought) he had no talent. He sought to cover up this fear by driving himself and by appearing extremely confident, sometimes to the point of alienating others who saw him as boastful and arrogant. He utilized alcohol simultaneously to relieve stress and to give himself the courage to act. He tended to date attractive women who made him "look good" and upon whom he lavished whatever money he had, but eventually became bored by and resentful of them.

Marvin achieved some success acting and accepted a position directing a small theater group, but his escalating alcoholism sabotaged his work, and he was forced to give up this job. He became sober with the help of AA and achieved recognition for his active role in the program over the years, but he did not return to the theater because he was afraid. Instead, he opted to make money in various aspects of the business world, but never attained his goal. Usually hating his jobs and employers, he felt he was too good for what he was doing and disappointed the management with his low productivity, inability to take even minor criticism, and surly attitude. He let several opportunities to switch careers pass by, and it was becoming more difficult for him to obtain work as he aged. He viewed his most recent position as his last chance to make money. His usual pattern of relationships with women continued over the years, although it was becoming increasingly difficult for him to attract the same caliber of women that he desired and he had little money to spend on them. He was becoming frightened of getting sick and dying alone.

Marvin attended psychotherapy sessions, but he felt so deeply humiliated and afraid to acknowledge his relapse to those who admired his apparently successful recovery from alcoholism that he could not bring himself to attend AA meetings and continued drinking, albeit in a somewhat more controlled fashion. He filled his therapy sessions with feelings of failure, hopelessness, and shame. He openly stated that he had been living in a dreamworld all his life and sustaining himself with fantasies of ultimately reclaiming the career he had wrecked with his early drinking. He realized he was not ever going to be a success and that he would never have the money to own anything of value. He felt bitter about not having his own family or any really intimate companion and acknowledged his inability to love anyone. He could not understand why he had allowed himself to waste his life and felt he had no one else to blame but himself. He felt he had nothing to show for all his years of drudgery and he envied all those around him who were young or successful or who loved their work.

Overwhelmed by the magnitude of Marvin's painful sense of remorse and hopelessness and helpless in the face of Marvin's resistance to returning to AA, the therapist tried unsuccessfully to identify and support Marvin's strengths and to hold out promise for a better future, to which Marvin responded with anger at the therapist's lack of realism. Not knowing what to do, the therapist referred Marvin to a psychiatrist, who prescribed antidepressants that did not seem to have a positive effect and that Martin eventually began to take erratically. When the therapist put more pressure on him to return to AA and stop drinking, Marvin dropped out of treatment.

Rose was a 70-year-old woman who attended a senior citizens' center in her community. She became known to the social worker there because a group at the center wanted to exclude Rose from numerous activities and trips. Although they were unsuccessful in excluding her, they refused to communicate with Rose, who, nevertheless, insisted on being present. Rose had alienated her associates by her incessant efforts to portray herself as special and superior to others, her disdain for and intolerance of those who were not as intellectual as she felt herself to be, her insensitivity to the feelings of others, and her refusal to help in the routine setting up and cleaning up that was necessary.

Rose had been the youngest of numerous, considerably older siblings in a financially successful, socially prominent, and competitive family. A somewhat frail child, she grew up in the shadow of the accomplishments of her brothers and sisters and witnessed the praise they received from her parents. Less involved with her than with their other children, Rose's parents delegated her care to household help, whom Rose often helped in their duties. Rose wrote poetry at a young age and spent hours listening to classical music and attending art museums. She became an attractive woman, but suffered from low self-esteem.

After attending college, Rose married a man who was a workaholic and self-absorbed but protective and financially secure, and they had two children. She did not enjoy the maternal role, so the children were raised largely with the help of a nanny, while Rose spent as much time as possible outside the home, usually attending courses or cultural events, generally by herself or with her husband with whom she shared many social activities. She did not easily maintain relationships with friends because of her hypersensitivity to perceived slights and her often-condescending attitudes. When her children became adults, they moved far from the family home and rarely visited after Rose's husband died when she was 65.

Her husband's death was a devastating blow, particularly because he had suffered severe economic losses on investments and, to her surprise and dismay, there were insufficient funds to support her customary life-style. She moved to a new community and missed what little social network she enjoyed. Lonely without her husband's protective presence, Rose was persuaded to attend the senior citizens' center to establish new contacts, but proceeded to antagonize those with whom she associated.

GOALS OF TREATMENT

Recognizing and Empathizing with Narcissistic Injury

A crucial goal of the treatment of elderly clients with narcissistic difficulties is to help them develop better ways of coping. To do so, however, helping professionals must look beyond these persons' sometimes annoying personality traits, bitterness, sense of entitlement, envy, and uncooperativeness to their narcissistic injury and feelings of worthlessness and hopelessness (Conway, 1988; Greene, 1986). Helping professionals must identify the characteristic patterns that these individuals have shown in their lives and the nature of the impact of the aging process, recent losses, illness, disability, changes, or other life events on the self and its compensatory structures. Even in the short run, the therapist, by relating to the person's subjective feelings of bitterness and despair, will enable him or her to feel understood, accepted, and less alone. In many instances, it is only against a backdrop of this type of empathy for the real despair that clients experience that the therapist can help them mourn the losses of the past, come to terms with their lives, master their feelings, remobilize, build up new compensatory structures, and find new gratifications in the external world. In some cases in which the narcissistic injuries stimulate profound weakness in the self, more reparative treatment may be indicated, even with this age group, that is focused on ameliorating early developmental arrests (White & Weiner, 1986).

Preserving and Strengthening the Self

Elderly individuals generally often lose the concrete evidence and symbols of their success or identity. Institutional environments further deprive them of their possessions, clothes, home, and status. The aging process and illnesses cause them to be less intact. Therefore, it is important to help those whose self-esteem is damaged to preserve as much of the reminders of their past achievements and life as possible. In many instances, doing so may extend to supporting what appears to be "magical coping," denial, and other defenses or seemingly unrealistic plans for the future or memories of the past that bolster the self-concept (Cohen & Eisdorfer, 1986; Furstenberg, 1989; Lazarus, 1980; Tobin, 1988).

Despite their grandiosity and sense of entitlement, narcissistic individuals not only show diminished self-esteem in the here and now, but they are extremely negative about themselves and their past experiences. They eradicate their history of achievement, which has no emotional meaning since they lack affirmation and recognition in the present. They forget previous successes. Their self-esteem can be enhanced by empathically helping them to retrieve memories, to review and reshape the way they view themselves and their past life experiences, and to identify and support their strengths and the ways and areas in which they can regain and retain control of their lives (Butler, 1963; Greenes, 1986; Grunes, 1982).

It is easier to accomplish these tasks when elderly persons have had areas of better functioning and success in their lives and when some avenues for self-expression, validation, and autonomy are still present. In the absence of these conditions, the therapist may join the client's pessimism or become too optimistic. The therapist's ability to strike a balance between his or her realism about past failures and current constraints and to hold out a positive vision of the person's past efforts and even small successes and future potential is vital.

Another avenue to restoring faltering self-esteem is through the therapist's actual functioning as an affirming or idealizable person to the client (Elson, 1986; White & Weiner, 1986). With narcissistic individuals who show such profound developmental arrests, therapists may need to meet their needs for applause or other forms of self-affirmation selectively at times, rather than to interpret their efforts to get their needs met as "manipulations" or as unhealthy attempts to obtain approval from the outside world. This does not mean that one always gratifies the clients' needs for mirroring. What is important is to provide a type of "optimal responsiveness" (Bacal, 1985) based on what will help the clients experience a renewed sense of self-esteem.

Mourning the Past and the Future

Since multiple losses of people, meaningful roles, opportunities, aspects of the self, creative outlets, a sense of control, and time itself are such core issues, helping elderly narcissistic individuals to mourn the past as well as lost future opportunities is a crucial part of the treatment process and must be actively encouraged. Their sense of remorse may be reality based, at least in part, since their pathology may have contributed to their occupational and relationship failures and to behavior that has damaged them or others, such as children, friends, spouses, or lovers, with whom they have been in close contact. At the same time, it is important to remember that narcissistic individuals have carried with them unrealistically grandiose, omnipotent, or perfectionistic expectations of themselves and what they should have accomplished in life that would be difficult for anyone to achieve. They need help to temper their sense of self-blame for not being able to control life or others and for having human limitations.

Intense countertransference reactions may be aroused in the therapist during the course of this grief work that can result in his or her attempts to suppress or close off the individual's pain, to minimize feelings of loss or failure, or to offer false reassurance about the future. The working-through process may take a long time, and the therapist must be able to sustain himself or herself during this arduous process.

Pointing out Maladaptive Defenses and Behavior

Within an overall atmosphere of empathy and acceptance, therapists may need to help narcissistic elderly clients recognize, limit, and modify their self-defeating and alienating behavior. A nonjudgmental attitude is needed as one attempts to relate empathically to the clients' experience of their own needs and to point out the negative consequences of certain traits and acts. An educational approach may be useful in helping narcissistic individuals to expand their awareness of the needs of others, to develop empathy for others, and to try out new ways of perceiving and relating to others.

Work with the Family and the Social Environment

The self-centeredness, depression, anger, and exhibitionism of narcissistic individuals is taxing for those around them, who, in turn, may withdraw, become angry, or otherwise cease to be supportive because of their own sense of loss. It is important to assess the mutual impact that elderly narcissistic persons and members of their family and social network are having on one another. Significant others need to be educated about the clients' difficulties and areas of vulnerability and helped to be more responsive. At the same time, attention must be paid to helping caretakers and others who are close to the client understand the client's impact on them, identify their own needs, and find supports that will help them be supportive without burning out. Although the provision of concrete services that relieve caretakers' burdens may play a crucial role, such services need to be accompanied by a greater focus on helping caretakers to recognize and deal with their own losses and needs and then to find substitutes or outlets for these losses without guilt.

Helping elderly clients to find opportunities in the social environment and actually restructuring certain aspects of the external world, when possible, so that they are more validating of the elderly clients' needs for self-esteem also are important during intervention. It may be possible to create a better fit between the individual and his or her environment that may be more affirmative.

IMPLICATIONS FOR STAFF AND AGENCY SETTINGS

In working with narcissistic vulnerability in the elderly, staff experience stress from multiple sources: (1) identification with the assaults to the self that elderly persons endure; (2) the impact of the clients' self-involvement, rage, depression, demandingness, entitlement, and hopelessness; and (3) the awareness of elderly persons' diminished opportunities for activities, roles, and relationships that affirm the self (Greene, 1986; Poggi & Berland, 1985). It is difficult for staff to be there emotionally for clients when they identify too deeply with the clients' pain and struggles, when they feel they have little to give, or when they are provoked by, rather than understanding of, what may appear to be annoying behavior. Stereotyped attitudes toward the elderly also may limit the staff's willingness to provide active treatment, their ability to provide hope, and their attempts to identify and create avenues for self-expression and self-affirmation. Consequently, staff training and support are essential in therapeutic settings.

The service delivery system also exerts a profound impact on staff members and facilitates or obstructs the helping process. Just as it is difficult for a parent to establish a good-enough holding environment for a child when he or she is feeling vulnerable personally or is surrounded by a nonnurturing and stressful environment, staff members cannot be optimally effective when they feel that the place in which they work is insensitive, neglectful, assaulting, or nonsupportive. A parallel process may occur in which they run the risk of passing along to clients what they experience from their surrounding work environment, which is affected by the wider society. The staggering effects of chronic illness and disability, poverty, death, budgetary cuts, overburdened health care systems, and the low priority for psychosocial services pose serious threats to providing humane and differential treatment for the elderly. Societal neglect affects the staff's healthy narcissism or own needs. Therefore, they must work to find ways to nurture themselves and, whenever possible, to work for changes in the nature of service delivery, so they can be there for others without burning out.

REFERENCES

Bacal, H. A. (1985). Optimal responsiveness and the therapeutic process. In A. Goldberg (Ed.), *Progress in self psychology* (Vol. 1, pp. 202–227). New York: Guilford Press.

Berezin, M. (1977). The fate of narcissism in old age: Clinical case reports. *Journal of Geriatric Psychiatry, 10*, 9–26.

Berezin, M. (1987). Reflections on psychotherapy with the elderly. In J. Sadovy & M. Leszcz (Eds.), *Treating the elderly with psychotherapy* (pp. 45–63). Madison, CT: International Universities Press.

Breslau, L. (1980). The faltering therapeutic perspective toward the narcissistically wounded aged. *Journal of Geriatric Psychiatry, 13*, 193–206.

Butler, R. (1963). The life review: An interpretation of reminiscence. *Psychiatry, 26*, 65–76.

Chessick, R. D. (1985). *Psychology of the self and the treatment of narcissism.* New York: Jason Aronson.

Cohen, D., & Eisdorfer, C. (1986). *The loss of self.* New York: W. W. Norton.

Conway, P. (1988). Losses and grief in old age. *Social Casework: The Journal of Contemporary Social Work, 69*, 541–549.

Cooper, A. M. (1986). Narcissism. In A. P. Morrison (Ed.), *Essential papers on narcissism* (pp. 112–143). New York: New York University Press.

Ellis, H. (1898). Auto-eroticism: A psychological study. *Alienist and Neurologist, 19*, 260–299.

Elson, M. (1986). *Self psychology in clinical social work.* New York: W. W. Norton.

·Freud, S. (1957). On narcissism: An introduction. In J. Strachey (Ed. and Trans.), *The standard edition of the complete psychological works of Sigmund Freud* (Vol. 14, pp. 111–140). London: Hogarth Press. (Original work published 1914)

Furstenberg, A. (1989). Older people's age self-concept. *Social Casework: The Journal of Contemporary Social Work, 70*, 268–276.

Goldfarb, A. I. (1959). Minor maladjustments in the aged. In S. Arieti (Ed.), *American handbook of psychiatry* (Vol. 1, pp. 386–394). New York: Basic Books.

Goldstein, E. G. (1990). *Borderline disorders: Clinical models and techniques.* New York: Guilford Press.

Greene, R. R. (1986). Countertransference issues in social work with the aged. *Journal of Gerontological Social Work, 9*, 79–88.

Greenes, J. M. (1987). The aged in psychotherapy: Psychodynamic contributions to the treatment process. In J. Sadovy & M. Leszcz (Eds.), *Treating the elderly with psychotherapy* (pp. 64–75). Madison, CT: International Universities Press.

Grunes, J. M. (1982). Reminiscence, regression and empathy—A psychotherapeutic approach to the impaired elderly. In S. I. Greenspan & G. H. Pollock (Eds.), *The course of life* (Vol. 3, pp. 545–560). Washington, DC: National Institute of Mental Health.

Hartmann, H. (1950). Comments on the psychoanalytic theory of the ego. *Psychoanalytic Study of the Child, 5,* 74–96.

Jacobson, E. (1964). *The self and the object world.* New York: International Universities Press.

Kernberg, O. F. (1970). Factors in the psychoanalytic treatment of narcissistic personalities. *Journal of the American Psychoanalytic Association, 18,* 51–85.

Kernberg, O. F. (1974). Further contributions to the treatment of narcissistic personalities. *International Journal of Psychoanalysis, 55,* 215–240.

Kernberg, O. F. (1986). Narcissistic personality disorder. In A. M. Cooper, A. J. Frances, & M. H. Sacks (Eds.), *Psychiatry: Vol. 1. The personality disorders and the neuroses* (pp. 219–230). New York: Basic Books.

Kohut, H. (1966). Forms and transformations of narcissism. *Journal of the American Psychoanalytic Association, 14,* 243–272.

Kohut, H. (1971). *The analysis of the self.* New York: International Universities Press.

Kohut, H. (1977). *The restoration of the self.* New York: International Universities Press.

Kohut, H., & Wolf, E. (1978). The disorders of the self and their treatment: An outline. *International Journal of Psycho-analysis, 59,* 413–425.

Lasch, C. (1978). *The culture of narcissism: American life in an age of diminishing expectations.* New York: W. W. Norton.

Lazarus, W. (1980). Self psychology and psychotherapy with the elderly: Theory and practice. *Journal of Geriatric Psychiatry, 13,* 69–88.

Poggi, R., & Berland, D. (1985). The therapist's reaction to the elderly. *The Gerontologist, 25,* 508–513.

Pollock, G. H. (1987). The mourning-liberation process: Issues in the inner life of the older adult. In J. Sadovy & M. Leszcz (Eds.), *Treating the elderly with psychotherapy* (pp. 3–30). Madison, CT: International Universities Press.

Pulver, S. E. (1986). Narcissism: The term and the concept. In A. P. Morrison (Ed.), *Essential papers on narcissism* (pp. 91–111). New York, New York University Press.

Reich, A. (1960). Pathologic forms of self-esteem regulation. *Psychoanalytic Study of the Child, 15,* 215–232.

Sadovy, J. (1987). Character disorders in the elderly: An overview. In J. Sadovy & M. Leszcz (Eds.), *Treating the elderly with psychotherapy* (pp. 175–229). Madison, CT: International Universities Press.

Thomas, G. (1989). *Emotional problems of aging.* Springfield, IL: Charles C
     Thomas.

Tobin, S. (1988). Preservation of the self in old age. *Social Casework: The Journal
     of Contemporary Social Work, 69,* 550–555.

White, M. T., & Weiner, M. B. (1986). *The theory and practice of self psychology.*
     New York: Brunner-Mazel.

14

Fear and Phobias

Robert L. Barker

A 79-year-old man was recently admitted to a psychiatric facility, seemingly in a state of terror. During the previous several months, he had grown increasingly fearful and was now reluctant to encounter people or situations beyond his four walls. Neighbors and family members, concerned about his health and well-being, initiated the admission in hopes that medical care would restore him to his warm and gregarious nature.

The man's diagnosis seemed obvious to the admitting physicians. The symptoms were those delineated in DSM-III-R for agoraphobia. The man had expressed strong but unreasonable fear about leaving his home and facing the world. He clearly indicated his fear of being in places or situations from which escape would be difficult and help would be unavailable in emergencies.

But the diagnosis was wrong. A physical examination revealed that the man had developed urinary incontinence. He had been staying home, not because of the intense fear seen in agoraphobics, but simply because he was too ashamed to be seen in public. Minor surgery restored his bladder control, and soon the man resumed his healthy and sociable walks throughout the neighborhood (Malatesta, 1989).

Social workers and other professionals who encounter psychopathology in older persons learn much from cases such as this one. The most important lesson is this: When assessing and diagnosing older people, one must always consider the entire gamut of biophysical, psychosocial, economic, and historical factors that inevitably influence the individual's behavior and circumstances. In work with a senescent client, a single diagnosis is usually an impediment to effective treatment (Blum & Weiner, 1979). When the most apparent symptoms suggest only that the client suffers from "nonorganic" psychopathologies as neurotic fears or anxieties, it is time to look deeper and wider for more complete explanations.

The case of the "agoraphobic" man also illustrates one of the most common unhealthy types of behavior seen in older people, that of increased social isolation. Physical and emotional health can never be optimal unless the older person is involved with others and engaged socially; conversely, when isolation becomes the predominant life-style, physical and mental illnesses are much more probable (Hooyman & Lustbader, 1986).

Finally, the case typifies the ease with which the label "agoraphobia" can be misapplied to an isolated older person. The man was not phobic; he was afraid. It is fear, rather than its distant cousin phobia, that is the major factor in the isolation of older people (Fry, 1986, pp. 20–27).

Fear is more likely to confine older people than is physical handicap, chronic pain, cognitive impairment, depression, organic brain disorders, or any other condition that receives so much attention in gerontology. Fear is present in virtually all the other disorders that afflict the elderly, and it exists in many older people who are free of other dysfunctions. Thus, every professional who works with older people needs to understand the nature, causes, consequences, and treatment of fear.

THE NATURE OF FEAR

Fear is defined as "the emotional and physical reaction to an identifiable or perceived source of threat" (Barker, 1991, p. 55). Fear is not necessarily psychopathological. In fact, it can be useful and essential to one's survival. All humans experience it at times, as apparently do most other animals. Fear may be constructive in that it helps mobilize the individual for effective defensive action. It arouses physiological responses, creating a sharpness of perception that may enhance the individual's performance and coping strategies. The reaction of Mrs. C is an illustration:

Mrs. C was 72 when she was mugged on her way home from the store. Her attacker pushed her from behind and ran off with her purse and packages as she fell to the ground. It took several weeks for her to recuperate from the injury to her knees and right shoulder, but much longer to recover from the psychic injury. Living alone, she wanted to continue her regular visits to the store. But every attempt to walk out her door was accompanied by fear of another incident. Despite an almost overwhelming desire to stay home and despite her quickened heartbeat, heavy breathing, and perspiration, she made herself walk the same route where the attack took place.

One day on such a walk, Mrs. C realized she was being followed. She quickly reviewed her options before deciding on the most prudent response. She abruptly stopped, turned, and looked directly at her pursuer. Then she dropped her packages and purse and stepped aside. The man hesitated for a moment as he decided whether to go after the woman or the packages. This gave Mrs. C more time to distance herself from the packages. As she anticipated, the man rushed to the packages, scooped them up, and sprinted away.

This time it was the mugger, not Mrs. C, who was distraught. She had taken the precaution of keeping her valuables in a hidden travel pouch, rather than in her purse. And her clear view of the thief enabled her to identify him to the police and help them convict him. Mrs. C is still fearful in her daily walks, but she remains alert and effective. She has organized a "walk-sharing group" among her older neighbors, who now take regularly scheduled walks together. Mrs. C still has justified fears, but rather than incapacitate her, they have contributed to positive results.

Unfortunately, fear doesn't always lead to positive outcomes. Fear responses are awakened not only when people are confronted by muggers or direct and immediate threats, but when they anticipate some unpleasant future event. Our fear responses are triggered by phenomena that have no effect on any other creature. No other animal seems afraid of becoming incapacitated, dependent, or old.

Physiologically, the focus of the fear response is generally the same in humans and in other animals: in the neuroendocrine system. An important element in this system are endorphins, part of a long polypeptide chain of amino acids. Endorphins transmit information between nerve cells at their synapses and release chemicals into the blood stream to influence target cells throughout the body. Through this action, the body enters the state of readiness to resist or escape imminent danger more effectively (Heckenmueller, 1985).

Although the physiological aspect of fear is useful and similar in all people and animals, there are widespread differences in the way people and animals respond when afraid and in the perceived catalysts of the fears. Unfortunately for urbanized humans, the fear response works better when the danger is an approaching hungry lion than when it is the long-term anticipation of socioeconomic or health problems.

The behavioral manifestations of fear may range from occasional mild and brief discomfort to continuous and intense panic. On the mild side of this continuum, one is barely aware of the existence of fear. At the other extreme, one may become immobilized and helpless. In normal and healthy fear, the intensity of the reaction is approximately proportionate to the degree of danger. In its unhealthy manifestations, it can be far out of proportion to the degree or imminence of the danger. One of these unhealthy manifestations is the type of fear known as "phobia," or "phobic disorder."

DISTINCTIONS BETWEEN FEAR AND PHOBIA

The terms *fear* and *phobia*, as used by mental health professionals, are not synonymous. Phobia refers to a specific type of fear whose etiology and treatment approach is different from other kinds of fear reactions. Although fear reactions may be of limited intensity or duration and tend to be based on more immediate and objective dangers, phobias involve more abstract and subjective phenomena. Phobias are characterized by (1) an excessive level of anxiety or fear, (2) a highly specified object or situation to which the fear is attributed, and (3) extreme efforts by the individual to avoid or escape the feared object (Thomlison, 1984).

A phobia may consist of a single episode of intense fear, while a phobic disorder is chronic. According to DSM-III-R, a phobic disorder, a form of anxiety disorder, is a chronic mental illness in which intense fear is omnipresent and requires constant efforts to resist it. Generally, the sufferer of a phobic disorder consciously recognizes that the fear is out of proportion to the danger, yet continues to devote psychic and physical energy toward diminishing it by avoiding the catalyst for it.

The person who suffers a phobic disorder tends to focus on one object or situation as a perceived source of danger. Theoretically, there are an infinite number of phobias, and thousands have been named, even though some have affected few, if any, individuals.

Since *phobia* comes from the Greek *phobos*, the specific surname of the fear also usually comes from the Greek term for that object or situation. For example, *agoraphobia* is derived from the Greek word *agora*, meaning marketplace. The condition was first identified in people who were afraid to go into shopping areas where they might be unable to retreat to their homes. Later it was also noted in people whose fear was already so intense that they would never enter a public place. Agoraphobia is the most common phobic disorder, especially in older people, but many other phobias are also seen in mental health centers. They include acrophobia (the fear of heights), aquaphobia (the fear of water), claustrophobia (the fear of enclosed areas), nyctophobia (the fear of darkness), thanatophobia (the fear of death), and zoophobia (the fear of animals).

Other than agoraphobia, the delineated phobias that especially affect older people include algophobia (the fear of pain), decidophobia (the fear of making decisions), pyrophobia (the fear of fire), and monophobia (the fear of being left alone). Another phobic reaction that is common to elders is xenophobia, the fear of strangers. This was the diagnosis given to Mrs. R:

Since Mrs. R was a toddler more than sixty-five years ago, she had been shy and ill at ease around people she didn't know. But now her "shyness" was becoming intolerable. When she was introduced to people or met unfamiliar shopkeepers and office personnel, her anxiety became so intense that she would feel faint and nauseous. Her physician, whom she had known for years, could find no cause for her phobia, despite a thorough physical and psychological evaluation. The symptoms had appeared gradually and imperceptibly, without any discernable catalyst. She had never been frightened by strangers and could remember no incidents connected to the problem.

Her physician, with the help of a consulting social worker, soon realized they were seeking answers to the wrong question. Instead of determining the cause of the phobia, they decided, they should be locating the cause of her general level of anxiety. Once they were on the right track, they ascertained that Mrs. R was concerned about her husband's declining health. With medication and some supportive psychosocial therapy, Mrs. R was able to control the anxiety. Soon she was meeting and dealing with unfamiliar people with increasing assurance and decreased fear, even though her husband's health continued to worsen.

In other words, despite the way the various phobias are named, anxiety is a more important contributor to phobic disorders than is any specific object or situation in the environment. The phobic individual is over-whelmed by general anxiety and reacts by displacing the resulting emotions onto an external object that will presumably be more tolerable and avoidable.

Behavioral theorists describe this problem slightly differently. They say that the phobic reaction is a learned pattern of behavior, the consequence of a chain of associations of various negative stimuli. For example, an elderly woman develops algophobia, the fear of pain, after hearing repeated stories from friends who suffered pain. The friends' pains were due to arthritis, surgery, and headaches, and while she had none of these ailments, she anticipated the day she might. She had learned to anticipate a problem and experience its results before its occurrence.

Although phobic disorders may be debilitating, the victim usually has reason to retain them. They seem to make anxiety tolerable by concentrating it onto the feared object or situation. Thus, the phobia persists despite efforts to see that the feared object is not really so terrible. Mental health professionals usually fail to convince their clients that the feared object is relatively harmless. They have more success when they help the clients overcome anxiety and look more rationally and confidently at the feared object.

In most adults phobic disorders are more debilitating than are other types of fear. But in older persons, fear itself is equally debilitating and difficult to treat. The fears of elders are based not only on abstract or subjective danger, but on actual or imminent threats (Fedinson, 1986).

Capacity to Cope with Fear

The normal fear response (that which excludes phobic disorders) should be commensurate with the seriousness of the perceived danger. When everything else is equal, the greater the amount of danger confronting an individual, the more intense will be the psychophysiological state of readiness. However, when any group of people is exposed to identical threats, some will be more afraid than will others because each individual not only determines the objective degree of danger but must assess his or her capacity for coping with it.

In healthy adults with appropriate self-esteem and flexible cognitive functioning, the capacity for coping is usually well developed (Birren & Zarit, 1985). Their coping skills are derived primarily from direct experience in successfully encountering similar risk situations, and, to a lesser extent, on observing how others have coped in such circumstances. Thus, a person with little experience with the threat will generally be more afraid than will one who has coped successfully on previous occasions.

Even when a threatening situation is outside the range of the individual's direct experience or observation, coping is possible when there is healthy self-esteem. Such a person will generally be less afraid of a given threat than will a person with low or fluctuating self-esteem. When one realistically recognizes one's strengths and limitations, it is easier to evaluate one's ability to deal with a threat than when such awareness is uncertain.

Finally, a person can still successfully cope without much experience, observation, or healthy self-esteem if he or she is able to consider alternatives rationally and to solve new problems. Adaptability in thinking permits one to encounter new situations with the confidence to figure out how to solve anticipated problems. Regardless of their level of intelligence, people who are more flexible in their cognitive functioning have a better chance of dealing with the threat and thus less reason to be afraid (Labouvie-Vief & Hakim-Larson, 1989).

OLDER PEOPLE AND FEAR

For these reasons it is understandable that older people tend to be more fearful. With diminishing controls over their lives, they face a wide range of unfamiliar experiences—changes in their physical, mental, and socio-economic circumstances with which they could have little direct experience coping. Many older people experience the loss of loved ones, declining perceptual acuity, the threat of serious handicapping illnesses, and a staggering array of socioeconomic changes, all within a relatively short period. They must confront these changes at a time when the resources on which they have relied throughout their lives are becoming less dependable (Harel, 1988).

If they can't rely on these resources, they would, at least, like to rely on their own time-tested abilities. Yet when they most need healthy self-esteem, many elderly people are relegated by society to roles of diminished worth. Eliminated from the work force, and all too often subjected to avoidance, ridicule, and overt age discrimination, they are at a time of life that is hardly propitious for developing good feelings about themselves (Hess, 1987). This is what happened to Mr. L:

As a passenger bus driver for over forty-five years, Mr. L had to depend on reasonably good eyes to do his job. But, as it was becoming apparent to his employers and customers, he was gradually experiencing seriously diminished visual acuity that proved to be uncorrectable. Even though he had won many accolades from his employers and compliments from his riders, he was asked to retire. With his wife deceased and his offspring living in various parts of the country, he felt isolated and unappreciated. He gradually grew more depressed and even suicidal.

Through his company's Employee Assistance Program, he was referred to a social worker. The assessment was prompt: "You've lost confidence in yourself; your sense of worth is damaged. You need to learn to feel better about yourself."

Mr. L shrugged and replied, "Sure, I know that. It's obvious. But how can I? I've lost my job, my family, and my health, and no one appreciates me anymore. Let's face it. What do I really have to feel good about?"

Unlike many older people in similiar situations, Mr. L found a happy answer. With the social worker's help, he got a job in the personnel department of a city transit company. There he advised the personnel people about which drivers should be hired, fired, and retrained. He instructed new drivers about how to deal with customers. After a few months on this job, his confidence and self-esteem were as healthy as ever.

Unfortunately, such solutions are not always available to older people who are forced out of the job market. These elderly people have to rely on other resources and adapt to different realities. However, doing so may be extremely difficult. Many older people become set in their ways and are increasingly resistant to change (Lezak, 1988). They tend to avoid all new problems that possibly can be avoided, rather than to seek innovative ways to solve them. They rely on that part of their cognitive functioning known as "crystallized intelligence," rather than on the "fluid intelligence" that is more useful in problem solving.

Cognitive Functioning in the Elderly

Crystallized intelligence refers to an individual's concrete aggregate experiences that are accumulated throughout a lifetime. It is the sum of all the factual information and effects of the socialization-acculturation process. This type of intellectual functioning continues developing throughout one's lifetime. It is why, on many tests of knowledge and intelligence, especially involving general information, verbal abilities, and arithmetic, older people generally do well.

It is in the realm of fluid intelligence that older persons' functioning is more likely to diminish. Fluid intelligence refers to the immediate adaptive ability to perceive relationships between objects and events, to reason, and to abstract. Since it depends on the biological and physiological integrity of the nervous system, under the relentless deterioration of the biological aging process, this aspect of the intellect is more likely to decline. Timed tests of cognitive functioning show a marked diminution of abstract reasoning and problem-solving abilities in most older people.

However, because there is only gradual deterioration in the nervous system, unless traumatic brain damage occurs, the resulting decline in fluid intelligence is also gradual. Thus the older person has time to find or develop compensatory mechanisms. And since crystallized intelligence goes on developing, most older people come to rely more heavily on it than on fluid intelligence. This may be the most significant reason why the thinking of older people often seems to be less flexible and more reliant on information than on innovation. Of course, there are great individual differences among the elderly, with some maintaining more fluid intellectual capacities than their younger counterparts ever had. It is only when the cognitive functioning of groups of younger people is compared with that of commensurate groups of elders that this phenomenon is apparent.

Catalysts of Fear

Because the degree of fear response is proportionate both to the intrinsic danger of the threat and to the capacity of the individual to cope, many older persons inevitably face fear. Their fears are not necessarily abstract or based on an overload of anxiety from intrapsychic sources, as in the case of phobic disorders, but are immediate and objective (Croake, Myers, & Singh, 1988). Older people are most afraid of falling, of sensory diminution, of mental decline or mental illness, of physical illness or handicap, of financial hardship, and of being victimized by abusive caretakers or criminals.

THE FEAR OF FALLING Nearly every older person has heard about a scene such as this one: A woman of advanced years falls while walking down some stairs or even while simply standing. The fall results in a broken leg or perhaps a broken hip. The treatment and recovery processes are agonizingly slow and full of setbacks. They seem to lead to the woman's decline, growing helplessness, and eventual death.

This scenario is not apocryphal. Falls leading to serious injury are common among elderly people, especially women. The U.S. National Safety Council (Bernstein & Schur, 1990) reported that while persons over age 65 constitute only about 11 percent of the population, they account for 25 percent of all deaths from accidents or injuries. The highest number of unintentional injuries among older people are due to falls. In one study, up to 38 percent of the subjects in a sample of people aged 65 or over acknowledged having had at least one fall in the past year, and 24 percent of those who fell suffered serious injuries (Tinetti, Speechly, & Ginter, 1988). What is even more alarming is that these figures may be too low. Older people characteristically underreport or deny such incidents, which makes it more difficult to establish precautions that may prevent the recurrence of accidents (Tideiksaar & Silverton, 1989).

The causes of these falls are becoming well known, even to those who are the most vulnerable. In addition to diminished perceptual acuity, declining musculature, and distractability, osteoporosis is a particular source of injuries from falls. Osteoporosis is a disorder of the bones associated with calcium deficiency and characterized by increasing porosity and brittleness and decreased density in the bone mass. The physiology of postmenopausal women, as well as women's initial smaller bone mass, makes them more vulnerable than men to osteoporosis.

Physicians attempt to deal with osteoporosis primarily by prevention because there is little chance of restoring bone mass once it is gone. However, there has been little success in decreasing the incidence of osteoporosis-related injuries through diet and exercise (Larson & Shannon, 1984). But primarily, extreme caution, education, and the reduction of hazards in the environment are still the most important means of decreasing this problem. Because the fear of falling is realistic and of immediate serious concern, many elderly people are led to assume life-styles of restricted movement and activity.

FEAR OF SENSORY LOSS Diminished acuity of the senses, especially in hearing and vision, can be frightening to older persons. In their classic study, Butler and Lewis (1973) reported that the fear of anticipated hearing loss is widespread among the elderly, 80 percent of whom lose some hearing. The elders' understandable fear is that they will lose the capacity to participate fully in society (Fedinson, 1986). When small signs of hearing impairment are noted, many older people begin to think they will soon be unable to carry on normal conversations, hear the radio and television, or participate normally in human interactions without caretakers. The loss of visual acuity may be equally frightening because it suggests the end of independent living activities, such as driving cars, walking, reading, and attending various types of performances.

The fear is not only of the loss of vision, hearing, or whatever other senses are involved, but of the ability to interpret the environment accurately. It is through our senses that we obtain the information we need to assess the environment and know how to respond effectively to it. If the information we are getting is incomplete or distorted, our resulting decisions will not be reliable. In other words, the fear of loss of sensory acuity goes far beyond the senses themselves. As in the example of Mr. L, the bus driver with failing eyesight, the loss of vision lowered his self-esteem. For others, such as Mrs. W, an aging professional social worker, the loss also affected her clients and colleagues.

Mrs. W had worked in a large family service agency for forty years. Her love of her job as a social worker had not diminished even though her hearing had. She planned to continue, but communicating with clients was a growing problem. Even with a hearing aid, she was no longer able to pick up on the subtle sounds and nonverbal vocalizations from her clients that had formerly given her so much valuable information. Hence, she began to make incorrect diagnoses and treatment plans. Some clients became impatient with her frequent requests to repeat louder what they had said. Clients' complaints and requests to transfer to other workers became more common. The tension between Mrs. W and her colleagues escalated as her caseload lightened and theirs increased.

Eventually Mrs. W had to consider retirement. Her agency colleagues recognized, however, that her rich experience and highly developed skills would be lost to the agency if she did so. She, herself, realized that she would become depressed and isolated if she left the agency. All the workers at the agency agreed to an alternative plan. Mrs. W would leave direct practice to become a consultant and administrator. Her hearing was still good enough for these more formal exchanges. The decision proved to be a good one. In her new role, Mrs. W continued her important work and regained the respect of her colleagues.

The fear of sensory loss that many elders have can be minimized by skilled intervention. Social workers and other professionals can help in several ways. First, they can facilitate whatever medical treatment is necessary to correct the existing problems. A good diagnosis and medical treatment often lead to marked improvements and a commensurate reduction of fear. Second, they can help the older person learn all that is available about the problem of diminished sensory acuity and how to deal with and compensate for it. Fear is assuaged when it is tempered by knowledge of what the problem actually is and what can be done about it. Finally, they can help the client avoid generalizing about the acuity problem. Some hearing or vision loss is unlikely to mean eventual deafness or blindness. And older persons need to know that they can still retain their autonomy and ability to make proper decisions even when there is some sensory loss (Goldmeier, 1985).

THE FEAR OF CRIME The elderly are constantly reminded of their vulnerability to crime in news stories of older people being mugged, raped, or swindled out of a lifetime's savings. The stories are emphasized in the media, not to alarm the elderly, but because they get attention and awaken our sympathy for the elderly victims and our outrage at the perpetrators. Some news stories, especially those that describe how older people were cheated in financial schemes, are probably well-intentioned efforts to keep the elderly ever vigilant (Orzek & Loganbill, 1985).

Nevertheless, these stories may be more a disservice than a help. Even though there is some evidence that the elderly are no more likely to be victimized by crime than are other groups in the population (Lagrange & Ferraro, 1987b), such news stories heighten the fears of older people. Even if they are not more likely to be victimized by crime, many elderly people believe they are. This fear is especially great among older women, minority elderly people, and previous victims of crime (Lagrange & Ferraro, 1987a; Taylor & Chatters, 1986; Warr, 1984). And the consequences of a crime to an older person are usually more destructive than they are to a younger one. The recovery from the physical, emotional, economic, and social harm is usually slower and less certain for the elderly. Although crime itself is harmful, the fear of crime also victimizes the elderly. It keeps many of them housebound at a time when they need social contacts and stimulation. It feeds their suspicion and apprehensions about people when they increasingly need to put their trust in others. The case of Mrs. D is an example.

Mrs. D, aged 85, had so many locks on her doors that it took several minutes to open them. Social calls became such a production for her friends and family that they rarely visited her. Telling her that the extra locks were of little value in deterring a determined burglar only increased her anxiety. Her family was concerned about her isolation and about the danger she faced if she needed to exit or enter rapidly. With social work help arranged by the family, Mrs. D finally overcame some of her fears, and her home became more inviting to her friends and family.

The social workers's role in assuaging the fear of crime is fourfold: educating the older client about what the risks actually are; showing the client how to minimize those risks; enhancing the client's self-confidence and coping skills; and mobilizing groups of older people so they can, together, achieve more social integration and become less vulnerable to criminal activity (Orzek & Loganbill, 1985). Of course, the social worker's long-term indirect role—to facilitate social conditions that reduce the rate of crime and that provide opportunities for people so they will not engage in crimes to meet their needs—is also important.

FEAR OF IMPOVERISHMENT Most people over age 65 in the United States have been profoundly influenced by the Great Depression of the 1930s, when jobs were scarce, food and shelter were uncertain, and retirement-income security was unheard of. The quest for economic well-being has been a major preoccupation of this generation ever since. And the aged have made considerable progress in this quest; personal savings, work-related pension programs, and governmental income-security programs now provide much more economic well-being for more elderly people than ever before (England, 1987). In the past fifty years, the income-based poverty rate among older people has dropped from 75 percent to 15 percent (Brody & Brody, 1987). Nevertheless, the fear of poverty still weighs heavily on many older people (Maldonado, 1987).

It is a fear that is not entirely unfounded. While 15 percent of our elders are poor, another 5 percent are nearly at the poverty line. The poverty rate is much higher among some groups in the elderly population, especially women living alone and minorities. The poverty rate for blacks is 38 percent and for Hispanics, 26.6 percent (Maldonado, 1987). In the United States, more than two-thirds of older black women who live alone are poor (Brody & Brody, 1987; Maldonado, 1987).

In the United States, older people have largely come to depend upon the social security system to protect them from impoverishment. Financial planners estimate that 64 percent of preretirement income is needed to maintain one's standard of living even when no catastrophic situations occur. For most older Americans, personal savings and work-related pensions do not provide this income (Kilty, 1989). Thus, various social security programs now provide about 40 percent of all the income received by those over age 65. For some groups of elderly people, especially minorities and people who were "working poor" during their younger days, the programs provide up to 100 percent of their income (Gallo, Reichel, & Anderson, 1988).

Because of this reliance on the social security system, the economic concerns of older people are closely tied to the apparent health of the system and the benefits that can be derived from it. Yet, for the past several years, older people have been warned that the social security system is going broke or that the funds in its reserve will have to be used to reduce the federal budgetary deficit (Waxman, 1990). More recently governmental initiatives have reduced cost-of-living allowances and raised the income tax on benefits (Dentzer, 1990). Fears about impoverishment are heightened in such an atmosphere.

When the additional threat of the costs of catastrophic health care are considered, the elderly person's fears are further intensified (Torres-Gil, 1990). The costs of health care have skyrocketed in recent years, while funds available to elderly people have remained stable. Medicare has helped considerably, but it pays, on the average, only 48 percent of the elderly person's medical costs, only 55 percent of physicians' bills, and only 2 percent of nursing homes' bills. (Holzman, 1989).

Nursing home bills are especially frightening to older people. Costs in these facilities now average more than $22,000 per year. Two-thirds of the elderly who live alone would run out of their savings in thirteen weeks in nursing homes (Gallo et al., 1988). Many elderly people try to protect themselves from these risks by purchasing supplementary insurance. Yet they have found that "Medigap" insurance programs are themselves risky. Several insurance companies have been found to be misrepresenting their benefits, and thousands of insurance salespeople are convicted annually for defrauding elderly clients. It is estimated that the elderly spend up to $3 billion annually on health insurance that fails to cover the promised costs of long-term care. These problems are illustrated in the following case of Mr. and Mrs. B.

Mr. and Mrs. B considered themselves too proud and independent to let themselves become dependent upon their children or to become wards of the state. So after years of carefully managing their funds and saving for their retirement, they felt financially secure when that time came. Then Mrs. B was diagnosed with Alzheimer's disease. Within a few years of costly home care and then nursing homes, their savings were gone. The nursing home costs were even greater than their Medicare allowance and supplemental insurance. Eventually, Mrs. B was transferred to a lower-cost, publically subsidized long-term-care facility, and Mr. B moved into a public housing apartment. Mr. B says he no longer fears destitution—he has nothing to lose.

The role of the social worker or other helping professional in assuaging the financial fears of older people is important. Bringing the elderly in contact with administrators of the social security system, financial advisers, and reputable insurance agents is a start. Helping older people develop networks among themselves, where sound financial advice and opportunities are shared, is another step. In the long run, advocacy for better programs and stricter scrutiny or existing ones is also essential for social workers and their elderly clients.

FEAR OF MENTAL DECLINE OR PSYCHOPATHOLOGY The view among some people, including the elderly, is that the loss of mental faculties is inevitable as one gets older. Some believe it is remarkable to avoid senile dementia, Alzheimer's disease, depression, or neurosis. Obviously, such a view is wrong, but it is so widespread that it must be considered a form of "agism" that is based on ignorance and insensitivity. In fact, most older people do not become afflicted with mental disorders. If they occur, most psychopathologies, including schizophrenia, retardation, depression, neurosis, and substance abuse, tend to originate when people are younger (Duensing, 1988; Klemmack & Roff, 1984).

Although some forms of memory loss are expected in older people (Crook, Johnson, & Larrabee, 1986), the onset of organic mental disorders, including senile dementia and Alzheimer's disease, is not inevitable. Neither is the decline in overall cognitive functioning. The declines that do occur, and which improperly get lumped in with the loss of cognition, are frightening to some, but not as debilitating as are organic mental disorders. As was noted, declines are more likely to occur in perception, reaction time, and "fluid" intellectual functions, rather than in cognitive processes (Ford & Jarvik, 1979).

One of the tragedies of fears of this type is that of the self-fulfilling prophecy. If the older person believes that the loss of cognitive functions is inevitable, he or she may give up and fail to take the steps that are necessary to remain emotionally healthy (Meeks et al., 1990). This is what happened to Mrs. P.

At age 68, Mrs. P still worked productively and happily as a department store clerk. Only when the store became very busy did she have any difficulties. Then she noticed that she was more forgetful. She sometimes had trouble remembering where goods were located and whether she had yet received money from customers. Convinced that she was becoming senile, she got a checkup from her physician and an evaluation from her employers. Both were positive about her health and effectiveness and recommended that she continue working. Nevertheless she decided to retire. Predictably, she became more reclusive and less effective under stress than before.

The important role for the social worker or other helping professional in cases like this is to educate older persons about the high probability of their continued cognitive functioning. This education should also be extended to younger people, especially those who equate aging with inevitable cognitive deterioration. The social worker also helps older persons maintain and develop known sources of healthy mental functioning. Physical and social activities, the pursuit of goals, and work toward the well-being of others are important components of efforts to maintain mental health.

FEAR OF ABANDONMENT AND HELPLESSNESS Many older persons indicate that they are more afraid of being abandoned in a state of helpless dependence than anything else, including poverty, death, or dementia (Hess, 1987). The fear is of being isolated from family or friends, reduced to embarrassment or indignity in welfare institutions, and being vulnerable to abusive caregivers. It is often triggered by the deaths of loved ones and decrements of the sensorium.

Such fears are often related to life in highly mobilized societies as in the United States and Canada. In such nations families frequently become separated through vocationally forced relocations and other job opportunities, as well as through the desire for changed life-styles (Mullins, 1989). The high rate of divorce and the greater longevity of women also mean that a high proportion of older people spend their final years essentially alone. This has become a norm in our society, despite the need for older people to maintain social involvement (Erikson, Erikson, & Kivnak, 1986) and the feeling of belonging (Hamm, 1989).

Fears of abandonment are further magnified by justified concerns about elder abuse and abusive caregivers. Many older people fear being forced into dependence in facilities where they will be harmed. Others fear becoming helpless and burdensome to family members who may mistreat them. With increasing frequency, these fears are justified. Many family members, as well as employees of hospitals, nursing homes, and aged care facilities, have been convicted of elder abuse (Scogin, 1989).

In elder abuse, "caregivers" harm their elderly charges through overt violence, threats, and neglect. The overt abuse may be physical, psychological, financial, legal, verbal, or sexual (Gallo et al., 1988). Subjecting elders to humiliation, whether intentional or not, is considered a form of abuse, as is treating them as children. The incidence of elder abuse is not known with much accuracy (Johnson, 1989). However, reports of its occurrence have increased greatly in the past decade, leading many older people to becoming frightened about the possibility of being placed in such situations. Unlike children, the competent elderly can take part in decisions about their own treatment, but often are afraid to do so (Korbin, Guttman, & Lee, 1989). They fear that their abusive family members will subject them to even more violence or place them in public facilities. From nonfamily caregivers, they fear neglect, isolation, and the embarrassment of needing help from strangers.

Reducing such fears is challenging for social workers and other helping professionals because it necessitates some form of help for or control over the caregiver. Studies show that the cause of elder abuse is related more to stress and emotional problems within the caregiver than to the behavior of the elderly person (Pillemer & Finkelhov, 1989). And unless the elderly person reports the abuse, the professional has little opportunity to help the abuser. The threat of retaliation probably keeps most victims quiet about their plights.

FEAR OF ILLNESS Closely associated with the fear of abandonment is the older person's concern about becoming physically ill. This is the fear of facing the pain, discomfort, indignity, financial hardship, inconvenience, and incapacitation of sickness. Although only 5 percent of the elderly are maintained in nursing homes or other institutions, 86 percent of all people over age 65 have one or more chronic health problems that require increasing hospitalizations, medical expenditures, and family caregiving to maintain their daily functioning (Walsh, 1989). For older people, even those who are relatively healthy, the threat of illness is a justifiable ongoing concern.

Some concern stems from the perceived inability to obtain a correct medical diagnosis and to receive the proper treatment. Most medical textbooks on treating the elderly indicate that it is necessary to take more time and evaluate more systems, even those that don't seem relevant to the identified symptoms (Gallo et al., 1988). The older person's impaired hearing, sight, mobility, and comprehension require a more patient and deliberate approach in the medical examination. Even so, studies show that physicians tend to spend less time with their older patients (Keeler, Manning, Newhouse, Sloss, & Wasserman, 1982).

Some physicians are indifferent to or feel helpless diagnosing and treating the elderly. To them it is normal for an old person to be sick. Perhaps this is why elderly people enjoy the story of the old man who complained about pain in his left elbow. After a brief examination, his physician shrugged and said, "Well, what do you expect for an 85-year-old man?" "But doctor," the man exclaimed, "my right elbow is 85 too, and it feels fine!"

HYPOCHONDRIASIS One reason older people get less medical attention than they need is related to hypochondriasis, a mental disorder that stems from an intense fear of physical illness. Hypochondriasis is the preoccupation with the details of one's bodily functions and concern about the possibility of having some disease. In DSM-III-R, it is classified as one of the "somatoform" disorders (a mental disorder with the appearance of a physical illness, but, lacking any known organic basis, is generally thought to be psychogenic). Of all the mental disorders that afflict the elderly, hypochondriasis is among the most prevalent (Bergman, 1978).

Hypochondriacal individuals of all ages present symptoms to physicians and medical care centers, but tend to distrust their physicians and the advice they are given. They are reluctant to accept reassurances of well-being and often go from one physician to another in quest of someone who will confirm their fears (Kellner, Abbott, Winslow, & Pathak, 1987). These hypochondriacal complaints, especially from older people, tend to provoke extremely negative feedback from physicians and others. Since part of the underlying reason for seeking the medical advice is attention and the reduction of anxiety, the resulting rejection is a catalyst for the formation of additional symptoms and efforts to get further medical attention.

When hypochondriasis or the extreme fear of illness arises for the first time late in life, it must be viewed with more concern and less antipathy than when it appears in younger people. Its appearance in older people often indicates actual physical or mental health problems that are unrelated to the presenting symptoms. It often indicates depression, the increased risk of suicide, or some serious underlying physical disease of which the older client is unaware (Bergman, 1978).

Hypochondriasis and the fear of illness may seem useful to some elderly people, temporarily at least, in serving a psychological function (Blum & Weiner, 1979). The fear of illness may be a displacement of anxiety away from a more fearsome object. These greater threats may include all the specific fears delineated earlier, plus those of death and rejection by society. Older people, especially those with strong religious beliefs, are more inclined to deny their fear of death than are younger people (Thorson & Powell, 1989; Westman, 1984). A more apparent fear, that of anticipated rejection by society, is what many older people expect because of their reduced proficiency, curtailed activity, declining social status, and exposure to agism. Another psychological function of hypochondriasis is to permit older persons to express anger at their caregivers and others in ways that seem less likely to result in abusive responses. The older person usually cannot fight back directly against actual or perceived mistreatment, but can cause the caregiver considerable inconvenience through the feigned illness (Blum & Weiner, 1979). The hypochondriac usually does so unconsciously, but sometimes is well aware of the motives for his or her hypochondriacal complaints. In the long run, however, such behavior results in even more stress in the caregiver, which increases the risk of abuse (Pillemer & Finkelhov, 1989).

PHOBIC DISORDERS IN OLDER PEOPLE

All the fears discussed thus far are based on actual and imminent threats that confront most older people. The phobic disorders, on the other hand, are a special type of fear, based not on direct or immediate threats, but on an overload of general anxiety that gets displaced onto a specific catalyst. They include the social phobias, the panic disorders, and agoraphobia.

Social Phobias

Social phobia is an intense fear of being observed, evaluated, or harmed in some social encounter. The anxiety is activated when one is compelled to enter any situation where poor performance in public will result in humiliation. Sufferers of social phobias most commonly fear public speaking, using public bathing facilities, dining in restaurants, or being embarrassed in front of others. Basically they are afraid to reveal how anxious they are, a concern that usually leads to the very outcome they feared.

Social phobia usually begins during one's sensitive and self-conscious preadolescent years. However, many people over age 65 become afraid of public scrutiny for the first time. Physicians, caregivers, and mental health professionals often note the high number of older people who become extremely modest and reticent about self-disclosure. Some elderly persons find it excruciatingly difficult to submit to physical or mental-status examinations or psychotherapy.

Social phobias are not thought to be incapacitating in younger people. For most, their worst effect is their interference with vocational advancement or achieving various goals in social relationships. However, in elders they may contribute to other problems that have serious consequences. These phobias prevent elders from presenting themselves for needed help. They cause caregivers to believe the elders are uncooperative. Needed physical examinations are avoided and when they finally do take place, the information disclosed is often minimal or inaccurate.

It is not difficult to understand why elderly persons develop social phobias. No one who experiences diminished self-esteem, uncertainty about new roles, and the distrust of one's senses and perceptions relishes being scrutinized by others and possibly judged negatively. But these newer sources of anxiety are added to those that already exist. Older persons have trouble displacing sources of new anxiety because many of their physical and psychological adaptive systems are already operating at or near capacity. When new stressors occur, additional burdens lead the adaptive mechanisms to find some form of escape. The most convenient form of escape is avoidance, especially in those realms where others may be observing.

Panic Disorders

Another type of fear-anxiety reaction are the panic disorders. The victims of this illness unexpectedly experience discrete periods of intense fear or discomfort for which there is no known overt source of threat or public scrutiny. The name is derived from the Greek god Pan, who was always nervous and moody; whenever he was unexpectedly disturbed, he'd jump and scream with such intensity that he and everyone who heard him were terrorized. Their resulting fear was called "panic." Nowadays, victims of this malady react similarly, with intense startle reactions that are far out of proportion to the presenting stimuli.

When panic occurs, a variety of physical symptoms are manifested. These symptoms may include shortness of breath, dizziness, faintness, palpitations, tachycardia, trembling, sweating, choking, nausea, hot flashes, chest pain, and the fear of dying or going crazy (DSM-III-R).

Panic disorders occur frequently in the general population, and some studies have found that up to 6.5 percent of patients in the medical care system could be diagnosed this way. Women with this diagnosis in the medical care system outnumber men three to one, although this ratio may be due more to men's greater reluctance to avail themselves of health services for anxiety-related symptoms (Katon, 1989). Among older people the incidence rates are proportionate to the general population.

Panic disorders develop in three stages. An older person may experience the first attack after confronting a series of life stresses or threats. Because it is new, unanticipated, and apparently unrelated to immediate environmental situations, the experience can be overwhelmingly frightening. After settling down, the elder hopes there will not be a recurrence and tries to forget about it. If it can't be forgotten, and usually if the stressors continue unabated, the second stage in the panic disorder occurs.

In the second stage, the panic attacks increase, and the elder begins to avoid situations in which such experiences may be anticipated. Fears about specific risks intensify and phobias develop. For example, the elder who has an attack while visiting his or her grandchildren may become anxious later when invited for a subsequent visit. Eventually the elder feels compelled to avoid other family members. Then friends, neighbors, and strangers are avoided, and the elder's life becomes progressively constricted (Katon, 1989).

In the third stage, the avoidance behavior becomes further intensified until the elder is almost completely housebound. For a while the older person can still do things, such as travel unaccompanied, but only if it is considered imperative to do so. Many older people give up their jobs at this point, rationalizing that it is time to retire anyway. They may seek treatment from physicians and therapists, but they often do not continue their treatment because it involves leaving home (Rapee & Barlow, 1988). Eventually, the avoidance behavior becomes so pervasive that the elder relies on others to perform needed public functions and then cannot leave home at all. This is the full-fledged state of agoraphobia.

Agoraphobia

The most common phobia is agoraphobia (Thompson et al., 1988). Among all people with phobic disorders, young and old, about half suffer from agoraphobia. It is difficult to know the extent of this disturbance in older people because professionals tend to attribute many other physical and mental disorders to it. Nevertheless, many housebound elderly people who fear entering the outside world are indeed agoraphobics.

For the diagnosis to be justified, it is first necessary to rule out all other possible causes of this behavioral pattern. It is especially important to consider somatic symptoms, such as hyperventilation, irritable bowel syndrome, muscle tension, headaches, and tachycardia (Fava, Kellner, Zielezny, & Grandi, 1988). When such symptoms reveal physical illness, rather than hypochondriasis, the elder may well be in self-imposed isolation for fear of personal catastrophe, such as having a heart attack or losing control of bowel or bladder function. If physical causes are eliminated, it is still necessary to rule out other forms of psychopathology. Depression and suicidal ideation often result in isolationist behavior (Krause, 1986; see also Chapters 10 and 20). Substance abuse disorders, post-traumatic stress disorder, and paranoid disorders also are frequently associated with homebound isolation (see Chapters 7, 16, 17, and 19). Only after any of these existing conditions are treated would it be worthwhile to undertake specific therapy for agoraphobia.

The onset of agoraphobia may be gradual or sudden. Even though the average age of onset is 26, many elderly people develop it for the first time (Luchins & Rose, 1989). When its development is gradual, the sufferer is likely to have had episodes of phobia or panic disorder at a younger age. When it occurs suddenly, it is likely to follow an identifiable precipitating event.

In the sudden onset of agoraphobia, common precipitating events may be sudden losses of loved ones or frightening experiences. Some studies have found an association between the recent loss of relationships with significant adults, which causes intense separation anxiety, and the onset of agoraphobia (Gittelman & Klein, 1985). More studies have associated its onset with such traumas as falling down in a publicly conspicuous place, forgetting where the car was parked and requiring help from passersby, or publicly experiencing somatic symptoms that alarm observers as well as the elder. The older person then goes home, ruminates about the episode, imagines horrific scenarios that may accompany similar attacks in the future, and eventually refuses to enter situations in which these experiences occurred or could eventually take place.

Most theorists believe that the episode, by itself, is not sufficient to cause the subsequent fear and isolation. Instead, the episode is the last straw following anxiety about other stressors and major life events, especially those involving separation and interpersonal conflict (Pollard, Pollard, & Corn, 1989).

TREATMENT APPROACHES FOR FEARS AND PHOBIAS

The treatment of fears and phobias in the elderly is similar but not identical to the treatment of these conditions in younger people (Myers & Salmon, 1984). In all age groups, the goals of treatment are to reduce anxiety and to instill in the client a sense of worth and meaning. When anxiety is replaced by self-esteem and the sense of continued purpose, fears and phobias will also be replaced (Roy-Byrne & Katon, 1987; Waters, 1984).

Therapists don't agree on the best ways to achieve these goals, especially in work with the elderly (Myers & Salmon, 1984). The major therapy orientations, including the existential, psychopharmacological, psychosocial-systems and cognitive-behavioral schools have different approaches. However, the disapprobation that once existed among these schools has lately given way to more reciprocal respect and even some exchange techniques (Michaelson, Mavissakalian, & Marchione, 1988).

The existential orientation has probably paid more attention to the treatment needs of the elderly than it has to other populations. Existentialists report success through such techniques as life review and reminiscence therapy, logotherapy, and finding ways to fill the "existential vacuum." An example of this approach is seen in the following account of existential social work with Mrs. A.

Mrs. A came to the social worker with crying spells, loss of energy, boredom, and the feeling that something was missing in her life. She said she had spent most of her time since retirement and her husband's death alone watching television. She had little social life and few interests and seemed only to be waiting to die. Although she had an adequate income, she was worried about the costs of therapy. The worker scheduled her for weekly treatment at a reduced fee provided she would "pay" for part of her treatment by doing volunteer work at a local settlement house. After only six sessions, Mrs. A terminated treatment, saying she needed more time for the settlement house. She had renewed energy and interests because meaning had been restored to her life by performing meaningful work (Lantz & Pegram, 1989).

In the psychopharmacological approach, the prevailing view is that there is a biophysiological and genetic predisposition in anxiety and that medication, combined with some form of psychotherapy, is most effective for countering any dysfunction. The National Institute of Mental Health identified three classes of effective medication for problems of this type. Tricyclic antidepressants, benzodiazepines (tranquilizers), and monoamine oxidase inhibitors (MAOs) all are efficient with some patients, if the dosages are correct and are maintained correctly and if the side effects are limited (Katon, 1989; Robinson, 1982). Because many fearful older people develop anticipatory anxiety, these medications may permit them to experience the dreaded stimulus in a relatively relaxed way. They gradually lose their fear of the discomfort around that stimulus and can devote their psychic energies to healthier endeavors.

In the psychosocial-systems orientation of treatment, the premise is that the underlying anxiety is the result of intrapsychic or interpersonal conflict that is reduced through catharsis, self-understanding, increased knowledge, better access to social resources, enhanced communication among family members, and environmental modification. In these treatment approaches the client dissipates his or her existing anxiety and wards off new sources of it by eliminating conflict and developing more effective defenses against new anxieties. The psychosocial treatment approach was chosen for Mr. G, as in the following case example.

Mr. G, a 73-year-old man, came to a mental health center because of his intensifying fear of pain and sickness. He was placed in a therapy group that consisted of seven other elderly people who shared similiar symptoms. Mr. G enjoyed the group and its discussions about the members' various life experiences. The group helped him remember his own childhood encounters with his grandmother who lived with his family. As his grandmother grew older, she suffered agonizingly painful arthritis until she died. Mr. G remembered hating his grandmother and wishing for her death. When she died, his guilt made the conscious memory intolerable, and it was

repressed for the next sixty years. Once the group helped him uncover his memory. Mr. G was able to look more rationally at his
current fears and control them more effectively.

Despite the results in this case, empirical evidence of the efficacy of the
psychosocial orientation has not been established, even though most of the
techniques used in this orientation are considered essential supplements in
the other orientations. For example, those who prescribe medication for
treating these anxiety-fear disorders indicate the need for accompanying
psychotherapy to help clients learn to cope with subsequent stress and to
improve their self-esteem (Thomlison & Rinehart, 1989).

In the cognitive-behavioral orientation, the success in treating phobias is
well established (Michaelson et al., 1988). Behaviorally oriented therapists say that overall anxiety is reduced by helping the client gain control
over the specific fear. Once this problem is extinguished, the client can
address other specific problems, if necessary, until the target goals are
reached.

The techniques that cognitive-behavioral therapists commonly use for
clients in all age groups include systematic desensitization, guided imagery,
progressive relaxation, modeling, flooding, and cognitive modification.
Clients of cognitive-oriented therapists deal with their fears by considering
them rationally, systematically looking at all components of the fear stimulus,
considering alternative behaviors that can lead to the resolution of their
fears, and implementing behaviors that have been chosen as being most
likely to achieve the desired results (Clark, 1986; Heimberg, Becker, Goldfinger, & Vermilyea, 1985).

The most frequently used behavioral technique in the treatment of phobic
disorders is systematic desensitization (Rapee & Barlow, 1988). The client
is first taught how to self-induce relaxation. Self-induced relaxation can be
achieved through progressive muscle relaxation, in which the client tenses
and relaxes muscle groups in a systematic pattern, and through guided
imagery, in which the therapist helps the client picture pleasant imaginary
scenes to be used when confronted with stress.

In the systematic desensitization procedure, the client rates the degree to
which various objects or situations that are relevant to the phobic stimulus
provoke anxiety. The therapist then exposes the client to these stimuli, while
using the relaxation and imagery exercises. For example, if the client is
afraid of heights over six feet, the therapist encourages the client to stand
on the lowest rung of a stepladder while imagining some pleasant experiences

long enough for anxiety to end at that level. This process is repeated slowly until the client is comfortable at levels higher than six feet.

A social worker with a behavioral orientation helped Mrs. Y by using systematic desensitization.

Mrs. Y presented with a diagnosis of pyrophobia, among other disturbances. This fear of fire was obviously related to her experience the previous year with a fire in her retirement apartment complex in which one of her fellow residents had been trapped and killed. The therapist helped Mrs. Y identify a reasonable goal, that of seeing and being around fire without undue discomfort. A gradual progression of steps toward this goal were identified. They included (1) watching a television program that showed a family by a fireplace, (2) watching a videotape of a fireplace (for increasing lengths of time), (3) holding an unlighted match, (4) lighting a match, (5) lighting a pilot light on a gas range, (6) building a fire in a fireplace, (7) watching a videotape showing a burning house, and (8) watching a videotape of firemen rescuing people from a burning building. Each step was accompanied by associations with pleasant stimuli. Movement to the next step was not undertaken until Mrs. Y had achieved a specified degree of comfort. Once she had overcome the intensity of this fear, the therapist went on to work with her on other presenting symptoms.

The behavioral approaches of modeling, flooding, and stress induction have also helped many clients, but they must be used cautiously in work with the elderly. In flooding and stress induction, the therapist brings the client into direct or imagined contact with the feared object. The client remains in this contact, without being able to withdraw, until he or she presumably is inured to the feared object or situation (Jacobs & Nadel, 1985). Such an aversive form of treatment may be useful for a younger, stronger, more supported client, but it may be more than many older people can tolerate healthily. Modeling, on the other hand, can be ideal for the older person. In this technique, the client is placed in situations with opportunities to imitate the behavior of other persons who have successfully coped with specified risks.

ADAPTING TREATMENT APPROACHES TO THE ELDERLY

Social workers and therapists who work with the fearful elderly find that they can use any of these treatment orientations with as much success as they achieve with younger people. However, they may emphasize certain aspects of their therapy and make some accommodations to suit the unique circumstances and needs of the elderly client (Woods & Britton, 1985). Some of the more important accommodations are as follows.

1. Before any kind of therapy is attempted, a thorough evaluation and accurate assessment are essential. Although a therapist may competently proceed to work exclusively on the fears and phobias of a younger person, such is not the case with older clients. It is almost inevitable that an older client who presents symptoms of fear or phobia is suffering from additional dysfunctions that may be physical or psychogenic (Blum & Weiner, 1979).

2. The focus of the assessment should not be confined to the client's potential mental and physical disorders, as it often is with younger, less fearful clients. Influences that may be as great or greater than the physiological and mental ones include personal values, economic factors, religious orientations, the family support system, and the client's sociocultural history.

3. In getting the information needed to develop an accurate assessment and treatment plan, the therapist should not rely only on the elderly client, but should acquire data from family members, friends, caretakers, physicians, and as many others as possible (Kane & Kane, 1981). Even if the fearful older client has an excellent memory and other cognitive functions, one cannot rely solely on the accuracy of the information thus obtained. The fearful older client will often be extremely modest and reticent about self-disclosure. When there are sensory losses, the older client may misunderstand the questions and try to conceal that fact by offering convenient but inaccurate answers.

4. The environment and circumstances in which fearful elderly clients are interviewed must take account of their special needs. Fatigue, distractability, and guardedness are likely in these clients. Thus, offices that permit little or no distraction are important. It would be even better to conduct the interviews in the clients' homes or similar familiar settings (Burton, 1985; Wasson et al., 1984). It is usually preferable to have shorter, more

frequent sessions than would be the case with younger, less frightened clients.

5. All the concerns expressed by the fearful elderly client should be addressed when raised. With clients who are fearful about illness, including hypochondriacs, considerable time should be devoted to explaining the exact meaning and nature of the symptoms. The client has the right to be told, when asked, exactly why the information is needed and to what use it will be put (Lezak, 1988).

6. Most of the fears faced by elderly clients do not indicate psychopathology or organic dysfunction. The same threats would be equally frightening to younger people. To seek to eliminate the fears by trying to improve only the elder's emotional well-being is to deny that such threats exist. It is a form of "blaming the victim."

7. In the treatment of older people's fears and phobias, group approaches have been shown to have considerable worth. Only older fearful clients who suffer dementias or who are still too distractable do not do well in groups (Waters, 1984). The therapy techniques that yield good results for older fearful people are usually done in groups of similar older people or sometimes mixed-generation groups. Forms of therapy of this type are life review, peer counseling, reality therapy, remotivation, milieu therapy, and multiple-impact family therapy.

8. In group or individual psychotherapy with the fearful older person, the professional supplements the intrapsychic therapy with efforts to enhance the client's social support system. There is considerable evidence that the fears and anxieties of an older person are assuaged more by the knowledge that he or she is still connected with others who care about them (Walsh, 1989).

GERONTOPHOBIA

One other type of phobia seriously affects older people, perhaps with more harm than all the other kinds combined. In this condition it isn't the elderly who seem afraid, but those who come in contact with them. The phobia has been called "gerontophobia," or sometimes "gerophobia." It is the fear of old people, of being around them, of being discomforted in any way by their mere existence. Of course, it stems, in part, from the individual's fear of growing old and from his or her attempts to deny that probability.

It is a disease that seems to afflict an increasing number of young people. It has the same root cause as that of prejudice and discrimination against other groups. The basic cause of prejudice against racial and ethnic minorities, homosexuals, women, and the elderly is ignorance, frustration about the inability to achieve goals and the accompanying wish to blame someone for it, and feelings of personal inadequacy.

Ignorance about any identifiable group is due largely to separation or isolation. A growing trend in Western society is the separation of and minimal communication among generations. Studies have found that adult children avoid conversations, especially, frank discussions, with their elderly parents (Synge, 1988). Rarely do families of more than two generations live together. Instead, there is the proliferation of apartments and whole towns exclusively for older people. Social events tend to be strikingly homogeneous as to the ages of participants. In the news-entertainment media, the recent trend is toward "narrowcasts," so that every age group has its own television and radio programs and printed matter.

Thus, people have fewer opportunities to gain from and enjoy the unique wisdom and experience of elderly people. Instead, they are confronted mostly with negative stereotypes. Those who are afflicted with gerontophobia come to think of the elderly only as people who are ugly, unpleasant, senile, unhealthy, and bothersome.

Treatment for this disease is as much the responsibility of social workers and other helping professionals as is the treatment of the other phobic disorders. It involves the same techniques that are used for the other phobias, including anxiety reduction, self-esteem building, education, gradual exposure to the fear stimulus, and encouraging more opportunities for interpersonal contacts among the generations.

BIBLIOGRAPHY

Barker, R. L. (1989). Anxiety states and related disorders. In F. J. Turner (Ed.), *Child psychopathology* (pp. 179–211). New York: Free Press.

Barker, R. L. (1991). *The social work dictionary* (2nd ed.). Silver Spring, MD: National Association of Social Workers.

Barry, J. (1988). Autobiographical writing: An effective tool for practice with the oldest old. *Social Work, 33,* 449–451.

Bergman, A. (1978). Neurosis and personality disorder in old age. In A. D. Isaacs & F. Post (Eds.), *Studies in geriatric psychiatry* (pp. 41–75). New York: John Wiley & Sons.

Bernstein, A. B., & Schur, C. L. (1990). Expenditures for unintentional injuries among the elderly. *Journal of Aging and Health, 2,* 157–178.

Birren, J. E., & Zarit, J. M. (1985). Concepts of health, behavior and aging. In

J. E. Birren & J. Livingston (Eds.), *Cognition, stress, and aging* (pp. 2–20). Englewood Cliffs, NJ: Prentice-Hall.

Blum, J. E., & Weiner, M. B. (1979). Neurosis in the older adult. In O. J. Kaplan (Ed.), *Psychopathology of aging* (pp. 167–195). New York: Academic Press.

Brady, A. B. (1985). Death is forever: Living is now. *Psychotherapy Patient, 2,* 135–138.

Bratter, B. (1986). Peer counseling for older adults. *Generations, 110*(3), 49–50.

Brody, E. M., & Brody, S. J. (1987). Aged: Services. In *Encyclopedia of social work* (18th ed., Vol. 1, pp. 106–122). Silver Spring, MD: National Association of Social Workers.

Burton, J. R. (1985). The house call: An important service for the frail elderly. *Journal of the American Geriatrics Society, 33,* 291–293.

Butler, R. N., & Lewis, M. (1973). Aging and mental health: Positive approaches. St. Louis, MO: C. V. Mosby.

Clark, D. A. (1986). Cognitive approach to panic. *Behaviour Research and Therapy, 24,* 461–470.

Croake, J. W., Myers, K. M., & Singh, A. (1988). The fear expresed by elderly men and women: A lifespan approach. *International Journal of Aging and Human Development, 26,* 139–146.

Crook, T., Johnson, B. A., & Larrabee, G. J. (1986). Age-associated memory impairment: Proposed diagnostic criteria and Measures of Clinical Change. *Developmental Neuropsychology, 2,* 261–276.

Dentzer, S. (1990, July 23). The elderly fight back. *U.S. News & World Report,* pp. 46–50.

Duensing, E. E. (Ed.). (1988). *America's elderly: A sourcebook.* New Brunswick, NJ: Center for Urban Policy Research, Rutgers, the State University.

England, R. (1987, March 2). Greener era for gray America. *Insight, 3,* 8–11.

Erikson, E. H., Erikson, J. M., & Kivnak, H. Q. (1986). *Vital involvement in old age: The experience of old age in our time.* New York: W. W. Norton.

Fava, G. A., Kellner, R., Zielezny, M., & Grandi, S. (1988). Hypochondriacal fears and beliefs in agoraphobia. *Journal of Affective Disorders, 14,* 239–244.

Fedinson, M. C. (1986). The distribution of distress among elderly people. *Journal of Gerontology, 41,* 225–233.

Ford, C. V., & Jarvik, L. F. (1979). Genetic aspects of psychopathological disorders in later life. In O. J. Kaplan (Ed.), *Psychopathology of the aging* (pp. 7–28). New York: Academic Press.

Fry, P. S. (1986). *Depression, stress and adaptations in the elderly.* Rockville, MD: Aspen.

Gallo, J. J., Reichel, W., & Anderson, L. (1988). *Handbook of geriatric assessment.* Rockville, MD: Aspen.

Gittelman, R., & Klein, D. F. (1985). Childhood separation anxiety and adult agoraphobia. In A. H. Tuma & J. J. Maser (Eds.), *Anxiety and the anxiety disorders* (pp. 167–187). Hillsdale, NJ: Lawrence Erlbaum Associates.

Goldmeier, J. (1985). Helping the elderly in times of stress. *Social Casework: The Journal of Contemporary Social Work, 66,* 323–332.

Hamm, A. O. (1989). Fear conditioning, meaning and belongingness: A selective association analysis. *Journal of Abnormal Psychology, 98,* 395–406.

Harel, J. (1988). Coping with extreme stress and aging. *Social Casework: The Journal of Contemporary Social Work, 69,* 575–583.

Heckenmueller, J. (1985). Cognitive control and endorphins as mechanisms of health. In J. E. Birren & J. Livingston (Eds.), *Cognition, stress, and aging* (pp. 89–110). Englewood Cliffs, NJ: Prentice-Hall.

Heimberg, R. G., Becker, R. E., Goldfinger, K., & Vermilyea, J. A. (1985). Treatment of social phobia by exposure, cognitive restructuring, and homework assignments. *Journal of Nervous and Mental Disease, 173,* 236–245.

Hess, N. (1987). King Lear and some anxieties of old age. *British Journal of Medical Psychology, 60,* 209–215.

Holzman, D. (1989, January 26). Closing Medicare's coverage gaps. *Insight, 5,* 52–53.

Hooyman, N. R., & Lustbader, W. (1986). *Taking care: Supporting older people and their families.* New York: Free Press.

Jacobs, W. J., & Nadel, L. (1985). Stress induced recovery of fears and phobias. *Psychological Review, 925,* 12–31.

Johnson, T. F. (1989). Elder mistreatment identification instruments: Finding common ground. *Journal of Elder Neglect and Abuse, 1,* 15–36.

Kane, R. A., & Kane, R. L. (1981). *Assessing the elderly: A practical guide to measurement.* Lexington, MA: Lexington Books.

Katon, W. (1989). *Panic disorder in a medical setting.* Rockville, MD: National Institute of Mental Health.

Keeler, E. B., Manning, W. G., Newhouse, J. P., Sloss, E. M., & Wasserman, J. (1982). Effect of patient age on duration of medical encounters with physicians. *Medical Care, 20,* 1101–1108.

Kellner, R., Abbott, P., Winslow, W. W., & Pathak, D. (1987). Fears, beliefs and attitudes in DSM-III hypochondriasis. *Journal of Nervous and Mental Disease, 120,* 25–31.

Kilty, K. (1989). Social security, private resources and the economic security of older Americans. *Journal of Aging Studies, 4,* 97–109.

Klemmack, D. L., & Roff, L. L. (1984). Fear of personal aging and subjective well-being in later life. *Journal of Gerontology, 39,* 756–758.

Korbin, J. E., Guttman, D., & Lee, S. (1989). Elder abuse and child abuse: A consideration of similarities and differences in intergenerational family violence. *Journal of Elder Abuse and Neglect, 1*(4), 1–14.

Krause, N. (1986). Life stress as a correlate of depression among older adults. *Psychiatry Research, 18,* 227–237.

Labouvie-Vief, G., & Hakim-Larson, J. (1989). Developmental shifts in adult thought. In S. Hunter & M. Sundel (Eds.), *Midlife myths* (pp. 69–96). Newbury Park, CA: Sage.

Lagrange, R. L., & Ferraro, K. F. (1987a). Assessing age and gender differences in perceived risk and fear of crime. *Criminology, 27,* 697–719.

Lagrange, R. L., & Ferraro, K. F. (1987b). The elderly's fear of crime: A critical examination of the research. *Research on Aging, 9,* 372–391.

Lantz, J., & Pegram, M. (1989). Casework and the restoration of meaning. *Journal of Social Casework, 70,* 549–555.

Larson, K. A., & Shannon, S. C. (1984). Decreasing the incidence of osteoporosis-related injuries through diet and exercise. *Public Health Reports, 99,* 609–613.

Lezak, M. D. (1988). Neuropsychological assessment. In L. Teril & P. M. Lewinsohn (Eds.), *Geropsychological assessment and treatment* (pp. 3–38). New York: Springer.

Luchins, D. J., & Rose, R. P. (1989). Late life onset of panic disorder with agoraphobia in 13 patients. *American Journal of Psychiatry, 14,* 920–921.

Malatesta, V. I. (1989). Misdiagnosis of geriatric agoraphobia: A case of urinary incontinence. *Clinical Gerontologist, 8*(3), 36–45.

Maldonado, D. (1987). Aged. In *Encyclopedia of Social Work* (18th ed., Vol. 1, pp. 95–106). Silver Spring, MD: National Association of Social Workers.

Meeks, S., Carstensen, L. L., Stafford, P. B., Brenner, L. L., Weathers, F., Welch, R., & Oltmeyers, T. F. (1990). Mental health needs of the chronically mentally ill elderly. *Psychology and Aging, 5,* 163–171.

Michaelson, L., Mavissakalian, M., & Marchione, K. (1988). Cognitive correlates and outcome of cognitive, behavioral and physiological treatments of agoraphobia. *Psychological Reports, 63,* 999–1004.

Mullins, L. C. (1989). Emotional and social isolation among elderly Canadian seasonal migrants in Florida: An empirical analysis of a conceptual typology. *Journal of Gerontological Social Work, 14,* 111–130.

Myers, J. E., & Salmon, H. E. (1984). Counseling programs for older persons: Status, shortcomings and potentialities. *Counseling Psychologist, 12*(2) 39–53.

Orzek, A. M., & Loganbill, C. (1985). Treatment strategies for fear of crime among the elderly. *Clinical Gerontologist, 4*(1) 17–29.

Pillemer, K., & Finkelhov, D. (1989). Causes of elder abuse: Caregiving stress vs. problem relatives. *American Journal of Orthopsychiatry, 59,* 179–187.

Pollard, C. A., Pollard, H. J., & Corn, K. J. (1989). Panic onset and major events in lives of agoraphobics. *Journal of Abnormal Psychology, 98,* 318–321.

Powell, W. E. (Ed). (1988). Life transitions in the elderly: A special issue. *Social Casework, The Journal of Contemporary Social Work, 69,* 539–592.

Rapee, R. M., & Barlow, D. H. (1988). Panic disorder: Cognitive-behavioral treatment. *Psychiatric Annals, 18,* 473–477.

Robinson, D. S. (1982). Monoamine oxidase inhibitors in the elderly. In C.

Eisdorfer & W. E. Fann (Eds.), *Treatment of psychopathology in the aged* (pp. 1–8). New York: Springer.

Roy-Byrne, P. P., & Katon, W. (1987). An update on the treatment of the anxiety disorders. *Hospital and Community Psychiatry, 38,* 835–843.

Scogin, F. (1989). Training for abusive caregivers: An unconventional approach to intervention dilemma. *Journal of Elder Abuse and Neglect, 1*(4), 73–86.

Synge, J. (1988). Avoided conversations: How parents and children delay talking about widowhood and dependency in later life. *Ageing and Society, 8,* 321–335.

Taylor, R. J., & Chatters, L. M. (1986). Patterns of informal support to elderly black adults: Family, friends, and church members. *Social Work, 31,* 432–439.

Thomlison, R. J. (1984). Phobic disorders. In F. J. Turner (Ed.), *Adult psychopathology: A social work perspective* (pp. 280–315). New York: Free Press.

Thomlison, R. J., & Rinehart, K. (1989). Phobic disorders. In F. J. Turner (Ed.), *Child psychopathology: A social work perspective* (pp. 213–237). New York: Free Press.

Thompson, J. W., Burns, B. J., Bartko, J., Boyd, J. H., Taube, C. A., & Bourdin, K. H. (1988). The use of ambulatory services by persons with and without phobia. *Medical Care, 26,* 183–198.

Thorson, J. A., & Powell, F. C. (1989). Death anxiety and religion in an older male sample. *Psychological Reports, 64,* 985–986.

Tideiksaar, R., & Silverton, R. (1989). Psychological characteristics of older people who fall. *Clinical Gerontologist, 8*(3), 80–83.

Tinetti, M. E., Speechly, M., & Ginter, S. A. (1988). Risk factors for falls among elderly persons living in the community. *New England Journal of Medicine, 319,* 1701–1707.

Torres-Gil, F. (1990). Seniors react to the Medicare Catastrophe Bill: Equity or selfishness. *Journal of Aging and Social Policy, 2,* 1–8.

Walsh, F. (1989). The family in later life. In B. Carter & M. McGoldrick (Eds.), *The changing family life cycle* (2nd ed., pp. 311–334). Boston: Allyn & Bacon.

Warr, M. (1984). Fear of victimization: Why are women and the elderly more afraid? *Social Science Quarterly, 65,* 681–702.

Wasson, W., Ripeckyj, A., Lazarus, L. W., Kupferer, S., & Force, F. (1984). Home evaluation of psychiatrically impaired elderly: Process and outcome. *The Gerontologist, 24,* 238–242.

Waters, E. B. (1984). Building on what you know: Techniques for individual and group counseling with older people. *Counseling Psychologist, 12*(2), 63–74.

Waxman, H. (1990). The forgotten catastrophe: Financing long term care. *Journal of Aging and Social Policy, 2,* 11–15.

Westman, A. S. (1984). Denial of fear of dying and death in young and elderly populations. *Psychological Reports, 55,* 413–414.

Woods, R. T., & Britton, P. G. (1985). *Clinical psychology with the elderly.* Rockville, MD: Aspen.

15

Antisocial Behavior in Old Age

Sondra Brandler

The suggestion that old age is a period of some eccentricity, of a break with social conventions, a view of just slightly off-center pixilated old ladies wearing somewhat bizarre costumes and saying, perhaps too forthrightly for societal tastes, what they mean, is intrinsic to our social myths. Our literature abounds with the often-ominous and sometimes reclusive old ladies with the peculiar bottles and flowerpots on their windowsills and with similarly threatening lascivious old men offering candy to sweet young girls in exchange for some favors. We have been fed on stereotypical images of senescence as a time when many folks are more than a little bit out of touch with what is normal and acceptable behavior; when many withdraw from social contact; and when others violate the rules, the norms, and even the laws of social interaction.

As social workers, some of us have had contacts with such people, and some of us have, regrettably, even reinforced the myths and approached clients with the biases and confusions of which even professionals are not totally free. Antisocial behavior is too often regarded as a natural function of aging—social conventions ignored as inhibitions decrease with mental deterioration. The truth is that individuals with antisocial personality disorders age just as everyone else ages and that some persons develop antisocial characteristics in old age that are partly in response to the aging process.

In DSM-III-R (p. 342) antisocial personality disorder is described as "a pattern of irresponsible and antisocial behavior in adults." Typical adolescent manifestations include early or aggressive sexual behavior, excessive drinking, and the use of illicit drugs. In adulthood, the behavior continues and manifests itself in an inability to sustain a consistent work performance or to function as a responsible parent. Interpersonal difficulties, and often accompanying depression, continue throughout life and interfere with the capacity to maintain lasting, close, warm, and responsible relationships.

Types of behavior that are common in the antisocial personality disorder include irritability and aggressiveness, sometimes leading to physical confrontations; conning; lying; cheating; the failure to honor financial obligations; impulsivity; recklessness; promiscuity; squandering money; and various sorts of criminality (such as pimping, prostitution, fencing stolen goods, and selling drugs). Some general features noted in the psychiatric literature are the lack of responsiveness in relationships, pathological egocentricity, the specific loss of insight, fantastic and uninviting behavior, poor judgment and the failure to learn by experience, unreliability, untruthfulness and insincerity, and inadequately motivated antisocial behavior (Hinsie & Campbell, 1974, p. 617). Sometimes viewed as one of the specialized borderline diagnoses, the antisocial personality disorder is a condition for which there is no evidence of organic etiology.

Although many of the most flagrant characteristics of the antisocial personality disorder tend to diminish or disappear in old age, so that there is far less criminality, promiscuity, and physical acting out than in younger populations, the diagnosis and treatment of clients who are dubbed "antisocial" becomes far more problematic, and the eccentricities associated with the myths become entangled in some of the assessments. The antisocial personality disorder in old age is not truly a distinct diagnostic entity. Some types of antisocial behavior are manifestations of organic problems or of depression, and all are complicated by the confluence of issues related to the developmental life tasks of aging, the most important of which are centered on loss and adaptation to change. Certain coping patterns may also result in what is commonly regarded as antisocial behavior. The successful practitioner must understand that antisocial behavior is both part of a lifetime characterological disorder that becomes exaggerated in old age and that it is manifested only in old age as a reaction to the aging process. The case of Sam illustrates some of the complications.

Sam: The Aging of the Antisocial Personality

Sam, a 71-year-old insurance salesman, approached a social worker at a senior citizens' center to request a private meeting. He stated that he was in a desperate state and needed to talk with someone immediately. Suspicious that someone would see or hear about his conversation with the social worker, Sam did not reveal his name or any identifying information until the session was nearly over.

Sam is a large and somewhat imposing man, who looks much younger than his years. His hair is dyed black and slicked back fashionably, and he sports a perfectly trimmed mustache. Sam dresses in a flamboyant, flashy manner, wearing a chain necklace, a silver bracelet, and several rings. The aroma of his cologne pervades the office. His story is told with some tears and many off-color remarks and jokes. As it unfolds, his tone of voice shifts from detached to hostile. At one point, he seems furious and out of control; the next moment he appears almost cajoling and then mournful. Throughout, he speaks quickly, eager to have it all out and before the social worker.

Sam has been married for forty-seven years, and he and his wife had two children, a daughter and a son. When the daughter was in her midtwenties, married and the mother of two sons, she died suddenly. Sam and his wife were devastated, and their marriage, which had never been satisfying for Sam (he later revealed to the social worker that he had numerous affairs in their early years together), deteriorated completely. Sam took to staying later and later at his business and making appointments for the evening hours rather than go home. He sought the company of other women, while his wife retreated more and more into her life at home. He lied about his whereabouts and acted in a manner he calls "shrewd and clever," descriptions he also uses to characterize his business dealings. As Sam saw it, his wife had elevated his daughter to a "saint" and was interested in nothing other than her loss. He felt "trapped" in his marriage, unable to free himself either financially or emotionally. He began to frequent the racetrack, where he gambled heavily (an activity he admits he engaged in all his adult life). Sam maintained some closeness with his grandsons, but as time passed, his son-in-law remarried and eventually moved out of town, and the boys, too, were lost to him. Robert, Sam's son, an angry, moody adolescent at the time of his sister's death, eventually completed college and married. He has a 9-year-old son, Jeffrey.

Sam says that he has come for help because of the current problems with Robert and Jeffrey. About three years ago, Robert was in a car accident and sustained a back injury, the treatment of which resulted in permanent disability and constant pain. Robert misses a great deal of work and has suffered financially as well as physically. Once a wealthy businessman living always slightly beyond his means, Robert blames Sam for bringing him to the physician who caused his difficulty. A several-million-dollar malpractice suit is currently in the courts, and Robert is already getting some payments through various insurances. In the meantime, Robert calls Sam and his wife daily, demanding money, being verbally abusive and threatening. He also comes to the house; forces entry; and flies into a rage, cursing and screaming. Sam thinks that all his neighbors are aware of the family's private business and is embarrassed by it.

Robert has also been restricting Jeffrey's visits with his grandparents, saying that Sam undermines Robert's authority with the child, gives too much unrequested advice, and is a bad influence. Robert also resents Sam's contact with and supposed support of Sam's other grandsons. Sam has been in close touch with one of his now-grown grandsons and says that he has made suggestions about the young man's career plans and has offered help.

In the second session, Sam reveals what appears to be a strikingly important piece of his story. For the past fifteen years, Sam had been leading a double life, having a relationship with another woman, Alice, a fact he contends was unknown to his wife but he suspects is known to Robert, who has made some oblique remarks. Until recently, Sam had been spending much of his time living with his divorced female friend, Alice, and her daughter. About six months ago, Alice died after a short illness. Alice's daughter, grown and married now, calls Sam "Daddy," and remains much attached to Sam, even since her mother's death. Sam has never been able to grieve openly over the loss of his companion or admit his ongoing relationship with her daughter. Since so much of his time over the past fifteen years was spent with Alice, he also finds himself with much time on his hands and no place to escape from his troubles at home with his wife and his son.

Assessment and Treatment

In therapy, Sam struggles to act appropriately, to impress the social worker with his cunning and charm, but his fading sexuality is played out in his telling and retelling of obscene jokes. In his discussions with the therapist, Sam expresses some of the anger he feels toward women, "the saint" of a daughter who punished him by dying and leaving him with his ever-mourning wife who never understood his needs and the lover who has now abandoned him to face the end of his life miserable and alone. Sam is overtly sexual with the social worker, interspersing his sad tale with obscene stories that bear little relationship to the content of the session. The social worker must struggle to accept the offensive behavior without personalizing it or becoming judgmental. Throughout each meeting, Sam comments on the worker's dress, facial expressions, and demeanor. Supposedly humorous, his remarks have a needling, biting quality. Sam's bitterness is felt in nearly every exchange. Antisocial behavior is a turnoff to social workers and interferes with an empathic helping response. With a client like Sam, the social worker needs to give feedback regarding behavior without the client sustaining further emotional injury, an extremely delicate process.

Although much of Sam's behavior is part of a lifelong pattern of antisocial behavior that includes lying, business maneuvering, womanizing, and gambling, his current situation is related to his life stage, as an older man who has lost a life partner; who is struggling to appear vigorous and young as he feels his powers waning; and who, on some level, regrets his past indiscretions and the payment they are now exacting in shame, guilt, and public humiliation. Treatment at this point must focus on issues related to Sam's aging, for it is Sam's inability to cope with them, rather than the larger pattern of dysfunctional and antisocial behavior, that has caused him to seek help. The contract can center only on attainable goals, and the social worker chooses a crisis intervention model, focusing on what Sam identifies as the two most difficult areas—dealing with Robert and adjusting to numerous losses, the most important of which is the death of Alice. Sam can accept the need for help in these two areas without feeling that his masculinity will be further undermined.

John: The Antisocial Personality Disorder in an Aging Family

John is a 66-year-old Irish Catholic client who has been living for thirty-five years with his sister, Mary, and brother-in-law, Tom. Tom and Mary are the parents of three married sons. A priest, in whom Mary confided, referred the family for counseling at a local family service agency. As Mary describes it, her situation at home is a "living hell." She and Tom own a small house where John has a basement room. Six years ago John, who was a heavy smoker, was diagnosed with lung cancer, which necessitated the surgical removal of a large portion of his lung. Since his surgery, John has had several bouts of pneumonia and has difficulty going outside in cold weather. He was no longer able to handle work as a loading-dock foreman, where he had been employed for several years, and was forced to retire early. He has been working a few early morning hours as a cleaning man in a bar, but most of the day, he is at home.

Tom is also retired from his job as a driver for a food company. For five years since his retirement, he has been nearly reclusive, leaving the house only to purchase beer or cigarettes and speaking only to members of his immediate family. Infrequent visits from his sons and their families are his only social contacts. His sons, aware that Tom was ailing, had to force him to go to a physician. Tom has been quite ill but follows none of the physician's orders. Tom's resistance to treatment infuriates Mary. Mary reports that Tom cares little about his appearance or hygiene and has no interest in anything. From what is described, it appears that Tom, who is depressed, may be an alcoholic as well. He and Mary have little conversation and no intimacy.

Mary has a social life outside the home; visits with relatives and friends; vacations with her sisters; plays bingo at her chuch; and attends mass, often with John, every week. She is fashionably dressed and visits the beauty parlor regularly. She says that she is particular about how her house is kept and is distressed that a serious back condition now prevents her from housecleaning. The family could afford some limited household help, but Tom opposes spending any money.

Mary's spinal arthritis finally resulted in major surgery and a long convalescence. John visited the hospital daily and was terribly distraught. For the past year, he has been doing all the shopping, laundry, yard work, and housekeeping. Although John and Tom appear always to have been rivals for Mary's affection, John's relationship with Tom has been deteriorating steadily; the two men are constantly bickering, John incensed that Tom does none of the housework. John has been drinking, staying at the bar after work and coming home inebriated and in a foul mood. Heated arguments between Tom and John have escalated to the point where John has become physically abusive. Though both men are of slight build, Tom, again as Mary reports, is frail and has been hit by John with enough force for Tom to be thrown to the ground. Mary suggests that John has had a lifetime of fighting, occasional drunkenness, and difficulty getting along. When he was working, however, this behavior was less of a problem at home. The drinking was limited to days off, but his fits of temper and verbal abusiveness were a source of difficulty at work and at home. John had several relationships with women, but they were always stormy and unsatisfactory, often ending in violent episodes.

When Mary sought the support of her priest, John's temper and drinking were both out of control. She said that she was afraid that John would kill Tom and that she had told John that he could not come into the house, had given him his clothes, and had sent him away. Mary knew that John was staying in a room behind the bar, sleeping on a cot in an unheated area, and managing without an appropriate kitchen facility. She had not seen him in ten days. She confided that she would have to sell her house because she was unable to attend to things; that Tom would not be of any help; that he would not even change his own linens when she left fresh ones on his bed; and that she was not wearing her back brace, necessary for her recovery, because Tom, unlike John, was never cooperative in helping her to put it on. John's dog was also creating problems. Mourning John's absence, the dog was wetting indoors, a situation that was unpleasant and that Mary was unable to handle. She had scheduled a vacation with her sister and thought that Tom would need John to look after him, but was afraid the two would get into trouble together.

Although John's old-age behavior is only a continuation of behaviors in which he has engaged throughout his life, the issues have changed as the members of his family have aged. He has temporarily sought refuge in a room behind the bar, but he could easily become homeless. He is in poor health and could not brave a winter living in a shelter. Neither could he afford other housing. While his drinking was always a problem, with the losses associated with retirement, it is now growing more out of control. John's health has deteriorated, and his difficulty managing the household tasks, particularly with his resentment of Tom who is immobilized by depression and unwilling to do his share, has increased.

Tom, who had been a responsible adult, according to Mary, always providing for his family and caring for his sons when she worked the evening shift at an ice cream factory, has responded to retirement by a complete withdrawal from life. Overnight, according to his family, he became a dilapidated unresponsive old man. Mary, the key to maintaining some emotional balance in the household, has also become disabled, and with less physical strength, she feels out of control, both physically and emotionally. After two weeks of keeping John away, and despite his crying and begging, refusing to allow him back, Mary considers John's promises of good behavior and agrees to have him return. The cycle begins anew.

Assessment and Treatment

An assessment of this family must include the recognition of the realities of poor health and limited income, both factors associated with aging. Most important, however, are the issues of self-esteem. Retirement, for both John and Tom, has exacerbated existing difficulties. Neither man feels fulfilled or competent; each, in some way, had been defined by his job. Without work and with few other social outlets, Tom has retreated from life, and John has coped by using the dysfunctional antisocial patterns of his past. Mary also feels inadequate because she too has aged and has experienced the loss of her former roles.

Any treatment plan with this family must develop in relation first to Mary. Mary is the one seeking help and is clearly in the strongest position in the family. If the social worker views Mary as the enabler of John, the alcoholic, the therapy can focus on mobilizing Mary to refuse to allow John to stay in her home unless he cooperates in some program. As a beginning, John needs to attend Alcoholics Anonymous. Mary's church houses an Al-Anon group, which would probably provide a supportive environment for her. John's participation in Alcoholics Anonymous would, at the least, occupy his time outside the house. Although the goal for John is recovery, the opportunity for him to socialize and have a break from his family is also important.

Mary is receptive to psychotherapy, eager to get away and talk with someone. John will also be able to benefit from psychotherapy when he is ready. The social worker should also support Mary's need for some household help to ease the burden on John and to allow for fewer sources of friction between Tom and John. If the social worker hopes to reach out to Tom, she will have to make a home visit, attempt to engage him, assess whether he too is an alcoholic, and help to move him in the direction of a medical evaluation. Tom's reclusiveness, his sudden and extreme withdrawal, may suggest organic changes complicated by depression. In treating this family, the social worker must be sensitive to the meaning of lifelong patterns, to characterological components, and to the changes people experience as they age.

ANTISOCIAL BEHAVIOR AS A GRIEF REACTION

Sometimes individuals who have never strayed from societally acceptable behavior respond to stress in old age with what may be thought of as deviant or antisocial behavior. Usually, such behavior is part of an adjustment reaction to a loss or a manifestation of depression. A fairly typical case is that of Marty.

Marty

Marty is a 76-year-old widower living in a retirement community in Florida. He had been happily married to Doris, his childhood sweetheart, for forty-five years. They decided to sell their small luncheonette, a business that they operated for over thirty years in New York City, to provide a down payment on a modest home in Florida. With their combined social security benefits and some bank interest, the two planned a relatively easy life. About six months after they moved to Florida, Doris began to have some health problems. The physician diagnosed ovarian cancer, and within two years Doris was dead. Marty was inconsolable, and his daughters were frightened by the intensity of his sadness.

The two daughters spent much time with Marty in the beginning, but eventually had to resume their other responsibilities. It was at this point that many of the lonely widows in Marty's community began to pursue him, and he was very much taken with his newfound friends and with the female attention. He took his dates to the most expensive night spots and wined and dined these women royally. He also treated his friends to expensive presents, the kind of gifts he would never have considered purchasing before.

Marty was living way beyond his income and had to dip into his savings to pay his regular bills. In short, his nest egg was cleaned out, and he was heavily in debt. Still his spending did not diminish; Marty had credit cards. Marty was involved in a relationship with a woman who had no sense of his financial limitations. He freely shared all his credit cards with her, and what he did not spend on extravagant purchases, she did. The creditors were pursuing him, and he was struggling to pay rent, utilities, and food expenses.

In desperation, Marty approached his daughters for help. At first, they helped willingly, unaware that he was squandering his savings and encouraged that he was again having a social life. The behavior was continuing, however, and Marty was now involved with loan-sharks. He was using the money from his daughters to stave off his creditors and to continue his lavish public life-style. At home, he was doing without food. His relationship with his female companion was also deteriorating, although he did not change his spending habits. Discovering that the refrigerator and cupboard were bare, his daughters finally confronted him. The story spilled out. His daughters decided to send food to ensure that Marty would eat, confiscated his credit cards, and brought him to a family service agency for assistance.

Assessment and Treatment

The social worker suggested several approaches for assisting Marty that considered the following factors: He was still openly grieving and had never dealt fully with the pain of losing Doris and the life-style they had planned together. He was also deeply ashamed of his behavior and, having worked and struggled his whole life, had nothing to show for it. His debts were so extraordinary that he could never hope to repay them, and he was thrust into dependence on his daughters, whose own resources were limited. The female companions he had sought had taken advantage of his supposed wealth and were not real friends; Marty still needed the company of other men and women.

The treatment plan for Marty focused on his emotional, financial, and social needs. Marty was seen for individual short-term treatment and in a bereavement group. Addressing the grief issues in a situation where he was not alone was a useful outlet for him. He was also helped to get some part-time work in a senior lunch program that provided him with some extra income and allowed him to socialize. Marty was a natural in the kitchen, calling upon all his old skills as a short-order cook. Thus, the job also addressed his strengths and capabilities, rather than his limitations and failings. Marty was referred to a money-management expert to help him budget and straighten out some of his financial affairs. The dysfunctional

patterns had emerged in response to the death of Doris, and while changing
his behavior was necessary, it was insufficient without a focus on the origins
of the problem—the profound loss Marty had suffered.

ANTISOCIAL INDIVIDUALS AND CAREGIVERS

Antisocial behavior is particularly difficult in situations that demand good
interpersonal skills. For older people who live in institutional settings or
those who need custodial care at home, handling social interactions successfully may be essential to receiving good-quality care. Behavior that
offends common good manners or that specifically insults caregivers results
in bad communication and often a return in kind. Again, the behavior may
be characterological or the individual's response to factors related to his or
her aging or often a little of both.

In a nursing home, the older person may also be traumatized by the
process of institutionalization and may exhibit various normally unacceptable types of behavior as a way of resisting change and expressing anger.
Formerly docile individuals, not necessarily mentally impaired, may bite
or scratch persons who are assigned to bathe them or to provide them with
medical treatment. Some patients spit out their food or purposely throw it
on the floor. The need for institutionalized persons to find an area of their
lives in which they are still able to maintain control and individuality, two
essentials to feeling alive, sometimes results in antisocial actions. The intrusiveness of institutional care may also be intolerable to some older persons.
The angry way in which some residents may express themselves, the cursing
and abusiveness, alienates them from other residents and service providers.
The inability to accept a situation in which one may have to wait one's turn
for care, acquiesce to some level of service different from one's expectations
when one was at home, or yield to schedules or other limits on getting what
one wants is difficult. The antisocial act may be a symbolic way of expressing
feelings; the social worker must help interpret the meaning of such behavior.

Commonly, residents of institutions develop attachments to a particular
chair, and vicious arguments may ensue when someone else tries to sit in
the favorite place. The difficulty in sharing is not truly about the chair,
although it appears to be, but about the process of sustaining a placement
in which one is seemingly "robbed" of one's possessions. In such a context,
the chair is elevated to much greater significance. One resident of a nursing
home was verbally abusive with other residents, accusing them of having
"stolen" her name. It turned out that the institution's laundry often misplaced clothing, and residents were given clothing to wear (marked with the

correct name tag) that belonged to other people. The sense that she had lost her identity in the institution was profoundly felt.

Alienating other residents is also a means of separating oneself from others, of showing that one is not truly like the others but different and better, that one has individual needs and qualities. In an attempt to maintain their identity, some residents may refuse to be grouped with other people, to attend any social functions in the facility, or to go along with any group plans. In general, the antisocial battling among residents is a symbolic statement about anger and loss.

Disputes about the cleanliness of residents in a setting where people are in close proximity to each other and where family members judge the care of their relatives based on concern with hygiene are frequent. Many residents refuse to take baths or showers. Even people who are being cared for in their own homes may object to being groomed or washed. Again the refusal to bathe, although an antisocial act, is related to the fears of dependence and intrusion. Persons who live alone may not wish help, but may also be afraid of falling or being unable to get in and out of the bathtub. Consequently, they simply refuse to bathe. Without a context, the failure to maintain cleanliness may be misunderstood.

A peculiar situation in which residents of nursing homes or those receiving home care have refused to shower occurs in some Jewish facilities where there are Holocaust survivors. These patients have the terrifying memory of the gas chambers and the showers that took millions to their deaths. In general, people who have been severely deprived or have suffered greatly may have special difficulties adjusting to institutional life—anxieties that are expressed in antisocial behavior. People who have lived through war or economic hardship may become hoarders, collecting leftovers off the plates of others, grabbing extra bread or condiments, and storing food in their rooms. This behavior is a terrible problem for facilities that attempt to provide a sanitary and vermin-free environment. The nature of institutional life demands sharing and cooperation. A patient's survival, both emotionally and physically, requires that service providers feel kindly toward him or her. Antagonizing such workers by aggressive, resistant, or abusive behavior often compromises the level of care.

Pauline: The Nursing Home Pariah

Pauline, an 88-year-old nursing home resident had so infuriated the

staff at the facility where she lived that, with her every hospitalization and return to the home, they drew straws to see who would be
unlucky enough to be assigned to her care. She managed to gather
her family together to support her contention that whatever was
done for her was done late, badly, or inappropriately and was constantly reporting staff members to the administration for the supposed failures in the performance of their jobs. Her relationships
with other residents were also difficult, so much so that she had to
be placed in a private room. All the staff, including the social workers, were obliged to devote an inordinate amount of time attending
to Pauline's needs.

Assessment and Treatment

The social worker's primary role was to help Pauline to vent the extreme
frustration she felt at having to be placed—to help her to express her feelings,
rather than to displace them onto other residents and the staff. The social
worker also needed to give Pauline fair feedback on the effect of her diatribes
on those around her and a reality-based warning of the ways in which she
was sabotaging her own care. The needs of Pauline's family also had to be
recognized. Pauline's anger was directed at them as the instigators of her
placement, and they, too, were struggling with ambivalent feelings regarding
their decision to place their mother. The social worker had to enlist the
support of the family in working to help Pauline to be more cooperative.
Throughout Pauline's stay at the nursing home, the social worker had to
give her ongoing support while negotiating with and reinterpreting for the
staff the issues with which Pauline was struggling. In many private facilities,
such a resident would be labeled a management risk—a person so destructive
to the routines of the institution and so troublesome in her dealings with
other residents and staff, that she might be asked to leave.

Caring for an antisocial individual in her own home, though less disturbing to other people, may also be troublesome. Attacking and unreasonable patients usually create a situation for themselves in which workers are
unwilling to stay on the job. If a person is unable to be cared for at home
and if a private institution cannot tolerate his or her behavior, the next stop
would likely be a state facility. Complicating the issues related to the disposition of such a case is the biochemical revolution that allows institutions
to respond to difficult patients by medicating them into submissiveness.
Drugs may control antisocial behavior by subduing patients. In addition to

the potentially deleterious effects of medications and the violation of patients' rights in being medicated for the purpose of institutional control, drugs treat the symptom, not the problem.

The importance of a therapeutic intervention in which social workers attempt to negotiate with other staff around patients' needs while helping patients to express their feelings in a more constructive manner cannot be minimized. Social workers must stay with such clients in a trusting relationship, provide supportive boundaries, and encourage the exploration of the meaning of the behaviors, as the case of Laura indicates.

Laura: The Need for Control

Laura, a 90-year-old patient who has some difficulty with her speech because of a stroke, was known to spit and scratch workers who were attempting to cut her fingernails. She repeatedly threatened that worms would come out of her fingers if her nails were trimmed. In other areas, Laura appeared mentally intact and tractable, but cajoling and bargaining with her about the grooming was impossible.

The social worker began to explore the issues with Laura, and a perfectly logical explanation emerged. Laura had been in several institutions before her placement at the current facility. At one nursing home, her nails had been cut so close that her fingers bled. In the throes of the manicuring procedure at the current location, with Laura's terror of being hurt and her difficulty in expressing herself, Laura could offer no explanation to caretakers and simply became irrational and unmanageable.

Assessment and Treatment

The social worker again had to negotiate with the staff to make Laura's behavior more understandable to those who were caring for her. The staff, in turn, tried to speak gently and reassuringly as they attended to Laura's needs. Also the social worker had to offer Laura support during procedures that were frightening to her: assuring her that no one would harm her, asking her to report any discomfort she was experiencing, and promising that the procedure would be stopped if she had any difficulty. In this way Laura was in control of the situation.

Laura's reaction to having her fingernails trimmed is not such an unusual one. Some routine grooming methods that are utilized in nursing homes and other institutions violate a patient's sense of individuality and privacy. Many residents fight haircuts that are forced on them without regard to style or taste. Defensive behavior is regarded as antisocial, and patients who exhibit it are dismissed as confused, uncooperative, or ill mannered. Mental asylums, prisons, concentration camps, and armies have long used cutting or shaving hair to create uniformity and reduce individuality. In nursing homes, even some severely mentally impaired older adults react unfavorably to having their hair cut. For women, in particular, for whom lovely long hair has often been a sign of beauty, the act of having their hair cut against their will is an affront to their sense of self. In general, whether older people are living in institutions or in their own homes, antisocial behavior is often a way of expressing underlying issues.

DISENGAGEMENT

Although thus far antisocial behavior has been described as acts that are contrary to societal norms, the term *antisocial* has been commonly used to refer to the withdrawal from others. Certainly, friends and family members report many instances of formerly socially active older people refusing to participate in social functions and of generally reducing their social contacts. In identifying antisocial behavior as a shunning of the society of others or as a general unresponsiveness in interpersonal relations, some theorists suggest that it is a healthy preparation for impending death. Disengagement theory, introduced in 1961 by Cummings and Henry (Hancock, 1987, pp. 2–3), suggests that the disengagement process is a biologically and psychologically intrinsic and inevitable response to aging—a "normal" healthy adaptation. According to this theory, healthy and satisfied elderly persons disengage from the pressures and responsibilities inherent in social interaction. These individuals accept their reduced functionality and importance and do not resist the changes in their status and activity levels that may lead them to become troubled, depressed, and frustrated (Hussian, 1981).

The empirical research on disengagement has not entirely supported the notion that disengagement, in itself, is a desirable and natural process; rather, it has found that disengagement is a process that is strongly influenced by cultural factors and individual personality. Examples of the different ways in which certain cultures view social withdrawal are important to any perception of clients' behavior. A Chicana client who seems to be withdrawing from intimate relationships with her children is likely to have greater problems than is a similarly aged Scandinavian American woman who reports minimal or lessening contact with her adult children and grandchildren (Birren & Schaie, 1977). The Chicano family's emphasis on family relationships and the expectation of help from children without any loss in status for the older person is quite different from the fiercely held value of independence that characterizes Scandinavian culture. Of particular interest in understanding certain cultures is that for some the disengagement of aged members is part of a normative pattern that demands certain behavior to accomplish life tasks. For example, one study (Birren & Schaie, 1977, p. 317) found that elderly Thai persons become preoccupied with themselves and remote, though polite, as they contemplate their transition to the next life in accordance with their Buddhist tradition.

Differences in individual personalities and changes in social networks also account for the degree of engagement a person maintains as he or she ages. Persons who were not particularly socially able in their early years obviously are not likely to be socially connected as they grow older. People who define themselves by their work roles and whose social contacts are made through work have to develop a whole new set of relationships when they retire; for them, work is the necessary vehicle for affiliations. Widows and widowers also experience changes in their perceptions of themselves as social creatures; the social circles of many of them also revolved around their partners and are now redefined by their single status. At a time in life when energy may be at its lowest, they must seek new friendships to stay socially involved.

In a more general sense, all people experience changes in their social environment as they, their friends, and their family members age. Through illness, moves to other communities, institutionalization, and death, an older person is likely to have lost many of those who are dear to him or her. The social world of elderly people, particularly the old-old, has contracted. Investing in new intimate friendships is risky, since these relationships may also result in losses. Some individuals feel too vulnerable to become as socially engaged as they might have been in the past.

The way in which older people see themselves, having internalized many of the societal notions about the aging process, contributes to the idea that it is time to withdraw from social interaction. Too much contact with adult children is regarded as interference, finding a companion of the opposite sex is humorous, staying on the job too long suggests an unwillingness to move over as one should to allow the next generation to take its rightful place. The loss of a positive self-image often accompanies physical changes and disabilities. One client, an officer on the board of directors of a senior citizens' center and an active member for many years, stopped attending the program after she had broken her hip and needed to use a walker. She was so ashamed of her appearance while utilizing the walker that she said she was not "up to" seeing any visitors at home. Other persons report that they do not leave the house because they have dentures that fit so poorly that they are embarrassed to be seen in public. Older people accept the kinds of portrayals of the elderly on television and in the movies as infirm, dilapidated, and unattractive. Although there has been some improvement in public images of older people, with the increase in the number of older consumers, older characters in programs and in advertising are most often still pictured stereotypically as laughable or as one dimensional. The men are likely to be wearing sweaters, while the women, in dresses with lace collars, are likely to be baking cookies.

Mental health professionals also should be aware that many people disengage from social contact as they age simply because health problems, which interfere with travel and safety, limit their capacity for social interaction. Problems with vision may result in the fear of falling outside the home or otherwise negotiating strange environments; for example, a blind man could not attend a senior citizens' program because he could not manage in the public rest room without help from a female aide who could not enter the men's room. Difficulties with ambulation may prevent the use of public transportation. Problems with hearing may interfere with full participation in organizational life or make it difficult to maintain a conversation. Podiatric problems, dental problems, and digestive difficulties may keep older people close to home and away from social contact. In short, culture, personality, perceived social status, and lack of opportunity for engagement combine with health factors to discourage social interaction for certain older people. The case of Joseph is an example.

Joseph: Finding Himself Alone

Joseph, an 85-year-old man, had recently been widowed, and his adult children applied in his behalf for many services, including housekeeping, Meals on Wheels, and a friendly visitor program. A social worker from a case-management agency was sent to evaluate Joseph's needs and to try to arrange for the appropriate plan. On the telephone the family had described their father as an ailing old man who could do little for himself and who needed comprehensive outpatient care if he was to avoid institutionalization. Therefore, the social worker was quite surprised when she actually met Joseph.

As Joseph related his story, a different picture emerged. Joseph had been the caregiver for his wife, who had been wheelchair bound for the last six years of her life as the result of a stroke. Joseph had bathed her, assisted with toileting, helped her eat, managed the household, cooked, cleaned, and shopped for both of them. Only in the last year, when his wife had become more severely disabled, did Joseph require some minimal assistance for a nurse's aide, who helped him lift his wife into her chair and then back to her bed. In good weather Joseph always brought his wife outside to sit in the sun with neighbors.

Joseph had been an outgoing person and enjoyed socializing, but was severely limited by his wife's disabilities. One or two mornings each week, when the aide would oversee his wife's care, Joseph would go to a senior citizens' program to play cards. About two months before his wife's death, when she was already in a guarded condition, Joseph stopped leaving the house for any activities other than marketing. He would not permit anyone to spell him in his care for his wife and kept her safe, clean, and well cared for in her own home until her death.

Immediately after his wife's funeral, Joseph was brought to his daughter's house, where he remained for several weeks, and then was taken to his son's home, where he stayed for several more weeks. He did not return to his own home for about two months. The family then decided to contact some community agencies. Before a complete evaluation was made, Joseph was placed on a list for home-delivered meals. Since the family understood that Joseph would be ineligible for the meals if they reported that he was also receiving homemaker service (three hours a day for three days per week), they instructed him to deny that he was receiving any help. He was also uneasy about leaving the house because doing so would indicate that he was not truly homebound and deserving of a meal. As he explained it, Joseph now spent much of his day sitting in his home alone waiting for his meal to arrive and engaged in a sort of clandestine play to ensure that the homemaker and meal deliverer would not meet. Fully capable of handling more of his own care but unhappy about displeasing his children, Joseph, immobilized by grief, went along with a charade that aggravated his discomfort. He had lost both his life partner and his reason for surviving. He had no role and nothing to do with his day and spent much of it just sitting and crying. Without daily structure, he seemed incapable of concentrating or focusing on anything.

Assessment and Treatment

The services he received actually contributed to Joseph's feeling useless and entrapped him in his home and away from social contact. His adult children had made their decisions about their father without consulting him, and, although well meaning, their assumptions about his capabilities were destructive. Some limited help with the housekeeping and frequent visits with the family might have been of assistance, but what was really needed was to re-engage him with his peers, perhaps at the senior citizens' center where he already had some connections and where he could also have his lunch meal in the company of others. Participation in a support group for widowed persons might also be useful for Joseph. After some time and some recovery, he might even find volunteer work involving people that would occupy more of his time in ways that he might find productive.

For Joseph, who had been socially active throughout his life, disengagement resulted from a combination of situational factors and his children's inaccurate understanding of the expectations for old age, some of which Joseph internalized. Joseph suffered from social isolation and accompanying depression. He needed social contact to return to functioning, but the programs to which he was referred denied him that contact. Commonly, however, individuals who become disengaged change more gradually, and significant problems that require treatment and are not natural and healthy adjustments to aging go undetected, as may be seen in the case of Rose.

Rose: Disengagement or Dysfunction

Rose, an 83-year-old widow, had been living alone in her New York apartment for twenty-five years since the marriage of her son, Dan. Convinced of his mother's independence, Dan approached Rose's old age with confidence born of ignorance. Although her son was attentive, he lived far away and was unaware of her daily difficulties. Rose had no use for dependent people and shared little of her personal concerns with her son. She had raised Dan on her own after her husband's death, had taught school for nearly forty years, and had always been fully capable of managing her own affairs.

Throughout her life, Rose had established few intimate relationships. She had one close female friend with whom she had weekly contact, a male companion with whom she went to dinner every few weeks, and a group of teacher friends with whom she visited a few times a year. A young neighbor, who regarded Rose as a sort of adopted grandmother, periodically stopped in to see if Rose needed anything, and Rose and this woman would visit. Rose had been an only child, and her only remaining family was a distantly related cousin. She was, however, closely allied with her husband's family, including one niece who was in regular contact with her, calling frequently and inviting her for holidays and family events. This niece, Linda, a social worker, noticed the subtle decline in Rose's functioning.

Linda's first clue came with the illness of Rose's one close friend. Rose made a few calls to the hospital to inquire about her friend, but did not visit her in the hospital or pursue her interest in her friend's care with the woman's family when her lifelong friend was too ill to respond. Rose learned of her friend's death, but did not attend the funeral. When Linda asked Rose why she did not go to the funeral, Rose simply said that it was too much for her to manage. Similarly, Rose's relationship with her male friend, a close companion for more than twenty years, ended with his institutionalization. Thereafter, Rose maintained no contact with him.

Linda continued to call and invite Rose, but Rose said she really was unable to visit because Linda's children, once favorites with Rose, were "too noisy" for Rose to tolerate. Rose was too "tired" for all the commotion. She canceled her annual visit to Dan's home for her only grandchild's birthday because this visit was also too stressful and tiring for her. Rose said that she had been seeing her physician and that everything was fine, but Linda thought that Rose was not as alert or oriented as she should be. The information about the medical appointments was vague, and Linda suspected that some of Rose's medications should be evaluated. Linda called Rose's physician, but the physician, who saw Rose in a hospital clinic, read the chart and saw no identified concern about Rose.

Most surprising to Linda was the fact that Rose seemed to be critical of the young neighbor she had once valued and complained that the neighbor was making demands on her. These demands focused on the neighbor's request that Rose hold a camp trunk in her home to be picked up during the day while the neighbor was at work. Rose seemed centered on a variety of petty criticisms. Fortunately, however, the neighbor continued to feel fondly toward Rose and to check on her well-being. Troubled by Rose's behavior, the neighbor called Dan, who telephoned his mother but detected nothing wrong other than the fact that his mother seemed more forgetful than usual and repeated herself.

When Rose said that she was unable to attend a holiday dinner with Linda's family, Linda decided to drop by Rose's apartment and investigate in person. She found Rose, always meticulous about her appearance, in a dirty nightgown and robe. The refrigerator and cupboards were empty, overdue notices on utility bills and rent were spread over the table, and bottles of prescription medications and pills without containers were strewn about. Rose seemed terribly confused and disoriented, had no idea of whether she had eaten, and could not say what she might like to eat. Linda immediately went marketing, bought provisions, and restocked Rose's kitchen. When Linda prepared the food, Rose ate ravenously. After clearing up some of the papers and removing the medications, Linda, uncertain about what drugs Rose had or had not taken, thought that Rose might be having a drug reaction. She helped Rose, who seemed exhausted, into clean nightclothes and then to bed.

Linda suspected that something was seriously wrong with Rose, who seemed strangely compliant with whatever was suggested. Withdrawn and submissive over the next few days, Rose ate what she was given, took her prescribed medications as Linda administered them, and then drifted back to sleep. Rose seemed to be sleeping most of the time. She had no interest in watching television, reading, or jewelry making, three activities she had previously enjoyed. Rose never asked about any of her family members and seemed disconnected from everyone. Perhaps she had suffered a stroke. Dan spoke with Rose's physicians and learned that Rose had missed her last few scheduled appointments. Rose was in the care of several specialists— a cardiologist who attended to her pacemaker, a hemotologist who monitored a blood condition, and an internist who dealt with her hypertension. The physicians were not in communication with each other. The clinic personnel took no responsibility for checking on Rose and did not inquire about Rose's missing appointments.

Assessment and Treatment

Rose's normally independent nature and her ability to function with limited social involvement had allowed her to withdraw completely from others without anyone really noticing that she was in serious trouble. Unable to admit difficulties in managing her affairs, she hid her situation from Dan and Linda. In part, Dan may not have been able to accept that his mother was failing, and he was fooled by Rose's presentation when they conversed by phone. Even when Linda called Dan to say that something was very wrong with Rose, Dan was incredulous. After all, he assured Linda, Rose had gotten a good report from her physicians. That Rose chose to stay home alone was not a serious issue; this was a lifetime pattern. That she had few friends was no worry; she had outlived her friends and did not require too much intimacy. However, that Rose had disengaged from her most precious relationships and was antagonistic or indifferent to her few remaining friends and relatives suggested a serious problem. Unable to accept that she was ill and unable to carry on without help, Rose distanced herself from everyone, avoiding visits with Linda and Dan and finding fault with her neighbor.

Dan took Rose to a geriatric physician, who examined Rose utilizing a holistic approach, assessing the prescription medications she was taking and the possible synergistic effects of these drugs. The physician discovered that Rose was suffering severe anemia, in part a side effect of one of her medications. In her confusion, Rose may actually have been taking more of the medicine than the prescribed dose. The anemia was so extreme that Rose had become too fatigued to purchase and prepare food and her nutrition suffered, contributing to a general decline in her health and increased disorientation. Rose was hospitalized for further investigation of the anemia; it was found that she had an operable stomach cancer that was treated surgically. She was given a blood transfusion and made a remarkable recovery. Her confusion cleared.

Rose's disengagement and withdrawal from friends and family was symptomatic of a problem but was easily dismissed as a natural part of her process of aging. If her neighbor and niece had not been alert, Rose surely would have died from what was a treatable condition. The physicians who prescribed medications without consultation and who trusted Rose to be able to take the drugs properly had some responsibility in contributing to the difficulty. The clinic personnel who did not investigate when a patient, who had regularly scheduled appointments, did not show up were also at fault. Dan, whose denial of the painful situation explained away his mother's forgetfulness and repetitiveness as a normal part of aging, also contributed to the problem.

In general, even with individuals who are not particularly socially active, any dramatic behavioral or personality change in social involvement is likely to indicate some problem requiring intervention. In Rose's case, although the primary difficulty was physical, it was played out in changes in her relationships. Withdrawal may result from a medical problem, from depression, as part of an adjustment reaction, or as a combination of these or other factors, but isolation and retreat from life are not normal to aging.

CONCLUSION

Antisocial behavior in old age may be a continuation of antisocial behavior earlier in life, or it may be symptomatic of a person's difficulty accepting and dealing with feelings related to the stresses of the aging process. Whether the antisocial behavior manifests itself in acting in defiance of social norms and conventions or in withdrawal from social interaction, it is an expression of internal struggles. To treat the client, the social worker must explore the source of the behavior. Since much antisocial behavior leads to dysfunction and clients' inability to meet their needs and feel productive, the social worker's goal should be to uncover the roots of that behavior and find positive ways to help clients express difficult feelings.

To assess any situation adequately and, in turn, to serve older clients, community agencies, social workers, clergy, physicians, nurses, and other health professionals must work cooperatively with each other and with families. Interventions may focus on medical concerns, adjustments to changes in roles, or finding social opportunities, but wherever the problem exists, real solutions are often best provided by a network of services. The mental health professional must evaluate the origins of antisocial behavior, however this behavior is manifest, by examining the biopsychosocial context, which includes culture, personality, health, and social environment, and by seeing all these factors as they are juxtaposed against the events in the developmental stage of aging.

REFERENCES

American Psychiatric Association. (1980). *Diagnostic and statistical manual of mental disorders* (3rd ed., rev.). Washington, DC: Author.

Birren, J. E. & Schaie, K. W. (Eds.). (1977). *Handbook of the psychology of aging.* New York: Van Nostrand Reinhold.

Brody, E. M. (1977). *Long-term care of older people*. New York: Human Sciences Press.

Busse, E. W., & Pfeiffer, E. (Eds.). (1965). *Behavior and adaptation in late life*. Boston: Little, Brown.

Butler, R., & Lewis, M. (1974). *Aging and mental health*. St. Louis, MO: C. V. Mosby.

Hancock, B. L. (1987). *Social work with older people*. Englewood Cliffs, NJ: Prentice-Hall.

Hinsie, L. E., & Campbell, R. J. (1974). *Psychiatric dictionary* (4th ed.). New York: Oxford University Press.

Hussian, R. A. (1981). *Geriatric psychology*. New York: Van Nostrand Reinhold.

Kimmel, D. C. (1980). *Adulthood and aging* (2nd ed.). New York: John Wiley & Sons.

16

Alcohol and Elderly People

Kathleen J. Farkas

Historically, gerontologists and addictions specialists have not been especially close colleagues. In fact, there is evidence to suggest that some saw their work as mutually exclusive (Kola, Kosberg, & Joyce, 1984; Kola, Kosberg, & Wegner-Burch, 1980). Gerontologists were not convinced that working with alcoholics-albeit-elderly-people was part of their professional responsibility, since alcoholism and alcohol-related problems certainly are not the most prevalent health and social problems among older people, whereas addictions specialists thought that the elderly were too small a part of their population to allocate much in the way of assessment and treatment resources (Whittington, 1988). The prevailing belief that alcoholism is a self-limiting disease (Drew, 1968) and the stigma toward both elderly people (Kosberg & Harris, 1978) and toward alcoholics reinforced the idea that elderly people do not have problems with alcohol.

The experience of both gerontologists and addictions specialists during the past twelve years, however, has shown that older people do experience significant problems with alcohol, and there is a growing body of clinical and research literature on the assessment and treatment of alcohol problems among elderly people (Atkinson & Kofoed, 1982; Atkinson & Schuckit, 1981; Glantz & Backenheimer, 1988; Gottheil, Druley, & Skoloda, 1985; Kofoed, Tolson, Atkinson, Toth, & Turner, 1987; Maddox, Robins, & Rosenberg, 1986; Meyers, Hingson, Mucatel, Heeren, & Goldman, 1985; Mishara & Kastenbaum, 1980; Sumberg, 1985; Williams, 1984). This chapter reviews the epidemiological literature on the extent of alcohol use and abuse among elderly people and discusses clinical issues in the assessment of alcohol problems, as well as treatment options and research on the effectiveness of these options with elderly people.

328

DEFINITIONS

Any discussion of alcohol use and alcoholism must deal with the issues of definition. As Cahalan (1987) pointed out, the presence of the phenomenon (alcohol use) or of the disease (alcoholism) is usually measured by the consequences, such as the incidence of alcohol-related illness, accidents, and crimes. However, the existence of these consequences does not *prove* that alcohol use or alcoholism is a causal factor. For this reason, Cahalan (p. 7) cited Knupfer's (1967, p. 974) definition of alcohol-related problems: "A problem—any problem—connected fairly closely with drinking constitutes a drinking problem." This definition makes no assumptions that drinking is the cause of the problem or that the problem is the cause of the drinking. Although it is a scientifically defensible position for epidemiologists, it is not especially helpful for practitioners who are interested not only in understanding the phenomenon, but in predicting and controlling it. However, the disease model of alcoholism offers the practitioner a set of diagnostic criteria to use in the assessment of alcohol abuse as an illness that can be diagnosed and treated.

The debate over the definition, etiology, and treatment of alcoholism and alcohol-related problems is beyond the scope of this chapter, but it revolves around the question of whether alcoholism is a disease or a behavioral problem. Babor (1981, p. xiii) suggested that there is not one disease or problem, but several related syndromes with the common characteristics of "drinking, dependence, and damage." It is important to note, as Wallace (1989, p. 325) did, that "neither a simple behavioral model nor a simple disease concept can adequately explain alcoholism," since alcoholism is "not merely a physical problem but a psychological and sociocultural problem as well." Jacobson (1989, p. 19) incorporated this broad approach in his definition of alcoholism:

> Alcoholism is a general term frequently used to indicate any of various types of alcohol use, misuse, abuse, or dependency problems, some of which may be progressive; may be of varying and multiple etiologies and may follow varying courses of development; may involve multiple organ systems to varying degrees; may pervade, to varying degrees, a variety of psychological, personal, interpersonal, occupational, spiritual, social, or other behavioral domains; may recur after attempted therapy; and may lead to declining health or death of the patient unless adequately and properly treated.

Jacobson's definition allows the social worker to address the health, social, and personal problems associated with the use of alcohol. Although the focus of this chapter is on alcohol and the problems associated with its use, some mention must be made of the fact that elderly people experience difficulties with other drugs, primarily prescription drugs and over-the-counter medications, but also illicit drugs to a small extent (Abrams & Alexopoulos, 1988; Coons, Hendricks, & Sheahan, 1988; Whittington, 1988; see also, Chapter 17).

ALCOHOL USE

Abstention

Two of the most reliable and salient findings from community-based epidemiological studies of alcohol use are that elderly people report significantly lower rates of alcohol use than do younger people and that the older the population the lower the rates of alcohol consumption (Barnes, 1979; Branch, 1978; Cahalan, Cissin, & Crossley, 1969; Gomberg, 1980; Robins, Helzer, & Przybeck, 1986; Warheit & Auth, 1984). Elderly people have higher rates of abstention from alcohol than does the general population; two-thirds of the people aged 60 and older report that they do not drink alcohol in any amount during the year, compared to one-third of the younger population. The largest proportion of abstainers in a sample of persons aged 60 and over was found to be 68 percent (Dunham, 1980). Since rates of alcohol consumption vary by region, ethnic group, gender, and socioeconomic status, it is not surprising that abstention rates also vary by these factors. Women aged 60 and older drink less often and consume less alcohol than do their male counterparts.

Why are prevalence rates of alcohol use lower for elderly people? A number of biological and social aspects of later life may explain this fact. For example, the increased risk of poor health in later life may dissuade people from drinking, since abstinence or reduced drinking is recommended for people who take certain medications or who have medical conditions that would be exacerbated by drinking alcohol (Brody, 1982). In addition, age-related physical changes that are unrelated to disease or illness may result in decreased physical tolerance of the effects of alcohol (Lamy, 1988; Salzman, VanderKolk, & Shader, 1975). For instance, because increases in the proportion of body fat decrease the volume of body water, which may result in higher blood-alcohol concentrations, elderly people feel the effects of alcohol more as they age. Other physical changes, such as changes in hormone levels and in rates of absorption, metabolism, and elimination, may affect the sensitivity of body tissue to alcohol in older people.

Social changes associated with age have also been implicated in the reduction of alcohol use and abuse (Blose, 1978; Brody, 1982). For example, the loss of roles, such as from the death of a spouse, may decrease one's social opportunities to drink. Retirement and reduced income may decrease the prevalence of alcohol use by the elderly as well. However, Ekerdt, DeLabry, Glynn, and Davis (1989) did not find support for the role of retirement in either increased or decreased drinking among newly retired people.

Meyers, Goldman, Hingson, Scotch, and Mangione (1981) asserted that changes in drinking habits are not necessarily related to age, but are the results of differences among cohorts or generations. Using retrospective accounts of drinking habits, they found evidence that today's older people are more likely to report lifelong abstinence and that the rates of lifelong abstinence are highest in the oldest respondents. They attributed this phenomenon to the continued influence of the Temperance movement and Prohibition on the drinking habits of older people, particularly older women. In cross-sectional and longitudinal analyses of alcohol intake in a sample of elderly people in the community, Adams (1990) found a statistically significant decline over time in the percentage of elderly people who drank alcohol. However, among those who continued to drink, only heavy drinkers significantly decreased the amount of alcohol they consumed.

Chatham (1986) offered several other possible explanations: that elderly people tend to hide or deny their drinking more than do other age groups, are unaware that they have a drinking problem, and do not associate symptoms of drinking with their use of alcohol and that physicians and families are unable or unwilling to recognize the indicators of alcohol abuse in elderly people.

Rates of Alcoholism and Alcohol-related Problems

Despite the trend toward abstention and the decreased use of alcohol in late life, many elderly people drink alcohol and some experience significant physical, social, emotional, and financial problems that are alcohol related. Bailey, Haberman, and Alksne (1969) found the highest rate of alcohol problems and alcoholism (23 per 1,000) in two age groups in a New York City study: those aged 65 to 74 and those aged 45 to 54. Since widowers were overrepresented in the alcoholic-drinking group, the study concluded that older men who have lost their spouses may be at a higher risk for alcohol-related problems.

Estimates of the magnitude of alcohol-related problems and of alcoholism among the elderly have varied from a low of 2 percent to a high of 49 percent (National Institute on Alcohol Abuse and Alcoholism, 1981; Schuckit & Pastor, 1978). Gomberg (1980) estimated that 10 percent of the population over age 60 experience problems with alcohol. The Ecological Catchment Area Program of the National Institute of Mental Health estimated the magnitude of alcoholism and alcohol-related problems among the elderly to be between 1.9–4.6 percent for men and .1–.7 for women (Maddox et al., 1986). Kermis (1986) challenged these figures as underestimates, saying that alcoholism among elderly people is a salient health issue that is neither recognized nor treated.

Not all alcohol use among elderly people is to be discouraged. To the contrary, there is evidence that the moderate use of alcohol may result in social and mental benefits for elderly people (Mishara & Kastenbaum, 1980; Volpe & Kastenbaum, 1967). Among the benefits that have been attributed to the moderate use of alcohol by elderly people, both in the community and in nursing homes, are increased morale, reduced worry, greater ease in falling asleep, and improved performance on a face-hand test (Kastenbaum, 1988). Goodwin et al. (1987) found that alcohol intake was positively associated with several measurements of cognitive status, but these correlations tended to disappear after income, education, gender, and age were controlled.

CLASSIFICATIONS OF DRINKING PATTERNS AND ONSET OF PROBLEMS

Elderly people with alcohol problems have typically been categorized by their age at the onset of the problems (Rosin & Glatt, 1971; Zimberg, 1974, 1978). Early-onset, or Type I, drinkers are people who began having problems with alcohol earlier in life and continue to drink abusively in old age. They reach old age despite their drinking behavior because of their strong social support systems or their strong physical constitutions.

Late-onset, reactive, or Type II drinkers were light or moderate social drinkers or perhaps abstainers in their younger years, but begin to experience problems related to drinking after they enter late life. They are thought to experience more reactive events, such as bereavement, loneliness, and stress, and to use alcohol to adapt and cope to these changes (Carruth, 1980; Rosin & Glatt, 1971).

A third onset category, intermittent problem drinkers, was suggested by Zimberg (1978) to capture people who had a brief period of abusive drinking in their earlier years, followed by years of abstinence or responsible use, only to experience alcohol-related problems in later life. Using the onset framework, several authors have estimated that two-thirds of elderly alcoholics are early-onset drinkers and the remaining one-third are late onset drinkers (Duckworth & Rosenblatt, 1976; Rosin & Glatt, 1971; Zimberg, 1974, 1978). Furthermore, Zimberg (1974) noted that these onset groups not only differ in etiology, but in the treatment strategies that are most effective for helping them.

The usefulness of onset typologies is not uniformly accepted among researchers and practitioners, however. Giordano and Beckham (1985) took issue with the late-onset classification and contended that more attention should be paid to male-female differences and family conflicts in addressing the needs of elderly people with alcohol-related problems. Parrella and Filstead (1988) accepted the importance of onset in the clinical course of alcoholism for people of all ages, but argued that the concept of onset has not been precisely defined or used consistently in research or practice. The following case study illustrates the use of onset in the assessment of alcohol-related problems and alcoholism among elderly people.

Mr. F, aged 69, spent his working life as the owner of a hardware store not far from his house. It was a profitable business, and he sold the store a year ago when he decided to retire. Six months after his retirement, his wife of forty years died suddenly. After her death, Mr. F's daughter noticed that her father was sleeping a great deal more than usual. She also noticed that he was spending more and more evenings at a bar in the neighborhood—something he had never done before—and that there were several bags of beer bottles in his trash each week. Initially, she thought that it was good for her father to socialize at the bar and that his increased sleeping was nothing more than the result of late nights and his mild depression after his wife's death. She thought that Mr. F might be drinking more than usual, but that he was entitled to some solace after all the losses he had encountered in the past year. Since she had not known that her father's drinking was a problem in the past, she was not concerned about it now and expected that, with the passage of time and as his grief lifted, he would cut back on his sleeping and drinking.

Mr. F's daughter casually mentioned these events to her father's sister, who became alarmed and recounted the many problems Mr. F had experienced with drinking in his twenties and how Mrs. F had struggled to get him to stop drinking after their marriage and the births of their children. The aunt said that Mrs. F had kept her husband's drinking in check during their marriage and often feared that he would go back to his old ways during holidays or other occasions when alcohol was present. When Mr. F's daughter asked her father about his visits to the bar and what he did there, he said that he spent most of the time drinking alone and several times had to be sent home in a taxi because he was too drunk to walk. He said that he was afraid that his drinking would get out of control now that his wife was not there to motivate and support him.

The fact that Mr. F's drinking increased and that he began to experience alcohol-related problems at age 69 after two significant losses could be seen as an example of late-onset problem drinking. His use of alcohol could be seen as a reaction to his recent life events. Family members and friends may tolerate this increased use of alcohol in the absence of work roles and interpersonal relationships that may define it as a problem. Indeed, family members often minimize the risks and problems associated with drinking because they believe that the older person is entitled to the pleasures or comfort of a drink. Only when the pattern of Mr. F's lifelong alcohol use was mentioned did his daughter begin to worry that his drinking might present a serious problem and addressed it with him. Mr. F had not been treated for his earlier drinking problem; he is at risk of experiencing alcohol-related problems now that some of the stabilizing influences—in his case, his wife's approval and the routine of his work—are no longer present.

Dunham (1981) argued that at least six patterns of alcohol use may be useful in work with elderly people and that one cannot understand the current use of alcohol outside the context of the lifetime pattern of use. These patterns are presented in Table 16.1.

Onset is a helpful concept in unraveling the causes and determining the treatment of alcoholism and alcohol-related problems among elderly people, but it is important to consider it and the problems related to drinking in the context of the person's lifetime patterns of alcohol use (Joyce, 1984).

The elderly are an underserved population in alcohol treatment services. Bloom (1983) estimated that only 15 percent of the alcoholics over age 60 receive treatment. A common barrier to treatment is the attitude of professionals, family members, and elderly people themselves that treatment is not effective or that the elderly are not suitable clients for treatment. On the contrary, the evidence shows that treatment for alcohol-related problems

TABLE 16.1
Lifetime Drinking Patterns*

Abstainers	People who do not currently drink alcohol and who never drank alcohol.
Rise and Fall	People who began to drink alcohol in their early twenties and were heavy drinkers for thirty or forty years, but then decreased their alcohol use completely or drank only infrequently.
Rise and Sustained	People who began to drink heavily in their twenties and continue to do so throughout their lives. Early onset or Type I.
Light throughout Life	People who became light drinkers in their earlier life and continue this pattern. These people may taper their use as they become older.
Light-Late Risers	People who began light drinking earlier in life and continue this use until later life when they increase to moderate drinking.
Late Starters	People who do not begin their alcohol use until midlife and then rise to moderate or heavy drinking. After 10 to 20 years, some of these people return to abstaining, but some continue moderate use. Late onset or Type II.
Highly Variable	People whose drinking repeatedly fluctuates between moderate to heavy drinking and infrequent drinking abstention. Intermittent drinkers.

*"Background Characteristics of Lifelong Abstainers and Drinkers" appeared in "Aging and Changing Patterns of Alcohol Use," by Roger G. Dunham, *Journal of Psychoactive Drugs*, 13 (2): 145 (1981), and is used with permission.

and alcoholism can be successful for older people (Dupree, Broslowski, & Schonfeld, 1984; Kofoed, Tolson, Atkinson, Turner, & Toth, 1984; Zimberg, 1984). However, the initial step in increasing the number of elderly people in treatment for alcohol-related problems is comprehensive screening and assessment.

SCREENING AND ASSESSMENT

Screening can take place in a variety of settings and can be done by a variety of professionals and service providers. The purpose of screening is not only to identify elderly people who are alcoholic, but to evaluate the role alcohol may play in other health and social problems. Older people who drink alcohol socially and occasionally may experience problems.

The attitudes of professionals, families, and elderly people themselves about alcohol and alcoholism may present barriers to effective assessment. Professionals, even those who work routinely with elderly people, see alcohol and drug problems as minor problems and the result of poor self-control and are often not aware that even a small amount of alcohol may have untoward effects and that elderly people may experience serious problems related to drinking (Brown, 1982). This lack of awareness is further complicated by the fact that many of the indicators of alcoholism and alcohol-related problems are seen as consequences of health problems that elderly people routinely experience. The following case example, taken from the records of a geriatric clinic that specializes in the general medical care of elderly people, illustrates this problem.

Mr. B, an 85-year-old white man, has been a patient of this clinic for the past three years. He came in today with complaints of a sore back after a fall in his home last week. He is in good health and appears to be well nourished and alert. He reports he has had several falls in the past two weeks. His neighbor reports that Mr. B has had at least two episodes or urinary incontinence. The neighbor also reports that Mr. B's speech has sounded slurred of late when she has called to check on him in the evening. Mr. B denies any problems other than the soreness in his back. A physical examination and laboratory studies ruled out urinary-tract infection and yielded no significant findings. The plan includes further observation and a home evaluation of safety hazards.

During the monthly review of cases, one of the team members remarked, "If he were younger, this would sound like a drinking problem." Indeed, Mr. B's falls and incontinence did turn out to be a drinking problem. Mr. B had received a case of beer from his nephew and had renewed his habit of having one or two beers during the evening, something he had given up after an episode of poor health about ten years earlier. Although nothing in his history would lead one to suspect that he is an alcoholic, the increased ingestion of beer and his body's decreased capacity to tolerate the effects of alcohol led him to have problems. Mr. B responded well to a discussion of the effects of alcohol and cut down from two beers to one glass of beer each evening. He did not experience any more episodes of falling, slurred speech, or incontinence. If Mr. B had been younger, it is reasonable to believe that the staff would have initially considered the role of alcohol use, rather than an illness or other health problem, to be the root of his problem.

The professionals in this case should not be judged too harshly for missing the role of alcohol in Mr. B's problems. As evidenced by the DSM-III-R criteria for Alcohol Intoxication (Table 16.2) there is much overlap in the diagnosis of alcohol problems and age-related physical problems.

These criteria capture the characteristics of persons who are intoxicated with alcohol. Aside from point A, they also capture the characteristics of an elderly person who may suffer from a physical illness, such as an infection or various organic mental impairments. Point D, in fact, suggests the possibility that other physical or mental disorders can result in these types of behavior and signs. Therefore, practitioners must rule out other physical or

TABLE 16.2
Diagnostic Criteria for Alcohol Intoxication (303.00)

A. Recent ingestion of alcohol (with no evidence suggesting that the amount was insufficient to cause intoxication in most people).

B. Maladaptive behavior changes (e.g., Disinhibition of sexual or aggressive impulses, mood lability, impaired judgment, impaired social or occupational functioning).

C. At least one of the following signs
   1. Slurred speech
   2. Incoordination
   3. Unsteady gait
   4. Nystagmus
   5. Flushed face

D. Not due to any physical or other mental disorder

SOURCE: Reprinted with permission from the *Diagnostic and Statistical Manual of Mental Disorders, Third Edition, Revised* (p. 128). Copyright 1987 American Psychiatric Association.

behavior and signs. Therefore, practitioners must rule out other physical or mental impairments to achieve an accurate diagnosis of alcohol intoxication. Given the increased risk of health problems in later life, it is not surprising that the signs and symptoms of alcohol use are frequently interpreted as physical or mental illnesses. The fact that professionals, families, and older persons themselves often are not sensitive to the problems of alcohol use and alcoholism in the elderly further complicates the assessment issues. In work with elderly people, it is more an issue of "ruling in" alcohol use or abuse than of ruling out other physical and mental problems.

Social workers and other health professionals who work with older people in hospitals or nursing homes have learned that the failure to ask questions about alcohol use may result in serious physical problems, so that many intake or admitting forms include questions about alcohol use. However, the method of interviewing about drinking can affect the way an older person answers. Consider the following case example:

Mrs. V is a 79-year-old woman who was admitted to the hospital for the removal of her gall bladder. She was admitted the night before the surgery, and early in the evening complained of insomnia and a slight headache. The physician prescribed a mild sedative, she slept well, and the operation was uneventful and successful. Mrs. V recovered speedily until late the first postoperative day, when her niece noticed that she was anxious and seemed depressed about her chances of recovery. Her blood pressure became elevated, and she felt nauseated and vomited several times. She had no history of previous illnesses, and there was no record of alcoholism or alcohol problems in her record. At this point the niece wondered aloud to the nurses whether it was important for them to know that her aunt routinely drank three or four glasses of sherry each evening to help her sleep.

Mrs. V was not experiencing problems related to her surgery or hospital stay; she was exhibiting symptoms of alcohol withdrawal. Without the information provided by her niece, it is likely that the medical staff would have explored other physical or mental illnesses as the root of her problems. The DSM-III-R criteria of uncomplicated alcohol withdrawal are presented in Table 16.3.

In this vignette, the admitting social history had included a question about alcohol use and alcohol problems. Mrs. V, who had grown up during

TABLE 16.3
Diagnostic Criteria for Uncomplicated Alcohol Withdrawal (291.80)

A. Cessation of prolonged (several days or longer) heavy ingestion of alcohol or reduction in the amount of alcohol ingested, followed within several hours by course tremor of hands, tongue, or eyelids, and at least one of the following.
  1. Nausea or vomiting
  2. Malaise or weakness
  3. Autonomic hyperactivity tachycardia, sweating, elevated blood pressure
  4. Anxiety
  5. Depressed mood or irritability
  6. Transient hallucinations or illusions
  7. Headache
  8. Insomnia
B. Not due to any physical or mental disorder, such as alcohol withdrawal delirium.

SOURCE: Reprinted with permission from the *Diagnostic and Statistical Manual of Mental Disorders, Third Edition, Revised* (p. 130). Copyright 1987 American Psychiatric Association.

Prohibition and the Temperance movement, had abstained from drinking any type of alcohol for most of her life. During the past several years, she had experienced problems sleeping and had tried, on the advice of her neighbor, a "tonic" of sherry to help her sleep. Gradually, she had increased her use to the point where she had several "tonics" each evening. When the social worker had asked, "Do you drink alcohol—beer, wine, or mixed drink?" Mrs. V had honestly replied, no. While the amount of alcohol she consumed was not great by the standards used for younger adults, her body's decreased ability to metabolize and increased sensitivity to alcohol had caused her to experience the symptoms of withdrawal.

Assessment Techniques

A common mistake in assessments of an elderly person's use of alcohol is to omit a short definition of what you mean by the word *alcohol*. For example, some people do not count beer as an alcoholic beverage. A reliable opening question might be phrased, "Do you ever have a glass of beer, a glass of wine, or a mixed drink like a highball?" By mentioning the different types of alcohol, you can evaluate the extent to which the older person understands your question. It also opens the door to a discussion of how much the person drinks, how often, and under what circumstances. Many people do not drink often, so you need to remind some of them of the occasions when alcohol is present. Especially with people who say that they never drink, it is important to respond with a statement such as, "That means that you don't ever have a glass of wine with Sunday dinner or at holidays or parties."

Elderly people may not link the problems they experience after drinking with the ingestion of alcohol. Most people interpret the term *alcohol problems* as large, serious events, such as losing a job or being arrested. They do not necessarily associate the upset stomach they have after two glasses of wine at the anniversary party as an alcohol-related problem. A thorough interviewer is specific not only about the types of alcohol used, but about the purposes, the situation, and the way the elderly person uses alcohol in his or her life.

Alcohol-related problems in younger people are often first noticed because of a behavioral consequence of alcohol use. An assessment of alcohol use may be triggered by behavior at work, at home, or in public. Work-related indicators include increased absenteeism or poor performance on the job. Interpersonal relationships of alcoholics and problem drinkers are often dysfunctional; families and friends call attention to problems. Although elderly people with alcohol problems also have dysfunctional interpersonal relationships, they are more likely to live alone, to be retired, and to have limited daily social interactions. Often there is not another person in the house to link the behavior with the ingestion of alcohol. Problems with the law, especially arrests for driving under the influence of alcohol and for public intoxication, are some of the primary ways that younger individuals with alcohol problems come to the attention of professionals. Elderly people, however, are less likely to be arrested for any alcohol-related crime and, therefore, their problems with alcohol may go undetected for a long time.

Behavioral indicators of alcohol-related problems must be adapted for use with elderly people. Alcohol use should be investigated as a possible factor in any significant changes in behavioral patterns, significant losses, or changes in health status experienced by older people. For example, have the person's nutritional habits changed? Is he or she not as hungry as usual? Could it be that he or she is too full after drinking to eat? Is the person spending less money on food? Is he or she using this money to buy alcohol? Does medication seem to be losing its effectiveness? Could another substance, such as alcohol, be present in the system? Does the person seem to be unusually forgetful? Does there seem to be a particular time of day when the forgetfulness is worse than at other times? Has the person had any unusual accidents? Is he or she falling or tripping more than usual? Does the house look different? Is it unusually dirty or disorderly? Certainly, alcohol is not always the cause of these changes in behavior among elderly people. However, alcohol can and does play a causative role for some elderly persons; therefore, drinking behavior warrants attention in the assessment of all health and social problems.

The previous case examples illustrated several summary points about assessment: (1) Professionals and family members who are not aware of alcoholism and alcohol-related problems in the elderly are likely to overlook signs and symptoms of alcohol use or to attribute them to physical illness. (2) Questions about drinking alcohol should be included in initial health-screening visits with older people. (3) Questions about drinking alcohol should be routinely asked in relation to changes in behavior, attitude, or physical functioning in older people. (4) Questions about alcohol use should address lifelong patterns and reasons for changes in drinking patterns, as well as the current use of, and problems with, alcohol.

Screening and Assessment Instruments

A variety of assessment instruments exist, some of which have been developed for research purposes and some of which are used primarily in clinical situations (see Jacobson, 1989, for a comprehensive review of the major screening instruments). Few instruments have been developed for use with elderly people, but most can be adapted to evaluate them. Three of the most common will be reviewed here: The CAGE test, The HEAT test, and the Michigan alcoholism Screening Test (MAST).

The CAGE questionnaire (Mayfield, McLeod, & Hall, 1974, p. 1122) is one of the quickest screening tools available. The acronym CAGE stands for the first letter of key words in the four questions that make up the questionnaire: "(1) Have you ever felt you should *cut* down on your drinking? (2) Have people *annoyed* you by criticizing your drinking? (3) Have you ever felt *guilty* about your drinking? (4) Have you ever had a drink first thing in the morning (an *eye-opener*) to steady your nerves or get rid of a hangover?" Although the brevity and the results of the validation studies support the utility of the CAGE for the general population, there are some issues in its use with older people. The fact that the questions are so straightforward may influence elderly people to answer in ways that minimize their problems with alcohol. Elderly women, especially, are prone to feelings of guilt and shame around problems related to drinking. Thus, sensitivity to the issues of guilt and shame will preclude the exclusive use of the CAGE as an assessment tool. Jacobson (1989, p. 22) questioned the lack of a temporal framework in the CAGE and suggested that the practitioner should ask, " 'When?' in response to any affirmative answer." The temporal framework is especially important in work with elderly people, who may reflect upon their use over their entire life in answering the CAGE questions. It may be helpful to ask an older person to answer the questions in reference to particular time frames (e.g., the past month, the past three months, the past year, at any time during your life) to understand that person's alcohol-use pattern.

A variation of the screening ideas implicit in the CAGE test is a rapid screening tool entitled HEAT (Willinbring & Spring, 1988, p. 28). The questions in the tool are "(1) *How* do you use alcohol? (2) Have you ever thought you used to *excess*? (3) Has *anyone* else ever thought you used too much? (4) Have you ever had any *trouble* resulting from your use?" Although the softer language of the HEAT gives it an advantage over the CAGE for use with older people, the time-frame issue is still a problem for the HEAT. Hence, a yes answer to any of the questions on the CAGE or the HEAT must be explored fully.

The MAST (Selzer, 1971; Selzer, Vinocur, & Van Rooijan, 1975) is a familiar and widely used instrument among both practitioners and researchers. It consists of twenty-five weighted items and can be used in an interview or as a pencil-and-paper test.

Interviews take about twenty minutes. The questions review the signs and symptoms of alcoholism; a score of 5 or more identifies a problem related to alcohol use. The scoring of the MAST is at issue for use with elderly people, since some studies (e.g., Jacobson, 1989) have found that using a cutoff point of 5 results in unacceptably high rates of false-positive rates. Jacobson suggested that using a cutoff point of 12 for the general population results in a more balanced rate of false-positive and false-negative rates. Johnson's (1989) review of assessment instruments for use with elderly people revealed that the MAST has excellent specificity and sensitivity in elderly men.

TREATMENT OF ALCOHOLISM AND ALCOHOL-RELATED PROBLEMS

Motivating Older People to Seek Treatment

Once a diagnosis of alcohol problems or alcoholism has been made, the next step is to motivate the person to seek and accept treatment (Miller,

1989). The same issues that color diagnosis and assessment may also influence an older individual's decision to seek treatment and to remain active in the treatment program. Especially salient in work with elderly people are the guilt and shame associated with alcohol use. Even though Prohibition and the Temperance movement no longer strongly influence this country's social mores, the principles of those times are often ingrained in the belief systems of older clients. A sensitive practitioner will explore the difference between denial of a problem and guilt and shame about the existence of a problem and the stigma of a label of alcoholism in helping an older person to accept treatment.

As with other health and mental health problems, older people may not feel that they are worth the help since they believe they do not play productive roles in society. Therefore, issues of self-esteem, self-worth, and potential are central in motivational work with the elderly person and his or her family (Rathbone-McCuan, 1988). The practitioner may be faced with such questions as "Why should I give up [or take away] drinking; it is my [his or her] last pleasure in life?" While drinking may be the only pleasure a person derives from life, it is the practitioner's role to point out the problems and risks associated with the continued use of alcohol. It is this issue of confrontation—making the implicit, explicit—in the assessment of problems and the development of motivation for treatment that requires detailed familiarity with the specific risks associated with alcohol use and the potentials of treatment for elderly people.

A variety of pressure points are useful in stacking the deck so the individual chooses treatment. In work with younger people, for example, addictions workers often use the possible loss of a job or the alienation of family members to tip the balance in favor of treatment. The facts of later life—retirement and widowhood—however, preclude these pressure points for many elderly people. Just as the behavioral indicators of the problem must be adjusted for older people, so must the motivational approaches. The message is not that elderly people are particularly unmotivated to seek treatment, but that their life circumstances give rise to different barriers that must be addressed.

As was mentioned previously, today's cohort of elderly people grew up in a time when alcohol use was illegal and sinful. The admission that they use alcohol may give rise to more shame and guilt in older people, especially older women, than in younger populations. Seeking treatment may only reinforce that shame and may be seen as another failure, since many older people believe that personal problems are not to be dwelt upon. Denial is a central issue in work with alcoholics and problem drinkers. However, stigma, shame, and guilt are also salient issues, and workers must evaluate and explore all these areas before labeling an elderly person unmotivated or resistant to treatment. Likewise, special concern is warranted in work with minority elderly people who may have been subjected to racism and discrimination throughout their lives. It is important for social workers to understand the meaning the elderly person attributes to drinking-related problems and then to place that meaning within the cultural context of the person's life. Few studies have examined the ethnic and cultural differences that are pertinent in the use of alcohol in later life.

Gerontological social workers are familiar with the usefulness of a home assessment and are accustomed to visiting their clients at home instead of seeing them in the office. This is not necessarily the experience of addictions workers, who are more often tied to institutional and agency settings. Therefore, the homebound elderly person in need of treatment may present a special motivational problem. Not only must the person accept the fact that he or she is in need of treatment and be willing to seek it, but the person must also be willing and able to leave his or her home. For a person who has been homebound because of physical or mental illness, the thought of leaving home and adapting to another place is a special barrier. Workers who are faced with homebound clients will do well to minimize the role of the denial of drinking problems until the issues of fear, adaptation, and stigma are addressed.

Older adults are a heterogeneous group. However, despite individual differences, they have common concerns: independence, health and health care, and finances. These common concerns may be used to motivate them to decide to stop drinking and to seek treatment. In general, elderly people are concerned about their health and do not want to be ill, debilitated, or dependent upon others. An emphasis on the negative effects of alcohol upon a person's health can make issues of use and abuse more salient. Since most elderly people take medication, the difficulties that arise when alcohol and prescription or over-the-counter drugs are mixed is a good place to start. If the person has a chronic health problem, point out the complicating health problems that may arise if he or she continues to use alcohol. For some conditions, the use of alcohol may be life threatening. Don't assume that physicians and other health care professionals have outlined the contraindications of alcohol; remember that many of them believe that elderly people do not drink and therefore do not address the issue.

Social workers can also capitalize upon elderly people's relationships with family members and friends to increase their motivation to seek treatment. Of special importance is the relationship to grandchildren or other younger family members or friends. If an older person can pinpoint a relationship in which he or she feels needed, the preservation of that relationship may be a strong motivating force for treatment.

The fact that people are in their later years has been used by some as a deterrent to treatment. Older alcoholics and problem drinkers may think they have lived their lives and do not have much in their future. However, a person's acceptance of the fact that he or she has limited time left can be used to undergird the decision to obtain treatment. The practitioner's role is to point out the opportunity to spend the remaining time as productively as possible and to present treatment for alcohol problems as a bridge to that goal. Certainly, this view may be seen in a developmental perspective of later life; the older adult attempts to review life's accomplishments as a way of giving meaning to his or her life and in reconciling hopes and reality to leave a legacy.

Treatment Levels and Options

Treatment for alcoholism and alcohol-related problems typically involves levels and options of services. Detoxification is the initial step into treatment for many people. The purpose of detoxification services is to withdraw people from the alcohol and other drugs in their systems. Because of the side effects of withdrawal, detoxification services are usually supervised by medical personnel and are located in hospitals. Typically, people stay in detoxification for three to five days. Elderly people may require a longer period of detoxification because their slowed metabolism increases the length of time that drugs remain in their systems. The presence of chronic and acute medical problems in, and the use of prescription drugs by, elderly people also warrant special attention during detoxification. However, the limited array of medical services offered by alcoholism treatment agencies and institutions may hamper the admission of older people, especially those with acute and chronic medical problems.

The next level of treatment is rehabilitation, which includes primary treatment, intermediate treatment, and aftercare services. After the alcohol is removed from the person's system, the goals of primary treatment are for the person to diagnose the problems alcohol has caused, to increase his or her knowledge of the effects of alcohol in all aspects of life, and to develop a personal plan of daily living without alcohol. Options for primary care include inpatient or residential care and day treatment. Intermediate care follows primary care and involves halfway-house or three-quarter-way-house programs. Aftercare services continue when the person completes the course of treatment and returns to the routines of daily life. Aftercare may continue for a year or longer and usually consists of weekly or monthly meetings. In the United States, the twelve steps of Alcoholics Anonymous are central to most rehabilitation programs. Participation in the fellowship of Alcoholics Anonymous undergirds the treatment and aftercare plans of most individuals who enter any phase of treatment.

CLINICAL ISSUES IN ALCOHOLISM TREATMENT WITH ELDERLY PEOPLE

Saunders (1983) outlined some of the common features of alcoholism treatment services that present barriers to full participation by older people. One is the emphasis on social and emotional problems that are experienced by younger people. Programs that are geared primarily toward the concerns of younger people may reinforce the older person's feeling that he or she is not worth treatment and will not benefit from it. The clinical component of most treatment programs consists of a mix of individual and group therapy. The philosophy of such a mix is that the clients need individualized counseling as well as to be part of a peer-support system. The needs and abilities of elderly people may warrant the modification of the mix of individual and group modalities.

Today's older generation came of age in a time when people were taught to hide their feelings and not to reveal personal information in public. Therefore, the focus on the recognition and discussion of personal feelings, which are common therapeutic techniques used in alcohol treatment, may be too painful or too foreign for some elders to tolerate. A respectful and gentle, yet firm and supportive stance with elderly people is preferable to direct, public confrontation. Another related, but separate point is the use of profanity and the graphic discussion of sexual topics by younger clients during the course of group treatment. Most professionals in the field become tolerant of this type of disclosure as part of their therapeutic work and forget the shocking effect these stories and language can have upon older people, especially women. In light of these special considerations, some have argued that the treatment needs of older people are best served in age-specific programs.

The fast pace of many programs may not permit the elderly person the time he or she needs to assimilate the content. Not only do many older people need additional time to comprehend and digest new information, they also may need a slower physical pace. A nap in the middle of the day's schedule may be viewed negatively for younger people, but it may be a functional addition to the therapeutic regimen for elderly people.

The audiovisual materials used in educational and therapeutic groups may not be suitable for older people with communication deficits. Large-print materials and amplification devices are not standard in most alcohol treatment programs. Literacy is another issue in that the level of literacy in the older population is generally less than that in younger groups.

The role of community and family supports in the treatment of alcohol problems in the elderly needs to be emphasized. Most treatment programs include an aftercare component that involves a weekly meeting to discuss the clients' experiences in living without alcohol or other drugs. For elderly people, the aftercare component may need to be more intensive and to focus on the development of social contacts and new social roles, since many are retired, widowed, or at risk of social isolation because of age-related social changes.

Age-specific versus Age-mixed Programs

The question of whether treatment for alcohol-related problems and alcoholism should be included in treatment programs with people of all ages or segregated by age is central to service delivery. Janik and Dunham (1983) analyzed data from 550 alcoholism treatment programs supported by the National Institute on Alcohol Abuse and Alcoholism to learn if elderly people fared as well in these settings as did younger people. They found few differences in treatment or outcome among age groups. However, the group aged 60 and older showed significantly greater improvement than did the 40–59 group. On the basis of these findings, Janik and Dunham supported the notion that elderly peple do as well in mixed-age treatment settings as do younger people. At least two groups of researchers have taken issue with this position (Kofoed et al., 1987; Moos, 1983). Kofoed and colleagues asserted that the central question is not whether elderly people do as well as do younger people in treatment, but "Do older alcoholics in elder-specific treatment do better than similar older alcoholics in typical mixed-age treatment?" (p. 46). Their argument and findings support a value-added description of age-specific treatment for older people. The benefits of age-specific peer interaction that they found in their small sample were increased levels of compliance with and completion of treatment.

There is a growing number of descriptions and evaluations of age-specific alcoholism treatment programs (Dupree et al., 1984; Gordon, 1988b; "Older Problem Drinker," 1975; Saunders, 1983; Schmall & Stiehl, 1984). All these programs view the older individual as being capable of change, but in need of specialized approaches to deal with stigma, to accommodate communication deficits, and to adjust educational and motivational materials to reflect relevant topics in the elderly person's life.

DIRECTIONS FOR PRACTICE RESEARCH AND POLICY

This chapter closes, in a way, where it began by talking about the partnership between professionals in the field of aging and professionals in the treatment of addictions. Who should take responsibility for the assessment and treatment of elderly people who experience problems with alcohol? That the elderly are not the largest or most vocal group needing alcohol treatment services and that alcoholism and alcohol-related problems are not the most prominent issues in gerontology have allowed both sets of professionals to assume that the other was providing the services. One can argue that both gerontologists and addiction-treatment specialists have a role to play with this population. For gerontologists, the role is one of increased sensitivity to the impact of any amount of alcohol use on the health and safety of older people. It is important that gerontologists be skilled in assessment techniques that facilitate a discussion of alcohol use among elderly clients and the relationship of this use to health and social problems. Many community settings, such as meals programs and recreational programs, conduct health and social assessments as part of their admissions process. These settings provide excellent opportunities for prevention and early detection of alcohol problems among elderly people who may not come to the attention of other service providers. Gerontological social workers must examine their attitudes toward alcohol and alcoholism, become skilled in the detection of alcohol-related problems, and develop service-referral linkages with alcohol treatment services.

On the other hand, practitioners in the field of addictions have much to learn about the treatment of elderly people with alcohol problems. Not only must particular aspects of treatment programs be adapted to accommodate the special needs of elderly people, but professionals must adjust their clinical stances to provide the additional motivational and educational support that is necessary. These practitioners must examine their attitudes toward aging and aged people to be effective with this group. Additional content on normal aging and the developmental context of aging in this society would be welcome additions to continuing education programs for addictions specialists who work with elderly people.

Fortunately, collaborative service models for elderly people exist. The work done in several states to address the issues of mental health problems among elderly people could be directly applied to the problems of alcohol abuse (Biegel & Farkas, 1989). Models in the field of addiction treatment dealing with the problems of dual diagnoses—mental health problems and addiction problems—can also be adapted for work with aging populations. Educational and training efforts that involve program planners and practitioners in both arenas are in order.

Creative approaches to service delivery must be coupled with equal attention to the development of knowledge and practice research. Certainly, the cohort-related questions about the use of alcohol and the willingness to use treatment services by different groups of elderly people are ripe for examination. A number of questions in the addiction treatment literature address the efficacy of treatment modalities, the role of relapse in treatment, the use of spirituality in treatment, and the process of recovery in light of other social and personal problems. The issues of women's recovery should be especially relevant to practitioners who work with elderly people, since an increasing number of women who have used alcohol throughout their lives will enter late life in the next decade. In addition, since the knowledge base on the treatment of minority elderly persons with alcohol problems is weak, there is a need to develop culturally sensitive outreach and treatment models.

In conclusion, there has been much progress in our knowledge of the nature of alcoholism and alcohol-related problems among elderly people during the past twelve years. The challenge for the future is to apply this knowledge in addressing the needs of older people who use and abuse alcohol. The fact that this society will experience a sustained growth in the number of people over age 65 warrants an investment of time and resources on effective strategies of prevention and treatment for alcohol problems in later life. We cannot safely assume that future cohorts of elderly people will exhibit the same patterns of decreased alcohol use and the small proportion of problems as has the group who has been influenced by the Temperance movement and Prohibition. The changes in the roles that older people play in society, in the norms and patterns of alcohol use, and in the attitudes that people hold toward aging and alcohol use will all have an effect on the nature of services and social work practice in the future.

BIBLIOGRAPHY

Abrams, R. C., & Alexopoulos, G. S. (1988). Substance abuse in the elderly: Over-the-counter and illegal drugs. *Hospital and Community Psychiatry, 39*, 822–829.

Adams, W. L. (1990). Alcohol intake in the elderly: Changes with age in a cross-sectional and longitudinal study. *Journal of the American Geriatrics Society, 38*, 211–216.

American Psychiatric Association. (1987). *Diagnostic and statistical manual of mental disorders* (3rd ed., rev.). Washington, DC: Author.

Atkinson, J. H., & Schuckit, M. A. (1981). Alcoholism and over-the-counter and prescriptions drug misuse in the elderly. In C. Eisdorfer (Ed.), *Annual Review of Gerontology and Geriatrics* (Vol. 2, pp. 255–285). New York: Springer.

Atkinson, R. M., & Kofoed, L. L. (1982). Alcohol and drug abuse in old age: A clinical perspective. *Substance and Alcohol Actions/Misuse, 3*, 353–368.

Babor, T. F. (1981). Evaluating the evaluation process. In R. E. Meyer, B. C. Glueck, J. E. O'Brien, T. F. Babor, J. Jaffe, & J. R. Stabenau (Eds.), *Research monograph No. 5. Evaluation of the alcoholic: Implications for research, theory, and treatment* (pp. x–xvi). Rockville, MD: National Institute on Alcohol Abuse and Alcoholism.

Bailey, M. B., Haberman, P. W., & Alksne, H. (1969). The epidemiology of alcoholism in an urban residential area. *Quarterly Journal of Alcohol Studies, 26*, 19–40.

Barnes, G. (1979). Alcohol use among older persons: Findings from a western New York State general population study. *Journal of the American Geriatrics Society, 27*, 244–250.

Biegel, D. E., & Farkas, K. J. (1989). *Mental health services for the elderly: Service delivery issues.* Cleveland, OH: Monograph Series, Western Reserve Geriatric Education Center, Case Western Reserve University.

Bloom, P. J. (1983). Alcoholism after sixty. *American Family Physician, 28*, 111–113

Blose, I. L. (1978). The relationship of alcohol to aging and the elderly. *Alcoholism Clinical and Experimental Research, 2*, 17–21.

Branch, L. (1978). *Boston elders: A survey of needs.* Boston: Commission on Affairs of the Elderly.

Brody, J. (1982). Aging and alcohol use. *Journal of the American Geriatrics Society, 30*, 123–126.

Brown, B. (1982). Professionals' perceptions of drug and alcohol abuse among the elderly. *The Gerontologist, 22*, 519–525.

Cahalan, D. (1987). *Understanding America's drinking problem: How to combat the hazards of alcohol.* San Francisco: Jossey-Bass.

Cahalan, D., Cisin, I., & Crossley, H. (1969). *American drinking practices: A national study of drinking behavior and attitudes* (Monograph No. 6). New Brunswick, NJ: Rutgers Center of Alcohol Studies.

Carruth, B. (1980). *An exploration of some subgroup differences among older alcoholics.* Ann Arbor, MI: University Microfilms International.

Chatham, L. R. (1986). Greetings from the National Institute on Alcohol Abuse and Alcoholism. In G. Maddox, L. Robins, & N. Rosenberg (Eds.), *Nature and extent of alcohol problems among the elderly* (pp. xi–xiii). New York: Springer.

Coons, S. J., Hendricks, J., & Sheahan, S. (1988). Self-medication with non-prescription drugs. *Generations, 12*(4), 22–26.

Drew, L. R. H. (1968). Alcohol as a self-limiting disease. *Quarterly Journal of Alcohol Studies, 29,* 956–976.

Duckworth, G., & Rosenblatt, A. (1976). Helping the elderly alcoholic. *Social Casework, 56,* 296–301.

Dunham, R. G. (1981). Aging and changing patterns of alcohol use. *Journal of Psychoactive Drugs, 13,* 143–151.

Dupree, L. W., Broslowski, H., & Schonfeld, L. (1984). The gerontology alcohol project: A behavioral treatment program for elderly alcohol abusers. *The Gerontologist, 24,* 510–516.

Ekerdt, S. J., DeLabry, L. O., Glynn, R. J., & Davis, R. W. (1989). Change in drinking behaviors with retirement: Findings from the Normative Aging Study. *Journal of Studies on Alcohol, 50,* 347–353.

Giordano, J. A., & Beckham, K. (1985). Alcohol use and abuse in old age: An examination of Type II alcoholism. *Journal of Gerontological Social Work, 9,* 65–83.

Glantz, M. D., & Backenheimer, M. S. (1988). Substance abuse among elderly women. *Clinical Gerontologist, 8*(1), 3–26.

Gomberg, E. L. (1980). *Drinking and problem drinking among the elderly: Usage and problems* (No. 1). Ann Arbor: University of Michigan, Institute of Gerontology.

Goodwin, J. S., Sanchez, C., Thomas, P., Hunt, C., Garry, P., & Goodwin, J. (1987). Alcohol intake in a healthy elderly population. *American Journal of Public Health, 77,* 173–177.

Gordon, M. (1988a, January–February). Addressing individual needs of older adult patients. *Alcoholism and addiction, 8*(1), 20–21.

Gordon, M. (1988b). Sage Crossing: A treatment program designed for elders. *Generations, 12*(4), 82–83.

Gottheil, E., Druley, K., & Skoloda, T. (1985). *The combined problems of alcoholism, drug addiction, and aging.* Springfield, IL: Charles C Thomas.

Hinrichsen, J. (1984, Spring). Toward improving treatment services for alcoholics of advanced age. *Alcohol Health and Research World,* 31–39.

Jacobson, G. R. (1989). A comprehensive approach to pretreatment evaluation: 1. Detection, assessment and diagnosis of alcoholism. In R. Hester & W. Miller (Eds.), *Handbook of alcoholism treatment approaches: Effective alternatives* (pp. 17–53). New York: Pergamon Press.

Janik, S. W., & Dunham, R. G. (1983). A nationwide examination of the need for specific alcoholism treatment programs for the elderly. *Journal of Studies on Alcoholism, 44,* 307–317.

Johnson, L. K. (1989). How to diagnose and treat chemical dependency in the elderly. *Journal of Gerontological Nursing, 15*(12), 22–26.

Joyce, K. (1984). *Alcohol use and event-related stress among community elderly.* Unpublished doctoral dissertation, School of Applied Social Sciences, Case Western Reserve University, Cleveland, OH.

Kastenbaum, R. (1988). In moderation: How some older people find pleasure and meanings in alcoholic beverages. *Generations, 12*(4), 68–73.

Kermis, M. D. (1986). The epidemiology of mental disorder in the elderly: A response to the Senate/AARP report. *The Gerontologist, 26*(5), 482–487.

Knupfer, G. (1967). The epidemiology of problem drinking. *American Journal of Public Health, 57,* 973–986.

Kofoed, L. L., Tolson, R. L., Atkinson, R. M., Toth, R. L., & Turner, J. (1987). Treatment compliance of elder alcoholics: An elder-specific approach is superior to "mainstreaming." *Journal of Studies on Alcohol, 48,* 47–51.

Kofoed, L. L., Tolson, R. L., Atkinson, R. M., Turner, J., & Toth, R. L. (1984). Elderly groups in an alcoholism clinic. In R. M. Atkinson (Ed.), *Alcohol and drug abuse in old age* (pp. 35–48). Washington, DC: American Psychiatric Press.

Kola, L. A., Kosberg, J. I., & Joyce, K. (1984). The alcoholic elderly client: Assessment of policies and practices of service providers. *The Gerontologist, 24,* 517–521.

Kola, L. A., Kosberg, J. I., & Wegner-Burch, K. (1980). Perceptions of the treatment responsibilities for the alcoholic elderly client. *Social Work in Health Care, 6,* 67–90.

Kosberg, J. I., & Harris, A. P. (1978). Attitudes toward elderly clients. *Health and Social Work, 3,* 67–90.

Kraft, P. G. (1988). Hopedale Hall: Geriatric drug and alcohol treatments in a community-based hospital. *Generations, 12*(4), 84–86.

Lamy, P. P. (1988). Actions of alcohol and drugs in older people. *Generations, 12*(4), 13–19.

Maddox, G., Robins, L., & Rosenberg, N. (Eds.). (1986). *Nature and extent of alcohol problems among the elderly.* New York: Springer.

Mayfield, D., McLeod, G., & Hall, P. (1974). The CAGE questionnaire: Validation of a new alcoholism screening instrument. *American Journal of Psychiatry, 131,* 1121–1123.

Meyers, A. R., Goldman, E., Hingson, R., Scotch, N., & Mangione, T. (1981). Evidence for cohort or generational differences in the drinking behavior of older adults. *International Journal of Aging and Human Development, 14,* 31–44.

Meyers, A. R., Hingson, R., Mucatel, M., Heeren, T., & Goldman, E. (1985). The social epidemiology of alcohol use by urban older adults. *International Journal of Aging and Human Development, 21,* 49–59.

Miller, W. R. (1989). Increasing motivation for change. In R. Hester & W. Miller

(Eds.), *Handbook of alcoholism treatment approaches: Effective alternatives* (pp. 67–80). New York: Pergamon Press.

Mishara, B., & Kastenbaum, R. (1980). *Alcohol and old age.* New York: Grune & Stratton.

Moos, R. H. (1983). Reaction paper. In G. Maddox, L. Robins, & N. Rosenberg (Eds.), *Nature and extent of alcohol problems among the elderly* (National Institute on Alcohol Abuse and Alcoholism Research Monograph No. 14, pp. 139–147). Washington, DC: U.S. Government Printing Office.

National Institute of Alcohol Abuse and Alcoholism. (1981). *A preliminary report on aging and alcoholism.* Washington, DC: National Institute of Alcohol Abuse and Alcoholism.

Older problem drinker. (1975, Spring). *Alcohol Health and Research World,* pp. 2–17.

Parrella, D. P., & Filstead, W. J. (1988). Definition of onset in the development of onset-based alcoholism typologies. *Journal of Studies on Alcohol, 49,* 85–92.

Rathbone-McCuan, E. (1988). Promoting help-seeking behavior among elders with chemical dependencies. *Generations, 12*(4), 37–40.

Robins, L. N., Helzer, J. E., & Przybeck, T. (1986). Substance abuse in the general population. In J. Barrett & R. M. Rose (Eds.), *Mental disorders in the community: Findings from psychiatric epidemiology* (pp. 9–13). New York: Guilford Press.

Rosin, A. J., & Glatt, M. W. (1971). Alcohol excess in the elderly. *Quarterly Journal of Studies on Alcohol, 32,* 53–59.

Salzman, C., VanderKolk, B., & Shader, B. I. (1975). Psychopharmacology and the geriatric patient. In R. I. Shader (Ed.), *Manual of psychiatric therapeutics.* Boston: Little, Brown.

Saunders, S. J. (1983, April 23). *Treatment program unique to the elderly alcohol and substance abuser.* Paper presented at the School for Addiction Studies Mini Conference on Substance Abuse and the Elderly, Toronto, Canada.

Schmall, V. L., & Stiehl, R. E. (1984). A workshop for family and friends. *Generations, 12*(4), 80–81.

Schuckit, A., & Pastor, P. A. (1978). The elderly as a unique population: Alcohol. *Alcoholism: Clinical and Experimental Research, 2*(1), 31–38.

Selzer, M. L. (1971). The Michigan Alcoholism Screening Test: The quest for a new diagnostic instrument. *American Journal of Psychiatry, 127,* 89–94.

Selzer, M. L., Vinokur, A., & Van Rooijan, L. (1975). A self-administered short Michigan Alcoholism Screening Test (SMAST). *Quarterly Journal of Studies on Alcohol, 36,* 117–126.

Sumberg, D. (1985). Social work with elderly alcoholics: Some practical considerations. *Journal of Gerontological Social Work, 8,* 169–180.

Volpe, A., & Kastenbaum, R. (1967). Beer, wine, and "TLC" in a geriatric hospital. *American Journal of Nursing, 67,* 100–103.

Wallace, J. (1989). A biopsychosocial model of alcoholism. *Social Casework: The Journal of Contemporary Social Work, 70,* 325–332.

Warheit, G. J., & Auth, J. B. (1984). The mental health and social correlates of alcohol use among differing life cycle groups. In G. Maddox, L. Robins, & N. Rosenberg (Eds.), *Nature and extent of alcohol problems among the elderly* (pp. 29–66). New York: Springer.

Whittington, F. J. (1988). Making it better: Drinking and drugging in old age. *Generations, 12*(4), 5–7.

Williams, M. (1984, Spring). Alcohol and the elderly: An overview. *Alcohol Health and Research World,* 4–8.

Willinbring, M., & Spring, W. D. (1988). Evaluating alcohol use in elders. *Generations, 12*(4), 27–31.

Zimberg, S. (1974). Two types of problem drinkers: Both can be managed. *Geriatrics, 29,* 135–138.

Zimberg, S. (1978). Alcohol and the elderly. In D. Peterson, F. Whittington, & B. Payne (Eds.), *Drugs and the elderly.* Springfield, IL: Charles C Thomas.

Zimberg, S. (1984). Psychosocial treatment of elderly alcoholics. In S. Zimberg, J. Wallace, & S. Blume (Eds.), *Practical approaches to alcoholism psychotherapy* (2nd ed., pp. 347–366). New York: Plenum Press.

17

Medication Problems and Drug Abuse

Edith S. Lisansky Gomberg

There can be little argument that in old age there is an increase in both acute and chronic illnesses and, accompanying such an increase, more use of medication. When drugs are classified as prescription medications, over-the-counter (OTC) medications, and legally banned substances, the elderly use a disproportionate amount of prescription and OTC medications. Although older people constitute 12 percent (AARP, 1986) of the population, it is estimated that they receive 30 percent (O'Malley, Judge, & Crooks, 1980) of all prescriptions written. Of the total personal health care expenditures in the United States, elderly persons represent 31 percent (Kane & Kane, 1990).

In addition to the obvious linkage between the use of psychoactive, mood-altering drugs and the mental health of older persons, a case can be made for a significant relationship between illness, medication, and the mental health of the elderly. Issues associated with medication and the elderly include prescribing practices, the costs of medication, optimal dosages, drug interactions, side effects, and the compliance of patients. This chapter discusses older people's response to drugs and usage of therapeutic and recreational drugs and some of the issues raised by medication use and makes some recommendations related to clinical practice and policy issues.

RESPONSE TO DRUGS

The *pharmacokinetics* of drugs involves the study of the time course of absorption, tissue distribution, metabolism, and the excretion of drugs and

355

their metabolites from the body. Nutritional factors alter the absorption, distribution, metabolism, and excretion of drugs (Lamy, 1980). Diet and nutrient components affect drug action, although the specifics of such nutrient-drug interactions are not always clear.

The study of age effects on pharmacokinetics contributes to the understanding of altered *pharmacodynamics* among older persons. Pharmacodynamics is concerned with the physiological and psychological response to a drug (Vestal & Dawson, 1985): There is a greater or lesser response in elderly persons to particular drugs, independent of pharmacokinetic effects. Different psychoactive drugs, for example, have different pharmacodynamic effects; for instance, the response of elderly persons to some of the benzodiazepines seems to be enhanced (McCormack & O'Malley, 1986). Although there is evidence of altered sensitivity to some drugs, the reasons for these changes are still not clearly understood. Older people show increased sensitivity to the depressant action of morphine, and it is hypothesized that the aging brain is more sensitive to drugs that depress the nervous system.

Almost everyone is familiar with the side effects of medications, and such awareness seems to be a major issue in patients' noncompliance. Although side effects may be positive, for the most part, they are adverse drug reactions, defined by the World Health Organization as "any response to a drug which is noxious and unintended, and which occurs at doses used in man for prophylaxis, diagnosis or therapy" (Stewart, 1987, p.7). Estimates are that about a million persons are hospitalized and 140,000 deaths occur annually from adverse drug reactions (Talley & Laventurier, 1974). According to the Food and Drug Administration (FDA) more than half the deaths and almost 40 percent of the hospitalizations related to adverse drug reactions in 1986 occurred among the elderly (*Medication Trends for Older Adults*, 1989).

Older people's adverse drug reactions may be related to the increased severity of disease, to the number of medications they take, and to drug interactions, among other reasons (Gomberg, 1990; Stewart, 1987). Whatever the reasons, older patients apparently are much more likely to develop problems from drug therapies than are younger patients (Vestal & Dawson, 1985).

It must be remembered that few drugs have precise and narrow ranges of pharmacological effects. Most health workers view aspirin as an analgesic and the benzodiazepines as anxiolytic, but each of these widely used drugs has multiple effects, and health care workers need to be aware that the patient's use of several drugs may produce antagonistic or interactional effects. Furthermore, the side effects of some drugs may "mimic senility" ("Senility by Prescription," 1988). Cognitive impairment, a drug side effect, may be manifest in forgetfulness, confusion, and slowed thought processes.

Although several classes of medication may have such side effects, sedative-hypnotic drugs, particularly the benzodiazepines, are most commonly associated with such impairment. In a discussion of adverse drug reactions reported by Health and Welfare Canada and in studies from the United States, the United Kingdom, and other countries, McKim and Mishara (1987) suggested that such reactions may not be related to age per se but to the number of medications and the dosages involved, and they stated that the risk of adverse drug reactions can be "diminshed by an appropriate adjustment of dose" (p. 37).

CATEGORIES OF DRUGS

Prescription Drugs

It is not particularly useful to search for the average number of prescription medications used by older persons. Studies show great variability in use that is related to at least two factors: whether the population studied is ambulatory, living in the community, living in housing for the elderly, or in institutions and which medications are included. Older people in hospitals or nursing homes are prescribed more drugs than are those living in the community. For example, Stewart (1987) described a study of nine hospitals that found an average of 8.7 drugs per person and a nursing home study that found an average of 6.1. Guttman's (1977) household survey of older persons showed an average of 1.6 medications, Ostrom, Hammarlund, Christensen, Plein, and Kethley's (1985) survey of people living in housing for the elderly noted an average of 3.0, and a study of the "ambulatory elderly" (Falvo, Holland, Brenner, & Benshoff, 1990) found an average of 2.5 prescribed medications reported by respondents. A recent survey of 58 residents of a retirement center, 49 women and 9 men, with an average age of 83, showed the mean number of medications (in response to the question, "What number of prescriptions do you have?") to be 3.0 (Gomberg, 1991). It is hardly surprising that older people who are relatively healthy and are living unassisted report fewer medications than do those who are hospitalized or in nursing homes.

Which medications are taken most frequently? A study by the Task Force on Prescription Drugs (1968) of the U.S. Department of Health, Education, and Welfare yielded the following list of the most frequently prescribed medication categories for the 65 plus age group:

cardiovascular
tranquilizers

diuretics
sedative-hypnotics
antibiotics
analgesics
hormones
antiarthritics
diabetic products
antispasmodics

The frequency of use of both prescribed and OTC drugs was found by May, Stewart, and Hale (1982) to be

vitamins
analgesics/antirheumatics
cardiovascular
antihypertensives
sedative-hypnotics
cathartics
diuretics
antacids
thyroid
anticoagulants

Approximately the same listing was reported by Venner, Krupka, and Climo (1980), and a recent report of responses by volunteer subjects at five senior citizens' centers (Falvo et al., 1990) found that the three most frequently cited were antihypertensives, cardiovascular, and psychotherapeutic drugs. Medications used by elderly Canadians are, in order of reported frequency, cardioactives, vasoactives and diuretics, analgesics and anti-inflammatory drugs, tranquilizers and hypnotics, laxatives, and vitamins (McKim & Mishara, 1987).

Women are generally found to be more frequent users of psychoactive drugs (Falvo et al., 1990; Ostrom et al., 1985; Venner et al., 1980), and this finding is consistent with what has been found in male-female comparisons in different age groups. Some questions have been raised, however, whether there is not a trend toward the greater use of antidepressants by elderly men.

An interesting pattern appears in that the use of prescription drugs peaks in the seventies and then declines. Kotzan, Carroll, and Kotzan (1989) reported that most medications were given to white, female patients over age 65.

OTC Medications

The frequency lists just cited include vitamins, analgesics, cathartics, and antacids, and it is safe to assume that these are bought frequently by older persons, as well as by people of all age groups. Guttman's (1977) community study reported that two-thirds of the respondents were using OTC drugs, and Simonson (1984) estimated that these drugs may be used by as much as 75 percent of the elderly. Are the elderly greater users of OTC medications? There is little agreement on this question.

Should there be special labeling on OTC medications to describe their effects on people over age 65, as the FDA has proposed for *prescribed* drugs? This is an issue that will be debated further. It is of interest to note that more information is available to consumers of OTC drugs on packages and in package inserts than to consumers of prescription drugs.

Although they are obviously not OTC medications, home remedies and folk remedies should be mentioned here. Herbal teas, chicken soup, and the like are not obtained by prescription and are easily available. Such home remedies may be helpful because of their pharmacological or placebo effects (or both). Perhaps it is a wise course to use the counsel of the medical and pharmaceutical professions and to supplement their recommendations with home remedies.

A last word: Nonnarcotic analgesics are the most commonly reported drugs of purchase by older persons both in the United States and in other countries (Gomberg, 1990).

Prescribed Psychoactive Drugs

Older persons have a higher rate of prescription and usage of psychoactive drugs. Psychoactive drugs are a special kind of prescription drug, designed to deal with mental and emotional conditions and usually having the potential for addiction. There is a fair amount of interest in "prescription drug abuse," which usually turns out to be dependence on *prescribed* tranquilizers or stimulants. Unlike purposeful drug abuse, it is possible to become dependent on such drugs unintentionally (although the question of a person's potential for drug dependence must be dealt with).

The question of prescribed psychoactive drugs is tied to the problem of psychiatric diagnosis in the elderly. Older persons who present with mental illness are likely to manifest sensory deficits, isolation, poverty, loss of social supports, and chronic illness, which compounds the difficulty of diagnosis. (Research linking hearing loss and paranoid thinking in the elderly is relevant; see Crook & Cohen, 1981.) Mental disorders that appear most frequently among the elderly include depression, dementia, paranoia, hypochondriasis, and iatrogenic drug problems.

The question of depression raises some important issues. The criteria for diagnosis are not agreed upon, although the incidence is estimated at 10 percent (Faun & Whelass, 1975). Clearly, illness, loss, and death enhance depression rates; yet it must be noted that older persons express more life satisfaction than do younger persons and that a sizable proportion of depression in the elderly may be environmentally based and amenable to help. The diagnosis of depression is further confused by malnutrition, apathy, memory loss, withdrawal, and self-devaluation (see Chapter 10).

National surveys that include the elderly living in the community show the high usage of psychoactive drugs, and 50 percent of elderly persons who use psychoactive drugs have reported that they could not perform their daily activities without the medication (Prentice, 1979). Insomnia, which is a frequent complaint of older persons, is often countered with sedative-hypnotic prescription drugs, and depressed affect with antidepressants. Some researchers think that psychoactive drugs are overprescribed for the elderly, while others believe that these medications make life more tolerable for this age group.

The use of psychoactive drugs in nursing homes has raised a number of questions. Many nursing home residents have not been psychiatrically diagnosed, but the use of such medications may make their care easier for the caretakers. The question is this: Are the drugs used for the long-term benefit of the patients or to facilitate the caretaking problems? There are also concerns about the extent to which psychoactive medication may contribute to the emotional and mental disorders of nursing home residents (Cooper, 1988).

Up to age 65, women are more likely to be users of psychoactive drugs than are men. An early survey (Mellinger, Balter, Parry, Manheimeder, & Cisin, 1974) found that more older men than women were users of antidepressants. In a recent report, Robbins and Clayton (1989) noted that in the 65-and-older age group, men are more likely than are women to report the prescribed use of sedatives, tranquilizers, and stimulants in the past year. Do older men have greater access to medical care and do they use medical facilities more than do older women? Are there gender differences in emotional disorders among older men and women that are being recognized?

Nicotine

The use of nicotine, although not prescribed, belongs in any discussion of psychoactive drugs. Tobacco is sometimes classified as a "recreational drug" or a "social drug." However classified, its use is a health issue, and the relationship between smoking and a variety of diseases is well documented. There is a high correlation between the use of alcohol and the use of nicotine, and a review of studies of the metabolism of drugs by elderly persons (Sellers, Frecker, & Romach, 1982) concluded that the effects of aging, smoking, and drinking are confounded.

In 1965, the National Center for Health Statistics found that 28.5 percent of older men and 9.6 percent of older women were current smokers; by 1987 these figures had become 17.2 percent and 13.7 percent, respectively (*Smoking, Tobacco and Health*, 1989). It is notable that there has not only been a convergence in the smoking rates of men and women aged 65 and older, but that the percentage of older women who smoke has increased (perhaps because the 1965 cohort of older women contained many who were socialized to view smoking as unfeminine behavior). It has been estimated that about 15 percent of older Canadians are current smokers and, here again, the figures for elderly men have declined while those for elderly women have remained stable. McKim and Mishara (1987) believe these percentages relate to the different mortality rates of smokers and nonsmokers and to the concerns of older people about their health. When the rates of the per capita consumption of cigarettes for all age groups are compared for countries for which data are available, Cyprus ranks first, the United States ranks fifth, and Canada ranks eighth (*Smoking, Tobacco and Health*, 1989).

An interview study with people aged 65 and over, conducted in Massachusetts, reported that respondents who lived alone or with their children, those in the oldest age group interviewed, and those who reported their health as "poor" or "fair" were *less* likely to be smokers (Branch, 1977).

Illegal Substances

When the term *drug abuse* is used, people usually think of banned substances, such as cocaine, heroin, and marijuana. Also available as street drugs are prescribed substances (usually opioid drugs) that are illegally diverted, sold, and used without medical sanction.

Generational differences in the use of illegal drugs are marked. The National Household Survey of Drug Abuse (National Institute on Drug Abuse, 1988) found that a relatively modest number of young people aged 12–17, the maximum number in the 18–34-year-old group, and a sharply lesser number of adults aged 35 and older reported "ever using" marijuana, hallucinogens, heroin, and cocaine. These differences in "lifetime prevalence" are also reported for persons in treatment for substance abuse, usually alcohol dependence, both males (Gomberg, 1982) and females (Gomberg,

1986). Patients in their forties and older patients have experimented with illegal substances much less frequently than have patients in their twenties.

Older people probably occasionally use drugs like marijuana and other hallucinogens socially, and some users of illicit drugs survive into old age. However, the information is limited and is confined to opiate-dependent persons.

Although it has been widely believed that narcotic addicts either die or "mature out" and do not appear in the elderly population, it turns out that some survive. Pascarelli (1985) reported that in 1974, only .005 percent of people in the New York City methadone maintenance program (methadone maintenance is an accepted therapeutic technique in which the drug-dependent person is maintained and monitored and given regular doses of methadone, a synthetic narcotic drug) were aged 60 and older, but that by 1985, this proportion had risen to 2 percent. There is no evidence of late-life onset or the recent development of drug dependence—the patients studied were long-term narcotic addicts. When DesJarlais, Joseph, and Courtwright (1985) examined an older cohort attending methadone maintenance clinics in New York City in 1979, they found 286 patients in the 55–59 age group, 262 in their sixties, 53 in their seventies, and 5 in their eighties. Patients with addictions of twenty years and longer were interviewed, and several factors emerged as major contributors to their longevity. They had long-lived parents, a genetic advantage, and they had lived by their wits, but avoided violence. They were able to keep supplied with narcotics and were careful to keep the needles clean, a critical caution in the era of AIDS, which is spread through the use of contaminated needles. They were able to hold drugs in reserve, which suggests a less-than-total loss of control, and they made moderate use of nonopiate drugs, particularly alcohol. Most of the older patients lived alone and used the methadone maintenance clinic as a community center, and many of them continued to conceal their use of drugs successfully. Ironically enough, most of the interviewees were in reasonable health, with the same health problems that are found in older cohorts in the general population; however, 90 percent of the older addicts had been heavy smokers, and smoking-related health problems were relatively frequent among those who were disabled. There was no information about the elderly addicts' dealings with the criminal justice system. Traditionally, elderly substance abusers who were a major concern of the criminal justice system were the alcoholic homeless, manifested in the term "the revolving door." However, the number arrested for public intoxication has decreased markedly (Petersen, 1988).

PROBLEMS ASSOCIATED WITH MEDICATION

In a time when a new "wonder drug" is front-page news, when people are living longer because of pharmacological advances, when disputes arise among physicians about whether chemotherapy is a safer alternative to coronary surgery, it is not surprising that the attention of the public, the media, legislators, and governmental agencies becomes focused at times on issues of medication and the proper uses of medication. On the one hand, those who are interested in the mental health needs of the elderly (Johnson, 1989) point out that the elderly are short changed in mental health care. On the other hand, medication-associated problems appear frequently in the media (Brody, 1990), which emphasizes "abnormal behavior" that can be drug related and indicates that the elderly are "most susceptible because they metabolize drugs more slowly" (p.B5). The misuse of medication is not confined to the elderly, of course, but may apply to all age groups. And blame for medication-associated problems may be spread widely, too: physicians, pharmaceutical companies, pharmacists, and patients all are responsible.

There is, first, the issue of *overmedication* and polypharmacy. When several different medications are prescribed for the same individual, we speak of *polypharmacy*. If it is the same physician who prescribes several medications and if he or she is well informed about the effects of the different medications, the situation is less worrisome. Unfortunately, that is not always the case. The issue of overmedication is an issue of prescribing practices, and here there is a line, not always clear, between overmedication and pharmacological Calvinism. These are issues that should be raised in medical education.

Clearly, more research is needed on the pharmacokinetics of drugs that are used for elderly patients. Basic research on drug-drug and drug-nutrient interactions is needed, as is more advanced research on adverse drug reactions. Studies of biochemical aspects, pharmacological variations, and psychological response are also necessary. The mental health and well-being of the elderly are strongly tied to issues of health and feelings of well-being. Maintaining the health of the elderly is a great contribution to their mental health.

Although the elderly apparently consume a disproportionate share of psychoactive drugs, the question of underreporting has been raised. It may well be that the disproportion is even greater than is currently estimated. The use of such substances raises psychological, ethical, and philosophical questions, such as these: If an elderly person is depressed, does one give an antidepressant, help deal with the depressed feelings, or do both? If an older patient complains of insomnia and fatigue, does one prescribe a sedative-hypnotic or try to foster a regime of exercise and activity, or both? The use of such medications in nursing homes raises other issues; a national survey conducted by the Department of Health and Human Services found that more than a quarter of U.S. nursing homes administer drugs with minimal medical attention and supervision (Tolchin, 1988). The conclusion of medical researchers, patients' advocates, and academics in medical ethics was, a decade after another federal study of the "serious overuse and misuse" of such drugs, that the practice has continued (Bishop, 1989). Cooper's (1986) two-year study of drug-related problems in nursing homes reported the extensive misuse of drugs, particularly related to "poor distribution systems." The second most common drug-related problem that Cooper found was adverse drug reactions and interactions, almost two-thirds of which were preventable.

Undermedication is another problem. Sometimes undermedication is a result of the high *cost* of medications. A comparison of current data from the National Medical Expenditure Survey with results from the 1980 survey of the noninstitutionalized elderly Medicare population

> indicates a far greater increase in average charges per prescription and in average annual prescription expenditures than in the percent of Medicare beneficiaries obtaining medicine or in the annual number of prescriptions per beneficiary (Moeller & Mathiowetz, 1989, p.4).

It is reported that a sizable percentage of the prescriptions that are written are not brought to pharmacies for filling, and it is a safe assumption that economic considerations loom large. There is a growing concern about increases in the prices of medications, which are far higher than is the current rate of inflation (Freudenheim, 1991).

A survey of the American Association of Retired Persons (AARP) (1984) found that the most frequent noncompliance behavior was patients stopping medication in "mid-process." There is also, physician-fostered under-medication and a phenomenon termed "opiophobia," when physicians are anxious about the treatment of cancer pain with Schedule II drugs (morphine, codeine, meperidine, etc.); these and other issues related to prescription problems are under discussion by the American Medical Association (Wilford, 1988a, 1988b) and by the Ministry of National Health and Welfare of Canada (McKim & Mishara, 1987).

The National Institute on Drug Abuse (NIDA) operates a Drug Abuse Warning Network (DAWN) that collects reports of drug abuse episodes from emergency rooms and medical examiners. The following 1989 data (NIDA, 1990) indicate the percentage of drug episodes for persons aged 60 and older who present at emergency rooms as a percentage of the total number of specific drug episodes:

Nonbarbiturate sedatives	7.1%
Tranquilizers	4.9%
Barbiturate sedatives	3.8%
Antidepressants	3.4%
Antipsychotics	3.2%
Nonnarcotic analgesics	1.7%
Narcotic Analgesics	1.4%
Amphetamines	.3%
Hallucinogens	.2%

In addition, codeine combinations constitute 3.6 percent and alcohol plus other drugs constitute 1.1 percent of the drug episodes for this group. It is of interest that since emergency room cases often tend to be adolescents and young adults that the most frequent drug episodes for *all* emergency room episodes are cocaine, alcohol in combination with other drugs, and narcotic analgesics. Among the elderly presenters for nonbarbiturate sedatives at emergency rooms, a high proportion have problems with "OTC sleep aids." Self-medication for insomnia obviously has its risks, and there are problems with the misuse of a variety of OTC drugs. Aspirin is the leading cause of hospitalization linked to overdose and to dangerous drug interactions (McKim & Mishara, 1987), although the excessive use of antacids, laxatives, decongestants, antihistamines, and the like also leads to hospitalization.

Gender patterns in the use and abuse of medications have been well reported. The NIDA has devoted a research monograph to women and drugs (Ray & Braude, 1986) several of whose chapters are concerned with elderly women. Braude (1986) discussed adverse drug effects based on drug interactions, changes in drug disposition with age, and increased sensitivity to drugs among elderly women, but pointed out that much of the curricula of the helping professions is "devoid of gender-related information." Barry (1986) described altered pharmacokinetics and gender differences in the metabolism of several psychoactive drugs. Glantz and Backenheimer (1988), reviewing what is known about substance abuse among elderly women, concluded that research support is available for these conclusions:

1. Alcohol and drug abuse are not currently widespread problems for elderly women, but are likely to increase as younger women alcoholics and illicit drug users age.

2. Elderly women are at risk of the misuse of self- and other-perpetrated drugs, including drug-drug and drug-alcohol interactions, and they may also be at risk of self-perpetrated abuse involving legal psychotropic drugs.

3. Elderly women are apparently at a greater risk of physician-perpetrated drug abuse involving prescription psychoactive drugs than are any other age-by-gender group.

A report of data gathered in a national household survey in 1982 (Robbins & Clayton, 1989) came to different conclusions than did Glantz and Backenheimer: Women aged 45–64 reported the greater use of prescription psychoactive drugs than did women aged 65 and older. In the 65-and-older group, men were more likely than were women to report the medical use of sedatives, tranquilizers, and stimulants during the past year. Since the total sample of women were more likely to report the use of medically prescribed psychoactive drugs during the past year, what was reported is an interesting reversal among the elderly. It has been speculated that such a reversal may be related to the increased use of medical care by older men or to a possible gender difference in psychiatric disorders among older men and women (Gomberg, 1990).

Little data are available about *ethnic differences*, but Robbins and Clayton (1989) presented comparative data on the use of medically prescribed psychoactive drugs reported during the past year (the nonmedical or illegal use of such substances was almost never reported by the elderly respondents) by drug categories and by reporting respondents aged 65 and older:

Sedatives: Black males 3%, White males 12% and Hispanic males 9%; Black women 4%, White women 8%, Hispanic women 0.
Tranquilizers: Black males 22%, White males 10%, Hispanic males 22%; Black women, 7%, White women 10%, Hispanic women 0.
Stimulants: Black males 3%, White males 2%, Hispanic males 0; Black women 0, White women 1%, Hispanic women 0.
Analgesics: Black males 10%, White males 7%, Hispanic males 0; Black females 20%, White females 15%, Hispanic females 0.(p. 212)

It is difficult to know what to make of these numbers: White men and women use sedatives more than do minorities, tranquilizers appear to be used by a sizable proportion of minority men, men in general use more stimulant drugs than do women, and women use more analgesic drugs than do men. Discussing ethnic differences among all age groups, Robbins and Clayton (1989, p. 215) stated: "Minorities are slightly less likely than whites to have used prescribed psychotropic drugs. This contrasts sharply with the overrepresentation of minorities in substance abuse treatment populations." It should be noted that what is described is "past year medical use," that is, respondents were asked if they ever had a drug of, say, the sedative class prescribed for them by a physician and when they had most recently used the drug. Ethnic variations in access to medical care, in physicians' prescribing practices, in patients obtaining a prescribed drug, and in compliance may all be involved. The role and significance of folk remedies among blacks, whites, and Hispanics should also be studied.

Noncompliance

The problem most often cited by physicians and gerontologists in connection with medication of the elderly is noncompliance. Although noncompliance is by no means confined to elderly medication takers, most of the interest has been in older persons' noncompliance. Since OTC drugs are purchased by or for older persons they are self-administered; however, little attention has been given to whether older persons comply with the directions on OTC packages or inserts.

There are different patterns of noncompliance. One major pattern is to obtain a prescription but not bring it to a pharmacist. Such nonuse may be related to apathy, but is often related to the financial status of the patient. As was noted earlier, Moeller and Mathiowetz's (1989) summary of the use of drugs by and expenditures of Medicare beneficiaries compared 1980 and 1987 data. It reported much larger increases in the average charge per prescription and the average annual expenditure for prescription drugs than in the percentage of Medicare beneficiaries obtaining medications or the annual number of prescriptions per beneficiary. In 1980, the average charge per prescription was $8.05, whereas in 1987, it was $16.89.

Other patterns of noncompliance include these:

Partial use: The patient begins but does not continue to take the medication.

Self-directed medication: The patient decides to modify the dosage.

Self-directed medication: The patient uses an OTC drug with the medication.

Incorrect dosage: The patient takes a larger dosage than was prescribed.

Incorrect dosage: The patient takes a smaller dosage than was prescribed.

Improper timing or sequencing of medications.

Shared medication: The patient is given or takes medication not prescribed for him or her.

Periodic noncompliance: The patient takes a "holiday" from drug therapy.

There are undoubtedly other patterns of noncompliance (Kendrick & Bayne, 1982; Raffoul, Cooper, & Love, 1981). A national survey by Gomberg (1990, p. 181) reported that the most frequent pattern of noncompliance was partial use, "when consumers stop taking a prescription drug mid-process." Forty percent of the respondents experienced side effects and 20 percent of those reported that neither physicians nor pharmacists discussed the potential side effects with them. In a sample of patients at a Veterans Administration outpatient clinic, the noncompliance most frequently reported was hoarding, which was clearly linked to the patients' concerns about access to medication (Gomberg, Hsieh, & Adams, 1990).

Lamy (1980) defined the issue in terms of "basic trust," pointing out that cooperation, rather than compliance, is needed and recommending that patients be educated to promote such cooperation. Young (1987), after stating that as many as 50 percent of prescriptions do not produce the desired results because "they will have been used improperly," recommended, on the basis of an FDA study, that more information about prescription medications should be given to patients. Young also suggested that health care practitioners seem to overestimate their communication skills.

Another recommendation for dealing with patients' noncompliance is reminder systems, such as the pharmacist sending a reminder to the patient that his or her prescription is due to be refilled (Lachman, 1987). In addition automated calling systems have been instituted, and interactive systems in which the patient responds are in development. Furthermore, the U.S. Office for Substance Abuse Prevention disseminates a consumer-oriented booklet (*Using your Medicines Wisely*, 1988).

Whether the education is to be given by the health care practitioner or is aimed directly at the consumer, there is obviously an advantage in people, elderly or otherwise, knowing about the medications they are prescribed. The lack of information about side effects, for example, appears to be related to the limited time that health care practitioners spend with patients and to the patients' passivity and lack of questioning. With an increasing proportion of the population being elderly and with the development of new chemotherapies almost daily, the issue of how to keep older persons informed about the medications that will be prescribed is a real problem.

Most discussions of elderly persons noncompliance with medications attribute the behavior to impairments including visual impairment, hearing loss, memory loss, or even "senility." Advertisements for drugs in medical journals and magazines frequently include a photograph of an enfeebled and bewildered-looking patient (usually a woman). Older patients are viewed as slow to understand directions. For some patients, there are indeed sensory and memory losses. The question is whether the approximately 40 percent of older patients who do not comply with directions are mentally impaired or whether other factors are at work. To what extent are matters of control, autonomy, and self-determination in decision making involved? To what extent, if any, are the denial of aging or self-destructive motives involved? One may also ask about the rapport between physicians and patients and whether physicians who have good rapport with their patients have the problem of their patients' noncompliance to the same extent as do other physicians. There are, then, a number of different factors in noncompliance, including patients' education and knowledge of side effects; the relationships between health care practitioners and patients; motivations like autonomy, denial of illness, and self-destructiveness; and the cognitive and sensory limitations of older patients.

Finally, it should be noted that we are describing the compliance-with-medication regimen, but compliance actually includes a broader range of behavior, such as directives about diet, exercise, and abstinence from alcohol. A study of social support and "patient adherence" among hypertensives (Caplan, Harrison, Wellons, & French, 1980, p. 1) defined *adherence* as being synonymous with *compliance*: "the patient's behavior as measured against a set of prescribed actions." An early study by Walton (1956) comparing two groups of cirrhotic alcoholics found that those who adhered to a strict regimen involving diet and abstinence from alcohol were more "emotionally mature" than were those who did not and who were described as more self-destructive and hostile. While alcoholics are viewed as psychopathological and hypertensives are not, the conditions related to them as patients and to the situations that promote their adherence to medical regimens may be similar.

MEDICATION ISSUES VERSUS MENTAL HEALTH ISSUES

The point hardly needs to be labored: The bedrock of aging successfully is good health. There are, however, many chronic diseases like hypertensive disorder that do not functionally impair those who are diagnosed with them. The relationship between good physical health and good mental health is obvious (people with chronic illnesses who maintain good mental health tend to be the exceptions), and the role of medication in maintaining productive activity is large. It is likely that the chemotherapy of many chronic and acute illnesses associated with aging will improve with new discoveries.

For an aging society, the goal is to have the benefits of chemotherapy with minimal adverse side effects. Although this goal is served, in part, by biochemists, a number of things need to be done to establish the maximum effectiveness and minimum negative consequences of medication:

1. Gerontological medical education and improved prescription practices by physicians.
2. An extended partnership between physicians and pharmacists in geriatric medication.
3. The inclusion of education for retirees on keeping their own medication profile of both prescribed and OTC drugs.
4. Training for home care providers, including family members, in the management of medications.

These recommendations were made by a Medication Working Group assembled for a surgeon general's Workshop on health promotion and aging (Abdellah & Moore, 1988).

Another fact of life is the physician's critical role in the prescription and management of medications. The prescribing physician needs to have the most current information on geriatric medicine, to be sensitive, and to have good communication skills. The discussion of noncompliance has, until recently, focused heavily on the limitations and shortcomings of patients in not following orders. However, patients are more likely to keep their physicians informed about side effects, the termination of medication, and other behavior if they have rapport with them.

Other health professionals, such as pharmacists, nurses, and social workers, can aid the process of maximizing the benefits of medication by having an understanding approach. The side effects of drugs may include confusion, depression, drowsiness, loss of appetite, ataxia, and gastrointestinal disorders. When older clients who are on medication report any of these symptoms health care professionals need to investigate whether there is a relationship between the medication and the reported behavior and inform the prescribing physicians. They are the patients' advocates.

Finally, there is the role of government and public policy. For a start, the FDA should encourage the use of older populations in clinical trials of drugs. The question of whether new drug labeling is needed (with directions for use by older groups) should be debated. And it seems obvious that it would benefit the elderly population if the government encouraged both basic science and drug evaluations in developing new medications for ailments of the elderly.

REFERENCES

Abdellah, F. G., & Moore, S. R. (Eds.). (1988). *Proceedings of the surgeon general's workshop, Health Promotion and Aging, March 20–23, 1988.* Washington, DC: U.S. Department of Health and Human Services.

American Association of Retired Persons. (1984). *Prescription drugs: A survey of consumer use, attitudes amd behavior.* Washington, DC: Author.

American Association of Retired Persons. (1986). *A Profile of Older Americans.* Washington, D.C.: Author.

Barry, P. P. (1986). Gender as a factor in treating the elderly. In B. A. Ray & M. C. Braude (Eds.), *Women and drugs: A new era in research* (NIDA Research Monograph No. 65, pp. 65–69). Washington, DC: U.S. Government Printing Office.

Bishop, K. (1989, March 13). Studies find drugs still overused to control nursing home elderly. *New York Times*, pp. 1, 8.

Branch, L. G. (1977). *Understanding the health and social service needs of people over age 65.* Cambridge, MA: Center for Survey Research, University of Massachusetts, MIT, and Harvard University.

Braude, M. G. (1986). Drugs and drug interactions in the elderly woman. In B. A. Ray & M. C. Braude (Eds.), *Women and drugs: A new era in research* (NIDA Research Monograph No. 65, pp. 58–64). Washington, DC: U.S. Government Printing Office.

Brody, J. E. (1990, June 14). Personal health: The elderly are most susceptible because they metabolize drugs more slowly. *New York Times*, p. B5.

Caplan, R. D., Harrison, R. V., Wellons, R. V., & French, J. R. P., Jr. (1980). *Social support and patient adherence: Experimental and survey findings.* Ann Arbor: Survey Research Center, Institute for Social Research, University of Michigan.

Cooper, J. W. (1986). Drug related problems in a geriatric long term care facility. *Journal of Geriatric Drug Therapy, 1*(1), 47–68.

Cooper, J. W. (1988). Medication misuse in nursing homes. *Generations, 12*(4), 56–57.

Crook, T., & Cohen, G. (Eds.). (1981). *Physicians handbook on psychotherapeutic drug use in the aged.* New Canaan, CT: Mark Powley Associates.

DesJarlais, D. C., Joseph, H, & Courtwright, D. T. (1985). Old age and addiction: A study of elderly patients in methadone maintenance treatment. In E. Gottheil, K. A. Druley, T. E. Skoloda, & H. M. Waxman (Eds.), *The Combined problems of alcoholism, drug addiction and aging* (pp. 201–209). Springfield, Il: Charles C Thomas.

Falvo, D. R., Holland, B., Brenner, J., & Benshoff, J. J. (1990). Medication use practices in the ambulatory elderly. *Health Values, 14*(3), 10–16.

Faun, W. E., & Whelass, J. C. (1975). Depression in elderly patients. *Southern Medical Journal, 68*, pp 468–475.

Freudenheim, M. (1991, May 11). Pressure grows for curbs on prices of prescriptions. *New York Times*, pp. 1, 27.

Glantz, M. D., & Backenheimer, M. S. (1988). Substance abuse among elderly women. *Clinical Gerontologist, 8*(1), 3–26.

Gomberg, E. S. L. (1982). The young male alcoholic: A pilot study. *Journal of Studies on Alcohol, 43*(7), 683–701.

Gomberg, E. S. L. (1986). Women and alcoholism: Psychological issues. In *Women and alcohol: Health-related issues* (pp. 78–120). Bethesda, MD: National Institute on Alcohol Abuse and Alcoholism.

Gomberg, E. S. L. (1990). Drugs, alcohol, and aging. In L. T. Kozlowski, H. M. Annis, H. D. Cappell, F. B. Glaser, E. M. Sellers, M. S. Goodrich, Y. Israel, H. Kalant & E. R. Vingilis (Eds.), *Research advances in alcohol and drug problems* (Vol. 10, pp. 171–213). New York: Plenum Press.

Gomberg, E. S. L. (1991). *Survey of medication compliance among residents in a retirement home.* Unpublished manuscript.

Gomberg, E. S. L., Hsieh, G., & Adams, K. M. (1990). Patterns of drug use in a general medical care clinic for veterans: A pilot study. In B. B. Wilford (Ed.), *Balancing the response to prescription drug abuse* (pp. 119–132). Chicago: American Medical Association.

Guttman, D. (1977). *A survey of drug-taking behavior of the elderly.* Washington, DC: Catholic University of America.

Johnson, J. (1989, March 6). Mental ills of elderly need help, panel told. *New York Times*, p. 8.

Kane, R. L., & Kane, R. A. (1990) Health care for older people: Organizational and policy issues. In R. H. Binstock & L. K. George (Eds.), *Handbook of aging and the social sciences* (3rd ed., pp. 415–437). San Diego: Academic Press.

Kendrick, R., & Bayne, J. R. D. (1982). Compliance with prescribed medication for elderly patients. *Canadian Medical Association Journal, 127*, 961.

Kotzan, L., Carroll, N. V., & Kotzan, J. A. (1989). Influence of age, sex, and race on prescription drug use among Georgia Medicaid recipients. *American Journal of Hospital Pharmacy, 46*, 287–290.

Lachman, B. G. (1987). Increasing patient compliance through tracking systems. *California Pharmacist, 35*(3), 54–58.

Lamy, P. P. (1980). *Prescribing for the elderly.* Littleton, MA: PSG.

May, F. E., Stewart, R. B., & Hale, W. E. (1982). Prescribed and nonprescribed drug use in an ambulatory elderly population. *Southern Medical Journal, 75*, 522–528.

McCormack, P., & O'Malley, K. (1986). Biological and medical aspects of drug treatment in the elderly. In R. E. Dunkle, G. J. Petot, & A. B. Ford (Eds.), *Food, drugs and aging* (pp. 19–28). New York: Springer.

McKim, W. A., & Mishara, B. L. (1987). *Drugs and aging.* Toronto: Butterworths.

Medication trends for older adults, 2(3). (1989). Reston, VA: National Pharmaceutical Council.

Mellinger, G. D., Balter, M. B., Parry, H. R., Manheimeder, D. I., & Cisin, I. H. (1974). An overview of psychotherapeutic drug use in the United States. In E. Josephson & E. E. Carrol (Eds.), *Drug use, epidemiological and sociological approaches* (pp. 340–359). New York: Hemisphere.

Moeller, J., & Mathiowetz, N. (1989). *Prescribed medicines: A summary of use and expenditures by Medicare beneficiaries* (National Medical Expenditure Survey Research Findings No. 3), Rockville, MD: National Center for Health Services Research and Health Care Technology Assessment.

National Institute on Drug Abuse. (1988). *National Household Survey of Drug Abuse: Main findings 1985.* Washington, DC: U.S. Government Printing Office.

National Institute on Drug Abuse. (1990). *Annual data from the Drug Abuse Warning Network (DAWN)* (Statistical Series 1, No. 9). Washington, DC: U.S. Government Printing Office.

O'Malley, K., Judge, T. G., & Crooks, J. (1980). *Geriatric clinical pharmacology and therapeutics.* In G. Avery (Ed.), *Drug treatment* (2nd ed. pp. 158–181). NY: Ach's Press,

Ostrom, J. R., Hammarlund, E. R., Christensen, D. B., Plein, J. B., & Kethley, A. J. (1985). Medication usage in an elderly population. *Medical Care,* 23, 157–164.

Pascarelli, E. F. (1985). The elderly in methadone maintenance. In E. Gottheil, K. A. Druley, T. E. Skoloda, & H. M. Waxman (Eds.), *The combined problems of alcoholism, drug addiction and aging* (pp. 210–214). Springfield, IL: Charles C Thomas.

Petersen, D. M. (1988). Substance abuse, criminal behavior and older people. *Generations,* 12(4), 63–67.

Prentice, R. (1979). Patterns of psychotherapeutic drug use among the elderly. In National Institute on Drug Abuse, *The Aging process and psychoactive drug use* (pp. 17–41). Washington, DC: U.S. Government Printing Office.

Raffoul, P. R., Cooper, J. K., & Love, D. W. (1981). Drug misuse in older people. *The Gerontologist,* 21, 146–150.

Ray, B. A., & Braude, M. C. (Eds.) (1986). *Women and drugs: A new era for research* (Research Monograph No. 65). Washington, DC: U.S. Government Printing Office.

Robbins, C., & Clayton, R. R. (1989). Gender-related differences in psychoactive drug use among older adults. *Journal of Drug Issues,* 19, 207–219.

Sellers, E. M., Frecker, R. C., & Romach, M. L. (1982). Drug metabolism in the elderly: Confounding of age, smoking and ethanol effects (Substudy No. 1219). Toronto: Addiction Research Foundation.

Senility by prescription. (1988, April 15). *Emergency Medicine,* pp. 124–126.

Simonson, W. (1984). *Medications and the elderly: A guide for promoting proper use*. Rockville, MD: Aspen Systems Corp.

Smoking, tobacco and health: A fact book. (1989). Washington, DC: U.S. Government Printing Office.

Stewart, R. B. (1987). Drug use and adverse drug reactions in the elderly: An epidemiologic perspective. *Topics in Geriatric Rehabilitation*, 2(3), 1–11.

Talley, R. B., & Laventurier, M. F. (1974). Letter to the editor. *Journal of the American Medical Association*, 229, 1043.

Task Force on Prescription Drugs: The drug users. (1968). Washington, DC: U.S. Government Printing Office.

Tolchin, M. (1988, September 2). U.S. nursing homes faulted in study over medications. *New York Times*, pp. 1, 10.

Using your medicines wisely: A guide for the elderly. (1988). Washington, DC: U.S. Government Printing Office.

Venner, A. M., Krupka, L. R., & Climo, J. J. (1980). Drug usage and health characteristics in noninstitutionalized retired persons. *Journal of the American Geriatrics Society*, 27, 83–90.

Vestal, R. E., & Dawson, G. W. (1985). Pharmacology and aging. In C. L. Finch & E. L. Schneider (Eds.), *Handbook of the biology of aging* (pp. 744–819). New York: Van Nostrand Reinhold.

Walton, D. (1956). *A study of selected personality factors in chronic alcoholics with portal cirrhosis undergoing medical treatment*. Unpublished doctoral dissertation, Adelphi University, Garden City, NY.

Wilford, B. B. (Ed.). (1988a). *Digest of controlled substances legislation*. Chicago: American Medical Association, Department of Substance Abuse.

Wilford, B. B. (Ed.). (1988b). *Use and abuse of psychoactive drugs: An annotated bibliography*. Chicago: American Medical Association, Department of Substance Abuse.

Young, F. E. (1987, October). Questions about your medicine? Go ahead—ask. *FDA Consumer*.

18

Psychosexual Issues and Aging

Pat Conway

When the topic of sexuality and aging was broached with a group of older persons working as senior companions, their first response was silence. Then, a variety of opinions about sexuality in old age emerged. One man talked poignantly about his relationship with his wife: how tied they were to each other, that single beds were the worst invention. He noted that they had twin beds because sleeping alone was more comfortable for his wife because of an illness. Then he grinned and stated that the twin beds did not stop him from sleeping with her; he liked to feel her next to him. The women in the group seemed more open to the potential of older persons enjoying an overtly sexual relationship than did the men. One man commented at the end of the meeting that the group was a "roomful of dirty old women."

The primary discussion, centered on what sexuality is and "how much is good," covered the range of opinions that have been voiced generally about the place that sexuality has in the lives of older persons. Many people think that older persons have no business expressing their sexuality (Brecher, 1984; Butler & Lewis, 1977; Jarvik & Small, 1988; Pfeiffer, 1978; Starr, 1985). As the author's 16-year-old daughter exclaimed upon hearing the topic of this chapter, "Ugh! Old people don't do it!" A segment of the television program *Carol and Company*, entitled "A Grandma Gets It On," broadcast on September 22, 1990, focused on a daughter's reaction to being called to a nursing home by the administrator, who was incensed that 82-year-old Grandma insisted on having sex; Grandma was ordered by her daughter to stop her unacceptable behavior or be moved to a nursing home for women only. LeShan (1990, p. 19), representing "older persons," berated "the Dr. Ruth Syndrome," the assumption that all persons, including

375

older persons, are very interested in sex: "I deeply resent the show-biz approach to the private lives each of us has a right to, and having started my adult life feeling guilty about too much sex I'll be damned if I'll end my days feeling guilty about too little sex." On the other hand, recent publications about sexuality and older persons are likely to include information about the advantages of sexuality for older persons (Doress & Siegal, 1987).

Which view is really representative of sexuality and aging? This chapter explores that question. To do so, it discusses the meaning of *old* and *sexuality*; explicates the factors that influence sexuality, such as gender, age, life satisfaction, organizational policies, depression, medication, and other health factors; and describes the level of sexuality of older persons. It concludes with implications for social work practice, from policy development to individual counseling.

This chapter is based on the assumption that sexuality is a normal component of all persons' lives, although the expression of sexuality may vary according to an individual's characteristics, psychosocial situation, physical health, and age. In addition, many of the sexual dysfunctions or dissatisfactions of people who are older are the result of health problems and medication, others' opinions about the appropriate sexuality of older persons, and the lack of access to partners—not the lack of interest.

DEFINITIONS

What Is *Old?*

Old age, characterized by the tasks of promoting intellectual vigor, coping with physical changes, adapting to role changes, accepting one's past life, and facing death, is difficult to define (Newman & Newman, 1987). Whether one is elderly varies by each organization's or person's goals and resulting definition. For instance, persons aged 50 or older are eligible for membership in the American Association of Retired Persons, and local Councils on Aging invite persons aged 55 and older to participate in their activities. According to the Older Americans Act, age 60 is old. Age categories, young-old (55–64 years), middle-old (65–74 years), old-old (75–84 years), and very old (85 years and over) are perhaps most useful when comparing differences and similarities by age (Atchley, 1987; Botwinick, 1984).

An environmental marker for old age is retirement, but this, too, is confusing. A person may retire from the military at age 42, which certainly is not old. Another may never work outside the home and therefore never retires. When do they become old? And the person who retires at the traditional age, 65 (set by the Social Security Act of 1935), may then enter another lucrative career for many more years of work outside the home, still old by chronological age but certainly not retired (Kaufman, 1986).

Asking for a definition from a person who is aged 55 and older leads one to believe that the definition of old is "no longer able to function"; one is old when one can no longer live life fully. "You are as old as you look." "A person who is two years older than I am is old." "When I can't dance any longer, I will be old." Given improved nutrition, living conditions, and health care, persons are living to be old (aged 55 and older) and are still experiencing good health and a satisfying quality of life. A definition of age by developmental, as well as chronological, markers considers not only age, but psychological, biological, emotional, and cognitive functioning in interaction with the environment.

Perhaps the assessment of age by a person's level of functioning, rather than by age, although.imprecise, is most useful for the practitioner. This article includes information about persons who are 55 and older, while still respecting each individual's ability to determine whether he or she fits the category of old. The many determinants of functional age provide important parameters for any discussion about sexuality and age and therefore are considered throughout.

What Is Sexuality?

Sexuality encompasses a broad range of activities, not just sexual intercourse or orgasm. A study by Brecher (1984) highlighted the variety of sexual experiences of people over age 50. In his study, sexuality included stimulation by all the senses—taste, sound, sight, smell, and touch. Although orgasm was considered vital by most participants, the desired frequency of orgasm and the means of achieving it varied. For some individuals, sexuality included touching, but orgasm was no longer desired.

Including a wide range of experiences, senses, and feelings in the definition of sexuality allows for continued pleasurable sexual expression in old age (Doress & Siegal, 1987; Malatesta, 1989). Pleasuring—any form of physical activity or arousal that feels good (Starr, 1985)—rather than any particular act, is now regarded as a better index of sexual activity, since it promotes sexual gratification.

FACTORS THAT INFLUENCE SEXUAL EXPRESSION

Nonhealth or Sexual Factors

DEMOGRAPHICS Currently, approximately 12 percent of the population in America is aged 65 and above; of that group, the old-old category is increasing most rapidly (Lowy, 1985; Myers, 1987). When one describes who older Americans are, one must remember that each cohort will vary, depending on the unique social, political, and economic forces that shaped its developmental process (Foner, 1986). Today, the old-old are more likely to be female, with reduced financial resources, reduced mobility, and reduced physical functioning. Surviving men are more likely than are surviving women to be married; women are more likely to live alone (Myers, 1987, p. 166). The ratio of men to women over age 60 is one to four; three-fourths of all married women will be widowed some time during their lives (Brecher, 1984). Brecher estimated that the rate of *available* single older men is even lower: one man for every five women.

Although death rates are higher for nonwhites than for whites who are younger than age 65, the rates are similar after age 65. "Above this age, there is little race difference in life expectancy and it has been small for decades. In fact, at age 75 to 79, deaths of nonwhites have occurred at later ages than they have for whites" (Botwinick, 1984, p. 9). Therefore, a smaller percentage of the population aged 65 and older are nonwhite, but those persons of color who reach age 65 can expect a long life span.

LIFE AND MARITAL SATISFACTION In spite of the potential for reduced life satisfaction, given the inexorable physical changes related to aging, older persons report higher life satisfaction than do younger persons, although they rate their happiness lower (George, 1980). Factors that contribute to life satisfaction in old age seem to vary by gender. In Botwinick's study (1984), predictors of life satisfaction for men were their own emotional and physical well-being and their wives' emotional characteristics, whereas predictors for women's life satisfaction were income and leisure time. Of particular importance to life satisfaction is the presence of a "confidant," according to this study. In Brecher's study (1984), people who were unmarried reported lower life satisfaction than did those who were married, and all persons, men and women, married and unmarried, who were sexually active reported higher life satisfaction than did those who were not sexually active (see also Traupmann, Eckels, & Hatfield, 1982). Although sexuality seems to be one factor that would be included when examining life satisfaction, it is frequently omitted from such measures (George & Bearon, 1980).

Brecher (1984) found that, other than sexuality, the quality of communication is the most important contributor to satisfaction with marriage for persons over age 60; other variables considered included gender, age, the "empty nest syndrome," place of residence, family income, education, retirement, religion, health, duration of marriage, remarriage, autumnal marriage, first marriage after age 50, and differences in the ages of the partners. Almost all persons who reported satisfaction with their level of communication were also happily married. The converse was not necessarily true; those who reported less satisfaction with communication might still report satisfaction with their marriages. Communication about sex was also correlated with satisfaction with sex. Starr (1985) found a much higher level of interest in sexuality in the study by Starr and Weiner (1981), which included the influence of communication, than in other studies, suggesting that communication is key, not only in marriage, but in the research process. Perhaps studies that ask for numbers, such as how often one reaches orgasm, understate the levels of sexual activity and interest of older persons. Questions about how much interest one has in sex, such as how often one would have intercourse if one could achieve an erection, would be a better indicator.

In summary, persons who are older have a higher life satisfaction than do younger persons. Satisfaction with marriage and with sex is enhanced by communication. Having a confidant, someone with whom to communicate is also essential.

EMOTIONAL AND PSYCHOLOGICAL FACTORS Both disturbances in emotions, such as depression and sadness, and intrapersonal psychological issues, such as lowered self-esteem as a result of changing health and biological functioning, influence sexual desire and sexual behavior (Butler & Lewis, 1977; Kaplan, 1974; O'Donohue, 1987; Rice, 1989; Travis, 1987). One single woman said that she was sexually active only when she could orchestrate the setting so her partner never actually saw her body; she was convinced that her "plump" body and sagging breasts and derriere, changes related to normal aging processes, would turn off any man. In addition, men become afraid of failure to perform as more stimulation to reach erection and more time between ejaculation is required. Losses, such as the loss of a breast through a mastectomy and the loss of fertility through menopause, may result in a changed view of oneself and a consequent grief response.

Depression and sadness may result from a variety of causes, the grief reaction to multiple losses, a symptom of an illness, a reaction to medication, or the presence of a lifelong depressive illness. Grieving, which may be more common in old age as the number of losses increases, includes a period—awareness of loss (Schneider, 1984)—typified by sadness and other depressive symptoms. Vegetative behavior, characteristic of this phase, leaves one with reduced energy and interest in life, including sexuality. Touching may be healing, but the grieving person lacks the ability to seek out relationships and may shun others. Partners may find themselves at odds during this time, since different persons move through the grief process at a different pace. One partner's rejection of sexual activity may be perceived by the other partner as a rejection of him or her. It may be difficult to distinguish among depression related to a loss (exogenous depression), depression that is ongoing throughout one's life and is not specifically related to life events (endogenous depression), and similar symptoms caused by other physical and emotional problems. Youst, Beutler, Corbishley, and Allender (1986) suggested that physical complaints that are seemingly unrelated to actual physical functioning are a good clue to depression in older persons and that depression leads to decreased pleasure in all areas of life, whereas dementia does not. Thus, intervention will vary, depending on the "cause" of the depressive symptoms (see Chapters 3 and 10).

ENVIRONMENTAL CONTEXT An older adult's environmental context influences his or her interest in sexuality and its expression indirectly through attitudes and directly by constraints or expectations placed on the older adult by caregivers (family and staff in institutions or those who provide home care), medical personnel, counselors, and other peers. Rice (1989) stated that women in institutions are expected not to be sexual; they have no privacy and no double beds.

Others expect that elderly widowed or divorced people should not be interested in a new relationship at their age. For example, when a man in his sixties, widowed for about a year, remarried a longtime friend, his adult children felt angry that he could, in their eyes, "forget" their mother so quickly and remarry.

Age and Health-related Biological Changes

Aging, illnesses, and medicines influence sexuality as one grows older (Barber, Lewis, Long, Whitehead, & Butler, 1989; Longenberger, 1980). Physical, social, psychological, and cognitive changes occur as a result of the aging process. Bodies develop arthritis, heart disease, high blood pressure, and sensory impairments, such as of taste, vision, and hearing. Even the loss of teeth can influence one's sexuality; for instance, a man approaching his sixties stated that he would have to quit kissing when he and his partner needed dentures because he found them so offensive. As LeShan (1990, p. 58) noted:

> Divorce after sixty is likely if one or both partners cannot accept the changes that come with age. A little arthritis here, a little heart trouble there, a hysterectomy that seems to have lowered the capacity for orgasm, lots of gray hair and lines. . . . in a desperate attempt to deny the aging process one still may search for greener fields to lift a less passionate libido.

Heart problems, more likely to be a problem for men aged 50–65 but equally a problem for men and women over 65, not only reduce physical functioning but may increase anxiety about sexual activity (Botwinick, 1984). The fear of dying during sexual excitement is caricatured in television shows. For example, in the October 18, 1990, segment of the sitcom, "Doctor, Doctor," a plane was left without a pilot because he died during sexual excitement; the characters joked about the pilot's physical state upon finding him with his pants down, shirt open, and penis erect. The same evening on another television show, "L.A. Law," a lawyer who experienced a heart attack was embarrassed when his wife asked the physician which types of sexual behavior are safe.

Strokes lead to partial erections, impotence, and impaired ejaculation in men and decreased lubrication in females and may also impair the ability to enjoy pleasuring (see Chapter 3). Degenerative diseases, such as arthritis, increase pain with movement and reduce flexibility. In addition to physical difficulties unrelated to sexuality, diabetes may lead to impotence and premature and retrograde ejaculation in men and decreased vaginal lubrication in women. Drugs may cause impotence and reduced sexual drive, as may other substances, such as alcohol and nicotine. Prostate surgery leads to impotence in some men; impotence may result from psychological forces as well (Longenberger, 1980; McCracken, 1988; Steffl, 1978). One study (McCracken, 1988) found, though, that men who were educated about the potential effects of surgery on sexual performance prior to the surgery did not experience any impotence other than that resulting from physiological changes. A hysterectomy may reduce sensations during intercourse and orgasm because of physical changes. This does not mean, however, that one gives up one's sexuality as a result of physiological changes (Brecher, 1984). As Botwinick (1984, p. 91) stated, "Although there is sexual aging, all experts agree that neither sexual needs nor sexual function ceases. People of almost all ages can and do have sexual lives."

Sometimes illnesses such as AIDS, that are unexpected in this age group decrease sexual satisfaction. A 70-year-old woman, Alice, contracted AIDS and subsequently participated in a support group for women with AIDS. Although much older than the other members, she did not hesitate to express great sadness at not being touched, kissed, or being able to participate in sexual intercourse as a result of her diagnosis. Although Alice's husband remained completely supportive, he had terminated all intimate touching.

In a training session about loss and grief for older persons who were being prepared to act as companions for homebound old persons, the group began to discuss losses related to sexuality. The only man in the group pooh-pooed the importance of sexuality for older persons. He asserted that it was not a loss that resulted in grieving because sex was no longer desired; it was inappropriate for older persons. Several women responded vehemently that he should speak for himself, since sexuality remained an important component of their lives. The trainer responded by speaking generally about the changes that occur as a result of treatments for illnesses that are more common as we age, such as high blood pressure. When the man heard that some medications cause impotence, he acknowledged that he was on high blood pressure medicine. He "saved face" when he became impotent, which he was unaware might be related to medication, by saying that he no longer desired any sexual activity.

Physical Changes Specific to Sexuality

MALE SEXUAL FUNCTIONING Men's sexual functioning peaks in late adolescence or the early twenties and declines thereafter. Thus, men require more stimulation to reach an erection and more time to ejaculate and between erections, ejaculate less, and experience less pleasure during ejaculation (Botwinick, 1984; Kaplan, 1974; O'Donohue, 1987). The level of sexual potency varies more across individuals than by age group; it is related more to the level of potency over one's whole life than to the level of other males of the same age.

FEMALE SEXUAL FUNCTIONING Women's sexual functioning is relatively constant from their late teens to their fifties or sixties; then it declines (Brecher, 1984; O'Donohue, 1987). Women experience physical changes such as a decline in hormones, hot flashes, and changes in mood, during menopause, which occurs at about age 50, that affect their sexuality (Pearson & Beck, 1989). The uterus, cervix, ovaries, vagina, labia majora, and clitoris decrease in size; the wall of the vagina thins, and glandular secretions decrease. Vaginitis is more frequent.

HOW SEXUALLY ACTIVE ARE OLDER ADULTS?

The level of sexual activity during old age seems to depend, first, on the level throughout one's life (Starr, 1985). Cohen (1988, p. 52) stated that the need for touch is constant throughout life: "If [a person] didn't like touch at 23 [he or she] won't like touch at 80." The availability of a partner, especially for women, influences the opportunity for sexuality. Health-related factors, attitudes about sexuality, external pressures (economic and career), the use of substances, and the lack of excitement in sexual partners may also effect the level of sexual activity.

The General Social Surveys (Smith, 1990), which included questions on sexual behavior, found that the rate of partners declined from 1.76 for those under to age 30 to .35 partners for those over age 70. It also found that the rate of sexual intercourse decreases by age, from 78 times per year for those under age 40 to 8 times per year for those over age 70. The decrease is most apparent in the unmarried. Few of the persons identified as widowed reported having intercourse, and since the population of women who are widows increases dramatically with increasing age, it is logical that their rate of intercourse would decrease.

Older men, although experiencing a biological decline in sexual functioning, report a higher level of sexual activity than do women. Although the rate of sexual activity for married men and women is similar, unmarried men, both heterosexual and gay, report a higher level of sexual activity than do unmarried heterosexual and gay women. Seventy-five percent of the unmarried men versus 50 percent of the unmarried women in Brecher's study (1984) said they were sexually active (including masturbation and having a partner); Brecher also noted that more men than women value sexuality in marriage. One study indicated that sexual activity for men increases from age 60 to age 70 (O'Donohue, 1987). Starr and Weiner (1981) found that men aged 60–69 had "sexual relations" about 1.5 times per week, comparable to the 1953 Kinsey study's findings (cited in Starr & Weiner, p. 268) for the rate of marital intercourse for men aged 40 and that the percentage of men who are sexually active in old age varies by study, from 50 to 80 percent. As Botwinick (1984, p. 101) stated, "Although the decline with age in sexuality is more apparent in men than in women, the sexual activities of men, for various reasons, are more frequent than those of women throughout most of their lives." However, half the men *and* women in their seventies and older in Brecher's study (1984) reported that they masturbated.

A heterosexual woman's rate of sexual activity varies by the level of sexual activity of her male partner (Botwinick, 1984; Brecher, 1984; Falk & Falk,

1980; Malatesta, 1989; Starr, 1985). For instance, Botwinick (1984) found that a woman's level of sexual activity varied by the age of her husband; she was less sexually active if married to an older man and more sexually active if married to a younger man. Sexual activity also varies by access to a partner. As women age, their number of same-age male partners declines. Thus the level of masturbation may be a better index of sexual activity for women than may sexual intercourse (Berezin, 1975). Although 50 percent of the women in Brecher's (1984) study reported masturbating, Christenson and Gagnon (1965) found that in both the married and nonmarried groups they studied, sexual activity (masturbation and sexual intercourse) waned after age 50 for women. Kehoe (1988) found a lowered rate of sexual activity for women who are lesbian, as well.

PSYCHOSEXUAL DISORDERS

The determination that sexual behavior is dysfunctional is dependent on the individual and couple being assessed; caution is recommended when labeling a behavior a "disorder." As long as an individual is satisfied with his or her level of sexual activity and is not intruding on another's, the behavior cannot be labeled dysfunctional. There are tremendous variations in the levels of sexual activity and in the ways that sexuality is expressed. Specific problems, such as impotence and vaginal pain during intercourse, can be identified and addressed. The inclusion of "psychosexual issues" in any assessment allows the determination about whether any issues around sexuality exist and which interventions may be appropriate that would enhance the quality of the person's life.

CONCLUSION

Butler and Lewis (1977, pp. 136–139) identified ten advantages of sexual activity in older age:

1. opportunity for expression of passion, affection, admiration, loyalty, and other positive emotions,
2. an affirmation of one's body and its functioning,
3. a strong sense of self,
4. a means of self-assertion,
5. protection from anxiety,
6. defiance of the stereotypes of aging,

7. the pleasure of being touched or caressed,
8. a sense of romance,
9. an affirmation of life, and
10. a continuing search for sensual growth experience.

Fifty to 75 percent of people over age 65 report being sexually active. People are more likely to have an interest in sexuality and to respond if they continue to be sexually active (Malatesta, 1989). Satisfaction with life, marriage, and sexuality are interrelated. Satisfaction with one's level of expressed sexuality is correlated with satisfaction with life and with one's partner. Women who are satisfied with their marriage are more likely to say that sexuality is important than are women who are unsatisfied. Women who masturbate but do not have a partner report dissatisfaction with the lack of a partner. Men continue to be interested in sexuality, regardless of biological changes, and unmarried men report higher levels of sexual activity than do unmarried women. Although there is little information about the sexual practices of people who are gay and lesbian as they age, it appears that women may be less active than men, at least in a partner relationship.

Implications for Social Work Practice

Flexibility in problem solving contributes to satisfaction with one's sexuality in old age. A wide range of couples arrangements, such as long-term marriage, multiply marriages, casual sex, extramarital affairs, same-sex relationships, and multiple sexual partners, are possible. Defining sexuality broadly as encompassing a wide range of sensuous experiences increases one's opportunities for sexual expression. Sexuality is expressed in a variety of ways—those that are overtly sexual, such as experiencing an orgasm during sleep, masturbation, and intercourse—and those that are nonsexual but that provide satisfaction—hugging, massage, and friendships.

Orgasm During Sleep

A daughter hesitantly described her mother's "crazy" behavior two years following the death of her husband. Ms. W told her daughter that occasionally Mr. W visits her at night; during these visits, Ms. W. experiences sexual satisfaction. Ms. W continues to function successfully at work, in her social contacts at church and in the community, and within her family. Education about the normalcy of "seeing" a deceased loved one in dreams and of experiencing orgasm during sleep allowed the daughter to redefine her mother's behaviors as acceptable, not requiring psychiatric intervention.

Assistance in problem solving, especially in offering alternatives from which to choose, may enhance an older individual's quality of life (Harbert & Ginsberg, 1990). It may involve changes to enhance an individual's situation, interventions with the family and community, preparation for the professional, and research.

CHANGES TO ENHANCE AN INDIVIDUAL'S SITUATION Sexuality is characteristic of human beings, whatever their age. However, interest in and the expression of sexuality vary dramatically from individual to individual, including the elderly. Therefore, it is unrealistic to make assumptions about the sexual behavior of all persons aged 65 and older. Since sexual interest and expression in older adults vary dramatically across individuals, they are probably more consistent with the behavior of an individual over his or her life than across individuals in any particular cohort. People who are sexually active are more likely to retain their interest in sexuality and ability to perform sexually.

Respecting an individual's choice about the level of sexual activity is paramount. Some may prefer no overtly sexual activities. As LeShan (1990, p. 18) pointed out:

And here we are now, told by Dr. Ruth and an assortment of other manic people that our hormones are not declining, it's all in our heads, and there is no reason why we shouldn't be gleefully rolling in the hay at least twice a week. . . . I'm here to tell you that if you get a group of ladies into the right state of relaxation, they will guiltily giggle the truth: they are really into hugging and cuddling more than you-know-what.

Since heterosexual women are likely to find themselves without a same-age partner in old age, they may decide to choose among other alternatives, such as involvement with a much younger person or a same-sex sexual partner and masturbation. Nonsexual activities that meet some needs for sexuality include massage, touching family members and friends that is not overtly sexual but takes care of "skin hunger," and caring for pets. Malatesta (1989, p. 106) suggested "spending time with one's children and grandchildren, kissing and hugging one's children and grandchildren, wearing attractive clothing, having your hair done, expressing one's spirituality, visiting friends and relatives, wearing lingerie, and physical activity."

Starr (1985, p. 105) answered the question, How do you handle normal sexual feelings? with "denial, compensation, sublimation, resignation, and feelings of persistent frustration, among others." It is hoped, though, that these are not the only alternatives for older persons who are interested in outlets for sexual expression. However, Barbach and Levine (1980, p. 364) noted that women may not be able to accept any alternative from a broad range of choices, given the messages they received while growing up about the unacceptability of "masturbation, younger male partners, female partners, nonmarital affairs, or sharing their male partners with other women."

Developing a belief system that helps one make sense out of loss, one's previous life, and one's future enhances one's ability to appreciate all aspects of life. An existential orientation to living is characteristic of this stage. As one older woman stated, "Tragedy is going to hit because we are born to die." This awareness of one's mortality may be a blessing. The fact that death is more present, with people in one's life more vulnerable, as is that person, and the process of making sense out of one's life, enhances appreciation for all parts of oneself, including one's sexuality (Barbach & Levine, 1980).

❑ ❑ ❑

Solutions to changes in physiology that accompany illness and aging vary with the concern. Using water-based lubricants to supplement naturally occurring vaginal fluids decreases unpleasant sensations during intercourse for women, but hormonal treatments are controversial and should be carefully considered. Changes in the type of lovemaking accommodate physical changes resulting from aging, illness, and disease. Both men and women can learn specific techniques to increase stimulation. Alternatives to stimulation, such as vibrators, can take the place of hands pained by arthritis. Women may exercise the pubococcygeal muscle to improve bladder control, increase support to the back, and contribute to increased sexual satisfaction, using Kegel exercises. When impotence is a concern, determining its possible cause (e.g., illness resulting in a colostomy or heart disease, medication, or alcohol ingestion) may result in treatment or adaptations (Bennett & Rivard, 1982). The advice of a trained physician is invaluable.

If the cause of impotence appears to be related to the relationship, then referral to a qualified couples or sex therapist may be advisable. Sex therapy includes attention to medical problems, training about intimacy, and psychotherapy (Thienhaus, 1988). Communicating what one prefers and what is unpleasant is crucial to continued sexual enjoyment as changes occur.

Paying attention to general psychological and physical health, through nutrition, medical care, and exercise, increases one's ability to live healthily in old age and enjoy whatever level of sexuality is desired. Books, such as *Worst Pills, Best Pills* (Wolfe, Fugate, Hulstrand, & Kamimoto, 1988), allow one to be a conscientious consumer of health care services and medications; they not only discuss the impact and interactions of medications, but provide a guide for examining one's own use of medicine. Sexual behavior can also be adapted to reduce the risk of infection; for example, concerns about sexually transmitted diseases may lead one to use condoms and foam to prevent disease even though one is no longer concerned about pregnancy.

Education about the normal aging process and the impact of illnesses and medicine on sexuality increases the older individual's options (Salamon & Charytan, 1984; Smith & Schmall, 1983); for instance, one may enjoy lovemaking without experiencing an orgasm. Reading about sexuality and disabilities provides helpful information about potential adaptations as well. *The New Our Bodies, Ourselves* (Boston Women's Health Book Collective, 1984), for example, provides not only education but a philosophy of how older women may live their lives. Unfortunately, popular books about sexuality and old age seem to be geared only to women. This situation is ironic, since older men may frequently limit their sexual behavior due to issues related to impotence (Starr, 1985).

Treating specific illnesses also increases one's ability to enjoy life. Rather than ignoring depression, assuming that it is "normal" for an older person, treatment can dramatically increase one's enjoyment of sex. The fear of sexual activity because of heart disease may be dealt with by obtaining information from the physician about one's general state of health and ability to exercise. As O'Donohue (1987, p. 106) pointed out, "A man and wife who are compatible, whose sexual patterns are very familiar, can achieve sexual intercourse with a minimum expenditure of energy and a minimum strain on the heart." O'Donohue stated that sexual activity is like climbing two flights of stairs; one can be sexually active if one can climb two flights of stairs.

FAMILY AND COMMUNITY Contacts with people outside the family decrease with increasing age, and family members become more important as supports and confidants, especially for men, who report few friends, even though they are involved in social support networks like clubs (Field & Minkler, 1988). The provision of education and resources to the family allows them to view the older family member as a whole person, including a sexual person (Brier & Rubenstein, 1979; Jarvik & Small, 1988).

Policies of agencies and institutions can recognize and respect the entire range of needs and emotions that an older person experiences. Allowing older persons to remain with their partners and to express themselves sexually enhances the quality of their lives. Providing private rooms for two and the establishment of other policies allows the person who is single to be active sexually as well. Wasow and Loeb (1978) found that 40 percent of the women in their survey who lived in nursing homes would be sexually active if they had partners.

Expanding acceptable communication between partners and between older persons and others in their environment, such as caregivers and professionals, is critical. Information from older persons indicates that being able to talk with their partners increases their satisfaction with the relationship and enhances their ability to enjoy their sexuality. To maintain flexibility, people must be able to talk openly with each other about what may be considered private and even unacceptable topics.

Little information is available about people who are older and who are gay and lesbian. Elderly gays and lesbians may have even more issues related to sexuality and aging owing to lowered self-esteem because of cultural attitudes and may be even more hidden than may younger generations, which limits their access to partners (Dunker, 1987; Lewis, 1984). Kimmel (1979) interviewed fourteen aging gay men and found that they all thought that sexuality was important, although it was less so than when they were younger. Addressing community attitudes about sexual orientation will expand options for persons who are gay and lesbian.

PREPARING THE PROFESSIONAL The goal of professionals who work with people who are older is to make their lives, including their sexual behavior, "less burdensome physically and more rewarding emotionally" (Harbert & Ginsberg, 1990, p. 277). Information about sexuality and aging is included in writings specifically about sexuality, but is limited in general books about aging. Unfortunately, the literature for professionals may view sexuality and old age only in the context of "problems." For instance, the only reference in the index of Social Work with the Aging (Lowy, 1985) is to "sexual problems," which indicates that sexuality is viewed only in the context of a complication, not as part of a person's whole life. And the advice given may be limited, in that sexual expression is viewed narrowly, in traditional terms. In Social Work with the Aging, Lowy stated: "It is important to be cautious in evoking sexual feeling if the person has little hope of finding a suitable partner" (211). Surely, sexuality can be expressed in many other ways, such as in nonsexual massage, masturbation, and the body's natural response of experiencing an orgasm during sleep.

Factoring in the issue of sexuality in any intervention, whether it is the development of a policy about sleeping arrangements in a nursing home or counseling a couple about acceptable physical exertion after a heart attack, is logical. To do so, social workers and other professionals must feel comfortable with their own sexuality and with allowing others to discuss their sexuality and have knowledge of the biological, social, cultural, and emotional developmental stages of old age (Barber, Lewis, Long, Whitehead, & Butler, (1989). Figuring out how to ask about sexual practices when the person in front of you looks like your mother takes special practice and preparation. Knowledge about when to refer a client to a medical specialist and who is best suited is critical. Access to resources for referral, such as a gerontological physician who can give appropriate medical advice to the older person about issues related to sexuality, may be particularly limited in rural areas.

Developing respectful policies for agencies and institutions that take into account each individual's desires, capabilities, and choices around sexuality is important, as long as those choices do not intrude on another person without his or her wish. The social worker assists clients to consider a wide variety of acceptable options and then helps them determine with whom it is appropriate to talk about sexuality. Finally, the social worker facilitates older persons' ability to talk about sexuality with physicians and other health care professionals, staff in nursing homes and in other congregate living situations, and mental health professionals.

RESEARCH Little is known about the types and levels of sexual expression by and the developmental tasks of different cultural groups and gay and lesbian people who are older. Research in these areas will also assist practitioners in determining the best intervention for older persons who are attempting to meet their developmental tasks.

Determining older persons' opinions about sexuality and the frequencies of particular sexual attitudes or activities is difficult because of problems in finding representative responses and with accurate reporting. Since many people choose not to respond to questions about sexuality, and others in their environment may disapprove of and discourage their participation, the information they present must be interpreted with these limitations in mind. Therefore, ways of gathering information need to be adapted to increase the reliability of the data that are gathered and the generalizability of results. Asking older persons about how they would behave if nothing prevented them, rather than how frequently they engage in intercourse, may result in more accurate information about their interest in sexuality. The inclusion of satisfaction with sensuality-sexuality in measurements of the life satisfaction of older persons results in more accurate measures of all imporant facets of life satisfaction.

Research identifying "normal" sexual behavior in old age and outlining the circumstances in which a person would benefit from intervention by a helping person would improve professional interventions. More knowledge about the impact of specific illnesses and medications and their impact on sexuality will increase the abilities of helping professionals to address the "whole" person.

BIBLIOGRAPHY

Atchley, R. C. (1987). Age grading and grouping. In G. L. Maddox (Ed.), The encyclopedia of aging (p. 150). New York: Springer.

Auer, E. T. (1982). Sex after 55. In T. G. Duncan (Ed.), Over 55: A handbook on health (pp. 435–442). Philadelphia: Franklin Institute Press.

Barbach, L., & Levine, L. (1980). Shared intimacies. Toronto: Bantam Books.

Barber, H., Lewis, M., Long, J., Whitehead, E., & Butler, R. (1989). Sexual problems in the elderly, 1: The use and abuse of medications. Geriatrics, 44(3), 61–64.

Bennett, A. H., & Rivard, D. J. (1982). Male impotence: New concepts in management. New York State Journal of Medicine, 82, 1676–1683.

Berezin, M. A. (1975). Masturbation and old age. Masturbation from infancy to senescence (pp. 329–347). New York: International Universities Press.

Borges, M. A., & Dutton, L. J. (1979). Attitudes toward aging: Increasing optimism found with age. In A. Monk (Ed.), The age of aging (pp. 42–50). Buffalo, NY: Prometheus Books.

Boston Women's Health Book Collective. (1984). The new our bodies, ourselves. New York: Simon & Schuster.

Botwinick, J. (1984). Aging and behavior: A comprehensive integration of research findings (3rd ed.). New York: Springer.

Bowling, A. (1989). Who dies after widow(er)hood? A discriminant analysis. Omega, 19, 135–153.

Brecher, E. M. (1984). Love, sex, and aging. Boston: Little, Brown.

Brier, J., & Rubenstein, D. (1979). Sex for the elderly? Why not? In A. Monk (Ed.) The age of aging (pp. 195–213). Buffalo, NY: Prometheus Books.

Butler, R. N., & Lewis, M. I. (1977). Sex after sixty. New York: Perennial Library.

Butler, R. N., & Lewis, M. I. (1986). Aging and mental health. Columbus, OH: Charles E. Merrill.

Carstensen, L. L., & Edelstein, B. A. (Eds.). (1987). *Handbook of clinical gerontology*. New York: Pergamon Press.

Christenson, C. L., & Gagnon, J. H. (1965). Sexual behavior in a group of older women. *Journal of Gerontology, 20,* 351–356.

Cohen, S. S. (1988). *The magic of touch.* New York: Harper & Row.

Davis, R. H. (1978). *Sexuality and aging.* Los Angeles: University of Southern California Press.

Dayton, B. I., & Antonucci, T. C., (1988). Reciprocal and nonreciprocal social support: Contrasting sides of intimate relationships. *Journal of Gerontology: Social Sciences, 43*(3), 65–73.

Doress, P. B., & Siegal, D. L. (1987). *Ourselves, growing older.* New York: Simon & Schuster.

Dunker, B. (1987). Aging lesbians: Observations and speculations. In Boston Lesbian Psychologies Collective, *Lesbian psychologies* (pp. 72–82). Urbana: University of Illinois Press.

Eisdorfer, C., Lawton, M. P., & Maddox, G. L. (Eds.). (1985). *Annual review of gerontology and geriatrics* (Vol. 5). New York: Springer.

Falk, G., & Falk, U. (1980). Sexuality and the aged. *Nursing Outlook, 28*(1), 51–55.

Field, D., & Minkler, M. (1988). Continuity and change in social support between young-old and old-old or very-old age. *Journal of Gerontology: Psychological Sciences, 43*(4), 100–106.

Finucane, T. E. (1990, March 20). Sexual behavior changes over time, but remains popular. *The State,* p. 3-D.

Foner, A. (1986). *Aging and old age: New perspectives.* Englewood Cliffs, NJ: Prentice-Hall.

George, L. K. (1980). *Role transitions in later life.* Monterey, CA: Brooks/Cole.

George, L. K., & Bearon, L. B. (1980). *Quality of life in older persons.* New York: Human Sciences Press.

Giambra, L. (1983). Daydreaming in 40 to 60-year-old women: Menopause, health, values, and sexuality. *Journal of Clinical Psychology, 39*(1), 11–21.

Harbert, A. S., & Ginsberg, L. H. (1990). *Human services for older adults: Concepts and skills* (2nd ed., rev.). Columbia: University of South Carolina Press.

Hendricks, J. (1987). Age identification. In G. L. Maddox, (Ed.), *The encyclopedia of aging.* New York: Springer.

Jarvik, L,. & Small, G. (1988). Sex: Do they really do it—now? *Parent care: A common sense guide for adult children.* New York: Crown.

Kaluger, G., & Kaluger, M. (1984). *Human development: The span of life* (3rd ed.). St. Louis: Times Mirror/Mosby College.

Kaplan, H. S. (1974). *The new sex therapy.* New York: Brunner/Mazel.

Kaufman, S. R. (1986). *The ageless self.* Madison: University of Wisconsin Press.

Kehoe, M. (1988). Lesbians and gay men over 60 speak out. *Journal of Homosexuality, 16*(3), 63–74.

Kimmel, D. (1979). Life-history interviews of aging gay men. *International Journal of Aging and Human Development, 10,* 239–248.

LeShan, E. (1990). *It's better to be over the hill than under it.* New York: Newmarket Press.

Lewis, M. (1984, November–December). Sexual activity in later life: A challenge issue for nurses. *Imprint,* pp. 48–49.

Longenberger, R. (1980). Sex and the elderly. *Journal of Long Term Care Administration, 8*(2), 13–30.

Lowy, L. (1985). *Social work with the aging.* New York: Longman.

Ludeman, K. (1981). The sexuality of the older person: Review of the literature. *The Gerontologist, 21,* 203–208.

Maddox, G. L. (Ed.). (1987). *The encyclopedia of aging.* New York: Springer.

Malatesta, V. J. (1989). Sexuality and the older adult: An overview of guidelines for the health care professional. *Journal of Women and Aging, 1,* 93–118.

McCracken, A. L. (1988). Sexual practice by elders: The forgotten aspect of functional health. *Journal of Gerontological Nursing, 14*(10) 13–17.

Mercer, R. T., Nichols, E. G., & Doyle, G. C. (1989). *Transitions in a woman's life.* New York: Springer.

Minkler, M., & Langhauser, C. (1988). Assessing health differences in an elderly population: A five year follow-up. *Journal of the American Geriatrics Society, 36,* 113–118.

Monk, A. (1979). *The age of aging.* Buffalo, NY: Prometheus Books.

Montagu, A. (1978). *Touching (The human significance of the skin).* New York: Harper & Row.

Moran, J. (1979). Sexuality: An ageless quality, a basic need. *Journal of Gerontological Nursing, 5*(5), 13–16.

Murrell, S., Himmelfarb, S., & Phifer, J. F. (1988). Effects of bereavement/loss and pre-event status on subsequent physical health in older adults. *International Journal of Aging and Human Development, 27*(2), 89–107.

Myers, G. C. (1987). Demography. In G. L. Maddox (Ed.), *The encyclopedia of aging* (pp. 164–167). New York: Springer.

Newman, B. M., & Newman, P. R. (1987). *Development through life: A psychosocial approach.* Homewood, IL: Dorsey Press.

O'Donohue, W. T. (1987). The sexual behavior and problems of the elderly. In L. L. Carstensen & B. A. Edelstein (Eds)., *Handbook of clinical gerontology.* New York: Pergamon Press.

Pearson, B. P., & Beck, C. M. (1989). Physical health of elderly women. *Journal of Women and Aging, 1*(1, 2, 3,), 149–174.

Pfeiffer, E. (1978). Sexuality in the aging individual. In R. L. Solnick (Ed.),

Sexuality and aging (pp. 26–32). Los Angeles: Ethel Percy Andrus Gerontology Center, University of Southern California.

Reisman, J. M. (1988). An indirect measure of the value of friendship for aging men. *Journal of Gerontology, 43,* 109–110.

Rice, S. (1989). Sexuality and intimacy for aging women: A changing perspective. *Journal of Women and Aging, 1*(1, 2, 3), 245–264.

Roff, L., & Klemmack, D. (1979). Sexual activity among older persons: A comparative analysis of appropriateness. *Research on Aging, 1,* 389–399.

Salamon, M., & Charytan, P. (1984). A sexuality workshop program for the elderly. *Clinical Gerontologist.* 2(4), 25–35.

Smith, M., & Schmall, V. (1983). Knowledge and attitudes toward sexuality and sex education of a select group of older people. *Gerontology and Geriatrics Education, 3,* 259–269.

Smith, T. W., (1990, February). *Adult sexual behavior in 1989: Number of partners, frequency, and risk.* Paper presented at the meeting of the American Association for the Advancement of Science, New Orleans.

Schneider, J. (1984). *Stress, loss, and grief.* Baltimore, MD: University Park Press.

Starr, B. D. (1985). Sexuality and aging. In C. Eisdorfer, M. P. Lawton, & G. L. Maddox (Eds). *Annual review of gerontology and geriatrics* (Vol. 5, pp. 97–126). New York: Springer.

Starr, B. D., & Weiner, M. B. (1981). *The Starr-Weiner report on sex and sexuality in the mature years.* New York: McGraw-Hill.

Steffl, B. M. (1978). Sexuality and aging: Implications for nurses and other helping professionals. In R. L. Solnick, (Ed.), *Sexuality and aging* (pp. 132–153). Los Angeles: University of Southern California Press.

Thienhaus, O. J. (1988). Practical overview of sexual function and advancing age. *Geriatrics, 43*(8), 63–67.

Tomb, D. A. (1984). *Growing old: A handbook for you and your aging parent.* New York: Viking.

Traupmann, J., Eckels, E., & Hatfield, E. (1982). Intimacy in older women's lives. *The Gerontologist, 22,* 493–498.

Travis, S. (1987). Older adults: Sexuality and remarriage. *Journal of Gerontological Nursing, 13*(6), 8–14.

Wagner, G., & Green, R. (1981). *Impotence: Physiological, psychological, surgical diagnosis and treatment.* New York: Plenum Press.

Wasow, M., & Loeb, M. B. (1978). In R. L. Solnick (Ed.), *Sexuality and aging.* Los Angeles: University of Southern California Press.

Wharton, G. F. (1981). *Sexuality and aging: An annotated bibliography.* Metuchen, NJ: Scarecrow Press.

Wolfe, S. M., Fugate, L., Hulstrand, E. P., & Kamimoto, L. E. (1988). *Worst pills, best pills.* Washington, D.C.: Public Citizen Health Research Group.

Yost, E. B., Beutler, L. E., Corbishley, M. A., & Allender, J. R. (1986). *Group cognitive therapy: A treatment approach for depressed older adults.* New York: Pergamon Press.

19

Post-Traumatic Stress Disorder

Joy Spalding

A REVIEW OF THE LITERATURE

What Is Post-Traumatic Stress?

It is generally recognized that old age is a period that is particularly fraught with change and crisis (Spalding, 1984). At other stages of the life cycle, crises are usually experienced sequentially and singly. In old age, however, what Brody (1977, p. 60) called "assaults" occur in clusters, abruptly and interact with age-related stresses: decrements in capacities; illnesses; and losses from death and of income, work, and social roles. Chronic and acute psychological symptoms often accompany these life crises (Burks & Barclay, 1985; Norris & Murrell, 1987; Spalding, 1984). Although these crises are stressful and may be traumatic for older people, they are not equal to the life-threatening experiences that precede post-traumatic stress disorder (PTSD). The stress is usually less severe in impact and is not experienced as painfully as with PTSD.

PTSD, according to DSM-III-R, describes symptoms that develop after a psychologically distressing event that is beyond the range of usual human experience. Typically, the event is experienced as a threat to an individual's life or body, but may also be a threat of the sudden loss or destruction of the self, home, environment, family members, or friends.

Some of the case material used in this chapter was provided by Kristi Williamson, M. S., Coordinator of Older Adult Services, Mount Hood Community Mental Health Center, Gresham, Oregon. None of the cases is currently in treatment; details have been changed to hide the identity of persons discussed.

Physical violence, crime, disasters, and accidents are some of the experiences—in one's own life or in others—that can cause post-traumatic stress. The most commonly cited examples of such events in the literature are the Holocaust (B. Kahana, Harel, & E. Kahana, 1988, 1989; Marcus & Rosenberg, 1989; Wilson, Harel, & Kahana, 1988), the Vietnam War, violent political repressions and those who have experienced disasters (Hendin & Haas, 1984; Marcus & Rosenberg, 1989; Wilson, 1989; Wilson, Harel, & Kahana, 1988). Special attention has been paid to the psychological impact of these experiences and the resulting stresses. These studies have helped us understand that problems are not always experienced immediately and that symptoms may not appear for many years.

Unfortunately, there is little specific information in the literature on other types of elderly victims of PTSD. Neither studies of adaptation and coping nor the focus on life events adequately addresses the elderly's responses to major life-threatening stressors, such as kidnapping, assaults, rape, accidental or natural disasters, or deliberately caused disasters. While life events, such as the loss of a spouse, friends, or a job, may be traumatic, they are not life-threatening or destructive and are within the range of expectable human experiences.

DSM-III-R does not indicate subtypes; DSM-III does. These subtypes are acute PTSD whose onset is within six months of the trauma and whose symptoms last fewer than six months, and chronic or delayed PTSD, the duration of whose symptoms is six months or more and whose onset of symptoms is delayed at least six months after the trauma. Chronic PTSD is especially relevant for older clients, who may never have resolved feelings created by traumatic experiences. The passage of years is no guarantee that the trauma will be resolved; growing older often intensifies the symptoms of PTSD (Nichols & Czirr, 1986).

People who undergo life-threatening traumas report terror and a sense of helplessness during the event. They are severely frightened. How an individual experiences the traumatic event affects the severity and type of stress symptom, so that a spectrum of behavioral and psychological responses are characteristic of post-traumatic stress. However, studies show that the disorder is more severe and longer lasting when the stressor is caused by people rather than by natural forces.

It is not unusual for depression, generalized anxiety, or sleep disturbances to accompany PTSD in the elderly, especially when PTSD is chronic or long lasting. Stressors associated with changes in an individual's life often cause these symptoms as well, symptoms that also occur with adjustment disorders (see Chapter 11). However, this reaction to changes does not last longer than six months, according to DSM-III-R.

For some persons, the symptoms of stress appear immediately; for others, major symptoms appear years later. DSM-III-R notes that generally the traumatic event is experienced recurrently and obtrusively through recollections and dreams or when the person is exposed to like events or related symbols. Such experiences can be particularly difficult when combined with challenging life circumstances in older age (Archibald & Tuddenham, 1965).

The reexperiencing of the trauma is a diagnostic criterion of the disorder. Since the fears reappear with the reexperiencing, victims of PTSD make persistent efforts to avoid thoughts or feelings, activities, or situations that recall the traumatic event. Feelings of numbness, psychogenic amnesia, and detachment are not unusual. Some persons report the inability to experience emotions; many are depressed and anxious. According to DSM-III-R, depressive disorders, or organic mental disorder may be diagnosed following the traumatic event (for a detailed listing of the criteria for a diagnosis of PSTD see DSM-III-R, p. 250–251).

Role of Social Workers

PTSD in the elderly is a relatively new concern for clinical social workers. Clinicians may ignore symptoms of PTSD because attention to the diagnosis and treatment of chronic and acute PTSD symptoms in the elderly is relatively scant in the clinical literature. They must, therefore, turn primarily to the PTSD literature on younger groups for knowledge and theory, which is not always applicable to the older group. In addition, Nichols and Czirr (1986) cited the widespread tendency of professionals to believe that PTSD symptoms are related to schizophrenia, alcoholism, antisocial personality disorder, or depression—if not to ignore them. They believe that clinicians who do not consider PTSD may fail to identify the primary problem of an elderly client. Nichols and Czirr (1986) accurately described PTSD as a "hidden syndrome in the elderly."

There are few examples in the literature to inform us in our clinical social work with the elderly PTSD clients, as B. Kahana, Harel, and E. Kahana (1989) and Marton (1988) noted. Davis and Brody (1979) discussed older women and sexual assault, but focused primarily on prevention and only briefly mentioned crisis intervention. Their rich bibliography contained few items about the treatment of PTSD following rape. There is even less material on minority ethnic and racial groups, including the ever-growing, ever-aging refugee population.

The focus in the gerontological literature has been primarily on adaptation and coping, rather than on the direct psychological impact of stressful or traumatic events and PTSD. The related clinical practice literature is more often concerned with adjustment disorders or anxiety.

A number of writers have addressed therapeutic approaches to the emotional stresses of later life, but largely their works are concerned with the changes and losses that are characteristic of old age. Although these stressors, such as relocation (Aldrich & Mendkoff, 1963; Borup & Gallego, 1981), may be acute and have a considerable impact, they are not the life-threatening stressors that are associated with the development of PTSD (Butler & Lewis, 1982; Chatters & Taylor, 1989; Harel, 1989; Osgood, 1985; Rzetelny, 1988; Spalding, 1984).

Stress symptoms have been identified in all segments of the population in varying degrees (Helzer, Robins, & McEvoy, 1987). Therefore, it isn't surprising that stress has been a major subject of works of popular psychology as the public, along with professionals, has become increasingly aware of negative aspects of stress. As a result there is a burgeoning of interest in the management and treatment of stress throughout the life cycle.

Coping styles and strategies determine how stressful situations are dealt with and are markers of mental health, and social work has played a role in underscoring the value of social supports, psychosocial treatment, and services for helping clients develop strategies for coping with stressful events.

Coping style as a reflection of an older individual's culture has drawn attention over the years. For example, elderly Chinese people have been found to use more coping strategies and of a different type than have other groups (Wong & Reker, 1985).

There are clear indicators that disadvantaged minority ethnic or racial groups are subjected to greater stress, so that the double jeopardy of aging is more than a hypothesis. Adaptation and coping vary with one's role perception within one's group, and there may be compensatory factors related to family life, morale, and life satisfaction (Dowd & Bengston, 1978; Markides, 1983).

Although studies such as these have helped social workers to understand more about how minority groups cope with stress, they have not included a broad range of post-traumatic stress subjects, which has created a gap in the literature and in our understanding. We need to close that gap as minority groups grow larger, more varied, and older. For example, the refugee community has cited the inadequacy of support services to teach culturally appropriate coping skills and the failure of professionals in the helping field to emphasize dependence versus independence and self-help for their elders (Fujiwara, 1985; Gozdiak, 1988). Thus, the aging of minority groups should be a major target for social work training and research if we are to serve the PTSD population.

This case shows what one Southeast Asian refugee family experienced:

Mrs. N, aged 73, came to the United States from Southeast Asia as a refugee, following a very difficult period of war in her country. Her family had managed to escape to a neighboring country, where they were put into a refugee camp. Life was again difficult, exacerbated by the fact that her husband died in the camp. Fortunately, one son and his family were in the United States, and Mrs. N was able to gain entry after a few months' wait.

Mrs. N stayed in the house alone while the family was in school and at work. Often she would cry all day and told her family that she couldn't forget what had happened during the war and the loss of her husband in the refugee camp. She paced the house at night, afraid to go to sleep. She was also afraid of people breaking into the house and killing her. Because her daughter-in-law often missed work to stay with Mrs. N, her daughter-in-law's employer suggested a community mental health center in the neighborhood. However, no one at the center could speak Mrs. N's language. Thus, her first visit to the center was her last visit. "How can I talk?" she said. "Besides, they think I'm crazy and they kept writing down things about me. I don't think they respect me, an old person. They don't know our ways."

Given the lack of appropriate treatment strategies for PTSD, social work clinicians must draw largely on general treatment modalities that are based on crisis intervention and cognitive and behavioral theories to treat symptoms of anxiety and depression or to alleviate the pain of reexperiencing and nightmares.

Slowly the field is moving beyond the combat-related emphasis. Although social work must continue to recognize the growing needs of the aging population of veterans, it is equally essential to understand how to treat elderly clients who suffer from trauma of all types.

SETTINGS FOR SOCIAL WORK WITH OLDER CLIENTS WITH PTSD

The mental health care of older people did not increase along with the growth of social services in the 1960s. Nor have the past few decades brought an increase. Social workers are still not providing sufficient mental health treatment for elderly clients in need.

Estimates of the rate of mental disorders in the elderly indicate that they exceed the estimated rate of 10 percent in the general population; the rate may be as high as 40 percent, depending on the criteria that are used to define psychological impairment. Thus, there is a substantial clientele that the profession could serve, including persons with PTSD (Finkel, 1981; Lebowitz, 1987; Romaniuk, McCauley, & Arling, 1983).

Most older people first consult their primary care physician or are referred by family members when they experience stress and anxiety problems that affect their well-being (Regier, Goldberg, & Taube, 1978). They are less prone to make self-referrals to mental health providers.

The family physician—especially one who has been educated about the elderly—may refer the person to a mental health center and provide the patient who is hesitant to seek clinical services with understanding and support. He or she may make a direct referral to a community agency or sometimes to a private clinic, when the degree of emotional difficulties warrants it. Each of these is a setting in which social workers treat older clients with PTSD.

Only half the community mental health centers (CMHCs) in the United States have services specifically for the aged. Since under 5 percent of the population aged 65 and over uses the services of these CMHCs, this group is not well served by social workers. According to Lebowitz (1987), although few data are available, the private sector is used even less.

Often an older person will talk to a cleric following a traumatic event or when experiencing stress and feelings of not being able to cope. As the clergy become more knowledgeable about the needs of the older members of a congregation, they increasingly make referrals to outside professionals. Some congregations maintain a roster of members who are social workers or are other mental health professionals, and others employ social workers who fulfill "parish duties," although many of the clergy now have a social work degree in conjunction with their religious credentials.

When a physician has hospitalized a patient because of physical symptoms and recognizes that a component of the illness is extreme stress, anxiety, or severe depression, particularly following a traumatic event, generally, he or she refers the patient to the social work staff. The primary tasks of hospital social workers are to assess the patient, diagnose the disorder, and develop an ongoing treatment plan for posthospital care.

In some instances, a client with PTSD may be admitted to a psychiatric facility for intensive treatment because of acute symptoms or when concurrent diagnoses make it advisable. The Veterans Administration medical center is an example of a setting in which an ever-growing number of combat-related PTSD clients are being treated by social workers. With new nursing home regulations in place, long-term-care facilities will be increasingly called upon for psychosocial assessment, treatment planning, and treatment.

When the disorder is identified, clients may be linked to social work settings through other services (such as aging services agencies that conduct case management and nutrition sites or senior citizens' centers with auxiliary services). Focal sites for service delivery provide links with appropriate mental health services. Community agencies are becoming more and more aware of mental health needs related to trauma, chronic or acute and recent.

The rise of crisis hot lines and services in communities has enhanced the opportunity for social workers to provide interventions for clients following rape, abuse, and other forms of trauma. These services provide direct intervention or referral twenty-four hours a day, as do 911 and the emergency rooms of hospitals. Social workers participate in these services.

Social workers are often seen as the front line for the elderly with PTSD of whatever degree because of the generally recognized need to work with the whole person and often with the family. However, we should keep in mind that elderly persons may be suspicious of the social work profession and think that mental health treatment will lead to institutionalization.

Over thirty years ago, Perlman (1957), following the lead of the functional school, emphasized the setting for social work treatment. Environment has become recognized as an important component of social work practice that is framed by a systems perspective. Turner (1978) stated that the setting is important to the therapeutic process and should be examined, evaluated, and used in a planned way, congruent with the psychosocial approach. It is especially necessary to consider the setting when referring older clients who are in need of treatment. What does the setting mean to them?

Any setting for social work must provide a supportive environment for elderly persons whose attitudes are barriers to undertaking and continuing treatment and who are experiencing the high level of anxiety that accompanies PTSD. A physically attractive setting, an oasis of peace and quiet, near transportation and in a safe area is essential for PTSD clients.

The elderly may be victims of their own attitudes about seeking help for psychological disorders. This cohort sees mental problems as a stigma and a sign of personal failure. They may believe, as do unschooled professionals, that you can't cure old people. They may be embarrassed about an accident or a rape or crime against them. Another barrier may be their perception of certain social services as "charity." A major task of any setting is to help overcome these ideas and attitudes, beginning with intake procedures and as part of the intervention process.

The type of social work intervention is determined by the methods used in the particular setting—individual, group, or family therapy—and that are appropriate for a particular individual in whatever combination the social worker prescribes. Because of the high levels of stress and anxiety in PTSD, ideally the agency or clinic will provide twenty-four-hour access to help, with rules clarified at the outset.

SOCIAL WORK TREATMENT

Current theories about human development attempt to explain patterns of change that take place throughout the life cycle. Each stage, including later life, is seen as a period not only of change but of growth, determined by biological factors that interact with psychological and social factors. Thus, when social workers treat the elderly, the use of this developmental perspective enables a client to make changes that enhance growth.

The resolution of the post-traumatic stress crisis may lead to a transition that marks maturity, increased adaptive capacity, and personal growth. By meeting the challenge of a trauma, the client can accomplish a crucial task of the last stage of life: integrity versus despair, according to Erikson's model (Erikson, 1956; Spalding, 1984).

The developmental perspective also emphasizes the interaction of the person, the broad social environment, and the personal environment. Resources are an important aspect of these systems. Clearly, the ecological approach of social work fits well with the demands of treatment for all elderly clients (Golan, 1987; Hartford, 1985).

Social work's dual emphasis on the person and the environment has special meaning for work with clients with PTSD whose symptoms affect their personal and social environments, which, in turn, affect the clients. Problems arise with interpersonal and family relationships. Also PTSD clients need to be linked with resources and services in their environment that will reinforce their ability to cope.

Intervention is, as Germain and Gitterman (1987, p. 495) said, "directed to improving people: environment relationships by facilitating self-management of the internal world of feelings, perceptions, thoughts, values, motivations, and attitudes and helping people to increase the responsiveness of the external world where necessary." The goal of the treatment of PTSD is to help the person manage that internal world while learning to make appropriate and advantageous use of the external world—his or her environment and resources.

When a client has suffered a traumatic experience, the first task is to meet the client's immediate needs, internal and psychological, external and environmental. One of the functions of the intake and assessment process is to determine what these needs are. The treatment plan will incorporate the needs, which differ depending on whether the PTSD is acute or chronic and whether the client is in a crisis situation.

The two categories of PTSD—acute and chronic—differentiate recent and immediate experiences that must be treated as a crisis and past or historical events for which the symptoms are of a long duration or the onset of symptoms is delayed; in some clients, the onset of acute symptoms is delayed for some time, and a crisis does not arise until recent and immediate experiences trigger one. Both are categorized as PTSD according to DSM-III-R, although, as was pointed out earlier, DSM-III separates the two categories as subtypes, but DSM-III-R does not. Treatment should be carried out differentially for the acute and chronic types.

TRAUMA AS CRISIS

Crisis and stress are usually linked with trauma. Stress is the emotional distress that events can produce; crisis is viewed as involving: "(1) a specific and identifiable stressful event, (2) the perception of the event as meaningful and threatening, (3) the disequilibrium resulting from the stressful event, and (4) the coping and interventive tasks that are involved in an adaptive or maladaptive resolution" (Parad, 1977, p. 230). Erikson's (1959) description of crisis serves well here: a period of psychological and behavioral tension precipitated by life hazards, accompanied by heightened demands on the individual—demands that the individual has difficulty meeting.

A recent, acute traumatic experience reflects the configuration of a crisis and, therefore, crisis intervention is appropriate. Accordingly, a client should be seen as soon as possible after the traumatic experience, bypassing any waiting list. Intake screening needs to be simplified so that treatment can begin during the client's first visit. Immediate help will diminish the impact of the stressful experience and provide "emergency emotional and environmental first aid" (Parad, 1977, p. 236). It will also provide support for the stressed client to enhance his or her coping skills and to manage the crisis period with some degree of understanding.

Assessment

The all-important assessment is carried out concurrently with crisis intervention. The collection of information and data is important for the client who has had a fresh, acute traumatic experience because it contributes to an initial, tentative diagnosis and understanding of the ecological system of the PTSD client. It also provides a base for the more complete assessment and later treatment.

Before developing an individualized treatment plan, the social worker should gather as much data as possible. Bloom and Fischer (1982) emphasized the need for consistent guidelines for the initial data collection. What is the trauma that has brought the client to ask for help? What is the degree of trauma? What are the psychological sequelae of the current trauma? Is it a recent, extreme trauma that constitutes a crisis? Are there persistent symptoms that were not present before the traumatic experience? What is the client's history—the past trauma and coping mechanisms used? What are the client's strengths, vulnerabilities, current ways of coping with the stress, and what are the client's resources?

The diagnostic criteria for PTSD identify the characteristic symptoms that follow a psychologically traumatizing event that is "outside the range of usual human experience" (American Psychiatric Association, 1987, p. 247). Associated features, such as depression or anxiety, may coexist to a degree that warrants their diagnosis as a separate disorder. In older people problems with memory, concentration, or vertigo may be confounded with mild dementia. The differentiating factor will be the trauma that has occurred, as is illustrated in the following case example:

Mrs. T, aged 73, was abducted from the yard of her isolated home by unknown assailants who sexually assaulted her and left her by the side of the road. She was found by a passing car and returned to her home, where the police were called.

The police found her to be in a confused state with little recall of the events. When she saw a physician a few hours later in the hospital emergency room, the physician perceived her as slightly demented. He diagnosed her "senile," ascribing her problems to dementia. He failed to incorporate into the assessment the recent severe trauma that she had experienced and did not meet her psychological needs at a time of severe crisis.

The initial assessment—whether part of crisis intervention or of the intake process for chronic stress—which is the basis for treatment planning, is shaped largely by the client's response to the trauma.

Individual responses differ in highly personal ways: experiences have meanings that are related to pre- and postevent translations. The resolution of this experience and its meaning are treatment goals, and any plan that is developed must take into consideration the individual's responses during the assessment. It is important, therefore, to understand clearly what the experience represents to the client.

Assessment is not only the collection of facts and data. It involves professional judgment and persistent thinking about treatment. It is selective, responsible, and developmental—a process for which social workers are accountable (Turner, 1978). How does the information collected inform us about the client's ability to cope and adapt to the traumatic experience? It must be evaluative of the client as a whole person and of his or her systems. It must have a psychosocial approach.

Sensitivity to the older client is especially important. Questions may seem to be an invasion of privacy, particularly by a generation who was socialized to keep their feelings to themselves or who are not oriented toward seeking help. Some types of trauma, such as rape or being a crime victim, may be embarrassing, and the client does not want to expose his or her raw vulnerability.

Meeting with the family, as well as the client, is effective for collecting the client's history and making an assessment before one develops a treatment plan. History taking can usefully be carried out in the client's home (Butler & Lewis, 1982; Herr & Weakland, 1979; Swanson, Frey, & Hyer, 1989), where additional information may be gained and there is an opportunity to observe family dynamics and interaction. The shape and strength of the family support system may be a major determinant of an older client's progress in developing coping skills.

The family is part of the client's human environment, which is made up of relationships with individuals or groups within the community. The human or social environment and the physical environment affect the adaptive and coping tasks a client faces and their outcome (Moos, 1986). Therefore, it is valuable to include information about these environments in developing the assessment and treatment plan.

Social work alone is concerned with the duality of the inner person and the person-in-environment, taking an ecological approach. To focus on the person and the problem in this way is especially appropriate for the elderly. As Brody (1977, p. 55) pointed out, "the aging phase of life brings into sharp focus the interlocking of physical health, mental health, social, economic and environmental factors."

Treatment Decisions

Treatment decisions begin from the first moment of contact with the client, when the assessment and diagnostic process is initiated. This is particularly true if the trauma is a recent life-threatening experience, such as rape or a similar event that meets the criteria for crisis intervention. The decision to use a crisis approach is appropriate, since high levels of stress and anxiety require immediate help with coping mechanisms and problem solving.

Not all crises are caused by recent experiences; some may represent a crescendo of feelings resulting from stress accumulated from a trauma in the distant past. Engulfed by acute distress and vulnerability, a client may become open to help and to finding new solutions for the first time.

The main goals of crisis intervention are (1) to alleviate symptoms and relieve suffering; (2) to help the client understand what has created the symptoms: anxiety, numbness of feelings, depression, forgetfulness, and so on; (3) to provide ways for the client to deal with these symptoms by supporting the client's mastery of affective, cognitive, and behavioral tasks; and (4) to restore the client to his or her precrisis level of adaptation (Wolberg, 1968).

These goals parallel those of short-term therapy and apply to PTSD intervention in general. Indeed, short-term therapy may be the treatment of choice for a variety of reasons, particularly for an older client (Sobel, 1980). To indicate that treatment will not be extended over a long period may be comforting to the client, who may see treatment as a sign of "sickness" and as discouraging and burdensome financially or emotionally. Sharing goals with the client and indicating a time boundary, with the opportunity to return later or intermittently as needed, may lessen the client's anxiety.

On the basis of the work of Parad (1965), Rapoport (1962), and Wolberg (1968), Strean (1978, p. 181) laid out these principles to follow:

Session 1: Attempt to establish a working relationship with the client while

getting as much information as possible. Provide the client with some explanation of the symptoms in understandable language. Explain that the
treatment period will be limited, depending on the amount of work the
client accomplishes.

Succeeding sessions: (1) The client is helped to find appropriate resources
in his or her social or physical environment—an attorney, physician, member of the clergy, police, and so on—who will reduce stress. (2) The client
learns to identify the ways of coping and adapting to stress that worked in
the past, as well as those that are maladaptive. The social worker helps the
client determine what may now be interfering with adjustment and coping
with the trauma and its effects. The client is encouraged to find and try
new ways of coping.

The move from crisis intervention to a model of ongoing treatment comes
when a client has developed some skills in managing the symptoms, so that
they do not interfere with everyday living and work. He or she is prepared
to move forward and build on the base of short-term crisis treatment to
reach new levels of resolution.

AFTER THE CRISIS

The kinds of formal and informal helping systems and resources that may
have been engaged during the crisis period are an important adjunct to the
social work role, no matter what modality is chosen for ongoing treatment.
How the systems are used in conjunction with treatment depends on the
practitioner's individual style and creativity.

The ongoing social work role involves the following: (1) legitimating the
client's feelings, letting the client know that his or her feelings are valid,
understandable, and acceptable, especially angry and hurt feelings; 2) ab-
solving the client of guilt, with recognition that the client had no other
choice; (3) supporting the client's efforts to cope by identifying with the
client what has worked in the past and new ways that can be tried (an older
person has developed good survivor's skills, but is not always aware of these);
(4) supporting the client's autonomy and decision making following the
trauma, which may have aroused feelings of helplessness and inadequacy;
and (5) building the client's self-esteem by ego support and fostering the
client's cognitive understanding of events related to the trauma and the
client's role (Rzetelny, 1988, pp. 149–150).

These tasks can be carried out through whatever method is chosen as
most appropriate to fulfill the goals of treatment and to meet the client's

needs. Most often treatment will be short term, chosen from a range of theoretical frameworks.

For PTSD clients, the goals usually focus primarily on the specific experiences that are at the root of the stress disorder. Treatment helps clients to integrate the emotional and cognitive aspects of their trauma and to get on with their lives (Hendin & Haas, 1984). Once this integration has taken place, the anxiety or depression and other symptoms generally abate. When there is another concurrent diagnosis, additional treatment, with new goals, may be called for after an integration process.

Individual Treatment

Hendin and Haas (1984) recommended a thorough exploration of the traumatic event or events. They noted that a number of different interventions may have to be used to carry out this step because of the client's defenses against the trauma: avoidance, amnesia, and focus on current problems. A reconstruction process that includes eliciting specific details about the setting, behavior, and surrounding feelings should be carried out so that the client and therapist understand the meanings and feelings accompanying the event.

Often dreams and nightmares about the experience yield information that is useful for treatment, unraveling details about the trauma as repressed details and feelings emerge. Hendin and Haas (1984) also suggested that linking day-to-day events that precipitate nightmares to the trauma demonstrates how current perceptions become distorted. Dreams are also a marker of progress, as are recurrent flashbacks.

Some therapists report that examining flashbacks and revisualizing and reliving a traumatic event can enhance the client's understanding of the experience (Hendin & Haas, 1984). Horowitz (1986) indicated that the client's personality style and stage of recovery should determine the parameters of the exploration of the experience.

Hendin and Haas included the role of personality factors in how an event is perceived and experienced. How the PTSD is expressed depends on the individual personality and provides clues about how the person functioned before the trauma. If the goal is to integrate the event with other life experiences, personality factors cannot be excluded from therapy.

Because of the intense emotional content of the work carried out in treatment, clients may be able to tolerate no more than two sessions per week. Several writers have reported than when painful experiences are encountered, clients will "forget" appointments; thus missed appointments may be a cue that sessions should be spaced further apart (Krystal, 1981;

Zetzel, 1975). The client's inability to tolerate the anxiety, anger, or ensuing depression may temper the pace of the treatment.

The use of medication for PTSD symptoms has been debated extensively (Roth, 1988) and requires medical consultation with professionals who are trained specifically in prescribing for the elderly. Hendin and Haas (1984) indicated that the findings of several studies have supported the use of psychological rather than pharmacological interventions because medication suppresses dreams and thoughts.

There are central areas of stress reactions to trauma that victims must work with in post-traumatic therapy (Ochberg, 1988). These areas include feelings of loss and bereavement around victimization, humiliation, and subjugation and death imagery and the specter of death. A number of other researchers and clinicians have also underscored these areas, adding the loss of self and self-continuity and vulnerability (Wilson, 1989). These feelings are not unlike the feelings identified by crisis theorists.

In what Horowitz (1986) described as "phase-oriented post-traumatic therapy," he listed twelve techniques of treatment: (1) structure events and organize information, (2) reduce the number of external demands, (3) structure periods of rest and recuperation, (4) provide a model for identification and permit temporary dependence and idealization, (5) facilitate cognitive reappraisal and interpret in educational ways, (6) facilitate understanding of the differences between the past and present self, (7) reduce exposure to situations that trigger associations with the trauma, (8) teach techniques for dealing with memories of the trauma, (9) provide support, (10) use desensitization and stress-reducing techniques, and (12) consider the use of antianxiety or other drugs when symptoms are so severe that they interfere with treatment. These techniques are congruent with social workers' repertoire, employing a mixture of psychosocial treatment, cognitive therapy, and behavioral techniques combined with the utilization of resources.

The discomfort of the client with PTSD often creates a high level of discomfort in the social worker, which may lead to the avoidance of heavily laden material and threaten the effectiveness of treatment. Working with a traumatized client is often painful and difficult, and countertransference may be overwhelming, as Nichols and Czirr (1986) pointed out. In addition, in working with an elderly patient, the social worker may be confronted with countertransference issues that arise from his or her feelings about age or about older family members. Consultation or supervision may be helpful when those feelings interfere with the progress of treatment.

Individual treatment is illustrated in the following case example:

Mr. S was anxious and depressed, preoccupied with fears and thoughts about his own death that had persisted following an accident where he was driving in which his wife died. He denied any suicidal intent. He presented symptoms of chronic PTSD, accompanied by depression attributable to the loss of his wife.

Interventions were designed to address (1) the trauma of the accident, (2) Mr. S's underlying unresolved guilt and grief, (3) his generalized fear and anxiety about his death, and (4) his impaired "vision" of himself and his capacities. Mr. S was supported and gently encouraged in his self-paced reconstruction and exploration of the details of the accident. Over time, he was able to express his feelings about the event more completely, partially let go of the guilt, and resolve the loss of his wife. He was able to resume earlier activities comfortably.

Dependence on the therapist became an issue, however, and the family was assembled to address ways in which Mr. S could shift his relationship to others. Other members of the family became more involved with Mr. S, and his social life broadened. Upon termination, he was still feeling some dysphoria, but appeared to have integrated the trauma.

Group Therapy

The use of groups is widely considered the preferred treatment after crisis intervention or in conjunction with individual psychotherapy (Lieberman, 1980; Osgood, 1985; Wilson, 1989). It is used consistently for combat-related PTSD. Brende and Parson (1985) and Hendin and Haas (1984) acknowledged the value of the group to share feelings and lessen the sense of isolation, but cautioned that individual therapy is needed to explore intense personal meaning of experiences.

Group work with older people is limited because of these clients' resistance to sharing emotions. The feeling of numbness and denial that can continue long after a trauma, combined with socialization that fosters hiding emotions, may make a group feel threatening. However, Butler and Lewis (1982) reported success with age-integrated group therapy that required the presence of a life crisis, within certain diagnostic categories, for participation. Older participants were able to express feelings and emotional catharsis within these groups.

Lakin (1987), substantiating other authors, indicated that group therapists must be able to challenge self-held negative stereotypes about old age. Conflicts among group members need to be controlled more carefully in groups of elderly people than in other groups, and the therapist generally has to be more active in initiating and structuring sessions. All evidence points to the value of group therapy with the elderly, especially in conjunction with individual treatment.

The decision to use group therapy depends on the makeup of the individual client, as determined through assessment, and the goals that the therapist and client have established. This is also true of family therapy (Turner, 1978).

Family Therapy

Work with families has long been part of social work's psychosocial orientation to practice. It is based on the premise that to understand the client's system, we need to understand the family dynamics and interactions with the client.

During the early crisis period, when the assessment process takes place, meeting with the family adds useful information about the client, as was emphasized earlier. Informing the family about resources and educating them about PTSD are early tasks for the social worker. In later meetings with the family the social worker facilitates decisions and actions that need to be taken with, and on behalf of, the elderly traumatized relative.

Although no controlled studies have been carried out to demonstrate the value of family therapy with older adults, case reports increasingly indicate positive outcomes. From a systems perspective, when one member of the family has a problem such as PTSD, the whole family is affected, and parts of the system must accommodate the other parts. If the family system can change positively, the impact on the PTSD victim can also be positive, diminishing his or her stress (Bowen, 1978; Minuchin, 1974).

Families can make changes that enable them to provide support for their elderly relative with PTSD; listen to the relative's painful memories when appropriate; and allow and understand expressions of emotion. Within the family, the relative can continue to integrate the trauma (Nichols & Czirr, 1986). Individual therapy sessions are not the only way to escape from a trauma; family therapy may be the necessary catalyst for it to occur. Families frequently must learn how to respond to the special problems of the older victim and meet his or her ongoing needs, both psychosocial and concrete (Davis & Brody, 1979).

The literature reports few studies about family therapy with PTSD victims, although there are indications that family education and support groups have been effective for the family members themselves. Social workers who treat PTSD clients may also be involved with these groups, including self-help groups that are often leaderless and problem focused.

Behavior Therapy

Anxiety, a major symptom of PTSD, may be treated with exposure techniques. Clients can be systematically desensitized through exposure to anxiety-producing trauma-related stimuli. Desensitization is usually carried out gradually and is combined with relaxation exercises (Beck & Emery, 1985; Wolpe, 1969).

Such techniques are valuable because they enable a client to develop a sense of mastery and provide a coping tool to use when he or she feels overwhelmed. However, behavior therapy deals mainly with one symptom and does not focus on the trauma itself, which is central to the therapeutic task with a PTSD client. Thus, it is useful as a complement to other forms of therapy.

Cognitive Therapy

Surveying the trends in psychotherapy, Smith (1982) concluded that the cognitive-behavioral therapies are one of the strongest emphases today. Yet, in a literature review, Storand (1983) found meager information about cognitive therapies with the elderly.

Ellis's (1962) rational-emotive therapy and Beck's cognitive therapy (Beck, 1973; Beck & Emery, 1985) work to correct faulty and distorted thinking. These therapies are appealing to social workers because they assume that people can shape their own lives and rationally determine their behavior. Another positive aspect of these therapies is that progress and outcomes are measureable (Werner, 1982).

The literature does not indicate a wide use of these therapies with PTSD clients. However, two aspects of Beck's work are clearly appropriate for PTSD symptoms of extreme anxiety and depression.

People who have experienced traumatic events are especially sensitive to reminders of the event. A range of stimuli may create anxiety that, coupled with unpleasant visual memories, may be as painful as was the original event (Beck & Emery, 1985) (Rado, 1948, called this phenomenon "traumatophobia.") PTSD victims develop fearful thinking, "catastrophizing" (Ellis, 1962) by focusing on the worst possible outcome of a situation. They selectively abstract from the whole view a skewed perspective of danger and self-vulnerability (Beck & Emery, 1985), and appraising situations as being fraught with danger (which Beck, 1973, called "false alarms"), constantly scan the environment fearfully.

Through tested strategies and techniques, clients can learn to restructure their thinking. Using logic and questions, the therapist can help PTSD clients cope with their fears. Again, cognitive restructuring is a way to deal with symptoms, and while it may help clients feel better, it does not fully resolve the trauma and bring about integration.

Depression is the second focus of Beck's work that many social workers rely on. The Beck Depression Inventory is a valuable tool to measure the depth of depression and to gauge progress in treatment. It is considered reliable and is generally usable with elderly people, although special testing techniques may be needed because of visual or cognitive problems.

Cognitive therapy has been demonstrated to be effective with depressed older adults (Steuer et al., 1984; Thompson, Gallagher, & Breckenridge, 1987). Cognitive therapy rests on three precepts: depressed individuals think negatively in a distorted way; consistently interpret new situations negatively; and make systematic cognitive errors that sustain their negative view of themselves, others, and the world. These precepts are congruent with problems encountered by depressed PTSD victims, who need to develop more accurate and balanced views of their circumstances and of themselves.

Cognitive therapy may be successful in work with the elderly if they are helped to understand why it does not fit their standard view of therapy, are taught how to carry out the tasks of cognitive therapy, and are provided with printed educational materials. Clients should be offered the chance to return for additional sessions, if necessary, following this short-term therapy (Thompson, 1987).

Werner (1982) suggested that cognitive therapy can be used in group and family therapy, as well as in individual therapy. He presented some excellent case studies that demonstrated the use of cognitive therapy in social work settings. Some of these studies are applicable to PTSD.

Summary

Social work has a broad range of therapies from which to choose to work with clients with PTSD. Each of these treatments has some value. Singly or together in various complementary combinations, they can help PTSD victims integrate the trauma into their lives or alleviate painful symptoms in that arduous process. Our major task as social workers is to use these methods to help PTSD clients escape from their trauma and to get on with their lives. The following case of an older PTSD client shows how different kinds of therapy can be used together:

Mrs. J was referred to the agency by her physician following the removal of a cancerous larynx. She was preoccupied with thoughts about her beloved son's final days in his struggle with cancer and found it difficult to think about anything else. She was clinically depressed and diagnosed as having PTSD. Her family had discouraged her from talking about her son's death and her own experience with cancer and urged her to "move on." Intervention began with consultation and education to encourage her adult children to allow their mother to explore her feelings with them.

Mrs. J spent much of her weekly visits going over the specifics of her son's death and identifying her feelings of anger and helplessness, which then became attached to her fear of her own death. Because of her high level of anxiety, she was taught to work with relaxation tapes to use at home. She was also helped to develop positive, happy images to replace the painful images. Finally, she was able to take part in a support group with other cancer patients. Gradually she resumed her normal activities.

RESEARCH: PTSD AND RELATED TOPICS

As interest in stress and the impact of stress has increased among the public and professionals, so has research. The demand for information about the negative effects of stress has brought new attention to research, as the need for knowledge about causes and treatment has moved the field forward (Goldberger & Breznitz, 1982).

Much research has focused on combat-related PTSD in an effort to understand the development of PTSD, individual ways of integrating or adapting to trauma, and differential treatment outcomes. Along with these studies has been work related to Holocaust survivors.

Few studies have examined the impact of trauma and non-combat-related PTSD in older age. Studies continue to examine the stressors that affect individuals and the impact of natural disasters, but few focus specifically on the elderly.

Cognition has become a major research area in PTSD (Goldberger & Breznitz, 1982; Lazarus, 1987). As researchers observe the vast human spectrum of responses to trauma, they try to understand how differences in cognitive style affect responses.

Just as traumas vary, so do people. Yet little research has been reported on the effect of personality on the impact of or recovery from trauma. Little in the literature deals with defenses, according to Marton (1988).

One of the problems with stress and PTSD research has been the lack of consistency in defining terms (E. Kahana, B. Kahana, Harel, & Rosner, 1988). *Stress* has multiple definitions, as have the related concepts of coping and adaptation, which are major focuses of of research on aging.

There are conceptual problems as well. Lazarus (1987) stated that age is not a useful variable, given individual and cohort differences in life history, events, and transitions. Therefore, any study of PTSD, coping, and adaptation will be distorted. Systematic observations of coping and successful adaptation by PTSD clients have yet to be conducted. Lazarus suggested that only longitudinal studies can provide the information that is necessary for intervention.

Stress and coping theory are essential for understanding responses to events (Figley & McCubbin, 1983; Lazarus & Folkman, 1984), but researchers have not gone far enough in examining broad economic and social variables (Vosler, 1990) that are important in aging. The relationship of environmental factors—social, economic, and physical—to the outcome of trauma has only begun to be studied (George, 1987). Also, we know little about the role of the utilization of resources in the environment as a mitigating factor in PTSD, beyond the value of social supports (Harel, 1989).

Gender-specific studies have the same problems as do age-specific studies: It has been impossible to carry out controlled studies. The vast differences among cohorts and the variance in stress responses confound research attempts. The continued examination of gender roles in relation to PTSD in the aged may give us some answers in the future (Barnett & Baruch, 1987).

As our large and varied refugee population grows older, studies can help us understand PTSD in these groups, who have gone "from dignity to despair" (Gozdiak, 1988). Now we have scant research findings to inform our intervention.

Ethnic culture and norms affect aging, as well as psychological adaptation to acute stress, underscoring the need for studies directed toward PTSD and aged ethnic groups. This is an area in which we have limited knowledge, apart from that about Holocaust survivors.

Research to fill the gaps in our knowledge would show us more effective ways to intervene with special groups who are suffering from PTSD. It would also enable policymakers to develop service systems that meet the particular needs of these groups.

Anxiety, a prime symptom of PTSD, is a major research interest. It is measurable (clients can provide self-reports of changes) (Beck & Emery, 1985; Goldberger & Breznitz, 1982), and it is clearly defined and differentiated.

Although clinical depression, a symptom of PTSD, is measurable by a number of instruments, researchers have tended not to focus on this area in PTSD. In the elderly depression is easily confused with other conditions, and symptoms often represent a range of non-PTSD factors. Thus, age-specific PTSD-related depression is scarcely explored.

One area of depression related to trauma that has been studied over the years is relocation trauma. Early reports showed dramatically negative findings for relocated older people (Aldrich & Mendkoff, 1963). Although this is the one area of post-traumatic stress and aging that has consistently received attention from researchers, findings have been inconsistent. However, there is considerable evidence to link relocation and acute post-traumatic stress (Coffman, 1983; Horowitz & Shulz, 1983).

Blazer (1987) pointed out that the demonstrated effectiveness of biological treatments for severe depression in later life has overshadowed attention to psychotherapy with the elderly. This has also been true for anxiety. Because of the acknowledged problems with medication for the elderly, biological treatment and many other types of physiological approaches warrant additional research on the genetic predisposing factors in depression and on the seasonal effects on depression. New areas of diagnosis and treatment are being opened up.

As we approach the next century, there are increasing indicators that we are on the verge of a new era of biological-physiological discoveries. For example, studies of the Yale-based National Center for Post-Traumatic Stress Disorder suggest that there may be permanent biological change in persons who have experienced severe trauma (Goleman 1990). This finding supports the links between stress and trauma made long ago by Selye (1980).

New ways of conducting research and new areas of research are creating changes in knowledge, but many areas still need to be studied. We do not have findings that are applicable to a broader ethnic population or to women. Social scientists have yet to address non-combat-related PTSD adequately, and more attention to elderly victims of PTSD is particularly needed. As the veterans group ages, a burgeoning number will need help. Unless research is expanded and enhanced to develop knowledge about PTSD in the elderly, we will be unprepared to meet these clients' needs.

Social workers have a unique opportunity to advance this research as they work with clients. By integrating practice and research, we can increase our knowledge about PTSD and be prepared to meet the future mental health needs of our clients and of our profession.

POLICIES AND PROGRAMS

To establish programs that meet the needs of older individuals who are experiencing PTSD, planners must first understand what these needs are through research and the assessment of needs. Services must be responsive to those needs and provide a range of alternatives that are appropriate to the various needs of older clients. In addition, planners should carry out ongoing evaluations and be prepared to change programs when outcomes do not fit the identified needs.

The need for certain services may be temporary, as with new immigrant groups, for example. Other programs may have to be redesigned as the target group changes. Community emergency plans should include provisions for older citizens who may suffer particularly painful sequelae following disasters.

Often education about PTSD is needed so the rationale for services that are specific to elderly people is understood. Education also brings clients into treatment and reinforces family members' participation, while it enlists community support and ongoing funding for a program.

Policies for PTSD clients are essential at the agency level. Crises require immediate assessment and treatment planning; timing is all important. Agency policies must ensure that clients are seen as quickly as possible and that agencies provide for immediate, individualized linkages with the appropriate services in the community.

Agency policies should be examined to identify which may exacerbate the anxiety and stress of clients. How do older clients perceive the agency? How do they experience the staff—the total staff—and the services?

An important ingredient of social work is recognition of the importance of the setting to clients. Since agency policies are prime determinants of the quality of help provided for PTSD clients, it is our responsibility to engage in the continual evaluation of settings and the impact of their policies.

BIBLIOGRAPHY

Aldrich, C. K., & Mendkoff, E. (1963). Relocation of the aged and disabled. *Journal of the American Geriatrics Society, 11,* 185–194.

American Psychiatric Association. (1987). *Diagnostic and statistical manual of mental disorders* (3rd ed., rev.). Washington DC: Author.

Appley, M. H., & Trumbull, R. (Eds.). (1986). *Dynamics of stress.* New York: Plenum Press.

Archibald, R. C., & Tuddenham, R. D. (1965). Persistent stress reaction after combat: A 20-year follow-up. *Archives of General Psychiatry, 12,* 475–481.

Barnett, R. C., & Baruch, G. (1987). Social roles, gender, and psychological distress. In R. C. Barnett, L. Biener, & G. K. Baruch (Eds.), *Gender and stress* (pp. 122–143). New York: Free Press.

Beck, A. T. (1973). *Diagnosis and management of depression.* Philadelphia: University of Pennsylvania Press.

Beck, A. T., & Emery, G. (1985). *Anxiety disorders and phobias: A cognitive perspective.* New York: Basic Books.

Blazer, D. (1987). Depression. In G. Maddox (Ed.), *The encyclopedia of aging* (pp. 169–170). New York: Springer.

Bloom, M., & Fischer, J. (1982). *Evaluating practice: Guidelines for the accountable professional.* Englewood Cliffs, NJ: Prentice-Hall.

Borup, J. H., & Gallego, D. T. (1981). Mortality as affected by interinstitutional relocation: Update and assessment. *The Gerontologist, 21,* 8–16.

Bowen, M. (1978). *Family therapy in clinical practice.* New York: Jason Aronson.

Brende, J. O., & Parson, E. R. (1985). *Vietnam veterans: The road to recovery.* New York: Plenum.

Brody, E. (1977). Aging. In J. Turner (Ed.), *Encyclopedia of social work* (17th ed., Vol. 1, pp. 55–78). Washington, DC: National Association of Social Workers.

Burgess, A. W., & Holmstrom, L. L. (1976). Rape trauma syndrome. In F. J. Turner (Ed.), *Differential diagnosis and treatment in social work* (2nd ed., pp. 692–702). New York: Free Press.

Burks, N., & Barclay, M. (1985). Everyday problems and life change events: Ongoing vs. acute sources of stress. *Journal of Human Stress. 11,* 27–35.

Butler, R. N., & Lewis, M. (1982). *Aging and mental health: Positive psychosocial and biomedical approaches* (3rd ed.). St. Louis, MO: C. V. Mosby.

Chatters, L. M., & Taylor, R. J. (1989). Life problems and coping strategies of older black adults. *Social Work, 34,* 313–319.

Coffman, T. L. (1983). Toward an understanding of geriatric relocation. *The Gerontologist, 23,* 453–459.

Davis, L. J., & Brody, E. (1979). *Rape and older women.* Washington, DC: U.S. Government Printing Office.

Dowd, J. J., & Bengston, V. L. (1978). Aging in minority populations: Examination of the double jeopardy hypothesis. *Journal of Gerontology, 33*, 427–436.

Ellis, A. (1962). *Reason and emotion in psychotherapy.* New York: Lyle Stuart.

Erikson, E. (1956). The problem of ego identity. *Psychological Issues, 1*, 101–164.

Erikson, E. (1959). *Identity and the life cycle.* New York: W. W. Norton.

Figley, C. R., & McCubbin, H. I. (Eds.). (1983). *Stress and the family: Vol. 2. Coping with catastrophe.* New York: Brunner/Mazel.

Finkel, S. (Ed.). (1981). *Task Force and the 1981 WHCOA of the APA.* Washington, DC: American Psychiatric Association.

Foa, G., & Foa, E. B. (1987). Rape victims: Post-traumatic stress responses and their treatment: A review of the literature. *Journal of Anxiety Disorders, 1*, 69–86.

Fujiwara, T. (1985). Developing culturally relevant services for minority elderly. Seattle, WA: Asian Counseling and Referral Service.

Gelfand, D. (1982). *Aging: The ethnic factor.* Boston: Little, Brown.

George, L. K. (1987). Life events. In G. Maddox (Ed.), *The encyclopedia of aging* (pp. 391–393). New York: Springer.

George, L. K. (1990). Gender, age and psychiatric disorders. *Generations, 14*, 22–27.

Germain, C. B., & Gitterman, A. (1987). Ecological perspective. In *Encyclopedia of social work* (18th ed., pp. 488–499). Silver Spring, MD: National Association of Social Workers.

Golan, N. (1974). Crisis theory. In F. J. Turner, (Ed.), *Social work treatment* (pp. 420–456). New York: Free Press.

Golan, N. (1987). Crisis intervention. In *Encyclopedia of social work* (18th ed., Vol. 1, pp. 360–372). Washington, DC: National Association of Social Workers.

Goldberger, L., & Breznitz, S. (Eds.). (1982). *Handbook of stress.* New York: Free Press.

Goldfarb, A. (1978). Psychiatry in geriatrics. In S. Steury & M. Blank (Eds.), *Readings in psychotherapy with older people* (pp. 173–181). Rockville, MD: National Institute of Mental Health.

Goleman, D. (1990, June 12). Key to post-traumatic stress lies in brain chemistry, scientists find. *New York Times*, B5.

Gozdiak, E. (1988). *Older refugees in the United States: From dignity to despair.* Washington, DC: Refugee Policy Group, Center for Policy Analysis and Research on Refugee Issues.

Harel, Z. (1989). Coping with extreme stress and aging. *Social Casework: The Journal of Contemporary Social Work, 69*, 575–583.

Harel, Z., & Kahana, B. (1989). The day of infamy: The legacy of Pearl Harbor. In J. P. Wilson (Ed.), *Trauma, transformation and healing: An integrative approach to theory, research and post-traumatic therapy* (pp. 129–158). New York: Brunner/Mazel.

Hartford, M. E. (1985). Understanding normative growth and development in aging. *Journal of Gerontological Social Work*, 8(3–4), 37–54.

Helzer, J. E., Robins, L. N., & McEvoy, L. (1987). Post-traumatic stress disorder in the general population. *New England Journal of Medicine, 26*, 1630–1634.

Hendin, H., & Haas, A. P. (1984). *Wounds of war*. New York: Basic Books.

Herr, J. J., & Weakland, J. H. (1979). *Counseling elders and their families*. New York: Springer.

Horowitz, M. J. (1986). *Stress response syndromes* (2nd ed.). Northvale, NJ: Jason Aronson.

Horowitz, M. J., & Shulz, R. (1983). The relocation controversy: Criticism and commentary on five recent studies. *The Gerontologist, 23*, 229–234.

Kahana, B., Harel, Z., & Kahana, E. (1988). Predictors of well-being among survivors of the Holocaust. In J. Wilson, Z. Harel, & B. Kahana (Eds.), *Human adaptation to extreme stress* (pp. 171–192). New York: Plenum.

Kahana, B., Harel, Z., & Kahana, E. (1989). Clinical and gerontological issues facing survivors of the Nazi Holocaust. In P. Marcus & A. Rosenberg (Eds.), *Healing their wounds* (pp. 197–211). New York: Praeger.

Kahana, E., Kahana, B., Harel, Z. & Rosner, T. (1988). Coping with extreme trauma. In J. Wilson, Z. Harel, B. Kahana (Eds.), *Human adaptation to extreme stress* (pp. 55–80). New York: Plenum.

Kinzie, J. D., Boehnlein, J. K., Leung, D., Moore, L., Riley, C., & Smith, D. (1990). The prevalence of post-traumatic stress disorder and its clinical significance among Southeast Asian refugees. *American Journal of Psychiatry, 147*, 913–917.

Krystal, H., & Niederland, W. G. (Eds.). (1981). *Psychic traumatization*. Boston: Little, Brown.

Lakin, M. (1987, Fall). Group therapies with the elderly: Issues and prospects. *Psychotherapy: Theory, Research and Practice, International Journal of Group Psychotherapy* (Special issue).

Lazarus, R. S. (1987). Stress and coping. In G. Maddox (Ed.), *Encyclopedia of aging* (pp. 647–649). New York: Springer.

Lazarus, R. S., & Folkman, S. (1984). *Stress, appraisal and coping*. New York: Springer.

Lebowitz, B. (1987). Mental health services. In G. Maddox (Ed.), *Encyclopedia of aging* (pp. 440–442). New York: Springer.

Lieberman, M. (1980). The effects of social supports on response to stress. In I. L. Kutash, L. B. Schlesinger, & Associates (Eds.), *Handbook of stress and anxiety* (pp. 764–783). New York: Jossey Bass.

Lieberman, M. A., & Tobin, S. S. (1983). *The experience of old age: Stress, coping and survival*. New York: Basic Books.

McCrae, R. R. (1987). Stress and stressors. In G. Maddox (Ed.), *Encyclopedia of aging* (pp. 649–650). New York: Springer.

Manson, S. M. (1984). Problematic life situations: Cross-cultural variation in support mobilization among the elderly. Washington, DC: Administration on Aging.

Marcus, P., & Rosenberg, A. (Eds.). (1989). *Healing their wounds.* New York: Praeger.

Markides, K. S. (1983). Minority aging. In M. W. Riley, B. B. Hess, & K. Bond (Eds.), *Aging in society: Selected reviews of recent research* (pp. 115–138) Hillsdale, NJ: Lawrence Erlbaum Asssociates.

Marton, F. K. (1988). Defenses: Invincible and vincible. *Clinical Social Work Journal, 16,* 143–155.

Melick, E., Logue, J. N., & Frederick, C. J. (1982). Stress and disaster. In L. Goldberger & S. Breznitz (Eds.), *Handbook of stress* (pp. 613–630). New York: Free Press.

Minuchin, S. (1974). *Families and family therapy.* Cambridge, MA: Harvard University Press.

Moos, R. (Ed.). (1986). *Coping with life crises: An integrated approach.* New York: Plenum.

Nichols, B. L., & Czirr, R. (1986). Post-traumatic stress disorder, hidden syndrome in elders. *Clinical Gerontologist, 5*(3–4), 417–433.

Norris, F., & Murrell, S. (1987). Transitory impact of life event stress on psychological symptoms in older adults. *Journal of Health and Social Behavior, 28,* 197–211.

Ochberg, F. (1988). *Post-traumatic therapy and victims of violence.* New York: Brunner/Mazel.

Osgood, N. J. (1985). *Suicide in the elderly: A practitioner's guide to diagnosis and mental health intervention.* Rockville, MD: Aspen Systems.

Parad, H. J. (Ed.) (1965). *Crisis intervention: Selected readings.* New York: Family Service Association

Parad, H. J. (1977). Crisis invervention. In J. Turner (Ed.), *Encyclopedia of social work* (17th ed., Vol. 1, pp. 228–237). Washington, DC: National Association of Social Workers.

Parad, H. J. (1985). Some principles of working with older patients. *Journal of the American Geriatrics Society, 33,* 44–47.

Perlman, H. H. (1957). *Social casework: A problem-solving process.* Chicago: University of Chicago Press.

Rado, S. (1948). Psychodynamics and treatment of traumatic war neurosis (traumatophobia). *Psychosomatic Medicine, 4,* 362–368.

Rapoport, L. (1962). The state of crisis: Some theoretical considerations. *Social Service Review, 36,* 221–217.

Regier, D. A., Goldberg, I. D., & Taube, C. A. (1978). The defacto U.S. mental health services system. *Archives of General Psychiatry, 35,* 685–693.

Romaniuk, M., McCauley, W., & Arling, G. (1983). An examination of the prevalence of mental disorders among the elderly in the community. *Journal of Abnormal Psychology*, 93, 458–467.

Roth, W. T. (1988). *The role of medication in post-traumatic therapy*. New York: Brunner/Mazel.

Rzetelny, H. (1988). Emotional stresses in later life. *Journal of Gerontological Social Work*, 8(3–4), 141–151.

Selye, H. (1980). The stress concept today. In I. L. Kutash, L. B. Schlesinger, & Associates (Eds.), *Handbook of stress and anxiety* (pp. 127–143). New York: Jossey Bass.

Smith, D. (1982). Trends in counseling. *American Psychologist*, 37, 802–809.

Snyder, C. R., & Ford, C. E. (Eds.). (1987). *Coping with negative events: Clinical and social psychological perspectives*. New York: Plenum.

Sobel, E. F. (1980). Anxiety and stress in later life. In L. I. Kutash, L. B. Schlesinger, & Associates (Eds.), *Handbook on stress and anxiety* (pp. 317–328). San Francisco: Jossey-Bass.

Spalding, J. (1984). Transitions of later life. *American Family Physician*, 29, 211–216.

Steuer, J., Mintz, j., Hammen, C., Hill, M., Jarvik, L., McCarley, T., Motoike, P., & Rosen, R. (1984). Cognitive, behavioral and psychodynamic group psychotherapy in treatment of geriatric depression. *Journal of Consulting and Clinical Psychology*, 52, 180–189.

Storand, M. (1983). *Counseling and therapy with older adults*. Boston: Little, Brown.

Strean, H. S. (1978). *Clinical social work: Theory and practice*. New York: Free Press.

Swanson, G., Frey, J., and Hyer, L. (1989). The strategic approach to unfreeze symptoms of PTSD. *Clinical Gerontologist*, 8, 83–86.

Thompson, L. W. (1987). Psychological assessment. In G. Maddox (Ed.), *The encyclopedia of aging* (pp. 54–99). New York: Springer.

Thompson, L. W., Gallagher, D., & Breckenridge, J. S. (1987). Comparative effectiveness of psychotherapies for depressed elders. *Journal of Consulting and Clinical Psychology*, 55, 385–390.

Turner, F. J. (1978). *Psychosocial therapy: A social work perspective*. New York: Free Press.

Turner, F. J. (Ed.). (1984). *Adult psychopathology: A social work perspective*. New York: Free Press.

Ulbrich, P. M., & Warheit, G. J. (1989). Social support, stress and psychological distress among older black and white adults. *Journal of Aging and Health*. 1, 286–305.

Ulman, R. B., & Brothers, D. (1988). *The shattered self: A psychoanalytic study of trauma*. Hillsdale, NJ: Analytic Press.

Vosler, N. R. (1990). Assessing family access to basic resources: An essential component of social work practice. *Social Work, 35,* 434–441.

Waskel, S. (1981). The elderly, change, and problem solving. *Journal of Gerontological Social Work, 3,* 77–81.

Werner, H. D. (1982). *Cognitive therapy: A humanistic approach.* New York: Free Press.

Wilson, J. P. (1989). *Trauma, transformation and healing: An integrative approach to theory, research, and post-traumatic therapy.* New York: Brunner/Mazel.

Wilson, J. P., Harel, Z., & Kahana, B. (Eds.) (1988). *Human adaptation in extreme stress: From the Holocaust to Vietnam.* New York: Plenum.

Wolberg, L. (1968). Short-term psychotherapy. In J. Marmor (Ed.), *Modern psychoanalysis treatment* (pp. 343–354. New York: Basic Books.

Wolpe, J. (1969). *The practice of behavior therapy.* New York: Penguin Press.

Wong, T., & Reker, G. T. (1985). Stress, coping and well-being in Anglo and Chinese elderly. *Canadian Journal on Aging—La Revue Canadienne du Veillissement, 4,* 29–37.

Zetzel, E. (1975). Affect tolerance. *Annual of Psychoanalysis, 3,* 179–219.

20

Suicide and the Elderly

Susan O. Mercer

B runo Bettelheim, a psychoanalyst and prolific writer who was world famous for his innovative treatment of autistic children, died by his own hand in early 1990 at the age of 86. Bettelheim was a survivor in many ways. He spent a year in the concentration camps of Dachau and Buchenwald before coming to the United States in 1939. He was described as a stubborn fighter, one of the first to articulate the process of mass behavior under extreme situations, such as the concentration camps. He headed the University of Chicago's Sonia Shankman Orthogenic School, where he put his theories into practice with severely disturbed children. He was quoted as saying that although he had a rewarding life, he could not get over his experiences in the concentration camps. Apparently life had not been so rewarding for him lately. His wife of forty-three years died in 1984. He had a stroke in 1987 that diminished his ability to write. There were rumors of his estrangement from one of his children. He had recently moved from his apartment on the West Coast to a retirement home in Washington, DC. At some point Bettelheim apparently decided he had enough; he took some pills and put a plastic bag over his head until death came. Bettelheim was also a member of the Hemlock Society, so named because it was Socrates who drank hemlock when he was condemned to death (Friedrich, 1990; Goodman, 1990).

When is enough enough? Are suicides among the young, the healthy, and the depressed considered a waste, whereas those among the elderly are understandable if the people are old enough and sick enough? Are there any good reasons for suicide? Can suicide be a rational decision that we can accept as other than tragic and wasteful? Are our attitudes toward suicide changing because of the advances in medical technology that balance the

425

miracle of survival with the agonies of respirators and feeding tubes? Does our fear of the dying process exceed our fear of death as a result of these medical advances (Goodman, 1990)?

There are no easy answers to any of these questions. However, this chapter was written for those who want to begin to understand why and how older Americans are committing suicide at a high rate. The issues and elements of elder suicide are examined in some detail: demographics, high-risk factors, suicidal intent and methods, and suicide in nursing homes. The purpose is to provide clear indicators of the high-risk factors associated with elders who attempt or commit suicide. The chapter concludes with a discussion of the relationship of suicide to depression, methods of assessment, and interventions.

DEMOGRAPHICS

Suicide is a large-scale social phenomenon that has attracted increasing attention. The world population is about 5 billion persons, and world suicide rates are about 13 per 100,000 (Battin, 1982). The primary sources of worldwide data on suicide are the official mortality statistics that most countries publish. However, the accuracy and comparability of worldwide suicide rates have been questioned for a variety of reasons. First, it is argued that differences in national rates of suicide are invalid because the countries' procedures for determining and reporting suicide differ. Second, critics say that statistics are unreliable and that suicide is underreported because the criteria for suicide vary from country to country, and perhaps even within countries. Nevertheless, epidemiologists have examined suicide rates across various countries (Sainsbury, 1986). Table 20.1 depicts the suicide rates for eleven countries, including the United States. It is presented for general information, although the data are old and far from complete in terms of a world perspective.

It is well established that suicide is a major mental health concern in the United States. It is the seventh leading cause of death for males of all ages, and the tenth for females. Public awareness and intervention efforts have consistently focused on adolescents and young adults and have largely ignored or overlooked suicide among the elderly (Osgood, 1985). Do policymakers and community leaders, consciously or not, consider elder suicide less tragic? Teenage and young-adult suicide is a serious problem, but elder suicide is also a major public health issue (Mercer, 1989).

Older Americans have a 50 percent higher suicide rate than does the

TABLE 20.1
Suicide Rates per 100,000 for Eleven Countries, 1959

Country	Suicide Rate per 100,000
Czechoslovakia	24.9
Austria	24.8
Germany, Federal Republic	18.7
Sweden	18.1
England and Wales	11.5
United States	10.4
Poland	8.0
Norway	7.8
Canada	7.4
Italy	6.2
Ireland	2.5
Mexico	2.1

SOURCE: Adapted from P. Sainsbury and B. M. Barraclough. "Differences between Suicide Rates." *Nature*, 220 (1968), p. 1252.

general population and are the group that is most at risk for suicide (Manton, Blazer, & Woodbury, 1987; Osgood, 1985; Osgood & McIntosh, 1986). The National Center for Health Statistics (1988) indicated that the number of suicide deaths for persons aged 15–24 was 5,120 and for persons aged 65 and older, 6,275 in 1988. Older Americans not only take their own lives in disproportionate numbers, but generally do it quietly, with few pleas for help.

Almost 30,000 persons in the United States chose to kill themselves in 1985. The National Center for Health Statistics (1988) reported an annual rate of 12 suicides per 100,000 persons in the general population, but 18.5 per 100,000 among persons aged 65–74, 24.1 per 100,000 for persons aged 75–84, and 19.1 per 100,000 for persons aged 85 or older. Many experts believe these rates are underreported. The elderly can easily commit "covert" suicide by starving themselves, terminating life-sustaining medications, or overdosing on prescribed medications. Elder suicides may also be disguised as fatal accidents. Even with the probable underreporting, elderly persons continue to commit suicide more frequently than do younger persons and have done so for as long as the U.S. government has maintained official suicide data. This finding also holds true for most other developed countries (McIntosh, 1987).

HIGH-RISK FACTORS

Sex

Older men commit suicide at a significantly higher rate than do older women. In fact, males of all ages commit suicide at a significantly higher rate than do females of all ages. Yet the dissimilarity of the rates of male and female suicide is more dramatic for the elderly than for any other group. Rates of suicide in males increase through the eighth decade, with those aged 80–84 having the highest rate, approximately 53 suicides per 100,000 persons. The rates of suicide in females increase until 45–55 and decline thereafter. Specifically, white men over age 65 have a suicide rate that is four times the national average—43.2 per 100,000 persons in 1987 (U.S. Bureau of the Census, 1988). The ratio of male to female suicides in the 65–69 age range is approximately 4:1, but by age 85, the ratio jumps to approximately 12:1 (McIntosh, 1985; Osgood, 1985).

Since 1950 there has been a noteworthy change in the suicide rates of elderly men. For example, the rate for white men, aged 65–74, has decreased 26 percent since 1950 (Osgood, 1985: Resnik & Cantor, 1970). Further research is needed to explain this declining rate of suicide among older white men. One suggested factor influencing the decline is economics. Marshall (1978) found a significant correlation between declining suicide rates for white men aged 65–74 and improved economic status among the group. It is important to keep in mind that although the rate for older white men has declined, this group still has the highest risk for suicide.

Race

Suicide rates among elderly whites are significantly higher than among elderly minorities of color. The rate for whites generally increases with age and peaks in old age, whereas the rate for minorities of color generally peaks in young adulthood and then declines (McIntosh, 1985; Osgood, 1985). The ratio of suicides of elderly whites to elderly minorities of color is approximately 3:1. The rate for black men aged 65 years and older is 12.9 per 100,000 persons (U.S. Bureau of the Census, 1988).

Although data are generally sparse on suicides among minorities of color, they demonstrate that there are considerable diversity among groups and unique characteristic patterns related to suicide. Thus, the widespread practice of grouping all nonwhites into a single category is misleading when examining suicidal behavior. For example, there are certainly tribal differences, but, in the main, Native Americans have the overall highest suicide rates of any racial-ethnic group in the United States. However, elderly Native Americans rarely commit suicide, so this ranking is attributed to the high rates of suicide among younger Native Americans. In fact, few Native Americans survive to old age. It is suggested that those who do survive are a selective, hardy group who may lack suicidal tendencies (McIntosh & Santos, 1981). Suicide rates among Native Americans aged 15–44 are two to four times higher than among the same age groups in the U.S. population. The concentration of suicides among young and middle-aged Indians may be attributed, in part, to their difficulty in coping with environmental stressors and the white culture. Separating etiological factors from precipitating factors is obviously complex (Dinges & Joos, 1988).

Suicide rates for African Americans are usually the lowest of any minority in the United States, in sharp contrast to those for Native Americans. The age patterns of the two groups, however, are essentially the same; suicide rates among African Americans peak in young adulthood and decline thereafter, with low rates for the elderly. The lower rate of suicide among older African Americans than among older whites is attributed to the greater involvement of African Americans in their families, churches, and other community systems (McIntosh & Santos, 1981). African Americans also appear to have a broader definition of an extended family. Perhaps older African Americans also receive more respect within their culture. Like Native Americans, older African Americans may also be a selective sample who have learned to manage cultural ambiguities in a mentally healthy manner.

McIntosh and Santos (1981) found peaks in suicide rates in old age in both Chinese and Japanese Americans and concluded that the rates for older persons in these Asian American groups exceeded those of the U.S. population and of whites. These rates were based on 1976 data and on a small number of deaths, however, and are subject to great fluctuations with even small changes. Compared to earlier published data, the suicide rates among the elderly in these Asian American groups, although highest within their own group, were decidedly lower than those previously reported. Possible explanations for the declines in suicide rates among older Asian Americans include the dying out of the immigrant population and their replacement by more acculturated elders.

There are no data on suicide rates among older Spanish-speaking persons. Clearly, more research is needed to define and understand the extent of suicide among different racial-ethnic groups and to determine the influence of their different histories, opportunities, and economic situations in the United States on their suicidal behavior (McIntosh & Santos, 1981).

Marital Status and Social Environment

As early as 1891, Durkheim (1891/1951) reported that the incidence of suicide varied not only by age and gender, but by marital status. His rationale for the greater proportion of suicides among widowers than among widows was that men benefit more from marriage than do women. More recent studies have confirmed Durkheim's theory by consistent reports that unmarried and widowed persons of all ages are more likely to commit suicide than are married persons and that elderly widowers are significantly more at risk of suicide than are elderly widows. Women generally assume the nurturing roles that maintain the links with family and friends, whereas elderly men are less involved with family, friends, and community and are among the most socially isolated individuals in our society (Osgood, 1985; Osgood & McIntosh, 1986). It is suggested that women are more social and have closer friendship networks, are socialized to have greater "survival skills" in caring for themselves through purchasing and preparing foods and housekeeping, are are more socialized and are expected to be the caregivers in our society—caregivers for children and for men. If suicide rates are an indicator, men have paid a high price for their alleged deficits in survival skills and connectivity to family and friends.

Other High-Risk Factors

Other important high-risk indicators of suicide among the elderly include social isolation and loneliness. A history of recent losses; experiences with illness and intractable pain; and changes in status related to income, employment, and independence are additional risks (McIntosh, 1985; Osgood, 1985). Osgood's (1985) review of the literature on the relationship between socioeconomic class and suicide noted that although some studies found that suicide is more prevalent in upper-class persons, the bulk of the research reported higher suicide rates for persons in lower socioeconomic strata, including poor elderly persons. Studies also demonstrated a correlation between suicide rates and the loss of self-esteem from such factors as the loss of a job, a reduction in job responsibilities, and stress from retirement, particularly if the retirement is mandatory (Osgood, 1985). Miller (1978) reported that the fear of institutionalization in a nursing home and the anticipated loss of independence are major precipitating events in elder suicide.

Aging may be defined in many ways, and the aging process has certain themes. Clearly, a major factor in aging is the accumulation of losses, which may lead to heightened stress and increased vulnerability. This incremental and often relentless vulnerability may lead to helplessness and hopelessness, which may increase the risk of choosing suicide.

SUICIDAL INTENT AND METHODS

When older persons decide to commit suicide, they are likely to complete the act. They predictably use more lethal methods, are generally more serious, and make fewer suicidal gestures than do other age groups. (The ratio of their nonfatal attempts to completed acts is about 4:1, compared to as high as 200:1 in the young [McIntosh, 1985].) McIntosh (1985) suggested that nonfatal attempts by elderly people are likely to be due to poor planning, not to the lack of determination. The poorer recuperative capacity of the elderly and the greater likelihood of social isolation are also contributing factors to the higher rate of completed suicides.

Firearms and explosives are considered more lethal than are poison or other methods. In the main, men choose more violent methods and women choose less violent, more passive means. Specifically, firearms are more likely to be used by males (73.6 percent) than by females (30.6 percent), although the use of firearms in completed suicides among all groups, including older women, has recently increased. Before 1982, poisons (prescription or over-the-counter drugs) were the primary method of suicide by females. The less lethal methods obviously increase the chances for discovery and provide more time for a change of heart and medical assistance (McIntosh, 1988; McIntosh & Jewell, 1986), whereas the use of firearms increases the chance of death.

Time's feature story ("7 Deadly Days," 1989) on the first seven days in May 1989, when, in one ordinary week, 464 Americans died by firearms, noted that of the 464 deaths, 75 men and 11 women, ranging in age from 55 to 87 years, killed themselves with guns. The article attached faces and details to the staggering statistics. The stories bring home some of the primary factors that contribute to a high rate of suicide among older persons—poor health, the loss of a spouse, depression, loneliness, and fear of going to a nursing home. Each of these older persons also had immediate access to a gun. The following disquieting case vignettes are representative of older persons who decide to kill themselves.

Billy H, aged 58, North Little Rock, Arkansas, had been depressed since his wife's death. He was a retired automotive-supply company employee and was known for his charity and volunteer work. He shot himself with a revolver.

Herbert K, aged 84, of San Francisco, suffering from Parkinson's disease, called a relative to say he intended to kill himself. He did so before the relative could reach him.

Mary Louise W, aged 77, of Portland, Oregon, was a housewife suffering from cancer. She shot herself in the head with a pistol while sitting in any empty bathtub.

Roy A, aged 61, of Brantly County, Georgia, urgently summoned the sheriff to his house a week after he buried his wife. The sheriff found his body and a shotgun in the backyard.

Carl H, aged 69, Albermarle, North Carolina, was a retired mill-worker who had agreed to accept counseling because of his suicidal intentions. However, he killed himself before the first counseling session.

Caroline H, aged 75, Wellborn, Florida, was depressed about the possibility of moving into a nursing home. She shot herself with a pistol in her car outside her mobile home.

Lawrence W, aged 65, Dade County, Florida, was beset by ill health. He excused himself from a visit with family members and went into his garage and shot himself with a revolver.

These vignettes also bring home the painful fact that more Americans die of gunshot wounds every two years than have died, to date, of AIDS. Similarly, firearms take more lives in the United States every two years than did the entire Vietnam War. Only car accidents exceed shootings as the leading cause of injury-induced fatalities ("7 Deadly Days," 1989). One in every other household has a gun. Some continue to argue that people, not guns, kill people; others insist that the pervasiveness of gun ownership in the United States is relevant. Suicide by a firearm is certainly more likely to result in death than is suicide by any other method. Osgood (1991) recommended that restrictions be placed on the ownership of firearms as a method of reducing suicide in persons of all ages. Her position is supported by Lester (1988), who reported that states with strict handgun controls experienced less of an increase in suicides.

ELDER SUICIDES IN NURSING HOMES

There are about 19,100 nursing homes in the United States with approximately 1.5 million beds. Eighty-eight percent of the nursing home residents are aged 65 or older. Nursing home residents are typically quite old and tend to be female and white. The use of a nursing home increases with advanced age for both females and males, although females are placed in nursing homes at a significantly higher rate than are men, regardless of their age. Nursing home residents are more likely to be older, sicker, and widowed than are older persons living in the community (Hing, 1987).

All these factors put nursing home residents at a high risk for suicide. However, little research has been done on the prevalence of suicide in nursing homes. To an older person, admission to a nursing home usually symbolizes the end of self-responsibility and control over her or his environment. Perceptions of hopelessness and helplessness are frequently the result of this loss of control, leaving the individual more vulnerable to illness and depression (Mercer & Kane, 1979). It is well established that there is a close relationship between depression and suicide, and the incidence of depression in nursing home residents is reported to be alarmingly high. Fry (1986) estimated that 25 percent of the elderly nursing home residents are depressed, and Blazer (1982) suggested that the figure is closer to 30–50 percent.

Osgood and Brandt (Osgood & Brandt, 1988; Osgood, Brandt, Lipman, 1989) completed the first national study of elder suicide in nursing homes in 1986. they mailed questionnaires to nursing home administrators in a computer-generated random sample of 1,080 institutions. The list included skilled and intermediate nursing care facilities; personal care or residential care facilities; and board-and-care homes, which have at least three beds and provide some kind of direct supervision of residents. The questionnaire included items on the facilities, staffs, and residents and information about the number of overt suicides, suicide attempts, incidents of "indirect life-threatening behavior" (ILTB), and deaths from ILTB during 1984–85. ILTB was defined as "repetitive acts of individuals directed toward themselves which result in physical harm or tissue damage and which could bring about a premature end of life" (p. 5). Examples of conscious and willful ILTBs included refusing medications or food, swallowing foreign substances or objects, self-mutilation, or having serious "accidents." When such behavior was related to a physical or cognitive condition, it was not considered an ILTB.

Suicidal behavior by residents in 1984–85 was reported by administrators in almost 20 percent of the facilities. Many nursing home residents apparently lost the will to live and took conscious steps to end their lives. Others quietly lost hope and refused to eat, drink, or take medications. A number of residents had experienced one or more major losses shortly before they engaged in the suicidal acts: the loss of a spouse or a child, the loss of a pet, and the loss of one or more areas of physical functioning (primarily hearing or eyesight or the ability to ambulate), or decreased cognitive functioning. Many suicides were reported as occurring soon after a hospitalization for a major illness. The loss of personal possessions also resulted in a sense of powerlessness and dependence. The medical records noted frequent somatic complaints and incidents of crying, fatigue, loss of appetite, and other expressions of depression and withdrawal in persons who attempted or completed suicide (Osgood & Brandt, 1988).

The rate of suicides in nursing homes is predictably lower than that among community-based elderly persons. This lower rate is attributed, in part, to the closer observation of residents in nursing homes and perhaps to inaccurate reporting that is intended to protect the suicides' families and the reputation of the facilities. Although the sample in their study was relatively small, Osgood, Brandt, and Lipman (1989) found that the prevalence of suicide among nursing homes residents is generally comparable to that in the general population, including a higher reported incidence among whites than among nonwhites and a higher rate for men than for women. Equally important, they found that the suicide rate is highest among the old-old, the physically frail, and those who engage in intentional life-threatening behavior because overt suicide is out of their reach.

PREVENTION AND INTERVENTION PROGRAMS

In October 1988, The American Association of Retired Persons sponsored a nationwide survey to determine what suicide prevention and intervention programs were available for older persons (Mercer, 1989). The survey examined the level of resources directed toward the problem of elder suicide and existing or pending legislation. The four types of organizations surveyed were 57 state units on aging, 54 state mental health commissioners, the 52 state legislative reference bureaus, and 116 crisis intervention hotline centers throughout the United States.

The survey found that few suicide prevention and intervention programs specifically target older persons. Little activity was reported in the areas of personnel training, the specific identification of elders who are at a high risk for suicide, or current legislative action. No respondent reported seeking additional funds for intervention programs.

Comments from many respondents representing the state units on aging indicated that states tend to see programs, such as adult protective services, Meals on Wheels, adult day care, senior activity centers, transportation, and the whole range of services for the elderly as basically addressing elderly suicide, although not through a direct program. The respondents also recognized that the self-neglect and noncompliance of elders with health regimens are forms of indirect suicide. Case-management programs and the states' long-term care ombudsmen programs were also reported as dealing with depressed and potentially suicidal elderly people. Some states reported that adult protective services are mandated to investigate all adults who attempt suicide. The survey clearly showed that the problem of elder suicide is recognized at the professional level. Some states have also engaged in research on elder suicide and established commissions to make recommendations that are based on the research findings.

In the main, the commissioners of community mental health reported that elder suicide is addressed within the context of other efforts, such as hot lines, alcohol and drug abuse programs, and routine evaluations and screening for suicide among older psychiatric admissions or intake interviews. Unfortunately, we must keep in mind that older persons are underrepresented in such programs and rarely call crisis hot lines. This fact was reinforced by the responses of the suicide-prevention and crisis-intervention agencies. Many crisis-intervention centers do not keep statistics on callers who are over age 21. Those centers that keep more detailed statistics by age generally reported that less than 5 percent of the callers were aged 60 or older.

Most respondents in all the categories seemed aware of the higher incidence of suicide among the elderly, although some stated they did not know how serious the problem really was, and their state had done nothing, to their knowledge, to address the issue. Most respondents strongly agreed that elder suicide is a problem and reported a lack of emphasis on this high-risk population. Some respondents were almost apologetic and perceived they were caught in the binds of cost containment, problems in the allocation of resources, increasing needs, and diminishing resources.

Although several noteworthy programs in San Francisco; Dayton, Ohio; and Spokane, Washington, target elder suicide, most centers generally focus on suicide in adolescents or young adults, and the statistics on older callers are low.

Some intriguing ideas emerged from the study. For example, the Spokane Gatekeeper program uses postal carriers, meter readers, apartment managers, and so forth, to identify high-risk elders who do not self-refer. Even on the rare occasions when the elderly seek help on their own, they generally present physical, social, environmental, and economic problems, rather than mental health problems (Raschko, 1985).

The San Francisco Suicide Prevention Center reported a range of geriatric programs, including a twenty-four-hour Friendship Line staffed by trained volunteers and a Geriatric Outreach Program that provides such services as reminders about medication, advocacy, support for transitions, and safety checks. It also conducts support groups to bring isolated elders together. The groups are staffed by fifty volunteers and meet once a week for ten weeks with transportation provided.

The Suicide Prevention Center in Dayton, Ohio, received a grant in 1986 to develop resources on elder depression and suicide. As part of its Gatekeeper Program, it developed an educational module for nursing home staff entitled A Season of Loss (Praeger, Stevens, Bernhardt, & Sattem, 1988) that consists of a training videotape and instructional manual and is available on loan to nursing homes in the area.

DEPRESSION AND THE ELDERLY

The association between suicide and depression is of considerable practical importance. Depression is a major illness among the elderly and is associated with increased morbidity and mortality (Mercer, Garner, & Leon, 1990). Fry (1986) reported that prevalence studies reflect that as many as 20 percent of all community-based persons over age 65 show significant symptoms of depression. Furthermore, the frequency of depression for those older persons who are institutionalized may be as high as 25 percent.

The concept of depression is an imprecise one that is frequently confusing to both the public and to professionals (Osgood, 1985). It is not surprising, therefore, that depression is commonly undiagnosed or misdiagnosed in older persons. The clinical symptoms are variable and generally atypical. Depression may present as an alteration in mood, chronic physical illness, grief, hypochondriasis, alcoholism, or a specific syndrome (Warshaw, 1982). Specific reported symptoms and feelings include the loss of self-esteem, feelings of helplessness, and complaints of cognitive deficits (Weiss, Nagel, & Aronson, 1986). When this mood change is connected to a physical illness, depression becomes a symptom of the disease. When older persons are depressed, their appetite, sleep, and thought processes are altered and they may appear to be cognitively impaired (see Chapter 10).

Depression includes many symptoms, but is usually defined as being a mood disorder, in which the mood is dysphoric or in which satisfaction with all or almost all usual activities is diminished. Depression can range from a mood of disquiet and restlessness to despair and thoughts of suicide (DSM-III-R, p. 222; Praeger et al., 1988).

The presentation of depression in the elderly is frequently atypical in comparison to younger persons. When depression exists, it is frequently difficult to distinguish somatic and psychological complaints (Rozzini, Bianchetti, Carabellese, Inzoli, & Trabucchi, 1988). Physical complaints, such as headaches, difficulty breathing, abdominal pain, and atypical pain are common. These somatic complaints may "mask" depression. Masked depression occurs when an elder is depressed, does not recognize it or cannot easily verbalize it, and so attempts to hide or "mask" the depressive symptoms. Goldfarb (1974) suggested that another common symptom of masked depression is the older person's tendency to be more critical and provoking toward a spouse or child; the behavior may be the person's ineffective way of appealing for supportive relationships. Apathy and self-isolation are typical, but an elderly person may deny experiencing a dysphoric mood. Feelings of guilt are less often reported, but a loss of self-esteem is usual. Chronic confusion, which may result in pseudodementia, is a frequent presentation. If heavy drinking or alcoholism is suspected, then it is necessary to probe for an underlying depression (Kane, Ouslander, & Abrass, 1984; Warshaw, 1982).

As was previously mentioned, depression may also be a symptom of a physical illness, such as cardiovascular disease, heart disease, nutritional deficiencies, cancers, infections, Parkinson's disease, and endocrine abnormalities. Many medications, including heart medications, blood-pressure drugs, sedatives, analgesics, antiparkinsonism drugs, steroids, hypnotics, and antipsychotics, are also associated with depression. Furthermore, an environment of isolation, sensory deprivation, and dependence may precipitate and exacerbate depression (Fry, 1986; Kane, Ouslander, & Abrass, 1984; Warshaw, 1982).

Depression may be the most common cause of confusion, disorientation, and forgetfulness in the elderly. It is important to differentiate between depression and dementia, since depression is usually treatable and reversible (see Chapters 3 and 10). A clinical assessment can help distinguish between the two. Table 20.2 outlines the differences. The assessment is more difficult in the early stages of dementia or in a mild depression.

Assessing Depression in an Older Person

A comprehensive psychosocial, environmental, medical, and pharmacological evaluation is essential. Assessment includes evaluating the primary source of the depression, the severity of the symptoms, and the mental and

TABLE 20.2

Guide to the Clinical Differentiation between Depression and Dementia

Symptom	Depression	Dementia
Family aware of problem	Yes	Not always
Person complains about memory	Common	Unusual
Social skills	Impaired	Retained
Personal distress	Marked	Little
Symptoms during P.M.	Seldom	Often
Previous history of depression	Common	Unusual

SOURCE: G. Warshaw, "Cognitive Impairment and Its Treatment in Later Years: Delirium, Dementia, and Depression," *Center Reports on Advances in Research*, 6 (2) (Durham, NC: Duke University Center for the Study of Aging and Human Development, November 1982), p. 5.

physical status of the person. It is important to determine if the person had any earlier depressive episodes and if there is a family history of depression. A thorough medical history is also needed, including the use of any prescription or over-the-counter drugs. The use of standardized measurement instruments is a valuable adjunct to the clinical assessment. Most paper-and-pencil instruments have limitations, however, and none can take the place of face-to-face personal interaction and empathic listening.

A number of rating scales can aid the assessment of the presence and severity of depression. The Beck Depression Inventory (Beck & Beanesden-fer, 1974) is a self-administered twenty-one item scale that has been tested extensively for reliability and validity. It takes five minutes or less to complete, discriminates between groups with different levels of severity of depression, and is sensitive to changes in the severity of depression. The maximum score is 63, and persons who score above 22 are probably depressed.

The Zung Self-Rating Depression Scale (Zung, 1965) is a twenty-statement Likert scale that has also been widely used with the elderly. It is a self-administered scale that requires approximately five minutes to complete, has been validated against other instruments, and is useful as a screening device. The Hopelessness Scale (Beck, Weissman, Lester, & Trexler, 1974) is a twenty-item true-false scale that may be self-administered or orally administered. It measures hopelessness, which is closely linked to depression, and is an aid in assessing the potential for suicide. There is one known study of the scale's use with a nursing home population (Mercer & Kane, 1979).

For reasons previously discussed, it is also important to assess the older person's mental status and the extent of any cognitive impairment. The Folstein Mini-Mental State Examination (Folstein, Folstein, & McHugh, 1975) is useful in quantifying cognitive skills and screening for cognitive loss. It measures cognitive impairment related to orientation, registration recall, attention concentration, calculations, language, and motor skills. The instrument has been extensively validated and twenty-four hour test-retest reliability has been documented. The thirty-one-item measurement is easy to administer and takes approximately fifteen minutes. The reader is referred to Kane and Kane (1981) and Lavizzo-Mourey, Day, Diserens, and Grisso (1989) for a more detailed discussion of the use of standardized measurement instruments with older persons.

ASSESSMENT OF SUICIDAL RISK IN OLDER PERSONS

In addition to assessing depression, it is important to assess the imminence of suicide and the potential for death. Persons who are in the most frequent contact with older persons—physicians, family members, social workers, the clergy, or pharmacists—play a critical role in the identification of elderly people who are most at risk for suicide. Older persons are most likely to turn to their physicians when they feel desperate. Studies have reported that over 75 percent of older persons who completed suicide had seen a physician shortly before their death. Frequently, these older persons presented the physicians with various somatic complaints; some saw the physicians with no obvious physical ailments but with a sense of something being wrong. Too frequently, the physicians did not recognize the suicidal intent (Foster & Burke, 1985; Miller, 1977; Osgood, 1985). Miller (1977) contended that physicians may fail to recognize the suicidal risk because they are not trained to recognize the danger signals and may, like others, be anxious and un-comfortable with the topic of suicide.

An accurate assessment of the risk of suicide requires knowledge of pertinent demographic variables; an understanding of the precipitating factors that may lead to the consideration of suicide; and knowledge of the individual's personal background and family life history; present and past crises; typical patterns of responses to crises; history of and present physical and mental illnesses; the quantity and quality of the person's relationships; and personal, financial, environmental, and social resources (Osgood, 1985). In addition, a thorough assessment of the risk of suicide involves an accurate knowledge and assessment of the person's suicide plans and the potential for death.

A number of researchers have documented the presence of verbal, behavioral, and situational clues in a majority of older persons who eventually kill themselves (Miller, 1978; Osgood, 1985; Shneidman, Farberow, & Litman, 1970). It is critical that mental health practitioners recognize and be sensitive to these clues as an initial step toward intervening with older persons.

Verbal clues to a potential suicide may be direct or indirect, and examples of such clues are as follows:

- "I am going to kill myself."
- "I am not the person I used to be."
- "My family would be better off without me around to worry about."
- "You will not be seeing me around much longer."
- "Ever since I retired, I've felt in the way and useless."
- "I can't take much more of this."
- "Life has lost its meaning to me."
- "Nobody needs me around anymore."
- "If ——— happens, I will take myself out of this pain."
- "I want to end it all very soon."
- "You won't have me to worry about much longer now."

Direct suicidal threats ("I am going to kill myself") and suicidal fantasies or ideations must always be taken seriously. A significant majority of older persons who threaten to kill themselves eventually complete the act. Indirect statements (such as, "Life has lost its meaning to me") are more veiled, but also must be taken seriously because they represent a red flag that indicates the older person's state of mind and loss of hope or discouragement (Osgood, 1985).

Behavioral clues to potential suicide may also be direct or indirect. Obviously, the most direct behavioral clue is a suicide attempt. As was stated earlier, older persons have a low rate of nonfatal suicide attempts, and most older persons who attempt suicide commit suicide within one or two years following a failed attempt (Osgood, 1985).

Behavioral clues include the following:

- A previous suicide attempt.
- Giving away personal items or money.
- Buying a gun.
- Putting personal affairs in order.
- Planning a funeral shortly after the death of a spouse.

- Making or changing a will.
- Writing a suicide note.
- A sudden, unexplained recovery from a severe depression.
- Any unexplainable change in a usual behavioral pattern.
- A sudden resignation from church, organizations, clubs, and so forth.
- Crying for no apparent reason.
- Self-destructive acts or an unreasonable number of accidents.
- Isolation of self from family or significant others.
- Stockpiling pills or medications.
- Making an appointment with a physician for no apparent physical problems or shortly after a previous visit to the physician (Osgood, 1985).

The following case example illustrates both verbal and behavioral clues that signal the potential for suicide.

Mrs. S, aged 71, was found slumped behind a fence on the outskirts of a residential area in which she lived, her body covered with plastic bags. She had been missing for ten days, and her death was ruled a suicide by the county medical examiner. She was later described by her son as a natural-born teacher who possessed a world of knowledge and an insatiable interest in learning. She was a language specialist with three master's degrees and spoke eight foreign languages and traveled extensively. She engaged in many volunteer activities in her community even though she was legally blind. The turning point seemed to be when Mrs. S became convinced that her mind was failing. She wrote her youngest son a letter four days before she disappeared, describing her fluctuating periods of disorientation and memory loss and explaining that she feared she was in the early states of Alzheimer's disease and had no intention of "hanging around for years as a mindless hulk." She asked him to help. Her son responded to her note, but it was too late. When the police investigated and searched her home, they found a note she had written that detailed a lethal combination of sleeping pills and alcohol. When she disappeared, she left no clues regarding her whereabouts for the police or her family. It seemed fairly certain that she did not want to be found.

In hindsight, Mrs. S's son said his mother gave clues to her later suicide. She had financed a family reunion the previous summer, during which she told one family member that the experience was "like having your funeral so you could attend it." Her family was not aware until after her death that she was a member of the Hemlock Society, the Los Angeles-based euthanasia group. She was also a card-carrying member of Americans Against Human Suffering (Keyes, 1989).

In a hindsight assessment of Mrs. S, it is apparent that the lethality potential was high. She gave both verbal and behavioral clues, she apparently had suicidal ideations, and a method of self-destruction was accessible to her.

SUICIDE PREVENTION

Social workers are uniquely trained and capable of responding therapeutically to older persons who are at risk of suicide. Unfortunately, the counseling of elderly persons has been hindered by the pessimism of some mental health professionals, who do not believe that an older person is flexible enough to make significant emotional and cognitive changes, and by the underutilization by elderly people of community mental health centers and counseling services. The reasons behind this professional pessimism and underutilization of services by the elderly are complex. The former may be related to persistent myths that the elderly are not good candidates because of their inflexibility toward learning, general intractability, lack of motivation, and irreversible disabilities. Mental health practitioners may also feel that dealing with disabilities, losses, and death are depressing and consider the elderly to be "low status" clients. Any of these attitudes may result in gerophobia, or the fear-avoidance of older persons (Butler & Lewis, 1982; Fry, 1986.)

Older persons may underutilize mental health practitioners because of their basic conservatism regarding money, a sense of privacy, and less comfort and familiarity with the predominantly expressive talk methods used in counseling (Glamser, 1974; McGee & Lain, 1977). A combination of these factors has led to stereotyping and a tendency to treat mental health problems of elders with institutional placement and pharmacological intervention without considering counseling a necessary and valuable contribution to the treatment process.

There are, however, many factors that favor older persons' use of counseling. Older adults have experienced a lifetime of adaption to stressful situations, and many have an immense reserve of resilience. Even minimal special time, attention, and counseling can help older adults reactivate these problem-solving capacities (Fry, 1986).

Intervention Strategies

The older person who is depressed or shows signs of potential suicide must be helped. The first step is to recognize suicidal clues and to assess the potential for death accurately. Swift assessment and intervention can save the life of an older person who is considering suicide who can then receive appropriate psychosocial intervention. Osgood's (1985) extensive review of the literature on counseling older persons in crisis offered the following suggestions.

Adapt the treatment to the resources of the older person. To intervene effectively, the practitioner must adapt the treatment to the resources of the individual. These resources include physical and psychological capabilities; memory; motivation; environmental factors; and support from family, friends, and the community. An in-depth knowledge of these resources is possible only if one completes a thorough social history and assessment, including the administration of appropriate standardized tests, meetings with the family, and efforts to connect with and engage the older person.

Take an active, direct approach. An active, direct approach is recommended for anyone in a crisis state. The practitioner must help define the problem and be active in generating solutions. An assertive, even authoritarian approach may be what is needed to interrupt and redirect the negative, downward spiral. Osgood (1985) suggested that sometimes just telling the older person not to kill herself or himself may be enough to prevent a suicide.

Be supportive. Older persons are quite responsive to active, empathic listening and expressions of caring, warmth, and support. A touch and an understanding attitude can help the older person feel he or she is not alone in the pain.

Be empathic. Empathy is a basic central ingredient of a therapeutic relationship and an alliance. It is the capacity to move beyond an objective recognition of the older person's feelings and behavior and to experience the world as the person does. Empathy and unconditional positive regard may be a healing force that can lead to positive change or may create receptiveness for further counseling and reeducation.

Maintain a brief, problem-centered focus. Deeper insight therapy may be less appropriate for an older person than may a brief, present-oriented, problem-centered approach.

Listen. Many older persons have a deep-seated need to tell—to express feelings of remorse, guilt, fear, or pain. A discussion of their past lives, as well as of their current problems and feelings, may be therapeutic.

Use nonverbal communication. Older persons frequently experience physical impairments in sight and hearing. Nonverbal communication can help bridge these gaps. It is also important to face the older person, to be comfortably close, and to be aware of speaking to the "best ear," if necessary. Facial expression, tone of voice, gestures, and encouraging nods are all important signals to the older person regarding how the practitioner is responding.

Treat the older person with respect. Respect involves a commitment by the practitioner to understand, to convey acceptance and a nonjudgmental attitude, and to affirm the older person's worth. It also involves attention to the physical arrangements of the interview, privacy, confidentiality, and courtesy. Last, it means addressing older persons by their full names and using appropriate titles, such as Ms., Mrs., or Mr.

Keep coping mechanisms intact. We all use defense mechanisms to help us cope. It is important not to attempt to remove the older person's coping mechanism until another one can take its place. It is important to assess the reasons for the coping mechanism and to work to facilitate more adaptive ones if necessary. Modeling appropriate behavior, healthy coping, and problem solving is a beginning step.

Incorporate special catalysts for intervention. Family photographs, scrapbooks, special movies, mementos, and a beloved pet can all serve as agents for the development of a relationship and intervention. Reminiscence can help reframe the content, experiences, and outlook of the person's life.

Group treatment. Older persons can be responsive to supportive, group treatment. There is increasing evidence about the value of support groups for cancer patients, heart patients, and the recently bereaved. For a detailed discussion of various group treatment options, the reader is referred to Osgood (1985) and Burnside (1978).

Early detection of and intervention for psychiatric disorders. Persons in gatekeeping positions, such as physicians, nurses, social workers, clerics, and pharmacists, must be alert to read the clues of possible suicide in older persons. Accurate assessment may prevent a suicide. The practitioner should memorize the major warning signals and be familiar with the standardized assessment instruments discussed earlier. The practitioner should also keep current referral resources. Frequent reassessment and vigilance are important to prevent suicide.

In addition to the strategies just outlined, practitioners must assess and understand other critical aspects of dealing with older persons who show signs of potential suicide (Hatton, Valente, McBride, & Rink, 1977; Osgood, 1985). For example, they must assess themselves and do the following:

1. Come to terms with suicidal feelings or impulses in themselves.
2. Avoid stereotyping older persons. Come to grips with any biases that may be connected to ageism, racism, classism, and sexism.
3. Handle any special resentment that may be directed toward older persons.
4. Overcome any fears of responsibility for making decisions that may encourage older persons to attempt suicide.
5. Avoid making subjective comparisons of older persons, with themselves or with other persons.
6. Deal with their feelings of professional inadequacy.
7. Handle any listening difficulties, so they can listen empathically and without distraction.
8. Develop skills to establish rapport and trust rapidly.

QUESTIONS TO ASK In interviews with older persons who have a high potential for suicide, it is a dangerous myth to believe that they should not be questioned directly about their suicidal ideations and plans. In fact, it is important to question them in a direct, specific manner. For example, the question may be phrased in the following way: "Do you sometimes feel so bad that you think of suicide?" If an older person responds yes or gives an ambivalent answer, then ask: "Have you thought how you would kill or harm yourself?" If the answer is yes, then determine what methods the older person has contemplated using and if these means are available or accessible. It is also important to inquire if the older person has ever attempted suicide before and what happened at that time.

Beck, Rush, and Emery (1979) outlined the following ten critical questions in suicide assessment:

1. How will you do it?
2. How much do you want to die?
3. How much do you want to live?
4. How often do you have these suicidal thoughts or wishes?
5. When you are thinking of suicide, how long do the thoughts stay with you?
6. Is there anyone or anything to stop you?

7. Have you ever attempted suicide?

8. Do you have a plan?

9. On a scale from 1 to 10, what is the probability that you will kill yourself?

10. What has happened that makes life not worth living?

Management Considerations

Interventions depend on the assessment of the older person's needs, capabilities, suicidal risk, and available resources. As a general rule, it is better to be overly judicious than to neglect the warning signs. If the person is in imminent danger of suicide, arrange for a family member, friend, or neighbor to stay with him or her. An elderly suicidal person who shows symptoms of severe depression or dementia should be assessed as being especially at risk and promptly hospitalized. Hospitalization, even for short-term observation, is an agonizing decision, but it provides an immediate way to control suicidal behavior and to encourage outpatient follow-up. Furthermore, antidepressant medication may be necessary to enable the older person to participate in counseling (Fry, 1986; Praeger et al., 1988). The following criteria for hospitalizing an older person who is contemplating suicide were adapted from Kirstein, Prusoff, Weissman, and Dressler (1975) and from Comstock (1977).

1. A well-defined plan for self-destruction.

2. A recent history of medically serious attempts.

3. Suicidal ideation that has evolved into gestures.

4. Social isolation.

5. The inability to respond to crisis intervention and repeated verbalizations about suicidal wishes without seeing alternatives.

6. Evidence of a well-defined suicide attempt.

7. Hallucinatory or delusional suicidal states.

8. Disappointment with one's inability to achieve gains from suicide attempts and inability to change behavior.

9. Moderate or severe depression, exhibited in self-rage, self-blame, or self-punishing thinking.

10. The inability to form a therapeutic alliance with others because of an inability to interact.

Contracting with the Suicidal Older Person

Contracts are recommended for older persons who have been assessed as being at either a high or a low risk of suicide. If the risk of suicide is low, the practitioner may contract with the older person to contact him or her if any emotional or environmental changes bring about further feelings of helplessness or hopelessness. The practitioner must remain available and accessible to the person. A contract with an older person who is assessed as a high risk for suicide is more specific and designed to gain more time and to delay the final decision to commit suicide (Praeger et al., 1988). Slaikeu (1984) outlined contract issues that have different levels of intrusiveness and directness.

1. The client will not commit suicide for the next several days.
2. The client will get rid of lethal means for the time being.
3. The client will not stay alone over the weekend.
4. The client will call for assistance if conditions or feelings worsen.

No-suicide contracts can build on the older person's ambivalence about dying and become a mechanism to motivate him or her to examine alternatives. The major goal of any intervention is to alleviate anxiety and to maintain or reestablish psychological functioning (Fry, 1986).

The following example demonstrates some of the management strategies presented.

An 83-year-old retired chemist and his 81-year-old wife lived in a housing complex for the elderly. Mrs. T kept house, and Mr. T volunteered at the local hospital and exercised at the YMCA. They often visited with their only son. Both were active intellectually and physically until Mrs. T suffered a stroke and lost her speech and some mobility. Upon her discharge from the hospital, the couple was referred to a multiservice agency who could evaluate the home situation and provide the necessary services. A clinical social worker assigned to the couple met with them regularly and arranged for the appropriate home care. Mr. T seemed afraid to leave his wife for any length of time and made no attempt to arrange for someone to be with her so he could continue his activities. Mrs. T's condition was stable, albeit at a compromised level of functioning. Mr. T's physical condition began to deteriorate. During his visits with the social worker, he mourned the loss of his wife as she used to be; her mobility and responsiveness were gone. Mr. T began to talk about death—his own and his wife's. At first, he spoke of it as a probability for people in their eighties, but soon his mood changed from the contemplation of the possibility to the wish for release from the present situation. He could not think of leaving his wife, so he began to ruminate on ways they could die together. He talked of shooting her first and then himself (adapted from Kress, 1982, p. 173).

The social worker assessed the situation as being serious and determined that Mr. T was at a high risk for suicide (and homicide). Mr. T was willing to negotiate a no-suicide contract with the social worker for one week. Arrangements were made for Mr. T's gun to be locked up in a friend's home. The son was informed of the risks and agreed to be involved and to keep in frequent contact with the couple, including spending nights in their home for a week. The physician was advised of the seriousness of the situation and of Mr. T's depression and agreed to evaluate Mr. T for an antidepressant medication. Hospitalization was not recommended for Mr. T because of his responsiveness to the interventions. Eventually, the couple agreed to move into a supervised residential setting, where they could maintain their own rooms, but have nursing assistance available for Mrs. T. The new facility also provided two meals a day that were served in a common dining room. Mrs. T was in a more protected environment. Mr. T did not resume his volunteer work or his exercise program, but he no longer perseverated about suicide and death. Mr. and Mrs. T were able to enjoy outings with their son and eventually made new friends in the residential facility.

Mr. and Mrs. T were not "cured" of old age or the physical disabilities that were permanent. They faced real losses that could not be erased. They were, however, treated with empathy and caring and directive problem solving that, at the same time, respected their need to maintain some control over their lives.

CONCLUSION

Researchers have made a range of suggestions for improving service networks to respond to older persons who contemplate suicide. Most of the suggestions relate to early detection and intervention, education, training, and the development of service networks. Osgood (1985) suggested that elders must be aggressively sought through contacts with physicians, pharmacists, the clergy, the police, community-based social service providers, social security offices, geriatric screening programs, and family and friendship networks. McIntosh, Hubbard, and Santos (1981) suggested establishing special centers to reach depressed or troubled elders, setting up separate hot lines for the elderly, training and utilizing other elderly people to form a type of "buddy system" to reach out to the vulnerable, and developing community-based outreach programs to locate high-risk elders. According to Fisk (1989), these linkage programs work to identify and coordinate community resources that can benefit older people and ensure that they get the support they need, regardless of where they enter the system.

Education and public awareness are also central ingredients in the prevention of suicide in the elderly. The educational videotape and training manual (Praeger et al., 1988), produced jointly by the Suicide Prevention Center in Dayton, Ohio, and Wright State University in Dayton are excellent examples of an education approach. The goals of educational efforts should be to recognize the symptoms of depression and the warning signs of suicide, as well as to gain increased understanding of the aging process and how to best to cope with aging. In other words, elder suicide is a health and mental health issue, but the phenomenon is also more. It is a reflection of generalized hopelessness with the circumstances of life and the environment. At the heart of all such recommendations are rigorous and creative outreach to the elderly at risk, case management, integrated programs, trained personnel, peer supports, appropriate intervention and follow-up. We cannot dissociate the prevention of suicide by the elderly from negative societal stereotypes and myths of the aged, social isolation, retirement-related stresses, and other factors that are correlated with elder suicide. Educational and public awareness efforts must be broadly targeted to include the elderly, mental health professionals, the clergy, law enforcement personnel, health care providers, volunteers, caregivers of the elderly, the media, and the community (McIntosh, 1987; Osgood, 1985).

Elder suicide will not go away. It is a social problem that is not going to "fix itself." Some even suggest that when the baby boomers reach age 65, we can expect an increase in suicide among the elderly. Blazer, Bacher, and Manton (1986) attributed this projected increase to the higher prevalence of depression among the baby boomers. Even if these projections are inaccurate, it is reasonable to assume that the actual increase in the number of older persons in the United States will inevitably lead to an increase in elder suicides in the decades ahead.

The high rate of suicide among the elderly is a waste of lives and a major source of family disruption, and the costs in human suffering are beyond calculation. The challenge is to raise collective consciousness and to develop innovative interventions, creative legislative actions, and comprehensive programs to address suicide among the elderly. The existing, albeit small, efforts to prevent elder suicide must be viewed as a beginning. The lack of programs, emphasis, and understanding must be seen as a window of challenge and opportunity that needs to be addressed (Mercer, 1989).

REFERENCES

Battin, M. (1982). *Ethical issues in suicide.* Englewood Cliffs, NJ: Prentice-Hall.

Beck, A. T., & Beanesdenfer, A. (1974). Assessment of depression: The Depression Inventory. In P. Pichot (Ed.), *Psychological measurements in psychopharmacology* (pp. 151–169). Basil, Switzerland: Karger.

Beck, A. T., Rush, B., & Emery, G. (1979). *Cognitive therapy of depression.* New York: Guilford Press.

Beck, A. T., Weissman, A., Lester, D., & Trexler, L. (1974). The measurement of pessimism: The Hopelessness Scale. *Journal of Consulting and Clinical Psychology, 42,* 861–865.

Blazer, D. G. (1982). *Depression in later life.* St. Louis, MO: C. V. Mosby.

Blazer, D. G., Bacher, J. R., & Manton, K. G. (1986). Suicide in later life: Review and commentary. *Journal of the American Geriatrics Society, 34,* 519–525.

Burnside, I. M. (1978). *Working with the elderly: Group process and techniques.* North Scituate, MA: Duxbury Press.

Butler, R., & Lewis, M. (1982). *Aging and mental health* (3rd ed.). St. Louis, MO: C. V. Mosby.

Comstock, B. S. (1977). Suicide events and indications for hospitalization. *Proceedings of the tenth annual meeting,* American Association of Suicidology, Boston.

Dinges, N. G., & Joos, S. K. (1988). Stress, coping and health: Models of interaction for Indian and Native populations. In S. M. Manson & N. G. Dinges (Eds.), *Behavioral health issues among American Indians and Alaska Natives: Explorations on the frontiers of the biobehavioral sciences* (Vol. 1, Monograph No. 1, pp. 8–64). Denver: University of Colorado Health Sciences Center.

Durkheim, E. (1951). *Suicide.* New York: Free Press. (Original work published in 1891)

Fisk, C. F. (1989). Programs and services help older Americans combat isolation and depression. *Aging Network News, 5*(10), 4.

Folstein, M. F., Folstein, S. E., & McHugh, P. R. (1975). Mini-mental state: A practical method for grading the cognitive states for the clinician. *Journal of Psychiatric Research, 12,* 188–198.

Foster, F. G., & Burke, W. J. (1985). Assessing and treating the suicidal elderly. *Family Practice Recertification*, 7(11), 33–45.

Friedrich, O. (1990, March 26). Dead by his own decision. *Time*, p. 65.

Fry, P. S. (1986). *Depression, stress, and adaptations in the elderly: Psychological assessment and intervention*. Rockville, MD: Aspen.

Glamser, F. D. (1974). The importance of age to conservative opinions: A multivariate analysis. *Journal of Gerontology*, 29, 549–554.

Goldfarb, A. I. (1974). Masked depression in the elderly. In E. Lesse (Ed.), *Masked depression* (pp. 236–249). New York: Jason Aronson.

Goodman, E. (1990, March 17). Bettelheim leaves us looking for meaning. *Arkansas Gazette*, p. 11B.

Hatton, C. L., Valente, S., McBride, S., & Rink, A. (Eds.). (1977). *Suicide: Assessment and intervention*. New York: Appleton-Century-Crofts.

Hing, E. (1987, May 14). *Use of nursing homes by the elderly: Preliminary data from the 1985 National Nursing Home Survey*. Hyattsville, MD: National Center for Health Statistics.

Kane, R. A., & Kane, R. L. (1981). *Assessing the elderly*. Lexington, MA: Lexington Books.

Kane, R. L., Ouslander, J. G., & Abrass, I. B. (1984). *Essentials of clinical geriatrics*. New York: McGraw-Hill.

Keyes, R. (1989, February 1). Lust for life forsaken in despair. *News-Leader* (Springfield, MO), p. 12A.

Kirsling, R. A. (1986). Review of suicide among elderly persons. *Psychological Reports*, 59, 359–366.

Kirstein, L., Prusoff, B., Weissman, M., & Dressler, D. M. (1975). Utilization review of treatment for suicide attempters. *American Journal of Psychiatry*, 132, pp. 22–27.

Kress, H. (1982). The role of the social worker. In E. L. Bassuk & A. D. Gill (Eds.), *Lifelines: Clinical perspectives on suicide* (pp. 152–178). New York: Plenum.

Lavizzo-Mourey, R., Day, S. C., Diserens, D., & Grisso, J. A. (1989). *Practicing prevention for the elderly*. Philadelphia: Hanley & Belfus.

Lester, D. (1988). Research note: Gun control, gun ownership, and suicide prevention. *Suicide and Life-Threatening Behavior*, 12, 131–140.

Manton, K. G., Blazer, D. G., & Woodbury, M. A. (1987). Suicide in middle age and later life: Sex and race specific life table and cohort analysis. *Journal of Gerontology*, 42, 219.

Marshall, J. (1978). Changes in aged white male suicide: 1948–72. *Journal of Gerontology*, 33, 763–768.

McGee, J., & Lain, M. (1977). Social perspectives on psychotherapy with the aged. *Psychotherapy: Theory, Research, and Practice*, 14, 333–342.

McIntosh, J. L. (1985). Suicide among the elderly: Levels and trends. *American Journal of Orthopsychiatry, 55,* 75–82.

McIntosh, J. L. (1987). Suicide: Training and education needs with an emphasis on the elderly. *Gerontology and Geriatrics Education, 4,* 125–139.

McIntosh, J. L. (1988, April). *Geographic changes in the U.S. elderly suicide.* Paper presented at the meeting of the American Association of Suicidology, Washington DC.

McIntosh, J. L., Hubbard, R. W., & Santos, J. F. (1981). Suicide among the elderly: A review of issues with case studies. *Journal of Gerontological Social Work, 4,* 63–74.

McIntosh, J. L., & Jewell, B. L. (1986). Sex difference trends in completed suicide. *Suicide and Life-Threatening Behavior, 16,* 16–27.

McIntosh, J. L., & Santos, J. F. (1981). Suicide among minority elderly: A preliminary investigation. *Suicide and Life-Threatening Behavior, 11,* 151–166.

Mercer, S. O. (1989). *Elder suicide: A national survey of prevention and intervention programs.* Washington DC: Public Policy Institute, American Association of Retired Persons.

Mercer, S. O., Garner, J. D., & Leon, J. (1990). *Geriatric case practice in the nursing home.* Newbury Park, CA: Sage Publications.

Mercer, S. O., & Kane, R. A. (1979). Helplessness and hopelessness among the institutionalized aged: An experiment. *Health and Social Work, 4,* 90–116.

Miller, M. (1977). The physician and the older suicidal patient. *Journal of Family Practice, 5,* 1028–1029.

Miller, M. (1978). Geriatric suicide: The Arizona study. *The Gerontologist, 18,* 488–495.

National Center for Health Statistics. (1988, September 30). *Monthly Vital Statistics Report, 36*(6), 25.

Osgood, N. J. (1985). *Suicide in the elderly: A practitioner's guide to diagnosis and mental health intervention.* Rockville, MD: Aspen.

Osgood, N. J. (1991). Psychological factors in late life suicide. *Crisis, 12*(2), p. 18–24.

Osgood, N. J., & Brandt, B. A. (1988, April 16). *Suicidal behavior in long-term care facilities.* Paper presented at the Annual Meeting of the American Association of Suicidology, Washington, DC.

Osgood, N. J., Brandt, B. A., & Lipman, A. A. (1989). Patterns of suicidal behavior in long-term care facilities: A preliminary report on an on-going study. *Omega, 19,* 69–77.

Osgood, N. J., & McIntosh, J. L., (1986). *Suicide and the elderly: An annotated bibliography and review.* New York: Greenwood Press.

Praeger, S., Stevens, F., Bernhardt, G., & Sattem, L. (1988). A *season of loss: A training manual for the prevention of elderly depression and suicide.* Dayton, OH: Suicide Prevention Center.

Raschko, R. (1985). Systems integration at the program level: Agony and mental health. *The Gerontologist, 25*(5), 460–463.

Resnik, H. L. P., & Cantor, J. M. (1970), Suicide and aging. *Journal of the American Geriatrics Society, 18*, 152–158.

Rozzini, R., Bianchetti, A., Carabellese, C., Inzoli, M., & Trabucchi, M. (1988). Depression, life events and somatic symptoms. *The Gerontologist, 28*, 229–232.

Sainsbury, P. (1986). The epidemiology of suicide. In A. Roy (Ed.) *Suicide* (pp. 17–39). Baltimore, MD: Williams & Wilkins.

Sainsbury, P., & Barraclough, B. M. (1968). Differences between suicide rates. *Nature, 220*, 1243–1252.

7 deadly days. (1989, July 17). *Time*, p. 31.

Shneidman, E. S., Farberow, N. L., & Litman, R. (1970). *The psychology of suicide*. New York: Science House.

Slaikeu, K. A. (1984). *Crisis intervention: A handbook for practice research*. Boston: Allyn & Bacon.

U.S. Bureau of the Census. (1988). *Statistical abstract of the United States: 1988*. Washington, DC: U.S. Government Printing Office.

Warshaw, G. (1982). Cognitive impairment and its treatment in later years: Delirium, dementia, and depression. *Center Reports on Advances in Research, 6*(2). Durham, NC: Duke University Center for the Study of Aging and Human Development.

Weiss, I. K., Nagel, C. L., & Aronson, M. K. (1986). Applicability of depression scales to the old, old person. *Journal of the American Geriatrics Society, 34*, 215–218.

Zung, W. W. K. (1965). A self-rating depression scale. *Archives of General Psychiatry, 12*, 63–70.

21

Family Issues and the Elderly

Susan Watt · Ahuva Soifer

Establishing parameters for the healthy functioning and behavior of elderly persons can be done reasonably only with reference to "the family" and the relationships of those involved. The elderly often belong to several families—past and present. Since families take different forms and are often divided about responsibility and decision making, as well as by distance and authority, and since the perceptions of reality and responsibilities vary so greatly, understanding the family and its significance is complex and essential, especially, but by no means exclusively, for the social work practitioner.

To understand families and the elderly, it is important to know what the mythologies are: what is "fact" and what is "factual myth." Factual myths are those myths, beliefs, "always" statements (as in families always care about their elders), or moral certitudes (as in good families care for their elderly members) that the elderly, families, and professionals may believe to be true without examining their authenticity. Until the increases in longevity in the mid-twentieth century, the elderly did not live long enough to become special burdens to their families. Eccentricities and brief periods of nurturing and caring were tolerated as hailing their imminent death. Now, with therapies and devices that prolong not only living but dying, the length of interaction between the elderly and their families, including the care of impaired elderly members, needs to be included in our understanding of family functioning (Garant & Bolduc, 1990).

FACTORS AFFECTING FAMILY FUNCTIONING

A number of factors—some idiosyncratic, others part of identifiable patterns—establish the interactions of families and their elderly members, conditioning behavior that may appear, appropriately or deceptively, to be healthy or unhealthy. With the rapidly growing interest in gerontology and competition among disciplines, there is a danger of the particularization of emphasis, as well as of generalized stereotyping. It is vital, therefore, that social workers, with their special perspective on the person in his or her situation, understand and convey to colleagues in other professions the need to appreciate the relationships that condition and color behavior.

For many elderly individuals and couples, the social milieu has been compressed with the losses of jobs and recreational activities and contacts, as well as friends and companions, so that whoever remains takes on added importance (Chappell & Havens, 1985). Thus, their families are especially significant. In this narrowed circle of social relationships, family members often carry added weight as lifelines. Even if distant, they often appear to the elderly to be the most significant parts of their emotional lives—the ones who do, will, or ought to care; the repositories of treasures (the family name, the family lore, and traditions, as well as the family wealth, if any); and the links to immortality.

Family members are invested with attributes, often based on a history that preceded their birth, and are depended on in ways that may appear to be unreal or disproportionate to outsiders. Even ancillary family members (nieces and nephews, stepchildren and grandchildren) are often considered participants by inheritance in old family feuds and debts and frequently accept responsibility for elderly persons.

The complexities of the internalized family relationships, which may encompass a unique and individual mixture of past and present, perception and reality, and experience that has subjectively adapted to remarkable changes, condition the behavior and responses of the elderly and of their various family members in ways that may appear healthy or somewhere on the way to problematic or pathological (Keith & Schafer, 1985).

Unless individually explored, understood, and put into perspective, neither behavior nor reactions can be honestly assessed or treated. Essential to such understanding are the skills to appreciate the complexities of each individual's interactions with widening circles of interrelated and often interdependent milieus.

The skilled social worker also needs to grasp and interpret special knowledge of the constants and rapidly changing cultures of the elderly, adequate time, and a keen awareness of ongoing demographic factors for colleagues and policymakers, as well as for families and elderly persons themselves (Foner, 1984; Fry, 1980).

It is necessary to remember, always, that families are as disparate as are the individuals of whom they are composed. An elderly couple represents one kind of complicated nuclear family; a widow or widower frequently sees himself or herself as part of the couple, bereft or relieved, and is often so seen by other members of the extended family (e.g., children or siblings of one or the other), with old memories and grievances vividly alive.

Demographic changes have affected the elderly and their family connections in major ways (Novak, 1985). For many, mobility in their lifetimes has meant immigration, away from roots and a known way of life, with adaptations to new circumstances that may have involved isolation, new affiliations and values, or terrible guilt (e.g., when families in the Old Country were wiped out by the Holocaust or by natural disasters). It has also meant, in many cases, the dispersion of children and distance from grandchildren, family celebrations, and so forth. Loneliness, resentment, and discordance have twisted expectations, often sowing confusion in the elderly about their own values and their worth and challenging faith and beliefs (Berman, 1987).

Changes in social alignments have also shaken the realities and belief systems of many elderly persons. Divorces, children born out of wedlock, blended families, and accepted homosexuality and promiscuity have left some with no grandchildren, some with various grandchildren from different combinations of families, some forbidden to have contact with blood relations, others expected to welcome changing partners and unrelated offspring. In the hurly-burly of changes within the family, as they know it, they are often excluded or overlooked. Their advice and family traditions are dismissed as not being pertinent, their wisdom is seen as out of date (Duff & Hong, 1981–82).

Given the rapid pace of living for their young, they are often isolated, even when cared for, and they themselves struggle to find a balance between independence and participation—trying to be helpful and not a burden, looking for ways to exercise a sense of self in the barrage of new ways about which they have—unasked for—opinions.

Similarly, family members who are struggling with their own adaptations to the many changes often find it difficult to accept the responses of their elderly members and find ways to adjust that may be destructive and problems for themselves and for others in the family, including their spouses and children and their elderly relatives.

New roles for women, new possibilities of leisure and retirement, economic shifts, and employment transfers also leave gaps in the family-care-providing structures that are still seen as the expected model by many, including professional policymakers and decision makers and caregivers. Nevertheless, most care giving for elderly persons is provided either totally or in substantial part by family members, usually female, often wives or daughters and daughters-in-law (Rosenthal, 1985, 1986).

Shifts, such as moves from cities to suburbs, affect families and their elderly members in different ways. Differences in life-style (e.g., no room for elderly relatives in small city apartments and difficulties in access to services in suburbs), problems in leaving familiar surroundings and people and in making new friends, and the loss of ethnic and religious supports loom differently for the elderly and their caring families. Obstinacies about not moving, about not allowing strangers in to help, and about continuing to do difficult chores or to do easy ones the hard way may prove highly troublesome to well-meaning families (who now feel obliged to make real sacrifices of time and energy to be sure "everything's all right") and to objective professionals. Such insistence may or may not represent "healthy" responses; only careful analyses of *all* that is involved, including family power struggles, can suggest a valid answer.

In our multicultural tapestry, the elderly from various ethnic and racial backgrounds, including native peoples, may present a particular puzzle. Many retain, or *return*, in their later years to habits and customs that they themselves decried earlier. To the dismay of their more assimilated family members, their behavior (e.g., the reliance on herbs and spells, rather than on physicians and medicine, lighting fires at a home shrine, or wearing a red string around the neck) may appear to be mere superstition; a loss of cognitive ability or memory; or totally out of character, bizarre, and even dangerous. To the unfamiliar professional, observed or described behavior— talking aloud to "familiars" or lapsing into a language that may sound like gibberish—may appear to be, without a thorough exploration, sure signs of problem behavior. Worried, embarrassed, or ignorant family members may contribute to this impression.

THE FAMILY AND THE ELDERLY AS OBJECTS OF SERVICE

The elderly and their families receive services through a variety of un-coordinated, discretely structured, and provider-driven organizations and programs that are often in competition for funds, professional resources, and control of aspects of the service sector. There is, for example, wide variance within and among the Canadian provinces and U.S. states as to the type, amount, and structure of services, including widely different interpretations of regulations regarding the types and amounts of services and criteria for the provision of both institutional and in-home care.

The perception that "something" is wrong, often framed in terms of medical frailty, usually prompts the family of the elderly to become "objects of service." The service may be either directed at the elderly person (e.g., personal care services), with the family occupying a secondary focus, or directed at the family, who is viewed as the primary recipient (e.g., family counseling and respite care), with benefits accrued to the elderly member. But becoming the object of service may, in and of itself, produce perceptions and behavior that create or reinforce the appearance of pathology. One key factor is that services are most often initiated in a period of crisis for the elderly and their families, with little understanding of preexisting dynamics, wishes, preference, and coping patterns. Services are superimposed, with little regard for the ability and willingness of the recipients to conform to the perceptions, methods, and demands of providers and little ability of providers to adapt services to the needs and preferences of recipients.

Urgency and Permanence of Service

Most commonly, service is initiated at a point of crisis for the individual or for the family because of a negative change in the health of either the elderly person or a significant caregiver. When illness causes significant shifts in the existing arrangements, trade-offs, and balances within the family, resolution of the crisis will often bring new arrangements and a new balance that may include the provision of externally provided services. Whether these services are introduced, and on what basis and to what extent, often depends upon the perceptions of the professionals who are involved in managing the health crisis, rather than on the professionals' knowledge of the particular family or their understanding of and response to the preexisting situations.

Like all relationships in families, the bonds and contracts between elderly members and the rest of the family are based on complex patterns and idiosyncratic arrangements that grow out of circumstances, promises, and feelings of loyalty and guilt, as well as out of the externals of proximity, moves, employment and unemployment, changes in the health status of family members, historic disagreements and alliances of family members, and the postponement of unpleasant or difficult decisions. In short, families and the elderly function like all other families; they generally take the course of least resistance, the course of the familiar or least difficult (Biegel & Blum, 1990). A crisis disrupts these balances and forces a reevaluation of existing arrangements, which opens up the potential for change. Change itself, and particular changes, may affect the elderly in ways that cause the appearance of problematic, unhealthy responses and behavior. Unless they are understood *in context*, these responses and behavior lead family members and professionals to inappropriate diagnoses.

One aspect of decision making for the elderly and their families that sets them aside from other family forms is that decisions have a sense of permanence, of finality, from which there is no retreat. For example, the elderly, their families, and policymakers talk about the use of institutions for elder care as one-way filters—once entered, there is no escape. Hence, quite reasonably, institutional care takes on a negative, "giving up" quality; institutions have become the refuge of last resort, rather that one of a range of services that can be used to help the elderly. Despair, withdrawal, rebellion, and a sense of betrayal and abandonment may lead to acting-out behavior that may appear dysfunctional or out of character and be incorrectly diagnosed and treated.

Most often the crisis that results in the introduction of services to the elderly and their families is precipitated by medical concerns. The health care system, which is structured and staffed to deal with acute and resolvable medical crises, is not geared to deal with the fallout of crises. It is designed to respond out of context and within a framework that has been developed to deal primarily with medical decision making for the young whose objective is cure. Even within that framework, questions related to the elderly and their families (e.g., euthanasia) are complex, and decision making is fraught with difficulties that health care professionals do not welcome (e.g., Who will make the decision?).

Recognizing and fearing the loss of control about decisions that will affect *whether* they live or die and where and how they will live and die are powerful stimulants to behavior by the elderly that seem inappropriate to younger family members and professionals. These fears are often realistic, and dealing with them openly is not encouraged, by anyone involved, unless careful social work is allowed and practiced.

Not only professionals and family members resist discussing surrogate decisions about heroic life-preserving measures, terminal diagnoses, funeral wishes, or even the implications of and choices to give up homes or to stop driving cars and to accept placement—the elderly themselves often demur and defer.

The reluctance of the elderly is often complicated by a strong sense of how they "should" be treated, based on real or mythological memories of what they have done to deserve such treatment, of how things were in "their" day, of how they themselves treated their elders, and so on. Though some elderly people are quite articulate—even repetitious—about their feelings, many consider it unseemly, unnecessary, or even dangerous to express their thoughts.

Danger may be in the fear of abuse or of exacerbating tense relationships (their own or those of a child and his or her spouse) or out of shame and hurt, and a desire to "protect" the feelings or the well-being of a family member. The complexities of these feelings and the dissonances they or their suppression engender may lead to seemingly bizarre behavior by the elderly and their families. The importance of a sensitive social work assessment is illustrated in the following case study:

Mrs. G, a 90-year-old widow, was admitted to the emergency department of a hospital after a fall in her home. She was accompanied by her great-grandson. She lives alone in a two-story house that she and her husband purchased sixty years ago and in which she raised her daughter, now aged 68, and her son, now aged 62. She was referred to the social worker when she appeared to be confused, insisting that she didn't have to use the bathroom; that she didn't know how to get hold of her children; and that someone, whose name she didn't know, visited every day to take care of her; she wanted to go home, period. She had no acute medical problems, had suffered some bruising from her fall, and would be unable to bear weight on her legs for several days. There was a reluctance to admit her to the hospital, since she was already viewed as a "discharge problem" and since no acute medical intervention was required.

The social work assessment revealed that the history that Mrs. G provided was, in fact, accurate. She was in receipt of daily in-home services, with different nurses, physiotherapists, and homemakers coming into her house. She had moved to the first floor of the house and had used, for several months, diapers and a commode instead of the upstairs bathroom. Her daughter, who saw her every day, was returning from a vacation in seventy-two hours, and her great-grandson would contact her and keep an eye on her until his grandmother returned. Sorting out this patient took several hours of listening, probing, seeing that she was fed, confirming community involvement, and arranging for an ambulance transfer home. Mrs. G avoided a hospitalization that she did not want and that was medically unnecessary because in an urgent but not-crisis situation, a social worker was able to understand her needs and supports in the context of her day-to-day life and her wishes for care.

Invasion and Clienthood

As a result of professionals' assessment of the nature of the crisis and the appropriate way in which the elderly, their families, and the service sector should respond, the purveyors of service frequently create a kind of client-hood that neither the family nor the elderly person has requested (O'Neill, 1985). Social workers have a signifcant role to play in understanding the nature of this kind of clienthood and interpreting it to service purveyors.

These services are often imposed or denied by a larger system whose objective is the cost-efficient provision of minimal interventions. By virtue of an elderly person's requiring some type of service (e.g., admission to a nursing home or the provision of in-home nursing services), the family often is subjected to the observations and judgment of professionals about their ability to provide care; their ways of interacting with one another; their life-styles; and their preferences, idiosyncrasies, traditions, and cultural patterns of elderly-family caring. It is common to hear professionals render judgments on the caring provided by families or the response of elders to family care-giving efforts: "If he were my father, I'd take him home," "She should be grateful to have such a caring family," or "I don't know how they have coped so long."

Frequently, services are seen to be for the family, rather than for the client: "They don't *need* a nurse; they could learn to change this catheter if they really wanted to." Services are equated with the failure of the family to take responsibility and to "really" care, for the elderly family member. Projections of what professionals fantasize they may be willing to provide for their own elderly family members form the basis of judgments about the suitability of providing services that the elderly and their families are expected to receive gracefully and with gratitude. In this regard, services are most often "dispensed," proffered by professionals as though they owned them, rather than as entitlements paid for by the general public (Callahan, 1988).

The availability of professional care does not always relieve the pain of isolation and alienation. As a substitute for the hoped-for family closeness, it often points up, by its very kindness, the loss or the gap. When perceived as useful, but not kind—impersonal, perfunctory, impatient—it accentuates the solitary state (Cohler, Groves, Borden, & Lazarus, 1989).

For many, becoming responsible for an elderly family member means becoming a secondary client. In addition to the information required, the forms and correspondence, the appointments scheduled and kept, there is a pervasive sense of being assessed, measured, and labeled by professional and service systems. Secrets, peripheral embarrassments, attitudes, and ignorance become exposed and are made subject to professionals' judgments and attempts at correction in the guise of "education." These issues are illustrated in the following case study.

Mr. W applied for admission to his local home for the aged, and as part of the admission process was required to bring in his "next of kin" for an interview, ostensibly to explain to them the services that were available, but also to sign a financial guarantee. Mr. W, who had not told his children—a son and daughter, both of whom live several hundred miles from Mr. W—of his intention to sell the family home and move into a more sheltered setting, had always been reluctant to share information about his finances. He was independent, hard working, and very lonely since the death of his wife five years ago. He liked his children, but didn't feel close to them; he saw them as having moved away in both a physical and social sense, including giving up their connections with the church and their European heritage. He believed that they were critical of him for "clinging to the past" and thought that they had forgotten their mother and really wouldn't care where he lived. Social work was called in when Mr. W abruptly left the interview calling the admissions officer a "damn busybody."

Disruption of Family Functioning

When change entails "moving to the children," additional, more personally painful adjustments may have to be faced. The mutual fond acceptance that has prevailed, based on occasional visits during holidays and other times of celebration, may become severely strained with the close juxtaposition of changed life-styles. The relationship itself may suffer strain, as adult children demonstrate unwelcome acceptance. Elderly parents may be critical of their children's child-rearing practices or perceived disrespect. Intergenerational conflict may become angry and mutually destructive as expectations of appropriate behavior are subject to great pressure in close quarters.

Whether families combine their living arrangements to include their elderly members or attempt to keep elderly members in their own residences, distance and distancing may become a serious issue. The lack of private respite, of time and space for oneself, becomes a problem for all when joint living and increased care are chosen. When separate households are selected, the physical, emotional, and financial strains of travel, managing another household with limited resources and permissions granted, and juggling a nuclear and natal family and their particular tugs-of-war, exact a great and increasing price for caregivers and receivers alike (Wister, 1985).

Both the elderly and their families often feel completely at the mercy of the continuation of care by those who are hired to provide it. Threats of leaving or their actuality frequently sow panic and further disrupt a precarious hold on caring. Thus, a desperate family member may "take sides" with an inadequate provider of care to avoid disruption and hence cause pain and anger to or retribution by an offended elderly complainant.

Shifts within the family in whatever balance of response to old and new interactions and external pressures and circumstances may create profound barriers to the expression of need and to the capacity to deliver care. New permissions have to be elicited mutually, in relation to dependence, the invasion of personal space, priorities, and the rights of others. Old biases, prejudices, and preferences may prove to be genuine obstacles or may be used as red herrings. Rational arguments about prejudices are no more effective with the elderly and their aggrieved families than they are with anyone else. Similarly, gratitude, no matter how real, does not overcome the pain of major disruptions, the tilting of family balances, or sadness associated with the loss of carefully worked out interdependences (Birkel, 1987; Horowitz, 1985; Montgomery, 1989).

Communication Issues

Communication with and within families of the elderly is subject to all the issues of style, interpretation, content taboos, and prescribed information providers. In addition, special consideration must be given to the more common problems of communication, such as the import of short-term memory loss that is different in nature, not just in amount, from significant gaps in functional memory. For example, repetition may be an essential adaptation of a style of communication for elderly members with short-term memory loss and must not be confused with the pathological symptom of perseveration.

For many elderly persons, isolation and loneliness create twin barriers to easy communication. Long periods of silence—in which their thoughts may turn inward and brooding, may move to the past or become circular around perceived slights, fears, or pleasant memories—make "surfacing" to the brisk pace of communication with others difficult. It is particularly difficult to do so under stress or when information must be exchanged and absorbed for decision making.

Analogously, in a world that has often shrunk significantly for the elderly, who have little involvement in or contact with functioning groups and activities, the desire to process information quickly may have receded, even more than the ability to do so. An elderly person who has developed the habit of savoring and reliving every bit of "news" may be reluctant to move swiftly from step to step or to condense information or summarize thinking. This reluctance may have made family members impatient and dismissive, and although their assessment of the mental capacities of their elderly relative may be incorrect, it may be readily accepted by the "efficient" professional.

The elderly and their families tend to use communication patterns and styles that are often drawn from another time and hence incorporate different meanings for common words (e.g., dinner was most often served at noon in previous generations; the evening meal was supper) or ascribe culturally specific meanings to different communications (e.g., in many cultures, it is considered rude to make eye contact with authority figures). In some families, old forms of address are given up, to the chagrin of the elderly, who see them as earned signs of respect and may refuse to respond without them.

Within the family some communications may be viewed as an expression of personal concern or closeness, while the elderly person may find familiarity in communication to be insulting. For example, the common North American practice of using first names among adults is often viewed as a derogatory practice by elderly persons, who view the use of social titles and last names (e.g., Mr. Smith or Mrs. Jones) as signs of respect.

Time frames also assume different meanings for the elderly and their families. What is recent for the professional is likely to be different for the elderly person who holds long-ago memories near and dear, placing them in the recent, rather than in the remote, past. Like all of us, the elderly have "fixed" special times and people, forever securing past events in the present. In any family, the entire concept of aging is marked with the experiences of long ago and with familial definitions, laced with shoulds and shouldn'ts, communicated from generation to generation.

Of particular note is the impact of professional jargon on the elderly and their families. Although the most common examples are found in medicine, all disciplines use jargon whose particular meaning is often unknown to families. Even basic designations, such as a nurse or a social worker, conjure up images that affect the ways in which families communicate. For example, it is common for families to assume that social workers are concerned only with their financial situation or to suspect that they are mistreating their elderly relatives.

It is important, therefore, that professionals recognize the context in which communication is taking place and that they modify their own communication strategies to take into account possible misunderstandings, unexpected interpretations, and lay comprehension of common jargon. Checking and rechecking the understanding of the elderly and their families is crucial for clear and meaningful communication.

At the same time, it is important to remember that dysfunctional communication, some of which may reflect truly pathological relationships, may be particularly well rooted in families of the elderly. By virtue solely of the length of time invested in these patterns, change will be difficult to effect and may come at an extraordinary price for everyone involved (Nussbaum, Thompson, & Robinson, 1989). The importance of clear and meaningful communication is illustrated in the following case example.

The local placement service received an urgent call from Mrs. T saying that she had to get her father into a nursing home right away. She was so distressed on the phone that the intake worker was unable to get any sense of what had precipitated this urgent call. All that Mrs. T could say was that her father had spilled his coffee. The social work consultant was called in to assess the situation. It was discovered that Mr. H had moved in with his daughter, son-in-law, and two children in their early twenties, both still in school, following the death of Mrs. H from cancer. Initially, the living arrangements had been satisfactory; everyone made adjustments in schedules, eating habits, recreational activities, and use of the television and stereo. However, Mr. H had become increasingly demanding of family members, complaining about their behavior and attitudes; he was especially critical of Mrs. T's children and their "disrespectful language." Recently, Mr. H had started taking long walks and was often gone for several hours. He seemed unable to recall where he had been or what he had been doing. Mrs. T felt under increasing pressure to be at home and to monitor her father's behavior. From her perspective, the more she tried to please him, the more demanding and difficult he became.

On the morning of her call to the placement service, she had taken Mr. H his breakfast in bed. After tasting his coffee he spilled it—all over Mrs. T—accompanied by accusations that she had never learned to cook and saying, what was she trying to do, poison him. Mrs. T had convinced herself that her father was developing Alzheimer's disease. Careful assessment disclosed that Mr. H had mixed feelings about living with his daughter; he found the busy household tiring, didn't like the behavior of his grandchildren or their parents' response to it, missed having friends his own age— anyone who remembered World War II and the Big Band sound. Mrs. T, on the other hand, increasingly resented her father's inter- ference in the running of the family, especially his constant compar- ison of her behavior to that of her late mother. She was frequently confronted by complaints from her husband and children about the need to compromise plans and promises to accommodate Mr. H. Mrs. T thought that she was responsible for her father's welfare, but resented the restrictions that "another child" placed on her free time. She vividly recalled a conversation between her parents, many years before, in which her father declared that he would die before he went to a nursing home because, after all, children who would "put their parents away" were just trying to "kill them off." No dis- cussion of alternatives had ever been broached between Mrs. T and Mr. H.

Judgment and Labeling

In many instances, the presence of strangers, no matter how helpful, is felt as an intrusion by the elderly and by their families. The new intimacy may be threatening to relationships or self-esteem and may reenforce old, un- resolved conflicts. The presence of an authorized stranger, such as a profes- sional, invades privacy and may elicit the strain of "proper" behavior. The professional's involvement, at whatever level, in the intimacies of body, purse, relationships, and plans, may be both requested and resented.

The elderly person or family members may feel deskilled or inadequate because of the judgments of the professionals. Old resentments may be displaced onto one or more of the professionals involved. The family may mobilize to do so together, sabotaging as a unit, or there may be painful divisions and disparate alliances with a particular professional. It is not surprising, for example, that the family member who pays—or who is of the same generation—is often the one with whom the professional caretaker consults, talks, or becomes accountable, perhaps to the distress of the elderly person who feels unheard or misunderstood. The fear of losing a caregiver may make a family member dismiss or ignore the complaints of the elderly relative in favor of keeping the peace or "understanding the other side." Intimidation, often subtle, becomes a weapon in the hands of the elderly person, family members, and professionals that can be wielded effectively in the name of reason, protection of the elderly, and exacting responsibility.

Service Entitlement

Historically, services to the elderly were predicated on the failure of the individual or family to meet economic or health needs and required the separation of the elderly person from the family as the price of service. Service was perceived as an act of charity to be received without question or challenge and with humility and gratitude. Not that long ago, the only option open to families who needed help in providing care was the poorhouse. Municipal homes for the aged were the more enlightened poorhouses, and hospitals were where people went to die.

Increased longevity, health status, wealth, mobility, and consumer rights have changed the face of caregiving and created a range of options for providing care both in institutions and at home. The provision of independent income to the elderly through Old Age Security and the Canada Pension Plan has minimized elderly people's economic dependence on their families. In some sectors, the elderly have amassed considerable wealth, often vested in property, which has resulted in their children remaining in an economically dependent relationship with them, similar to that of the traditional agrarian family. The impact of possible inheritance must be included in understanding the relationships among family members. Both the elderly and their heirs may view their economic relationship, often quite differently, as important in making decisions about care. For example, the daughter who stays home to care for her aging parents may believe that she is more entitled to inherit the estate of her parents than are her other siblings. Elderly parents may turn over their homes and wealth, King Lear style, with the expectation of being cared for, but not having to give up control.

The provision of universally accessible medical care without reference to the income of either the elderly person or his or her family also changes the patterns of economic dependence often experienced by American families. Care can be sought and received without worrying that the financial costs will force or rupture family relationships.

Apart from their families, the elderly have developed their own image that has been generated, in part, by larger social conditions. In their own right they have become, collectively, a consumer group of considerable power that retailers and service providers have to reckon with. Concessions have been made to this group in the form of senior citizens' discounts, privileges, and passes, and they are mass purchasers of travel services, forms of entertainment, recreational activities, and gifts. They have also, on occasion, organized and exercised political clout (Gifford, 1990).

Remarriage, women in the work force, forced retirement, and retirement planning have provided options for the elderly separate from their families. The elderly's traditional roles as "senior statesmen"; doting grandparents; and transmitters of family traditions, customs, and skills are being replaced by the development of new interests, attachments, and life-styles. As documented in other aspects of family formation and reformation, the elderly are shaping new roles and new relationships that professionals must learn to understand, assess, and accommodate in their work. New norms are being established, new customs are emerging, and the range between health and pathology is taking on new twists and turns.

WHERE THE ELDERLY AND THEIR FAMILIES ENCOUNTER SOCIAL WORKERS

The elderly and their families encounter social workers in a variety of institutional and community settings. It is important to differentiate whether they are seen in the context of a familiar or unfamiliar setting, since the significance of cues from familiar surroundings is often more crucial for the elderly than for most other groups. For the elderly "home" may be someone else's house; the meaning of the situation in which social workers are called to serve the elderly is a first ingredient in understanding the context of the client.

The categorizing of the settings in which social work service may be found is easy for professionals and generally reflects, in the Canadian context, who is paying for the service and hence who has the authority to require, permit, or deny the service. Whether social work is present in each of these settings varies from jurisdiction to jurisdiction (Watt, 1985). These distinctions generally are not meaningful to the elderly and their families, who bring to their encounters with social workers, whether in institutions or in the community, whatever preconceived ideas, beliefs, and values they have acquired in their past experiences. This is a second contextual factor that must be taken into account by social workers, since the elderly often have seen social workers only as people "dealing with the poor" or "putting people away."

Institutional Settings

One of the most common first encounters among social workers, the elderly, and their families is in the acute care hospital. Usually precipitated by concerns about discharge planning, the social worker will be required to assess, most often in a short time, the needs and resources of the individuals and their families to provide posthospital care.

The discharge-planning function is a complex one that involves the efforts of an interdisciplinary team, the patient, and the family, with the social worker taking the lead role in matching the patient's needs with resources drawn from the patient's and the larger community environment. Often the discharge plan includes the transfer of ongoing responsibility to another social worker in either the community or an institutional setting. Therefore, the patient and his or her family may have to deal with a number of social workers over the course of one admission for a major medical problem that results in moves within an acute care hospital, rehabilitation or convalescent services, and long-term care in institutions or in the community (Ciotti & Watt, 1990).

Most long-term care institutions, including chronic care hospitals, palliative care units, geriatric rehabilitation programs, and some nursing homes, have social workers on staff or available for consultation. In these situations, although discharge planning may be part of the role, the focus of social work intervention is more likely to be the adjustment of the patient and his or her family to the losses and limitations associated with long-term care. In addition, in progressive institutions, social work will be one of the disciplines in any multidisciplinary team that plans and evaluates the outcome of the care program with the patient and his or her family. A range of social work interventions, including bereavement counseling, may be used in specific settings.

Community Settings

Social workers increasingly are encountering elderly clients in social work agencies as the primary clients or through families who seek assistance. In the latter case, the elderly family member may be identified as the source of the family's problem or may merely appear as one of the family members involved with the difficulty for which the family has sought help.

A range of community programs and institutions serving the elderly employ social workers, often as the primary mental health professionals on their staffs. Home care programs, respite care programs, residential settings (e.g., homes for the aged and senior citizens' residences), geriatric day care centers, specialty clinics and facilities (including psychiatric outpatient facilities), and family physicians' practices are among the community settings that provide social work services.

SOCIAL WORK SERVICES TO THE ELDERLY AND THEIR FAMILIES

Excluding primary social work settings, the elderly and their families are referred to social workers either as a result of some other professional identifying a problem that she or he believes warrants social work intervention or through categorical or programmatic standards for referral. For example, in some homes for the aged, all applicants are initially screened by the social work staff to ensure the suitability of their application. In geriatric assessment programs, social work assessment is an integral part of the total assessment process and involves all patients and their families. An example of a categorical referral is an automatic or routine request for the assessment of any patient over age 75 who is admitted to an acute care hospital with a diagnosis of dementia.

Four factors will determine the quality of the referral for the elderly person and his or her family. Quality will vary according to the meaning of the referral to the elderly person and his or her family members. The attitude of both the referring and receiving professionals will set a tone for the referral. The mix of skills and approaches used by the specific social worker will also influence the quality. Finally, the loss of control, the diffusion of the original agreement about intervention as the referral moves out and through the care system, will have an impact upon the client's perception of the quality of care provided.

In secondary settings, social work is often precariously positioned. Social workers are constantly interpreting their roles not only to patients and their families but to a steady stream of ever-changing professionals upon whom they depend for their referrals. The degree to which this interpretation is heard, absorbed, and acted upon will dramatically influence the opportunities for service to the elderly and their families, both in institutions and in the community. This situation is particularly critical in relation to mental health issues, since social workers frequently function as the gatekeepers for the elderly to other mental health professionals.

The professionals who refer elderly clients often have preconceived solutions or resolutions that may not have been shared with any two parts of the system, let alone with the client system as a whole. When the referring agent has already decided on both the nature of the problem and the appropriate solution, the referral to social work is intended either to persuade the client to agree to the definition of and solution to the problem (or at least to the latter) or to fact find to support the definition and solution that is to be prescribed.

An alternative expectation about referral may best be described as a "throwing up of hands" referral. In these instances, common to all types of professional referral, the referring agent simply wants to be rid of the "problem." Most professionals, who have a powerful tendency to take sides and to project our own attitudes and values, have little incentive to invest in the complex planning of treatment options for elderly clients. Other than in specialized geriatric services, the elderly are a problem for the service system, since they have special needs and consume valuable and expensive resources (e.g., acute treatment beds) that professionals often believe should be used for younger clients. Thus, referrals to social workers have the underlying intent of solving a systemic problem, a problem for the professionals.

The elderly person and various members of the family come to the referral with a range of expectations that often parallel those of the referring professional. The elderly, by experience, have come not to expect much investment by professionals, which, in turn, conditions their response to social workers, including predisposing them either to act out or to withdraw; such behavior may then be interpreted as pathological unless it is understood in the context of this complicated referral process.

THE UNIQUE PERSPECTIVE OF SOCIAL WORKERS

Social workers bring a unique perspective to work with the elderly and their families. They understand the individual and his or her behavior in a context that includes the family. Understanding clients as they are and not as interested parties wish they would be allows social workers to evaluate objectively the strengths and deficits of both elderly persons and their environments and allows for unconventional resolutions of their problems. The application of this perspective begins with the social work assessment.

Assessment

Assessment of the elderly can be done only in the context of their families, even if their family members are not physically present. We all develop our own definitions of appropriate aging behaviors that are based heavily upon the norms of our families. The family reflects cultural norms and values even if only through its rejection of them.

The family gives meaning to the history provided by the elderly person. Family members may provide critical details that an impaired elderly relative may have forgotten or present a different perspective through the details they convey.

There is almost always a perceptual gap between the elderly and their families about past events. Understanding these disparities is part of a competent assessment. The impact of different value systems may be reflected by different memories; this gap is often a reflection of the difference between what "ought to have been" and "what was." Gaps may also be a response to perceptions of power and of people in power asking questions that are considered to be invasive; different generations perceive power differently and have a different stake in their relationship to people who they think have power. For example, the social worker may be viewed by both the elderly person and his or her family, who disagree about plans for posthospital care, as the one who determines the discharge plan. For the elderly person, the social worker's power is a threat, the threat of placement in a nursing home, a power to be countered. For the family, the social worker's power is an opportunity to enforce their wish for alternative care, a power to be courted and convinced.

The elderly also may develop an unfamiliar sense of entitlement, conditioned by often-inaccessible cultural norms, that may present as bizarre behavior to professionals and family members. For example, they may demand more personal care (e.g., bedpans, meals in bed, and assistance with dressing) than may younger people with a comparable degree of disability.

The psychosocial implications of loss and change, characteristic of this phase of the life cycle, feed into a history of long-term family dynamics that are alive and well long after many of the actors have died. Lost spouses, old lovers, siblings, and parents continue to influence the response of the elderly. Understanding this context is also part of the social work assessment.

Finally, social workers bring to the assessment process the ability to synthesize and convey these complex facts and factors. They counterbalance popular and professional cultures and mythologies by conveying the complexities and individualities of a particular elderly person in the context of his or her family and their broader social, psychological, and cultural experiences (Watt & Soifer, 1991).

Intervention

Social workers bring to intervention with the elderly the knowledge and skills to intervene with the family as a unit, not as separate components. While members of other disciplines have developed specific family-oriented techniques, social workers use the theory and practice of family interventions as part of their basic set of interventions.

Social workers also bring a biopsychosocial perspective to intervention, including an appreciation of time and relationships, that permits them to distinguish between a psychosocial crisis that demands immediate, skilled intervention and a situation in which the needs of others produce pressure to act quickly. For example, discharge from a hospital is not a crisis; the urgency often associated with referral to social work has more to do with the needs of the hospital as a system than with any crisis for the patient. Therefore, in such a situation, there is no justification for taking over the patients' and their families' responsibilities for problem solving simply to expedite freeing a bed.

Social workers bring to interventions the ability to deal with the fallout of interventions with the elderly, including the ability, based on their knowledge of the biopsychosocial reality of the elderly, to anticipate the realities that constrain the goals of intervention. In addition, although they have the knowledge and skills to mobilize community resources, social workers are only too aware of the limitations, of both quantity and quality, of these much-needed resources.

Group work skills, part of social workers' "bag of tricks," permit intervention with groups of elderly persons, family groups (including family conferences), and multidisciplinary teams.

Finally, social workers in the best tradition of the profession, support the right to self-determination of the individual in the face of decisions that may have negative outcomes. These advocacy skills can be used to ensure that physically and even mentally impaired elderly people have a strong voice in a system that values unquestioning compliance with authority and the least troublesome solution for the system (Holosko & Feit, 1991).

Other Types of Services

The value of indirect services for the elderly and their families is included in the perspective of social work. These services include advocacy for services, the development of social policy, and community development to enhance the quality of the lives of the elderly and their families. The evidence gathered from case-by-case involvement is a powerful tool in innovating and shaping services.

Social workers have a role to play in case management for the elderly. As professionals, they are ideally suited to develop, with the elderly person, professionals in the community, and family members, a plan that optimizes the resources of the individual, the family, and the community in the provision of care (Moxley, 1989).

Issues and Problems

There are a number of pitfalls in working with the elderly and their families; some are unique to the situation of the elderly and some are merely exaggerations of problems that are endemic in the human services. An example of the latter dilemma is that of "taking sides."

More time is needed to assess and intervene with the elderly because of the complexities already described. In most agencies, social workers must fight for adequate time to provide these services. Similarly, the urgent need for indirect advocacy and policy-building services is time consuming and usually is not a popular activity from the vantage point of agencies or the government.

Stereotyping is a common pitfall; "the elderly," the "old-old," the "frail elderly," and the "cognitively impaired" are designations that carry culturally (both community and institutional cultures) determined stereotypes. There is a real danger of acting on these stereotypes, since there is little incentive to differentiate one elderly person from another. Eligibility for services is commonly defined by age; resources can rarely be individualized to the needs of the client, and the rewards for the tremendous work involved to individualize services are few. Similarly, families are subjected to stereotyping. The likelihood that professionals are, in their private lives, members of families with elderly relatives, increases the probability of projection and identification in response to the situations of clients. These factors reinforce the tendency to stereotype the elderly and their families, both to deal with the demands of the system and to cope with providers' reactions to the situations they encounter (Novak, 1985).

Blockages and shortages within the formal caregiving systems, both health and social service, also present pitfalls for social workers in dealing with families. Considerable pressure is exerted on families to be responsible for the systems' failures, to take responsibility that has been vested in the formal caregiving system but is not being exercised (e.g., the availability of long-term care beds and inadequate homemaking services as part of community-based care). Since social workers are largely employed by the same system that is failing to provide services in proportion to the needs of the elderly, there are strong forces pressuring them to align themselves with the system's, rather than the client's, best interests.

The lack of status and power of social work in many of the care systems for the elderly exacerbates the problems of "taking the client's side." High turnover rates and a high degree of frustration and "burnout" characterize social work practice in settings where these deficiencies exist. The results can be devastating for the provision of services.

The trend from doing home visits as part of social work may be especially difficult in dealing with the families of the elderly. Similarly, the lack of flexibility and creativity in the provision of resources, including the provision of social work services, is another practice pitfall.

The lack of social work research on issues of aging, families of the elderly, and service options for the elderly and their families is leaving social workers dependent upon the perspectives of other disciplines and professions to define roles, interventions, and strategies for improving care. This lack also predisposes social work to both fads and aversions in the care of the elderly. One example is our approach to elder abuse; on the one hand, we are reluctant to believe that elder abuse exists, while, on the other hand, we find it everywhere.

Finally, it is important to remember that the elderly have almost become a reflection of the problems of modern, industrial society in North America (Olsen, 1982). The negative mental health effects of these problems can be seen in the elderly and their families to encompass larger social issues, such as social structure, poverty, isolation, unplanned change, and technological advances. We could learn a lot about mental health in general from a careful examination of the mental health issues of the elderly and their families.

BIBLIOGRAPHY

Berman, H. J. (1987). Adult children and their parents: Irredeemable obligations and irreplaceable loss. *Journal of Gerontological Social Work*, 10(2), 21–34.

Biegel, D. E., & Blum, A. (1990). *Aging and caregiving: Theory, research, and policy*. Newbury Park, CA: Sage.

Biegle, D. E., Sales, E., & Shulz, R. (1991). *Family caregiving in chronic illness*. Newbury Park, CA: Sage.

Birkel, R. C. (1987) Towards a social ecology of the home-care household. *Psychology and Aging*, 2, 294–301.

Callahan, D. (1988). Families as caregivers: The limits of morality. *Archives of Physical Medicine and Rehabilitation*, 69, 323–328.

Chappell, N. L., & Havens, B. (1985). Who helps the elderly person: A discussion of informal and formal care. In W. A. Peterson & J. Quadagno (Eds.), *Social bonds in later life: Aging and interdependence* (pp. 211–228). Beverly Hills, CA: Sage.

Ciotti, M., & Watt, S. (1990). Discharge planning and the role of the social worker. In M. J. Holosko & P. A. Taylor (Eds.), *Social work practice in health care settings* (pp. 469–488). Toronto: Canadian Scholar's Press.

Cohler, B., Groves, L., Borden, W., & Lazarus, L. (1989). Caring for family members with Alzheimer's disease. In E. Light & B. Lebowitz (Eds.), *Alzheimer's disease treatment and family stress: Directions for research* (pp. 50–105). Bethesda, MD: National Institute of Mental Health.

Connidis, I. A. (1989). *Family ties and aging*. Toronto: Butterworths.

Duff, R. W., & Hong, L. K. (1981–82). Quality and quantity of social interactions in the life satisfactions of older Americans. *Sociology and Social Research*, 66, 418–434.

Foner, N. (1984). *Ages in conflict: A cross-cultural perspective on inequality between old and young*. New York: Columbia University Press.

Forbes, W. F., Jackson, J. A., & Kraus, A. S. (1987). *Institutionalization of the elderly in Canada*. Toronto: Butterworths.

Fry, C. L. (Ed.). (1980). *Aging in culture and society*. New York: Bergin.

Garant, L., & Bolduc, M. (1990). *Family caregiving: Myths and realities*. Quebec City: Ministre de la santé et des services sociaux du Quebec.

Gee, E. M., & Kimball, M. M. (1987). *Women and aging*. Toronto: Butterworths.

Gifford, C. G. (1990). *Canada's fighting seniors*. Toronto: James Lorimer.

Holosko, M. J., & Feit, M. D. (Eds.). (1991). *Social work practice with the elderly*. Toronto: Canadian Scholar's Press.

Horowitz, A. H. (1985). Family caregiving to the frail elderly. In M. P. Lawton & G. L. Maddox (Eds.), *Annual review of gerontology and geriatrics* (pp. 194–246). New York: Springer.

Keith, P. M., & Schafer, R. B. (1985). Equity, role strains, and depression among middle-aged and older men and women. In W. A. Peterson & J. Quadagno (Eds.), *Social bonds in later life: Aging and interdependence* (pp. 37–50). Beverly Hills, CA: Sage.

Montgomery, R. J. V. (1989). Investigating caregiver burden. In K. S. Markides & C. L. Cooper (Eds.), *Aging, stress and health* (pp. 201–218). New York: John Wiley & Sons.

Moxley, D. P. (1989). *The practice of case management*. Newbury Park, CA: Sage.

Novak, M. (1985). *Aging and society: A Canadian perspective.* Scarborough: Nelson Canada.

Nussbaum, J. F., Thompson, T., & Robinson, J. (1989). *Communication and aging.* New York: Harper & Row.

Peterson, W. A., & Quadagno, J. (Eds.). (1985). *Social bonds in later life: Aging and interdependence.* Beverly Hills, CA: Sage.

Popenoe, D. (1988). *Disturbing the nest: Family change and decline in modern society.* New York: Aldine de Gruyter.

Olsen, L. K. (1982). *The political economy of aging: The state, private power, and social welfare.* New York: Columbia University Press.

O'Neill, O. (1985). Between consenting adults. *Philosophy and Public Affairs, 14*(93), 252–277.

Rosenthal, C. J. (1985). Kinkeeping in the familial division of labour. *Journal of Marriage and the Family, 47,* 965–974.

Rosenthal, C. J. (1986). The differentiation of multigenerational households. *Canadian Journal on Aging, 5,* 27–42.

Watt, S. (1985). Social work in the health care field. In S. Yelaga (Ed.), *An introduction to social work practice in Canada* (pp. 166–181). Toronto: Prentice-Hall.

Watt, S., & Soifer, A. (1991). Conducting psychosocial assessments with the elderly. In M. J. Holosko & M. D. Feit (Eds.), *Social work practice with the elderly* (pp. 31–46). Toronto: Canadian Scholar's Press.

Wister, A. V. (1985). Living arrangement choices among the elderly. *Canadian Journal on Aging, 4,* 127–144.

22

Psychosocial Problems and the Needs of the Elderly in Mental Health

David Guttmann · Ariela Lowenstein

I n *Reflections on My Eightieth Birthday*, Bertrand Russell (1956, p. 220) wrote:

> On reaching the age of eighty it is reasonable to suppose that the bulk of one's work is done, and that what remains to do will be of less importance. The serious part of my life ever since boyhood has been devoted to two different objects which for a long time remained separate and have only in recent years united into a single whole. I wanted, on the one hand, to find out whether anything could be known; and, on the other hand, to do whatever might be possible toward creating a happier world.

This quote from the famous scientist-philosopher seems especially relevant today. Russell wrote of completing the bulk of one's work at age 80—which leaves a good number of years of constructive work well beyond the customary age of 65 years as a time of life for taking leave of one's major life accomplishments. Russell echoed ideas that many elderly people sense: the need to come to terms with one's age, make peace with oneself, accept responsibility for things that happened in one's life, and recognize the significance of one's contributions to others. These are all part of this quest, which is basically spiritual or, as Hertz (1990, p. 192) said: "You are as young as your faith, as old as your doubts, as young as your self-confidence, as old as your fears, as young as your hopes, as old as your despair."

Given favorable conditions and encouragement, the elderly also construct a new self—just as people do in adolescence, "a self that both adds to and subtracts much from the old personality of our prime" (Hall, 1922, p. 411). Senescence, like adolescence, has its own feelings, thoughts, and wills, and their regimen is as important as that of the body. As Hall (1922, p. 100) stated: "Individual differences here are probably greater than in youth."

There are, of course, differences in the perception of psychosocial problems and needs of the elderly from one culture to another, from one ethnic group to another, and sometimes even within the same ethnic group or within the various social classes of a certain culture (Gelfand & Fandetti, 1980; Guttmann, 1973).

Despite past and present attempts to "melt the umeltable ethnics," ethnicity is the mysterious and powerful element in our lives that, however ignored and suppressed, comes back to haunt us the more we advance in years. Ethnicity may be defined as historically derived cultural uniqueness consisting of a shared symbolic system of meanings. It is expressed chiefly through attitudes and values commonly held by a group of people in formal and informal communications, as well as in body language, and by a sense of a common core that binds together people from similar cultural environments. These elements provide people with a sense of identity, which may serve as a source of strength in old age.

Aging is as much a universal biological phenomenon as is any other stage in the life cycle. Yet, it is also a cultural phenomenon. Each ethnic group has developed over the centuries its unique patterns of coping with the problems of aging and its own attitudes toward the aged. These patterns and attitudes influence significantly whether aging will be a time of joy, wisdom, and integration into society or a time of despair, destitution, and depression.

Attitudes toward income security, illness, pain, the use of leisure time, retirement, widowhood, death, and bereavement, to name but a few of the commonly experienced issues in old age, are all colored and seen through the cultural prisms that represent ethnicity. We all are familiar with stories about old folks who revert to their native language the nearer they draw to death. No matter how long they have been in the United States or Canada, no matter how well they learned English or how frequently they used it in their daily communications, no matter whether they have been absorbed into the majority culture, no matter whether they attempted to forget their roots and assimilated the external aspects of social class and the corresponding life-styles, in their old age they embark on a journey backward toward their early beginnings.

As Baroni (1979) stated: "Americans are the most racially, culturally, ethnically and regionally different people in the world, and there must be tolerance for diversity because it's a key to our survival."

The full understanding and acceptance by policymakers in this society of cultural attitudes to aging are basic conditions for effective policies and programs aimed at the problems of aging. In a pluralistic society, attention must be paid to the fact that there are millions and millions of elderly people who belong to well over a hundred different ethnic groups. For these people, their ethnic group membership, including their established and time-honored ways of life, is a critical factor in their overall well-being. Yet, significantly, there is still a lack of information about the similarities and the differences in adjustment to and coping with socioenvironmental demands by elderly members of ethnic groups that must be taken into consideration by those who serve them. Nor are there functional models for the delivery of services to reach the needy among the ethnic aged. There are many elderly "ethnics" who do not use political assertiveness and lobbying to achieve their interests, but who, nevertheless, are as concerned about their own well-being as are their more vocal and active counterparts.

The processes, problems, and needs of older life are complex. In fact, most of the vital issues concerning the well-being of the elderly tend to cut across disciplinary lines. Even within a specific discipline, a multifaceted perspective may be useful.

From the onset, we have to state that in this chapter we cannot address all subjects connected to the psychosocial problems of the aged in our modern society. We are limited by this recognition to certain topics. Consequently, we will not deal, for example, with such problems as Alzheimer's disease, mental retardation, addictions, or crime. What we present here is applicable to the situation of the elderly today and is based on present knowledge. Therefore, we will address the following: (1) theoretical perspectives in social gerontology, (2) the psychosocial needs of the elderly, and (3) social work interventions and roles.

THEORETICAL PERSPECTIVES IN SOCIAL GERONTOLOGY

Gerontology is the systematic study of the aging process—a process that involves biophysiological, psychological, and social factors. Each of these factors is interdependent. One's physical condition affects social behavior, and vice versa.

The physical, psychological, and social changes that accompany advancing age often place older people under stress. Antonovsky (1980), a researcher in the area of medical sociology, questioned why a substantial number of subjects who experience crises do not become ill. Or, in other words, what is the difference between a pathological and a nonpathological response to stress or to a stressful life event? The answer is *resistance resources*. Antonovsky defined resistance resources as the power that can be applied to resolve a tension expressive of a state of disturbed homeostasis. Central to this power is the concept of tension management, meaning the *rapidity* and the *completeness* with which problems are resolved and tension is dissipated.

All the psychosocial theories of aging attempt to explain ways in which the psychosocial needs, which are the basis of the stress that elderly people experience, may be alleviated. The most discussed theories of aging in the gerontological literature are the psychosocial theory of development, disengagement theory, activity theory, continuity theory, exhange theory, and network theory.

THE PSYCHOSOCIAL THEORY OF DEVELOPMENT Erikson (1963), who had perhaps the greatest impact on aging through his conceptualization of human development, postulated that development occurs through a series of eight stages—from childhood to old age. Each stage mirrors a crisis or conflict in development and marks a major adjustment that people must make to their social environment. Each stage is also expressive of the major psychosocial needs of an individual who is experiencing it. The critical factor is how people adjust to each problem area because some resolution of each age-specific task, or conflict, must be made before a new stage can begin and a new task is presented to the developing ego.

Erikson postulated that the last stage of life should be devoted to the final establishment of ego integrity, meaning the ability to accept the facts of one's life and to face death without great fear. What is important to remember in this regard is that development is never static. It continues throughout the entire life cycle, for the "individual continues to establish new orientations to self and the social world" (Freiberg, 1987).

DISENGAGEMENT THEORY Over thirty years ago, Cumming and Henry (1961) postulated the major changes that retirement brings to the life of older people. This concept has become known in gerontology as disengagement theory (see Atchley, 1971; Crawford, 1971; Cumming, 1975; Hochschild, 1975).

This theory contends that as people reach old age, they become less involved in the organized structures of society, reduce their psychosocial interactions and roles, and thus withdraw from social life. The major psychosocial need, according to this theory, is to find meaningful activities and roles that will substitute for the previously held statuses and roles. In other words, the psychosocial need of the disengaged person is to accept disengagement gracefully and to find new channels to satisfaction with life. When the withdrawal is voluntary and successful, the result is a heightened sense of satisfaction with one's life.

ACTIVITY THEORY Other gerontologists maintained that the major psychosocial need of the elderly is to continue the same level of activity to which they were accustomed before retirement. They postulated the activity theory of aging, which is based mainly on concepts borrowed from Erikson. The maintenance of a certain level of activity is, indeed, a psychosocial need that can be met by involvement in many social roles and interactions (Atchley, 1977; Havighurst, 1968; Hendricks & Hendricks, 1977; Lemon, Bengston, & Peterson, 1972; Longino & Kart, 1982; Maddox, 1963; Neugarten, 1968, 1977; Palmore, 1968). However, this theory assumes that people can maintain the same level of activity as they were used to in middle age and disregards the natural decline in energy, stamina, power, and strength with advancing years.

CONTINUITY THEORY Continuity theory claims that older people as a whole continue to have social and psychological needs that are similar to those they had in middle age and that previous life-styles, habits, and patterns of activity continue into the post-retirement years. It is basically an attempt to combine the two theories just discussed (Atchley, 1977; Butler & Lewis, 1982; Chen, 1980; Hazan, 1980, 1984). The shortcoming of this theory is that it tends to disregard the need for personal growth that always implies change.

EXCHANGE THEORY Exchange theory is based on the nature and structure of the social, psychological, economic, and legal interactions between the generations. The various transactions of parents and children constitute a flow of activities that ideally should work in both directions, namely, from the children to the parents, and vice versa, for the benefit of both parties. Each party makes a unique contribution to the transaction. When the exchange is perceived by both parties as satisfactory, then the psychosocial need of having achieved a "fair deal" is met (Dowd, 1975, 1978, 1980; Lee & Ellithorpe, 1982; Sauer & Coward, 1985).

NETWORK THEORY Research in social gerontology has shown that the majority of disabled elderly people live in the community and are cared for by their families (Brody, 1985; Emerson, 1976; Gonyea, 1987; Shanas, 1979; Sussman, 1976).

During the past decade, social gerontologists found that human longevity has reached a point at which a large number of elderly people become dependent on various sources of support for the maintenance of their daily lives. Consequently, they emphasized the role of social support networks in the gerontological literature. They clearly recognized the importance of the informal social support network that provides assistance during times of crises (Biegel & Blum, 1990; Brody, 1985; Cantor, 1983; Hooyman, 1983). Social networks provide two kinds of assistance to needy elderly people: governmental and public services and sources of aid and help given by families, friends, neighbors, and volunteers (Killilea, 1982; Sauer & Coward, 1985).

The fundamental conclusion of gerontologists is that a breakdown in the social support system of an individual greatly increases the likelihood that stressors will have serious detrimental effects on his or her mental health. Stated more positively, the availability of a supportive social network seems to enhance significantly the ability of an individual to cope with both physical and psychological stressors (McCubbin, Sussman, & Patterson, 1983).

THE PSYCHOSOCIAL NEEDS OF THE AGED

Needs are defined in the *Social Work Dictionary* (Barker, 1987, p. 105) as "physical, psychological, economic, and social requirements for survival, well-being, and fulfillment." According to *Webster's* (1986, p. 1512) a need, as opposed to a wish, indicates "a lack of something requisite, desirable, or useful, . . . [or] a condition requiring supply or relief" for the maintenance of the homeostasis of an organism. A need also means "a lack of the means of subsistence," or an obligation or necessity (*Webster's*, 1986, p. 790). And psychosocial needs are needs involving both psychological and social aspects, combining clinical, psychological, and social services, and relating social conditions to mental health.

Needs have many dimensions and many connotations. Concepts such as "welfare," "standard of living," and "socioeconomic condition" basically express objective perceptions of needs, whereas, "well-being," "quality of life," and "sense of security" may be considered both subjective and objective feelings regarding needs.

In social policy, for example, there is a "need" to combine the needs, wishes, and aspirations of the people concerned with the most recent scientific theories and methods that can define and measure objectively the psychosocial needs of the elderly for their welfare. An evaluation of other than the concrete needs of aging is a complex undertaking, especially when one has to deal with personal and subjectively felt needs in relation to the quality of a given service. No wonder, then, that these needs seldom are the subjects of measurement (Guttmann, 1987).

The psychosocial needs of the aged constitute two main groups: the external and concrete ones, which are more readily open for scientific observation and measurement, and the emotional and subjective ones, which at times are hard to identify, not to mention alleviate. The gerontological literature on needs attests to the difficulty that formal support networks and systems of services have in responding adequately to both the objectively and subjectively felt needs of the aged.

The overall psychosocial needs of the elderly can be roughly divided into five groups: psychological needs, spiritual needs, social needs, personal needs, and environmental needs.

Psychological needs center on the ability to choose among various alternatives: having a positive self-image, perceptions of life as meaningful, the maintenance of an optimistic outlook on life, the satisfaction of emotions, autonomy, feelings of belonging, and satisfying relationships with "significant others" (Neugarten, 1977; Wan, Adler, & Lewis, 1982; Weinberg, 1987).

Spiritual needs include a religious-philosophical outlook on life, a personal philosophy and values, hope, meaning, identity (both personal and social-cultural), wisdom, and love (Erikson, 1950; Rabinowitz, 1985).

Social needs emphasize connection and connectedness to family members, friends, neighbors, and organizations, as well as social interaction and involvement in social-political affairs and obtaining support and assistance from the community as the need arises (Sullivan, 1986; Yehudai, 1985).

Personal needs are geared toward the satisfactory maintenance of daily activities; the expression of creativity through work (volunteer and paid), hobbies, and crafts; housing and living arrangements; and the like (Lawton, 1987; Rosenberg & Hribets, 1985).

Environmental needs are connected to the quality of the neighborhood; to physical beauty; and to meeting the need of the elderly for comfort, safety and security, easy access and mobility to major life-supporting services, and useful information from and communication with service providers (Churchman, 1981; Yehudai, 1985).

Responses to the objective and subjective needs of the elderly in all five areas of life mean the strengthening of their capacity to cope with the stresses that life brings to all of us, whereas the lack of response indicates the existence of the need and a consequent sense of disruption of the homeostasis. Rosow (1967), in a tongue-in-check statement, mentioned that the needs of the elderly are basically of two kinds—those that the elderly themselves see as needs and those that gerontologists identify as needs.

In a classical work in cultural anthropology and aging, Clark and Anderson (1967) stated that successful adaptation to old age necessitates that the primary values of the culture be dropped and alternative values be substituted, so that the need for conservation will replace the need for acquisition and self-advancement and cooperation with and concern for others will replace the control of others. They also listed six major perceived needs that the elderly must satisfy in old age for good mental and social health:

1. Sufficient autonomy to permit continued integrity of the self;
2. Agreeable relationships with other people;
3. A reasonable amount of personal comfort in body, mind and physical environment;
4. Stimulation of the mind and imagination in ways that are not overtaxing of physical strength;
5. Sufficient movement to permit a variety of surroundings; and
6. Some degree of passionate involvement with life, to escape preoccupation with death (Clark & Anderson, 1967, pp. 232–233).

Although few of us would argue with this concept of psychosocial needs, we also have to consider the more subjective, personal, emotional, and spiritual needs of the elderly that significantly affect their mental health.

Aside from the major role the family plays in the care of the elderly, a less commonly explored social network consists of religious organizations. Along with the ethnic voluntary associations of clubs, fraternities, and "societies," these organizations constitute the bulk of social networks that are critical for meaningful existence in old age. In its broadest sense, religion encompasses spiritual well-being and is one of the most significant and, surprisingly, one of the least explored factors that affects ethnic elderly people. Churches, synagogues, temples, and mosques are centers of socioreligious networks of the highest importance for large segments of the elderly population, not only with regard to the religious calendar of holidays and observances, but with regard to the centers' traditions and rituals. The religious foundation permeates actions and provides strength, while the concomitant social attitudes maintained by the ethnic community as a social network regulates the behavior of its members.

The importance of religion in the general welfare of people has been documented by numerous studies on demographics, such as the various Gallup polls (Gallup Opinion Index, 1978) and the President's Commission on Mental Health (1978). Baum and Baum (1982) found that religion has the strongest influence on the psychomoral health of those aged 68–72 who have already undergone the scrutiny of their past lives, but that this influence can lead to integrity or despair, depending on which mechanisms are operating, while the innermost needs of old people are simply ignored. Chief among these needs is the need for a sense of security and reassurance that the elderly will not be ridiculed, degraded, or despised once their mental capacities decline with the onset of senility and that they will not be abandoned, forsaken, or warehoused when their strength fails them (Fecher, 1982).

This innermost need was recently discovered by a surprisingly large number of young people as well. In the January 28, 1986, segment of the Phil Donahue television show "CBS Morning Show" in the United States, young, well-to-do, famous, and supposedly successful women disclosed in public their innermost fears of being turned into "bag ladies" in old age. If this fear is so great for such people, imagine how elderly people who experienced the Great Depression, the two world wars, the Holocaust, and other calamities feel about what may happen to them when their funds and the generosity of society and family run out!

Forty-six years ago, Simmons (1946) found two other important needs or universal interests of the aged in many cultures: the need to extend life as long as possible and the need to withdraw from life, when the time comes, without too much suffering and pain and with good prospects for an attractive hereafter.

Towle (1952), a noted educator in social work, pointed out that all needs take on different meanings at different stages of life under different circumstances. And these needs must be taken into consideration in any professional intervention.

UPROOTEDNESS

In our perception, the major psychosocial problem of the aged in our time is uprootedness, which has reached massive proportions since World War II. Uprootedness is defined as the "state or quality of being uprooted or a sense of insecurity resulting from that state" (Webster's, 1986, p. 2518).

The mass uprootedness of elderly people from many different cultures is a commonly ignored phenomenon in modern society. The most disadvantaged elderly people are the victims of technological advances, urbanization, the constructions of super highways and new cities, and desertion by their social-climbing offspring and those who have been displaced by wars, famine, massive unemployment, and related social and political ills. For example, native-born Japanese Americans who are in their sixties, seventies, and eighties and who lived in the United States during World War II were the victims of political uprootedness and placement in internment camps by the U.S. government.

Erikson (1964, p. 84), the noted psychoanalyst and a leading developer of the theories of human development, and himself an immigrant, highlighted the problem of uprootedness with his characteristic and profound insight: "The mental health of individuals torn away from their homes, their work and their country in forced migration has repeatedly been a special concern of international meetings." He cited a study by Lerner (1958), who asked Turkish villagers where they would go if they had to emigrate. "Many were too horrified even to think of alternatives: it would seem 'worse than death,' they said" (quoted in Erikson, 1964, p. 84).

Uprootedness in old age has serious consequences for the mental health of the individuals concerned and for their families and communities. We have selected two major areas of life for illustration: (1) retirement—uprootedness from the world of work—and (2) changes in family life and institutionalization—uprootedness from the social world.

Uprootedness from the World of Work

Retirement at age 65 (or earlier) is a relatively recent phenomenon, especially in its institutionalized form. Most people tend to associate retirement with physical and emotional deterioration followed by decreased morale—the combination of which often results in low satisfaction with life and increased vulnerability to stress. The fear of retirement is related to the difficulty in accepting change in the accustomed ways of perceiving and dealing with the world—especially with the world of work, long viewed as a critical component of mature, adult functioning. According to sociologists and educators Friedman and Havighurst (1954), work has a fivefold meaning. It is (1) a source of income, (2) a life routine and major use of one's time, (3) a source of personal status and identity, (4) a source of social interaction, and (5) a source of meaning and creativity.

Work, as Terkel (1974, p. xi) so eloquently said, is "a search for daily meaning as well as daily bread; for recognition as well as cash; for astonishment rather than torpor; in short for a sort of life, rather than a Monday through Friday sort of dying. Perhaps immortality too is part of the quest." No wonder, then, that retirement, especially when it is involuntary, is looked upon as a stressful life event.

In meeting the psychosocial needs of the aged in retirement, both the internal and the external environments of the aged play critical roles. A flexible social environment is one that adapts itself to the changing needs of the aged, as expressed by their growing dependence on outside help. A major internal psychosocial need of the aged is to make the necessary preparations for the inevitable decline and infirmities of old age early enough in life, and preferably during middle age, *before* problems of daily living reach crisis proportions.

Beaver (1983, p. 194) cited the following case for illustration:

> A well-groomed and recently retired man, age sixty-six, sought treatment because of his feelings of dissatisfaction with the way he was running his life. He began to explain in the early sessions that instead of feeling better he was feeling worse. During the sessions the worker would try to draw him out in an effort to deal with his discomfort. The worker was aware that her client missed his job very much, and that he was experiencing difficulty in filling his time with meaningful activities. He seemed to be drifting and uncertain about what to do with himself and his time. But he avoided discussing his feelings about retirement and what it meant for him to give up his job. After each session with the worker, he would experience headaches, and prior to sessions he would experience high levels of anxiety.

WHEN DOES RETIREMENT EQUAL UPROOTEDNESS? Some old people do not successfully adapt to retirement. Those who are forced to retire on a small pension experience a drastic reduction in their standard of living, and some may experience poverty for the first time in their lives. Many actively seek new jobs, but few are successful. Those who did not develop self-satisfying leisure or nonwork interests during their preretirement years usually do not adapt satisfactorily. Often they have based their self-worth and identity on the status of work and the virtue of productivity and find it difficult to justify a life of leisure activities. Atchley (1977) noted that they tend to have a strong negative attitude about the meaning of retirement in general. This group of poorly adapted retirees frequently experiences depression, apathy, and social withdrawal.

Some people are unhappy and restless after they retire, not because they are negativistic about retirement, but because they are simply bored and don't know what to do with much of the time that is available to them. These individuals need to be provided with structured opportunities for meaningful social participation.

Uprootedness from the Social World

With the shift from a family system based on consanguine values to one held together by bonds of conjugality and sentiment, the obligations and influences of kinship have been minimized and the older generation has been placed outside the children's circle of privatized domesticity (Hareven, 1986). As a result, the normative definitions of the roles of adults and older family members are not clearly delineated.

The family continues to be the major source of support for the elderly (Lee, 1980). It has been well documented that older people are not abandoned by their children but typically live near at least one child, interact frequently with their children, and are often involved in the exchange of mutual aid with their offspring (Cicirelli, 1983; Guttmann, 1990; Lee & Ellithorpe, 1982; Lowenstein & Cibulski, 1989; Shanas, 1979; Thompson & Walker, 1984).

As elderly parents move along the aging continuum, from the "young-old" to the "old-old" to the "very-old" (Neugarten, 1977), the asymmetry in parent-child relations becomes more evident (Rosenmayr, 1978). Their impaired health strains family interactions and the caregiving role and has a negative impact on intergenerational relationships (Danis & Silverstone, 1981; Robinson & Thurhner, 1979). No factor has a greater negative impact on intergenerational relationships than institutionalization, symbolizing the failure of the family to support an aged member. The elderly and their families often hold similiar negative views, so that institutionalization, which equals uprootedness from family life, becomes the least desirable alternative when an elderly person begins to require support and assistance (Gonyea, 1987; Kahana, 1971).

Researchers have identified the events that precede institutionalization: the death of a spouse or of children, multiple physical disabilities, mental confusion, the aging of adult children, changing neighborhoods, and the exacerbation of old family conflicts (Branch & Jette, 1983; Shanas, 1979; Stoller & Earl, 1983). The following case illustrates these problems:

Maria, a 71-year-old divorced woman, currently lives with her boyfriend. She has no children from her previous marriage, but her boyfriend has two children from his previous marriage. Maria is currently in poor health, having recently undergone surgery for the removal of a cancerous tumor from her stomach. As a result of her deteriorated health, her relationships with her boyfriend and his children have undergone negative changes. His children demand that their father cease to live with her and throw her out of the house, which belongs to him, despite the fact that Maria has taken care of her boyfriend, who is ten years older than she.

Maria has no family to turn to and lives in constant anxiety that she will be chased out of her boyfriend's home. She is extremely dependent on this man and is afraid of institutionalization.

Uprootedness in the family life of the elderly occurs when the family decides to institutionalize the vulnerable older member. The decision, however, is often a family process (Lieberman, 1978), guided by what Blenkner (1965) termed "filial crisis."

Montgomery and Borgatta (1982) suggested that families seek to institutionalize their elderly relatives when they perceive an incongruence between their own resources and the psychosocial problems and needs of their elderly relatives. The importance of the elderly relatives' medical, physical, and functional characteristics, as well as of family relations and family functioning, in differentiating nursing home and community placements is evident in the literature (Brody, 1985; Cantor, 1983; Gonyea, 1987; Lowenstein, 1989). The main reasons for deciding on institutional placement are related to both the parents' and children's psychosocial needs, mainly health problems; the social isolation of the elderly; and health and personal restrictions on the children's daily and family functioning.

All the mixed feelings that characterize close human relationships may surface during this process. It is a time of potential crisis in which everyone involved becomes aware that, if placement is implemented, it may be the last move that the older person will make. It is this form of uprootedness from the world of the family that most elderly people and their families dread. It is exacerbated by negative attitudes and feelings toward long-term care institutions. Shanas (1962, pp. 102–103) summarized it as follows:

> Almost all older people view the move to a home for the aged or to a nursing home with fear and hostility. . . . All old people—without exception—believe that the move to an institution is a decisive change in living arrangements, the last change [they] will experience before [they] die]. . . . Finally, no matter what the extenuating circumstances, the older person who has children interprets the move to an institution as rejection by his [or her] family.

Uprootedness from the world of the family and admission to an institution encompass physical and social environmental changes that influence the status, self-image, self-esteem, and functioning of the elderly person. The relationship of this environmental change to mortality and morbidity has been extensively studied, and the gerontological literature is filled with descriptions of the institutionalized elderly as disorganized, disoriented, and depressed (Goldsmith et al., 1986; Gottesman, 1974; Lawton, 1974; Lemke & Moos, 1984; Mercer & Kane, 1979; Palmore, 1976; Tobin & Lieberman, 1976).

Tobin and Lieberman (1976) offered three sources of problems that are inherent in this type of uprootedness: relocation, preadmission effects, and the totality of institutions (see also, Goffman, 1961; Goldsmith et al., 1986; Lawton, 1974; Lemke & Moos, 1984).

SOCIAL WORK INTERVENTIONS AND ROLES

The elderly are in many ways a heterogeneous group with different types and degrees of need. Some require only limited support and services to continue living independently in their own homes. Others require extensive health and social care in an institutional setting. What is the role of the social worker in the various services whose aim is to meet these different and varied needs?

The answer to this question should be considered within the framework of the society of which the social services are part because social policies, programs, and professional practice are shaped by the society and reflect a particular historical, political, and cultural context. Political structure and the heterogeneity of the population are also determinants of policy emphases and shape the form of service delivery (Hokenstad, 1988).

The basic goals of service delivery to the elderly in our modern society include enabling people to maintain maximum self-sufficiency, to live in as normal a setting as possible, and to participate actively in the society. Even long-term care of the frail elderly has shifted from early institutionalization to continuity of the person's life-style in a normal environment.

In recent years, the social network functions of the family have played an increasingly larger role in professional interventions on behalf of elderly clients. In Miami, for example, attempts were made to develop both the concept and the corresponding methodology of the "neighborhood family," which operates on the principle of shared responsibility in obtaining and using resources (Ross, 1978). Staff members serve as "regular family members," volunteers provide free labor, and the elderly—including those with various degrees of functional impairment—are able to maintain themselves in the "family" for long periods. Similar models were developed in Michigan (Silverman, 1978) and elsewhere. Rueveni (1979), on the other hand, used social network as a theoretical frame of reference in therapy, while Sussman (1978) investigated the feasibility, circumstances, and conditions under which the family network may be used as an alternative to institutionalization by providing care and a home environment for its elderly members.

Two of the most important issues in service delivery are the targeting and coordination of services. Targeting concerns the degree to which services are specifically directed at the elderly and to specific groups in the older population in accordance with a known need. Coordination concerns the linkages among different types of services, particularly between health and social services.

Social work practice is concerned with the interactions between individuals and their social evnironments. Its focus is on helping people use their social environment to meet their needs. People are complex beings. Their social environments are also complex. A major concern of social work, then, is to enhance older people's problem-solving and coping capacities, to link them with appropriate resources, and to promote more effective relationships between them and societal resource systems. In other words, the roles of social workers are the *locator* of resources; the *enabler,* to help the client utilize the resources; the *mediator,* who acts as a conciliator to reconcile differences between the client and an unresponsive resource; the *advocate*; and the *educator,* who performs a teaching role. There should be a judicious and careful interplay between each of the various roles.

The roles of social workers in the provision of services to the elderly differ from country to country. In some countries social workers are central to the delivery of social services and are actively involved in the provision of health services. In others, social workers have limited, or even peripheral, roles. Their roles are determined by two factors: (1) the stage of development that the profession has reached in a given country and the corresponding definition of professional roles and (2) the amount of training that social workers have in the field of gerontology. Social work's own definition of professional priorities and the practice preferences of social workers are also important factors in determining service roles (Aviram & Katan, 1989).

Social work roles and activities vary greatly according to the field of social welfare, its pattern and type of auspice, and the range and type of other occupations also employed (Lawrence, 1976). Social work interventions in the field of gerontology cover *casework, the mobilization of resources, community work and service planning, coordination,* and *administration.*

Social casework in any setting implies a focus on work with and on behalf of individuals and families to promote the well-being of the clients. A key function of the social worker in working with families who care for an aged member is to maximize the effectiveness of their help, while realizing the costs of caring to both the family and to society.

The health field in Australia, for example, has the longest history of providing casework services to elderly people. In that country, social workers in the health services assist elderly people and their families to grapple with the social and emotional problems and needs that complicate ill health and disability both as cause and effect (Brennan, 1988).

The provision of direct service to elderly clients in institutions by social workers deserves special consideration. It usually occurs in three phases: the first, prior to entry—to help the client and family make the decision to relocate; the second, during the stay—to help the client adjust and function in the new environment and to ensure that the client makes full use of his or her rights and personal potential; and third, severance—to help in situations involving the client's transfer from the institution, return to the community, and death.

Group work with the elderly has become an increasingly popular form of treatment since World War II. As more people began to seek professional help and as fewer trained people were available to help them, group work became a viable method of service. Current group procedures range from relatively traditional group psychotherapy, patterned after individual treatment approaches, to creativity-growth groups. The latter may or may not have a leader and may incorporate a wide range of specific techniques, for example, finger painting or photography (Goldberg & Deutsch, 1977).

Miller and Solomon (1979, pp. 87–88) pointed out that, from the social worker's point of view, the purposes of groups may be

> to help elderly people to develop new and caring relationships, to maintain and enhance feelings of self-worth through continuity of social roles and the development of new ones, and to exert control over their lives through confronting and engaging some of the problems of living in the institutions or in the community.

In general, group work with the aged involves a directive approach (Corey & Corey, 1977); leaders must take an active role in giving information, answering questions, and sharing themselves with the group members (Burnside, 1978). Furthermore, the group members may be actively involved in solving their own problems.

In many service systems social workers are part of a team of professionals who are responsible for the delivery of services. The team approach is especially emphasized in the health field.

In the area of *resource mobilization*, an important function of social work with the elderly is to act as liaison between them and the local or central health services and between them and other community services (Kahn, 1978). To achieve this function, the social worker performs as a *broker* and *advocate*.

A broker links individuals and groups who need help and do not know where it is available with community services. The need to act in the brokerage role has developed in conjunction with the growing network of services for the elderly that operate through different organizations within the same neighborhood or community. For example, in Israel half the community centers (sixty centers) operate a variety of services for the aged, including volunteer work, personal social services, counseling, and referral (Lowenstein & Bergman, 1988). Social workers in health settings, especially in hospitals, act as brokers when they activate community services on behalf of discharged patients or their families, sometimes together with social workers from the local welfare offices.

Cutbacks in the allocation of resources by the government affect social services in many countries, and the needy elderly are especially vulnerable. Thus it is necessary for the social worker to act as an advocate to influence social priorities, as well as to protect the rights and serve the needs of individual clients. Social workers also are aware of the necessity to cooperate with other human service professionals to fight for the rights of clients.

The shift toward case management reflects a change in the philosophy of working with the elderly. Rather than emphasizing cure, social workers are trying to care for them by mobilizing and bringing together various services that the client needs.

Case management is a role in which social workers have begun to engage in recent years, especially as the emphasis in service development shifted to community-based services. This role requires skills in the mobilization of resources. In social work it is still an entrepreneurial role. In an experiment in England, it proved to be successful (Sinclair, 1988), but it is not widely practiced there as yet. In Israel, it has been encouraged since the creation (in 1969) of the National Association for Planning and Development of Services for the Aged. There, social workers serve as service coordinators and managers as members of local community interdisciplinary professional teams, as well as on teams of various home care units operated by the health care systems (Lowenstein & Bergman, 1988).

In England, the Barclay Report (1983) on social work roles and tasks distinguished two main roles—counseling and social care planning—and emphasized the importance of social work involvement in what it termed "community social work."

Community work with the elderly generally has three major components: community development, social planning, and social action. In the Netherlands, for example, it is performed in three major areas: (1) in person-to-person relationships that include social counseling, casework counseling, home help, home nursing, and the organization of local voluntary work; (2) in the community, where it is done with and for the benefit of a group or category of persons and includes the organization of neighborhood centers, social animation, community organization, and education; and (3) in *social work administration*, which is performed in the service of the national, provincial, or municipal government and primarily includes the financing, inspection, and planning of welfare provisions (Driest, 1988).

One may also distinguish between brief social work services, in which the emphasis is on investigation, assessment, and the mobilization of resources, and long-term social work, which concentrates on the greater frailty of the clients and the need to sustain them and solve their problems (Black et al., 1983; Sinclair, 1988).

CONCLUSION

In assessing the importance and usefulness of social work practice in gerontology, we must note that working with the aged and responding to their many complicated needs requires a multidisciplinary and multitheoretical approach. Professionals (including social workers) who work with the elderly are still far from reaching a consensus on their respective domains, but they are more and more aware that the knowledge explosion is not the property of any one discipline.

Care of the elderly is, to a large extent, an area in which social philosophy, caring skills, and professional health and welfare expertise must be closely interwoven. If social workers are to meet their professional responsibilities, they must place themselves in a position to demonstrate their knowledge, competence, and involvement in all the components of effective practice in gerontology.

What does the loss of status and prestige among the elderly mean for helping professionals? It suggests that multiple skills and intervention strategies are essential on a variety of levels to meet the specific needs and problems of older people effectively.

Social workers must also understand the importance of support networks as resistance resources to stress (Antonovsky, 1980). Their main contribution to the well-being of the elderly is to learn how to create, maintain, develop, and activate the networks and how to identify the hidden resources of the elderly themselves and of society. Today more services are available to the elderly than ever, but many of them are not used by the elderly and their families, simply because these clients are unaware of their existence. Thus, social workers need to educate the community in how to utilize resources.

Older potential clients may be characterized as having a certain amount of wisdom gained through years of experience, as having lived through a span of history different from that of younger persons and with different influences on their socialization, and as wishing to maintain their independence for as long as possible. Older adults have an identity, a history, a long-range perspective on time. During their lives they have probably passed through various transitions and role changes, learned certain coping skills, and experienced and observed many things. Therefore, the most important factor in meeting the needs of elderly people is a true knowledge of the circumstances of their lives.

As social workers, we must remember that life's worst enemy is not death, but the waste of precious moments—the neglect of opportunities to learn, to act, to teach, and to be helpful. Indeed, the worst enemy of life is the failure to use life in the purpose of maturing and growing—in effect, of growing older (Wolf, 1990).

BIBLIOGRAPHY

Antonovsky, A. (1980). *Health, stress, and coping*. San Francisco: Jossey-Bass.

Atchley, R. (1971). Disengagement among professors. *Journal of Gerontology, 26*, 476–480.

Atchley, R. (1977). *Social forces in later life*. Belmont, CA: Wadsworth.

Aviram, U., & Katan, J. (1989). Professional preference of social work graduates in Israel: Populations, services and roles (in Hebrew). *Society and welfare, 1*, 3–16.

Barclay Report. (1983). *Social workers: The role and tasks*. London: Bedford Square Press.

Barker, R. L. (1987). *The social work dictionary*. Washington, DC: National Association of Social Workers.

Baroni, G. (1979). Keynote address, presented at the Symposium on Older Americans of Euro-Ethnic Origin, Catholic University of America, Washington DC.

Baum, M., & Baum, R. C. (1982). Psycho-moral health in later years: Some social network correlates. In D. E. Biegel & A. J. Naparstek (Eds.), *Community support systems and mental health* (pp. 54–72). New York: Springer.

Beaver, M. L. (1983). *Human service practice with the elderly*. Englewood Cliffs, NJ: Prentice-Hall.

Beaver, M. L., & Miller, D. (1985). *Clinical social work practice with the elderly.* Homewood, IL: Dorsey Press.

Bergman, S., & Lowenstein, A. (1988). Care of the aging in Israel: Social service delivery. In *Gerontological social work: International perspectives* (pp. 97–116). New York: Haworth Press.

Biegel, D. E., & Blum, A. (Eds.). (1990). *Aging and caregiving.* London: Sage.

Black, J., Bowl, R., Burns, D., Critcher, C., Grant, G., & Stockford, D. (1983). *Social work in context: A comparative study of three social services teams.* London: Tavistock.

Blenkner, M. (1965). Social work and family relationships in later life, with some thoughts on filial maturity. In E. Shanas & F. F. Streib (Eds.), *Social structure and the family* (pp. 46–61). Englewood Cliffs, NJ: Prentice-Hall.

Branch, L. G., & Jette, A. M. (1983). Elders' use of informal long-term care assistance. *The Gerontologist, 23,* 51–56.

Brennan, A. (1988). Perspectives on Australian social service delivery and social work practice in gerontology. In *Gerontological social work: International perspectives* (pp. 17–40). New York: Haworth Press.

Brody, E. M. (1981). "Women in the middle" and family help to older people. *The Gerontologist, 21,* 471–480.

Brody, E. M. (1985). Parent as a normative family stress. *The Gerontologist, 25,* 19–29.

Brody, S. (1978). The family caring unit: A major consideration in the long-term support system. *The Gerontologist, 18,* 556–564.

Burnside, I. M. (1978). *Working with the elderly—Group processes and techniques.* North Scituate, MA: Duxbury Press.

Butler, R., & Lewis, M. I. (1982). *Aging and mental health* (3rd ed.). St. Louis, MO: C. V. Mosby.

Cantor, M. (1983). Strain among caregivers: A study of experience in the United States. *The Gerontologist, 26,* 579–584.

Chen, P. (1980). Continuing satisfying life patterns among aging minorities. *Journal of Gerontological Social Work, 2,* 199–211.

Churchman, A. (1981). Planning of neighborhood and housing for the aged (in Hebrew). *Gerontologia, 18,* 41–49.

Cicirelli, V. G. (1983). Adult children's attachment and helping behavior to elderly parents: A path model. *Journal of Marriage and the Family, 45,* 815–825.

Clark, M., & Anderson, B. G. (1967). *Culture and aging.* Springfield, IL: Charles C Thomas.

Corey, J., & Corey, M. (1977). *Groups: Process and practice.* Monterey, CA: Brooks/ Cole.

Crawford, M. P. (1971). Retirement and disengagement. *Human Relations, 24,* 255–278.

Cumming, E. (1975). Engagement with an old theory. *International Journal of Aging and Human Development, 6,* 187–191.

Cumming, E., & Henry, W. (1961). *Growing old: The process of disengagement.* New York: Basic Books.

Danis, B. G., & Silverstone, B. (1981). *The impact of caregiving: A difference between wives and daughters.* Paper presented at the annual meeting of the Gerontological Society, Toronto.

Dowd, J. J. (1975). Aging as exchange: A preface to theory. *Journal of Gerontology, 30,* 584–594.

Dowd, J. J. (1978). Aging as exchange: A test of the distributive justice proposition. *Pacific Sociological Review, 21,* 351–375.

Dowd, J. J. (1980). Exchange rates and old people. *Journal of Gerontology, 35,* 596–602.

Driest, P. F. (1988). Social services and the elderly in the Netherlands. In *Gerontological social work: International perspectives* (pp. 153–167). New York: Haworth Press.

Emerson, R. M. (1976). Social exchange theory. In A. Inkeles, J. Colman, & N. Smelser (Eds.), *Annual review of sociology* (Vol. 2). Palo Alto, CA: Annual Reviews.

Erikson, E. H. (1950). *Childhood and society.* New York: W. W. Norton.

Erikson, E. H. (1963). *Childhood and society* (2nd ed.). New York: W. W. Norton.

Erikson, E. H. (1964). *Insight and responsibility.* New York: W. W. Norton.

Fecher, V. J. (1982). *Religion and aging: An annotated bibliography.* San Antonio, TX: Trinity University Press.

Freiberg, K. (1987). *Human development: A life span approach.* Boston: Jones & Bartlett.

Friedman, E. A., & Havighurst, R. J. (Eds.). (1954). *The meanings of work and retirement.* Chicago: University of Chicago Press.

Gallup Opinion Index. (1978). *Religion in America.* Princeton, NJ: American Institute of Public Opinion.

Gelfand, D. E., & Fandetti, D. (1980). Urban and suburban white ethnics: Attitudes towards care of the aged. *The Gerontologist, 20,* 588–594.

Goffman, E. (1961). *Asylums.* Garden City, NY: Doubleday.

Goldberg, S. R., & Deutsch, F. C. (1977). *Life-span individual and family development.* Monterey, CA: Brooks/Cole.

Goldsmith, H. F., Jackson, D. J., Kramer, M., Brenner, B., Stiles, D. I., Tweed, D. L., Holzer, C. E., & MacKenzie, E. (1986). Strategies for investigating effects of residential context. *Research on Aging, 8,* 609–635.

Gonyea, J. G. (1987). The family and dependency: Factors associated with institutional decision-making. *Journal of Gerontological Social Work, 9,* 61–77.

Gottesman, L. (1974). Nursing home performance as related to resident traits, ownership, size, and source of payment. *American Journal of Public Health, 64,* 269–281.

Guttmann, D. (1973). Leisure time activity interests of Jewish aged. *The Gerontologist, 13,* 219–233.

Guttmann, D. (1979). Use of informal and formal supports by the white ethnic aged. In D. E. Gelfand & A. J. Kutzik (Eds.), *Ethnicity and aging: Theory, research and policy.* New York: Springer.

Guttmann, D. (1986). Book review essay: Specialized bibliographies. *Journal of Cross-Cultural Gerontology, 1,* 317–323.

Guttmann, D. (1987). Ethnicity in aging: Perspectives on the needs of ethnic aged. *Social Thought, 13,* 42–51.

Guttmann, D. (1990). Filial responsibility—A logotherapeutic view. *Journal of Aging and Judaism, 4,* 161–180.

Hall, G. (1922). *Senescence, the last half of life.* New York: D. Appelton.

Hareven, T. K. (1986). American families in transition: Historical perspectives on change. In A. S. Skolnick & J. H. Skolnick (Eds.), *Family in transition* (pp. 39–56). Boston: Little, Brown.

Havighurst, R. (1968). Personality and patterns of aging. *The Gerontologist, 8,* 20–23.

Hazan, H. (1980). Continuity and change in a tea-cup: On the symbolic nature of tea-related behavior among the aged. *Sociological Review, 28,* 497–516.

Hazan, H. (1984). Continuity and transformation among the aged: A study in the anthropology of time. *Current Anthropology, 25,* 567–578.

Hendricks, J., & Hendricks, C. D. (1977). *Aging in mass society: Myths and realities.* Cambridge, MA: Winthrop.

Hertz, R. C. (1990). Reflections on old age. *Journal of Aging and Judaism, 4,* 191–195.

Hochschild, A. (1975). Disengagement theory: A critique and proposal. *American Sociological Review, 40,* 553–569.

Hokenstad, M. C. (1988). Cross-national trends and issues in social service provision and social work practice for the elderly. In *Gerontological social work: International perspectives* (pp. 1–16). New York: Haworth Press.

Hooyman, N. R. (1983). Social support networks in services to the elderly. In J. K. Whittaker & J. Garbarino (Eds.), *Social support networks: Informal helping in the human services* (pp. 134–166). New York: Aldine.

Kahana, E. (1971). Emerging issues in institutional services for the aging. *The Gerontologist, 11,* 51–58.

Kahn, H. (1978). *Services for the aged.* Jerusalem: State of Israel, Ministry of Labour and Social Affairs.

Killilea, M. (1982). Interaction of crisis theory, coping strategies, and social support systems. In H. C. Schulberg & M. Killilea (Eds.), *The modern practice of com-*

munity health: A volume in honor of Gerald Caplan (pp. 163–214). San Francisco: Jossey-Bass.

Larson, R. (1978). Thirty years of research on the subjective well-being of older Americans. *Journal of Gerontology, 33*, 109–125.

Lawrence, J. (1976). Australian social work: In historical international and social welfare context. In P. Boas & J. Crawley (Eds.), *Social work in Australia: Responses to a changing context* (pp. 1–37). Melbourne: International Press and Publications.

Lawton, M. P. (1974). Social ecology and the health of older people. *American Journal of Public Health, 64*, 257–260.

Lawton, M. P. (1987). *Environment and need satisfaction of the aging.* Philadelphia: Philadelphia Geriatric Center.

Lee, G. R. (1980). Kinship in the seventies: A decade review of research and theory. *Journal of Marriage and the Family, 42*, 193–204.

Lee, G. R., & Ellithorpe, E. (1982). Intergenerational exchange and subjective well-being among the elderly. *Journal of Marriage and the Family, 44*, 217–224.

Lemke, S., & Moos, R. H. (1984). Coping with an intra-institutional relocation: Behavioral change as a function of residents' personal resources. *Journal of Environmental Psychology, 4*, 137–151.

Lemon, B., Bengston, V., & Peterson, J. (1972). Activity types and life satisfaction in a retirement community. *Journal of Gerontology, 27*, 511–523.

Lieberman, G. L. (1978). Children of the elderly as natural helpers: Some demographic differences. *American Journal of Community Psychology, 6*, 429–449.

Longino, C., & Kart, C. S. (1982). Explicating activity theory: A formal replication. *Journal of Gerontology, 17*, 713–722.

Lowenstein, A. (1989). *Institutional placement decision-making and impact on family relations of the elderly—A filial crisis.* Paper presented at the Annual Symposium of the European Behavioral and Social Science Research Section of the International Association of Gerontology, Dubrovnik, Yugoslavia.

Lowenstein, A., & Bergman, S. (1988). Social work practice in gerontology in Israel. In *Gerontological social work: International perspectives* (pp. 117–131). New York: Haworth Press.

Lowenstein, A., & Cibulski, A. (1989). Differential resources of the elderly and patterns of intergenerational exchange. Unpublished.

Maddox, G. L. (1963). Activity and morale: A longitudinal study of selected elderly subjects. *Social Forces, 42*, 195–204.

McCubbin, H. I., Sussman, M. B., & Patterson, J. M. (1983). *Social stress and the family: Advances and developments in family stress theory and research.* New York: Haworth Press.

Mercer, S., & Kane, R. A. (1979). Helplessness and hopelessness among the institutionalized aged. *Health and Social Work, 4*, 91–116.

Miller, I., & Solomon, R. (1979). The development of group services for the elderly. In C. B. Germain (Ed.), *Social work practice: People and environments* (pp. 74–106). New York: Columbia University Press.

Mitchell, J. C. (1969). The concept and the use of social networks. In J. C. Mitchell (Ed.), *Social networks in urban situations* (pp. 105–130). Manchester, England: Manchester University Press.

Montgomery, R. J., & Borgatta, E. F. (1982). *Family supports: A preventive approach.* Unpublished manuscript.

Neugarten, B. (1968). The awareness of middle age. In B. Neugarten (Ed.), *Middle age and aging* (pp. 93–98). Chicago: University of Chicago Press.

Neugarten, B. L. (1973). Patterns of aging: Past, present and future. *Social Service Review, 47,* 571–580.

Neugarten, B. (1977). Personality and aging. In J. Birren & K. Schaie (Eds.), *Handbook of the psychology of aging.* New York: Van Nostrand Reinhold.

Palmore, E. (1968). The effects of aging on activities and attitudes. *The Gerontologist, 8,* 259–263.

Palmore, E. (1976). Total chance of institutionalization among the elderly. *The Gerontolgoist, 16,* 504–507.

President's Commission on Mental Health. (1978). *Report to The President* (Vol. 3, pp. 139–235). Washington, DC: U.S. Government Printing Office.

Rabinowitz, M. (1985). *The ages of man* (in Hebrew). Tel-Aviv: Am Oved.

Robinson, B., & Thurhner, M. (1979). Taking care of aged parents: A family cycle transition. *The Gerontologist, 19,* 586–594.

Rosenberg, D., & Hribets, F. (1985). *A five year communal plan for meeting the needs of the Jewish aging, 1985–1989.* New York: Federation of Jewish Philanthropies of New York.

Rosenmayr, L. (1978). The family—A source of hope for the elderly? In E. Shanas & M. Sussman (Eds.), *Family, bureaucracy and the elderly* (pp. 132–157). Durham, NC: Duke University Press.

Rosow, I. (1967). *Social integration of the aged.* New York: Free Press.

Ross, H. R. (1978). *How to develop a neighborhood family: An action manual.* Miami, FL: Northside Neighborhood Family Services.

Rueveni, U. (1979). *Networking families in crisis.* New York: Human Services Press.

Russell, B. (1956). *Reflections on my eightieth birthday.* New York: Simon & Schuster.

Sauer, W. J., & Coward, R. T. (Eds.) (1985). *Social support networks and the care of the elderly.* New York: Springer.

Shanas, E. (1962). *The health of older people: A social survey.* Cambridge, MA: Harvard University Press.

Shanas, E. (1979). Social myth as hypothesis: The case of the family relations of old people. *The Gerontologist, 19,* 3–9.

Silverman, A. G. (1978). *As parents grow older: An intervention model*. Paper presented at the 31st Annual Meeting of the Gerontological Society, Dallas.

Simmons, L. W. (1946). Attitudes toward aging and the aged: Primitive societies. *Journal of Gerontology, 1*, 72–95.

Sinclair, I. (1988). Social work and personal social services for the elderly in Great Britain. In *Gerontological social work: International perspectives* (pp. 77–97). New York: Haworth Press.

Stoller, E. P., & Earl, L. L. (1983). Help with activities of every day life: Sources of support for the noninstitutionalized elderly. *The Gerontologist, 23*, 64–70.

Sullivan, D. A. (1986). Informal support systems in a planned retirement community. *Research on Aging, 8*, 249–267.

Sussman, M. B. (1976). The family life of old people. In R. Binstock & E. Shanas (Eds.), *Handbook of aging and the social sciences* (pp. 218–243). New York: Van Nostrand.

Sussman, M. B. (1978). *A reconstituted young-old family: Social and economic supports in family formation*. Paper presented at the symposium on Informal Supports—Implications of Research for Practice and Policy at the 31st Annual Meeting of The Gerontological Society, Dallas.

Terkel, S. (1974). *Working*. New York: Pantheon.

Thomae, H. (1980). Personality and adjustment to aging. In J. E. Birren & R. B. Sloane (Eds.), *Handbook of mental health and aging* (pp. 285–309). Englewood Cliffs, NJ: Prentice-Hall.

Thompson, L., & Walker, A. J. (1984). Mothers and daughters: Aid patterns and attachment. *Journal of Marriage and the Family, 46*, 313–321.

Tobin, S., & Lieberman, M. (1976). *The last home for the aged*. San Francisco: Jossey-Bass.

Towle, C. (1952). *Common human needs*. New York: American Association of Social Workers.

Wan, T. H., Adler, B. G., & Lewis, D. T. (1982). *Promoting the well-being of the elderly: A community diagnosis*. New York: Haworth Press.

Webster's third new international dictionary of the English language—Unabridged. (1986). Springfield, MA: Merriam-Webster.

Weinberg, J. K. (1987). Aging and dependence: Toward a redefinition of autonomy. *Social Casework, 68*, 522–532.

Wolf, A. (1990). Thoughts on growing older. *Journal of Aging and Judaism, 4*, 215–219.

Yehudai, M. (1985). *The needs of the aged in the kibbutz* (in Hebrew). Tel-Aviv: Association of Kibbutz Movement.

23

An Overview

Francis J. Turner

I have never been sure whether it is more difficult to write the first or the last chapter for a book such as this. I do know that the two tasks each have different demands. In beginning a collaborative book, one writes about what one hopes the book is going to be, why it is being written, the rationale behind its structure, and the perceived unifying conceptual base that will guide the contributors.

However, when it comes time to write the final chapter, one is profoundly aware that, as the editor, you are no longer fully in charge. The book has taken on a life of its own. Your colleagues have done what you expected of them, but they have added something of themselves as well. They have all addressed their assigned topics from the perspective of their individual practice wisdom, knowledge, values, and experience. In their doing so, you as the editor have been shaped and changed.

As this particular task comes to a close and I seek to develop a retrospective overview, several things are clear. Certainly, there is much in the chapters that those experienced in this field have long known. Thus, there is much of what one expected to find. But there are also many new ideas and points of view. I have been marked by the ideas of these experienced colleagues and impressed that they have contributed much to our knowledge.

Overall I am pleased. There is much in these pages that needs to be carefully addressed by all components of the profession, indeed by colleagues in the other human service professions. In particular, there is a sense that in our work with the elderly, we still have a lot to learn. As experienced colleagues, the authors have risked speculating on new directions. Because some of this material is based in idiosyncratic practice wisdom, there may well be content with which some colleagues may disagree. In the spirit of the quest for knowledge, it is hoped that such differences will be brought forward to be examined and discussed. It is in this way that knowledge is built. Hence I will end this chapter with a plea for ongoing evaluation and research to advance and enrich our knowledge.

THEMES

As I have read and reread the material, I have noticed seven areas, or themes, that permeate the spectrum of topics: attitudes toward and about the elderly, knowledge and sociology of the elderly, diagnosis, treatment, services, social policy, and the future.

Attitudes toward and about the Elderly

In virtually all the chapters, we are reminded that, as professionals, our values and attitudes toward the elderly influence our perception of them as clients. In particular we are reminded of the serious implications of "over pathologizing" the various presenting situations we meet in our practice with this group of clients. As those who are frequently the primary professional caregivers, it is essential that we be aware of the various forms of problem functioning, including psychopathology of all types, that we will meet. But we should also remind ourselves that many components of our society still tend to view the very fact of being elderly as a problem situation. In such an attitudinal climate, it is easy for us to see only pathology or to believe we see it where it does not exist. Indeed, as was mentioned in the preface, even before the book was begun, there were strong admonitions from the publishers and the consultants with whom they had discussed the book that this was an issue.

The authors of the various chapters have done well in identifying the range and types of problems and pathology we meet in our elderly clients. Of equal importance, they have also reminded us that it is easy to misunderstand and to see problems in behavior that are a form of adequate adjustment to difficult situations. We are severally reminded of the temptation to find psychiatric-based explanations for behavior that is best and more appropriately understood from other life-system perspectives.

But a balanced view is needed. In our enthusiasm for "depathologizing" situations, we must not go too far. In so doing, we could miss what are situations of pathology in the most traditional sense of the word. The need is for highly developed differential diagnostic skills in situations in which the number of variables and potentially impinging conditions are vast.

Knowledge and Sociology of the Elderly

It is evident that as we have become more interested in, sensitive to, and concerned about the elderly, our knowledge base of this stage of the human adventure has been enriched and expanded. An important aspect of this knowledge development relates to the concept of history. In several chapters, we are reminded of the importance of understanding the life stories of our elderly clients from their perspectives. We need to listen more sensitively to our clients' stories to understand the origins of many of their current problems and the significance of such problems for them now. This knowledge also helps us identify the potential for strength that can be found in their histories. We need to be especially sensitive to the potential impact of history in view of some of the dramatic and overwhelmingly powerful events that many of our elderly clients have survived and of the forms of scarring that such events may have left on their psychosocial functoning.

As important as is this renewed sensitivity of the place of history in work with this population, it should also help us to look again at the importance of history in working with all clients. For a long time, the concept of history in the helping professions tended to be viewed principally in psychodynamic terms and thus was associated with a particular theoretical orientation. Hence, as some components of the profession distanced themselves from psychodynamic traditions, the importance of history in practice was minimized.

Accompanying this renewed appreciation of the critical need to understand history in our practice, there has been a corresponding awareness that we have had a too-narrow perception of what was essential in history. We are learning that history needs to be understood in a broad manner—to include the total gamut of a person's experiences—rather than to focus only on the traditional history of a client's personality development, as significant as it is.

In seeking to understand the totality of our client's situation, we are reminded of the important role that a person's cultural and ethnic history plays throughout life. In our work with the elderly, an understanding of a client's ethnicity and its significance in earlier years can help us understand much about a person's values, attitudes, roles, and life views. In addition, it can help us understand a client's perceptions of problems and the types and sources of help and solutions that are appropriate.

A particularly important component of this need to be ethnically sensitive is the awareness that our ethnic identity, complex as it may be, takes on different degrees of importance in our lives at different life stages. Frequently, it is in our later years that some of our ethnic heritage has a much greater significance than in an earlier stage of life and hence needs to be given much more attention by involved professionals. Significant persons in our clients' lives may well be surprised and puzzled at the importance that some of these issues have for their elderly family members and view these issues as signs of deterioration and regression, rather than as an existential wish to reidentify with significant components of their past. Another aspect of this area, which is sometimes tied to early neurological changes, is that many elderly clients forget English if they learned it as a second language and thus are able to communicate only in their original tongues.

Although several authors referred to ethnicity as an important variable, there was not as much detail on this topic as I would have anticipated. We may be at a point where we do not as yet have sufficient information or experience with this component of our clients' realities to do more than identify it as an important area of practice with the elderly and may need to wait for ongoing research and practice to develop it with more specificity.

Another interesting component of history, identified by several authors, is that some areas of problem functioning in the elderly are the result of their successes, not of their less-positive experiences. Hence, we are reminded that problems with such things as alcohol or diet that began late in life are sometimes the result of an affluent life-style that permitted clients' access to the good life, rather than to experience deprivation.

In addition to learning more about the elderly, we are, of course, increasing our awareness of what we do not know. An interesting demographic question mentioned in several chapters was whether some groups in our society are differentially represented among the elderly and if so, what may be some of the reasons for this fact. If there are indeed marked differences among groups from the perspective of who does and does not have a better chance to surive to late life, we need to be aware of some of the policy implications for long-term planning.

Throughout the chapters, there is much emphasis on the important role that the family plays in the successful or unsuccessful journey through our later years. This, of course, is not a new insight. Anyone who has worked with the elderly is aware that the presence or absence of family is frequently a critical variable in a satisfying biopsychosocial adjustment.

However, there are two themes that may be viewed as emerging developments in this understanding of the family. One is the growing appreciation of the complexities of role functioning within families as various members move through various developmental stages. In many aspects of general family work, we have to help parents come to terms with their transitional roles as their children mature through various life stages into adults and their need to relate to their children as equals, rather than as dependents.

What many families are now experiencing is a new set of role demands that go beyond this need. Now there are many instances in which the parents become the new dependents as their biopsychosocial problems increase. This reality frequently requires a new and often highly complex realignment of roles and dynamics in families. Thus, some family members who have just begun to experience the challenges and satisfactions of emancipation from the family find themselves faced with a new set of demands to care for older family members and their awareness that this care may well last as long as two decades.

It may well be that this phenomenon will reshape the concept of the extended family, a societal system that much untested professional wisdom presumed was no longer important. We are already seeing a growing societal expectation that persons, such as nieces and nephews and even more distant relatives, will play a role with elderly family members. Evidently, perceptions about these persons' responsibilities will be partially influenced by ethnic and cultural traditions. However, value shifts in the larger social system may bring about changed role perceptions even in groups with long-held traditions that minimized such responsibilities. It is interesting to note that several of the case examples in the various chapters spoke of nieces, nephews, grandchildren, and even great-grandchildren as the significantly involved others.

The second theme is our growing awareness of the highly complex and influential reality of intersystemic influences. Thanks to the insights of systems theory, we have increased our sensitivity to this reality in all aspects of our practice. However, in work with the elderly, the concept that a change in one system or subsystem can have effects on all systems becomes essential. Such apparently minor things as a one-day delay in the delivery of a pension check, a missed phone call, and an unexpected change in the weather may have critical implications for a person whose homeostatic balance is tenuous. These apparently minor changes can result in dramatic changes in the client's biological, psychological, social, and interpersonal functioning.

In particular we social workers are rapidly becoming aware that we have not paid sufficient attention to the biological realities of our clients. In the elderly, tenuous balance is frequently maintained between highly satisfying functioning and highly problematic functioning that hinges on slight changes in their biological systems. In this regard a slight alteration in medication or the failure to perceive the interinfluence of medications may spell the difference between being able to function well or being seriously ill.

In several chapters we are reminded of the need for more experience with and knowledge about groups who hitherto did not live into the later decades and hence for whose needs as elders we know little. This is especially so in regard to some of the developmentally limited or deficit elderly members of society. Therefore, we social workers are challenged to be open to a perception of the elderly that is broader than the societally defined concept of 65 years. That is, who is to be considered elderly may vary from group to group. For example, our Down's syndrome clients, most of whom used to die before they reached age 65, may be a group who age at a differential rate. There are probably other examples of both biologically and culturally different rates of aging.

Mobility is still another variable that may have important implications for service to the elderly. It appears that we are moving into an era of world history in which the reality of extensive and at times sudden geographic moves by large population groups will be increasingly common. Even now millions of people on our planet are on the move for a variety of political, cultural, environmental, and historical reasons. This type of mobility frequently means that whole families find themselves relocated, on short notice, in parts of the world that are very different from their locales of origin. In many of these events, elderly family members are commonly a part of the group on the move, especially since some of our immigration practices are becoming more attuned to the advantages of keeping families together.

Hence, many of our elderly clients may be faced with the challenges of readjustment to a different culture and life-style only in their later lives. This reality creates interesting challenges for the provision of services, funding for services, and the development of policies.

Over and over again, we are reminded by the authors that much of what is being said about working with the elderly is not based on reasearch or even on a rich accumulation of practice experience. Rather it is an extrapolation of ideas that stem from practice with younger clients with similar problems. Thus, many of the authors may have been highly tentative in their observations.

Diagnosis

A theme that permeates the preceding chapters is the importance of accurate diagnosis in working with the elderly. As was mentioned earlier, there is strong insistence that we must avoid overpathologizing situations. We are reminded of the complexities of situations and of the temptation to move too quickly to standard diagnostic categories. But this caveat in no way argues for an abandonment of diagnostic categories in the manner of the trendy decrying of the use of labels. Rather, it is a warning that we need to be constantly aware of the complexities of our cases, of the possibility of misassessing the critical interconnections of various components of a client's life, and of the risks of oversimplifying complex problems and of overcomplicating simple ones.

A part of this diagnostic challenge relates to the aforementioned theme that rapid and at times dramatic changes may take place in an elderly person's life that necessitate a need to rediagnose and reassess the client over and over again in view of such changes. Thus, diagnosis must, as always, be a continuous process, as well as a fact.

As a process, diagnosis needs to go on all through our work with the elderly and their significant others, so we are constantly aware of the shifts and developments that are taking place. As a fact, it requires that we regularly set out for ourselves and our colleagues our judgments about what we consider critical to the situation and the basis on which we are making judgments that lead us to take or not to take some pattern of interventions.

Treatment

One of the important themes emerging from these chapters, which ought to have implications for the whole field, is the need for a broadened concept of the term *treatment*. Since such things as a slight shift in medication by a skillful physician, an assurance that a neighbor will phone daily, an understanding visit by a volunteer, or a skillful piece of short-term therapy with an upset family member may all have dramatic effects on the overall functioning of a person, we need to consider all such interventions as being of equal value and as requiring the same degree of diagnostic acumen. Too long have we struggled with determining what kinds of intervention were of more worth than were others—whether family therapy was more prestigious than was supportive therapy, whether "real" therapy was insight oriented and work with the significant environment "only supportive," and on and on.

The test of the value of our interventions needs to be its impact on the client and the skill required to diagnose the situation, to assess what is needed, and to see that it is provided. Certainly, a volume such as this will not change our inter- and intraprofessional sociology in any drastic way. However, more experience with the complex and intersystemic needs of elderly clients may help us perceive the futility of some of our struggles over turf and prestige, but, more critically, the harm that can be done to clients, either through omission or commission, when professional boundaries obfuscate the clients' needs.

One particular area of intervention that is rarely addressed in work with the elderly is the role of the client's spirituality as a component of satisfying adjustment. This may well be an instance in which we are uncomfortable about crossing professional boundaries. A client's faith is frequently a way in which the client learns to deal appropriately with many of the challenges of this stage of life. Sometimes it involves a search for significance in one's final years or a rediscovering of one's roots. However, it may also be the source of some anxiety and guilt related to some aspect of a client's life and in an area where we can help build the appropriate networks that will permit the client to face these issues.

Services

It is clear from the content of the various chapters that one of the satisfying challenges of practice with this age group is to create and coordinate a broad range of highly flexible services. These services can be as complex as are some highly technological resources that will permit the distant computerized monitoring of medication to ways of ensuring that Mrs. Murphy's cat will be fed for the two days she is in the hospital. Again, these realities raise age-old questions for our profession, and indeed for most professions, of the multiplicity of services, of conflicting jurisdictions, of the clarity or lack thereof of the profession's mandate, of interprofessional rivalries, of differential assessments of what constitutes treatment, and of levels of decision making.

Too often we have found in practice that it is easier to obtain highly expensive services that don't really help when we cannot get what is really needed because it doesn't come under someone's mandate. The challenge to us as a profession is how to use the rich creativity that is part of most professionals to link, in highly individualized ways, those clusters of persons, technologies, professional expertise, services, policies, and volunteer resources in the community that really do represent the very best treatment for an elderly client. Our authors did not give us the final answers to these many challenges, but the issues they raised underscore the tasks to be addressed.

A particular issue in work with the elderly is that the network of significant others in the client's life is often beginning to shrink and to be less available just when it is most needed. Thus, an overall goal of policy and practice is to emphasize the concept of networking, both as a community responsibility and as an objective of individualized treatment.

An important component of this diversity of needs relates to various legal issues that clients need to face in regard to their lives and of the legal questions around who can make decisions for elderly persons when they are not in a position to do so for themselves.

Social Policy

Our work with the elderly reminds us that we cannot separate policy from practice; the two are inextricably interconnected. This reality, one that we keep remeeting in our profession, also challenges our schools of social work to prepare students for this component of practice. We need, of course, highly skilled clinicians, but of a kind that consider it their responsibility to use the knowledge gained from practice to struggle for the requisite social policies that will ensure optimum services and resources for the elderly. In addition, we need highly skilled policy experts who respect the skills and knowledge of clinicians and who will draw on the body of clinical knowledge as the basis of emergency social policies.

This work also leads us as a profession to ask some important questions. One is an interesting policy challenge related to our perception of who are the elderly in our profession. Are we comfortable letting colleagues practice as long as they want to in the profession, or do we question a colleague's competence as he or she becomes older? In a similar way, knowing that networks are important to the elderly, what kinds of networks should we be considering as professionals to ensure that our elderly colleagues in social work have appropriate access to what they need in their postpractice years? Do we have to develop new professional roles for ourselves as part of enhancing services to our own elderly members?

The Future

In conclusion, we can be comfortable that there is much we know about how to respond best to the needs of the elderly and their significant others. But there is much we do not know as well. However, overall there is an awareness that we cannot know everything. As our knowledge grows, so, too, does our awareness of the gaps in our knowledge. We appear to be over the period when we seemed always to have to have the final solution. This will never be!

There will not be dramatic breakthroughs in the quality and effectiveness of our services to the elderly. Progress will be by small incremental steps, achieved by careful, responsible testing of our knowledge and skills. We have made dramatic strides in the past three decades in learning to use research as a tool to advance knowledge. Nowhere is research more needed than in our practice with the elderly.

The content of these chapters should fill us with awe. We need to appreciate the immensity of our body of knowledge to date. We need to understand how complex and changing is this field of practice. We also need to accept humbly the vastness of our lack of knowledge.

We know that the demands on us to serve elderly persons better are going to continue. We know that they will increase in quantity and severity. But we also know that by responsibly and humbly accepting our commitment to test knowledge and develop new ideas and approaches, we can make steady progress. This progress will ensure that, to the best of our society's knowledge and abilities, we will strive to make use of our theories and practices to enhance the biopsychosocial realities of this important component of society, the elderly. Perhaps in closing it would be good to paraphrase the words of Pogo: "We have met the elderly, and they is us."

Acknowledgments

My family has always been involved in many different ways in the various phases of writing and editing our books. During the process, I am continuously aware of a sense of appreciation to them. This awareness is even stronger when a new book is completed. Thus, once again, I want to thank them and acknowledge their differential help and support. When this book began to develop almost everyone in the family—Joanne, Anne-Marie, Sarah, and Francis—was a student (and most still are, although the possibility of graduation is now a hoped-for proximate reality in a couple of instances). Duffy, the least scholarly and singularly disinterested of the gang, was very elderly herself when it began and has now left us. I am appreciative to all!

I am most grateful as well to my friend and colleague Dr. Naomi Golan for agreeing to write the Foreword. She has made major contributions to the social work literature, and her support of this work is an honor to me.

Once again, through this process I have come to know some new colleagues and to reconnect with former friends. I do not recall ever having had such prompt and enthusiastic responses to a project as I had to this one. The first group whom I approached were most helpful in identifying other potential scholars, and their suggestions are appreciated.

Once begun, my challenge was not to find appropriate authors, but to select from among many. It is evident that social workers do play and are going to play in the future a major role, if not the primary role, in the care of and service to the elderly. It is a privilege for me to assist in making the rich wealth of knowledge about our contribution to this highly significant and important group in our population available to my own colleagues and to those in other professions.

Francis J. Turner
York University, Toronto, Canada

513

Index

I wish to acknowledge my appreciation for the assistance of Kathleen Lidbetter, Brigitte Mertins-Kirkwood, Anne-Marie Turner, and Joanne Turner in the preparation of this index—F. J. T.

515